PUBLIC PERSONNEL SYSTEMS

Third Edition

Robert D. Lee, Jr., PhD
The Pennsylvania State University
University Park, Pennsylvania

AN ASPEN PUBLICATION®
Aspen Publishers, Inc.
Gaithersburg, Maryland
1993

Library of Congress Cataloging-in-Publication Data

Lee, Robert D.
Public personnel systems / Robert D. Lee, Jr. — 3rd ed.
p. cm.

"An Aspen publication."
Includes bibliographical references and index.
ISBN 0-8342-0392-8
1. Civil service—United States. 2. Civil service—United States—States.
3. Local officials and employees—United States. 4. Civil service—
United States—Personnel management. I. Title.
JK765.L43   1993
353.006—dc20
93-7743
CIP

Editorial Resources: Lenda Hill
Ruth Bloom

Library of Congress Catalog Card Number: 93-7743
ISBN: 0-8342-0392-8

Printed in the United States of America

1 2 3 4 5

To students—past, present, and future

Table of Contents

Preface v

Acknowledgments ix

Chapter 1—Introduction 1
    Public and Private Sector Comparisons 1
    Magnitude and Growth of Bureaucracies 4
    Personnel Systems 9
    Summary 13

Chapter 2—Patronage and the Merit Principle 15
    Patronage and Reform in Perspective 15
    Merit and Organizational Responsibilities 25
    Summary 36

Chapter 3—Organizational and Job Design, Position
           Classification, and Personnel Planning 43
    Organizational and Job Design 43
    Position Classification 49
    Operational Problems of Classification 57
    Personnel Planning 60
    Summary 69

Chapter 4—Pay and Employee Benefits 75
    Pay 75
    Employee Benefits 88
    Summary 102

Chapter 5—Recruitment, Examination, and Selection **109**
    Recruitment 109
    Examination 114
    Selection 129
    Summary 132

Chapter 6—Probation and Performance Evaluation **139**
    Probation 139
    Performance Evaluation or Appraisal 144
    Management Evaluation 158
    Merit Pay for All 160
    Summary 162

Chapter 7—Careers and Career Development **169**
    Careers in Government 169
    Career Executives 175
    Training and Education 182
    Summary 189

Chapter 8—Employee Rights and Responsibilities **195**
    Ethical Standards and Ambiguities 195
    Civil Rights 209
    Employee Accountability 217
    Summary 228

Chapter 9—Equal Rights and Affirmative Action **239**
    Minorities, Women, and Older Workers 240
    Outlawing Discrimination 243
    Discrimination in Various Aspects of Personnel
       Administration 250
    Affirmative Action 264
    Summary 273

Chapter 10—Motivation Theory **283**
    Determinations of Personality 284
    Content Theories 288
    Process Theories 292
    Summary 297

Chapter 11—Motivation in Daily Operations **303**
    Individual Workers and Autonomy 303
    Groups and Leaders 311
    Performance and Organizational Change 319

Limitations on Motivation 332
Summary 336

Chapter 12—Labor–Management Relations **347**
The Emergence of Unions and Bargaining 347
Collective Bargaining and Processes 353
Managing under Collective Bargaining 369
Summary 377

Critique **385**
A Negative View 385
Unresolved Issues 389
The Future 394
Closing Comment 401

Appendix A—A Research Guide to Personnel Literature **407**

Index **411**

Preface

This is a general book about public personnel systems. It surveys the emergence of these systems, their current status, and their possible future directions. Special attention is given to whether each aspect of personnel administration contributes to or deters effective and efficient government operations.

Personnel administration is examined within a systems context. The components of the system are considered along with the relationships among these components. The discussion covers whether the components of personnel systems are well integrated with each other and whether the systems are integrated within the broader governmental organization.

The book blends the new with the old. Traditional topics such as recruiting, testing, and selecting are considered. In recent decades, however, new forces have influenced public personnel systems. These include the rise of public sector collective bargaining and equal employment opportunity for minorities and women. The book emphasizes the role of judicial decisions in personnel systems. In recent years courts have become major instruments for determining what may and may not be done in personnel administration. The reader should be careful, however, not to assume that judicial decisions constitute the whole story. Neither laws nor judicial opinions by themselves account for the operations of personnel systems. For instance, although employment discrimination based on race and sex clearly is prohibited, such discrimination still continues in some places in government.

The book attempts to provide a balanced discussion of personnel systems, avoiding both outright condemnation and unqualified endorsement of existing operations. The reason for this approach is not timidity on the part of the author. Instead, the problem lies in the competing values that public personnel systems are expected to serve. One recurrent theme throughout, for example, is the appropriate balance between what government rightfully should expect of its workers and what workers rightfully should expect of government, juxtaposed with what citizens should expect from their governmental system. Many of the issues are discussed in pro and con terms, with readers having to judge which set of arguments is more persuasive. Choosing one side over the other depends on the relative weights an individual assigns to various values. As discussed in the last chapter, society has been unable to reach a consensus on the relative importance of many values that impinge on public personnel systems.

The discussion also is balanced in that it reviews state, local, and federal personnel systems. Emphasis on state and local systems is appropriate, especially considering the dramatic growth in the number of employees at those levels in recent decades. Great variation exists among these levels of governments and within them. Therefore, the reader should avoid overgeneralizations. What exists in any one government does not necessarily exist in other governments.

Personnel systems are treated in a broad context that is not limited to activities performed by personnel administrators. The reason is that an understanding of human behavior in government requires looking beyond traditional personnel functions. Therefore, the discussions include motivation theory along with specific techniques such as flexitime, management by objectives, organization development, quality circles, and total quality management.

The first two chapters serve as an overall introduction. The first chapter, "Introduction," differentiates public from private personnel and discusses how personnel systems are part of the larger governmental organization. Chapter 2, "Patronage and the Merit Principle," explains how and why personnel systems emerged and the organizational arrangements that have developed for furthering the merit principle.

The next five chapters are sequenced according to major personnel processes. Chapter 3, "Organizational and Job Design, Position Classification, and Personnel Planning," shows how bureaucracies can be structured and how jobs are established within bureaucratic units. The focus is determining what work is to be done in each job and the categorization of jobs into classes and series. Attention is given to forecasting future needs for personnel. The assigning of pay to groups of jobs and individual jobs is discussed in Chapter 4, "Pay and Employee Benefits." Chapter 4 also is concerned with employee benefits as a form of compensation. With positions having been defined and pay assigned to them, attention turns to "Recruitment, Examination, and Selection" in Chapter 5, with emphasis on the validity of testing programs. Chapter 6, "Probation and Performance Evaluation," discusses what happens to individuals after they become public workers. The concept of merit pay is given extended treatment. Chapter 7, "Careers and Career Development," focuses on promotion procedures and training as a vehicle for career development; career executives are of special concern.

The second half of the book deals with special problems associated with personnel systems. Chapters 8 and 9 concentrate on employee rights. Chapter 8, "Employee Rights and Responsibilities," discusses such critical matters as employee ethical responsibilities, loyalty and security problems, political rights of workers, and rights in adverse action proceedings. Chapter 9, "Equal Rights and Affirmative Action," identifies the numerous ways in which people have been discriminated against and the individual and collective remedies that have emerged. Chapter 9 emphasizes judicial interpretations of equal opportunity in employment and discusses the controversial topic of comparable worth.

The next two chapters deal with topics that usually are considered the responsibility not of personnel administrators but of line administrators. Chapter 10, "Motivation Theory," discusses why people behave as they do from the perspective of theories relating to individual motivation. Chapter 11, "Motivation in Daily Operations," reviews the opportunities and limitations of applying motivation theories. Daily management problems provide frequent obstacles to motivation.

Labor–management problems are reserved for the last substantive chapter, although this significant subject is kept in view throughout. Chapter 12, "Labor–Management Relations," pulls together those earlier discussions, explains the processes of collective negotiations, and discusses the implications for governmental operations.

Finally, "Critique" looks to the future. With earlier chapters having cited numerous strengths and weaknesses of contemporary personnel systems, this one considers the extent to which substantial changes are needed and whether appropriate changes are likely to occur. Of special concern is the need for a newly stated set of internally consistent concepts that can help guide the future development of public personnel systems.

This book is intended for a wide audience. For those contemplating careers in government, the material provides a general background on how personnel functions are carried out at all levels of government and how personnel systems affect the lives of public employees. A sensitivity to the techniques and issues associated with personnel administration is essential for all government employees. Another audience consists of those who have a career objective of being personnel administrators; the discussion can serve as a starting point in such a study. Another audience is current government workers in both personnel and nonpersonnel jobs; the discussion can serve as a review of some familiar issues as well as an update on current trends. Ideally, all readers will gain from this book an increased awareness of the immense importance of personnel systems in government.

Acknowledgments

I am thankful for the encouragement I have received from friends and colleagues throughout the United States. Numerous scholars and practitioners have asked about a new edition of the book, and I hope this third edition meets their expectations. I also appreciate the support I received from the Department of Public Administration of The Pennsylvania State University. Miriam Fultz and Beth Ondo typed the manuscript and made the seemingly endless corrections needed in the process of revising and editing.

I deeply appreciate the encouragement and support that I have received, but the final product ultimately is my responsibility.

Robert D. Lee, Jr.

Chapter 1

Introduction

A government is not just what exists on the printed pages of a constitution and in statute books. Although these documents are extremely important in setting the framework for what a government does, documents by themselves do nothing. People must make decisions about what government should and should not do. People must make decisions about how government services are to be provided, and people—not laws and regulations—provide those services. Citizens benefit not from the dollars spent on public programs but from the services provided by public workers.

This is a book about people in government, but not all government personnel are considered. Generally beyond the scope here are legislatures and their staffs, courts and their staffs, and chief executives. The focus here is career personnel and, to a lesser extent, noncareer personnel who work for the executive branches of federal, state, and local governments. The concern is the methods by which human resources are managed in governments.

This chapter has three sections that:

1. differentiate public personnel systems from those in the private sector
2. consider the growth of public bureaucracies and the magnitude of personnel in government
3. discuss the characteristics of systems and how personnel systems are parts of larger systems

PUBLIC AND PRIVATE SECTOR COMPARISONS

Both government and industry hire millions of workers, but the two are different in their basic missions and the ways in which they manage human

1

resources. One basic difference in missions is that the private sector is profit oriented, but the public sector is not. Profits result from selling goods and services at prices that are higher than costs. Costs are minimized to maximize profits. Industry, therefore, has an incentive to hire only those people it needs. Industry avoids overhiring and has an incentive to hire individuals who will be productive. Private sector employees whose productivity declines tend to be demoted or dismissed, although so-called deadwood is to be found in both sectors. Government, of course, is concerned with providing quality services with as few resources as possible, but it lacks the profit incentive that encourages keeping personnel costs low.

Competition is another aspect of a market economy based on the profit motive. A corporation attempts to keep process and production costs low to have a competitive advantage over other firms. If personnel costs push prices upward, the firm's sales will fall and so will profits. On the other hand, government in most instances operates as a monopoly rather than as part of a competitive market economy. A city fire department has a monopoly on its services, so that consumers do not have a choice about quality and cost. Government also has the option of raising tax rates and borrowing extensively to offset high operating costs. Although a corporation might be forced out of business if personnel costs rise excessively, government is not under such a constraint. Rapidly rising expenditures coupled with tax increases can result in taxpayer revolts and can lead to bankruptcy or near-bankruptcy, as in the case of New York City in the 1970s; nevertheless, governments are not threatened with extinction. The suggestion has been made that government programs should become more competitive and entrepreneurial, which presumably will foster increased efficiency in the use of human resources.[1]

The public sector is labor intensive. Industry uses raw materials and machines that turn those materials into finished goods. Government, in contrast, typically provides services and not products, and in most instances those services must be provided by people rather than by machines. Industry frequently has a choice between people and machines. If the cost of labor increases, industry will replace expensive workers with less expensive machines. The profit incentive encourages such shifts in personnel utilization. Much of what government does, on the other hand, defies mechanization. For example, mail-sorting machines may be able to replace some workers, but people still are required for mail delivery. Similarly, there are limits on the ability to substitute machines for teachers, road repair workers, and firefighters.

In some respects, society probably expects more of government workers than it does of private workers. High ethical standards are expected of public employees. Although some private sector practices may be shrugged off with "that's just business," those same practices in government would arouse public outcry. Government workers serving the commonweal are expected to avoid conflicts of interest in which special interests and personal benefits might be furthered at the expense of the public interest. On the other hand, the public probably believes that private sector employees are more efficient and productive than government workers. Neither generalization invariably holds true.

Managers in the private sector may have greater freedom in personnel matters than public managers. A corporation has considerable flexibility in how it hires and fires people. By comparison, public administrators frequently feel bound by bureaucratic red tape on personnel actions. This distinction between the two sectors, however, should not be overdrawn. State and federal laws affect many private sector personnel matters. Private sector occupational safety, pension system laws, unemployment compensation, equal employment opportunity, and labor relations are regulated by government. Indeed, government sets many of the rules by which industry must operate.

Authority is more structured in the private sector than in the public. In a corporation, an employee rarely is uncertain about who is the boss. In government, authority is more dispersed. Not only are there sometimes conflicting lines of authority within the executive branch, but there also are great uncertainties over the relative powers of the executive and legislative branches vis-à-vis public employees. Workers are expected to be responsive both to their administrative superiors and to legislators. Public employees may find themselves in positions in which they are responsible for implementing a statute that has strong legislative support but is basically opposed by the political leadership in the executive branch.

Another contrast is that the executive branch of government is led by amateurs/ politicians with short tenure, whereas the private sector has longer-term, experienced executives. A departmental secretary is appointed by and serves at the pleasure of the chief executive. Continuity of leadership in departments and major agencies is rare in any large government. Politically appointed executives obtain positions in part because of their roles in partisan politics, whereas private sector executives are more likely to be chosen because of their technical and managerial capabilities. This is not intended to suggest that politically appointed managers are incompetent and that private sector managers always are well qualified but rather to indicate that different sets of criteria are applied in selecting executives in the two sectors.

One other distinguishing feature is the single purpose served by personnel in the private sector compared with the multiple purposes served by those in the public sector. Industry uses people to make products and deliver services. Government uses people for these functions but for other reasons as well[2]:

- Government jobs have been used to reward the politically faithful; patronage has been—and continues to be—a common characteristic of all governments.

- Government employment is used to aid veterans, who are favored in being hired and promoted.
- Government employment sometimes is used to stimulate the economy; unemployed persons are hired by governments as a device for increasing consumer spending. Public employment then becomes a disguised form of welfare.
- Government jobs have been handed out by regional quota systems. Until 1978 the federal government set quotas on the mix of its workers in the Washington, DC area. By setting limits on the number of people hired from each state, it was thought that the bureaucracy would be more representative of the population.

In addition to contrasts, there are similarities between government and the private sector. One is a wide range in the nature of jobs. Both have jobs that greatly affect the general citizenry. Both also have many intrinsically dull jobs. Industry has the assembly line, where people often seem to be appendages of machines. Government has paperwork; workers may complain about the tedium of forms processing, yet those forms are what provide their jobs.

Both sectors have units that range from small to large. There are "Mom and Pop" stores and "Mom and Pop" local governments. The private sector has giants such as General Dynamics, General Electric, and General Motors, and the public sector has giant city governments such as those of Los Angeles, Philadelphia, and Detroit. State governments range from comparatively small to large employers. The federal government is the largest single employer in the country.

MAGNITUDE AND GROWTH OF BUREAUCRACIES

Government employment has grown from a minuscule number of employees to constitute a major segment of the labor market.[3] As of 1990, one of every six jobs in the country was in government. Under the Articles of Confederation the federal government had few employees, but with the adoption of the Constitution in 1789 an executive branch was created, from which the present giant bureaucracy eventually emerged.

Growth originally was slow. As late as 1816 there were fewer than 5,000 full- and part-time civilian employees in the federal service. After the Civil War, the number of federal employees increased exponentially, for example from more than 50,000 in 1871 to 100,000 in 1881. The period of most rapid growth was from the Depression through World War II. In 1931 there were only 610,000 employees, but by 1945, the peak of the wartime economy, the number had climbed to nearly 4 million. Within a year, this was reduced to less than 3 million.

Although the U.S. budget has grown dramatically since World War II, from $35 billion in 1947 to $1,500 billion ($1.5 trillion) in 1993, federal employment has remained relatively constant. Figure 1–1 shows that it has remained between 2 and 3 million; only once during this period (in 1950) has it dropped below 2 million.

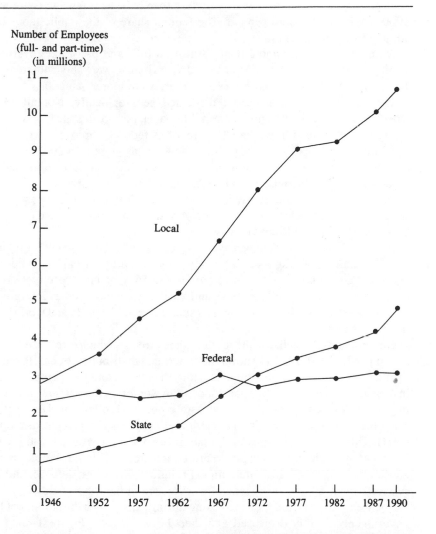

Figure 1–1 Federal, State, and Local Employment, 1946–1990. *Sources*: *Historical Statistics on Governmental Finances and Employment*, U.S. Census Bureau, U.S. Government Printing Office, 1985; and *Public Employment*, U.S. Census Bureau, U.S. Government Printing Office, selected years.

State and local employment, on the other hand, has shown dramatic growth. State employment just after World War II was equal to about half the federal total, but state employees now outnumber those in U.S. service (in 1990, 4.5 million compared to 3.1 million). Local government employment leaped from less than 3 million in 1947 to close to 11 million in 1990. After World War II, such employees accounted for slightly less than half the public work force; by 1990 they constituted 60 percent. The federal share of the public labor force slipped from 34 percent to less than 20 percent.

Altogether, there are more than 18 million full- and part-time government workers in the United States. After World War II, there were about 400 for every 10,000 persons in the country; by 1990, there were more than 600.

These workers, of course, are dispersed geographically. Not all federal workers are in the Washington metropolitan area, nor do all state workers work in their state capitals. Less than 15 percent of federal employees work in the Washington metropolitan area; California alone has more than 300,000 federal civilian workers. The federal government has workers concentrated in regional cities such as San Francisco and Philadelphia, but other workers are dispersed throughout the country at such facilities as military installations and post offices. State employees similarly are dispersed. A state such as Illinois needs offices in Chicago, Peoria, and Rockford as well as in Springfield.

Personnel are the most expensive components of a government's operating budget; salaries and wages constitute about one third of current costs. For state and local governments, the figures are 39 and 54 percent, respectively (these calculations exclude capital outlays and various transfers such as intergovernmental expenditures, benefits programs such as Social Security and welfare, and interest on debt).

Governments specialize in the services they provide, which is reflected in their use of personnel. Table 1-1 shows the functional distribution of employees for the three main levels of government. More than half of all local employees are in education, as are almost 40 percent of state workers. These figures reflect the importance of local school districts and state-operated colleges and universities. The other major state function is health and hospitals (18 percent of employment). Other local functions are small in comparison with education; only 7 percent of employment is in police protection. Federal civilian employment is concentrated in two fields: international relations, including defense, and mail service. About 60 percent of federal workers are in these two fields.

Local employment has been increasing during a time when the number of local governments sharply decreased and then began to rise (Figure 1-2). Local governments declined from more than 140,000 in 1942 to about 78,000 in 1972. Between 1972 and 1992 they increased to 87,000, largely as a result of growth in the number of special districts. The overall loss of 60,000 governments between 1942 and 1972 is explained largely by state-mandated school district

Table 1–1 Percentage Distribution of Employment by Level of Government and Function, 1990

Function	Total	Federal (Civilian)	State	Local
National defense and international relations	6	33	0	0
Postal service	4	26	0	0
Education	43	*	37	55
Highways	3	*	7	3
Health and hospitals	10	9	18	8
Police protection	5	3	2	7
Natural resources	2	7	4	*
Financial and other government administration	5	5	5	4
Other	22	17	27	23
TOTALS	100	100	100	100

*Less than 1 percent.

Source: *Public Employment: 1990*, U.S. Census Bureau, U.S. Government Printing Office, 1991.

consolidations; the number of districts dropped from 109,000 in 1942 to fewer than 15,000 in 1982. Since then, there have been relatively small changes in the number of local governments. The number of counties, cities, townships, and school districts is largely stable, although the number of special districts has increased from only 12,000 in 1952 to 33,000 in 1992, making them the most common form of local government in the United States.

Employment is distributed unevenly among the various types of local government. Table 1–2 indicates that school districts account for nearly half of all local employment and are followed by municipalities at 25 percent. Special districts, although the most numerous type of local government, hire only 5 percent of all such personnel. Counties have the largest average work force (712 employees) and school districts the second largest (340). The high figure for counties is explained in part by the fact that many counties operate schools and some have community colleges. About 25 percent of county government employment is in education.

These average figures should be interpreted with care because they can obscure the great variation in size among governments of the same type. Although cities have an average of about 140 employees, some are far above that figure and others are far below. The City of Los Angeles, for example, has about 51,000 employees, a figure that is greater than the population of many cities in the country. These variations must be kept in mind, for they greatly influence the

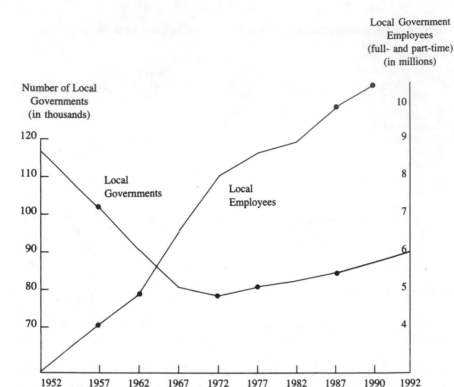

Figure 1-2 Number of Local Governments, 1952–1992, and Local Employees, 1951–1990. *Sources: Historical Statistics on Governmental Finances and Employment*, U.S. Census Bureau, U.S. Government Printing Office, 1985; and *Public Employment*, U.S. Census Bureau, U.S. Government Printing Office, selected years; and *Government Units in 1992: Primary Report*, U.S. Census Bureau, U.S. Government Printing Office, 1992.

---

nature of specific public personnel systems. Small jurisdictions tend to have less formalized personnel procedures than large ones.

The public work force always is undergoing change. One change that did not occur in the 1970s and 1980s, however, was a reduction in the number of employees. "Cutback management" and "retrenchment" were popular terms, but efforts to reduce the size of these bureaucracies simply did not materialize. Instead, growth continued, although it was expected to do so at a comparatively slow pace for the remainder of the century. One forecast suggested that public employment between 1990 and 2005 would grow at about the same rate as total employment, with much of the growth occurring in state and local government and the field of education.[4] The increased need for teachers was expected to result from the "echo effect" of post–World War II baby boomers having children.[5]

Table 1–2 Local Government Units, 1992, and Employees, 1990

Government Unit	Number of Governments	Full- and Part-Time Employees Number (000)	Percent	Average Number of Employees
Counties	3,043	2,167	20	712
Municipalities	19,296	2,642	25	137
Townships	16,666	418	4	25
School Districts	14,556	4,950	46	340
Special Districts	33,131	585	5	18
TOTALS	86,692	10,760	100	124

Sources: Public Employment: 1990 , U.S. Census Bureau, U.S. Government Printing Office, 1991; and *Government Units in 1992: Preliminary Report*, U.S. Census Bureau, U.S. Government Printing Office, 1992.

Growth in public employment could be slowed through greater use of contracting for services or privatization. All levels of government are making greater use of private firms in the delivery of public services. Contracting out solves many personnel problems because workers are employed by private employers, not government. It should be recognized, however, that this constitutes a disguised form of public employment in that many thousands of private jobs exist because of government contracts.

The public work force is changing not only in its size but also in its composition. Later chapters of this book explore changes in the age, sex, and racial composition of that work force. Another change to note is the mix of full- and part-time employees. About a quarter of both state and local workers hold part-time jobs; in the federal government, about 4 percent of the workers have part-time jobs and another 3 percent have intermittent jobs.

PERSONNEL SYSTEMS

Before delving into the core subject of this book, some terminology must be clarified. "Human resource management" is a popular term but generally is not used here.[6] The reason is that treating people as "resources" seems to connote that they are like other materials used in government such as paper, pencils, asphalt for roads, and guns for police officers. "Public personnel" is the term used here.

Identifying what is a public personnel system is difficult. If people make government run—and this book is a study of people in government—then seemingly all aspects of government are germane to the discussion. The focus needs to be narrower, however, and this is accomplished by using the concept of a system, defined simply as a "set of units with relationships among them."[7]

A social system is composed of organizations, individuals, the values they hold, and the relationships among these units and values. A system can be thought of as a network typically consisting of many different parts, with messages flowing among the parts. Systems have boundaries that distinguish them from other systems; these can be considered subsystems, which are parts of larger systems. Personnel systems, then, can be viewed as components or subsystems of the larger governmental/political system.

One way of defining a personnel system is to limit it to personnel-related agencies. Job-testing agencies, training bureaus, boards that hear appeals from employees facing dismissal, and other similar units would constitute the system. A related approach would be to set boundaries by limiting the system to what personnel administrators do. Among other things, they recruit and test people for public jobs and are involved in promotions and disciplinary actions. This has been described as a "maintenance" system or a subsystem that is not directly related to the main function of the organization.[8] In other words, personnel systems can be seen as facilitating the continuation of the organization through supplying needed workers, but that process in itself is only ancillary to the entity's main goals and objectives. Personnel systems can be viewed as providing facilitative functions and not immediately serving such ends as combating crime, mental illness, or illiteracy.

The focus here, however, is broader in that it is concerned more generally with how employees perform in, and are treated by, government. Managers necessarily are included. For example, disciplinary actions against workers are initiated not by personnel departments but by line managers. Motivating workers to perform efficiently and effectively is less the responsibility of personnel administrators than of line managers, who work closely with their subordinates on a daily basis. The personnel system must be defined to include line managers because they influence behavior in organizations. Chapters 10 and 11 consider various motivation theories and their potential for application by government managers.

Individual government workers surely must be considered part of personnel systems. Involved here are difficult value issues about the rights of individuals who choose to work for government. On the one hand, people do not relinquish their citizenship when accepting government jobs, and it can be argued that they should retain all personal freedoms. On the other hand, government can claim that it has a right to insist upon certain standards of conduct. Conflict between individual and government rights is particularly acute in matters of free speech, political participation, and collective bargaining and the right to strike.

Unions that represent groups of workers in collective bargaining constitute another important set of elements of public personnel systems. Unions usually are organized on a national basis, and their national policies affect state and local personnel systems as well as the federal system. Collective bargaining in the public sector gained considerable ground in the 1960s and 1970s, but by the 1990s major problems remained as to how to integrate that process with the other components of personnel systems.

Politically appointed executives need to be included in the system, as do career executives. A critical relationship exists between career employees, who have obtained their jobs on the basis of merit, and political executives, who have received their positions through partisan activities. Political executives frequently are amateurs, having less substantive knowledge about their agencies' programs than their subordinates. These executives have neither broad public support nor continuous, strong backing from their own chief executives. Personnel systems often seem to block political executives from taking actions they consider essential.[9,10]

The boundary of a personnel system must be extended even farther to include chief executives and aspects of the judicial and legislative branches of government. Legislative bodies must be considered, at least in terms of the laws that have established parameters for personnel actions. For example, such laws set standards for the dismissal of incompetent workers. Chief executives must be included because they issue executive orders that establish ground rules for many forms of personnel activities. For example, collective bargaining in the federal government was established initially by a presidential executive order. Courts—both state and federal—are part of the personnel system in that they interpret constitutional provisions and statutes that affect government workers.

Intergovernmental relationships are another aspect of personnel systems. Local governments have been created by their respective state governments and must follow their state's statutes. State and local governments are required to adhere to the U.S. Constitution and pertinent national laws. Local personnel systems are not independent but rather are subject to extensive controls by federal and state governments. In recent years one of the greatest influences on state and local personnel systems has been the federal court system.

Many nonprofit organizations influence the character of public personnel systems.[11] Universities train many of the people who serve in governments and impart standards of conduct to varying degrees in their instructional programs:

- The National Association of Schools of Public Affairs and Administration represents higher education programs that are major providers of administrators for government.
- The American Association of Collegiate Schools of Business provides students with business training that can lead to careers in government.

- The International Personnel Management Association is especially concerned with personnel.
- The American Society for Public Administration and the Association for Public Policy Analysis and Management are involved with furthering professionalism in government management.
- The National Association of State Budget Officers is an example of the more specialized professional groups.
- The Council of State Governments, the National League of Cities, the International City/County Management Association, and the National Association of Counties deal with improved management practices, including personnel practices, for their respective constituencies.
- Many other organizations from time to time are involved with aspects of personnel systems. Veterans organizations, civil rights groups, and other associations have been important lobbyists on state and federal laws affecting public personnel.

The general citizenry also is part of public personnel systems. Citizens make demands upon the bureaucracy and complain frequently that government workers are insensitive to the needs of the people they serve. A particularly difficult problem is balancing citizens' rights with those of government workers, who also are citizens. For instance, to what extent should workers be insulated from citizen and client pressure, especially from liability suits?

Public personnel systems should be viewed as dynamic processes involving group efforts to win acceptance of their values. Superseding all other values in the effort to reform personnel systems has been the merit principle, which maintains that personnel decisions should be based on criteria relating to how well an individual performs a job. Chapter 2 explores that principle in conjunction with the reform effort to oust patronage from government personnel systems. Many of the proponents of the merit principle have argued that it is incompatible with other values such as preferences for veterans, minorities, and women and the rights of workers to organize and bargain collectively. These conflicts on values are cast in terms of issues such as who should set personnel policies, what those policies should be, who should execute them, and how they should be translated into daily operations.

There is no single public personnel system; instead, there are many. Any one government may have several personnel systems in that different groups of workers are influenced by different agencies. Some units within a government may have authority for recruiting and selecting their own employees, whereas others must fill positions through a central personnel agency such as a civil service commission.

Although fragmentation may best describe what currently exists, at the same time all personnel systems—federal, state, and local—are related to each other.

Changes made in one system are felt in others. Because of the numerous systems and the numerous parts that constitute them, the student of public personnel must be careful not to become myopic.

Chapter 2 helps clarify the relationship between personnel functions and agencies. That chapter and those that follow, however, should not be considered independent discussions but rather as being integrally related to each other. The chapters organize the discussion to provide clarity, but given the multiplicity of people, organizational units, and values associated with public personnel systems, each chapter's discussion cannot be an airtight compartment.

In the following chapters, perspective is provided in terms of how personnel systems developed and how they currently operate. Attention is given to perceived problems, options for dealing with these problems, and the impetus for reform.[12] A concern for the future of personnel systems is evident throughout the discussion.[13–15]

SUMMARY

Important distinctions exist between public and private sector personnel systems. The profit motive in the private sector encourages the minimization of personnel costs, but government does not operate under such an incentive. Competition in the private sector also encourages efficient and effective use of personnel. Government is labor intensive and has fewer opportunities to mechanize operations than industry. Higher ethical standards are imposed on public workers. Private sector managers may have greater freedom in making personnel decisions. Lines of authority are distinct in the private sector, whereas public sector workers are subject to conflicting channels of authority. Unlike the private sector, the public sector uses personnel for reasons unrelated to the provision of services; these factors include patronage, aid to special groups such as veterans, and economic stimulation.

Government employment is a major segment of the nation's economy. The number of federal employees has grown from virtually none in the 1780s to 3 million in the 1990s. Since World War II, employment at the federal level has been largely unchanged but has grown rapidly at state and local levels. Federal employment is concentrated generally in defense and mail service, and state and local employment is heavily committed to education. Local employment has been increasing during a period when the number of local governments decreased and then plateaued. Among local governments, counties have the largest average work force followed by school districts and cities.

Personnel systems are part of the larger governmental system. A personnel system is not restricted to personnel agencies but must include the employees affected by those agencies and their supervisors. Legislative bodies, chief executives, courts, and the general citizenry are important components of the systems, as are intergovernmental relations, labor organizations, and professional and governmental associations. At stake are major value issues, especially how the merit principle should be applied in personnel decisions.

NOTES

1. D. Osborne and T. Gaebler, *Reinventing Government: How the Entrepreneurial Spirit Is Transforming the Public Sector* (Reading, Mass.: Addison-Wesley Publishing Company, 1992).

2. Subcommittee on Civil Service and General Services, Senate Committee on Governmental Affairs, *Repeal of Apportionment Requirement: Hearings*, 95th Cong., 1st sess. (Washington: U.S. Government Printing Office, 1977).

3. The data for this section are from the following Census Bureau publications via the U.S. Government Printing Office: *Historical Statistics on Governmental Finances and Employment* (1974 and 1985); *Historical Statistics of the United States: Colonial Times to 1970* (1975); *Governmental Finances in 1989–90* (1991); *Public Employment in 1990* (1991); *City Employment: 1990* (1991); and *Statistical Abstract* (1991).

4. R.E. Kutscher, New BLS projections: Findings and implications, *Monthly Labor Review* 114 (November 1991): 3–12.

5. V.A. Personick, A second look at industry output and employment trends through 1995, *Monthly Labor Review* 109 (November 1985): 26–41.

6. C.J. Lindley, Putting "human" into human resource management, *Public Personnel Management* 13 (1984): 501–510.

7. J.G. Miller, Living systems: Basic concepts, *Behavioral Science* 10 (1965): 200.

8. D. Katz and R.L. Kahn, *The Social Psychology of Organizations* (New York: John Wiley & Sons, 1978), 156–157.

9. H. Heclo, *A Government of Strangers: Executive Politics in Washington* (Washington: Brookings Institution, 1977).

10. L.E. Lynn, Jr., *Managing the Public's Business: The Job of the Government Executive* (New York: Basic Books, 1981).

11. R.D. Lee, Jr., Participants in the public personnel management process, *Policy Studies Journal* 11 (1982): 261–270.

12. J. Matzer, Jr., ed., *Personnel Practices for the '90s: A Local Government Guide* (Washington: International City Management Association, 1988).

13. Hudson Institute for U.S. Office of Personnel Management, *Civil Service 2000* (Washington: U.S. Government Printing Office, 1988).

14. U.S. General Accounting Office, *The Changing Workforce: Demographic Issues Facing the Federal Government* (Washington: U.S. Government Printing Office, 1992).

15. _____, *The Public Service: Issues Confronting the Federal Civil Workforce* (Washington: U.S. Government Printing Office, 1992).

Chapter 2

Patronage and the Merit Principle

The practice of appointing friends or political associates to public jobs has been characteristic of governments in the United States. Although patronage has been under strong attack for more than a century and the reform effort to eliminate it has been successful in many respects, vestiges of the practice remain. The merit principle has been advocated as the appropriate alternative to patronage. As this chapter shows, a concise definition of merit does not exist, but for the moment merit can be considered making personnel decisions based on the qualifications or capabilities of individuals rather than on their political allegiances or friendships.

This chapter discusses:

1. the rise of political patronage and the attempts to eliminate it
2. alternative organizational arrangements that have been used in furthering the merit principle

PATRONAGE AND REFORM IN PERSPECTIVE

One approach to the history of government appointments is to suggest that there were three main periods:

1. The period extending from the presidency of George Washington through that of John Quincy Adams was characterized by appointments to government based largely on the qualifications of individuals.
2. The period beginning in 1829 with the administration of Andrew Jackson saw the patronage or spoils system flourish.
3. The period that began in 1883 with the passage of the Pendleton Act reaffirmed the principle of merit and created the U.S. Civil Service Commission.[1]

(Important volumes on civil service reform aside from those cited separately throughout this section are listed at the end of the chapter.[2-11])

Such an interpretation is technically correct but overly simplistic in that it ignores the vast changes that have occurred since the adoption of the Constitution. A review of American history, of course, is beyond the scope of this book, but it should be recognized that the rise and fall of patronage occurred in the context of major societal and governmental changes. Events of the first era, which lasted until 1829, included substantial growth in the geographical size of the country (especially through the Louisiana Purchase), the War of 1812, and the increasing use of slaves. By 1830 there were more than 2 million African-Americans in the country, constituting 18 percent of the population.[12] The period from 1829 to 1883 included westward movement of the population, the end of slavery, the introduction of railroads, extensive industrialization, and a large influx of immigrants.

The years following the Declaration of Independence were truly formative ones for government. A major issue was determining what should be the relative powers of the national and state governments. The initial decision, incorporated in the Articles of Confederation, called for strong states and a weak national government. The Articles created a U.S. Congress but no executive branch to implement the legislation it adopted. This distribution of powers was not changed until 1789, when the Constitution was adopted, and in the interim states experimented with new governmental forms. States wrote constitutions that provided for the separation of powers among legislative, executive, and judicial branches; these documents included a bill of rights to protect the citizenry against abuses that had been prevalent during colonial rule.

One common requirement in early state constitutions was rotation in office through fixed terms with limitations on reelection. That practice continues today, with many governors being allowed to serve only two consecutive terms (the same is true for presidents). Several states in 1992 adopted additional term limitation measures. The original justification for rotation was that it provided a means of educating people in the operations of government. In time, rotation came to be justified as preventing the rise of a king; tyrannical government could not emerge because officeholders were required periodically to relinquish their positions.[13]

Information about the early application of the rotation principle to appointed state officers is sketchy. There are no accurate records for that period as to how many people worked for state or local governments. It seems likely, however, that the type of patronage that emerged in the mid-1800s could not have existed earlier because there were relatively few government jobs to be filled then.

With the adoption of the Constitution, attention was focused on the method of appointing officials of the new executive branch. The Constitution grants

Congress, and not the president, the power to decide how "lesser officers" are to be appointed, namely whether they are to be appointed by the president, the courts, or department heads.[14]

George Washington was well aware that, as first President of the United States, he could establish a pattern to be followed by his successors. He used the standard of "fitness of character" in making appointments. "Fitness," however, did not mean technical competence but rather was related to personal integrity and social standing. In other words, Washington sought honest individuals from the elite of society. Throughout the period before 1829, persons appointed to high government positions usually were wealthy, had considerable landholdings, and were far better educated than the general public. Another characteristic was that they often were related to one another. Nepotism, the appointment of relatives to government positions, was common, even under Thomas Jefferson, who officially deplored the practice.[15]

One of the most important developments of the prepatronage period was the emergence of national political parties. Parties did not exist when Washington was first elected, and many thought they were a European institution that should be avoided in the new government. Nevertheless, parties had emerged when Washington was elected for a second term. He and his successor, John Adams, were of the Federalist party, which was deposed in the election of 1800 by Jefferson, who was a Democratic-Republican. Upon taking office, Jefferson found that most government positions were held by Federalists and announced that he would use the appointment power to bring "balance" to the composition of the executive branch. For this reason, he sometimes is considered the "father" of political patronage, but that probably is an inappropriate label in that he did not engage in patronage on a wide scale.

The controversy over John Adams' "midnight appointments" is less important to the history of patronage than it is to constitutional history. When Jefferson became president, he found that Adams had appointed persons to judgeships in the last hours of his administration. The necessary paperwork had not been completed, and Jefferson's secretary of state, James Madison, refused to execute the appointments. The case was carried directly to the Supreme Court in *Marbury v. Madison*.[16] The Court, led by John Marshall, who was one of Jefferson's opponents, feared that the Jefferson administration would ignore a ruling on behalf of the office seeker, yet siding with the new administration would seem to suggest that the Court was impotent. The solution: The Court ruled that it had no power to handle the case. The Constitution specifies what cases can be brought directly before the Supreme Court, and the Court held that Congress unconstitutionally had expanded the Court's original jurisdiction by passing the Judiciary Act of 1789. The case established the power of judicial review, setting the Court as the main interpreter of the Constitution. This power now allows the Court to overrule the actions of Congress, the president, and state governments.

Open use of political patronage was introduced in 1829 by President Andrew Jackson. In his first inaugural address, he said:

> The recent demonstration of public sentiment inscribes on the list of Executive duties, in characters too legible to be overlooked, the task of *reform*, which will require particularly the correction of those abuses that have brought the patronage of the Federal Government into conflict with the freedom of elections, and the counteraction of those causes which have disturbed the rightful course of appointment and have placed or continued power in unfaithful or incompetent hands.
>
> In the performance of a task thus generally delineated, I shall endeavor to select men whose diligence and talents will insure in their respective stations able and faithful cooperation, depending for the advancement of the public service more on the integrity and zeal of the public officers than on their numbers.[17]

One era had closed and another had begun. Turnover of federal workers in the Jackson administration was not as great as might have been expected, but widespread firings and replacements by the politically favored were characteristic of subsequent administrations. "Polk (1845–49) removed more incumbents than any of the ten presidents who preceded him."[18] Patronage became equally prominent at the state and local levels.

Democratization must be credited or blamed for the rise of patronage. The size of the electorate expanded greatly, and so did the rate of voter participation. In the 1824 election of John Quincy Adams, there were 356,000 voters—27 percent of the electorate. By the 1840 election of William Henry Harrison, in contrast, 2.4 million persons voted—80 percent of the electorate. In those intervening 16 years, the electorate increased from 1.3 million to 3.0 million, a growth of 126 percent, and the number of persons voting soared by 575 percent.

These increases cannot be accounted for in terms of population growth. The white male population, the electorate of the era, grew by only 82 percent between 1820 and 1840. What had occurred was the lowering of barriers to voting, such as requirements to own property and to pay poll taxes. Persons previously disenfranchised not only could vote but did vote. From 1840 to the close of the century, 70 to 80 percent of the electorate voted in presidential elections.[19]

The introduction of mass voting necessitated strong party organization to win elections. From the parties' perspectives, voters needed to be informed about which candidates and parties could best serve their interests. Many voters could not read newspapers because of illiteracy or inability to read English. Party workers, therefore, were required to disseminate information. This periodic, labor-intensive activity created a pool of individuals who sought government jobs as a reward for their efforts. Jackson did not invent patronage but instead had it thrust upon him.

Political patronage as practiced in the 1800s had both advantages and disadvantages. On the negative side, patronage resulted in high turnover of personnel, thereby making government inefficient because of constant staff changes and lack of continuity. Inefficiency also stemmed from deliberate featherbedding, in which two political associates were hired when only one really was needed. On the other hand, turnover was a protection against elitist government and the rise of a monarchy. The patronage system provided an important route of upward mobility for people from the lower class. It also provided a simple mechanism for removing so-called deadwood.

Patronage has been attacked for resulting in incompetent people running government. Individuals received government jobs because of political ties, despite their lack of the skills and knowledge required by the jobs. This argument would be persuasive if it were applied to the type of work carried out by today's government, but it is not fully so in terms of the 1800s. Nontechnical jobs largely characterized that early period, and patronage proponents could contend that virtually anyone could carry out the duties of most jobs. Patronage, at least at the federal level, seems to have been restricted to nontechnical jobs; agencies involved in technical work, such as the Patent Office, were largely insulated from patronage.[20]

Patronage has been condemned for what it does to employees. Workers who prefer to stay out of politics are required to contribute part of their wages to the party in power and are required to campaign for the reelection of politicians. Low morale can result from such political pressures. Patronage also can be seen as precluding career development in that workers are removed from office whenever a new political party wins control of the government. This line of attack, however, should not be overextended. Patronage as practiced in the 1800s was rotational: One group of workers was dismissed with a change in administration but later was reinstated when their party regained control. Career workers existed in government under the patronage system.

One of the strongest sets of arguments in support of patronage is that it made the bureaucracy responsive to political leadership and helped coordinate the executive and legislative branches of government. Chief executives needed patronage to obtain legislative approval of proposed policies and programs. For example, a mayor could win legislative votes by appointing the friends of city council members. Patronage encouraged government workers to be responsive to the demands of the chief executive. In the words of President Jackson, "faithful cooperation" from workers was likely when they knew they could be dismissed.

Political patronage, however, did not make the bureaucracy as responsive as proponents of the system have suggested. Executives, by appointing political friends of legislators, in many instances named people who were not in agreement with them. To win election, a person needed the support of all factions or wings of the political party and, once elected, was obligated to appoint individuals from all wings of the party.

Another criticism of patronage is that it was excessively time consuming. Chief executives complained that they were too busy with appointments and dismissals and had little time left for policy considerations. President Harrison died during his fourth week in office, and "the opinion of many historians is that the real cause was the spoils system."[21] President Lincoln complained of the many people who sought jobs from him. "Once, when Lincoln was suffering from an attack of smallpox, he asked an assistant to invite the jobseekers in, for at last he had something he could give to all of them."[22]

Reform proceeded piecemeal and in small steps at the federal level. In 1853, an amendment to an appropriations bill required "pass examinations" for the selection of clerical workers. Although the process frequently was abused or ignored, the law was important because it initiated the examination process in the federal government. Nearly 20 years later, in 1871, an amendment to another appropriations bill allowed the president to set rules for personnel actions. Using this authority, President Ulysses S. Grant appointed a civil service commission that drafted regulations that would have greatly reduced the role of patronage, but the panel went out of existence in 1875 when Congress refused to appropriate money for the new system.

Pressure for reform continued to mount and became particularly intense after the assassination of President James A. Garfield by a disgruntled jobseeker in 1881. In January 1883, Congress passed the civil service reform law titled "A Bill To Regulate and Improve the Civil Service of the United States," better known as the Pendleton Act, named after Senator George H. Pendleton (Democrat of Ohio).[23] President Chester A. Arthur signed the bill.[24]

The main features of the new law included competitive examination requirements, security from dismissal for political reasons, and protection from being coerced into political activities. A bipartisan Civil Service Commission was created to oversee the process (the structure of personnel systems is discussed in the next section). Coverage was limited under the new law. At the outset, only about 10 percent of all workers were protected, mostly clerical workers in Washington, DC and employees in large post offices.

State and local governments followed the federal lead. In 1883 New York passed a law similar to the Pendleton Act. Massachusetts acted the next year. But from then until 1905, there was little reform at the state level. Then several states acted to reduce or eliminate patronage: Wisconsin and Illinois in 1905, Colorado in 1907, New Jersey in 1908, and Illinois in 1911.[25]

Civil service clean-up must be viewed in the context of broader governmental reform.[26-31] Many people had been repelled not only by favoritism in the appointment of workers but by widespread corruption at all levels of government. Scandals were common. Lucrative government contracts and franchises were awarded to favored corporations. Looting from the public treasury was extensive. The press played an important role in bringing these scandals to public attention.[32] Much of the corruption was tolerable as long as budgets operated in the black, but by the late 1800s and into the early 1900s financial situations tightened, and budget surpluses turned to deficits.

Structural reforms were introduced at the local level beginning in the late 1800s and at the state level starting around 1910. One thrust of these actions was to concentrate powers in the hands of the chief executive and to hold that person answerable for the administration of government.[33] The movement toward a short ballot was one approach. City charters were rewritten to allow for the election of only a few administrative officers instead of many. Under the strong mayor form of government, the mayor is responsible for appointing department heads. Should those officers engage in dishonest or unethical activities, the mayor is accountable and presumably would be voted out of office. Nonpartisan elections were expected to eliminate corrupt party influences. The council-manager form was introduced with the hope of bringing professional management to city government (one exception to these reforms was the commission plan, in which each elected commissioner operated one of the city's departments).

Financial reforms also were part of this movement. Budget offices were established, usually under the direction of the chief executive. Restrictions were imposed on accounting for revenues and expenditures. Competitive bidding was made mandatory for large government contracts. Audit agencies, independent of the executive, were created to watch for corruption.

The leaders of this reform movement were not average citizens. The civil service reformers generally were Protestant and often from old families and ranged from the economically comfortable to the wealthy. "They were lawyers, editors, clergymen, professors, and mercantile and financial, rather than industrial, businessmen."[34] When the Grant civil service commission was disbanded in 1875, patronage opponents formed the New York Civil Service Reform Association, which later became the National Civil Service Reform League, an active lobbyist for improvement at all levels of government. The individuals involved had little to gain personally from reform but saw their mission as cleaning up government to free the common citizen.[35]

Forces other than reformers helped end the period of spoils. One major factor was that ending patronage was good politics. Many of the members of Congress who voted for the Pendleton Act in early 1883 were lame ducks, having been defeated in the election of November 1882. President Arthur was Republican, and the Senate was basically in the hands of Republicans. The House of

Representatives, as a result of the 1882 election, was scheduled to change from Republican to Democratic control. Therefore, it was good politics to freeze the Republican workers into office. The Republicans also would be able to campaign in 1884 as reformers. In the Senate debate on the Pendleton Act, there was a brief, not entirely facetious, effort to change its name to "A Bill To Perpetuate in Office the Republicans Who Now Hold the Patronage of the Government."[36]

The merit principle has been used by legislative bodies and chief executives for their political advantage. Chief executives who have the power to bring positions under merit coverage by issuing executive orders have used that power before leaving office, thereby blanketing in political appointees. Congress has used the alternative of legislation. Passage of the Hatch Acts of 1939 and 1940 (see Chapter 8), which restrict government workers from participating in politics, was in part politically motivated. These acts blocked President Franklin D. Roosevelt from mobilizing government workers to oppose members of Congress who had not cooperated with his administration.[37-39] Many years later, members of the Nixon administration complained about the extensive use of freezing or blanketing in of political appointees. For example, of the 115,000 jobs in the Department of Health, Education, and Welfare, only 47 were not protected by the merit system.[40] During the transition periods from one political administration to another, representatives of the newly elected administrations at all levels of government frequently complain about their limited abilities to control the bureaucracy because of civil service restrictions.[41,42]

Several other forces can be identified as encouraging the demise of patronage. A rapidly expanding private economy with well-paying jobs made government jobs less attractive. Workers in the private sector not only were paid better but were not required to kick back part of their salaries to the political party (the practice of macing). Various pieces of social legislation limited the role of political machines as entities for helping the needy. Government jobs became increasingly specialized, making it impractical to hire the politically faithful when they were unskilled.[43] In recent years, unions have played an important role in reducing patronage; organized labor, in protecting its membership, opposes dismissals for political reasons (see Chapter 12).

The U.S. Supreme Court became a new factor in the patronage controversy in 1976, when in *Elrod v. Burns* it faced the issue of whether an incoming Democratic sheriff could remove non–civil service workers appointed by the previous Republican sheriff.[44] Five justices, a bare majority of the Court, decided in favor of the workers, but there was no majority opinion, leaving in doubt whether the ruling might be overturned in a future case. Three of the justices in the majority wrote an opinion based on the First and Fourteenth Amendments to the Constitution. The First Amendment provides for freedom of speech and implicitly for the freedom of belief, and the Fourteenth Amendment protects these rights from actions of states and, indirectly, their local governments. The opinion held that patronage restricted freedom of belief and that requiring government workers to contribute to a political party would have the effect of starving the opposition party. The opinion found that there was no evidence that keeping the Republican workers in their jobs should result in subversion of the new administration or in reduced efficiency and effectiveness. The view was that political considerations in removing and appointing government workers should be restricted to policymaking positions.

The dissenting opinions were strong. One said that the case involved an issue that should be decided by each state and that, if such an issue arose in the federal government, Congress, not the court system, should handle the problem. Chief Justice Warren Burger labeled the Court's ruling "a classic example of trivializing constitutional adjudication." The dissenters observed that patronage was "as old as the Republic" and had "contributed significantly to the democratization of American politics." The justices noted an earlier state supreme court ruling in favor of patronage in which a union attempted to protect its members from political dismissals: "Those who, figuratively speaking, live by the political sword must be prepared to die by the political sword."[45]

A few years later the Court dealt more definitively with the issue. In *Branti v. Finkel* (1980), it held (six to three) that the issue of patronage and dismissal was not whether jobs were of a policymaking or confidential nature.[46] Instead, the majority maintained that a political administration would need to prove that a specific party affiliation for a worker was necessary for effective performance. The ruling imposed a major legal burden on any administration that would like to engage in widescale political dismissals, thus greatly curtailing the use of patronage.

More recently, the Court held that political patronage in basically all aspects of public employment violates the freedoms of speech and belief guaranteed under the First Amendment to the Constitution. In *Rutan v. Republican Party of Illinois* (1990), the Court ruled five to four that hiring, promotion, transfer, and removal decisions could not be based upon political party affiliation except when a "vital government interest" could be shown.[47-49]

As a consequence of history, merit coverage is extensive at the federal level. More than 90 percent of all federal jobs are under a merit system. The largest group falls under the Office of Personnel Management (OPM), followed by the quasi-independent U.S. Postal Service. Other separate merit systems involve the Tennessee Valley Authority and the Foreign Service of the State Department.

Political jobs in the executive branch of the federal government are of several types.[50] The Executive Level I through V pay system covering cabinet members, deputy and assistant secretaries, and other high-ranking officers accounts for only about 500 positions. Below the executives are noncareer executives in the Senior Executive Service (SES). About 700 people are in this category; according to law, no more than 10 percent of the SES may be noncareerists. There are

Schedule C positions, ranging downward from GS-15; these involve either confidential work or policymaking.[51] Confidential workers include clerical employees and chauffeurs. Schedule C accounts for about 1,700 jobs. Political considerations sometimes influence decisions involving the hiring of temporary experts and consultants.[52] Political appointees in the executive branch, however, are a relatively rare breed compared with all 3 million federal civilian employees (Chapter 4 discusses the pay grades involved in these varying types of positions).

OPM has the authority to exempt positions from merit coverage on a case-by-case basis. Schedule A, B, and C exemptions are made under Civil Service Rule VI. Schedule A and B positions involve work that is neither confidential nor policymaking. Schedule A jobs, which number about 140,000, pertain to cases where an examination would be impractical, such as in the hiring of rehabilitated drug addicts to assist in a drug rehabilitation project. Schedule B jobs (more than 12,000) relate to cases where a competitive examination would be impractical but a noncompetitive examination is required. Other exemptions are made under Civil Service Rule VIII, which covers jobs outside the United States held by noncitizens (about 120,000 positions). When employees hold these types of positions and then are granted career appointments, suspicion arises that workers with political connections are being favored in appointment to merit positions.[53]

Considerable variation in merit coverage exists at the state and local levels. The variations involve not only the number of employees covered but also numerous aspects of coverage, such as politically motivated decisions about civil service test results and worker layoffs. Some local personnel systems may be merit in name but political in practice; gaps exist between what protection employees officially have and what they really have. Some jurisdictions protect almost all employees from patronage pressures; in some cases, only a handful of non–civil service positions exist in a government. A 1989 survey found that merit systems existed in 65 percent of cities with 10,000 population or more and in 58 percent of counties with 25,000 population or more.[54]

Politicial elections create periods of uncertainty and confusion for both patronage and career employees. As an election approaches, some political appointees resign their positions for private employment, others quit to work in an election campaign, and those who remain jockey for appointments to the newly vacated positions. After an election, widespread resignations or removals may occur, especially if the chief executive changes and even when the new executive is of the same political party as the outgoing executive. In these situations, merit employees are unsure of how policies are to be pursued and in many situations are unsure of who is in charge in their agencies. An executive transition is one of the most unsettling times for public agencies.[55,56]

MERIT AND ORGANIZATIONAL RESPONSIBILITIES

A definition of the merit concept has been avoided up to this point. Now the problem must be addressed. Merit is not the same as civil service. In one sense, civil service refers to all appointed civilian workers in government whether they are protected by the merit principle or not. "Civil service" in everyday discussion, however, tends to refer to merit-protected employees, particularly those who come under the protection of a civil service commission. In other words, the concept of merit tends to be confused with the organizational responsibility for promoting the concept. This confusion stems from the fact that civil service commissions were created in response to patronage.

Further confusion is added by a tendency to think of merit as the opposite of patronage, but the two are not simple antonyms. Patronage is nonmerit in that persons may be appointed to positions for reasons other than their capabilities; political loyalty is one of the main considerations. The two terms are not opposites in the sense that one results in the hiring of competent workers and the other of incompetent workers. Given today's political system, patronage or political appointees need to be capable of fulfilling the duties of their positions because incompetence is likely to have unfavorable political ramifications, particularly for those who select them.[57] Appointing "hacks" is unlikely to be in the best political interest of a chief executive. Since passage of the Pendleton Act of 1883 and similar state and local actions, the field of personnel administration has been groping for a definition of merit that is distinct from being simply the antithesis of patronage. Nonmerit activities may involve activities other than political patronage, as in the case of managers favoring their friends or people of particular races in personnel decisions rather than basing those decisions on the qualifications of personnel.[58]

In 1978 Congress passed the Civil Service Reform Act, which greatly altered the federal personnel system. The law identified nine principles of merit:

1. Recruitment should be from qualified individuals from appropriate sources in an endeavor to achieve a work force from all segments of society, and selection and advancement should be determined solely on the basis of relative ability, knowledge, and skills, after fair and open competition which assures that all receive equal opportunity.
2. All employees and applicants for employment should receive fair and equitable treatment in all aspects of personnel management without regard to political affiliation, race, color, religion, national origin, sex, marital status, age, or handicapping condition, and with proper regard for their privacy and constitutional rights.

3. Equal pay should be provided for work of equal value, with appropriate consideration of both national and local rates paid by employers in the private sector, and appropriate incentives and recognition should be provided for excellence in performance.

4. All employees should maintain high standards of integrity, conduct, and concern for the public interest.

5. The Federal work force should be used efficiently and effectively.

6. Employees should be retained on the basis of the adequacy of their performance, inadequate performance should be corrected, and employees should be separated who cannot or will not improve their performance to meet required standards.

7. Employees should be provided effective education and training in cases in which such an education and training would result in better organizational and individual performance.

8. Employees should be—
   A. protected against arbitrary action, personal favoritism, or coercion for partisan political purposes, and
   B. prohibited from using their official authority or influence for the purpose of interfering with or affecting the result of an election or a nomination for election.

9. Employees should be protected against reprisal for the lawful disclosure of information which the employees reasonably believe evidences—
   A. a violation of any law, rule, or regulation, or
   B. mismanagement, a gross waste of funds, an abuse of authority, or a substantial and specific danger to public health or safety.[59,60]

The law provides not only this list of principles but also a list of prohibited personnel practices that basically restates the principles in a negative sense.

When the wording of the nine merit principles is compared with the wording of the principles enunciated in an earlier law, changes in philosophy as to how personnel systems should operate become evident. The Intergovernmental Personnel Act of 1970 had six principles.[61] Both laws emphasize recruiting qualified workers, but the 1978 Act includes recruiting from "all segments of society," reflecting the value that the bureaucracy be representative of society as a whole.[62,63] Both laws support equal pay for equal work, but the newer one emphasizes the use of pay as an incentive and recognition for "excellence in performance." The two laws adhere to the principles of training workers and removing incompetent workers. Nondiscrimination provisions are in both laws, with the 1978 Act extending coverage to marital status, age, and handicap. The laws are opposed to partisan influences on merit employees.

Three additional principles are included in the 1978 Act:

1. Employees are to have "high standards of integrity, conduct, and concern for the public interest." This in part is a response to various scandals.
2. Employees should not be penalized for disclosing information about violations of law, mismanagement, and abuses of authority. In other words, "whistle blowers" in government are to be protected.
3. Employees are to be used efficiently and effectively. This concept is positive, in contrast to the negative aspects of merit, such as preventing partisan and other non-job-related considerations from being used in personnel decisions.

The efficiency and effectiveness provision reflects a growing concern that personnel systems are replete with red tape that hinders rather than encourages effective administration. Personnel administration has been seen as "the triumph of techniques over purpose."[64] The people who work full time in personnel administration constitute a small fraction of the public work force, yet it sometimes seems that personnel administrators have tied the hands of line administrators. For example, OPM and the Merit Systems Protection Board (MSPB) together have about 7,000 employees.[65] They do not begin to reflect the total personnel administration work force, however; thousands are employed by personnel units in line agencies. At the state and local levels, personnel administration also is a comparatively small activity as gauged by the number of workers and expenditures. Emphasis is being shifted away from neutral competence and toward positive administration that meets the public's wishes through the efficient and effective delivery of services.

Criticism of merit systems may be camouflage for a more severe problem in government. Merit systems may simply provide a convenient rationale for managerial ineffectiveness. The chair of the Municipal Manpower Commission of the 1960s said:

> We found in over 600 interviews that in many cases the blame for the inability to make any progress programmatically was placed by management on the civil service system, when in fact the management did not know where it wanted to go, what it wanted to do, and as a result what kind of people it wanted. So it tended to make the system the scapegoat.[66]

What becomes obvious is that merit principles impinge on all aspects of personnel administration. Personnel actions are decisions affecting individuals. These decisions include determining the score of an employment examination, selecting someone for a job, deciding who will attend a training program, and removing an incompetent employee. The merit concept also prescribes how workers are to perform regarding integrity, efficiency, effectiveness, and like concerns. As is demonstrated in subsequent chapters, however, the merit principle frequently is difficult to apply to specific situations. Sweeping generalizations are used to define the merit principle, but the world of personnel administration is detailed, not general. Public personnel systems each day produce specific decisions that affect the lives of government workers, people who would like to acquire such jobs, and the general citizenry.

Assigning organizational responsibility for the various aspects of personnel administration has been a controversial subject ever since the reform movement began in the 1800s.[67] Much of the problem stems from the fact that the function involves legislative, administrative, and judicial responsibilities:

- The legislative process involves the preparation and promulgation of administrative rules and regulations to interpret civil service laws.
- The administrative activities involve such matters as conducting civil service tests and selecting workers for jobs. Another aspect of administration involves enforcement activities to ensure that the regulations are followed.
- Judicial activities include interpreting regulations and reaching decisions about whether particular actions have conformed with those regulations; the judicial role, for instance, involves reviewing appeals of employees who claim that they have been dismissed in violation of merit standards.

How these legislative, administrative, and judicial functions are carried out vis-à-vis the chief executive has been a fundamental issue.[68] As mentioned earlier, the government reform movement of the late 1800s and early 1900s was aimed largely at strengthening the chief executive so that one individual could be held accountable, but the personnel reform effort is a major exception. Rather than strengthening the power of the president, governor, or mayor, early personnel reformers attempted to limit that control.

The device chosen was a civil service commission, usually consisting of three to seven individuals appointed by the executive with the advice and consent of the legislative body. At the federal level, the three-member commission was appointed by the president with the approval of the Senate. Civil service commissions usually are bipartisan, and only a bare majority may be from one political party. Commissioners' terms of office overlap and usually are for a period longer than the executive's term. For example, a governor may have a 4-year term and the commissioners 6-year terms; this also was the case at the federal level.[69–71]

The civil service commission, then, was designed to be largely independent of the chief executive in the hope that such an organizational configuration will prevent political considerations from entering into personnel matters. In this structure, the civil service commission serves as the policymaking body and oversees the operations of the personnel system. Daily operations are the responsibility of an executive director, who is a career employee selected by the merit process who reports directly to the commission as a whole.

Does such an arrangement protect against political influences, and are there disadvantages of this structure? The answer to the first question is, "not necessarily," and to the second, "yes." The National Civil Service League in 1970 made this harsh judgment of independent civil service commissions: "The claim that these commissions are insulating the system against pressures is often unfounded. Experience in many jurisdictions has shown that the deliberations of so-called independent commissions frequently reflect political expediency rather than the requirements of good public personnel administration."[72] The Nixon administration demonstrated an ability to circumvent the merit principle. It prepared an unofficial *Federal Political Personnel Manual* to suggest to political appointees methods for ousting career employees and replacing them with people loyal to the administration. In effect, departments were told to find jobs for party members with the assumption that some civil service rules would need to be bent to accomplish the task.[73,74]

An independent commission can hamper the chief executive in taking positive actions toward personnel management because authority resides in the commission. A situation can develop in which the executive must plead with the commission to adopt regulations and procedures that affect the personnel for whom the executive ultimately is responsible. A common criticism has been that civil service commissions assume a largely negative role, instituting bureaucratic red tape to prevent a resurgence of patronage. The National Civil Service League made this criticism:

> Such commissions are often much more concerned with keeping people out of the public service than in developing new techniques to attract persons into public employment. The roadblocks that these commissions have managed to erect have, in numerous instances, managed to frustrate thoroughly and to cut the effectiveness of some of our most competent and responsible administrators.[75]

President Jimmy Carter voiced a similar sense of frustration: "The system has serious defects. It has become a bureaucratic maze which neglects merit, tolerates poor performance, permits abuse of legitimate employee rights, and mires every personnel action in red tape, delay, and confusion."[76]

Another weakness of the traditional commission structure is that it makes no provision for strong leadership in personnel management. Although the commission has a chair, that individual basically has powers no greater than those of the other commissioners. The group's executive director is equally limited in performing a leadership function in that that individual must answer to the commission. What can result is a languishing system that seems to have little sense of purpose other than the overriding concern of keeping spoils out of personnel matters. At best, the system may be as effective as an automobile in neutral, and procedures can become ends.

An alternative to the traditional model is the structure that existed in the federal government until the 1978 reforms. The president had much more power than he did under the traditional model, including the power to prescribe what would be done in the competitive service, and the commission was required by law to aid him.[77] Commissioners could be removed by the president without regard to their terms of appointment. An incoming president could designate the commissioners so that he need not be compelled to work with a panel selected by his predecessor. The chair, moreover, was not just one of three individuals but instead was the chief executive and administrative officer of the commission. The chair selected the executive director on a merit (competitive) basis in consultation with the other commissioners.

This type of structure brings the merit system under greater control by the chief executive while retaining the relative independence of the commission in acting as a watchdog over the personnel system. A criticism, on the other hand, is that the chair (and the other commissioners to a lesser extent) assumes the role of advisor to the chief executive, which is a policymaking function, while simultaneously performing administrative and judicial functions. This blending of powers can lead to abuses; for that reason, a common prescription has been to separate these functions, particularly the judicial function, from each other.

The debate over the desirability of having an autonomous civil service commission or one more closely linked with the chief executive has continued since the 1800s, but during that time further considerations have been added. One is the rise of budgetary processes and budget agencies, a reform that has strengthened the executive's powers.[78,79] Beginning about 1910, governments began to establish budget offices that were answerable directly to the chief executive. At the federal level, this occurred with the passage of the Budget and Accounting Act of 1921. That legislation not only created the Bureau of the Budget, which was reconstituted in 1970 as the Office of Management and Budget (OMB), but also established the General Accounting Office (GAO) as an agency of Congress responsible for auditing the accounts of federal agencies.

Tensions between budget and personnel offices are inevitable. Part of the problem is historical in that budgeting is openly political and the personnel movement is deliberately apolitical. The tradition of budget offices is that they serve the needs of the elected executive, whereas personnel offices serve the cause of merit. Issues arise in that the budget office and line managers may be eager to move quickly on a given problem and feel frustrated by having to abide by civil service regulations.

Organizational turf is at stake. A personnel agency will tend to claim all personnel matters within its jurisdiction, as a budget office will claim all financial matters. The two conflict on personnel costs. One area over which budget offices have gained control is proposed legislation. When agencies wish to put forward legislation, it must be cleared through the budget office. The purpose of this clearinghouse function is to avoid having administrative units support bills that would require budget expenditures contrary to the chief executive's wishes.

Salary levels and hiring are other personnel areas in which budget offices play important roles. Given the importance of personnel costs in every government's budget, there obviously is concern that pay rates not be set excessively high. Total personnel expenditures can be controlled by limiting the number of hires. This process is known as complement control, meaning that an agency must obtain budget office approval to fill a vacancy or to create a new job or position.

In addition to the rise of budgeting, two other themes or principles have emerged to complicate the issue of organizational responsibilities for personnel functions: equal employment opportunity and collective bargaining. Proponents of merit have readily accepted the notion that women, minorities, and other groups should not be discriminated against, but they have had difficulty accepting affirmative action that might lead to giving preference in hiring to women because of their sex and to minorities because of their skin color (see Chapter 9). Similarly, merit proponents have had difficulty accepting the idea that some aspects of personnel administration are subject to negotiations between management and organized labor (see Chapter 12).

A consequence of budgeting, collective bargaining, and equal employment opportunity is that personnel systems involve many agencies and not just a civil service commission. Figure 2–1 shows how the federal personnel system is structured. OMB is part of the Executive Office of the President and normally is in close communication with the president. The Civil Service Commission was abolished in 1978–1979, and its functions were reassigned to OPM and the Merit Systems Protection Board (MSPB).

The Office of Personnel Management answers directly to the president but is not part of the Executive Office of the President.[80] The director of OPM is appointed by the president for a 4-year term with the advice and consent of the Senate; if the president wishes to retain a director beyond the 4 years, reconfirmation is required. The director is responsible for advising the president on personnel administration. OPM, under the supervision of the director, issues rules and regulations for personnel procedures to be followed by departments and agencies. OPM has an oversight function for ensuring that departments and agencies adhere to merit principles and regulations.[81]

The MSPB consists of three members appointed by the president for 7-year overlapping terms with the advice and consent of the Senate. No more than two

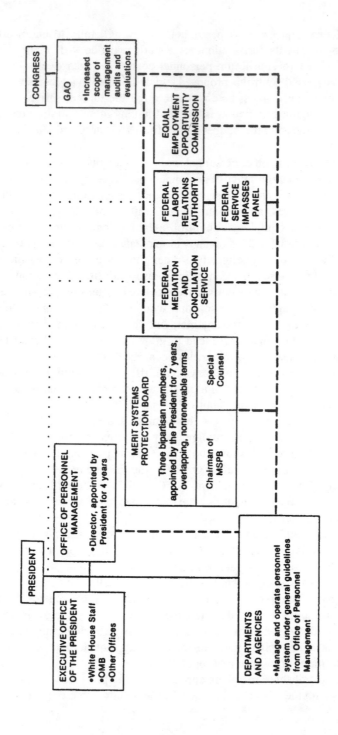

Figure 2–1 Federal Government Organization for Personnel Management. *Source:* Adapted from *Final Staff Report,* p. 244, Personnel Management Project, U.S. Government Printing Office, 1977.

board members may be from the same political party. The members' independence from the president is strengthened by permitting their removal "only for inefficiency, neglect of duty, or malfeasance in office." The president appoints one of the board members as chair with Senate approval; the chair is the "chief executive and administrative officer" of the board. The special counsel is appointed by the president for a 5-year term with the advice and consent of the Senate. The special counsel, who must be an attorney, also may be removed by the president "only for inefficiency, neglect of duty, or malfeasance in office."

Labor–management relations, which before 1978 had been regulated by presidential executive orders, are prescribed by the Civil Service Reform Act. The reform legislation established the Federal Labor Relations Authority (FLRA), which comprises three members appointed by the president to overlapping terms of 5 years. As with the MSPB, no more than two of the FLRA members may be from the same political party, and their appointments require Senate approval. FLRA members have the same protection from removal as the members of the MSPB. The general counsel is appointed by the president for a 5-year term with Senate approval and serves at the pleasure of the president. The general counsel is the chief administrative officer of the FLRA.

As in the earlier system, the Federal Mediation and Conciliation Service can assist in resolving impasses in negotiations, and such impasses may be resolved by the Federal Service Impasses Panel, which is a unit within the FLRA. The panel consists of at least seven members, appointed by the president, who can be freely removed by him. One of the main changes made in 1978 was the transfer of many duties previously administered by the assistant secretary of labor in this field.

Other changes stemming from the 1978 Act pertain to equal employment opportunity. The Equal Employment Opportunity Commission, which was created in 1964, was given an expanded role in the federal personnel system (those changes are discussed in Chapter 9).

The GAO, an arm of Congress, has gained increased responsibilities in the personnel field. Before the reforms, the GAO had broadened its financial audit role to include evaluations of governmental programs. By the mid-1970s, the GAO frequently was issuing reports dealing with personnel administration. Under the reform legislation, the GAO was charged with submitting to Congress an annual report on OPM and the MSPB. The law specifically charged the GAO with considering whether OPM was abiding by the merit system principles. The GAO also is responsible for assessing procedures used to appraise worker performance.

The changes involving labor–management relations and equal employment opportunity were far less controversial than the break-up of the Civil Service Commission into the OPM and the MSPB. Alan K. Campbell, chair of the Civil Service Commission at the time and the first director of OPM, emphasized the need for change given the perceived widespread public dissatisfaction with the existing federal bureaucracy as well as federal managers' unhappiness.[82] At the core of the issue was the familiar fear of political encroachment into personnel affairs. Proponents of the reorganization claimed that the then existing system was incapable of preventing partisan considerations and sometimes encouraged abuses. The red tape that blocked efficiency was seen as an invitation to managers to find shortcuts that might be contrary to merit. The proponents maintained that the political system had matured to the point that reversion to patronage was unlikely. Others were not completely convinced that the concept of merit was sufficiently established to entrust personnel administration to a personnel director who was directly answerable to the president.

Safeguards against nonmerit actions are built into the reformed system. As noted earlier, the law not only identifies merit principles but also includes a list of prohibited practices. The director of OPM, the MSPB, its special counsel, and the GAO all have roles in furthering merit in the personnel system. The MSPB, for example, is authorized to conduct personnel studies and may have access to agency personnel records. The law provides, "Any member of the Board, the Special Counsel, and any administrative law judge . . . may issue subpoenas requiring the attendance and testimony of witnesses and the production of documentary or other evidence." The MSPB may invalidate OPM rules and regulations that do not conform with merit. The special counsel can act as an ombudsman for employees seeking to reverse adverse actions against them that they deem unwarranted. When the counsel is convinced that prohibited personnel practices have occurred, the counsel may file a complaint against an individual employee and/or the agency before the MSPB, which has the authority to order corrective action.

Despite these safeguards, there were concerns in the 1980s about increased politicization of the federal personnel system by OPM's second director, Donald J. Devine, who served during the first years of the Reagan administration. One of his most controversial acts was to name five director's representatives, who were political appointees responsible for conveying the director's views to the career officers who headed OPM's ten regional offices. Later, Devine became embroiled in problems surrounding his confirmation for a second term and withdrew his name from consideration. The director's representative positions then were eliminated (see Chapter 8).

In other situations there have been concerns that political leaders, rather than politicizing administration, simply have bypassed or ignored career executives and managers. This approach, perhaps common during the Reagan administration, stemmed in part from political appointees' concern that careerists could not be trusted—that they would sabotage initiatives by such tactics as foot-dragging or leaking information to the media. Laws do not prohibit such bypasses and cannot force political appointees and career officers to work harmoniously.[83-88]

Not only have the safeguards failed to eliminate political influences, but these protective measures have created some potential for administrative and judicial controversy. The director of OPM has the authority to request a court of appeals to review MSPB decisions; controversies between these two units could become substantial and involve extensive litigation. Disputes also could emerge between the MSPB and its special counsel. The counsel is officially part of the board but is appointed independently and is protected from removal. President Carter's reorganization plan, which provided for the new organizational structure, and the original bills in both the House and the Senate were silent on the removal of the special counsel.[89] The House bill was amended to stipulate that the counsel must receive notice and a hearing before being removed; that provision was dropped from the final version. The law limits cause for removal to "inefficiency, neglect of duty, or malfeasance."

Given that the terms of the MSPB members and the special counsel are longer than the term of the president, and given their overlapping terms, it is conceivable that at some time substantially different views might exist among the individuals holding these positions. For instance, the special counsel might be particularly active in bringing before the board complaints that it considered inconsequential. Moreover, the special counsel has the right to intervene in any case before the MSPB, even though the panel might prefer to handle the case on its own. By providing for the relative independence of the special counsel, Congress may have created the potential for a situation similar to what developed between the National Labor Relations Board (NLRB) and its general counsel after passage of the Taft-Hartley Act in 1947. In that instance, the general counsel not only brought cases to the NLRB that the board did not care to consider but also sought judicial review of its decisions in the hope of their being overturned.[90,91] The Civil Service Reform Act, however, does not grant the MSPB special counsel authority to seek judicial review of board decisions.

One other organizational aspect of the federal system that warrants attention is the extent to which personnel functions are delegated to departments and agencies.[92] The 1978 legislation permitted the director to "delegate, in whole or in part, any function vested in or delegated to the Director." The main restrictions are that OPM must administer competitive examinations for administrative law judges and for positions common among federal agencies. OPM also must prescribe rules and regulations for personnel functions of departments and agencies. This authority to delegate functions provides an opportunity for eliminating much of the red tape that develops when systems are centralized and for granting agency flexibility that encourages more efficient and effective operations. Skeptics are concerned that decentralization can lead to unintended or deliberate abuses of the merit principle.[93]

If the federal structure is complex, the situation is no less so at the state and local levels. Agencies at those levels include civil service commissions; central personnel offices under the chief executive; and units responsible for administering collective bargaining, representing management in the bargaining process, making patronage and political appointments, and furthering the principle of equal employment opportunity. Political concerns are as prevalent at these levels of government as at the federal level.[94]

State and local systems may be considered even more complex than the federal system because of intergovernmental relations.[95] State governments, because they impose standards on local personnel operations, are part of local systems. Federal agencies are part of both state and local systems. Federal agencies in making grants to those governments require them to have merit systems and to be equal opportunity employers. As is discussed in later chapters, federal courts also have assumed prominent roles in state and local personnel systems.

A critique of the efforts to establish and maintain merit in personnel systems is inappropriate at this point in that many topics remain to be discussed in subsequent chapters. Nevertheless, some observations are appropriate.[96] Studies conducted at the federal level have yielded both encouraging and discouraging findings. On a positive note, federal personnel officials when surveyed reported almost unanimously that they had not "observed employees being pressured to contribute to a political campaign or participate in political activity."[97] On the other hand, results from a survey of former career executives were less encouraging. Only 15 percent said that they thought noncareer executives supported and upheld merit principles, and 44 percent said that one of their reasons for leaving federal service was the politicization of their organizations.[98] In another survey, 93 percent of career executives reported that they thought career executives were objective in making "grant, contract, and loan decisions" but only 55 percent thought political appointees were objective.[99] The National Commission on the Public Service, better known as the Volcker Commission, issued its report in 1989 expressing grave concern about numerous aspects of public service and the personnel system at the federal level.[100] The GAO has expressed concern about the quality and effectiveness of the public service and the leadership being provided by the OPM.[101,102] Some observers have concluded that "the federal government's merit system does not work."[103]

SUMMARY

The rise of political patronage is understandable when it is seen in perspective with the major societal changes that were occurring at the time. In the early years of this nation, appointments to government positions were based largely on individual qualifications, which tended to produce an elitist system. With the development of political parties and a rapidly expanding electorate, government jobs became attractive means of rewarding persons who had been effective campaigners.

Patronage had both strengths and weaknesses. Inefficiency may have increased with the appointment of political friends with minimal qualifications, but government of the early 1800s was comparatively nontechnical, so that many jobs could be filled with unskilled individuals. Patronage may have discouraged career development, although many workers moved in and out of office as the parties rotated in power. Coordination between the executive and legislative branches may have been furthered by patronage, and that system may have encouraged the bureaucracy to be responsive to political leadership. On the other hand, chief executives complained about the excessive time they had to devote to patronage matters.

Civil service reform occurred in the context of a larger governmental reform movement. At the local level, strong mayor and council-manager systems developed. Short ballots and nonpartisan elections were introduced along with restrictions on financial matters, including the development of budget processes.

Patronage declined because of legislation and other forces. Blanketing in of employees under a merit system was politically expedient. Economic growth made government jobs less attractive. Patronage was more difficult to use as jobs became increasingly technical. In recent years unions have been important contributors to the demise of patronage.

Merit is not simply the opposite of patronage, and the merit principle is applicable to all personnel actions. Merit involves dealing with people on the basis of their knowledge, skills, and other capabilities rather than extraneous or non–job-related characteristics. Personnel administration involves legislative, administrative, and judicial activities, and a persistent problem has been finding appropriate organizational locations for these activities, particularly in relation to the powers of the chief executive. The traditional model was to have a civil service commission that was insulated from the chief executive. That system has not guaranteed the elimination of political influences and has been criticized for blocking effective management.

Public personnel systems have become increasingly complex with the emergence of new values and governmental functions. Budget offices have been created and have acquired important powers in personnel administration. More recently, equal employment opportunity and collective bargaining have become important concerns.

In 1978, the federal government undertook a major restructuring of its personnel system. The Civil Service Commission was eliminated and its functions assigned to the new OPM, MSPB, and the latter's special counsel. The process for labor–management relations was written into the Civil Service Reform Act, which provided for an FLRA to administer that system. The reconfiguration was designed to increase the leadership and administrative responsibility of the president through the director of OPM while furthering the concept of merit and protecting against partisan and other non–job-related influences.

This chapter has presented the values and cast of characters found in public personnel systems. Subsequent chapters consider the interplay among those values and characters in relation to specific personnel functions.

NOTES

1. National Civil Service Reform League, *The Civil Service in Modern Government: A Study of the Merit System* (New York: National Civil Service Reform League, 1936).

2. L. Gulick, ed., Improved personnel in the public service, *Annals* 189 (1937): 1–198.

3. A. Hoogenboom, *Outlawing the Spoils: A History of the Civil Service Reform Movement, 1865–1883* (Urbana, Ill.: University of Illinois Press, 1961).

4. R. Maranta and D. Schultz, *A Short History of the United States Civil Service* (Lanham, Md.: University Press of America, 1991).

5. F.C. Mosher, *Democracy and the Public Service* (New York: Oxford University Press, 1968).

6. C.E. Prince, *The Federalists and the Origins of the U.S. Civil Service* (New York: New York University Press, 1977).

7. C. Schurz, *The Spoils System* (Philadelphia: Altemus, 1896).

8. M.B. Taylor, *History of the Federal Civil Service: 1789 to the Present* (Washington: U.S. Government Printing Office, 1941).

9. L.D. White, *The Federalists: A Study in Administrative History* (New York: Macmillan Publishing Co., 1948).

10. _____, *The Jeffersonians: A Study in Administrative History, 1801–1829* (New York: Macmillan Publishing Co., 1951).

11. _____, *The Republican Era, 1869–1901: A Study in Administrative History* (New York: Macmillan Publishing Co., 1958).

12. U.S. Bureau of the Census, *Historical Statistics of the United States: Colonial Times to 1970* (Washington: U.S. Government Printing Office, 1975), 14.

13. C.R. Fish, *The Civil Service and the Patronage* (New York: Longmans, Green, 1905), 79–85.

14. U.S. Constitution, Article II, Section 2.

15. S.H. Aronson, *Status and Kinship in the Higher Civil Service* (Cambridge, Mass.: Harvard University Press, 1964), 11–12, 140–157.

16. *Marbury v. Madison*, 5 U.S. 137 (1 Cranch 137) (1803).

17. A. Jackson, "First Inaugural Address (1829)," in *Inaugural Addresses of the Presidents of the United States* (Washington: U.S. Government Printing Office, 1965), 57.

18. U.S. Civil Service Commission, *Biography of an Ideal: A History of the Federal Civil Service* (Washington: U.S. Government Printing Office, 1973), 24.

19. U.S. Census Bureau, *Historical Statistics of the United States: Colonial Times to 1970*, 13, 1072, 1074.

20. D.H. Rosenbloom, *Federal Service and the Constitution: The Development of the Public Employment Relationship* (Ithaca, N.Y.: Cornell University Press, 1971), 53–55.

21. U.S. Civil Service Commission, *Biography of an Ideal*, 22.

22. D.R. Harvey, *The Civil Service Commission* (New York: Praeger, 1970), 6.

23. A Bill To Regulate and Improve the Civil Service of the United States (Pendleton Act), Ch. 27, 22 Stat. 403 (1883).

24. House Committee on Post Office and Civil Service, Subcommittee on Manpower and Civil Service, *History of the Civil Service Merit Systems of the United States and Selected Foreign Countries*, report prepared by Congressional Research Service, 94th Cong., 2d sess. (Washington: U.S. Government Printing Office, 1976), 87–173.

25. J.M. Mathews, *Principles of American State Administration* (New York: D. Appleton and Company, 1927), 195.

26. A.E. Buck, *The Reorganization of State Governments in the United States* (New York: National Municipal League and Columbia University Press, 1938).

27. R.S. Childs, *Civic Victories: The Story of an Unfinished Revolution* (New York: Harper & Brothers, 1952).

28. T.C. Devlin, *Municipal Reform in the United States* (New York: G.P. Putnam's Sons, 1896).

29. W.L. Riordon, *Plunkitt of Tammany Hall* (New York: E.P. Dutton, 1963).

30. M.H. Schiesl, *The Politics of Efficiency: Municipal Administration and Reform in America, 1800–1920* (Berkeley, Calif.: University of California Press, 1977).

31. J.C. Teaford, *The Municipal Revolution in America: Origins of Modern Urban Government, 1650–1825* (Chicago: University of Chicago Press, 1975).

32. L. Steffens, *The Shame of the Cities* (New York: McClure, Phillips, 1904).

33. P.S. Tolbert and L.G. Zucker, Institutional sources of change in the formal structure of organizations: The diffusion of civil service reform, 1880–1935, *Administration Science Quarterly* 18 (1983): 22–39.

34. Rosenbloom, *Federal Service and the Constitution*, 72.

35. P.P. Van Riper, *History of the United States Civil Service* (Evanston, Ill.: Rowe, Peterson & Company, 1958), 78–86.

36. House Committee, *History of Civil Service Merit Systems*, 164–173.

37. H. Kaufman, "The Growth of the Federal Personnel System," in *The Federal Government Service*, ed. W.S. Sayre (Englewood Cliffs, N.J.: Prentice-Hall, 1965), 54–55.

38. G.M. Kammerer, *Impact of War on Federal Personnel Administration, 1939–1945* (Lexington, Ky.: University of Kentucky Press, 1951).

39. L.D. White, ed., *Civil Service in Wartime* (Chicago: University of Chicago Press, 1945).

40. House Committee on Post Office and Civil Service, Subcommittee on Manpower and Civil Service, *Final Report on Violations and Abuses of Merit Principles in Federal Employment Together with Minority Views*, 94th Cong., 2d sess. (Washington: U.S. Government Printing Office, 1976), 579.

41. H.G. Rainey and B. Wechsler, eds., Symposium on executive transition in government, *Public Productivity Review* 12 (Fall 1988): 43–105.

42. The U.S. General Accounting Office prepared a series of transition papers in 1988 in anticipation of a new administration in 1989. See U.S. General Accounting Office, *Transition Series: The Public Service* (Washington: U.S. Government Printing Office, 1988).

43. F.J. Sorauf, The silent revolution in patronage, *Public Administration Review* 20 (1960): 28–34.

44. *Elrod v. Burns*, 427 U.S. 347 (1976).

45. *American Federation of State, County, and Municipal Employees v. Shapp*, 443 Pa. 527, 280 A.2d 375 (1971).

46. *Branti v. Finkel*, 445 U.S. 507 (1980).

47. *Rutan v. Republican Party of Illinois*, 497 U.S. 62 (1990).

48. M.H. Brinkley, Despoiling the spoils: *Rutan v. Republican Party of Illinois, North Carolina Law Review* 69 (1991): 719–740.

49. C. Daniel, Constitutionalizing merit? Practical implications of *Elrod, Branti,* and *Rutan, Review of Public Personnel Administration* 12 (January–April 1992): 26–34.

50. U.S. General Accounting Office, *Federal Employees: Trends in Career and Noncareer Employee Appointments in the Executive Branch* (Washington: U.S. Government Printing Office, 1987).

51. _____, *Personnel Practices: The Department of Energy's Use of Schedule C Appointment Authority* (Washington: U.S. Government Printing Office, 1990).

52. _____, *Federal Workforce: Inappropriate Use of Experts and Consultants at Selected Civilian Agencies* (Washington: U.S. Government Printing Office, 1991).

53. _____, *Personnel Practices: Propriety of Career Appointments Granted Former Political Appointees* (Washington: U.S. Government Printing Office, 1992).

54. S.F. Fox and C.J. Fox, Merit systems and personnel appraisals in local government, *Baseline Data Report* 22 (November/December 1990): 1–12.

55. H.G. Rainey and B. Wechsler, eds., Executive transition in government, *Public Productivity Review* 12 (Fall 1988): 43–116.

56. U.S. General Accounting Office, *Transition Series, 1988* (Washington: U.S. Government Printing Office, 1988).

57. D. Olshfski, Politics and leadership: Political executives at work, *Public Productivity and Management Review* 13 (1990): 225–243.

58. C. Ban and H.C. Redd III, The state of the merit system: Perceptions of abuse in the federal service, *Review of Public Personnel Administration* 10 (Summer 1990): 55–72.

59. Civil Service Reform Act, P.L. 95-454, 91 Stat. 1111 (1978).

60. Personnel Management Project, *Final Staff Report and Appendices to Final Staff Report* (Washington: U.S. Government Printing Office, 1977).

61. Intergovernmental Personnel Act of 1970, P.L. 91-648, 84 Stat. 1909 (1971).

62. D.G. Carnevale, Recruitment strategies in the federal government: Missing links and representative bureaucracy, *Review of Public Personnel Administration* 11 (Fall 1990–Spring 1991): 112–120.

63. F. Gottfried, *The Merit System and Municipal Civil Service: A Fostering of Social Inequality* (New York: Greenwood Press, 1988).

64. W.S. Sayre, The triumph of techniques over purpose, *Public Administration Review* 8 (1948): 134–137.

65. U.S. Office of Personnel Management, *Pay Structure of the Federal Civil Service* (Washington: U.S. Government Printing Office, 1985).

66. A.E. Pritchard, Jr., as quoted in N.R. Peirce, "Civil service systems experience 'quiet revolution,'" *National Journal* 7 (1975): 1,675.

67. House Committee, *History of Civil Service Merit Systems*, 465–492.

68. P.W. Ingraham and D.H. Rosenbloom, Political foundations of the American federal service: Rebuilding a crumbling base, *Public Administration Review* 50 (1990): 210–219.

69. Council of State Governments, *The Book of the States* (Lexington, Ky.: Council of State Governments, biennial).

70. D.L. Andrews and G.B. Jackson, Structure of local government personnel administration, *Baseline Data Report* 17 (June 1985): 1–12.

71. The same considerations are important in other countries. See R.C. Kearney, Political responsiveness and neutral competence in the developing countries, *Review of Public Personnel Administration* 8 (Spring 1988): 66–80.

72. National Civil Service League, *A Model Public Personnel Administration Law* (Washington: National Civil Service League, 1970), 5.

73. Subcommittee on Manpower and Civil Service, "Federal Political Personnel Manual," in *Final Report on Violations and Abuses of Merit Principles*, 573–811.

74. F.C. Mosher, et al., *Watergate: Implications for Responsible Government* (New York: Basic Books, 1974).

75. National Civil Service League, *A Model Public Personnel Administration Law*, 5.

76. J. Carter, *Message from the President of the United States: Civil Service Reform*, 95th Cong., 2d sess., H. Doc. 94-299 (Washington: U.S. Government Printing Office, 1978), 1.

77. 5 U.S.C. §1101 (1978).

78. R.D. Lee, Jr., and R.W. Johnson, *Public Budgeting Systems*, 4th ed. (Gaithersburg, Md.: Aspen Publishers, 1989).

79. G.C. Cornia, et al., Cooperation between personnel and budget offices during position requests and reclassifications, *State and Local Government Review* 17 (1985): 180–187.

80. L.M. Lane, The administration and politics of reform: The Office of Personnel Management, *Policy Studies Journal* 17 (1988–89): 331–351.

81. U.S. Merit Systems Protection Board, *Civil Service Evaluation: The Role of the U.S. Office of Personnel Management* (Washington: U.S. Government Printing Office, 1992).

82. A.K. Campbell, Civil service reform: A new commitment, *Public Administration Review* 38 (1978): 99–103.

83. J.P. Burke, *Bureaucratic Responsibility* (Baltimore, Md.: Johns Hopkins University Press, 1986).

84. P.W. Ingraham and C.R. Ban, Models of public management, *Public Administration Review* 46 (1986): 152–160.

85. P. Lorentzen, Stress in political–career executive relations, *Public Administration Review* 45 (1985): 411–414.

86. W.A. Niskanen, Jr., *Bureaucracy and Representative Government* (Chicago, Ill.: Aldine-Atherton, 1971).

87. J.P. Pfiffner, Political appointees and career executives, *Public Administration Review* 47 (1987): 57–65.

88. R.F. Durant, Beyond fear or favor: Appointee-careerist relations in the post-Reagan era, *Public Administration Review* 50 (1990): 319–331.

89. Reorganization Plan No. 2 of 1978, *U.S. Code of Congress & Administration News*, no. 5 (1978): 1387–1395; H.R. 11280 and S. 2640.

90. R.L. Gabriel, The role of the NLRB general counsel, *Labor Law Journal* 26 (1975): 79–87.

91. K. McGuiness, Effect of the discretionary power of the general counsel on the development of the law, *George Washington Law Review* 29 (1960): 385–398.

92. U.S. Merit Systems Protection Board, *Delegation and Decentralization: Personnel Management Simplification Efforts in the Federal Government* (Washington: U.S. Government Printing Office, 1989).

93. U.S. General Accounting Office, *Delegated Personnel Management Authorities: Better Monitoring and Oversight Needed* (Washington: U.S. Government Printing Office, 1982).

94. R. Hoogland DeHoog and G.P. Whitaker, Political conflict or professional advancement, *Journal of Urban Affairs* 12 (1990): 361–377.

95. A. Freedman, Doing battle with the patronage army: Politics, courts, and personnel administration in Chicago, *Public Administration Review* 48 (1988): 847–859.

96. P.W. Ingraham and D.H. Rosenbloom, eds., Symposium on the Civil Service Reform Act of 1976, *Policy Studies Journal* 17 (1988–89): 311–447.

97. U.S. Merit Systems Protection Board, *Federal Personnel Management since Civil Service Reform: A Survey of Federal Personnel Officials* (Washington: U.S. Government Printing Office, 1989), 5.

98. _____, *The Senior Executive Service: Views by Former Federal Executives* (Washington: U.S. Government Printing Office, 1989), 10 and 20.

99. U.S. General Accounting Office, *Senior Executive Service: Opinions about the Federal Work Environment* (Washington: U.S. Government Printing Office, 1992).

100. National Commission on the Public Service (NCPS), *Leadership for America* (Washington: NCPS, 1989).

101. U.S. General Accounting Office, *The Public Service: Issues Affecting Its Quality, Effectiveness, Integrity, and Stewardship* (Washington: U.S. Government Printing Office, 1989 and 1990).

102. _____, *Managing Human Resources: Greater OPM Leadership Needed To Address Critical Challenges* (Washington: U.S. Government Printing Office, 1989).

103. P.W. Ingraham and D.H. Rosenbloom, The State of Merit in the Federal Government, (Occasional paper prepared for the National Commission on the Public Service, 1990).

Chapter 3

Organizational and Job Design, Position Classification, and Personnel Planning

Given that a personnel system is part of a larger governmental system, personnel administration inevitably is associated with and limited by larger considerations. These obviously include the objectives or purposes of governmental programs. Such programs are established to meet societal needs and demands, with personnel administration being expected to facilitate meeting those needs and demands. Similarly, personnel administration often is limited by decisions about how services will be provided.

This chapter has four sections:

1. organizational and job design, including limitations imposed by the structure of organizations and efforts that have been made in designing individual jobs
2. how jobs or positions are grouped into classes, a process usually justified on the grounds that it furthers the objective of equal pay for equal work
3. operational problems encountered in the use of position classification
4. the use of personnel planning to enable government to fill the positions that are created

ORGANIZATIONAL AND JOB DESIGN

"Top down" and bottom up" are terms commonly used in the design of organizations and programs. The issue involved is whether to begin at the top or the bottom in designing an organization. The top-down approach involves starting at the top of the organization and determining what units and, in turn, what subunits to create. For example, if a state was planning to create a state department on environment and energy, the following questions would be asked:

1. What responsibilities are to be assigned to the department?
2. What bureaus should be created within the department?
3. What offices, divisions, or sections should be developed for each bureau?
4. How is management to identify the jobs or positions to be established in each of the lowest organizational units of the department?
5. How are specific tasks to be allocated to each position (including how they are to be performed and in what sequence)?

The bottom-up method is the reverse. The purposes or objectives of the organization are assumed, and attention is focused first on designing individual jobs. Once these are defined, they are clustered into organizational units that in turn are clustered into larger units, such as bureaus. The major weakness of the bottom-up approach is its premise that the work to be performed is readily understood and that there is a known relationship between the performance of tasks and the achievement of objectives. In designing a job, an analyst may seek the most efficient method of processing a form on the assumption that form processing is essential for meeting the objectives of the total organization. The danger of such an approach is suboptimization, in which work may be performed efficiently but is nonproductive in meeting objectives. The pure form of the bottom-up approach probably is rarely used, but this section later focuses on the extensive efforts put forth in job design.

The top-down approach, which is more popular in the design of organizational structure, has one major danger: There may be a tendency to focus on structure without considering purpose. Organizational charts are common in all large organizations, both private and public. Boxes are drawn showing what units report to what higher-level units. Shuffling the boxes from time to time is a popular sport. A common response to problems is reorganizing. When a department is not achieving what is expected of it or seems to be operated haphazardly, there may be a tendency to move boxes around on the chart; two boxes may be merged while another is divided into two new ones.

Much energy, time, and tax dollars can be consumed by reorganization. New working relationships must be developed between managers and their employees. Substantial costs result from having to print new stationery, issue new personnel and function directories, and physically move furniture and equipment from one set of offices to another. Frequent reorganizations are likely to produce chaos. Employees do not know from time to time who their supervisors are, few people seem to know who is responsible for what, and citizens seeking information or some other assistance from the department become bewildered and angered. In other words, reorganization is not a panacea, although it can serve a useful purpose when used judiciously.

Numerous issues arise as to the rules to follow in the design of organizations.[1] A full discussion of these issues is beyond the scope of this book, but they can be identified briefly as follows:

- How many levels in the hierarchy should be used?
- Should there be only bureaus within a department, or should bureaus be further subdivided?
- What is the appropriate span of control, that is, the number of persons reporting to a superior? For example, should five, ten, or more department heads report to a mayor?
- How should the staff functions of personnel, budgeting, and planning be located within the governmental structure?
- For larger jurisdictions, such as state governments and the federal government, how should functions within a department be related to geography?
- Should there be regional offices, and if so, how are they to relate to units at departmental headquarters?
- How is work to flow from one unit to another within a department and between departments?
- To what extent will centralization or decentralization policies be pursued?
- What authority will organizational subunits have, and what authority will be retained by higher units in the department?
- What will be the relative roles of specialists and generalists within the department?
- To what extent should government do the work, and to what extent should the work be contracted out to the private sector, both for-profit and nonprofit firms?

Government policies can be achieved in a variety of ways, with the direct delivery of services being only one. For instance, government organizations can be kept comparatively small if many public services are provided by private firms under contract with government; the process is known as privatization.[2,3] Other policies can be achieved by regulation, grants, and tax incentives or tax expenditures, in which the government forgoes tax revenues to achieve a policy objective.[4] Important functions can be handled through individual consultants or consulting firms that can recruit numerous experts to work on any given problem.[5]

Issues of these types typically are not the direct concerns of the personnel administrator; for better or for worse, they are resolved by others. Organizational structure or design may be largely mandated by the legislative body. City governments may be required by state law to have specified departments, even though some other configuration may be more appropriate for a given municipality. Cities with home rule charters may determine their own departmental configurations, but they too may be restricted by their charters, which may impose organizational structure. Changing the structure under a home rule charter would require voter approval.

Flexibility in changing organizational structure may be available to a chief executive. Presidents have had limited authority to reorganize agencies subject to veto by either the House of Representatives or the Senate. Some governors also have this type of authority.

Personnel units, however, may be largely outside the reorganization process. Instead, a blue ribbon committee composed of distinguished persons from the private sector and former government officials may be created to make recommendations for reorganizing a state department, a private consulting firm may be used for the same purpose, or a central staff unit other than personnel may have continuing responsibility in this area. The unit may be responsible for so-called organization and management (O&M) studies, which include analysis of work flow as well as organizational design.

Personnel systems, then, are greatly limited. A personnel organization typically must work within an agency structure that has been imposed by others. The personnel office may be required to focus on individual jobs when the problems of a department have more to do with its structure and the programs that are administered.

Although organizational design is likely to be beyond the scope of the personnel office, job design may be its responsibility, at least in part. Job design involves arranging tasks or work to be performed by an individual. The paramount criterion is efficiency. The job should be designed to minimize resource consumption and to maximize outputs of work. Work is to be designed simply because more complex approaches to the same task consume more employee time and therefore are more expensive. Tasks are to be defined in detail, and all persons performing the same tasks are to use the same procedures. Standardization of operations is to be imposed once an efficient method of performing a task has been identified. If all workers were permitted to operate as they saw fit, some would use less efficient procedures than others.

The school of scientific management is known for some of the most significant research on job design. Observing that workers assigned identical duties often performed at different rates and below what management expected, participants in this school of thought concluded that a systematic approach to designing work could increase employee productivity. The term "scientific management" was used to emphasize that work should not be organized haphazardly and that instead each aspect of work should be studied carefully to determine the "one best way" of doing it. An assumption was made that a single ideal method existed for performing any given task. Therefore, scientific management sought through research to discover that one best way.

Frederick W. Taylor, beginning in the late 1800s, was able to make substantial improvements in the design of work. One of Taylor's most celebrated accomplishments was achieved in working with pig iron handlers at the Bethlehem Steel Company. These handlers were required to pick up pigs of iron weighing about 90 pounds and load them onto railroad cars. In a day, the average worker loaded 12 to 13 tons, but Taylor developed a procedure that enabled an individual to load nearly 50 tons.[6-8]

Much of the work of Taylor and others focused on avoiding fatigue. Workers who were tired were less able to perform at the expected level. In the iron handler case, Taylor prescribed when the worker was to lift and when to take a rest. By resting, the worker was able to avoid excessive fatigue. Similarly, Taylor studied the size of shovels and the proper load of coal per shovel in stoking furnaces. Few pounds per shovel load tended to waste much body movement, and a heavy load required excessive exertion.[9]

Frank B. and Lillian M. Gilbreth also made great improvements in designing jobs. In one instance, bricklayers were able to increase the number of bricks laid in an hour from only 120 to 350. The Gilbreths and others focused on the motions used by workers and the time required to perform each movement. In other words, scientific management introduced motion and time studies.

Therbligs (an anagram of the name Gilbreth) were developed by Frank Gilbreth to categorize the types of hand movements used in work. Each of the seventeen types of therbligs involves a specific function, such as grasp, position, use, assemble, and search for a part. Work, then, can be defined by sequencing therbligs into the most efficient pattern. At a more detailed level, work can be specified for each hand and all other parts of the body, including the eyes. The following is a portion of the specifications for operating a lathe: "Pick up part and move to machine, place medium part in chuck, tighten independent chuck 18-inch lathe, tighten chuck with pipe on wrench, true up part on chuck, pick up aligning bar from floor."[10]

Scientific management developed a detailed set of guidelines or principles in defining work. For example, work was to involve the use of both hands because a person would be working at only 50 percent capacity when one hand was idle. Similarly, work should begin and end for both hands at the same time. Movements by both hands should be similar, and hand movements should be rhythmical and not jerky or necessitating abrupt changes in movement.

Job design through motion and time studies now is a highly developed science or art. Elaborate experiments are conducted in which different approaches to performing a task are assessed. Stopwatches are used in evaluating alternative approaches to work, as are movie and videotape cameras, which record both the time consumed and the motions used.

Body motions now constitute only one set of considerations in designing a job. Although researchers continue to seek more efficient use of the body in work, they also are concerned with the tools and the arrangements of the workplace, the process or steps in the job, the design of the product being made, and the selection of the raw materials used.[11] Instead of adjustments being made in the worker's motions, the product design may be changed, thereby eliminating the need for some movements. If a product is redesigned to eliminate a given component, savings are gained in body movements previously required in handling that unit. All this still is based on the original premise of one best way.

Of particular relevance to governments is research being conducted on office settings. The field of human factors engineering or ergonomics is concerned with the relationship between people and the equipment they use.[12–14] Word processing equipment with its video displays is being analyzed for worker fatigue along with the extent to which users readily understand software packages.

The conduct of motion and time studies and human engineering research has been more common in the private sector than in government. One reason may be that corporations consider such research an investment in that it can reduce costs and thereby increase profits; governments generally are not motivated by the profit incentive. Another reason has been resistance by government workers. Successful lobbying by employees has yielded legislation in some cases that has prohibited the use of stopwatches in government facilities. Employees have feared that such studies are intended to increase production by making them work increasingly harder with no boost in pay.

Nevertheless, research of this type has been helpful in government, particularly research involving repetitive work such as the numerous routine services provided by local governments. For example, research has been conducted on how to staff a garbage truck and the appropriate combination of personnel for a given type of truck. Procedures have been set on how to fill potholes in roads. Job design has been helpful in prescribing how many firefighters to use at a fire and how they should function.

Where job design may face limitations is in less repetitive or more innovative work. It is possible to prescribe for clerical secretaries how to arrange their desks, where to store bond paper, and how best to insert paper into a typewriter or word processing printer. It is less obvious how to prescribe other procedures for them, however, such as coping with irate telephone callers and handling the various clerical needs of professional workers in the office. This problem of not being able to specify procedures is even greater for managers and professional employees who are expected to cope with situations for which solutions are not known.

In both government and industry, the applicability of job design research may be limited by the nature of the workers. Scientific management to a large extent considers the individual much as a machine or an appendage to a machine. By defining each step of a job, little initiative or imagination is expected of the individual; it is as if computer programs were written for a group of robots. Extensive research on motivation suggests that workers may be more productive when given greater freedom in organizing their work (see Chapters 10 and 11). If various motivation theories are accepted, the search for one best way is unwarranted because a job design that is appropriate for one employee would not necessarily be fitting for others.

This is not to suggest that job design is antithetical to the needs of employees. Taylor and others saw scientific management as being compatible with the interests of both workers and management. Not only would management obtain benefits in increased productivity, but so would workers. Employees would increase their earnings and, in Taylor's terminology, would increase their self-respect by becoming "high-priced men." The "surplus" achieved through greater productivity would be distributed to both labor and management. Taylor envisioned a "mental revolution" in the ways people thought about work, and he should not be regarded simply as one who wanted to turn people into gears in a giant machine.[15]

Although technology has always greatly influenced the methods by which work is conducted, recent and anticipated changes in technology may create new opportunities and challenges in the design of work and organizations.[16–19] Computers, fax machines, and cellular phones are three relevant examples. As the work of government is increasingly conducted by computers, workers may become appendages to machines. On the other hand, as the availability of computer technology increases, work can be conducted in numerous locales, including employees' homes. Similarly, fax machines and cellular phones allow both workers and their managers to be physically removed from an agency's office and to be mobile throughout the course of the workday. Innovations in technology could lead to radical changes in organizational structures and individual jobs.

POSITION CLASSIFICATION

Job design concentrates on structuring the work situation; position classification accepts the job situation as a given. Position classification entails examining the work performed in various jobs and then grouping similar jobs or positions into classes.[20–23]

Although there are many reasons for the use of position classification, the paramount one is that it can be used to treat employees equitably. Position classification itself is not a pay plan (see Chapter 4), but the classification plan is used in developing the pay structure. In other words, when positions are classified, all persons performing similar or identical work are paid the same amount. The common phrase is "equal pay for equal work." Regardless of differences in education, social background, or political connections, two individuals performing the same type of job are entitled to the same pay. Similarly, position classification allows for treating differently any positions that diverge in skill requirements or level of responsibility. Managers, therefore, are classified separately from clerical workers.

Position classification also is justified on the grounds that it facilitates testing, career development, and employee evaluation. Testing programs can be devised for classes of jobs that cross agency lines. Equity is served by qualifying those who have the required skills and disqualifying all others. Without position classification, presumably there would be no fair way of developing tests. Classification further advances the equity principle by ordering or ranking positions so that employees know in advance what career opportunities exist. By specifying work requirements, position classification allows for assessing employee performance, or whether the individual is working at the expected rate and level of competency.

The hows and whys of the emergence of position classification are varied. One account is that in the early 1900s the Chicago Civil Service adopted position classification and that the idea quickly spread, in part because of that city's central geographic location in the United States.[24,25] Although Chicago apparently deserves substantial recognition, the concept of position classification actually stems from several different sources.

One was the scientific management school (and Taylorism in private enterprise). An outgrowth of job design was to classify like positions into groups. E.O. Griffenhagen, a private consultant based in Chicago, worked with private corporations in classifying positions. He began with the Commonwealth Edison Company in Chicago and went on to aid banks, insurance companies, and other firms.[26-29] A type of cross-fertilization resulted as both private enterprises and governments adopted position classification systems.

Divergences emerged, however, as corporations tended to restrict classification plans to manual labor and clerical positions, leaving higher-level positions unclassified; governments, on the other hand, tended to apply classification to most or all positions. Industry's presumed justification for lack of full usage was that higher-level positions involved more varied work, making classification difficult, and that variations in performance should be reflected in employee wages and salaries. The disadvantage was that, without some standardization of positions and pay, secrecy and distrust would or could arise. Employees do not want their pay revealed to fellow workers on the assumption that their rates are better than what others are receiving. Yet, even though all workers may think they are faring better than others, they also may all think they are doing worse.[30]

Inequities in pay constitute another factor that led to position classification. Indeed, that was one of the main stimulants in Chicago's adoption of such a system. Some workers were considered underpaid and others overpaid; when wage increases were being approved, there was no simple system for determining which positions should be awarded what pay boosts.

Although such inequities had long existed, the problem at the federal level was worsened by World War I. During the war, the federal bureaucracy often added employees at wage rates equal to or above rates being paid persons with considerable experience in government. This led to low morale and high turnover. Between 1917 and 1920, for example, one unit in the Bureau of Standards had 216 scientific employees, and 110 of those left.[31]

Variations in job titles abounded, again making difficult or impossible any consistency in setting salaries and wages. Titles for a federal senior file and record clerk included apprentice graphotype operator, assistant file clerk, bookkeeper, copyist, searcher, and even dictator, trouble chaser, special expert, and special agent.[32] In many cases, positions bearing dissimilar titles should have been treated the same because of the nature of the work performed, and conversely not all jobs with similar or identical titles should have been treated the same because their work varied.

More generally, position classification became popular because it complemented a larger reform movement in government. The economy and efficiency movement of the 1910s and 1920s brought many changes to government.[33] Budget surpluses vanished at all levels, stimulating concern for better planning and management. Emphasis was given to bringing greater order to the ways in which government operated. The Taft Commission on Economy and Efficiency in 1912 issued its report recommending the use of a structured budget process.[34,35] During the 1910s many state and local governments adopted such systems, although it was not until 1921 that Congress passed the Budget and Accounting Act, creating the Bureau of the Budget (now Office of Management and Budget) and the General Accounting Office.[36] A common slogan of the day was that government should be more businesslike, so that government officials and reformers turned to industry for possible innovations that might be adopted.

Position classification, then, blended well with the general reform movement. By classifying positions, government could reward workers appropriately for the work they performed. Savings could be achieved by not overcompensating them. Government could become more efficient by taking a systematic approach rather than a haphazard one to how work was assigned to employees.

Position classification has come to be recognized as a fundamental aspect of public personnel systems. At the federal level, the system was launched by the Classification Act of 1923, which applied only to workers in Washington, DC. The Ramspeck Act of 1940, as well as some earlier legislation, extended coverage to field personnel, and the Classification Act of 1949 updated and replaced the 1923 legislation. Virtually all states use some form of classification for at least part of their staffs. Less is known about local governments, but it can be assumed that most, if not all, large cities use some form. Smaller local governments may be more casual in their personnel operations and may have only the rudiments (if those) of such a system.[37]

A position classification plan is an organization or categorization of job types according to the nature of the work performed. A jurisdiction may have a separate plan for each general class of workers or for each separate pay plan in that often several pay plans may exist in a jurisdiction (see Chapter 4). For example, separate position classification plans may exist for such groups as executives; administrative, professional, and technological (APT) workers; clerical, office machine operation, and technical workers; and trade, craft, and manual laborers. White collar jobs in the federal government are part of the GS ratings and include executives, APT employees, and clerical workers. Blue collar workers are covered by the Federal Wage System (also explained in Chapter 4). Other workers, such as those in the Foreign Service, the Tennessee Valley Authority, the Postal Service, and selected health workers in the Department of Veterans Affairs, are in separate systems.[38]

Position classification plans typically are organized according to occupational groups. The Office of Personnel Management (OPM) uses twenty-two groups, such as a group for social science, psychology, and welfare; another group for engineering and architecture; and another group for medical, hospital, dental, and public health occupations.[39] Each occupational group contains series that further define the occupational area and recognize variations in the level of work performed within an occupation, namely from entry level to the highest level in a series.

A series is a set of jobs that are similar in content but different in level of factors or criteria applied. Each job in the series has the same basic title but usually has a numerical suffix reflecting the level of skill, knowledge, and the like. Within the health-related occupational group just mentioned for the federal government, separate series exist for medical officers, nurses, autopsy assistants, rehabilitation therapists, and medical records administrators. Agronomist positions in a state might range from Agronomist I for an entry-level position to Agronomist V for an experienced professional. The use of job series is said to enhance career development. The new employee, starting as an Agronomist I, quickly can determine what constitutes the promotion ladder.

When classes, occupational groups, and series are considered as a whole, the position classification plan is a set of abstractions or statements about "typical" or "benchmark" positions within the government. The plan describes these positions and the work that they entail, and the job of position classifiers is to take existing jobs and place them within the appropriate sections of the plan.

The development of a position classification plan begins with setting criteria for measuring work. Two positions cannot be compared unless standards exist for measuring their scope and content. Without such standards, the first position might be characterized in one way and the second in a different way, thereby presenting an apples-and-oranges problem. For example, one analyst might emphasize that a clerical secretary had to interact extensively with a wide range of persons both in and outside the organization, whereas another analyst considering a similar position would emphasize the extent of word processing.

Usually, four to ten clusters of measures are identified. One set of such criteria could be the following: (1) difficulty of duties, (2) supervisory responsibility, (3) nonsupervisory responsibility, and (4) requisite qualifications.[40] An alternative could be as follows: (1) subject matter, (2) difficulty and complexity of duties, (3) nonsupervisory responsibilities, (4) supervisory and administrative responsibilities, and (5) qualification standards.[41]

Although there is no obvious ideal number of factors, what is important is to establish criteria within each factor so that positions may be measured. If the factor of "job requirements" is to be used, what kinds of measures or standards might be applied? How is "job requirements" to be distinguished from other factors, such as responsibility? A beginning step is to describe in words the meaning of the factor. For example, job requirements might be restricted to the subject matter of the job, whereas responsibility would deal with the extent to which a person in a position was expected to act independently and/or to direct the activities of others.

The federal government uses the Factor Evaluation System (FES), which consists of nine factors[42]:

1. knowledge required by the position
2. supervisory controls
3. guidelines
4. complexity
5. scope and effect
6. personal contacts
7. purpose of contacts
8. physical demands
9. work environment

The first five of these factors are divided into subfactors. The knowledge factor, for example, has the subfactors of (a) kind or nature of knowledge and skills needed and (b) how the knowledge and skills are used in doing the work. This system, mandated by the Job Evaluation Policy Act of 1970, was developed in response to criticisms that a narrative system that was being used was insufficiently precise and led to low reliability. The complaint was frequently made that any given position might be classified differently depending upon who did the classification of the position.

Under the FES, a range of possible points is established for each of the factors. For instance, it is possible to award as many as 1,850 points for the knowledge factor; the maximum for the work environment factor is only 50. Table 3–1 illustrates the standards used in assigning points for medical records administration positions. As can be seen from the table, the minimum number of points on the guidelines factor for this type of position is 275, and the maximum is 650. Once points are assigned for each factor, they are totaled, and the result is used to determine the GS pay rating (see Chapter 4).[43,44]

Criticisms of position classification systems are abundant. One generic complaint is that these systems are extraordinarily complex and result in unnecessary rigidities at a time when flexibility is needed. For instance, the National Academy of Public Administration (NAPA) has recommended that the twenty-two occupational groups of the federal system be regrouped into ten.[45]

Table 3-1   Range of Points for Medical Records Administration Positions, Factor Evaluation System

		Range of Points	
Factors		Minimum	Maximum
1.	Knowledge	950	1,550
2.	Supervisory Controls	275	650
3.	Guidelines	275	650
4.	Complexity	150	325
5.	Scope and Effect	150	325
6. & 7.	Personal Contacts and Purpose of Contacts	30	330
8.	Physical Demands	5	5
9.	Work Environment	5	5
Total		1,840	3,840

Source: Compiled from FES Position-Classification Standard: Medical Records Administration Series GS-669, U.S. Office of Personnel Management, pp. 1–20, U.S. Government Printing Office, 1991.

A related criticism is that job series are often too narrowly defined. When a series is defined narrowly and has only a few levels, an employee may rise to the top level quickly and have no further opportunities for advancement in that specialty. At that point, the individual must forgo further advancement or seek to enter a different series. Because qualifying for other series often requires education and experience of specified types and duration, few opportunities may exist for changing series. Excessively narrow series definitions thus thwart career advancement. Narrow definitions often stem from values society places on various occupations. Clerical work, for example, has a generally low value, and opportunities for advancement through clerical series are limited. The complaint that employees are pigeonholed into narrowly defined series is common.[46] It is not difficult to find in many jurisdictions class titles that have only two or three positions. A person who accepts one of these positions may be unable to qualify for advancement to other series.

Use of numerous levels within a series can be equally disadvantageous. Arbitrary distinctions can emerge between each level of jobs within the series. In a city planning office, the jobs of Planner I, II, and III may have only a few practical distinctions but may have real differences in pay. The individuals in Planner I positions are likely to complain that they are doing the same work as all other planners in the office yet are being paid far less. The NAPA report recommended that three broad bands of jobs be established within series: development, full performance, and senior/expert.

Descriptions or specifications are prepared for positions. These job descriptions often are the bases for classifying specific positions. A job description for most jobs can be done in a page or two. The formats all include the title of the job and a statement of the type of work performed. Often a statement of the knowledge and skill required to perform a job will be included. The job description may follow the format of the factors used in classifying a position; for example, a section would explain the interpersonal aspects of the job. OPM recommends that four types of information be provided in position descriptions: introduction, major duties and responsibilities, controls over the position, and special qualification requirements.[47] Position controls refer to the extent of supervision and guidance over the position, and special qualifications entail "knowledge, skill, education, certification," and other requirements.

The systems used for evaluating positions and placing them within the classification plan are open to severe criticisms. Establishing measures or standards is easier for some factors than for others. In evaluating a supervisory position, it is easy to determine the number of workers supervised and their geographical dispersion: Do they all work in the same office? Another consideration is whether the supervisor is in charge of both day and evening shifts. The nature of the supervision, however, is more difficult to gauge. Where employees must operate by a procedure manual that prescribes virtually every possible situation, the extent or intensity of supervision is not as great as when problems frequently arise that require a supervisor to intervene.

Any point system, such as the FES, is subject to criticism on at least two counts:

1. The standards and point ranges may be inappropriate; that is, a classifier should be able to assign fewer or more points to a factor than those officially allowed.
2. Classifiers frequently misjudge situations and tend to award too few points to a position.

All this is much more than an academic exercise, given that workers' pay is set by the number of points awarded. Under the FES, only five points separate any two grade or pay levels.

Once a classification structure is established, it must be applied to the positions in the organization. Various techniques are used for classifying specific positions. A position classifier may conduct a desk audit, in which the individual in the position is observed for a period of time—from a few hours to perhaps several days—to determine what work is being performed. From such an audit, the classifier can learn how much time the worker spends alone and with peers, subordinates, and superiors. For a clerical position, it would be important to know whether the work was limited largely to typing form letters or was more varied, including taking dictation, answering telephones, and operating office machines. Although the desk audit is useful, it is expensive and cannot be applied to all positions. Another drawback is that it presumes that the classifier can interpret appropriately what work is being done simply by observing an employee. In actuality, the use of observation alone may not be enough to allow the classifier to grasp the types of problems involved. An additional problem is that classifiers' judgments can be influenced by how information is presented to them.[48] One response to this problem is to use a team approach rather than relying on a single classifier to evaluate a position. The Oliver classification system, named after Philip M. Oliver, uses the team approach.[49]

Other techniques rely on the descriptions and judgments of persons knowledgeable about the position. The incumbent is asked to complete a form that asks questions about the position, such as "What machines and equipment do you use in your job?", "What percentage of your time is spent using each of these machines?", and "To what extent is your work reviewed by your supervisor?" Open-ended questions such as these also may be submitted to the supervisor of the position being classified and to subordinates as well. One study of these alternative methods found that subordinates either overrated or underrated the superior's position. Incumbents tended to underrate their jobs, and supervisors tended to do best in properly describing a subordinate position.[50,51] Still, all three types of descriptions may be used as checks against each other.[52]

In addition to the government personnel offices that classify positions, there are private consulting firms that can assist governments in designing systems and in classifying specific positions. These firms are particularly useful for smaller jurisdictions that do not have the internal capability for devising classification plans or undertaking major revisions in existing ones. A potential disadvantage is that a consulting firm may apply its own standardized system on all customer governments, even though modifications are needed.

A common practice is to include minimum education and experience requirements. In theory, position classifiers derive those requirements from examining the work performed. The assumption is made that persons without the requisite background will not perform well and, conversely, that those with it will. This practice is defended as facilitating a fair examination process, screening out persons with inappropriate backgrounds.

The education criterion works best for highly technical jobs: Not everyone can be a nuclear physicist or surgeon. The education requirement is less obvious for other jobs: Can only persons with master's degrees in social work be capable social workers? Can only persons with master's degrees in public administration, business administration, or education administration be competent administrators? Does the nature of a manual labor position really require a high school education, or would sixth grade be sufficient? Education requirements that are set arbitrarily can establish barriers to employment or promotion. They also can serve as a form of credentialing; that is, they can serve to protect from competition those individuals holding the credential. Of particular concern is that such standards can discriminate against minorities and can benefit middle-class whites.

The experience requirement can be criticized on the same grounds. Simply because an individual has held a position for 3 years does not necessarily mean that there has been much growth. The person may have learned most of what there was to learn in the position in 1 year and have spent the next 2 years simply performing the job. Yet a person with 3 years of experience might be eligible for promotion to higher-level positions, whereas someone with only 1 year would not be eligible.

OPERATIONAL PROBLEMS OF CLASSIFICATION

Numerous problems arise in the use of position classification on a daily basis. One set of problems relates to keeping the position classification plan and job classifications themselves current.

The position classification plan actually is a set of abstractions about the types of work performed. As government assumes new responsibilities or performs work differently to meet its changing responsibilities, the plan must be adjusted to reflect those changes. A state government that takes on a new responsibility for approving or disapproving the installation of septic tanks for sewage disposal will create new positions requiring expertise in water pollution, soils, and related fields, but the classification plan may not reflect such a cluster of skills in any one type or group of jobs. It thus becomes necessary to alter the plan.

Line managers and professional organizations sometimes seek the creation of special classifications. Professional groups want to aggrandize their own specialties in the system. In the example of septic tanks, there may be pressure for a new job series of Septic Tank Regulators when an adequate series called Water Quality Engineers already exists. This may be done to overemphasize the technical knowledge required to deal with septic tanks so as to boost the pay level above that for Water Quality Engineers. If the plan is allowed to be modified often without genuine need, it becomes no plan at all.

The other side of the issue is whether positions are kept classified properly over time. Jobs change. What a given worker does now is not necessarily the same as what was being done a year or two previously. A filing clerk may have been assigned more duties as the amount of work increased; over time, the clerk's job has been upgraded informally (but not formally) to a secretarial position. Because wages are tied to the position classification plan and not to the work performed, inequity can result. The employee simply is not being paid adequately for the work performed. A study of the federal system found that 70 percent of the qualification standards in use were at least 10 years old and that 42 percent were at least 20 years old.[53]

Employees tend to request upgrading of their positions; obviously, few will ever recommend a downgrading. This produces the problem of classification inflation, or grade creep, and there are few incentives for managers to resist such inflation. The line manager, being constantly concerned with employee morale, may see upgrading the positions as a way of rewarding industrious workers and generally keeping them happy. Higher-level jobs will enlarge the organization's budget, which in turn may be seen as bringing greater prestige to the unit and its manager. Conversely, in times of budget restraint, top management usually will reject such proposals immediately, which can damage the manager in the eyes of both superiors and employees. Upgrading lower-level positions may serve eventually as justification for upgrading the manager's position and pay, so that the manager may gain a monetary benefit by helping subordinates.[54]

Still another issue is who should be responsible for classifying positions. When the work is done by a central personnel department or civil service commission, complaints arise over the time required in classifying and reclassifying jobs. There may be complaints that the central entity is not adequately aware of the unique characteristics of agencies and their jobs, so that the resulting classifications are faulty.

Given the complaints about central classifiers and the large workload involved in any sizable government, decentralization of position classification is common. This is the case at the federal level and in many states. Each department has its own personnel unit responsible for classifying. The central personnel department or civil service commission sets classification standards that are used by the department personnel offices. The decentralized approach may facilitate faster action. A potential disadvantage is inconsistency from department to department. Under a decentralized system, for example, administrative assistant positions might be classified differently among the departments. Some observers have been concerned that decentralization may allow for abuses in which some employees with connections to higher-ups are able to have their jobs upgraded even though there is no justification for doing so. Well-defined classification standards and selective audits conducted by the central personnel unit can limit such abuses.

When administrators are under pressure by their employees to upgrade their positions—a condition that may prevail much of the time—and when classification is decentralized, the potential for grade creep is greatest. During the 1980s, there was much concern that such grade inflation had become rampant in the federal government. The President's Private Sector Survey on Cost Control, better known as the Grace Commission, found that the government had 50 percent more personnel in midmanagement ranks than the private sector. The Congressional Budget Office, a staff unit of Congress, has estimated that misgrading of positions costs the government $2 billion a year. Beginning in 1984, the federal government took steps to correct the situation, with major emphasis on reviewing and, where appropriate, revising all positions that become vacant, such as when employees retire, resign, or are transferred.[55-59]

Grade inflation, however, remains a problem. One study of federal employment found that the most important factor explaining grade creep was the changing occupational mix of the federal work force. As the government hired persons with greater skills than were required earlier, average grade ratings increased. Declining pay comparability with the private sector was cited as a less important reason for the increase.[60]

Although upgrading positions may be beneficial to managers, they may find that other aspects of classification create problems. Managers may well prefer extensive flexibility in dealing with personnel matters, but classification blocks them. Employees cannot be rewarded or penalized financially by their supervisor by a unilateral edict because pay is structured according to the classification system. When positions need to be reclassified, managers complain that they are expected to wait patiently for the personnel system to make the appropriate changes; red tape seems to abound, producing almost endless delays.

Subordinates sometimes use classification as a weapon against their supervisors. "It's not in my job specs" may be the retort when a manager assigns new duties to an employee. Workers claim they are responsible only for duties described in the classification. As public employees become increasingly organized and even militant, this refusal to accept duties seems to increase. Managers see themselves in a situation in which they are expected to produce results but are not given sufficient authority to do so.

One of the most important criticisms of position classification systems is that they may be structurally biased against occupations held by women. This criticism has led to demands that workers be paid according to their comparable worth or contribution to organizations and that jobs be classified accordingly (see Chapter 9). As a consequence, personnel administrators are increasingly concerned with evaluating classification plans in terms of their potential or actual gender bias.[61,62]

Another problem of position classification involves the appeals procedures available to employees. Complaints are especially likely to arise when positions are reclassified downward. When this occurs, the incumbents usually are permitted to stay at the original salary level, but any new appointees will be paid at a lower rate. Problems also occur when employees are denied an upgrading of their positions. In a large government there can be several levels of appeals within a department, after which appeals can be made to a central personnel agency, such as a personnel department or civil service commission. If the employee still is not satisfied, a legal suit may be possible.

Such complaints suggest that personnel experts should consider possible alternatives to existing classification systems.[63] The Civil Service Reform Act granted authority to the Office of Personnel Management to approve selected experiments. Since 1981 the Navy, under OPM supervision, has been conducting experiments in this area at facilities in San Diego and China Lake, California.[64] Under the experimental system, broad levels of classifications permit managers to promote high-performing workers, including increasing their salary levels significantly. In response to results of these experiments, OPM Director Constance Horner in 1986 recommended to Congress sweeping reforms that would establish this Simplified Management System, as it is called, as an alternative to the traditional classification system.[65] These recommendations would establish broad career paths that would provide greater flexibility in classifying jobs and assigning work. The proposals also included significant changes in pay systems (see Chapters 4 and 6).

Finally, when considering all the complaints about position classification systems, one must question whether the systems' benefits outweigh the problems they generate. The seeming arcane nature of classification systems defies comprehension and breeds cynicism about their validity, reliability, and efficacy. In an era when technological advances are dramatically changing the ways in which work is conducted, a strong argument can be made for providing managers with the freedom to redesign jobs at will and to expect workers to adjust to the new demands made upon them. If the categories of classes, occupational groups, and series are combined or even collapsed into only a few categories, then greater opportunities can be offered to workers to advance within the bureaucracy.[66,67] When citizens demand that government be efficient in the use of resources, the claim can be made that managers should have considerable discretion in setting pay levels to reward highly productive employees and should not be bound by rigid pay systems that are set according to position classification plans.

PERSONNEL PLANNING

With positions having been created, the problem arises of how to identify the people needed to fill the positions. Indeed, in the creation of positions, a concern is always whether sufficient numbers of qualified individuals can be recruited. This concern is the responsibility of personnel planners. In general, four characteristics are found in most definitions of planning:

1. emphasis on rationality in choice selection
2. attention to goals and objectives of society and/or organizations
3. focus on deriving means for the attainment of these goals and objectives
4. orientation toward the future

Planning entails making a forecast of what will happen and devising strategies either for meeting that projected situation or for averting it.

Macrosocioeconomic planning has not been accepted in the United States. The idea was rejected during the Depression of the 1930s, which severely tested the nation's economic system, and again in the 1980s and 1990s as the country struggled to endure what has been called "deindustrialization."[68,69] Although society has been willing to accept considerable governmental intervention in the economy, there has been an unwillingness to grant powers to control the economy.[70] In simple terms, that type of planning is viewed as totalitarian, a simplistic view that has been reinforced by dictatorial governments relying heavily on national planning. Macroplanning has been seen as a device by which tyrants restrict individual freedoms.[71,72]

Although macrolevel planning is not practiced, macrolevel forecasting is. Forecasts are made of economic trends and of labor or personnel requirements. The Bureau of Labor Statistics (BLS) in the U.S. Department of Labor projects the availability of persons with certain types of skills and indicates expected shortages or surpluses. The BLS publishes the annual *Occupational Outlook Handbook* and the journal *Occupational Outlook Quarterly*. These can be useful for employers and for persons contemplating various occupations. Employers can prepare to confront problems in recruiting persons with needed skills where shortages are expected; individuals can avoid occupations where there already is an oversupply of workers.

Making these kinds of forecasts is extremely difficult in that what ultimately will happen in the future will be the product of millions of decisions. Because the United States does not have a centralized decision system determining which individuals will enter which fields, forecasts must be based on judgments as to what various segments of society and the economy are likely to do. For instance, one of the greatest forecasting problems in recent years has been predicting the extent to which women will enter the labor market. More women may choose to enter the market, and others already employed may remain in their jobs where in an earlier time they might have resigned to become full-time homemakers. Being in the labor market is not the same as being employed. A person who is employed or seeking employment is part of the labor market. An interactive process exists: People look for employment, but if they are unsuccessful for an extended period, they stop their search and drop out of the market. Similarly, if the outlook improves, they are likely to reenter the job market.

These forecasts also involve predictions of economic and technological changes:

- What industries can be expected to expand, and what will be their personnel needs?
- Will there be a boom in manufactured goods, and if so, what types of persons will be needed to manufacture these items?
- Will there be technological changes reducing the need for some skills and increasing the need for others?

Since World War II, automation obviously has had great impact on the mix of skills required in the labor market. Educational institutions also are important in influencing the occupational mix and, as with the economy, are not controlled centrally. Colleges and universities have difficulty in adjusting their output to meet demands. One of the best illustrations is the "production" of school teachers. During the late 1960s and 1970s, there was an oversupply of teachers given enrollment trends; in the 1980s and 1990s, a partial reverse pattern developed, with some types of teachers being in scarce supply. Rather than having a controlled system that allows only a predetermined number of people to enter a field, the existing system permits individual freedom of choice but, as a result, creates shortages in some occupations and surpluses in others.

Colleges and universities are subject to labor market pressures and frequently attempt to respond to those demands. When enrollments are threatened, these institutions seek to develop or enlarge programs that will attract students. The emergence of new public administration degree programs in the 1960s and 1970s is an example of schools responding to markets. Overproduction is an ever present danger, again because there is no central control. Each institution, recognizing government's need for administrators, establishes its own program, resulting in far more people seeking government positions than there are jobs available. Although some state educational systems attempt to control the number of public administration students (as well as other types of students) in their public institutions, there is no central control of all public and private institutions in the country.

Particularly troubling during the late 1980s and into the early 1990s were forecasts about the work force by the turn of the century. The Hudson Institute, working for the U.S. Department of Labor (DOL), prepared a 1987 report forecasting that the labor pool of young workers would shrink; that women, minorities, and immigrants would dominate the new entrants into the labor market; and that future jobs would require highly skilled employees.[73] That report was followed up in 1988 by the reports *Civil Service 2000* and *Opportunity 2000*, sponsored by OPM and the DOL, respectively.[74,75] These reports, taken together, suggested that all employers would face a difficult situation by the year 2000. The demand for highly trained employees (presumably young workers) would be at a peak level at a time when only low-skilled workers were in abundance. On a positive note, employers would be able to recruit minorities and women in furtherance of affirmative action objectives, but recruiting minorities and women with skills would be a difficult task. Government was seen as facing particularly severe challenges in that workers with needed skills would gravitate to the private sector, where salaries and wages were higher.

The initial response to these reports was alarm, with some employers taking measures to improve their competitiveness in coming years.[76] OPM adopted a strategic plan that concentrated on five factors that were considered critical in attracting and retaining employees:

1. opportunity to belong to a highly regarded work group which performs challenging and important work
2. competitive and fair compensation
3. opportunity for professional growth and development
4. opportunity to influence work assignments and work processes, to make an individual difference
5. an environment which respects the individual, provides due process, and protects the individual from discrimination, retaliation, harassment, partisan political pressures, and other conflicts[77]

In regard to the second factor, fair compensation, the federal government proceeded to restructure drastically its main pay system to improve its ability to recruit needed workers (see Chapter 4).

Doubt developed about the Hudson Institute's forecasts.[78] Although critics agreed that the work force would include greater numbers of minorities and women, this change was seen not as something dramatically new but rather as the continuation of a trend that did not require any precipitous action.[79] Additionally, critics suggested that the technical nature of jobs, especially those in government, was not going to increase at such a rate that employers would be unable to recruit sufficient numbers of adequately trained employees.

In contrast to macrolevel personnel forecasting, personnel planning within a jurisdiction can be defined as providing for "the right numbers and the right kinds of people at the right places and the right times."[80] The concern is to employ neither too many nor too few workers, either of which would reduce efficiency. The importance of avoiding overhiring is perhaps greater in the public sector than in the private sector because the former relies heavily on salaried workers. A private corporation that finds itself overstaffed can reduce personnel costs by cutting back on the number of hours worked by each employee. For the public jurisdiction, whose staff is largely salaried, reducing personnel costs may require the drastic action of furloughing workers through a process known as reduction in force. Major disadvantages of layoff policies are that those employees affected may encounter severe economic problems and that government may be unable to hire back employees once revenues return to a higher level. As a consequence, governments in the 1980s and 1990s increasingly turned to partial layoffs, such as requiring most or all employees to take unpaid leave 1 day a week for an extended period.

Personnel planning begins with a forecast of personnel requirements.[81-84] As can be seen in Figure 3–1, the forecast can be short range (covering a year or two), intermediate, or long range (10 years). The short-range forecast can be more accurate than the others because there are fewer uncertainties. One has a better chance of predicting what will happen tomorrow than what will happen 10 or 15 years in the future.

A weakness of the short-range forecast is that options for response necessarily will be restricted, whereas a long-range forecast provides greater lead time for devising and implementing response strategies. An important aspect of the needs forecast is making the projection on the basis of occupation and job level. The same specificity in forecasting is needed in the next step, the assessment of what will happen to current employees.

Position classification systems can be used as the structure for such forecasts, although alternative methods may prove more useful. Because under a merit system recruitment is geared to the position classification plan, it is appropriate to forecast needs on the basis of that plan. A problem, however, is that position classification systems may fragment skills or not highlight them sufficiently. In the first instance, two positions involving similar work may be placed in different parts of the classification plan. Alternatively, the classification might not reflect adequately the range of skills required. A labor economics analyst position, for example, might require knowledge of computer programming, but that skill might not be identified in the classification plan. Another aspect of the forecast should be whether positions involve managerial or supervisory roles.

The process of forecasting changes in current personnel is depicted in the box in the upper right corner of Figure 3–1. Experience data are used to project future changes or personnel flows.[85] During any year, some employees will remain in their positions while others will be promoted (or demoted) or will change their occupations (perhaps moving from a clerical or an administrative aide position). Others will leave the jurisdiction through resignation, retirement, dismissal, or death. The personnel planner needs to assess whether past and current trends are likely to continue. The fact that a given set of jobs has had a high turnover rate may be because promotion opportunities have been unusually great or because openings in the private sector have been numerous. The question is whether those competing situations are likely to continue.

Such analysis is facilitated by the widespread use of computerized personnel systems or human resource information systems (HRIS). Off-the-shelf computer software exists for a variety of personnel subjects such as job evaluation, salary survey analyses, and affirmative action and, more generally, for establishing an overall HRIS, which provides computer support for most aspects of the personnel system. Off-the-shelf computer programs or packages have the distinct advantage of governments not having to spend large sums for the development of the software.[86–88] Computer technology advances are resulting in the emergence of expert systems in which computers can engage in reasoning with qualitative knowledge rather than quantitative data.[89] These expert systems have the potential for analyzing position descriptions, labor contracts, and the like.

Drawbacks, of course, exist in the application of computer technology. Computer systems may be established for operational purposes such as payroll but may not be well designed for research purposes. As a result, a personnel

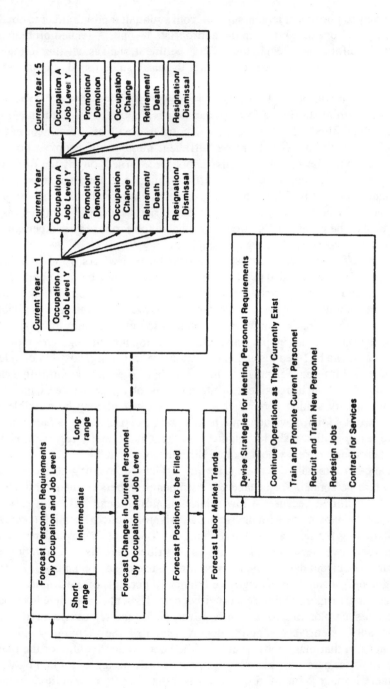

Figure 3-1 Personnel Planning Model.

planner may require considerable support from a computer programmer to obtain the right data from the system in the appropriate format. A related problem is whether the information kept in the HRIS is pertinent, such as whether it retains historical data about employees or whether the data can be found only in paper record archives.

By a comparison of the forecasts of personnel requirements and expected changes in current staffing, a forecast can be developed for the net number of positions to be filled. That forecast then is compared with an assessment of the external labor market. Will there be sufficient numbers of people who can be attracted to fill the vacant positions? Labor force projections by the BLS can be helpful. It is possible, however, for sufficient numbers of persons to be in the labor market but not be willing to accept government jobs. Engineers with job experience may prefer to work in private enterprise, where pay is higher; as a consequence, the public jurisdiction may be able to recruit only inexperienced engineers who completed college recently.

Once these forecasts are made, strategies can be devised. As is shown in Figure 3–1, it may be concluded that there is no need to change current operations. If forecasts indicate that ample personnel will be available, then no new action is required. Should there be a projected gap between needed and available personnel, then a strategy might be adopted to increase training programs to upgrade the skills of current personnel, thereby filling jobs through promotions. Positions also can be filled through more extensive recruiting, possibly coupled with increased training for new employees. Where it seems doubtful that the needed personnel can be recruited, an alternative is job redesign (see Chapter 9). If enough highly skilled persons cannot be recruited, it may be possible to redesign work so that few such individuals are needed. Another strategy is to devolve lesser-skilled tasks to volunteer workers and thereby reserve higher-skilled tasks for workers who are more difficult to recruit.[90]

Still another alternative is to contract for services, alleviating altogether the need to hire personnel. For instance, if sufficient numbers of medical doctors cannot be recruited because of low salaries in government, a fee-for-service arrangement can be made with physicians in private practice. Both job redesign and contracting for service involve revising the forecast of needed personnel.

Comprehensive personnel planning, as described here, is not common in government. Current data are nonexistent on the use of such planning, but it is likely that only a small percentage (well under 10 percent) of governments use such planning, primarily because it is neither cost efficient nor feasible for most. To attempt such planning for an entire government requires considerable staff and probably extensive computer support. Much of the planning would be superfluous in that many jobs would be filled automatically. One of the main justifications for personnel planning is that it devises strategies for coping with personnel shortages, but if few shortages exist then that benefit does not materialize. For that reason, personnel planning probably should be restricted largely to administrative, professional, and technical (APT) positions, disregarding most of the clerical and laborer levels. Even with APT positions shortages may be minimal, although some aggregate forecasting of all types of personnel is useful because of budgetary implications.

One of the most severe weaknesses of personnel planning involves forecasting future requirements. One approach is to make straight-line projections. For example, if APT positions have been increasing by 1 percent a year, the assumption would be that that pattern would continue in the future. Such an assumption obviously can be faulty, so other approaches are used. An alternative is to canvass administrators as to what they expect their personnel needs to be. This requires time, which translates into additional costs for both planners and administrators. In some cases the process has been even more elaborate; in these cases the Delphi technique has been used, in which various experts make forecasts and then review each other's forecasts, ultimately developing a consensus forecast.

If left to operate by themselves, personnel planning systems can result in putting the cart before the horse. Plans should be prepared about the future of government programs before beginning to plan for the personnel needed to implement the programs. Program planning sets forth recommendations on how programs are to be modified in the future. Decision makers, then, are presented with alternative futures. Once a decision is made to modify a program or to retain it in its current format, future personnel needs can be derived.

Numerous governments and corporations engage to varying degrees in strategic and program planning.[91-94] Strategic planning, as the name suggests, is concerned with the fundamental directions and purpose of an organization. Program planning can include lesser concerns in addition to those involving basic goals and objectives. Program planning often is linked with the process known as program budgeting. Agencies in their budget requests report projected needs for services and projected costs, which necessarily include those for personnel.[95]

Linking program planning with personnel planning is difficult because of their differing data requirements. The budget process cannot be expected to collect all data needed for personnel planning. Budget offices are more concerned with aggregates, such as how many additional technical workers will be needed if a proposed program change is approved, and less concerned with detailed personnel information. Personnel units, in contrast, are involved with specific types of technical positions. Budget processes are already complicated, involving as they do the preparation of numerous forms, and to add more forms requiring detailed information about personnel could add to the frustration of line administrators.

A possible solution to this problem is to require aggregate personnel projections in program planning through the budget process and to provide detailed personnel planning only for selected areas. Rather than attempting to devise personnel plans for all types of positions throughout a government, planners might focus on known or specific anticipated problems.[96] For example, a simple computer search of personnel files may identify some agencies in which a large percentage of the staff is approaching retirement age. In such cases turnover can be anticipated, and the personnel planner can assist in meeting the expected change. Similarly, personnel planning can be useful for agencies that are to be reorganized, where some employees may find that their positions have been eliminated; the planner can help plan for finding jobs for those who are displaced. This limited type of planning is useful in cases where a new agency is to be created, substantially increased in size, or decentralized so that central office positions will be reduced while regional office jobs are increased. Personnel planning, of course, can be useful for selected occupations where shortages are common. The federal government has had chronic problems recruiting sufficient numbers of engineers, and state and local governments have had difficulty acquiring attorneys and medical personnel. The latter problems, however, have eased as attorneys and physicians in the nation have increased in number; recruiting nurses remains a problem in many locales.

Other uses of personnel planning include the following:

- analyzing why some agencies have high turnover rates
- devising procedures for recruiting minorities and women as part of affirmative action programs
- familiarizing personnel with new technology such as word processing
- assisting employees who are laid off because of program cutbacks or contracting out, in which a government decides to contract for a service rather than provide it directly
- assisting employees to handle new responsibilities in situations where other workers have been furloughed

Problems exist even with this limited type of personnel planning. Planning that focuses on individual employees and how they will develop within an agency can result in the crown prince or heir apparent syndrome. Line administrators will not necessarily welcome the assistance of personnel planners. Such administrators may feel under enough pressure to cope with current problems and may be unwilling or unable to contemplate future ones. The personnel administrator may be viewed as not having any relevant expertise. A police chief might ask, What does a personnel planner know about law enforcement or traffic control? Planning also may be hampered by inadequate databases and information systems.

Planning may be difficult to undertake because of financial constraints. If a jurisdiction's budget is tight, any increased funds are more likely to be provided for delivering services than for what may be viewed as the luxury of personnel planning. Even personnel plans that actually are devised may not be implemented because of budgetary problems. Agencies may receive authorizations for new positions, but the budget office then imposes a freeze on all hiring to cut costs. Major economic downturns, such as the recessions of the early 1980s and 1990s, result in lost revenues and personnel layoffs despite any plans for personnel increases.

Personnel planning, along with many other functions of personnel administration, requires considerable amounts of information that is best handled by computers. Software programs known as database managers can keep detailed information on each employee and can compile information in a variety of formats. Computers can identify employees who are approaching retirement age and thereby provide information to planners regarding likely vacancies that will develop in agencies. Routine functions of keeping track of pay owed employees, vacation days accrued, and the like are readily handled by high-speed computers. As technology advances, the need for careful planning in the acquisitions of computer hardware and software has become increasingly apparent. The federal government has developed a strategic plan to help guide it in making automation decisions.[97]

SUMMARY

Organizational design typically is beyond the jurisdiction of personnel administrators, yet it will greatly influence the structuring of work and the arrangement of jobs. Job design, in contrast, may be partially the responsibility of personnel administrators. Highly developed techniques are used to determine how work can be conducted to minimize worker fatigue and maximize output. Having emerged from the scientific management school, however, job design may overlook employee motivation as an important contributor to productivity.

Position classification is one of several aspects of personnel administration intended to further the equitable treatment of employees. The position classification movement was part of a more general governmental reform movement of the 1910s and 1920s. In this system clusters of factors or aspects of work are identified, and positions are arranged in a plan according to the types of work being done. Often, points are assigned to positions according to the work performed: The greater the demands of a position, the greater the number of points. Technical problems abound, such as the appropriate number of classes to use, when and when not to create a job series, how to obtain information for classifying a specific position, and how to determine the education and experience needed.

Position classification problems also persist in the daily operations of governments. Keeping both the plan and the classification of specific jobs current is difficult. Classification inflation pressures can destroy the rationale of a plan.

Managers often feel thwarted by classifications. Central administration of the system can produce consistency and an unbiased approach but also can lead to excessive delays and red tape. Decentralization may aid in faster classification procedures, but it can result in nonstandardization of positions from department to department.

Planning for the future may be a well-accepted ideal, but personnel planning in government is not a well-established practice. Personnel planning begins with forecasting future needs by occupation and job level and projecting what will happen to current personnel in promotions, transfers, and separations. New personnel needs are compared with projected labor markets, and then strategies are devised to meet future needs. Comprehensive personnel planning systems probably are too expensive for most jurisdictions. Such planning perhaps should be restricted to occupations where shortages exist and to special situations, such as when agencies are expanding, declining, or decentralizing. Personnel planning would be greatly facilitated if more jurisdictions engaged in program planning linked with their budgetary systems.

NOTES

1. U.S. Office of Personnel Management, *Organizational Study and Design* (Washington: U.S. Government Printing Office, 1986).

2. R.H. Carter, Examining the premises of contracting out, *Public Productivity and Management Review* 13 (1989): 27–39.

3. M.J. Levine, Subcontracting and "privatization" of work: Private and public sector developments, *Journal of Collective Negotiations in the Public Sector* 19 (1990): 275–282.

4. L.M. Salamon, ed., *Beyond Privatization: The Tools of Government Action* (Washington: Urban Institute, 1989).

5. U.S. General Accounting Office, *Federal Workforce: Inappropriate Use of Experts and Consultants at Selected Civilian Agencies* (Washington: U.S. Government Printing Office, 1991).

6. F.W. Taylor, *The Principles of Scientific Management* (New York: Harper & Row, 1911), 42–48.

7. J.E. Kelly, *Scientific Management, Job Design and Work Performance* (New York: Academic Press, 1982).

8. C.D. Wrege and R.G. Greenwood, *Frederick W. Taylor: The Father of Scientific Management* (Homewood, Ill.: Business One Irwin, 1991).

9. Taylor, *Principles of Scientific Management,* 64–67.

10. S.M. Lowry, et al., *Time and Motion Study* (New York: McGraw-Hill Book Company, 1940), 388.

11. B.W. Niebel, *Motion and Time Study,* 8th ed. (Homewood, Ill.: Richard D. Irwin, 1987).

12. E.J. Lovesey, *Contemporary Ergonomics* (New York: Taylor & Francis, 1990).

13. C. Perrow, The organizational context of human factors engineering, *Administrative Science Quarterly* 28 (1983): 521–541.

14. See the following journals: *Applied Ergonomics, Ergonomics,* and *International Journal of Man–Machine Studies.*

15. F.W. Taylor, *Taylor's Testimony before the Special House Committee* (New York: Harper & Row, no date), 27.

16. P. Cressey and V. DiMartino, *Agreement and Innovation* (Englewood Cliffs, N.J.: Prentice-Hall, 1991).

17. C.E. Grantham, ed., *Managing the Human Computer Environment* (New York: Taylor & Francis, 1991).

18. M.L. Tushman and R.R. Nelson, eds., Special issue: Technology, organizations, and innovation, *Administrative Science Quarterly* 35 (1990): 1–210.

19. I. Winfield, *Organizations and Information Technology* (Cambridge, Mass.: Blackwell Science Publications, 1991).

20. M.S. Frank, Position classification: A state-of-the-art review and analysis, *Public Personnel Management* 11 (1982): 239–247.

21. S. McConomy and G. Ganschinietz, Trends in job evaluation practices of state personnel systems, 1981 survey findings, *Public Personnel Management* 12 (1983): 1–12.

22. H. Suskin, ed., *Job Evaluation and Pay Administration in the Public Sector* (Chicago, Ill.: International Personnel Management Association, 1977).

23. U.S. Civil Service Commission, *Job Analysis for Improved Job-Related Employee Development* (Washington: U.S.Government Printing Office, 1976).

24. I. Baruch, *Position-Classification in the Public Service* (Chicago, Ill.: Civil Service Assembly, 1941), 8.

25. C.L. King, ed., Competency and economy in public expenditures, *Annals* 113 (May 1924): 1–366.

26. V.S. Wilson, The relationship between scientific management and personnel policy in North American administrative systems, *Public Administration* 51 (1973): 200.

27. E.O. Griffenhagen, "Job analysis for position classification," in *Handbook of Business Administration*, ed. W.J. Donald (New York: McGraw-Hill Book Company, 1931), 1,135–1,144.

28. S.E. Bennis, et al., *Job Analysis: An Effective Management Tool* (Washington: Bureau of National Affairs, 1983).

29. S. Gael, *Job Analysis: A Guide to Assessing Work Activities* (San Francisco: Jossey-Bass, 1983).

30. G.A. Graham, "Personnel practices in business and governmental organizations," in *Problems of the American Public Service*, ed. C.J. Friedrich, et al. (New York: McGraw-Hill Book Company, 1935), 381–385.

31. Congressional Joint Commission on Reclassification of Salaries, *Report*, 66th Cong., 2d sess., H. Doc. 686 (Washington: U.S. Government Printing Office, 1920), 34–36.

32. Congressional Joint Commission, *Report*, 46–47.

33. W.E. Mosher and J.D. Kingsley, *Public Personnel Administration* (New York: Harper & Brothers, 1936), 33–34, 354–355.

34. W.H. Taft, *Economy and Efficiency in the Government Services*, H. Doc. 458 (Washington: U.S. Government Printing Office, 1912).

35. R.D. Lee, Jr., and R.W. Johnson, *Public Budgeting Systems*, 4th ed. (Gaithersburg, Md.: Aspen Publishers, 1989), 8–9.

36. Budget and Accounting Act, P.L. 67-13, 42 Stat. 20 (1921).

37. Classification Act of 1923, 42 Stat. 1488; Ramspeck Act of 1940, 55 Stat. 613; Classification Act of 1949, 63 Stat. 954; and Job Evaluation Policy Act of 1970, 84 Stat. 72.

38. U.S. Merit Systems Protection Board, *The Title 38 Personnel System in the Department of Veterans Affairs: An Alternate Approach* (Washington: U.S. Government Printing Office, 1991).

39. U.S. Office of Personnel Management, *Handbook of Occupational Groups and Series* (Washington: U.S. Government Printing Office, 1991).

40. W.G. Torpey, *Public Personnel Management* (New York: D. Van Nostrand, 1953), 44.

41. Baruch, *Position-Classification*, 92.

42. U.S. General Accounting Office, *Description of Selected Systems for Classifying Federal Civilian Positions and Personnel* (Washington: U.S. Government Printing Office, 1984).

43. C.H. Anderson and D.B. Corts, *Development of a Framework for Factor-Ranking Benchmark System of Job Evaluation* (Washington: U.S. Civil Service Commission, 1973).

44. U.S. Civil Service Commission, *How To Write Position Descriptions under the Factor Evaluation System* (Washington: U.S. Government Printing Office, 1978).

45. National Academy of Public Administration, *Modernizing Federal Classification: An Opportunity for Excellence* (Washington: National Academy of Public Administration, 1991).

46. T.A. DiPrete, *The Bureaucratic Labor Market: The Case of the Federal Civil Service* (New York: Plenum Press, 1989), 161–196.

47. U.S. Office of Personnel Management, *The Classifier's Handbook* (Washington: U.S. Government Printing Office, 1991).

48. C.T. Kulik, The effects of job categorization on judgments of the motivating potential of jobs, *Administrative Science Quarterly* 34 (1989): 68–90.

49. R.H. Scheele, et al., An experimental study of reliability in evaluating benchmark descriptions using the Oliver system, *Review of Public Personnel Administration* 9 (Fall 1988): 61–69.

50. L.L. Epperson, The dynamics of factor comparison/job evaluation, *Public Personnel Management* 4 (1975): 38–48.

51. S.B. Silverman, et al., The effects of age and job experience on employee responses to a structured job analysis questionnaire, *Public Personnel Management* 13 (1984): 355–359.

52. J.G. Veres, III, et al., A practical rationale for using multi-method job analyses, *Public Personnel Management* 16 (1987): 153–157.

53. U.S. Merit Systems Protection Board, *OPM's Classification and Qualification Systems: A Renewed Emphasis, a Changing Perspective* (Washington: U.S. Government Printing Office, 1989).

54. M. Penner, How job-based classification systems promote organizational ineffectiveness, *Public Personnel Management* 12 (1983): 268–276.

55. President's Private Sector Survey on Cost Control (Grace Commission), *Report on Personnel Management* (Washington: U.S. Government Printing Office, 1984).

56. Congressional Budget Office, *Reducing Grades of the General Schedule Work Force* (Washington: U.S. Government Printing Office, 1984).

57. W.G. Bailey, Restructuring the federal establishment, *Public Personnel Management* 14 (1985): 105–129.

58. U.S. General Accounting Office, *Compendium of GAO's Views on the Cost Saving Proposals of the Grace Commission*. Vol. 2 (Washington: U.S. Government Printing Office, 1985), 948–1,044.

59. _____, *How Certain Agencies Are Implementing the Grade Reduction Program* (Washington: U.S. Government Printing Office, 1986).

60. S.L. Durst, et al., Impacts of traditional explanatory factors on average grade increases in U.S. cabinet-level departments, *Public Administration Review* 49 (1989): 362–370.

61. C.T. Lewis and C.K. Stevens, An analysis of job evaluation committee and job holder gender effects on job evaluation, *Public Personnel Management* 19 (1990): 271–278.

62. R.W. Scholl and E. Cooper, The use of job evaluation to eliminate gender based pay differentials, *Public Personnel Management* 20 (1991): 1–18.

63. J. Cayer, Classification in the federal service: New looks at alternative approaches, *Public Administration Review* 52 (1992): 217–220.

64. E. Babcock and J. Meriwether, Reactions to a demonstration project: The Navy's experiment with pay and classification, *Management* 2 (Summer 1981): 14–17.

65. Proposal contained in a letter from Constance Horner, OPM Director, to the Honorable George Bush, President of the Senate, July 7, 1986.

66. DiPrete, *The Bureaucratic Labor Market*.

67. T.F. Lewinsohn and F. Dieckhoff, Yesterday's solution becomes today's problem: Consolidating clerical classes, *Public Personnel Management* 19 (1990): 25–30.

68. A. Schlesinger, Jr., *The Coming of the New Deal*. Vol. 2 (Boston, Mass.: Houghton Mifflin, 1957).

69. B. Bluestone and B. Harrison, *The Deindustrialization of America* (New York: Basic Books, 1982).

70. National Commission for Employment Policy, *Workforce Futures: Strategic Planning in the States* (Washington: U.S. Government Printing Office, 1990).

71. J. Burnham, *The Managerial Revolution* (Bloomington: Indiana University Press, 1941).

72. F.A. Hayek, *The Road to Serfdom* (Chicago, Ill.: University of Chicago Press, 1944).

73. Hudson Institute for U.S. Department of Labor, *Workforce 2000* (Washington: U.S. Government Printing Office, 1987).

74. Hudson Institute for U.S. Office of Personnel Management, *Civil Service 2000* (Washington: U.S. Government Printing Office, 1988).

75. Hudson Institute for U.S. Department of Labor, *Opportunity 2000* (Washington: U.S. Government Printing Office, 1988).

76. S.W. Hays and R.C. Kearney, State personnel directors and the dilemmas of workforce 2000: A survey, *Public Administration Review* 52 (1992): 380–388.

77. U.S. Office of Personnel Management, *Strategic Plan for Federal Human Resources Management* (Washington: U.S. Government Printing Office, 1990).

78. U.S. General Accounting Office, *The Changing Workforce: Demographic Issues Facing the Federal Government* (Washington: U.S. Government Printing Office, 1992).

79. P. Barnum, Misconceptions about the future U.S. work force: Implications for strategic planning, *Human Resource Planning* 14 (1991): 209–219.

80. J.W. Walker, Trends in manpower management research, *Business Horizons* 11 (August 1968): 37–46.

81. E.B. McGregor, Jr., The public sector human resource puzzle: Strategic management of a strategic resource, *Public Administration Review* 48 (1988): 941–950.

82. R.H. Meehan and S.B. Ahmed, Forecasting human resources requirements: A demand model, *Human Resource Planning* 13 (1990): 297–308.

83. R.E. Sibson, *Strategic Planning for Human Resource Management* (New York: AMACOM, 1992).

84. J.W. Walker, *Human Resource Strategy*, rev. ed. (New York: McGraw-Hill Book Company, 1992).

85. L.T. Pinfield and M. Morishima, Taking the measure of human resource management flows, *Public Personnel Management* 20 (1991): 299–318.

86. E.B. McGregor, Jr., and J. Daly, The strategic implications of automation in public sector human resource management, *Review of Public Personnel Management* 10 (Fall 1989): 29–47.

87. G.B. Siegel and J.R. Marshall, The use of PC software in teaching public personnel administration, *Public Personnel Management* 20 (1991): 61–69.

88. J.M. Stevens and R.P. McGowan, *Information Systems and Public Management* (New York: Praeger, 1985).

89. P.C. Chu, Developing expert systems for human resource planning and management, *Human Resource Planning* 13 (1990): 159–178.

90. J.L. Brudney and W.D. Duncombe, An economic evaluation of paid, volunteer, and mixed staffing options for public services, *Public Administration Review* 52 (1992): 474–481.

91. B. Bozeman and J.D. Straussman, *Public Management Strategies: Guidelines for Managerial Effectiveness* (San Francisco, Calif.: Jossey-Bass, 1990).

92. J. Koteen, *Strategic Management in Public and Nonprofit Organizations* (New York: Praeger, 1989).

93. E.B. McGregor, Jr., *Strategic Management of Human Knowledge, Skills, and Abilities: Workforce Decision-Making in the Postindustrial Era* (San Francisco, Calif.: Jossey-Bass, 1991).

94. P.C. Nutt and R.W. Backoff, *Strategic Management of Public and Third Sector Organizations: A Handbook for Leaders* (San Francisco, Calif.: Jossey-Bass, 1992).

95. Lee and Johnson, *Public Budgeting Systems*.

96. J.W. Walker, Human resource planning, 1990s style, *Human Resource Planning* 13 (1990): 229–240.

97. U.S. Office of Personnel Management, *Strategic Plan for Personnel Automation* (Washington: U.S. Government Printing Office, 1992).

Chapter 4

Pay and Employee Benefits

The compensation provided to public employees is necessarily an important concern in government. The cost of pay and benefits is the largest single item of a government's operating budget, excluding transfer payments such as welfare and Social Security benefits and intergovernmental grants. Compensation is equally important to the individuals employed by government; obviously, their livelihood and standard of living are at stake when salaries and wages are set.

This chapter discusses two topics:

1. pay for employees and the procedures used in determining pay levels
2. employee benefits or so-called fringes

Although these subjects are treated separately here, they must be considered together in understanding the total compensation that is provided to employees.

PAY

There are no absolute standards that can be applied in setting pay levels. From a government's perspective, pay must be sufficiently high to attract the necessary number of persons with requisite skills.[1] The 1989 Volcker Commission was concerned with the "federal compensation crisis," namely that pay was regarded as below what was needed to recruit and retain high-caliber personnel.[2,3] Neither the number of workers nor their skill levels are fixed, however, because jobs can be redesigned to adjust the skill requirements and thereby alter the number of employees needed. For example, a state mental hospital can adjust the relative mix of psychiatrists, psychologists, and counselors, depending upon the availability of persons in these occupations and the salaries necessary to attract them.

In seeking employees, a government competes in the labor market not only with industry but also with other governments. Individuals may be dedicated to working in government but are not necessarily dedicated to any one government. As a result, school districts compete with other school districts, cities with other cities, and states with other states. Competition also exists among levels. In any given locale there may be federal, state, county, city, and school offices, with all those governments being somewhat in competition with each other for personnel. Because governments are well aware that they compete with one another and the private sector in recruiting personnel, governments use a variety of sources of information to keep abreast of current trends in wages and salaries. The International City/County Management Association makes available pay and fringe benefit data obtained from national surveys of local governments.[4]

At the opposite end of the spectrum from pay being high enough to attract workers is the need for pay to be low enough for government to be able to afford them.[5] It could be that, to attract qualified mechanics to service police patrol vehicles, a wage level must be set so high that the government effectively is prevented from hiring a sufficient number of mechanics. If the mechanics example is weak, that of medical doctors surely is not. The incomes that physicians command in the private sector make it difficult for governments to afford large numbers of these professionals. As salaries are increased to compete with those offered in the private sector, the costs of personnel increase; a not infrequent response to raising salaries is to reduce the number of employees. Police departments in some instances have been forced to reduce their staffs because wage rates have increased faster than available revenues.

There is no simple balance between government's obligation to its employees and to its clients and taxpayers. Much rhetoric has been heard about government's obligation to treat its employees fairly, that is, that good performance is deserving of good pay. Few would take issue with such a position (although it may be overly paternalistic), but there are competing legitimate claims of taxpayers for low taxes and of clients for good services. Raising compensation levels to be fair to employees can raise the ire of taxpayers. Raising salaries by cutting back on the number of employees can result in worker opposition and taxpayer dissatisfaction with reduced services.

Traditionally, government salaries were lower than those for equivalent positions in the private sector. The standard explanation was that government employees traded money for security and fringe benefits. In recent years, however, public salaries have increased substantially, with some jurisdictions striving to maintain full comparability with the private sector. At the same time, job security has been reduced. Whereas layoffs or reductions in force (RIFs) once were rare, governments frequently turn to such cutbacks when budgets shrink as a result of tax revenue declines stemming from recessions.

Public sector wages for government blue collar workers and some lower-level white collar workers generally have been equal to or even better than those for similar employees in the private sector. There are differences among locales, however. Public sector clerical salaries may be higher than those in the private sector in smaller communities but lower than those in large cities. On average, federal salaries are generally higher than state and local government salaries.[6,7]

The public sector consistently has had difficulty keeping salaries competitive for administrative, professional, and technical personnel. The problem is particularly acute in recruiting individuals with computer skills. Some states have adopted legislation that allows substantially higher salaries for personnel in information resource management (computers) than normally would be permitted. The federal government has had a similar program since the mid-1980s and launched a more comprehensive special rate program beginning in 1990 (see below). Problems in keeping public salaries competitive are common in other countries, too.

Salary levels, of course, vary among governments. As might be expected, larger jurisdictions tend to have higher pay levels, and central cities tend to pay more than suburbs, except for the wealthier ones. Unionized government workers tend to be paid more than the nonunionized, although the threat of unionization may force up the latter's earnings.[8] Within the federal government, wages set through collective bargaining tend to be higher than those set administratively.[9] In recent years, on the other hand, some state and local unions have granted concessions in bargaining over pay.

The approaches to setting pay in government are diverse. During the height of the patronage era, salaries depended largely on the political ties of jobholders. As late as the 1920s, it was common for a government to have no systematic method for setting pay rates. One study of state government in that period found four common practices: (1) State legislatures set salaries by statute, (2) department heads set salaries with the approval of the governor, (3) department heads set salaries without needing gubernatorial approval, and (4) a board or commission set salaries.[10]

In many state and local governments, budget documents listed the names of employees and their compensation. The purpose of publicizing salaries was to avoid having some persons receive undue compensation. Table 4–1 is an example from the State of Washington's budget for 1939 to 1941. Such publicity presumably tended to encourage equal pay for equal work. Salaries of individual employees rarely are published now, except for those of high-level officials such as department heads and other cabinet-rank officers. In the federal service and many state and local governments, however, salary information about any employee is available to the public on request.

In any large government, several pay systems or pay plans may exist. The vast bulk of federal white collar employees are part of the General Schedule or "GS" system, but higher ranks are covered by the Performance Management and Recognition System, the Senior Executive Service, and the Executive Level that covers cabinet officers and their immediate subordinates. Blue collar workers are

Table 4–1 Political Science Salaries and Wages, University of Washington, 1939–1941 (Monthly Rate)

Occupation	Name of Present Employee	Salary Present (May 1938)	Salary Requested	Number of Months Employed or on Duty	Amount Requested from State Appropriations
Professor	Martin, C.E.	$510.00	$536.00	20	$10,642.00
Professor	Cole, K.	360.00	389.00	20	7,693.00
Professor	Levy, E.		150.00	3	450.00
			158.00	17	2,686.00
Professor	Mander, L.A.	350.00	389.00	20	7,663.00
Professor	Wilson, F.G.	380.00	399.00	20	7,923.00
Associate professor	Spellacy, E.	330.00	357.00	20	7,059.00
Associate professor	None		342.00	21	7,182.00
Assistant professor	Von Brevern, N.	260.00	284.00	20	5,608.00
Instructor	Biesen, C.	180.00		3	540.00
Research assistant	Epstein, J.	150.00	185.00	24	4,440.00
Research fellow	Jonas, F.	75.00		18	1,350.00
Research fellow	None		75.00	18	1,350.00
University fellows	Various			18	5,850.00
Graduate and under-graduate assistants	Various			18	540.00
Secretary	Christensen, V.	100.00	105.00	24	2,460.00
Stenographer (half-time)	Clyde, E.	40.00	50.00	24	1,200.00
Secretary	Foster, D.G.	100.00	105.00	24	2,460.00
Total political science					$77,096.00

Source: Reprinted from *Governor's Budget Compiled for the Twenty-Sixth Legislature, for Biennium 1939–41*, part 2, pp. 496–497, 1939.

in a separate system, as are some agencies, such as the Postal Service, and some workers in agencies, such as administrative law judges. Separate pay systems exist for administrative law judges, law enforcement officers, and other selected executive branch positions. Workers in the legislative and judicial branches are part of other personnel pay systems.

Pay plans generally have replaced the less structured approach to salary determination. A pay plan usually consists of a number of grades and steps within grades that are integrated with the classification of jobs existing in the government. The merit principle presumably is served by providing equal pay for equal work. Because the nature of work varies from job to job, some translation is necessary so that eventually two seemingly dissimilar jobs may receive the same pay. Chapter 3 discusses the use of points in classifying positions. A comparison of two jobs may reveal that one requires little technical knowledge and substantial interpersonal skills but that the other requires just the opposite. Under a point system, both jobs may receive the same number of points and therefore the same pay. Accordingly, budget and personnel analysts may receive the same pay, or a given type of clerical worker will be paid the same as a laborer, or a high-level clerical worker may earn the same as an administrative aide.

Under the pay plan, jobs are assigned to pay grades. At the federal level the main civilian set of pay grades is the GS system, ranging from the lowest grade, GS-1, to the highest, GS-15; the GS system is for white collar workers only. As already noted, other pay plans exist, and these often have various numbers of pay grades. For example, the Executive Level has five grades, and the Senior Executive Service has six.

Congress has defined the differences between grades, although its language is extremely broad and subject to varying interpretations. The description for GS-1 includes the statement that such positions involve "the simplest routine work"; GS-15 positions involve "work of outstanding difficulty and responsibility" performed "under general administrative direction, with very wide latitude for the exercise of independent judgment."[11]

It should be kept in mind that jobs are joined with the pay plan regardless of the individual employees involved. A federal worker might refer to himself or herself as a GS-12 when in actuality he or she is not. The worker simply holds a position that has been assigned the pay grade of GS-12.

One issue in establishing a pay plan is the appropriate number of grades to include. As noted, the federal GS system has fifteen grades, but some state and local governments use forty or even more, and others use far fewer. The advantage of using several grades is that differences in pay can be assigned according to variations in the demands of jobs. A system that had only four grades would require that all employees be placed in one of the four. This may be workable in a small local jurisdiction with few employees, but it would present great problems in a large one responsible for a variety of services and having employees with a wide range of skills. The disadvantage of numerous grades is that the system may become needlessly complex. Grades that require splitting hairs are of little use.

Because positions are assigned to pay grades, employees naturally want their positions reclassified upward and assigned to higher paying levels. As discussed in Chapter 3, classification inflation, or grade creep, is a continuing problem in all jurisdictions, particularly in the federal government in the GS-11 through GS-15 range. Part of this problem can be explained by the government greatly expanding its scientific responsibilities with a justified increase in grade levels. Nevertheless, unwarranted grade escalation also is a factor.[12]

Pay steps within each grade are used in most pay plans. In other words, not all persons within the same pay grade will receive the same pay. As few as four steps can be used, or as many as ten. There usually is some standard percentage or dollar increase from one step to another. As with grades themselves, there is no ideal number of steps, but a general rule of thumb has been that the highest step in any grade should be approximately 25 or 30 percent above the lowest.

The use of grades and steps is presented in Table 4–2 for the federal GS system. Ten steps are used for the fifteen grades, with the highest step in grades 3 through 15 being 30 percent above the lowest and a generally constant dollar difference between steps within each grade. It also should be noted that pay grades overlap. The pay for the fourth step of each grade is about the same as that at the first step at the next higher grade through GS-11, after which it widens.

Movement from one step to the next typically requires satisfactory performance on the job and a minimum period of time in each step (usually at least 3 months and often more). In the federal system, the minimum time is 1 year. The rationale for this approach is that the longer workers hold a position, the more productive they become, so that the movement to the next step is a merit increase. Officially, step increases are not automatic; satisfactory job performance is required. In practice, however, step increases in many jurisdictions are virtually automatic for all employees.

Critics contend that the automaticity of these increases fails to provide an incentive to workers, leading them to become lazy and to sit back and relax, secure in the knowledge that the pay raises will continue. An alternative would be a highly developed performance appraisal system to determine whether an employee would receive a raise and the amount. The Reagan administration proposed such a plan in 1986, with pay for groups of employees within broad bands. The difficulties of such a system, however, are substantial because of the problems involved in performance appraisal itself (see Chapter 6).

Although there may be some truth in the argument that automatic step increases provide few incentives, it also should be asked whether any system based on steps can provide incentives. Research has indicated that wages often

Table 4–2 U.S. General Schedule Pay Rates Effective January 1993

GS	1	2	3	4	5	6	7	8	9	10
1	$11,903	$12,300	$12,695	$13,090	$13,487	$13,720	$14,109	$14,503	$14,521	$14,891
2	13,382	13,701	14,145	14,521	14,683	15,115	15,547	15,979	16,411	16,843
3	14,603	15,090	15,577	16,064	16,551	17,038	17,525	18,012	18,499	18,986
4	16,393	16,939	17,485	18,031	18,577	19,123	19,669	20,215	20,761	21,307
5	18,340	18,951	19,562	20,173	20,784	21,395	22,006	22,617	23,228	23,839
6	20,443	21,124	21,805	22,486	23,167	23,848	24,529	25,210	25,891	26,572
7	22,717	23,474	24,231	24,988	25,745	26,502	27,259	28,016	28,773	29,530
8	25,159	25,998	26,837	27,676	28,515	29,354	30,193	31,032	31,871	32,710
9	27,789	28,715	29,641	30,567	31,493	32,419	33,345	34,271	35,197	36,123
10	30,603	31,623	32,643	33,663	34,683	35,703	36,723	37,743	38,763	39,783
11	33,623	34,744	35,865	36,986	38,107	39,228	40,349	41,470	42,591	43,712
12	40,298	41,641	42,984	44,327	45,670	47,013	48,356	49,699	51,042	52,385
13	47,920	49,517	51,114	52,711	54,308	55,905	57,502	59,099	60,696	62,293
14	56,627	58,515	60,403	62,291	64,179	66,067	67,995	69,843	71,731	73,619
15	66,609	68,829	71,049	73,269	75,489	77,709	79,929	82,149	84,369	86,589

Source: Adjustments of Certain Rates of Pay and Allowances, E.O. 12826, 57 *Federal Register* 62,909 (1992).

are not the main motivator of good job performance and that nearly automatic increases practically never are (see Chapters 10 and 11). Moreover, step increases may be so small that they could hardly be expected to have any effect. As Table 4–2 demonstrates, a GS-5 moving from step 1 to step 2 would receive a 3.3 percent raise—$611 extra per year, or $51 a month. Because some of this gain would be consumed by federal, state, and local taxes and increased retirement contributions, the new actual take-home pay would be well under that $51. Whether such increases serve as strong incentives is highly debatable.

An employee who remains in any grade eventually runs out of step increases and can look forward only to general, across-the-board raises for all employees, that is, changes in the pay table itself. The rationale is that an employee's productivity improvement eventually reaches a plateau. The individual has learned basically all that is to be learned in that job and is not increasingly more productive than others of comparable rank. Reaching that final step may serve as an incentive to seek a more demanding position at a higher level.

Some jurisdictions mitigate this situation by providing pay increases based solely on length of service. Longevity increases are defended as rewarding employees who have been "faithful" to the jurisdiction but have been criticized for rewarding laziness and retaining deadwood. From a purely rational standpoint, it may not be necessary to provide longevity increases to retain long-term employees; those who are at the top step in a grade and have been with that government for more than 15 years are not likely to resign. On the other hand, projected shortages of trained personnel may encourage governments to make greater use of longevity pay as a means of helping retain workers.[13]

How pay plans are adjusted over time varies greatly among governments. Collective bargaining at the state level, and especially at the local level, is used extensively in adjusting pay (discussed in detail in Chapter 12). Salary increases at those levels often are made simply in terms of the constraint of available revenues. Because these governments have substantial limits on their ability to incur debt, they must adjust salaries upward no higher than they can cover with expected revenues. It is not uncommon for jurisdictions in any given year to provide only token increases (or even no increases) because of expected revenue shortfalls. A government may be faced with the unpleasant choice of providing no salary increases and thus possibly losing employees or approving increases but furloughing many workers because of the lack of funds.

At the federal level, much attention has been focused on the method by which General Schedule salaries are set.[14,15] The Federal Salary Reform Act of 1962[16] and the Federal Pay Comparability Act of 1970[17] firmly established the principle that white collar federal workers should be compensated on a par with private workers. The federal government, however, was unable to match private sector pay rates. One study of twenty-two metropolitan areas found that in nine of these areas federal pay lagged behind private pay by more than 25 percent.[18]

The problem of setting pay on a par with the private sector is compounded for the federal government in that compensation for specific types of jobs varies widely from one locale to another.[19] A private sector entry-level accounting clerk in San Francisco, for instance, typically will receive double the pay of a similar clerk in Champaign-Urbana, Illinois.[20] If the federal government sets a national pay rate for its accounting clerks between the rates of these two cities, then federal workers in San Francisco will be underpaid in terms of the market and workers in Champaign-Urbana will be overpaid (it should be noted that this problem also exists at the state level, where standard state pay plans typically pay above market rates in smaller communities and below market rates in large metropolitan areas).

Given these problems and the need to be able to recruit talent throughout the country, the federal government took a major set of actions in 1990 as embodied in the Federal Employees Pay Comparability Act.[21,22] Although the GS system with its various grades and steps will continue, the pay rates for these are to vary according to locality. Starting in January 1994, the system provides for a nationwide adjustment based on what is called the Employment Cost Index, or ECI, a national index that examines nonfederal pay throughout the United States and is prepared by the Bureau of Labor Statistics in the Department of Labor. Adjustments then are made for specific localities as they vary from the national average. Over a period of several years, federal pay is expected to close the gaps that exist in federal pay being above or below nonfederal pay. When workers move within the federal system from one locality to another, their pay will be adjusted upward or downward, depending upon the prevailing locality rates. During the phase-in period, special wage increases were approved for workers in the New York, Los Angeles, and San Francisco areas. In these three areas, federal agencies encountered severe problems in recruiting and retaining staff because of comparatively low federal pay rates.

Under the 1990 legislation, adjustments in pay are recommended by the pay agent to the president, who has limited discretionary authority to modify those recommendations. The pay agent has consisted collectively of the secretary of labor, the director of the Office of Management and Budget, and the director of the Office of Personnel Management (OPM). Before making its recommendations, the pay agent must consider the advice of the Federal Salary Council, a nine-member body consisting of personnel experts and representatives of employee organizations.

The foundation for this entirely new system is the use of wage surveys conducted in localities throughout the United States, and the system's success will depend in part on whether those surveys are valid and reliable.[23,24] The earlier system used to make national adjustments in the GS system relied on the Professional, Administrative, Technical, and Clerical Survey, a survey that was widely criticized for its coverage in terms of the types of employers, the range of employers in terms of size, and the sampling techniques used to examine various classes of jobs.

In addition to establishing this locality-based pay system for the GS system, the Federal Employees Pay Comparability Act of 1990 contains several other provisions that strengthen the government's hand in attracting and retaining personnel. Bonuses are permitted to recruit people for hard-to-fill positions. Special pay rates may be set for up to 800 critical positions, and special rates may be paid for other workers whose skills are important.[25] Federal agencies may pay the travel expenses for candidates coming to federal offices for pre-employment interviews. New appointees to federal positions may receive moving expenses and may receive advances in pay in situations where they need funds until their first paycheck is awarded. In addition to moving expenses, bonuses may be paid to federal workers who agree to relocate to other geographic areas. Retention allowances may be paid workers whose skills are considered important and who agree to remain as federal employees. Workers may have time off with pay as an incentive for superior performance.

The 1990 law also made changes in the upper levels of the federal bureaucracy. GS-16, GS-17, and GS-18 classifications, known as the supergrades, were eliminated and replaced by a broad pay band known as the Senior Level. Banding allows for awarding specific pay rates for individuals within a salary range or band.

Turning to blue collar employees, locality pay has long been used at the federal level. The prevailing rate system, as it is known, is under the direction of OPM, which has designated about 135 geographic wage areas. The entity with the largest number of blue collar employees in an area, usually the Defense Department, is designated as the lead agency and is responsible for conducting the wage survey in cooperation with a wage committee consisting of agency and labor representatives. The Federal Prevailing Rate Advisory Committee provides advice to OPM on the overall operations of the system. Some 500,000 employees, including both workers and supervisors, are covered by the prevailing rate system.[26]

At the other end of the spectrum are executives. Compensation for public executives never has been comparable with that in the private sector, and it never will be. Six-figure incomes and higher are common in the private sector but not in the public. To some extent, low pay for top-level executives has been converted to a political virtue. Undoubtedly, the public is wary of large salaries for government executives, especially if there is a belief that these officials do little and therefore deserve little compensation. As a result, executives who leave private enterprise to become cabinet- or subcabinet-level officers often must take cuts in income. The compensation they receive typically is set by statute and is structured in terms of the compensation of the government's chief executive and legislators. In a state, cabinet officers' salaries typically are kept below the salary of the governor.

This ceiling on cabinet salaries in effect imposes limits on lower-level officials because it would be inappropriate for a department's assistant secretary to earn more than the secretary. Here, politics become important. Particularly in election years, politicians are reluctant to pass major salary increases. Quid pro quos must be developed whereby the legislators and executives both win raises. The issue is so sensitive that several years may pass before legislation to raise those salaries is initiated, while the rest of the government's employees receive annual increases.

The result is a compression of salaries among career executives and managers. A limit, known as a pay cap, is set to ensure that career employees do not have base salaries greater than their superiors' salaries. When this occurs, several layers of career executives and administrators may all earn the same pay regardless of the extent of their responsibilities. As would be expected, pay capping leads to low morale and may encourage some of the government's most talented workers to seek employment outside the government. During the early 1980s, many members of the federal Senior Executive Service earned the same pay, regardless of their responsibilities, because of the pay cap.

Paying workers based on their performance is a long-standing concept in the field of compensation for both public and private sector workers, but putting the concept into practice has been somewhat slow in the public sector.[27] As has been seen, pay has been assigned to positions independent of the individuals who hold those positions. The criticism surfaces that workers are usually paid their full salary regardless of their performance and that superior performers receive little financial recognition for their accomplishments.

Congress attempted to implement the "pay for performance" concept by including in the Civil Service Reform Act of 1978 a provision for what was called the Merit Pay System covering managerial and supervisory positions in the GS-13, GS-14, and GS-15 ranks. The law required agencies to devise systems for appraising the performance of these workers (see Chapter 6) and awarding pay increases accordingly.

Criticisms abounded when the Merit Pay System was implemented.[28-30] One area of complaint was the elaborate appraisal system that some agencies devised. Another was that the supervisors and managers were not assured of receiving the annual pay comparability adjustment that other workers received routinely. In response, Congress in 1984 replaced the Merit Pay System with the Performance Management and Recognition System (PMRS), which set ground rules for appraisal systems and guaranteed the supervisors and managers pay comparability if their work performance was judged to be "fully successful" or better. Further amendments were passed in 1991 in response to continuing criticisms (see Chapter 6).

The Federal Employees Pay Comparability Act of 1990 provided for a strengthening in the linkage between pay and performance throughout the civil service. The law provided for a Pay-for-Performance Labor–Management Committee to work with the director of OPM in developing a proposal for reforming the pay system. Legislative changes probably would be necessary to bring about any appreciable change in the existing system.

Beyond wages and salaries, there are several types of supplements to pay. Special compensation may be paid to employees who work evening and night shifts. Overtime pay at time and a half may be used, except that it typically is not provided to executive, administrative, and professional employees.[31] Where overtime pay is not provided, compensatory time is sometimes used; for example, an employee who works late several evenings or comes in on a weekend will be entitled to equal time off. Holiday pay is common among service areas that must operate around the clock throughout the year; fire, police, and hospitals are examples. Differential pay rates for different shifts of a workday are common, as is special pay for being on call.[32] Workers are entitled to pay for sleeping when their shifts are less than 24 hours. Extra compensation is paid by the military for employees in combat and by state and local governments for those in other hazardous duty. Differential pay may be provided to federal workers overseas and in Alaska and Hawaii. Special housing and clothing allowances may be provided, particularly for uniformed employees.[33,34] Extra compensation may be paid for extra work, such as the high school teacher who coaches the debate or soccer team after regular school hours.

Incentive pay or bonuses are used to retain workers and to encourage them to be highly productive.[35] The military provides bonuses for selected individuals to encourage them to remain in service.[36] Some school districts provide extra compensation to teachers willing to serve in schools in poor neighborhoods. Both the PMRS and Senior Executive Service have cash awards programs to recognize excellence in performance. Productivity gainsharing is used by some governments as a group incentive system, in which workers together receive extra pay for measurable improvements in their performance.[37]

Limits on the total amount of pay may be set to avoid some lower-level workers from being paid more than the highest ranked managers. At the federal level, for instance, total pay may not exceed the pay rate for Executive Level I ($148,400 in 1993).[38] The total pay limit should be distinguished from the pay cap noted above, which pertains to base pay.

There are important intergovernmental and economic policy concerns with regard to pay. To attract qualified employees, governments must have wage scales comparable with those in the private sector and other governments. Organized labor sometimes has been successful in gaining wage increases by taking advantage of the layering of governments. Under collective bargaining, teacher unions could negotiate salary increases in one school district after another. But there is a simpler and possibly more effective approach: If the union can persuade the state legislature to pass a minimum wage law for teachers above what generally is the existing wage rate, that law will have the effect of adjusting all teachers' salaries upward.

The same approach was taken at the federal level when in 1974 Congress extended the Fair Labor Standards Act (FLSA) to state and local governments. Not only was the national minimum wage to be applied, but also state and local governments were expected to meet maximum hour standards. This feature particularly troubled municipalities regarding their firefighters, who spend far more than 40 hours a week on their jobs, although much of that time is spent sleeping in fire stations. The U.S. Supreme Court, however, ruled in 1976 in *National League of Cities v. Usery* that the law could not be applied to "traditional" or "integral" functions of state and local governments.[39,40] In the 1960s, the Court had allowed the extension of the FLSA to state hospitals and schools.[41,42] In the years that followed, legal problems arose over what was and was not "traditional." The issue was resolved in 1985 when the Supreme Court in *Garcia v. San Antonio Metropolitan Transit Authority* overturned its earlier decision and held that Congress had almost unlimited power to impose restrictions on state and local governments.[43,44] The five-member majority held that the traditional/nontraditional distinction was unworkable.

The immediate impact of *Garcia* was a major financial threat to state and local governments. Several hundred million dollars a year would be required to pay overtime to workers, and many volunteers in government would come under the FLSA. In late 1985, Congress came to the rescue by passing the Fair Labor Standards Amendments, which specifically allowed governments to use compensatory time in lieu of overtime pay and exempted volunteers, including those who receive expenses and some other payments.[45,46] Since the extension of the FLSA to state and local governments, numerous issues and court cases have arisen regarding when employees are and are not covered under the law. For instance, if being a professional employee is defined as not having pay deducted for time away from work, then most state and local professionals would not qualify and therefore would fall under the FLSA and be entitled to overtime pay. In 1991, the U.S. Department of Labor adopted regulations that specifically exempted state and local governments from this test. As discussed later in this chapter and in others, the *Garcia* decision has far-reaching implications and was not simply overturned by the 1985 legislation.

As for economic policy, both the size of public employment and pay levels are important. It should be noted that government pay rates are especially important during inflationary periods. Because public employment has become a major portion of the total job market, pay increases for such jobs can stimulate private wage boosts, eventually resulting in higher costs for all goods and services. Public wages also are thought to have important psychological effects on private pay. Particularly at the federal level, it is thought that holding wage increases to a minimum can set an example for private employment. Therefore, presidents on occasion have reduced or blocked proposed federal salary increases even though available data justified such raises for comparability purposes.

Restrictions on state and local pay can be imposed by the federal government. In *Fry v. United States* (1975), the Supreme Court dealt with the power of the federal government to limit wage increases for state employees in Ohio.[47] The wage increases that would have gone into effect were higher than those approved by the Federal Pay Board. That board, operating under the Economic Stabilization Act of 1970, sought to limit wage increases to reduce inflation.[48] The Court ruled that while the employees were within a single state the increase would have an impact on interstate commerce and that, therefore, the federal government was empowered to set ceilings on wage raises. The Court found this to be an emergency measure that did not infringe on state sovereignty.

A final concern regarding pay involves the fact that some classes of jobs in government tend to be dominated by women and that these jobs tend to have lower pay ranges than other job classes. The contention is that when the value of the work performed in the women-dominated classes is compared with that in other job classes the women are not being adequately compensated, that women are not being paid according to their comparable worth.[49] This topic is discussed in Chapter 9.

EMPLOYEE BENEFITS

There is no such thing as a fringe benefit. Although people often speak of fringe benefits, these "fringes" are a form of compensation that employees consider an integral part of their work relationship, and the fringes involve substantial dollar outlays by government. For lack of a better term, "employee benefits" is used here.[50-52]

The preceding section discussed efforts to make pay in the public sector comparable with that in the private sector. If comparability is the stated objective, however, pay and benefits need to be viewed as a total compensation package. It is quite possible that salaries for some positions in the public sector are lower than those for comparable positions in the private sector, but this differential may be more than offset when benefits are taken into account. This section reviews the various types of benefits afforded to public workers and then addresses the issue of compensation comparability between the public and private sectors.

One of the most important nonmonetary price tags of public employment has been job security. Public employees are less likely to be furloughed, although RIFs do occur. This was amply evident during the early 1980s, when the federal government chose to cut back domestic programs and personnel and state and local governments were forced to reduce their programs as a result of losses of federal aid, restrictions on revenues such as Proposition 13 in California, and the recession that curtailed revenues drastically. Although these RIFs occur, they are less frequent in government than in the private sector, where firms are forced to reduce staff because products and services are not selling at expected levels. This means that the typical career of a private sector worker will include intermittent periods of unemployment during which income is reduced.

Work hours and workdays constitute another set of employee benefits. The 12-hour day and the 6-day week have long disappeared from both private and public sectors, although long hours may be expected of executives and other high-level officials in both sectors. The 40-hour work week generally is standard, although in recent years some state and local jurisdictions have reduced it to fewer hours, often as part of collective bargaining agreements. Assuming no change in the amount of work to be done or the productivity of workers, shortening the work week requires the hiring of additional employees and produces higher personnel costs. It also should be noted that some jurisdictions alter the work week over the course of the year; some cities have shorter operating hours during the summer.

Coffee and lunch breaks affect the total working day. At one extreme, an employee's hours may be from 8 A.M. to 5 P.M. with two 10-minute coffee breaks and an hour for lunch or, as in other cases, two 15-minute coffee breaks and 75 minutes for lunch. Sometimes employees are required to take such breaks. In other situations, the approach may be more flexible: An employee might work during lunch and then quit for the day an hour early.

Featherbedding exists in both private and public sectors, and there are no reliable data that indicate where it is more prevalent. Simply defined, featherbedding is a situation in which there is not enough work to fill the employees' time. Sometimes this results from overstaffing, with too many people to do the required work. This results in such absurd situations as a work crew of five being dispatched to fill one small pothole in a street. In other situations, the employees reduce their effective work time by taking unauthorized long lunch hours and rest breaks. It is not unusual to find employees who use the first half hour or so of each day to "prepare" for work. For instance, some clerical workers may take considerable time in the morning getting out paper, sharpening pencils, watering plants in the office, and the like, with a comparable ritual being performed at the end of the day. Practices such as these reduce the length of the workday and may necessitate the hiring of additional employees.

Government generally is liberal in giving days off for holidays.[53] As with industry, Christmas, New Year's Day, Presidents' Day (Lincoln's and Washington's birthdays combined), Veterans Day, Thanksgiving, Memorial Day, Independence Day, and Labor Day are legal holidays for most government employees. Other holidays also are common in government but less so in the private sector (e.g., Lincoln's birthday and Columbus Day). Many states release employees for part or all of Good Friday and for each general election day. Federal employees, on the other hand, do not have these as holidays.

Vacations are liberal in government. Many years ago, granting a vacation was largely at the discretion of administrative officers; an employee who was considered to have worked hard might be given up to 2 weeks of paid vacation. Since then, provisions for vacations typically have been embedded in statutes and administrative regulations. The method for calculating vacation or annual leave varies greatly among and sometimes within jurisdictions.

A person who begins a job is likely to have to work at least 6 months before becoming eligible for a vacation. The length of the vacation may be a function of the years of service, so that new employees may receive 2 weeks (10 working days) and those with 10 years or more of experience may get 3 weeks (15 working days). Vacation days, like the other factors discussed here, need to be considered in the issue of private–public comparability in compensation.

Table 4–3 lists many of the benefits that may be available to public employees. Of course, many of the items listed there and included in the following discussion are unavailable to large numbers of government workers. Within any government, some benefits may be provided to selected groups of workers and not others, such as different retirement benefits being available to police and firefighters as distinguished from other workers. One restriction, however, is that employers may not unduly favor highly compensated employees.[54] Jurisdictions are increasingly moving to flexible or cafeteria benefit plans, which allow workers options in the benefits they receive. Such cafeteria plans allow employees to customize their benefits to meet their specific needs, so that the benefits afforded to a single worker may be substantially different from those afforded to a married worker with two children.

Health

Programs involving employee health are one of the most important to workers and constitute a major expense for government. Because paying for the illnesses of workers is expensive, some governments have established wellness programs intended to encourage "healthy living."[55,56] These programs are designed to help workers avoid practices that can lead to health problems, such as overeating, having nutritionally inadequate diets, and smoking tobacco. Some jurisdictions provide exercise facilities and instructional exercise programs free of charge or at a nominal cost. Other activities include stress management courses that are intended to help workers cope with the demands of their jobs and their private lives.[57] Periodic physical examinations at no cost to employees or more specialized examinations, such as blood pressure and colorectal cancer screening, may be available.

Table 4–3 Forms of Employee Benefits

Holidays and annual leave

Health
  Wellness programs
    Diet improvement and weight loss
    Smoking cessation
    Exercise facilities and programs
    Stress management
    Periodic medical examinations
  Employee assistance programs
    Drug and alcohol abuse
  On-site infirmary
  Sick leave and compensation for
    unused leave
  Health insurance for employee, for
    dependents
    Health maintenance organizations
    Preferred provider organizations
    Prescription drug cards
    Long-term care insurance
  Dental and eye care plans
  Workers' compensation
  Disability benefits and retirement

Retirement and death
  Life insurance/death benefit
    Accidental death benefit
  Pension plan
  Social Security
  Deferred compensation

Financial security
  Financial advising
  Preretirement planning
  Credit union
  Unemployment insurance
  See, "Health" and "Retirement and
    death"

Family-related benefits
  Dependent care—Children and elder
    dependents
  Family leave—Maternity, parental,
    medical
  See, "Health"

Other
  Job training
  Educational benefits
    Repay student loans
    Free tuition or tuition discounts for
      employees, for dependents
    Educational leave
  Transportation
    Free parking or reduced parking
      rates
    Commuting allowance
    Coordination of car pools
  Flexible work hours and flexible
    workplace
  Job sharing

Employee assistance programs (EAPs) are related to wellness programs in that they too attempt to encourage healthful habits.[58–60] EAPs, however, focus upon employees who are experiencing problems on the job. An EAP may be used to help employees who report for work intoxicated or who are repeatedly absent because of their drinking problem. In such situations, participation in the EAP is mandatory, not voluntary, with the workers being expected to correct their behavior under the threat of being dismissed.

Other health-related benefits include on-site infirmaries and sick leave. By having infirmaries available to employees, health care costs can be reduced, and workers may be able to return promptly to work after receiving minor medical care. Sick leave is essential in that from time to time nearly everyone can be too ill to work. Government employees typically are entitled to 10 to 15 days of paid sick leave each year. Sometimes employees feign illness, call in sick, and stay home, thereby gaining additional vacation days. To avoid such abuses, governments have created incentive plans that allow workers to convert unused sick days into retirement benefits and other benefits.[61-63]

Governments and their workers have confronted the same rising costs in health care as other employers and workers. Full-time public workers are typically covered under group health plans, often with government paying the full cost of the coverage for the employees; when coverage is extended to dependents, then workers typically are expected to contribute to the plan.[64] As the nature of families changes in the United States, governments are having to re-evaluate their benefit packages. Domestic partners, including homosexual couples, may need to be covered in addition to spouses.[65] In an effort to contain mounting health insurance costs, governments employ several techniques, including requiring second opinions for surgeries, incentives to have some surgeries performed on an outpatient basis, and investigating for cases of fraud.[66,67] Blue Cross–Blue Shield is the most common insurer among state employees. Some governments have established or have subscribed to health maintenance organizations (HMOs); in these organizations, employees receive care from designated clinics and hospitals that have negotiated costs with the government employer. In preferred provider organizations (PPOs), employees obtain care from a variety of physicians, clinics, and hospitals that have agreed to reduce their fees.[68] Similar plans are available for dental and eye care.

Upon taking office in January 1993, the Clinton Administration set as one of its top priorities the development of a national health program that would provide broad coverage to most Americans and at a reasonable cost to be borne by individuals, private employers, and government. Emphasis was given to managed competition in which health insurance purchasing cooperatives, representing citizens in regional areas, would negotiate with various health plans regarding benefits and costs. Health providers would have an incentive to reduce their charges as a means of attracting enrollees in their plans.[69]

Other benefits pertaining to health involve situations in which employees are unable to work. Workers' compensation insurance protects employees in instances of accidents and illnesses (such as from fumes) on the job; in addition to covering medical costs, the program provides income maintenance protection for workers who are unable to work because of their injuries or illnesses. State and local workers are covered under their respective states' compensation programs; federal workers are in a different program created by the Federal Employees' Compensation Act of 1916.[70,71] Group disability insurance covers nonoccupational accidents, such as falling down stairs at home, or illnesses such as heart attack. Disability insurance is substantially less common than workers' compensation in most jurisdictions.

An employee who becomes disabled may be eligible for disability retirement. In virtually all cases, the individual must have worked for the government for some minimum period of time before becoming eligible for such a retirement;

at the federal level the minimum is 5 years, a typical waiting period. This type of retirement program is expensive, so governments need to be alert to potential abuses.[72]

One of the most severe criticisms of the disability retirement program is that it often is used for nondisability reasons. The charge is that supervisors counsel some of their employees into taking a disability retirement as a means of getting rid of deadwood. Rather than attempting to fire incompetent or troublesome workers—a task that is both difficult and unpleasant in many merit systems—supervisors may encourage employees to retire early using the disability route. Although physical disabilities are not easily faked, nervous disorders are more easily manufactured or exaggerated. The extensiveness of this practice is anyone's guess.

Retirement and Death

Several benefits pertain to retirement and death. Life insurance, which provides benefits to dependents in the case of the employee's death before or after retirement, usually is the group term type as distinguished from whole life and other endowment policies, in which premiums become a form of investment as well as provide financial protection in the event of death. The insurance program is handled by a private carrier or sometimes by a consortium of such carriers, as in the case of the federal government. The amount of coverage usually varies by compensation, with high-level employees being insured for greater amounts than those at lower levels. These plans often allow employees to purchase additional insurance. Who pays for insurance varies by jurisdiction, from all of it being paid by government to all of it being paid by the employee.

These term insurance plans can present problems to employees upon retirement. Life insurance usually expires upon resignation and sometimes upon retirement. In other cases, the amount of insurance drops drastically at retirement. Persons in their 60s attempting to buy life insurance find it extremely expensive and sometimes are denied coverage. The federal government provides free life insurance to its retired employees. Beginning at age 65, however, the amount of coverage is reduced.[73]

General retirement is one of the most expensive and troublesome benefits afforded employees. Depending on one's view, retirements can be regarded as government rewards to employees who have served faithfully for many years or as benefits they have earned and not as mere charitable contributions. The early view of pensions was that they constituted gifts from government and were not rights of employees. The U.S. Supreme Court in 1883 held, "No pensioner has a vested legal right to his pension. Pensions are the bounties of Government, which Congress has the right to give, withhold, distribute or recall, at its discretion."[74]

From a humane standpoint, it is undesirable to force an elderly employee to work simply because the person cannot afford to be without a source of income. Not only would that be inhumane, but it would mean retention of superannuated, less productive workers. Back in 1870, U.S. Senator Francis M. Cockrell, Democrat of Missouri, advocated a federal retirement system to get rid of "the fossils infesting the departments and performing no real service."[75] Another early justification for public employee retirement systems was that wage and salary rates in government were so low that employees had little choice but to use all income for daily survival and could not save for their retirement. Perhaps the most persuasive reason for these systems is that they encourage employees to remain with government and to develop careers. Without such retirement programs, workers would be more attracted to private sector careers, where retirement benefits are available.

Despite many early efforts to provide public retirement benefits, these programs were slow in being adopted. The federal government did provide various retirements to its employees early in the nation's history, but it was not until 1920 that Congress adopted the first generally applicable retirement program, the Civil Service Retirement Law.[76] Since that time the law has been amended many times, providing expanded coverage and increased benefits for employees. Military personnel are covered by separate legislation.

State and local governments have followed a similar route of gradually expanding the number of employees covered and increasing the benefits provided. There are more than 2,500 of these state and local systems, with the vast majority (about 90 percent) being administered locally. Most of the systems are small, having fewer than 100 members (about 1,700 systems); 95 percent of all employees, however, participate in one of the 170 largest systems that have 5,000 or more members. The smallness of state and local systems is a result of many jurisdictions having separate retirement systems for special types of workers; the police and fire programs, for example, often are independent of each other and those of other municipal workers.[77] The largest pension funds, as measured by assets, are California Public Employees, New York State and Local, New York City, California State Teachers, and New York State Teachers.[78] In addition to the state and locally administered plans, thousands of other small plans exist involving annuities with private insurance carriers.

Retirement benefit rates usually are based on the employee's salary and years of service. The higher these are, the higher the benefits will be. "Final average salary" often is used in the calculation. This may be an average of the employee's salary for the last 3 to 5 years. The figure is multiplied by the years of service and then multiplied by a percentage, usually between 1 and 2 percent. For example:

30 (years of service) × $35,000 (final average salary) × 0.02 (2 percent) =
$21,000 annual retirement benefits per year

Of course, great variations exist among jurisdictions. Some average the salaries of all years of service instead of just the last 3 years, and others average the three consecutive highest salaries, which need not be those of the last years. Some plans give proportionately increasing amounts as the number of years of service increases. Using the above example, 1.5 percent might be applied to the first 10 years of service and 2 percent only for subsequent years, which could save employers substantial amounts over time. Some retirement systems once applied different benefits or contribution rates to men and women based on the fact that women's longevity is greater than men's, but the Supreme Court in rulings in 1978 and 1983 found such practices discriminatory.[79]

Vesting is an important aspect of most public retirement plans and is common in private plans. Vesting allows employees to quit their jobs and receive retirement benefits when they normally would become eligible (such as at age 60 or 65). To become vested, employees normally must work for the government for some minimum number of years; 5 and 10 years are the most common standards. Upon quitting, they of course must leave their retirement contributions in the fund. The advantage to the employees is that they will be entitled to the benefits earned not only from their contributions but also from the government's contributions.

Reciprocity in retirement plans sometimes is available for those who change employers. Reciprocity (or portability) allows workers to take their retirement "credit" with them when changing employers. These types of agreements have the effect of allowing workers to enhance their careers by changing jobs without jeopardizing their financial positions during their retirement. Of course, there is no problem of reciprocity when an employee moves from City A to City B or to the state government when all state and local employees are part of a single state retirement plan.

The use of private, nonprofit retirement funds is another method that enables employees to change from one public employer to another without jeopardizing retirement benefits. The Teachers Insurance and Annuity Association (TIAA) is one example. A school district or university may provide for a retirement program through TIAA, so that there would be no problem should the teacher change employers.

In response to inflation, which can erode retirement benefits, governments have provided methods for adjusting annuities upward after the employee has retired. This can be accomplished by linking benefits to the Consumer Price Index, so that as prices rise benefits also rise. Another method is to grant retirees the same annuity increase that is provided to current workers; if the workers receive an across-the-board 5 percent salary raise, then the retirees will receive a 5 percent pension boost.

Where does the money come from to pay for retirement benefits? In most instances the employee and employer contribute approximately equal sums into the retirement fund, commonly 5 to 10 percent of the worker's salary. These monies are invested so that contributions plus earnings on investments are expected to cover the employee's eventual benefits. Such systems are said to be actuarially sound.

State and local systems invest their retirement funds in a variety of ways. Of the approximately $652 billion these systems had in cash and securities in 1991, 21 percent ($134 billion) was invested in corporate bonds and another 32 percent ($211 billion) in corporate stocks. The remainder of the funds' assets was in federal securities ($175 billion), mortgages, and other private and public investments.[80]

The adequacy of the funding of public retirement systems has long been a concern. In the 1920s some envisioned a "day of reckoning," when the federal retirement system would not be able to meet its obligations to retirees.[81] In 1963, the Advisory Commission on Intergovernmental Relations concluded that many state and local systems were "operating on an unsound financial basis."[82] This concern has persisted into the 1990s.[83,84] Simply stated, employee and government contributions plus earnings on investments are not adequate to meet the future obligations of most retirement systems.

Public employees have exerted great influence over their retirement benefits.[85] Federal workers have lobbied effectively before Congress. State and local employees have used collective bargaining to raise not only salaries but also retirement benefits. In the bargaining process, the management side sometimes has preferred to grant retirement increases rather than to raise wages. The reason is simple: Wage increases have a greater immediate impact on the current budget than retirement boosts. When the day of reckoning comes, the result will be (and is) large outlays for retirement benefits. In 1991, state and local governments combined paid nearly $40 billion in retirement benefits to former employees and their survivors.

The ramifications of underfunding retirement plans are debatable. One argument is that full funding is needed far more in private plans, where, if it is not adequate, retirees will not receive the promised level of benefits. Because governments, unlike any individual corporation, are not threatened with being forced out of business, public systems can expect to have continued support and therefore do not need to be funded fully. An alternative to full funding is pay as you go, in which current revenues are used to meet current retirement costs.

The other side of the argument is that public decision makers, if required to make full funding contributions when benefit increases are granted, would be more cautious in granting those benefits. From an economic standpoint, government should pay for resources when they are consumed, and personnel services are consumed when individuals are employees, not when they are retirees. Underfunding has the effect of postponing paying for current consumption. In other words, a hidden form of debt is being accumulated. In the future, local governments on a pay-as-you-go system may face severe problems in trying to meet retirement costs along with operating expenses and payments on the principal and interest on debt from bond issues.

Action has been taken to move retirement systems toward full funding, and further steps are being considered. Both the federal government and some states have accelerated contributions to their respective retirement programs. Some funds are entering into venture capital pools that finance corporate projects; although the risks may be high, the return on investment can be exceptionally high, thereby closing some of the gap in underfunding.[86,87] In 1974, Congress passed the Employee Retirement Income Security Act (ERISA), which requires actuarial funding for private pension plans.[88,89] Public employee labor unions have expressed support for a similar law for state and local systems, with governments at those levels generally being opposed. Whether this legislation, if passed, would be upheld in the courts is in doubt, although the 1985 *Garcia* decision (see above) can be construed to permit such congressional action.

Not only are investments of retirement funds expected to generate sufficient funds to pay retirees, but these investments may be expected to further social, ethical, and economic development objectives. State pension systems, for example, may favor in-state investments that foster economic growth. Pension systems for ethical reasons have avoided investments in South Africa.

Benefits under a public retirement system are not necessarily the only ones available. An employee can qualify for more than one retirement program. Some systems are structured to encourage early retirements. An employee can work for 20 years, earn a comfortable retirement, and then obtain a new position and earn a second retirement. Retired U.S. military personnel often find civilian employment in the federal government (a practice known as "double-dipping") or work for state and local governments. The Civil Service Reform Act of 1978 provided that the combined pay and retirement benefits to new double-dippers could not exceed the salary rate of Executive Level V.[90] At the state and local levels, employees may accrue better retirement benefits by earning the minimum in two or more jurisdictions. For example, fewer years of work may be required to earn two $10,000 retirements from two jurisdictions than to earn one $20,000 retirement from one jurisdiction.

At the federal level, there has been increasing concern that retirement programs are becoming too costly. As of 1992, retirement expenditures constituted 25 percent of federal personnel costs.[91] Possible changes include raising the retirement age and/or reducing benefits, increasing employee contributions, and delaying cost-of-living increases in benefits.

Social Security is still another factor. Participation by state and local governments has been voluntary, and when they do participate they usually provide an additional retirement program for their workers. When integrated, the two systems are intended to provide a comfortable retirement. The trend was toward increasing coverage until the late 1970s, when some jurisdictions began withdrawing from Social Security. Investment opportunities are one reason for withdrawing from Social Security. Some state and local jurisdictions and their employees thought their contributions could be invested to yield higher benefits than would be provided under Social Security.

Another reason for these withdrawals was the structure of both types of systems. For example, retirement plans for police and fire personnel often are geared to 20 years of service with compulsory retirement at age 50 or 55; their early retirement is justified because of the type of work they perform. Upon retirement, they can obtain other jobs that will qualify them for at least minimum Social Security benefits.

Federal workers, who have been outside the Social Security system, also availed themselves of this opportunity. Employees were attracted to early retirement to seek other employment where they would earn credit toward Social Security benefits.[92] Minimum rates under Old Age, Survivors, Disability, and Health Insurance were intended to aid lower-income workers so that benefits were not proportional to the number of years of work and the amount of contributions to Social Security. The result has been a more than comfortable life for some workers who have been able to qualify for both federal retirement and Social Security benefits.

The Social Security funding situation reached a crisis stage in 1983, and in response Congress made sweeping changes. State and local governments were prohibited from withdrawing. Jurisdictions that had chosen to withdraw had done so with the understanding that they never could reenter, but that was reversed. A provision was added to prevent windfall benefits for those who entered Social Security late in their careers. This was expected to encourage nonparticipating state and local governments to join Social Security.[93] The provision prohibiting withdrawal was upheld by the Supreme Court in 1986.[94] That decision, coupled with *Garcia*, granted strong powers to the federal government, powers that were used in 1990 when Congress passed the Omnibus Budget Reconciliation Act.[95] That voluminous piece of legislation included a provision requiring state and local government employees to join Social Security unless they were participating in a pension plan.

Federal employees also have come under Social Security. All employees hired on or after January 1, 1984 are covered by the Social Security system. This change, vigorously opposed by federal workers, was defended in part as helping improve Social Security's solvency by increasing contributions to the fund. Other changes included covering the president, vice president, members of Congress, federal judges, most political appointees, and employees of private tax-exempt organizations.

In 1986 Congress established the Federal Employees Retirement System (FERS), which covers employees hired since 1984 and other federal workers who opt to join.[96-99] The plan has three tiers: (1) Social Security, (2) a supplemental pension program that does not require employee contributions, and (3) an optional tax-deferred savings plan. Employees may contribute up to 10 percent of their salary to this plan, which is similar to 401-K plans in the private sector; this income is taxed later when benefits are paid. This option, known as "deferred compensation," is becoming increasing popular among state and local government employers.

As noted in the discussion of Social Security, retirement plans have important intergovernmental aspects. One problem that arose in this area in the 1980s was whether governments could tax the retirement income of employees from another government. Specifically, Michigan tax law provided for taxation of federal employee retirement benefits but not the benefits of retired state and local government workers. The U.S. Supreme Court held that the law violated the principle of intergovernmental tax immunity.[100]

Financial Security

Financial security benefits come in a variety of forms. Some, such as disability insurance, disability retirement, and retirement plans, have already been mentioned above. Other benefits pertaining to financial security include providing employees with advice in dealing with family budgets, avoiding excessive credit purchases, and planning investments. Special assistance is available for planning for retirement and includes nonfinancial advising, such as planning for the effective use of leisure time and coping with boredom stemming from not working. Credit unions are available through many large employers.

Unemployment insurance is one of the most important benefits regarding financial security. In an earlier time, being laid off by government was a rarity, but since the 1980s governments have found themselves periodically having to reduce their staffs because of falling revenues. If private employees are laid off for no fault of their own, they are entitled to unemployment compensation, but this has not always been the case for public workers. It was not until 1976 that Congress amended the unemployment compensation law to require this benefit for state, city, and county workers effective in 1978.[101] The law, of course, was supported by organized labor. The act later was upheld by the Supreme Court.[102-104]

Family-Related Benefits

Starting in the 1980s, governments became increasingly concerned with providing benefits that assist workers' families. The concern is that employers should help their employees meet both their work obligations and their family obligations.[105,106] Not only is dependent health insurance available as noted above, but so are many other benefits. As single-parent households have increased in number along with double-income families in which both husband and wife work outside the home, the need to provide care to other family members has increased. Child day-care benefits, including on-site child-care facilities, are increasing in popularity.[107,108] Public employers also are evaluating the need for benefits to care for elderly dependents; some private employers now provide respite day-care for elderly dependents.

Family leave provisions have become of major importance to workers. As is discussed in Chapter 9, women workers are protected from discrimination when they become pregnant. The Family and Medical Leave Act, signed into law by President Clinton in 1993, provides important protections to men and women working in both the private and public sectors.[109] An employee of a firm that hires at least 50 workers is entitled to 12 weeks of unpaid leave to care for

- a newborn or adopted child
- a seriously ill child, spouse, or parent
- oneself, when seriously ill

Leave can be denied for the highest paid employees, when they are considered to perform functions essential to the operations of the employer. While the law only requires unpaid leave, some employers continue to pay their workers when on extended family leave.[110–112]

Other Benefits

The range of other benefits that may be available to workers is immense. Governments routinely provide job training to improve worker performance and to help them qualify for promotions. Some jurisdictions provide educational benefits, such as covering tuition for college courses; universities often provide employees and their dependents with free or reduced tuition. Employees may be eligible for educational leave, which allows them to attend college on a full-time basis. In some instances, governments may consider repaying student loans as a means of recruiting employees with particularly needed knowledge and skills.

Some benefits involve transportation. Free or reduced parking rates may be available, or a commuting allowance may be paid. Many governments help coordinate employee car pools; a transportation allowance may be available on those occasions when employees must work late and are unable to commute home in their car pools. Some employees may have use of a government automobile, including one equipped with a cellular telephone.

Other benefits pertain to work schedules. Flexible work schedules or flexitime allow workers to adjust their working hours to accommodate their responsibilities in caring for family members (see Chapter 11). Flexible workplace plans allow employees to work at home, typically being linked to their employers through computers. Job sharing, in which two employees share a job, may be used.

In addition to all these benefits, some governments offer their workers still others:

- subsidized meals and paid meal breaks
- free or low-cost legal services
- personal use of offices, telephones, computers, and other facilities
- travel opportunities to governmental installations and to attend conferences
- administrative leave for jury duty, military leave, time off for blood donations, and the like
- free housing, uniforms or uniform allowances, cash for suggestions, moving expenses, and other benefits

An important benefit that is difficult to gauge is the increased salary a person can obtain in the private sector as a direct result of having worked for government.

One area deserving governments' attention is whether appropriate benefits are being provided to part-time workers, who constitute a growing segment of the public work force. In many instances, these workers unjustifiably are denied benefits. In 1990, almost all (93 percent) full-time state and local government employees received health insurance compared with only 38 percent of part-time employees.[113]

In-Kind Benefits

Tax laws greatly affect total compensation (pay plus benefits) in that in-kind benefits are generally tax free. For example, there is a difference between employee A who receives a $20,000 salary and a given amount of life insurance, health insurance, and other benefits and employee B who receives a total salary of $20,000 plus the sum required to purchase the same amount of benefits received by employee A. Employee B's full cash income generally is subject to federal income tax, whereas employee A does not pay tax on the free benefits. Employee A, therefore, actually is receiving higher compensation than employee B.

Public and Private Compensation

Finally, the question must be raised as to whether total compensation in the public sector is comparable with that in the private sector.[114] The question poses severe analytical problems. One problem is comparing like employers because one would not expect a small firm to be able to offer the types of benefits that are provided by large employers, both private and public. Another problem is gauging the benefits of retirement programs, which are extraordinarily important in any benefits package. Given the wide variety of possible features in these programs, objective comparisons obviously are difficult.

There also is the problem of determining what benefits to include in the analysis. If the benefits of job security and mobility (being able to change job locations without relinquishing benefits) are taken into account, federal compensation may be equal to or greater than compensation provided to workers by large private sector employers. Depending upon what benefits are included in the analysis, public sector benefits can be above, equal to, or below private sector benefits.[115-117] On the other hand, it should be recognized that government workers, especially executives, do not have other benefits frequently provided their counterparts in industry: stock options, country club and luncheon privileges, paid spouse travel expenses, and company-paid apartments.

During the 1990s and into the 21st century, governments will need to adjust their compensation plans to maintain their competitiveness with the private sector. Where scarcities occur in personnel, private and public sector employers will necessarily compete with both lucrative pay and benefits. Failure to be competitive will result in being able to fill positions only with mediocre talent or not being able to fill positions at all.

SUMMARY

Personnel compensation typically is the largest portion of any jurisdiction's operating budget. The pay plan, integrated with the position classification plan, provides a series of grades and steps within grades. The procedures used attempt to provide comparability in compensation between the private and public sectors. Considerable controversy has been generated over how the procedures for determining compensation levels in the private sector are used in ascertaining public levels. Comparability has been largely achieved for low- and medium-level positions; in some instances, public pay may be greater than private pay for similar jobs. Where comparability has not been achieved, and never will be, is at the executive level; for these jobs, private pay is considerably higher.

Public employees have numerous benefits other than pay. The 40-hour work week with rest and lunch breaks generally is standard. Numerous holidays are provided along with lengthy vacation and sick leave allowances. Life insurance, health insurance, workers compensation, and disability insurance are provided. Disability retirement has stirred some concerns that employees may abuse this benefit and that supervisors use it as a way of getting rid of deadwood.

General retirement benefits are increasing in cost and have stimulated fears of a future crisis in funding. Benefits typically are based on an employee's final average salary and years of service. Both employees and government contribute to retirement plans, with the funds being invested in corporate bonds and stocks. Annuities often are adjusted upward to compensate for rises in the cost of living. The result is that many retirement plans may not be actuarially sound. Proposals for the federal government require actuarial funding of state and local plans.

Achieving comparability between the private and public sectors requires considering both direct compensation and other benefits. The two groups of workers may be comparable in pay but not necessarily in benefits. Because it is extremely difficult to determine the real value of tangible and intangible benefits to public and private workers, a firm conclusion cannot be reached about the relative compensation levels of federal and private workers. There is agreement, however, that state and local compensation levels tend to be below those of industry.

NOTES

1. J.E. Annable, Jr., A theory of wage determination in public employment, *Quarterly Review of Economics and Business* 14 (Winter 1974): 43–58.

2. National Commission on the Public Service (Volcker Commission), *Leadership for America: Rebuilding the Public Service* (Washington: Volcker Commission, 1989).

3. U.S. General Accounting Office, *Recruitment and Retention: Inadequate Federal Pay Cited as Primary Problem by Agency Officials* (Washington: U.S. Government Printing Office, 1990).

4. International City/County Management Association (ICMA), *Compensation 92* (Washington: ICMA, 1992).

5. W.C. Lawther, et al., Compensation control mechanisms in the American states, *Public Personnel Management* 18 (1989): 325–338.

6. A.B. Krueger, *Are Public Sector Workers Paid More Than Their Alternative Wage?* Working Paper No. 2500 (Cambridge, Mass.: National Bureau of Economic Research, 1988).

7. D. Belman and J.S. Heywood, Government wage differentials: A sample selection approach, *Applied Economics* 21 (1989): 427–438.

8. R.G. Ehrenberg and G.S. Goldstein, A model of public sector wage determination, *Journal of Urban Economics* 2 (1975): 223–245.

9. U.S. General Accounting Office, *Comparison of Collectively Bargained and Administratively Set Pay Rates for Federal Employees* (Washington: U.S. Government Printing Office, 1982).

10. C.L. King, How shall salaries of state employees be fixed? *Annals* 113 (May 1924): 202–206.

11. Classification Act of 1949, P.L. 81-429, 63 Stat. 954.

12. S.L. Durst, et al., Impacts of traditional explanatory factors on average grade increases in U.S. cabinet-level departments, *Public Administration Review* 49 (1989): 362–371.

13. R.C. Kearney and K.S. Morgan, Longevity pay in the states: Echo from the past or sound of the future, *Public Personnel Management* 19 (1990): 191–200.

14. U.S. Office of Personnel Management, *Reforming Federal Pay: An Examination of More Realistic Pay Alternatives* (Washington: U.S. Government Printing Office, 1984).

15. President's Panel on Federal Compensation, *Report* (Washington: U.S. Government Printing Office, 1975).

16. Federal Salary Reform Act of 1962, P.L. 87-793, 76 Stat. 841.

17. Federal Pay Comparability Act of 1970, P.L. 91-656, 84 Stat. 1946.

18. U.S. General Accounting Office, *Federal Pay: Private Sector Salary Differences by Locality* (Washington: U.S. Government Printing Office, 1991).

19. C. Fay, et al., Locality pay: Balancing theory and practice, *Public Personnel Management* 20 (1991): 397–408.

20. U.S. General Accounting Office, *Federal Pay: Comparisons with the Private Sector by Job and Locality* (Washington: U.S. Government Printing Office, 1990).

21. Federal Employees Pay Comparability Act of 1990, P.L. 101-509, 104 Stat. 1427.

22. H. Risher and C. Fay, Federal pay reform: A response to an emerging crisis, *Public Personnel Management* 20 (1991): 385–394.

23. L.S. Hartenian and N.B. Johnson, Establishing the reliability and validity of wage surveys, *Public Personnel Management* 20 (1991): 367–383.

24. D. Belman and J.S. Heywood, The effect of establishment and firm size on public wage differentials, *Public Finance Quarterly* 18 (1990): 221–235.

25. U.S. General Accounting Office, *Federal Pay: Special Rates* (Washington: U.S. Government Printing Office, 1990).

26. U.S. Merit Systems Protection Board, *Federal Blue-Collar Employees: A Workforce in Transition* (Washington: U.S. Government Printing Office, 1992).

27. J.R. Schuster and P. Zingheim, *The New Pay: Linking Employee and Organizational Performance* (New York: Lexington Books, 1992).

28. J.L. Pearce and J.L. Perry, Federal merit pay: A longitudinal analysis, *Public Administration Review* 43 (1983): 315–325.

29. J.L. Perry, Making policy by trial and error: Merit pay in the federal service, *Policy Studies Journal* 17 (Winter 1988–89): 389–405.

30. G.T. Milkovich and A.K. Wigdor, eds., Committee on Performance Appraisal for Merit Pay, National Research Council, *Pay for Performance: Evaluating Performance Appraisal and Merit Pay* (Washington: National Academy Press, 1991).

31. *County of Kern v. Abshire*, 908 F.2d 483, *cert. denied* 111 S. Ct. 785 (1991).

32. K.J. Boyd and S.S. Dickerson, Local government personnel compensation and fringe benefits, *Baseline Data Report* 22 (May/June 1990): 1–14.

33. U.S. General Accounting Office, *Comparisons with Civilian Compensation and Related Issues* (Washington: U.S. Government Printing Office, 1986).

34. _____, *Military and Federal Civilian Disposable Income Comparisons and Extra Pays Received by Military Personnel* (Washington: U.S. Government Printing Office, 1984).

35. N.W. Clark, Incentive programs in government: Why aren't they being used? *Public Personnel Management Journal* 12 (1983): 181–185.

36. U.S. General Accounting Office, *Millions Spent Needlessly in Navy and Marine Corps' Aviation Bonus Program* (Washington: U.S. Government Printing Office, 1982).

37. K.C. Naff and R. Pomerleau, Productivity gainsharing: A federal sector case study, *Public Personnel Management* 17 (1988): 403–419.

38. "Aggregate Limitation on Pay," 5 CFR Part 530.

39. *National League of Cities v. Usery*, 426 U.S. 833 (1976).

40. W.J. Kilberg and L.B. Fort, *National League of Cities v. Usery*: Its meaning and impact, *George Washington Law Review* 45 (1977): 613–631.

41. *Maryland v. Wirtz*, 392 U.S. 183 (1968).

42. U.S. General Accounting Office, *Department of Labor's Enforcement of the Fair Labor Standards Act* (Washington: U.S. Government Printing Office, 1985).

43. *Garcia v. San Antonio Metropolitan Transit Authority*, 469 U.S. 528 (1985).

44. U.S. General Accounting Office, *The Fair Labor Standards Act: Extending the Act to State and Local Government Employees* (Washington: U.S. Government Printing Office, 1988).

45. Fair Labor Standards Amendments of 1985, P.L. 99-150, 99 Stat. 787.

46. V.R. Johnston and M. Kurtz, Handling a public policy emergency: The Fair Labor Standards Act in the public sector, *Public Administration Review* 46 (1986): 414–422.

47. *Fry v. United States*, 421 U.S. 542 (1975).

48. Economic Stabilization Act of 1970, P.L. 91-379, 84 Stat. 799.

49. R.W. Scholl and E. Cooper, The use of job evaluation to eliminate gender based pay differentials, *Public Personnel Management* 20 (1991): 1–18.

50. Employee Benefit Research Institute, *Fundamentals of Employee Benefit Programs*, 4th ed. (Washington: Employee Benefit Research Institute, 1990).

51. R.C. Kearney and C.J. Sears, Planning fringe benefits for the work force of the future, *Public Administration Quarterly* 9 (1985): 291–299.

52. J. Matzer, Jr., *Pay and Benefits: New Ideas for Local Government* (Washington: International City Management Association, 1988).

53. W.J. Woska, Pay for time not worked: A public-sector budget dilemma, *Public Administration Review* 48 (1988): 551–556.

54. Tax Reform Act of 1986, P.L. 99-514, 100 Stat. 2091.

55. J.W. Busbin and D.P. Campbell, Employee wellness programs: A strategy for increasing participation, *Journal of Health Care Marketing* 10 (December 1990): 22–30.

56. V. Carver and C. Ponee, eds., *Women, Work, and Wellness* (Toronto, Ontario: Addiction Research Foundation, 1989).

57. D.L. Nelson and C. Sutton, Chronic work stress and coping: A longitudinal study and suggested new directions, *Academy of Management Journal* 33 (1990): 859–869.

58. B. Mani, Difficulties, assumptions, and choices in evaluating employee assistance programs, *Review of Public Personnel Administration* 12 (September–December 1991): 70–80.

59. A. Moriarty and M.W. Field, "Proactive intervention," a new approach to police EAP programs, *Public Personnel Management* 19 (1990): 155–161.

60. R.W. Perry and N.J. Cayer, Evaluating employee assistance programs: Concerns and strategies for public employers, *Public Personnel Management* 21 (1992): 323–333.

61. H.L. Kroesser, et al., Selected factors affecting employees' sick leave use, *Public Personnel Management* 20 (1991): 171–180.

62. L.E. Peek, et al., State of Illinois sick leave incentive policy: University employees' dysfunctional behavior, *Public Personnel Management* 20 (1991): 325–338.

63. U.S. General Accounting Office, *Retirement Credit Has Contributed to Reduced Sick Leave Usage* (Washington: U.S. Government Printing Office, 1986).

64. C.J. Yaggy, Cost increases continue for state employee health plans, *Pension World* 27 (August 1991): 20–24.

65. M. McDonald, Domestic partner benefit changes, *Business and Health* 8 (October 1990): 11–12.

66. P. Moore, Health care cost containment in large American cities, *Public Personnel Management* 18 (1989): 87–100.

67. U.S. General Accounting Office, *Fraud and Abuse: Stronger Controls Needed in Federal Employees Health Benefits Program* (Washington: U.S. Government Printing Office, 1991).

68. T. Rice, et al., PPOs: The employer perspective, *Journal of Health Politics* 14 (1989): 367–382.

69. J. Rovner, Clinton has Rx for reform: Will Congress take the cure, *Congressional Quarterly Weekly Report* 50 (1992): 3,714–3,716.

70. W.J. Nelson, Jr., Workers' compensation: Coverage, benefits, and costs, 1987, *Social Security Bulletin* 53 (April 1990): 2–11.

71. Symposium on the Federal Employees' Compensation Act, *Monthly Labor Review* 114 (September 1991): 3–33.

72. U.S. General Accounting Office, *Most Civil Service Disability Retirement Claims Are Decided Fairly, but Improvements Can Be Made* (Washington: U.S. Government Printing Office, 1983).

73. *United States v. Clark*, 445 U.S. 23 (1980).

74. *U.S. ex rel. Bernett v. Teller*, 107 U.S. 64 (1883).

75. F.M. Cockrell, as quoted in J.T. Doyle, The Federal Service Retirement Law, *Annals* 113 (May 1924): 332.

76. Civil Service Retirement Law of 1920, P.L. 66-215, 41 Stat. 614.

77. U.S. Census Bureau, *Finances of Employee Retirement Systems of State and Local Governments* (Washington: U.S. Government Printing Office, annual).

78. A. Lamphere, Top 50 public pension funds, *City and State* 9 (February 10–23, 1992): 19.

79. *City of Los Angeles, Department of Water and Power v. Manhart*, 435 U.S. 702 (1978) and *Arizona Governing Commission for Tax Deferred Annuity and Deferred Compensation v. Norris*, 463 U.S. 1073 (1983).

80. U.S. Census Bureau, *Finances of Selected Public Employee Retirement Systems (June 30, 1991)* (Washington: U.S. Government Printing Office, 1991).

81. Doyle, The Federal Service Retirement Law, 337.

82. Advisory Commission on Intergovernmental Relations, *Transferability of Public Employee Retirement Credits among Units of Government* (Washington: U.S. Government Printing Office, 1963), 20.

83. B.R. Marks, et al., Toward understanding the determinants of pension underfunding in the public sector, *Journal of Accounting and Public Policy* 7 (1988): 157–183.

84. P. Zorn, Survey of state and local government employee retirement systems, *Government Finance Review* 8 (February 1992): 40–43.

85. D.R. Kemp, Major unions and collectively bargained fringe benefits, *Public Personnel Management* 18 (1989): 505–510.

86. T. Ring, State systems try out venture-capital pools, *City and State* 2 (December 1985): 13, 17.

87. F.G. Hayden, Public pension power for social investments, *Journal of Economic Issues* 23 (1989): 1,027–1,045.

88. Employee Retirement Income Security Act, P.L. 93-406, 88 Stat. 829 (1974).

89. U.S. General Accounting Office, *Pension Plans: Labor and IRS Enforcement of the Employee Retirement Income Security Act* (Washington: U.S. Government Printing Office, 1989).

90. Civil Service Reform Act of 1978, P.L. 95-454, 92 Stat. 1111.

91. U.S. Office of Management and Budget, *Budget of the United States Government* (Washington: U.S. Government Printing Office, 1992).

92. G. Burtless and J. Hausman, "Double Dipping": The combined effects of Social Security and civil service pensions on employee retirement, *Journal of Public Economics* 18 (1982): 139–159.

93. A.H. Robertson and R.W. Kalman, Social Security reform: Now and later, *Governmental Finance* 12 (September 1983): 29–34.

94. *Bowen v. Public Agencies Opposed to Social Security Entrapment,* 477 U.S. 41 (1986).

95. Omnibus Budget Reconciliation Act of 1990, P.L. 101-508, 104 Stat. 1388.

96. Federal Employees Retirement System Act of 1986, P.L. 99-335, 100 Stat. 514.

97. See Civil Service Retirement Spouse Equity Act of 1984, P.L. 98-615, 98 Stat. 3195 and Federal Employees Benefits Improvements Act of 1986, P.L. 99-251, 99 Stat. 14.

98. U.S. General Accounting Office, *Federal Retirement: Implementation of the Federal Employees Retirement System* (Washington: U.S. Government Printing Office, 1988).

99. _____, *Federal Retirement: Use of Contractors To Implement the Federal Employees Retirement System* (Washington: U.S. Government Printing Office, 1989).

100. *Davis v. Michigan*, 489 U.S. 803 (1989).

101. Unemployment Compensation Act Amendments of 1976, P.L. 94-566, 90 Stat. 2667.

102. *Los Angeles County v. Marshall*, 442 F. Supp. 1186 (1977), *cert. denied* 449 U.S. 837 (1980).

103. W.L. Hansen and J.F. Byers, eds., *Unemployment Insurance: The Second Half-Century* (Madison, Wis.: University of Wisconsin Press, 1990).

104. W. Vroman, *Unemployment Insurance Trust Fund Adequacy in the 1990s* (Kalamazoo, Mich.: W.E. Upjohn Institute, 1990).

105. U.S. Merit Systems Protection Board, *Balancing Work Responsibilities and Family Needs: The Federal Civil Service Response* (Washington: U.S. Government Printing Office, 1991).

106. L.E. Crawford, *Dependent Care and Employee Benefits Package* (Westport, Conn.: Quorum Books, 1990).

107. E.L. Suntrup, Child-care delivery systems in the government sector, *Review of Public Personnel Administration* 10 (Fall 1989): 48–59.

108. Y.T. Abraham and J.S. Bowdidge, Work-Place Child Care Act: A prototypical portrayal of potential public policies, *Public Personnel Management* 19 (1990): 411–418.

109. Family and Medical Leave Act, P.L. 103-3. (1993).

110. K. Doherty, Parental leave strategies for the 1990s, *Business and Health* 8 (January 1990): 21–23.

111. J.S. Hyde and M.J. Essex, eds., *Parental Leave and Child Care* (Philadelphia: Temple University Press, 1991).

112. U.S. General Accounting Office, *Parental Leave: Estimated Cost of Revised Parental and Medical Leave Act Proposal* (Washington: U.S. Government Printing Office, 1988).

113. D. Hedger, Benefits in state and local governments address family concern, *Monthly Labor Review* 115 (March 1992): 32–37.

114. U.S. General Accounting Office, *The Changing Workforce: Comparison of Federal and Nonfederal Work/Family Programs and Approaches* (Washington: U.S. Government Printing Office, 1992).

115. P. Moore, Comparison of state and local employee benefits and private employee benefits, *Public Personnel Management* 20 (1991): 419–439.

116. W.J. Wiatrowski, Comparing employee benefits in the public and private sectors, *Monthly Labor Review* 111 (December 1988): 3–8.

117. L.M. Lovejoy, The comparative value of pensions in the public and private sectors, *Monthly Labor Review* 111 (December 1988): 18–26.

Chapter 5

Recruitment, Examination, and Selection

Getting the appropriate people into government obviously has an impact on the quality of services provided. Placing workers in jobs for which they are unqualified can be expected to produce disappointing results for both government and the individuals involved. A worker who is dismissed for being unable to perform a job may find it difficult to obtain another position. The need for an effective intake process in which the knowledge, skills, and abilities of individuals are matched with the demands of jobs is hardly debatable, but the gap between aspiration and practice often is significant.

This chapter examines the following processes by which individuals are brought into public service:

1. methods of recruitment
2. the controversial field of civil service testing
3. the procedures by which individuals are selected from among qualified applicants to become public servants

The focus is entry into government rather than promotion and reassignment (see Chapter 7).

RECRUITMENT

Recruitment in the public sector often is not well planned, in part because somewhat conflicting purposes are at stake. Although all recruitment efforts are intended to obtain sufficient numbers of employees, there are differing views on the extent to which individuals with high qualifications should be sought. One view is that government should seek only those with the best skills; accomplishing this would require an extensive recruiting program, which would bring large numbers of persons under consideration. Because extensive recruiting is expensive, jurisdictions often are satisfied with somewhat less than the best; they may settle for superior but not necessarily outstanding workers. A commonly held view is that in recent times government has been unsuccessful in recruiting superior workers, resulting in a general reduction in the quality of the public work force.[1]

Of course, what constitutes a superior worker is highly debatable. Examination systems (discussed in the next section) may be unable to differentiate between persons with satisfactory skills and those with superior skills.

Another factor that sometimes enters into recruiting is the concept that government job opportunities should be available to a wide spectrum of persons as a democratizing aspect of the public service. Finding satisfactory or even superior personnel, then, is not all that is intended. The recruitment program thus may be aimed specifically at minorities, and in some cases goals may be set to attain a representative mix.

Recruiting involves getting people to apply for public positions, and inducing them to take that step may depend largely on the public sector's image in general and the jurisdiction's image in particular. People who think government work is dull, full of red tape, and pays little are unlikely to apply. Similarly, if government is seen as being corrupt and/or ineffectual, applicants may be few. If nonwhites think government deliberately discriminates against them, they may not apply. A study of community attitudes after the 1972–73 Watergate scandal that resulted in President Nixon's resignation found that two of five respondents (38 percent) had become more negative toward federal officials and that one third (35 percent) were not surprised by what had happened, a rather cynical view of the integrity of federal officials.[2] During the latter half of the 1970s and through most of the 1980s, Presidents Jimmy Carter and Ronald Reagan frequently criticized what they seemingly considered rampant incompetence in government administration. This "bureaucrat bashing," as it came to be called, added further tarnish to the image of the public service. Major public problems, including the widespread failure of savings and loan institutions and the 1992 riots in Los Angeles, gave the impression that public officials were incompetent at best.

Recruitment is likely to be successful if a government is perceived as a place in which employees perform interesting work, make real contributions to solving societal problems, have opportunities for developing productive careers, and enjoy substantial pay, benefits, and job security.[3] The Task Force on Recruitment and Retention of the National Commission on the Public Service (Volcker Commission) listed as its first recommendation the need to "make an exemplary public service a national priority."[4]

Recruiting for some political positions, as distinguished from merit positions, sometimes can be particularly difficult because the jobs can be perceived as excessively demanding with few accompanying benefits. These so-called prune jobs, in contrast with plums, include such positions as the director of the Food and Drug Administration and the director of the Federal Highway Administration.[5-7]

Of particular concern has been the ability of government to recruit administrative, professional, and technical (APT) workers. There often is an overabundance of unskilled or semiskilled applicants but a scarcity of highly trained individuals. Government typically is at a disadvantage in competing for medical doctors, attorneys, and engineers, considering the pay differentials between the private and public sectors. Moreover, professions often involve nonbureaucratic work, so that a medical doctor may well prefer to have a private practice rather than have to cope with red tape as a government employee.

This concern for APT employees has led to suggestions for careful personnel planning (see Chapter 3). One line of thinking has been that in the near future the pool of highly qualified talent will diminish as a result of demographic trends at a time when the technical demands of government jobs increase, thereby creating a major recruiting problem.[8,9] Alternative views suggest no such problem, however. Cutbacks in the defense industry have resulted in surpluses of some skilled workers. Periodic downturns in the economy regularly result in people previously employed in the private sector seeking government positions. Colleges and universities periodically "overproduce" many types of graduates, creating surpluses in skills and forcing individuals to turn to the public sector for possible employment. The leading role taken by the federal government in many scientific fields (for example, space and medical research) has made it comparatively easy to recruit top talent in many areas. Dire forecasts of recruiting problems have been criticized as being founded on weak analyses of demographic data and having assumed government jobs on average to demand far more technical knowledge than is the case.[10]

Regardless of whether a crisis looms in recruiting APT personnel, some jurisdictions have established special recruiting programs directed at entry-level professionals. The U.S. Office of Personnel Management (OPM) operates the Presidential Management Internship Program, which recruits graduate students from college campuses for 2-year paid internships that lead to permanent employment.[11] A significant aspect of this program is its reliance on schools to nominate their best graduates for consideration. This approach enlists schools as active components of the recruiting process rather than their being simply passive facilitators that allow recruiters to contact students. Several states and some cities have similar programs.

The success or failure of recruitment is a function of such factors as pay, whether individuals are willing to relocate and/or change employers, and other factors related to work and family needs. Low salaries compared with those of private sector jobs and the high cost of living in such locations as San Francisco and Washington discourage people from accepting government job offers.[12–15] Young people, especially the unmarried young, are more likely to be willing to move to another city to take a government job than older persons with families and homes. Persons already employed in the private sector may be unwilling to forfeit their seniority to take a public job; as shown in Chapter 4, retirement programs may discourage such a change. Applicants considering government employment are concerned about whether flexible work schedules are possible, child care is available, and leave policies are ample.[16]

Recruitment techniques are varied. All jurisdictions issue public announcements of job vacancies and scheduled examinations. These advertisements may appear in the classified section of newspapers as well as in poster form in government buildings, community centers, and such places as municipal transit lines. This shotgun approach is intended to reach a wide range of the population, albeit many will not be interested or will be unqualified to take the examination. When one is seeking professionals and administrators, a more directed approach is to advertise in newsletters and journals of their associations, such as in the newsletter of the International City/County Management Association.

Brochures and pamphlets covering general career opportunities are used. Sometimes governments publish career directories intended to provide general information about job opportunities in their jurisdictions. Such printed materials are sent to libraries, high school counselors, and college placement offices.

Job information centers, telephone hot lines, computer assisted information systems, and job fairs are used. The federal government has about 100 job information centers throughout the country, although only about 40 are open on a walk-in basis.[17] Toll-free 800 numbers or toll-call 900 numbers may be used, allowing a person to call at any time of the day for information about how to apply for a job. Mechanisms such as these have the advantage of providing a personal touch, but they can be counterproductive if inquiries are given cold and abrupt treatment or elicit sketchy information. OPM makes available a personal computer system known as the Federal Occupational and Career Information System (FOCIS), which helps current and prospective employees identify possible job openings; information also is available on a toll-call basis through OPM's Career America Connection at (912) 757-3000. Job fairs are held in which prospective workers may come to one location and speak with a variety of employers or employing agencies.

One of the most expensive forms of recruiting is in person. Recruiters interview applicants at job placement centers established at state and national professional conventions. Recruiters are sent to college placement offices and to specific departments of colleges and universities.[18] A city government may send recruiters to particular sections of town, such as to low-income/nonwhite neighborhoods. Whether the recruiter is trained in interpersonal relations can have a major influence on the interviewee's deciding to pursue job opportunities with that jurisdiction. A common constraint on the recruiters is that they can only explain job opportunities; they cannot make commitments because the individuals still must pass civil service tests.

Private search firms sometimes are used to design and execute search processes for key executive positions.[19] These firms can be particularly helpful in being sure that minority candidates are recruited into the applicant pool and can save innumerable hours of studying the credentials of possibly hundreds of applicants. The financial costs of these services can be high, however, and government leaders must be careful to avoid relinquishing control of the recruiting and selection process.

When government gives high priority to increasing the representative nature of its work force, that is, having its workers reflect the characteristics of the general population, special recruiting techniques and job redesign practices may be appropriate. For example, apprenticeship programs can be established that allow people to learn on the job; this type of program can help recruit people who otherwise would be barred from positions because of not meeting such requirements as having a college degree.[20]

Several other techniques are possible. Governments are giving consideration to the creation of special higher education scholarships that would commit recipients to government service. Governments also could pay off student indebtedness for new employees.

On the whole, government recruitment often is haphazard. Although many recruiting techniques are available and some jurisdictions are exceptionally thorough in their search processes,[21] jurisdictions frequently do not carefully plan their recruiting strategies. Ideally, a separate strategy should be planned for each job type, or at least for each job series, but funds to support such an effort usually are unavailable. Despite the paucity of data on the subject, it can safely be said that governments spend only a small amount on recruitment, in contrast with expenditures for other personnel functions such as testing and position classification.[22] Failure to recruit extensively sometimes results in no qualified applicants being available for some types of jobs. When that happens, line agencies may be forced to conduct their own recruiting to compensate for the inadequacies of the civil service commission's effort. Haphazard and slow recruiting processes can discourage applicants, especially better qualified applicants who may have job opportunities with other employers.[23] Direct hire authority, when granted to agencies, allows them to cut through red tape and promptly hire qualified candidates, a process that may lead to successful recruiting of people who otherwise would have been lost by the slow pace of recruitment and selection.[24]

Retention must be considered integral to the recruitment process. If the recruitment process is successful in attracting highly qualified individuals into government employment, then conditions need to be established to retain those individuals. All aspects of a job contribute to an employee's decision to stay or resign.[25] One study found that leave benefits were particularly important in encouraging federal workers to remain with the government.[26] If jobs lack a variety of attractive features, government may be engaged in a revolving door process in which workers are recruited with great frequency because of constant turnover.

Perceived low pay and limited opportunities for advancement can be major factors in government failing to retain its workers.[27,28] In a 1989 survey of 16,000 federal workers, "only about half of the respondents *would* recommend the Federal Government as an employer, while over one-fourth say they definitely would *not*."[29] One observer has suggested that the federal bureaucracy is characterized by anomie that casts career employees adrift with little sense of direction.[30,31]

EXAMINATION

Testing or examining is an essential aspect of the merit principle. According to that principle, people obtain government positions on the basis of their capacity to perform certain job duties, and the examination process is designed to determine that capacity. This section considers the types of tests used, test validity, and test administration. It is essential to understand that the term "test" does not necessarily mean a set of questions that candidates must answer; tests involve a wide variety of measurement devices.

Types of Tests

Testing essentially is a predictive process. A test is intended to screen out persons who would not perform well on a job. It preferably not only will screen out inappropriate individuals but also will allow for gradations in skills among qualified applicants. A worker with a high score on an examination should perform not only satisfactorily but in a superior fashion.

In developing a testing program for a given type of position, jobs are analyzed to identify what knowledge, skills, and abilities are required and at what levels. City police officers, for example, must have general police knowledge, such as an understanding of the law, and must be able to deal with peers and the public, to care for and use equipment, to attend to detail, and to make decisions.[32] Each of these in turn must be operationalized. The ability to make decisions obviously is too broad a concept to be a useful guide to testing an applicant for a police position. Should a police officer, confronted with a situation in which persons are being held hostage, be able to decide how to handle the situation or only know that a superior should be called in? The point is that the test should be geared to the type and extent of decision making required by the job.

Once characteristics have been defined, it is possible to consider what techniques to use in testing the candidates. As will be seen in this discussion, the techniques available are almost limitless, and as a consequence, decisions must be made regarding which techniques to use in any given situation. Test administrators need to apply test methods that have been found through research to be useful.[33]

All testing programs begin with an application; a candidate provides basic information, such as name and address, and job-related information, such as education and experience. At the federal level, Standard Form 171 is used to collect much of this type of information, although a separate, more specific application also may be required. The candidate describes experience related to each job held, including job title, pay, length of service, immediate supervisor, and a description of the work performed. Information also is provided about education. Persons with college educations applying for entry-level jobs include information about courses taken along with credit hours. The application is important in determining whether an individual meets minimal educational and experience requirements and can be used to screen out clearly unacceptable persons at the outset. The application also can be used in predicting whether the candidate has had the appropriate mix of experience to be able to cope with the job.

How critical formal education is to a given job is debatable. As noted in Chapter 3, education may be a good predictor of performance in highly technical fields. Credentialism—the practice of delineating a specific education as a prerequisite for a certain job—can unfairly exclude some persons, however. For federal jobs, the law specifically prohibits minimum education requirements except for science, technology, and professional jobs; even then, these requirements apply only when OPM has ruled that such education is necessary.[34] Meta-analyses conducted by OPM have found that grade-point average is moderately related to work performance in that as grade-point average increases, worker performance tends to increase.[35,36]

Verification of information on the application is important. Candidates may have a tendency to overstate their education and experience. Verifying education is relatively simple; all that need be done is to require a formal transcript from the school or schools. A more difficult task is assessing job experience beyond simply verifying employers and jobs held. How varied was the work performed? How much judgment did the candidate have to exercise? If an applicant previously held a position of "administrative aide," was the person really a clerical worker, a bookkeeper, or a trouble-shooter for the supervisor? Similarly, in comparing two workers who have been administrative aides, one for 1 year and the other for 2 years, should the assumption be made that 2 years is better?

Letters of recommendation and structured evaluation questionnaires can be used. Because the information may be of doubtful reliability, however, their value is limited. Some letter writers tend to be extremely or excessively positive, and others attempt to be more objective and therefore write less glowing reports. Almost all references are positive because candidates for jobs are unlikely to submit names of persons who would not write good recommendations.

Confidentiality of reference information is an important factor. The Family Educational Rights and Privacy Act of 1974, better known as the Buckley Amendment, sought to protect individuals from persons who wrote unwarranted negative or derogatory reference letters.[37] As a result of the legislation, letters of recommendation are available for inspection to the job applicant unless the candidate waives that right. Letters marked "confidential" can be expected to be afforded greater credibility by evaluators than nonconfidential ones. Material obtained from qualifications investigations also is subject to release to candidates under the Privacy Act, although identity of informants usually may be kept confidential.

Sometimes the application will be the only part of the testing program for a given set of jobs. Evaluators will determine points to be assigned to each type of education and training and then will calculate a total score. This is called an unassembled examination because the applicants do not come together or assemble to take a test. One prominent concern about education and training examinations is whether they are valid, that is, whether there is a link between education and training requirements on the one hand and eventual job performance on the other.

Assembled examinations are of two types: written and performance. Written examinations probably represent the most commonly used measurement technique. The exact nature of a test for a particular purpose is, again, a function of the qualities sought. For a trainee type of position, aptitude, learning capability, and other potential qualities are important. What the applicant knows actually may be less important than how well the person can be expected to learn. Closely associated with aptitude tests are intelligence tests. However, IQ tests are often challenged as being weak predictors of job performance. An individual can be an excellent worker in many types of jobs even though his or her IQ is not particularly high.

Aptitude and personality tests attempt to gauge whether a person's emotional and mental make-up will be compatible with a given type of work. Personality tests may be able to separate those who would become bored with a routine job from others who perhaps might find it satisfying. In private enterprise, the assembly line is an example of a situation in which high intelligence is not necessarily a positive attribute but the ability to maintain a continuous routine is. One possible flaw with using personality tests is that candidates may answer questions in a way they think will result in a high score; in other words, they can fake the examination.

Integrity tests have gained in popularity, especially in the private sector but also in the public sector. These tests often focus upon job applicants' honesty and can be considered an alternative to polygraph tests. The tests may ask whether a person considers taking small items home from work a form of theft. Other test items not focusing upon ethical standards may ask about the candidates' perception of themselves regarding their being sensible or adventurous.[38,39] Tests of this type can involve unwarranted invasion of applicants' privacy.[40]

Other paper-and-pencil tests are aimed more specifically at the substance of jobs. A common controversy about these tests is whether the questions are truly job related. An accounting test that is geared specifically to the accounting system of a jurisdiction might be appropriate when the required depth of information is so extensive that an inexperienced person would need months of training before becoming a productive employee. On the other hand, such a test, if focusing on trivial items peculiar to the jurisdiction's system, gives unwarranted advantage to current employees and raises artificial barriers to outsiders.

How much job information or knowledge is expected is equally important. A forest ranger test might ask questions about tree diseases, insect classifications, animal species, and soil types, but unless such knowledge is needed on the job, these questions should not be included. Similarly, reading skill may be regarded as essential, but should the test concentrate on reading speed, vocabulary, reading for detail, or reading for general comprehension?[41]

One frequent criticism of paper-and-pencil tests is that they are biased in terms of language skill achievements. A person may score low not because of lack of knowledge, skill, or capability but because of the language used in the test. If all that is necessary to perform a given job is a ninth-grade reading capability, tests written at levels above that grade clearly are inappropriate.

Up until 1982, one of the most important tests used at the federal level was the Professional and Administrative Career Examination (PACE), a test that blended some of the techniques just discussed. PACE covered professional and administrative jobs at the GS-5 and GS-7 levels (see Chapter 4 for an explanation of GS ratings) and was introduced in 1974 to replace the Federal Service Entrance Examination, which had been criticized as not being sufficiently job related.[42]

The use of PACE was discontinued as a result of OPM's signing a consent decree in response to a U.S. district court suit alleging the examination to be invalid and possibly discriminatory. This action occurred at a time when many federal workers had been displaced as a result of reductions in force (RIFs; see Chapter 8) caused by budgetary cutbacks; numerous positions that would have been covered by PACE were filled during this period by laid off or RIFed workers. Where agencies were unable to fill positions in this manner, however,

OPM allowed them to make appointments through Schedule B (see Chapter 2). A major drawback of this arrangement was that there was no central entry point for persons seeking federal employment; individuals had to contact each agency that might have a job opening. The use of Schedule B authority, however, did result in an increase in the proportion of minorities hired.[43,44]

In 1990, OPM introduced a new testing program to replace the Schedule B procedure, a stop-gap measure that was used for 8 years. Known as Administrative Careers with America (ACWA), this system consists of several tests rather than one. Separate tests exist for:

- health, safety, and the environment
- writing and public information
- business, finance, and management
- personnel, administration, and computers
- benefits review and tax and legal areas
- law enforcement and investigation

In the first year of operations, the ACWA tests were taken by more than 100,000 people. The tests share a common format. They have multiple-choice questions dealing with vocabulary, reading comprehension, tabular completion (calculating missing numbers in tables), and arithmetic reasoning. Reading questions are based upon paragraphs included in the tests. Arithmetic problems are of the following type: "An interagency task force has representatives from three different agencies. Half of the task force members represent Agency A, one-third represent Agency B, and three represent Agency C. How many people are on the task force?"[45]

A controversial additional component of the ACWA tests is the Individual Achievement Record (IAR). This portion of the test asks about applicants' educational experience (such as grades and participation in clubs) and work experience. OPM has been careful not to release sample questions of this portion of the examination. The Individual Achievement Record is analogous to integrity tests (see above discussion).[46]

Written tests used in public personnel systems usually are "objective." Multiple-choice, true–false, matching, and fill-in-the-blank questions are used. These types of tests are relatively easy to score and are less subject to varying interpretations by test evaluators. Tests can be of the answer-until-correct type, in which the examinee cannot proceed to the next test question until successfully answering a question. The examinee selects an answer and then sees whether the answer chosen is correct by erasing a coded area. If the answer is incorrect, another option must be chosen. Another approach is to use computer adaptive testing (CAT), in which progressively more difficult questions are given to the examinee. The examination ceases once the examinee reaches a point where he or she consistently incorrectly answers questions.[47]

On the other hand, some tests are of the essay type, requiring candidates to write a paragraph or more on a given problem. Candidates may be provided with an organizational scenario and supporting data that are to be used in preparing a position paper or memorandum.

Nonwritten tests can measure physical capabilities, skills, or aptitudes. Paper-and-pencil tests can be used to test motor skills such as the ability to trace lines. These types of tests are used mostly in industries, where products are made, rather than in government.

Government can use aptitude tests for jobs involving physical activities. Fire personnel, for example, need to be able to make hydrant connections, ascend ladders, lift equipment, walk through debris-laden buildings, and climb through windows. Therefore, tests are designed to determine the ease with which candidates can achieve these tasks.[48,49] Physical achievement tests, as distinguished from the aptitude variety, cover typing and other machine operation skills.

Oral examinations are one of the most common forms of nonwritten tests. It is important to understand that the oral examination is not the same as a job interview (discussed later). Job interviews are conducted by line supervisors and their staffs and can occur before or after a test has been given. In contrast, the oral examination is part of the formal testing program conducted by a personnel department or civil service commission. This test is used to examine qualifications not easily measured by other types of tests. General oral communication skill is tested along with abilities to think under pressure and to deal effectively with others in a face-to-face situation.

The formats of orals vary greatly. Candidates may be examined individually or in groups. Group interviews are useful in identifying interpersonal relations skills and leadership potential. In group orals, the candidates are given a problem to discuss and resolve within a specified time. Some group orals involve role-playing simulations in which examinees have assigned organizational positions and must deal with a problem facing the organization.[50] In individual orals, a standard set of questions is often given to each candidate. One question for a personnel analyst oral examination could be: "If an administrator in one of the line agencies had requested an upgrading of the classification of a position, how would you deal with that administrator in reevaluating the position?" This question would allow exploration of interpersonal relations skills and substantive knowledge of position classification techniques. Follow-up probe questions will vary and are used to determine the candidate's depth and breadth of substantive knowledge. Another form of oral examination is to present the examinees with a problem and some data and expect each of them to make a presentation before a board, which may have authority to ask probe questions. The oral can be conducted by one person, but a three-person board often is used.

In the oral examination process it is difficult to maintain consistency of standards from one candidate to another and from one board to another. At the state level, two or more boards dealing with the same testing program might convene in the state capital or might be dispersed geographically. The board usually consists of substantive experts who, while knowing their field of work (such as law enforcement), often are not well trained in conducting tests. As a result, board members unintentionally can be unfair to some candidates. Some examiners undoubtedly are biased for or against candidates' clothing, hairstyles, and mannerisms. Racial and sex biases are other common complaints.

Candidates usually are graded by oral examiners on scales, such as 0 to 6 points. Unless these scales are behaviorally anchored—that is, unless they have behavioral descriptions associated with each point on the scale—there can be wide inconsistencies from one board member to another and among boards. Some boards, for example, may reserve the highest level for only the truly outstanding candidates. The result is that they rarely if ever use the highest score, so that a scale of 0 to 6 becomes 0 to 5. Other boards, in contrast, may use the highest score more freely. This problem is analogous to performance evaluation scales (see Chapter 6 for a more detailed discussion).

Beyond these tests are physical examinations and background investigations (BIs). Physical examinations are particularly important in jobs involving manual labor, such as sewer, water, and road maintenance jobs. The BI is used for sensitive positions, especially in the military and other national security jobs.[51] BIs vary in their intensity; some involve extensive interviewing of the candidate's friends, former employers, relatives, and current and former neighbors. The BI should be distinguished from the qualifications investigation. The latter is concerned with whether a person has the necessary skills and knowledge for a position, whereas the BI is concerned with whether a person is loyal and not a security risk (see Chapter 8).

Other controversial tests include pre-employment drug screenings and polygraph (lie detector) tests, genetic tests, and screening for acquired immunodeficiency syndrome (AIDS). The Employee Polygraph Protection Act of 1988 basically prohibits employers from using lie detector tests. Genetic testing has been proposed as a means of determining a job applicant's likelihood of contracting diseases and other conditions that could result in major expenses for employers' health insurance plans.[52]

The examinations discussed can be used in combination with each other. When two or more techniques are to be used, the successive hurdle approach is applied. Candidates who do not clear one hurdle are not allowed to attempt the next one. This approach is economical in that more expensive forms of testing are reserved for later hurdles, when the number of candidates is smaller. For instance, candidates might be required first to pass a review of their education and experience and then a written test before being eligible to take an oral examination.

Test Validity

The concept of test validity is complex, but its main thrust is that the test must measure what it is designed to measure.[53,54] It is obvious, of course, that a test used in the employment process must be designed to measure some characteristic required by the job to be filled. If, for instance, candidates for drivers of municipal buses were given a typing test, the test probably would not be valid for such a job. Although the test may differentiate among skills—some candidates would pass and some would fail—it would have no bearing on applicants' capabilities as bus drivers. Validating a test provides guidance as to what interpretations or inferences may be properly made about test scores.

The issues of validity and job relatedness have become particularly important in recent years because screening devices have tended to limit the access of some groups to public jobs. Although the discussion of discrimination is reserved for later, it should be recognized here that charges of discrimination have resulted in substantial efforts to make certain that tests are valid and job related. One problem, for example, is constructing examinations that do not discriminate against handicapped applicants[55] (see Chapter 9 for an analysis of legal provisions and court decisions about test validity).

A superficial appearance of relevance is known as face validity. Some tests may appear to be valid but, when carefully scrutinized, are found not to be. Measurement experts do not attach any importance to face validity. Rather, they have devised several ways of determining the genuine utility of measuring devices.

Content Validity

Validity can be demonstrated in a number of ways. Content validity assesses whether the test measures subject matter needed in the target position and whether it appropriately samples the subject matter. In other words, the test covers a representative sample of tasks in the job. A personnel analyst test that asked no questions about labor–management relations would not meet content validity requirements (assuming that the personnel analyst had to deal with such relations). Even if a test covered all aspects of personnel, it would not necessarily be content valid because there could be an overabundance of questions dealing with one aspect of the field while other aspects received little emphasis (that is, it might overemphasize collective bargaining and underemphasize position classification). Moreover, the questions might be pitched at the wrong level of expertise for the target population.

A problem with the content validity test is that there is no easy way of determining the appropriateness of the questions that sample a given field. Complicating the problem is the fact that several testing devices are available for use. The sampling issue, then, arises not only for the mix of questions on a written examination but for the mix between a written and oral examination plus any others, such as physical and performance examinations.

The typical content validity procedure is to use "experts," either individuals currently holding positions or outside authorities, to define the area and level of expertise. In the case of the personnel test, personnel analysts in the jurisdiction might be used along with personnel "experts" from other governments and professors who teach personnel administration courses. These persons would be asked to review the content of the examination to determine whether appropriate questions had been included. Fairly rigorous methodologies have been developed to assemble the judgments of experts, but the methodologies cannot overcome the fact that the validity test rests upon composite judgments or opinions. Had a different set of experts been used in validating a test, the outcome could be substantially different.[56]

Criterion-Related Validity

Criterion-related validity is another alternative. This technique uses statistical analyses to determine the relationship between test scores and job performance. The test is valid if scores are related to job performance; high job performers, for example, generally earn high scores. Either concurrent or predictive validity may be used.[57] The concurrent validity approach involves administering the test to incumbents and comparing their test scores with appraisals of their job performance. Predictive validity, on the other hand, compares test scores of new job appointees with their performance measured at some later date. Both approaches involve correlation analysis.

Criterion-related validity can be understood by studying Figure 5–1. The horizontal axis indicates test scores, and the vertical axis measures job performance. Each dot on the graph represents an individual's score and job rating. A horizontal line has been drawn arbitrarily to represent the demarcation between high and low performance. The diagonal line is a regression line based on a least-squares criterion. The vertical broken lines A, B, and C represent possible cutoff points on hiring.

If only those with scores of A or better are hired, the test will virtually guarantee that all new hires will be high performers. If the cutoff is at the B level, however, some of the new hires will be low performers. The concept of probability is then employed: In the case of the B cutoff, there could be a

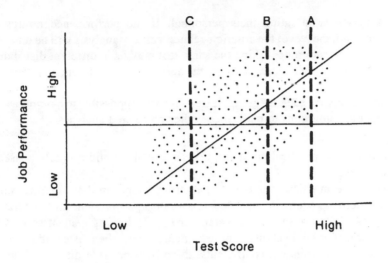

Figure 5-1 Relationship between Test Scores and Job Performance.

---

70 percent probability that each new hire will be a high performer. At the C cutoff, the probabilities worsen so much that low performers might outnumber high performers.

Taylor-Russell tables have been used for decades to assess the effects of various cutoff points.[58] The test in this example would be generally valid because there is a relationship between test scores and performance. The degree of validity, however, is affected by the cutoff point used. Many measurement devices are valid at extremely high or low scores but much less so in the middle range.

Although criterion-related validity seems an attractive solution to the problem of measuring validity, there are at least three problems in using it:

1. Only test scores for persons who have been hired can be considered because job performance can be measured only for such individuals. The validity measurement, then, cannot indicate how the persons who were rejected might have performed. It is conceivable that the test screened out the potentially best workers. One method of overcoming this problem would be to appoint at random a substantial sample of all applicants and then compare their performance with test results. Most governments would not be prepared to undertake such an experiment.
2. Measures of job performance are not necessarily valid or reliable themselves. As is seen in Chapter 6, great inconsistencies exist among

supervisors in rating their personnel. If the performance ratings are unsound, the rest of the criterion-related validity analysis will be unsound.

3. Different subgroups taking the same test may have different distribution patterns on test scores; that is, the test may be differentially valid for different groups. To check the validity of the test, results must be analyzed separately for each subgroup. It frequently is impossible to assemble large enough subgroups to make these criterion-related analyses.

Because of these practical problems, criterion-related validity rarely is used in public personnel systems.

Besides the practical problem of gathering subgroup data for differential validity, there has been extensive debate over the appropriateness of differential validity itself. Part of the problem stems from a lack of agreement about what constitutes differential validity. One argument is that, when differential validity is restricted to correlation coefficients, there may be little difference among subgroups, and the alleged problem is only a "pseudoproblem." Rather than concentrating on differential validity, this view holds, the focus should be differential prediction, namely, how test results are used in predicting performance. The issue is highly technical and necessarily couched in statistical terminology.

Construct Validity

Construct validity is another alternative. A construct is a hypothetical concept. In personnel testing, the constructs usually are traits that are hypothetical in that they cannot be measured directly but nevertheless are presumed to exist. It may be extremely difficult to pin down definitions of these constructs. They can include such traits as intelligence, industriousness, creativity, and aggressiveness, to name a few. Construct validity, then, gauges the extent to which test scores vary with a particular construct. For example, do scores on a given test rise with increases in creativity on the job? Construct validity often considers how one test relates to previously existing tests that are accepted as measures of the construct. For instance, does the new test that purports to measure industriousness correlate with other tests of industriousness?

A problem of construct validity for personnel testing is that it is necessary to demonstrate that the traits being measured are job related. Because the constructs themselves are hard to define, it is extremely difficult to show that they are indeed required. Construct validity, therefore, requires the use of criterion-related validity as part of the overall strategy. Content validity also may be needed. As a result, construct validity is more difficult to undertake than either of the two others.

Summary

Much confusion has existed over the specific steps to be used in any one of these validation strategies and whether one of the three is preferred. The issue is particularly acute when it relates to equal employment opportunity (see Chapter 9). In 1978, the major federal agencies concerned with employment discrimination agreed upon the Uniform Guidelines on Employee Selection Procedures.[59] The agencies were the Equal Employment Opportunity Commission, the Civil Service Commission (now OPM), the Department of Justice, the Department of Labor, and the Commission on Civil Rights. The guidelines give major emphasis to content and criterion-related validity and warn of the "extensive and arduous effort" associated with construct validity. Differential validity is not mentioned. The guidelines are consistent with the American Psychological Association's *Standards for Educational and Psychological Tests.*[60]

Given the complexity of the validation field, a jurisdiction would be ill advised to develop testing programs without having a staff suitably trained in validation techniques. One alternative, however, is to use examinations that have been prepared by organizations equipped to handle the validation problem. The International Personnel Management Association, which has provided test services since the 1950s, has tests available in such fields as police, fire, corrections, and office work. According to test vendors, their products are generally valid independent of specific organizations or governments.[61] Clients of these test services, however, should be careful to use the tests as originally intended and not for other purposes; a test for police officers, for instance, should not be used for park rangers, even though rangers have important law enforcement duties.[62]

Test Administration

Test administration usually is the responsibility of civil service commissions both in setting standards and in the actual conduct of examinations. Whereas functions such as position classification may be the responsibility of a civil service commission or personnel department, with actual classification of jobs being delegated, the examination process often is not delegated. There have been significant exceptions to this, especially at the federal level with the reforms of 1978. Issues develop with the decentralization of testing, however.[63] Some claim that decentralization allows agencies to abuse merit principles by discriminating. Other critics say that would-be government employees are forced to contact numerous agencies in search of job vacancies rather than needing to contact only the central personnel agency.

Examinations constitute one of the major work load fields for personnel offices. In any testing program, tests must be prepared, and that process consumes much time. Once tests are administered, they must be scored. If pigeonhole position classification is common (see Chapter 3), numerous different tests must be prepared. The greater the number of job series, normally the greater the number of tests that will need to be prepared. The use of a single entrance-level examination covering many series can greatly reduce the test preparation work load. Such tests may run into problems of job relatedness, however. Given the amount of work that must be done, heads of testing offices often feel understaffed and underbudgeted.

Civil service personnel usually must work with the agency staff in designing a test program, a process that can lead to tension between the two. With civil service staff members presumably having expertise in testing and agency personnel having substantive expertise, a symbiotic relationship should (but does not always) develop. Consultation between the two may occur in the course of establishing content validity (see above); department personnel, particularly key supervisors, may be consulted. The commission staff, however, being concerned about the security of the test, often will be reluctant to allow department personnel to see test questions; there may even be specific statutes, ordinances, or regulations that prohibit disclosure. An unfortunate situation can develop in which, after the test has been given and information about the questions leaks back to the supervisors, the supervisors conclude that many questions were not germane to the job and could have had the effect of screening out excellent candidates.

The location for assembled examinations will depend on the type of jurisdiction. Local governments may have only one test site; states may have several. Wide dispersal of sites provides easy access to persons who wish to take civil service tests. That can limit the types of tests that can be provided, however. Written tests are conducted easily almost anywhere, but that is not the case with performance tests.

Industry and, to a lesser extent, governments are moving toward greater use of assessment centers. Some of these are just new names for testing offices, but in other cases real changes have emerged. The assessment center consolidates much of the testing activity so that special, more costly facilities and techniques can be provided. If role-playing or some other type of group oral is to be used, the assessment center can provide special rooms, equipment, and materials for the test.[64] National standards provide that assessment centers must use multiple testing techniques, simulations, and multiple assessors who are properly trained and must engage in validation procedures.[65] The use of multiple assessors is thought to improve reliability and validity of testing.[66,67]

Considerations of timing are important. For many tests, if a candidate does not apply by a given date, there may be a wait of several months before the tests are given again. Other tests are continuous; in many jurisdictions, clerical tests are scheduled daily. When a large number of candidates have passed a test and the number of job vacancies is expected to be small, the testing program may be closed for an indefinite period. There would seem to be little need for continuing to accept new applicants when there are hundreds or even thousands of already qualified persons and only a few jobs that are likely to become vacant.

The frequency with which tests are given will depend also on available resources. Again, pigeonhole classifications lead to excessive numbers of examinations, and the staff may be unable to provide frequent tests within each job series. When this occurs, the number of "real" eligibles dwindles as the list ages; many persons on the list find employment elsewhere. When a test for a job series is offered frequently, limits may be imposed on candidates' retaking it. A person who hopes to raise a score may have to wait 6 months or more to retake the examination.

Another timing factor is the waiting period between different portions of a testing program. The hurdle approach, explained earlier, may require an applicant to wait several weeks between filing an application and receiving a score on experience and training, more weeks before taking a written examination, and several more weeks before the oral. The hurdle approach, therefore, can discourage many persons by lengthening the time required to become eligible for a public job.

Objective tests, of course, are the easiest to score. Many jurisdictions use optical scanners that read the answer sheets, score them, and provide raw and final scores. Computer programs are available for providing item analyses, which compare responses to one question with overall test performance. These analyses enable examiners to identify weak questions, namely those that overall high-scoring candidates get wrong and that low-scoring applicants get right.

Scoring an unassembled examination obviously is more time consuming and has far greater potential for unreliable results. A reliable test device is one that can be given several different times to the same individual with the same results. Unassembled test scoring—that is, rating of training and experience—is done by people, not machines, which increases the chances of differences in scorers' judgments.

For other tests with multiple components, a weighting is determined for each part, and a final score then is calculated. Portions of the test may be weighted so that, for instance, the oral portion counts 40 percent and experience and training count 60 percent. The weighted score is converted to a final score. The conversion, as often required by law, adjusts all grades to some set range, such as 60 to 100, with 70 being the minimal passing score. Therefore, a rating of 100 does not mean that all questions were answered correctly.

One of the most controversial aspects of the public service examination process has been veterans preference.[68] In 1865, Congress passed legislation giving preference to disabled veterans over others in appointment to positions. Ohio was the first state to adopt comparable legislation (1875), and by 1913 fourteen states had veterans preference laws.[69] Congress rewrote the legislation in 1919 to include World War I veterans and in 1944 passed the Veterans Preference Act.

How veterans preference applies to examinations has varied over time. In the 1930s, the U.S. Civil Service Commission conducted separate examinations for disabled veterans; those who passed were placed automatically at the top of eligibility lists even though numerous nonveterans might have scored much higher. Today, at all levels of government, the typical procedure is to require veterans to take the same test as all others, and if a veteran passes five points are added to the score (or ten points in the case of a disabled veteran).

Contrary to recommendations by President Carter, in 1978 Congress not only retained the point preference system but strengthened preference for disabled veterans. Those with a 30 percent disability or more may be hired noncompetitively, meaning that they need not compete with others through a competitive testing program. Should the agency choose to pass over a disabled veteran and select someone else, it must provide a written reason for this action to OPM. Despite the strong preference afforded veterans, they often are passed over for selection, and sometimes no one is selected to fill vacancies, at least in the short run. Another important feature of veterans preference legislation is that it is not limited to veterans. At the federal level, preference also is extended to widows of veterans, mothers of veterans who lost their lives, wives of disabled veterans, and mothers of unwed disabled veterans.[70,71]

Veterans preference is defended on several grounds:

- It is seen as rewarding individuals for their patriotism and/or their willingness to risk their lives in combat.
- It helps compensate for the years of low pay received in the armed forces.
- It helps veterans readjust to civilian life.

That last argument, however, fails to provide any justification for lifelong veterans preference. A veteran not only receives five or ten points for the first public job but also has this advantage every time he or she applies.

On the negative side, veterans preference distorts examination scores, so that the most qualified people do not necessarily receive the highest marks. Of course, this presupposes that tests are sufficiently discriminating that a person with a score of 95.8 can be expected to perform at a level superior to one with a score of 90.8. Advocates of preference would counter by claiming that veterans, having experienced what they did, are more mature or have other highly positive personality characteristics that make them better qualified than nonveterans.

Veterans preference also can be criticized for treating public jobs as a form of welfare assistance. Rather than doing this, would it be preferable to provide a lifetime financial benefit to veterans, assuming that some form of extra compensation was considered appropriate? Still another criticism has been that veterans preference tends to discriminate against women. In rejecting this argument, courts have reasoned that veterans preference applies to both sexes even though men are the primary beneficiaries (refer to Chapter 9).[72] This may dispose of the matter legally, but it does not alter the fact that veterans preference operates to the disadvantage of the majority of women. Political realities are such that veterans are likely to retain preference.

SELECTION

Once examinations have been taken and scored, eligibility lists are established. Candidates are ranked by score, and, as noted earlier, 70 often is the cutoff for passing. Large jurisdictions usually establish lists by region. A state may have ten regional eligibility lists for each job series; these are needed because many applicants are willing to work only in a particular area in the state. Eligibility lists often are longest for the state capital area and major metropolitan centers; for the same types of jobs the lists may be short or even nonexistent for small towns and rural regions.

Separate lists may be maintained for different types of applicants. A promotion list may be used for current employees, with these persons having preference over "outsiders" (see Chapter 7). Persons previously employed by the jurisdiction may be on a separate list and receive preference over other "outsiders." This preference often is provided to employees laid off or temporarily disabled. A third list would be for persons not previously or currently employed by the jurisdiction. Some governments require all applicants to compete with each other and rank them on a single list.

Names usually remain on a list for 1 or 2 years, after which the individuals must be re-examined or at least must reaffirm their interest in the job series and grade covered by the list. The government's personnel director or head of the civil service commission frequently has the authority to determine the length of time that the list will be maintained. If a list is kept for only 1 year, then the jurisdiction must have an active testing program to establish a new list. The reason for the time limit on eligibility lists is that the employment status of eligibles changes over time. An individual scoring high on two or more civil service tests may have accepted employment through one testing program while his or her name remains on other lists.

The selection process is triggered by an agency request to the civil service commission for a list of eligible candidates to fill a job vacancy. Before an agency may request this list, it often must obtain approval from the central personnel department, the central budget office, or a department of administration. Complement control is used to limit the number of governmental employees. When a jurisdiction is facing severe financial constraints, it may impose a rule such as requiring that for every four vacancies that occur only two or three may be filled.

Once the commission receives the agency's request, it prepares a list of eligible names.[73] This is known as the certification process. The list is supplied to the agency within a couple of weeks, or more quickly when the process is computerized. The amount of information that the commission supplies to the agency about each candidate may be minimal, such as name, examination score, and a few other essential pieces of information, or it may be extensive.

The employing agency usually will receive only a few names rather than a complete list of all eligibles. The most common practice is the "rule of three," which limits the agency to hiring from the top three names on the list. The rule of three was established at the federal level by the Veterans Preference Act of 1944. The justification for this limitation is that agencies should not be allowed to pass over the top candidates for less qualified individuals. The rule is criticized severely, on the other hand, because it assumes a precision in the measurement process far beyond what realistically is possible.

Of course, jurisdictions vary on this practice. Some state and local governments use the rule of ten, others the rule of one, which gives agencies a take-it-or-leave-it choice. Some jurisdictions, rather than the top three or so names, use the top three scores. This can produce an eligibility list with dozens of names on it because a number of candidates may have the same score. When two or more agencies draw from the same eligibility list, a government using the rule of three may certify the first three names to one agency and the next three to the second agency. Individuals in the first group will not be certified to another agency until the first agency has completed its review of them. In other jurisdictions, the top three names on the list may be sent simultaneously to two or more agencies.

The preference system assists veterans in the examination and selection processes. At the federal level, for most examinations, disabled veterans are placed at the top of the eligible list regardless of their earned ratings; other veterans are listed ahead of nonveterans with the same score. An agency that passes over a veteran to hire a nonveteran must supply to OPM a written statement explaining why this was done[74] (this same preference applies to mothers or wives of disabled or deceased veterans). Veterans also can be hired noncompetitively through Schedule B or Veterans Readjustment Authority or if they are at least 30 percent disabled. Those provisions obviously have the effect of forcing agencies to give veterans careful consideration. Pennsylvania has absolute preference. In that state, if the third-ranked person on a list of three certified eligibles is a veteran, only that person may be hired.

Once the certification list has been received, the agency conducts its own investigation of the candidates and arranges for job interviews. Candidates' former teachers, professors, and employers may be contacted by telephone or letter. Candidates usually are expected to pay their own expenses in traveling to the job interview, although at the federal level, agencies are authorized to pay travel expenses according to provisions in the Federal Employees Pay Comparability Act of 1990. When the certification list is long, there may be two rounds of interviewing. The first, using relatively short interviews, screens out the majority of candidates, and the second round questions the remaining individuals more intensively.

The job interview can be compared with the oral examination but usually is far more intensive and extensive. The oral format requires a standard set of questions, but there is no such requirement for the interview. The oral may seem to be a routine process for the examiners, but the agency is likely to take the interview process far more seriously because the person hired may remain there for several years. The candidates can anticipate being exposed to a variety of situations in a full day of interviewing, ranging from rigorous grilling sessions conducted by one or more agency staff members to casual luncheons. Many interviewers use situational problems in which candidates are asked how they would deal with a difficult set of circumstances.[75,76] Dominating the selection process is a concern for how well candidates' characteristics match the dominant culture of the organization because hiring misfits can be expected to result in endless problems.[77]

Considerable tension exists between the employing agency and the civil service commission over the selection process. The commission is concerned with potential abuses of the merit principle. Many jurisdictions have long histories of patronage or political cronyism, which personnel departments fear can be reasserted all too easily. Undoubtedly, many agency managers would like to hire their friends, but not necessarily only because they are friends but because they consider them well qualified. Agency managers frequently lack confidence in the testing program and are not convinced that the top three people on an eligibility list are indeed the three most qualified. Sometimes an agency has specially recruited an individual only to find that the person is not "within reach" on the eligibility list.

Agencies use various tactics to circumvent the rule of three (or whatever number). One right the agency has is to hire no one. If all three certified individuals are unacceptable, the agency can leave the position unfilled. If other agencies are drawing from the same eligibility list, the first agency can wait until the unacceptable candidates at the top of the list have found employment in one of the other agencies. Other eligibles then become "reachable." This practice, however, has two disadvantages: The agency's work load may be of such magnitude that it cannot function well without a full complement, and the agency takes a risk that the vacancy will be "collapsed" by some central unit, thereby prohibiting filling it in the future.

Other tactics are less aboveboard and are proscribed by law and/or administrative regulations. The agency can encourage certified eligibles to decline a job offer. This can be accomplished by explaining to them that the job requires working nights and weekends, that the prospective employee's office will be no larger than a closet, that there will be virtually no opportunity for promotions, and that the agency's director is nothing less than an evil demon. Once the three have declined, the agency may request a new list of eligibles. It should be stressed that these and other tactics are illegal in that they can be used systematically to discriminate against groups of applicants.

Another tactic is to ask for a reclassification of a position. The job might be reclassified as a politically sensitive one, not subject to the civil service examination process. An alternative is to request the creation of a new job classification that by definition would not have a standing eligibility list. Still another approach is to ask for a reclassification where it was known that the eligibility list for that class had expired. In that case, the agency would be free to hire anyone as a "provisional." Once the civil service commission has established a testing program for that job series, the provisional employee will be required to take the test. The advantages are that the provisional would have a better chance of scoring high because he or she would have been working on the job for a period of time and that the provisional is required only to pass the test, not score the highest, to retain the job.

When other tactics fail, there is at least one more. If a jurisdiction has a rule of one and the agency considers the top person a dullard at best, it may decide to hire that person. Once on the job, the individual's life is made as unpleasant as possible in hope that he or she will resign. If a resignation is not forthcoming, the individual may be dismissed relatively easily during the probation period (see Chapter 6). Once resignation or dismissal has removed that person, the agency is free to ask for a new certified candidate.

SUMMARY

Recruitment is one of the weakest functions performed in personnel systems. Part of the problem stems from conflicting or at least divergent values as to the purpose of recruiting. Is government to seek the best or be satisfied with those who are simply qualified? To what extent should there be a commitment to recruiting from a wide range of persons, including a mix of races, income groups, and the sexes? Whether people apply for public employment will depend in part on government's image, and that has not always been the best.

The techniques of recruitment include newspaper advertising, job and examination announcements sent by mail and posted in public places, general brochures and pamphlets, information centers, hot lines, and individual recruiting. Given these varied techniques, recruitment rarely is planned systematically.

Examination strategies are based on job analyses. A standard application form is used, on which candidates list their relevant education and experience. When candidates do not come together to take an examination, it is called an unassembled one. Written reference letters are used, although these often are difficult to assess. Most paper-and-pencil tests are objective, but some jurisdictions use essay tests. Physical aptitude tests (such as agility) and achievement tests (such as typing) also are used. Oral examinations are important for testing applicants for professional and administrative positions. The hurdle approach may be used when a testing program involves two or more separate measures.

Especially because of concern over possible discrimination, evaluating the validity of tests has become important. Content validity involves designing a testing program that samples the job's main aspects or subject matter. Criterion-related validity relates test scores to job performance. Construct validity involves identifying the traits needed to perform a job (for example, a leadership trait) and designing a testing program that examines candidates for those traits. A construct validity strategy includes criterion-related validity and may include content validity.

Test administration usually is the exclusive responsibility of a civil service commission. Examinations may be given in one central location or at several (in the case of states) or even hundreds (in the federal government). Machine scoring is used for objective tests. Evaluation of experience and training is subject to varied interpretation and threatens test reliability. Veterans preference adds five or ten points to veterans' test scores. The practice has been criticized widely but is not likely to be abandoned.

Selection begins with the establishment of eligibility lists and an agency's request for certification of eligibles. The rule of three is used frequently to limit agencies in their choice of employees. The practice is intended to encourage hiring on the basis of merit but often is criticized by line agencies as being too restrictive. Veterans preference applies in the selection process as well as in the examination process. Job interviews tend to be more extensive and intensive than oral examinations. Agencies, seeking freedom to hire individuals who are thought to be superior candidates, use various tactics to circumvent civil service procedures. These tactics include deliberate discouraging of certified candidates, position reclassification, and hiring and then firing unacceptable candidates.

NOTES

1. U.S. Merit Systems Protection Board, *Working for America: A Federal Employee Survey* (Washington: U.S. Government Printing Office, 1990).

2. R.D. Lee, Jr., Watergate and the image of the federal service revisited, *Public Personnel Management* 3 (1974): 111–114.

3. U.S. Merit Systems Protection Board, *Attracting and Selecting Quality Applicants for Federal Employment* (Washington: U.S. Government Printing Office, 1990).

4. National Commission on the Public Service, *Leadership for America*, Task Force Reports (Washington: National Commission on the Public Service, 1989), 76.

5. J.H. Trattner, *The Prune Book: The 100 Toughest Management and Policy Jobs in Washington* (Lanham, Md.: Madison Books, 1988).

6. J.H. Trattner and the Council for Excellence in Government, *The Prune Book: The 60 Toughest Science and Technology Jobs in Washington* (Lanham, Md.: Madison Publishers, 1992).

7. U.S. House of Representatives, Committee on Post Office and Civil Service, *U.S. Government Policy and Supporting Positions*, 100th Cong., 2d sess. (Washington: U.S. Government Printing Office, 1988).

8. Hudson Institute for U.S. Office of Personnel Management, *Civil Service 2000* (Washington: U.S. Government Printing Office, 1988).

9. S.W. Hays and R.C. Kearney, State personnel directors and the dilemmas of WorkForce 2000: A survey, *Public Administration Review* 52 (1992): 380–388.

10. U.S. General Accounting Office, *The Changing Workforce: Demographic Issues Facing the Federal Government* (Washington: U.S. Government Printing Office, 1992).

11. G. Johnson, *Recruiting, Retaining, and Motivating the Federal Workforce* (New York: Quorum, 1991).

12. U.S. General Accounting Office, *Federal Recruiting: Comparison of Applicants Who Accepted or Declined Federal Job Offers* (Washington: U.S. Government Printing Office, 1992).

13. A.B. Krueger, *The Determinants of Queues for Federal Jobs*, Working Paper No. 2499 (Cambridge, Mass.: National Bureau of Economic Research, 1988).

14. P.J. Haas and D.S. Wright, Administrative turnover in state government, *Administration and Society* 21 (1989): 265–277.

15. U.S. General Accounting Office, *Recruitment and Retention: Inadequate Federal Pay Cited as Primary Problem by Agency Personnel* (Washington: U.S. Government Printing Office, 1990).

16. _____, *The Changing Workforce: Comparison of Federal and Nonfederal Work/Family Programs and Approaches* (Washington: U.S. Government Printing Office, 1992).

17. _____, *Federal Employment: Poor Service Found at Federal Job Information Centers* (Washington: U.S. Government Printing Office, 1992).

18. _____, *Federal Recruiting: College Placement Officials' Views of the Government's Campus Outreach Efforts* (Washington: U.S. Government Printing Office, 1992).

19. D.N. Ammons and J.J. Glass, *Recruiting Local Government Executives* (San Francisco: Jossey-Bass, 1989).

20. D.G. Carnevale, Recruitment strategies in the federal government: Missing links and representative bureaucracy, *Review of Public Personnel Management* 11 (Fall 1990–Spring 1991): 112–120.

21. R.L. Armacost and R.L. Jauernig, Planning and managing a major recruiting project, *Public Personnel Management* 20 (1991): 115–126.

22. A.L. Brock, "Planning the Recruitment Program," in *Recruitment and Selection in the Public Service,* ed. J.J. Donovan (Chicago: Public Personnel Association, 1968), 84–99.

23. U.S. Merit Systems Protection Board, *Attracting and Selecting Quality Applicants for Federal Employment* (Washington: U.S. Government Printing Office, 1990).

24. U.S. General Accounting Office, *Federal Recruiting and Hiring: Making Government Jobs Attractive to Prospective Employees* (Washington: U.S. Government Printing Office, 1990).

25. _____, *Federal Employment: How Federal Employees View the Government as a Place To Work* (Washington: U.S. Government Printing Office, 1992).

26. U.S. Merit Systems Protection Board, *Federal Personnel Policies and Practices: Perspectives from the Workplace* (Washington: U.S. Government Printing Office, 1987).

27. _____, *Why Are Employees Leaving the Federal Government? Results of an Exit Survey* (Washington: U.S. Government Printing Office, 1990).

28. _____, *Who Is Leaving the Federal Government? An Analysis of Employee Turnover* (Washington: U.S. Government Printing Office, 1989).

29. _____, *Working for America: A Federal Employee Survey* (Washington: U.S. Government Printing Office, 1990), i.

30. A. Wildavsky, Ubiquitous anomie: Public service in an era of ideological dissensus, *Public Administration Review* 48 (1988): 753–755.

31. Also see R.B. Denhardt and E.T. Jennings, Jr., Image and integrity in the public service, *Public Administration Review* 49 (1989): 74–77.

32. W.W. Ronan, et al., Prediction of job performance dimensions: Police officers, *Public Personnel Management* 6 (1977): 173–180.

33. M.A. McDaniel and F.A. Schmidt, Computer-assisted staffing systems: The use of computers in implementing meta-analysis and utility research in personnel selection, *Public Personnel Management* 18 (1989): 75–86.

34. U.S. General Accounting Office, *Federal Recruiting.*

35. R.D. Bretz, Jr., College grade point average as a predictor of adult success: A meta-analytic review and some additional evidence, *Public Personnel Management* 18 (1989): 11–22.

36. S.S. Ariss and S.A. Timmins, Employee education and job performance: Does education matter, *Public Personnel Management* 18 (1989): 1–9.

37. Family Educational Rights and Privacy Act, P.L. 93-380, 88 Stat. 571 (1974).

38. U.S. Office of Technology Assessment, *The Use of Integrity Tests for Pre-Employment Screening* (Washington: U.S. Government Printing Office, 1990).

39. T.J. Bergman, et al., The evolution of honesty tests and means for their evaluation, *Employee Responsibilities and Rights Journal* 3 (1990): 215–223.

40. K.H. Decker, Employee privacy rights challenge employer screening techniques for the 1990s, *Journal of Individual Employment Rights* 1 (1992): 105–114.

41. R.J. Park, et al., The selection and validation of a reading test to be used with civil service employees, *Public Personnel Management* 14 (1985): 275–284.

42. U.S. General Accounting Office, *Appointments to Professional and Administrative Career Positions* (Washington: U.S. Government Printing Office, 1984).

43. C. Ban and P.W. Ingraham, Retaining quality federal employees: Life after PACE, *Public Administration Review* 48 (1988): 708–718.

44. U.S. Merit Systems Protection Board, *In Search of Merit: Hiring Entry-Level Federal Employees* (Washington: U.S. Government Printing Office, 1987).

45. U.S. Office of Personnel Management, *Administrative Careers with America: Background Information and Sample Questions for the Examination for Careers in Personnel, Administration, and Computer Occupations* (Washington: U.S. Government Printing Office, 1990). The answer to the question is 18.

46. R.J. Lavigna, Predicting job performance from background characteristics: More evidence from the public sector, *Public Personnel Management* 21 (1992): 347–361.

47. M.E. Giffin, Personnel research on testing, selection, and performance appraisal, *Public Personnel Management* 18 (1989): 127–137.

48. M.A. Hughes, et al., A content validation methodology for job related physical performance tests, *Public Personnel Management* 18 (1989): 487–504.

49. R.D. Arvey, et al., Validation strategies for physical ability testing in police and fire settings, *Public Personnel Management* 21 (1992): 301–312.

50. V.S. Kaman and C. Bentson, Roleplay simulations for employee selection: Design and implementation, *Public Personnel Management* 17 (1988): 1–8.

51. U.S. General Accounting Office, *Security Investigations: State Department Employees Investigation Practices Can Be Improved* (Washington: U.S. Government Printing Office, 1988).

52. J.D. Bible, When employers look for things other than drugs: The legality of AIDS, genetic, intelligence, and honesty testing in the workplace, *Labor Law Journal* 41 (1990): 195–213.

53. A.S. Faught, Employment tests in the public service, *Annals* 113 (May 1924): 311–321. This is an early study of test validity.

54. R.S. Barrett, Content validation form, *Public Personnel Management* 21 (1992): 41–52.

55. M.A. Nestor, Employment testing for handicapped persons, *Public Personnel Management* 13 (1984): 417–434.

56. W.C. Lawther, Content validation: Conceptual and methodological issues, *Review of Public Personnel Administration* 6 (Summer 1986): 37–49.

57. L.S. Kleiman and R.H. Faley, The implications of professional and legal guidelines for court decisions involving criterion-related validity, *Personnel Psychology* 38 (1985): 803–883.

58. H.C. Taylor and J.T. Russell, The relationship of validity coefficients to the practical effectiveness of tests in selection: Discussion and tables, *Journal of Applied Psychology* 23 (1939): 565–578.

59. "Uniform Guidelines on Employee Selection Procedures," 29 C.F.R. § 1607 (1978).

60. American Psychological Association, *Standards for Educational and Psychological Tests* (Washington: American Psychological Association, 1974).

61. Giffin, Personnel research for testing, selection, and performance appraisal.

62. A. Anastasi, Ability testing in the 1980's and beyond: Some major trends, *Public Personnel Management* 18 (1989): 471–485.

63. U.S. Merit Systems Protection Board, *Delegation and Decentralization: Personnel Management Simplification Efforts in the Federal Government* (Washington: U.S. Government Printing Office, 1989).

64. P.E. Lowry, The assessment center: Effects of varying consensus procedures, *Public Personnel Management* 21 (1992): 171–183.

65. Seventeenth International Congress on the Assessment Center Method, Guidelines and ethical considerations for assessment center operations, *Public Personnel Management* 18 (1989): 457–470.

66. P.E. Lowry, The assessment center: Reducing interassessor influence, *Public Personnel Management* 20 (1991): 19–26.

67. J. Pynes and H.J. Bernardin, Mechnical vs. consensus-derived assessment center ratings: A comparison of job performance validities, *Public Personnel Management* 21 (1992): 17–28.

68. S.S. Manela, Veterans preference in public employment: The history, constitutionality, and effect on federal personnel practices of veterans preference legislation, *George Washington Law Review* 44 (1976): 623–641.

69. J.F. Miller, "Veteran Preference in the Public Service," in *Problems of the American Public Service,* ed. C.J. Friedrich, et al. (New York: McGraw-Hill Book Company, 1935): 243–334.

70. 5 U.S.C. § 2108.

71. U.S. General Accounting Office, *Federal Hiring: Does Veterans' Preference Need Updating?* (Washington: U.S. Government Printing Office, 1992).

72. *Attorney General of New York v. Soto-Lopez,* 476 U.S. 898 (1986).

73. C.D. Saso and E.P. Tanis, *Selection and Certification of Eligibles* (Chicago: International Personnel Management Association, 1974), 10–23.

74. 5 U.S.C. §3318.

75. G.T. Gabris and S.M. Rock, Situational interviews and job performance, *Public Personnel Management* 20 (1991): 469–483.

76. M. Komter, *Conflict and Cooperation in Job Interviews* (Philadelphia: J. Benjamin Publishers, 1991).

77. C.A. O'Reilly, III, et al., People and organizational culture: A profile comparison approach to assessing person–organization fit, *Academy of Management Journal* 34 (1991): 487–516.

Chapter 6

Probation and Performance Evaluation

Once a government position has been offered and accepted, testing continues. During the initial weeks, months, or years, the individual is in a probationary status in which skills are tested on the job. The examination process may have been faulty in general or may have been in error in qualifying any one individual. The person may be well qualified from the standpoint of substantive knowledge but not qualified in being able to perform a given job on a daily basis. For example, severe personality problems may prevent a person from working effectively with peers. Probation allows the worker to be tested on the job, during which time the individual has limited security. How the person handles the job is recorded through the performance evaluation process. The performance assessment is used for determining whether that individual will continue to be employed. Periodic performance evaluations continue throughout the career of each person working in the government.

This chapter is an extension of the preceding ones, which discussed the design and classification of positions, the establishment of pay plans, and the processes of recruiting, examination, and selection. Now that a person has a job, what happens next? The first section of the chapter considers the probationary period, and the second discusses performance evaluation. The chapter concludes with a discussion of how managers are evaluated and whether the merit pay concept should be applied to all workers from entry through executive levels.

PROBATION

Once appointed, the government worker routinely is placed on probation, which may last several weeks to several years, the latter as in the case of a college faculty member. At the federal level, an individual in effect may have two probationary statuses[1]:

1. If appointed as a career-conditional employee, the person must serve 3 years before qualifying as a career employee. During the first of those 3 years, the person has an official probationary status.
2. If appointed as a career employee, as distinguished from career-conditional, the individual must serve a 1-year probation.

At all levels of government, periodic performance evaluations are completed by the worker's supervisor during the probationary period (these evaluations are the subject of the next section). The vast majority of workers successfully complete probation, but some are dismissed as not suitable (about 4 percent in the federal service).

The probation experience is not the same for everyone. Some people are hired at middle or senior levels of responsibilities. Others enter at more junior levels and come directly from high school, a baccalaureate program, or a professional graduate education program such as public or business administration. From the first day on the job, these persons may be expected to perform as all other workers. Some may be assigned to work with experienced employees, who act as coaches. Depending upon the agency, a team approach may be utilized at all times so that new employees never are expected to operate independently.

Regardless of whether the coach or team approach is used, some form of orientation will be provided. In a large department, the central staff may provide several hours or days of orientation for all new employees. This type of orientation is used to explain rules, regulations, procedures, and the like as well as to provide some familiarity with the names and faces of key personnel in the department. The direct supervisor also provides a type of orientation, explaining duties and operating procedures and often warning against certain practices. The orientations of the supervisor and central staff can differ, with central staff emphasizing some matters and the supervisor discounting their importance and emphasizing other matters.

New employees may go through what can be called a preprobationary status. Some persons enter government through internships, which last 1 to 2 years. The Office of Personnel Management (OPM) administers the 2-year Presidential Management Internship Program.[2] The presidential internships and some at the state and local levels can involve rotational assignments from one office or agency to another and sometimes, for federal and state programs, from one geographical location to another.

The internship enables both an agency and its interns to assess their capabilities and interests. An intern may find that certain types of work are more interesting than others, and the agency may find that the intern excels more in some types of tasks than in others. The interns also gain familiarity with the scope of the agency's responsibilities and with the individuals involved; that familiarity is expected to facilitate intra-agency communication and work flow.

Not all internships, however, are this systematic. Some interns are not rotated among positions or are not rotated among units within a department and receive virtually no training on the job. Instead, they are expected to perform basically as all other workers, although typically they are compensated at a substantially lower rate.

At the end of an internship, a public agency usually has no continuing commitment to the individual. In the case of long-term internships of a year or more, however, governments attempt to find permanent employment for the interns, a policy that is warranted considering the training time invested in them. Implementing such a policy is difficult during periods when budgets are being cut and hiring freezes are in force or when reductions in force (RIFs) are being implemented.

An alternative to the internship is to place the new employees in an intensive training program. There, all new employees are brought together for an extended period rather than being integrated with other employees. For example, in basic training in the military, recruits are trained together and after training are dispersed to various units. City and state police academies perform a similar function.[3] Some federal agencies that use nonuniformed personnel, such as the Federal Bureau of Investigation, have somewhat analogous training programs.

Successful completion of the extended training program or internship is required for continuing in government service, but it may not be a guarantee of continuing employment. The person who fails in the police academy obviously will not be retained, but success in the academy may provide no security because there may be more graduates than the police department needs. Assuming that a job is provided at the end of the training or internship program, the individual then is in a probationary status. The police rookie, having completed training at an academy, is a probationary employee.

The influences on a probationary worker can be understood by using socialization theory, which is concerned with how "an organizational member learns the required behavior and supportive attitudes necessary to participate as a member of an organization."[4] Four stages can be identified in the socialization process: anticipatory socialization, accommodation, role management, and outcomes.[5]

Anticipatory socialization entails the expectations individuals gain before obtaining employment. A student of social work may anticipate being able to work closely with impoverished families to help them resolve their problems but, once on the job, may find such accomplishments are difficult to achieve because of unwillingness on the part of the poor to accept counseling. The social worker also may feel unable to provide the counseling because of a large caseload and perceived excessive red tape requirements of the bureaucracy.

Expectancy theory deals with the relationships between what an individual expects and what actually occurs and how the differences can influence behavior (see Chapter 10). One view is that expectations should approximate reality to avoid disillusionment and undesired behavior. Sometimes supervisors "over-sell" jobs to candidates in the job interview. That can lead a person to accept a position only to become dissatisfied once on the job.

Socialization involves what the new employee anticipates coupled with perceptions of what occurs on the job. Accommodation is the process of learning about the job, the organization, and the people in it. Role management refers to the process of adapting; one individual may play different roles both within the organization and at home. Outcomes include satisfaction or dissatisfaction with the job, job motivation or the lack of it, and work productivity or its absence.

There is no extensive literature about what usually happens to probationers during the first weeks or months on the job.[6-8] The one classic study on the subject is Kaufman's 1960 study of forest ranger recruitment and probation.[9,10] Not much is known about how supervisors handle new employees. Some supervisors may assume a parental role; others act more as friends. Some may be harsh when a probationer makes an error; others may be either positive by sympathetically explaining the problem or indifferent because of being engrossed in other agency matters. An extremely busy bureau chief will have little time to explain procedures patiently and to correct problems involving a low-level worker. Another aspect about which little is known is the extent to which supervisors use the appointment of a new person as an opportunity to reassign responsibilities among subordinates.

The probationer's coworkers also play important roles, but again there is no extensive literature that describes those roles or the interplay between them and the probationer. Some employees may regard the probationer as a potential threat and as a result are aloof or even hostile. Others may act as a friend, a big brother or sister, or a parent. The probationer is thrust into a situation that has been evolving over time, a situation with all the complexities and nuances of any social order. Determining the organization's "pecking order" often is an initial task for the probationer. The person hired as a first-level professional will attempt to assess the relative influence or power of other professionals as well as clerical workers. For example, how important is gaining favor, or at least avoiding conflict, with the boss's secretary?

Integration of these supervisory and coworker influences is complicated by other factors, such as the substance of the job itself and the individual's personal life. The new job may be demanding, involving long hours, including some evenings and weekends; these demands may come as a major shock to the person recently graduated from high school or college. The demands of the job can disrupt family routines. Moreover, the new job may have involved moving to a new city, requiring the probationer and family to make a wide range of adjustments.

Role conflict and ambiguity can be consequences of the process. In the case of role conflict, competing demands are made on the individual. The person's family may expect special attention to getting settled, and the supervisor may expect dedication to the new position. Conflicting role expectations between supervisor and peers can develop all too easily, with the supervisor expecting dedication and peers expecting less commitment to the job. Role conflict also develops between what the probationer thinks is appropriate behavior and what conduct the organization seems to reward. The individual's profession may prescribe one type of behavior while the organization insists on another type.

Ambiguity refers to an absence of clearly stated expectations. The supervisor may have given little direction about what types of behavior are considered appropriate or may be mercurial, seemingly expecting one type of behavior one moment and a different type later. Such ambiguous situations obviously complicate the problem of developing behavior patterns that will meet with approval.

The result of this myriad of forces will be varying behavior patterns. Some workers become conforming and timid; others become rebellious. Some feel free to discuss problems with their supervisors, and others are intimidated. Ultimately some workers will adapt, and others will resign.

How these influences affect job performance is not obvious. The discussion of motivation in Chapters 10 and 11 indicates that there are many influences on behavior besides the experience during probation. It is safe to assume, however, that the probationary experience can have lasting effects on an individual's performance. Work habits, good or bad, may be established firmly during this period. Persons who have strong demands made on them during probation may tend to be more productive and successful (as measured by job status and pay) than other persons.[11]

If completion of probation is unsuccessful, resignation or dismissal is the possible outcome. No testing system can be expected to be able to select uniformly successful employees. For that reason, managers need flexibility in determining whether a probationer should continue. Procedural rights are substantially more limited for probationary employees than for permanent ones (the issue of adverse action against permanent or tenured employees is discussed in Chapter 8). At the federal level, the bureau chief or supervisor first must give written notification that a probationary employee is being considered for removal. The employee has a right to provide a written reply, which must be considered by the agency, but has no right to an oral presentation. The final step is the formal notice of removal, which must include the reasons for the action.[12]

Both lack of use and abuse of the dismissal procedure are problems in government. Some supervisors may delay taking the steps to remove an employee until that person automatically gains permanent standing at the end of the probationary period. This can result in the agency's having to cope with an incompetent employee for many years. The delay may be caused by other pressing demands on the supervisor's time or a desire to avoid an unpleasant situation. Dismissal not only affects that person but also can lead to low morale among other workers. Abuses, on the other hand, occur in the dismissal of employees because of race, sex, handicaps, or other extraneous matters. A personality clash between the supervisor and probationer can result in dismissal, even though the probationer is highly qualified. As noted in Chapter 5, supervisors sometimes accept persons at the top of eligibility lists and then encourage them to resign by making their jobs as unpleasant as possible.

Probationers may be dismissed for only vague reasons, and their right to appeal through administrative and judicial channels is greatly restricted. At the federal level, a probationary employee may be removed when "work performance or conduct . . . fails to demonstrate his fitness or his qualifications for continued employment" or when removal would "promote the efficiency" of the agency.[13] For instance, a federal poultry inspector was removed for "foul and abusive language."[14]

Probationers have limited, if any, rights to work at their assigned jobs and demonstrate their competencies. Judicial review of probationary employee dismissals is greatly limited. As one court has stated, "Dismissal from federal employment is largely a matter of executive agency discretion. Particularly is this true during the probationary period. The scope of judicial review is narrow."[15] The courts generally have not required that probationers be given an opportunity to appear at an administrative hearing to rebut charges brought against them. One protection afforded probationary as well as tenured employees is that they cannot be dismissed for exercising a constitutional right; the First Amendment right to free speech has been particularly important in this respect (see Chapter 8). Dismissal of probationers because of discrimination or the exercise of civil rights also is prohibited and reviewable by courts (the discrimination issue is considered in detail in Chapter 9).

PERFORMANCE EVALUATION OR APPRAISAL

Performance evaluation or appraisal is to be found in most governments. Federal laws require that employees be evaluated on a regular basis, and the same is the case with most states. A survey of local governments found that 79 percent of cities and 72 percent of counties have performance appraisal systems.[16] The following discussion considers the purposes of appraisals, the techniques used, and the problems associated with appraisals.

Purposes

Employee performance evaluations, appraisals, or efficiency ratings serve several purposes.[17-19] The topic is covered here because one of the primary uses of performance evaluation is to determine whether an employee should be retained beyond the probationary period. This is one of the most common uses of evaluations in state, city, and county governments. The second most common use of performance evaluation is for promotion purposes; persons with weak evaluations probably will not be promoted.

More generally, evaluations can be used to judge employees' potentials not only in terms of higher-level positions through promotion but also in terms of the assignment of duties. Evaluations are used for determining which employees will be laid off because of reductions in force (RIFs). Performance evaluations were used for this purpose by the federal government after World War II, when the size of the bureaucracy was reduced sharply, and evaluations still carry some weight in RIF decisions stemming from budget cutbacks.[20]

One of the more controversial uses of performance evaluation is for compensation purposes. Proponents suggest that employees should be rewarded financially for high performance. This practice has been less common in government than in industry, where flexible pay policies allow awarding extra compensation for superior performance, although collective bargaining agreements may restrict some of that flexibility.

There are conflicting views in both the private and the public sector on whether performance evaluations should be used in setting pay. On the positive side is the argument that wage increases can be used as incentives to improve productivity. Proponents contend that employees will accept systems that provide differing levels of pay based on varying levels of job performance. This assumption was the basis for the pay reforms Congress made in 1978.[21] Pay is linked with performance appraisal for persons in the Senior Executive Service and by the merit pay/Performance Management and Recognition System (PMRS) for supervisory and managerial positions. The Senior Executive Service is discussed in Chapter 7 and the PMRS later in this chapter.

Appraisal systems have been criticized as being invalid, that is, as not accurately gauging worker performance.[22] To base pay on invalid measures would produce inequities of either overcompensation or undercompensation. Workers often complain that their supervisors do not exercise care in the rating process and that, as a result, the ratings are flawed and should not be the basis of pay decisions.[23]

A more equitable approach than basing pay on merit, some critics say, is basing it on job evaluation; that is, pay should be set according to the work required by a job and not how well a person performs.[24] If the worker does not perform as well as expected, then either performance should be brought up to standards or the individual should be removed from the job.

It has been suggested that the use of performance evaluation in pay, promotion, and dismissal/retention decisions furthers the merit principle. Important personnel decisions are based on objective measures of worker performance rather than on political allegiances and cronyism. Theoretically, this improves workers' morale because they understand that their contributions to government will be recognized and rewarded suitably.[25] Performance appraisal systems are cited as important vehicles for communication between supervisors and their subordinates.[26]

Another purpose of performance evaluation is to provide a basis for employee development.[27] By requiring supervisors to assess periodically the strengths and weaknesses of each subordinate, performance evaluation systems can serve as the basis for devising a strategy for assisting each employee to improve.

Most evaluation systems these days require the supervisor to meet with each employee to discuss the evaluation. In some cases, workers must sign the rating form as proof that they have seen the documents, not as evidence that they necessarily concur with the ratings; in fact, in many cases they can write on the form that they do not agree, which can trigger an appeals or grievance procedure. The supervisor–subordinate meeting can be the occasion for planning improvements and for discussing why deficiencies exist. From this perspective, the supervisor serves as a coach or counselor. The result of the meeting may be an agreement that duties should be reassigned or that an employee should be sent to a special training program.[28,29] The evaluation also can be used as a vehicle for evaluating whether training received by workers has led to improved performance.

This approach is credited not only with furthering the individual's self-growth through improved motivation but also with facilitating organizational self-renewal and fostering increased productivity of the agency as well as the individual.[30] It is contended that supervisors need to be concerned not only with individual worker performance but also with how that performance relates to the overall operations of the agency. One suggestion is that it is possible to determine the dollar return on increased productivity stemming from an effective appraisal system.[31,32]

The primary argument against the coaching method is that it is sharply at variance with the other purposes of performance evaluation. Those other purposes involve negative as well as positive incentives. Poor performance, if linked with pay decisions, results in little or no compensation increase. Poor performance also results in the denial of promotion and can lead to dismissal either during the probationary period or later. In other words, the supervisor is required to assume the role of judge. Critics of the coaching method claim that a supervisor cannot successfully perform the roles of both judge and counselor.

Some organizations attempt to use both the judging and the counseling aspects of performance evaluation by having supervisors conduct separate interviews with employees for each of these different purposes. In one interview, performance is reviewed along with plans for improving performance; in the other interview, performance is related to salary decisions. The two interviews can be separated by two or more weeks. The results of this procedure have been mixed. The two-interview approach may be able to divorce the roles, but that may be doubtful given expectancy theory (see above). If the counseling interview occurs first, the employee will anticipate the outcome of the second session on pay. The same type of anticipation will occur if the order is reversed.[33]

The evaluation process can serve as a vehicle for informing employees about how well they are doing. That is particularly important for probationers so that, in the event of dismissal, they will not be surprised. Explaining deficiencies to probationers can provide an atmosphere of fairness and openness and can help avoid complaints over dismissal. Employees then cannot complain that they were unaware their work was substandard.

Existing evidence, however, suggests that performance evaluation tends to be more of a negative than a positive influence on behavior. In meeting with an employee, the supervisor is likely to focus on deficiencies in order to identify how improvements can be made. Unfortunately, subordinates often interpret these comments as harsh criticisms. Even extensive praise by the supervisor may be largely ignored by the subordinate, who says mentally, "Yes, you said I am a good worker, but . . . ." The employee may complain of receiving only a good rating when an excellent rating would have been more appropriate. In other words, performance ratings can produce negative attitudes that have negative influences on behavior.

Given the different purposes of performance evaluation and, as will be seen, the difficulties in devising such systems, it should be no surprise that performance appraisal has an uneven history. In the federal government, the process dates back to the 1840s, when Congress required service reports from each department, but the requirement soon was ignored more than it was heeded. In the early 1900s, appraisal became popular at all levels of government and in private enterprise, but the systems that were introduced tended to be abandoned over time.

One observer in the 1930s wrote, "Regardless of the nature of the form and the character of the organization, there is remarkable agreement in experience with rating systems. Most of the efforts to measure efficiency . . . have been failures."[34] Yet efforts to evaluate employees persist and will continue. As noted, each federal agency is required by law to have one or more evaluation systems.[35] State and local governments make extensive use of evaluation systems, although small local governments may be infrequent users.[36]

Appraisal Techniques

Performance evaluation, like position classification and the establishment of a pay plan, necessarily is based on a set of assumptions about the work involved in any job. Just as job analysis is essential to the classification of positions, so is it vital to performance evaluation. Without an understanding of the work involved in a position, a supervisor cannot assess how well an individual is performing in that job. Therefore, any performance evaluation system created independent of job analysis is likely to be inappropriate.

Performance appraisal includes three types of data: objective, personnel, and judgmental.[37,38] Objective data refer to the work accomplished by an employee. These might be the number of letters typed by a secretary, the number of traffic citations issued by a police officer, or the number of students taught by a school teacher. Personnel data include information about tardiness, absenteeism, commendations, and disciplinary actions; these data usually are to be found in a worker's personnel file. Although both the objective and personnel data are valuable in assessing an employee's performance, they do not provide a complete perspective on the individual. For that reason, judgmental data also are used. Judgmental data are the assessments of a rater about how well a worker performs. Rating systems, then, are basic tools of performance appraisal.

An initial concern must be what items are to be rated. There are three possible groups of items:

1. traits, such as initiative, imagination, and loyalty (see Chapter 5)
2. behavior and/or performance as the evaluation of a behavior[39]
3. the result of a behavior or performance

To illustrate the differences among these types, a worker might be highly motivated (trait), work extra hours without compensation (behavior), yet rarely complete an assignment correctly or on time (result). Appraisal systems that rely on traits assume a linkage between the trait and the eventual result; for instance, loyalty to the organization will produce results. Trait ratings once were popular but now are considered a poor method of evaluation. The behavior/performance system assumes that a particular behavior will produce desired results. In some instances, the behavior is intrinsically desirable (e.g., "always on the job when needed").

Most rating systems do not use the results orientation. Indeed, ratings by supervisors might be an inappropriate technique for gauging results. If it is necessary to know whether an employee completes work on time, a records system would need to be maintained and each individual's record rated periodically. Such a system would work best for jobs in which employees work independently of others and produce tangible items, perhaps as in the case of a tool-and-die maker in industry.

If the employee works with others, then the product is a joint one, and difficulties arise over assessing the relative contributions of each individual. If an item is not produced on time, should the fault be assigned to worker A, B, or C? This type of problem is common in government. It is easier to gauge performance when work is expected to yield tangible items, but government jobs typically involve providing a service rather than making tangible products.

What, for example, would be the direct product of a day-shift prison guard as distinguished from the products of other day-shift guards as well as those of evening and night guards?

The main thrust of performance evaluation has been in the area of attempting to describe what types of behaviors are needed in each position, as distinguished from traits and performance results. The distinction between traits and behaviors, however, is not always obvious when applied to actual situations. The literature seems to be replete with internally conflicting examples of what should and should not be regarded as a trait. For instance, should decisiveness, cooperation, and adaptability be considered traits or behaviors?[40] Is the behavior "handling stressful and emergency situations" little more than a more elaborate way of stating "adaptability," which can be considered a trait? Indeed, a blending has resulted in which researchers have devised descriptions of behavior for traits such as initiative, attitude, and communication.

Since passage of the Civil Service Reform Act in 1978, the federal government has devised appraisal systems based on critical elements. Every job is likely to have numerous aspects, but the federal system directs attention at those aspects that are essential (critical) and must be performed at a satisfactory level. A person could perform exceptionally well in all but one aspect of the position, but if that one aspect or element is critical, then overall performance must be judged to be inadequate. OPM has used the following as examples of critical elements for a secretary: "types correspondence and other material, takes and transcribes dictation, and receives telephone calls and visitors."[41,42]

Once the elements or items to be rated are established, the next step is to devise a rating form. One of the most popular forms of the 1920s was the Probst Service Report.[43] The Probst municipal rating form included such items as "lazy," "too old for the work," "usually pleasant and cheerful," and "drink is one of the principal failings."[44] The rater simply went down the list of more than seventy items, checking those that applied. Other systems have allowed for positive, negative, and neutral ratings. For example, the federal government in the 1930s used a plus for a positive evaluation, a minus for a negative one, and a check for average. The rater would use one of these in assessing such items as acceptability of work, thoroughness, and amount of work accomplished.[45] The federal Performance Rating Act of 1950 required using the categories of outstanding, satisfactory, and unsatisfactory as overall evaluations of each employee.

The checklist or the three gradations of plus, minus, and check have the advantage of simplicity, but a complaint is that they do not allow for distinguishing among variations in performance. As a result, scales have long been used. Figure 6–1 provides five sample scales. The first, which uses letters, once was common but has been largely abandoned. The second provides only the key words *high, medium,* and *low* with twenty gradations from which to select. The third uses a point system ranging from 0 to 25. The fourth provides worker

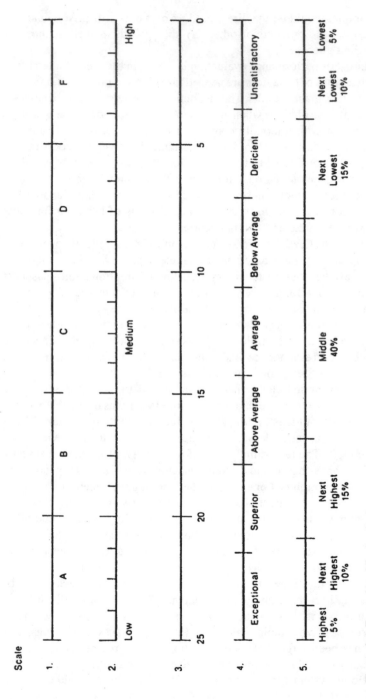

Figure 6–1 Examples of Rating Scales.

descriptions ranging from exceptional, superior, and above average down to unsatisfactory. The last scale uses a percentage distribution, with 40 percent in the middle and smaller percentages above and below.

Criticism of these types of scales is common. The letter grade system is regarded as too simplistic. Both that scale and the high-medium-low scale provide the rater with little guidance on what is meant by each gradation. The twenty gradations on the second scale may be overly detailed: What is the difference between one and two notches above middle? The point system has the same weakness. Sometimes the point system is used in combination with the word descriptor scale; a superior rating might be equivalent to between 20 and 25 points. The description and percentage scales do not indicate the standards being applied. Is the individual "superior" in comparison with current employees, all employees known by the rater, or some ideal standard? Similarly, on the percentage scale, what is meant by the middle 40 percent? The middle 40 percent, and all other employees below the middle, might be considered unsatisfactory by the rater.

In response to these criticisms, personnel researchers have turned to methods of identifying benchmarks along rating scales. Behaviorally anchored rating scales (BARS) provide work descriptions of behavior for various steps on a scale. The technique is related to the Probst rating system and a test developed by Thurstone as adapted in the 1930s by Beyl and Kingsley.[46,47] A five-step process is used in developing BARS[48,49]:

1. Persons having experience with a given type of work are asked to describe real examples of effective and ineffective behavior. These sometimes are called critical incidents.
2. The researchers group the incidents under several headings, which will become the main dimensions of behavior around which scales will be devised.
3. Another group of experienced persons provides judgments about whether the listed incidents are typical examples of positive and negative behaviors. This is called "retranslation." Agreement must be substantial for any item to be used. For instance, the researchers might require that at least 60 percent of the experts agree that the incident of "rarely argues with coworkers" is a measure of worker interpersonal behavior.
4. The researchers rank the incidents, often on a 7- or 9-point scale. This step also is done by a panel of experts, who need to agree on the point value if an item is to be retained. If "rarely argues," for instance, is given a point rating of 2 by 30 percent of the experts and a rating of 6 by 40 percent, the item would be discarded.
5. The researchers select a subset of the tested incidents and develop the final instrument.

A behaviorally anchored rating scale for a supervisor of sales personnel is shown in Figure 6–2. The behaviors range from an example of the best behavior (item 9) to an example of the worst (item 1). Item 5, reminding employees to wait on customers, presumably is a positive supervisory function, as are items 6, being courteous to employees, and 7, holding weekly staff training sessions and instructing staff members about what is expected of them. If item 7 were chosen by a rater, there would be a presumption that items 5 and 6 also applied.

A potential weakness of BARS is that the scale may not be unidimensional; that is, two or more dimensions may be included on the same scale. Thoroughness and accuracy of work, for example, are not necessarily the same type of behavior. A clerical worker could be thorough in processing forms, such as ensuring that all blanks have been completed and that the correct number of copies of each form has been made, but could be highly inaccurate in completing the forms. Another example would be a combined behavior of "planning and executing"; an individual could be an excellent planner yet an unsatisfactory executor[50] (whether this type of problem exists in the BARS in Figure 6–2 should be considered).

The federal government's approach to anchoring rating scales has been to establish performance standards for each critical element. The standard is a measure of achievement in terms of "quantity, quality, timeliness, manner, method, or cost."[51,52] Table 6–1 indicates suggested minimally and fully satisfactory standards for the secretarial elements mentioned earlier. OPM oversees the decentralized Performance Management System, which provides basic rules for the evaluation of employees in GS-1 through GS-15 positions. Federal agencies must use between three and five rating levels and must use the ratings of "unacceptable," "fully successful," and "outstanding."[53]

Appraisal Problems

Numerous problems exist with all appraisal systems.[54–56] One problem common to all systems is rater leniency. Supervisors tend to be lenient in rating their subordinates, in part because of a willingness to give them the benefit of the doubt, to encourage their efforts at self-improvement, and to avoid unpleasant situations. Because it is likely that the rating will have to be discussed with each employee, the supervisor may not wish to have to explain or defend negative judgments. Another reason for leniency is that unsatisfactory performance ratings may reflect poorly on the supervisor. The frequent result is that few employees are ranked below the midrange scale and most are rated high. The First Hoover Commission observed, "In two agencies examined, fewer than 3 in 1,000 employees were marked 'unsatisfactory' over a year," and a study in the 1980s had similar results.[57,58]

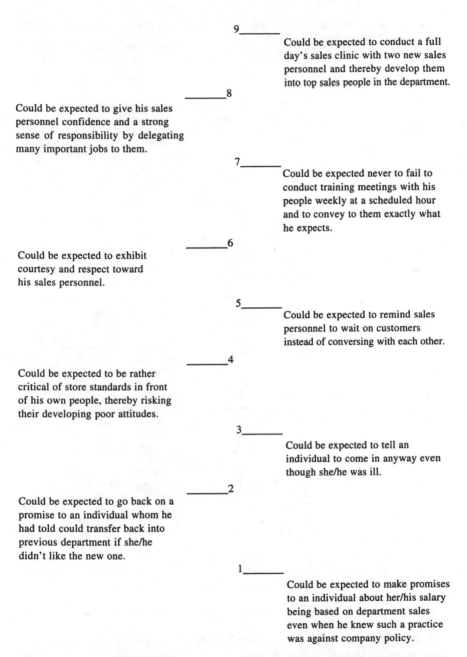

9_____

Could be expected to conduct a full day's sales clinic with two new sales personnel and thereby develop them into top sales people in the department.

_____8

Could be expected to give his sales personnel confidence and a strong sense of responsibility by delegating many important jobs to them.

7_____

Could be expected never to fail to conduct training meetings with his people weekly at a scheduled hour and to convey to them exactly what he expects.

_____6

Could be expected to exhibit courtesy and respect toward his sales personnel.

5_____

Could be expected to remind sales personnel to wait on customers instead of conversing with each other.

_____4

Could be expected to be rather critical of store standards in front of his own people, thereby risking their developing poor attitudes.

3_____

Could be expected to tell an individual to come in anyway even though she/he was ill.

_____2

Could be expected to go back on a promise to an individual whom he had told could transfer back into previous department if she/he didn't like the new one.

1_____

Could be expected to make promises to an individual about her/his salary being based on department sales even when he knew such a practice was against company policy.

Figure 6–2 BARS for Supervisor of Sales Personnel. *Source:* Reprinted from John P. Campbell et al., "The Development and Evaluation of Behaviorally Based Rating Scales," *Journal of Applied Psychology* Vol. 57, p. 17, with permission of the American Psychological Association, © 1973.

Table 6–1 Selected Critical Elements and Performance Standards for a Secretarial Position (GS-5)

Performance Element	Unacceptable Performance	Minimally Satisfactory	Fully Satisfactory	Out-standing
1. Types correspond-ence and other material.		Typed material is neatly arranged in appropriate format and proofread before submission to writer. Typographical errors are clearly corrected. Work is completed within requested timeframes *with no more than one undetected error.*	Typed material is free of errors, neatly assembled with all supporting documents correctly attached. Completed work is submitted well within requested timeframe.	
2. Takes and transcribes dictation.		Takes dictation with some interruptions requesting assistance with spelling, punctuation or grammar. Transcribes all material in draft for review by writer before typing final copy.	Takes dictation without interrupting speaker. Transcribes all but very complex, technical material in final form, without preparing draft copy. Consults dictionaries, thesaurus, secretarial handbooks to avoid errors in spelling, punctuation and grammar.	
3. Receives telephone calls and visitors.		Answers inquiries with assistance of others in office, screens and refers visitors and telephone calls accurately and courteously. No more than _____ legitimate complaints are received and no instances of discourtesy noted.	Maintains desk notes concerning data frequently requested for use in answering inquiries; screens and refers visitors and telephone calls appropriately, accurately and courteously. Volunteers to assist inquirer, using known office protocol. No legitimate complaints or discourtesies are noted.	

Source: Reprinted from *Performance Standards Handbook: A Reference for Managers and Supervisors* by G.A. Bullock (ed.), p. 1–16, U.S. Office of Personnel Management, U.S. Government Printing Office, 1981.

Some techniques have been instituted to make it impossible for managers to be excessively lenient. The percentage distribution technique allows the supervisor to place no more than a specified proportion of employees in a given category (see rating scale 5 in Figure 6–1). This forced distribution is relatively easy to administer when one overall rating is used for each employee, but not when a dozen or more scales are used. The percentage approach also is arbitrary, assuming that it is possible to identify the top 5 percent of the workers and so on. The percentage approach is based on the unwarranted assumption that workers are distributed according to the decreed distribution. The rating system may allow for only 5 percent in the highest category when in reality 10 percent of the workers are equally of the highest caliber.

An alternative is to use the person-to-person comparison method. The rater is expected to rank subordinates from highest to lowest. This can be done for the performance of employees considered as a whole or on the basis of traits or behaviors. For example, employees might be ranked according to initiative and industriousness. A given worker might rank third on initiative but twentieth on industriousness. The ranking method has the disadvantage of being time consuming and arbitrary, especially in the midrange. Although it may be possible to identify one set of subordinates as being more cooperative than another set, the workers in the midrange may seem equally cooperative, making it impossible to rank one worker higher than the others. Moreover, the rating is relative, not absolute. The very best worker might not be very good, or the worst one might be quite good.

A related problem is what is commonly called the "halo effect."[59] This refers to the tendency for employees to receive the same rating on all items being rated, such as all 7s on a 9-point scale for numerous different traits. Raters tend to have difficulty differentiating qualities in workers. A supervisor who regards an employee as generally poor will give a negative rating on all items, even though that person may have significant strengths in some areas.

Other problems include what might be called the "human nature" of raters. Some raters have biases that result in discrimination against employees of a given sex, age, race, religion, or ethnicity.[60–62] Raters are likely to be affected by the recency of events and the general context of the work environment.[63] If the day before a rating a worker makes a serious error on the job, the supervisor is likely to be harsh in rating. When a supervisor is particularly annoyed with the behavior of one employee, other subordinates are likely to receive higher ratings than would otherwise be the case.

Still another problem is that rating systems may require judgments for which the supervisor has insufficient information. A rater may be asked to assess the extent to which a subordinate consults peers in dealing with problems when the rater has not observed the individual sufficiently to make any such judgment. The rater simply may not complete this portion of the rating sheet; in some instances, rating forms provide a space to indicate "not observed." Serious errors can result if the rater makes a determination without much information.

One general prescription for raters' problems is that they need to be trained in the rating process.[64] Some advocate not merely rater training but also rater involvement in the development of the rating system itself. The standard interpretation is that raters are more likely to accept a system they helped develop. A mere 5-minute briefing of raters on the halo effect can substantially reduce such results.[65,66]

Training of raters should not be regarded as a panacea. Some raters, no matter how extensive their training, may have difficulty in social differentiation, which is the opposite of the halo effect. Even when it is shown that the rater tends to rate a person consistently on one scale after another, the rater may be unable to compensate for that tendency. A supervisor who consciously blocks a halo tendency can become arbitrary, dispersing ratings simply for the sake of dispersion.

Besides these problems involving raters, there are several other more general ones associated with performance evaluation. One involves the number of traits or behaviors to be assessed for each employee. Some rating systems not only require that various items or elements be ranked in terms of unsatisfactory, minimally satisfactory, fully satisfactory, and the like but also expect raters to provide short sentences or phrases describing the employee's assets and weaknesses. Obviously, the longer the rating form, the more time will be required to complete it, the more likely raters will be to complain of needless paperwork, and the more likely it is that they will be rushed and therefore careless when they rank subordinates.

Another issue involves whether persons other than the supervisor should be part of the rating process. Ratings by peers may be useful in providing a different perspective or second opinion.[67] Self-ratings may encourage workers to think more carefully about the different aspects of their activities on the job. One of the most sensitive suggestions is the use of subordinates and clients to rate superiors. Here, intimidation is possible. Welfare clients may fear reprisals if it becomes known that they gave low ratings to their social workers, as would social workers fear reprisals for giving low ratings to their bosses. Nevertheless, subordinate and client ratings are used sometimes. A prominent example has been the use of faculty evaluations by students as one source of input in tenure and promotion decisions.

Standardization versus decentralization is another issue. Some jurisdictions use a standard rating system for all employees throughout the government, and others allow agencies to develop their own systems. The Civil Service Reform Act of 1978 eliminated standard categories and permitted agencies greater latitude in devising systems that best met their needs.

Some agencies have chosen to use individually tailored rating forms in which each employee may have a unique set of critical elements and performance standards. Other agencies have used "generic elements" that have been applied to large groupings of employees. State and local governments vary greatly, with some using a standard system for specified jobs across department lines and others not.

Should there be an overall rating for each employee, and how is it to be derived? The argument for a single rating is that it condenses the evaluation into easily understandable terms: Employee A is "satisfactory," and employee B is "outstanding." The argument against this is that human behavior is too complex to simplify into a single overall rating. Indeed, double talk may be the result, as in this example from the U.S. Navy: "The existence of a satisfactory performance rating will not in itself be considered to be evidence of an acceptable level of competence since an employee's performance may be satisfactory in a marginal way but not of a nature to warrant an increase of pay."[68] In other words, satisfactory performance may not be satisfactory for pay increase purposes.

As an alternative to the supervisor's providing a summary rating, a composite may be calculated by averaging the scores on the various scales of the rating sheet.[69] Weights can be assigned to scales so that, for example, behavior associated with knowledge about the nature of the job might have greater weight than punctuality. The greatest potential flaw of either an averaged or a weighted total rating is that misjudgments may have been made in devising the system. Perhaps only fourteen of the sixteen behaviors on a rating sheet were really important, or perhaps one of the most important behaviors was omitted.

Given the potential for faulty overall ratings, they should be used with great caution, if at all. Supervisors and other raters should not assume that an employee with an average rating of 7.62 is superior to one with a 7.48 or, for that matter, a 6.00 average. Mosher and Kingsley, writing in the 1930s, said that the use of percentages, letter grades, and the like had been thoroughly discredited.[70] Although that observation may have been correct, the practice continues. One of the primary reasons is that personnel decisions often are binary: yes or no. There is a temptation to use overall ratings in making critical personnel decisions, such as dismissals, promotions, and layoffs.

Another problem with performance appraisal is that it is used infrequently or, in some instances, not at all. Frequent monitoring of worker performance can help in encouraging positive aspects of workers and in correcting weaknesses.[71,72] Supervisors, however, often avoid completing required evaluations according to announced schedules because of an aversion to evaluating personnel.

A cluster of problems exists regarding how top management supports performance appraisal and how appraisal is used in helping workers improve their performance. Simple rhetorical endorsement of performance evaluation systems by top management means little when a supervisor is working diligently with a subordinate to correct his or her performance. The supervisor needs backing by higher-level executives when it becomes necessary to remove an employee who has had unsatisfactory performance ratings and has been unwilling or unable to correct deficiencies.[73,74]

Today's personnel administrators, in implementing performance evaluation systems, must cope with labor unions. At the federal level, OPM and the Federal

Labor Relations Authority (FLRA) have been at odds with each other to some extent. In particular, the FLRA has ruled that unions have some role in performance appraisal systems. Although management does not need to negotiate as to the substance of critical elements and performance standards, procedures leading up to the establishment of those factors are negotiable, along with how they are communicated back to employees. OPM has provided "negotiation guidance" to agencies on these issues.[75]

Another concern with performance evaluation is that its focus is allegedly misplaced; namely, evaluation should be made of organizational results and not of individuals' work. Performance measurement of organizations, a longstanding set of concepts, gained increased attention starting in the late 1980s. Advocates contend that government can best be held accountable by linking the results of activities with their costs.[76-78] Similarly, management approaches such as total quality management emphasize group or team approaches to work and oppose measures that tend to highlight what individuals accomplish (see Chapter 11).[79,80]

MANAGEMENT EVALUATION

Although measuring the performance of any type of employee can be difficult, the task is particularly challenging when the performance of managers and executives is being reviewed. These persons are more likely to make a lasting impact on an organization than any one road crew worker or clerical secretary, so the need for performance evaluation can be assumed to be greater for them than for others. Measuring the activities of managers is complicated in that the direction and supervision they provide influence the work performed throughout the organization. The results of managerial work are the total outcomes of the organization.

Given the difficulty in assessing the linkage between a given manager's actions and the organization's productivity, most evaluation systems avoid a results-oriented rating system and concentrate on traits and/or behaviors. Many jurisdictions may use the same types of scales for managers and subordinates but provide additional scales for the managerial functions of supervising, budgeting, planning, and the like.[81,82]

One of the most important and most controversial innovations of the Civil Service Reform Act has been what was initially called the Merit Pay System in 1978 and is now known as the Performance Management and Recognition System.[83-85] (The Senior Executive Service is discussed in Chapter 7.) The system covers some 138,000 midlevel managers and supervisors who are designated General Management (GM) 13 through 15. More than 90,000 positions remain as GS-13 through GS-15. To be included in the GM framework, a position must entail either supervision of subordinates or managerial work. The system bases pay on the results of a performance appraisal system that relies on critical elements and performance standards, as discussed earlier. In passing the legislation, Congress had no intention of increasing the overall cost of paying these supervisors and managers. Therefore, the pay ranges of GS-13 through GS-15 set minimum and maximum limits on the PMRS, so that total compensation can be no greater than what would have been paid in terms of base pay, annual adjustments for pay comparability with the private sector, within-grade step increases, and quality step increases.

Within an agency, a pool is created with these step increase monies. Until 1985, the pool consisted of half the money that would have been used for comparability adjustments. The other half went more or less automatically to each member of the system. For instance, if federal employees overall were receiving a 4 percent pay adjustment, those in PMRS were assured only 2 percent. The monies in the pool then were distributed according to how high each worker's rating was for that year. In addition, the system provided cash awards or bonuses to highly rated personnel.[86]

One of the least popular aspects of the system was the guarantee of only half the annual pay comparability adjustment. A common complaint was that managers and supervisors supposedly had to work exceptionally hard to earn what they perceived to be a cost-of-living adjustment while their subordinates received such increases automatically. In response to these complaints and at the urging of OPM, Congress in 1984 amended the Act to provide that anyone in PMRS who earned a fully successful rating or higher would receive the comparability increase.

The legislation, in response to criticisms that rating systems used by some agencies were excessively complex, set five standardized levels of performance: unacceptable, minimally successful, fully successful, exceeds fully successful, and outstanding. Anyone receiving a fully successful rating or better also was assured some or all of a step increase, depending upon how high the rating was and the individual's step in the pay plan. Anyone receiving an outstanding rating was guaranteed a cash award of 2 to 10 percent of base pay.

The familiar complaint of some raters being more lenient than others applies to PMRS. This is particularly important because the variations in ratings can influence how much money a person receives. One partial solution to this problem might be to move toward more generic elements and standards. OPM suggested four critical elements for management: organizational planning, program direction and communication, human resources management, and program monitoring and evaluation.[87] A more dramatic solution would be to scrap altogether the critical elements and standards approach to evaluation. Congress authorized such action on an experimental basis in 1991.[88]

Many managers in the system question its fairness. Some learn about their performance standards 6 months into the rating period, perhaps too late in the year for them to meet these expectations. Sometimes managers and supervisors are satisfied with their ratings but then learn the ratings were lowered by higher authorities attempting to obtain a more balanced set of ratings among those in a pay pool. In other cases, Schedule C political appointees have been included in pay pools with merit employees and frequently receive higher ratings and therefore higher pay adjustments, leading to allegations of possible political influences on decisions. In a General Accounting Office study, 78 to 84 percent of respondents said the pay system did not motivate them to increase their performance.[89]

Information is generally unavailable as to whether the Performance Management and Recognition System has had any effect, positive or negative, on productivity, motivation, leadership, and the like. There also is no information about how expensive its implementation has been; clearly, its operation has required many thousands of person-hours. A key question is whether the system has generated morale problems. Performance bonuses were seen as being too small and as being awarded on bases other than high performance.[90] If managers are told they should be concerned/motivated by pay and if increases are slight, then dissatisfaction may result. The use of noneconomic incentives may be worth further investigation.[91] Because government probably never will be able to compete with managers' and supervisors' salary scales in the private sector, an alternative approach would be to enhance other aspects of public employment such as increased use of training, rotational job assignments, and a formal recognition system for exceptional performance.[92] An advisory committee, mandated by the 1991 amendments, concluded that "PMRS is neither fair nor effective."[93]

MERIT PAY FOR ALL?

The idea of merit pay or pay for performance has spread well beyond federal supervisors and managers. All types and levels of government exhibit keen interest in such systems as applied to some or possibly all of their workers.[94-98] The concept is particularly controversial in public education. Critics of elementary and secondary schools contend that teachers would be more diligent if their pay was determined by how well they taught.[99,100] Similarly, pay systems linked with performance evaluations are being developed for colleges and universities.[101,102]

The Civil Service Reform Act granted OPM authority to engage in personnel experiments. One that was undertaken was a demonstration merit pay system at two Navy laboratories: the Naval Weapons Center in China Lake, California and the Naval Ocean Systems Command in San Diego, California.[103-105] In the experiment, the traditional form of position classification with elaborate job descriptions was replaced with broad occupational or career paths; for example, scientists, engineers, and computer specialists were grouped together. Broad pay bands were established that included the equivalent of two or more GS pay grades. Workers could be hired within these bands at competitive salary rates, unlike the situation with the more rigid grade and step system. Workers also could move within the bands—upward or downward, depending on their performance—so that there was no assurance of receiving step or pay comparability increases. Overall, the system was well received by the naval workers, although skeptics suggest that one reason for their satisfaction is that pay rose faster in these facilities than in the control laboratories in Pennsylvania and Virginia.

In 1986, OPM sent Congress a proposal for a Simplified Management System modeled after the naval experiments.[106] Congress, however, failed to act on the proposal, being concerned about what would be the positive and negative outcomes of such a major change in the procedure by which most salaries are set in the federal government. Although no action was taken on the 1986 proposal, Congress did include an important provision in the Federal Employees Pay Comparability Act of 1990 (see Chapter 5). The law set pay for performance as national policy and instructed OPM to establish a labor–management committee to provide advice on designing such a system.

Wherever pay-for-performance systems are installed, several problems must be confronted.[107] Productivity gainsharing, in which workers share collectively the savings made through increased productivity, is advocated in some instances over systems that base pay decisions on whether a worker earned a satisfactory or outstanding rating.[108] A related problem is what goals and objectives are to be pursued; namely, are the purposes of governmental programs clearly defined, so that progress can be readily measured? Will organized labor support or oppose pay for performance?[109] Unions at the federal level have contended that pay-for-performance systems should be subject to collective bargaining.

In closing this discussion, concerns about the effectiveness of performance evaluation must be revisited. Any pay-for-performance system is by definition grossly inadequate and therefore inequitable if the performance evaluation system fails to measure accurately workers' performance. Expectations about what a performance evaluation system can accomplish need to be realistic, and the reality of the situation may be disappointing.[110] A survey found that a substantial majority of federal personnel specialists thought performance appraisal systems had had no impact or a negative impact on their agencies' effectiveness[111] (Table 6–2). This view applied to appraisal of executives, managers, and supervisors in PMRS and other white collar workers in the GS system.

Table 6–2 Personnel Specialists' Perceptions Concerning Performance Management Systems

"In Your Opinion, What Impact Has Each of the Three Performance Appraisal Systems Had on Your Organization's Effectiveness?"

System	Percentage of Respondents Who Said:		
	Greatly or Somewhat Improved	No Impact	Greatly or Somewhat Impeded
Performance Management System	29	44	28
Performance Management and Recognition System	27	39	35
Senior Executive Service	25	54	21

Source: Data from *Federal Personnel Management Since Civil Service Reform*, p. 11, U.S. Merit Systems Protection Board, U.S. Government Printing Office, 1989.

SUMMARY

Upon appointment to a government position, a new employee is placed in probationary status. Some persons, such as interns and police academy cadets, first must successfully complete a preprobationary period. Probation can be viewed as the final step in a testing program in which workers are tested on the job.

During the probationary period, which may extend from a few weeks to several years, the probationer is socialized into the organization. Expectations acquired before entering government can influence greatly whether the new worker successfully completes probation; unrealistic expectations can result in disillusionment. Role conflict and ambiguity can thwart successful socialization.

In the event that a supervisor is not satisfied with the performance of a probationer, that worker can be dismissed with relative ease. Although official reasons for dismissal must be given, these often are vague, and the probationer has limited rights to administrative and judicial appeal. Violation of constitutional rights and dismissals based on discrimination are the primary areas for judicial review.

Performance evaluation is used not only for determining whether an employee successfully completes probation but also for other purposes throughout the worker's career. Evaluations are used for judging workers' potential, making RIF decisions, deciding who should be promoted, and, to a limited extent, determining pay increases. Another purpose, somewhat in conflict with the others, is the furthering of worker effectiveness through coaching or counseling.

Most evaluation systems now use scaling techniques that focus on traits and/ or behaviors. Trait ratings, although popular, are not highly regarded by experts in performance appraisal. Behaviorally anchored rating scales (BARS) attempt to specify behaviors to provide clear standards for raters. Despite the extensive research devoted to BARS, technical problems remain. More general problems, such as rater leniency and the halo effect, apply to all rating methods. Rater training may assist in minimizing some of these problems. Other questions involve the number of traits or behaviors to be rated, the use of peers and subordinates in the rating process, standardization versus decentralization of evaluation systems across departmental lines, the use of summary or overall ratings, and the difficulty of evaluating midlevel and top-level managers.

Merit pay or pay for performance is being used selectively in governments. These types of pay systems are intended to provide financial incentives to workers. Serious problems persist in devising suitable performance evaluation procedures that can be the basis for making pay decisions.

NOTES

1. U.S. Office of Personnel Management, "Career and Career-Conditional Employment," in *Federal Personnel Manual* (Washington: U.S. Government Printing Office, updated annually), chap. 315.

2. K.E. Newcomer, et al., The Presidential Management Internship Program: Looking backward and moving forward, *Public Administration Review* 49 (1989): 372–386.

3. J.J. Ness, The relevance of basic law enforcement training, *Journal of Criminal Justice* 19 (1991): 181–193.

4. J. Van Maanen, Police socialization: A longitudinal examination of job attitudes in an urban police department, *Administrative Science Quarterly* 20 (1975): 207.

5. D.C. Feldman, A contingency theory of socialization, *Administrative Science Quarterly* 21 (1976): 433–450.

6. N.J. Allen and J.P. Meyer, Organizational socialization tactics: A longitudinal analysis of links to newcomers' commitment and role orientation, *Academy of Management Journal* 33 (1990): 847–858.

7. J.P. Wanous, *Organizational Entry, Recruitment, Selection, Orientation and Socialization of Newcomers*, 2d ed. (Reading, Mass.: Addison-Wesley Publishing Company, 1992).

8. J.P. Wanous, et al., The effects of met expectations on newcomer attitudes and behaviors: A review of meta-analysis, *Journal of Applied Psychology* 77 (1992): 288–297.

9. H. Kaufman, *The Forest Ranger: A Study in Administrative Behavior* (Baltimore, Md.: Johns Hopkins Press for Resources for the Future, 1960).

10. T. Tipple and J.D. Wellmon, Herbert Kaufman's forest ranger thirty years later: From simplicity and homogeneity to complexity and diversity, *Public Administration Review* 51 (1991): 421–428.

11. D.E. Berlew and D.T. Hall, The socialization of managers: Effects of expectations on performance, *Administrative Science Quarterly* 11 (1966): 207–223.

12. 5 U.S.C. § 3321 and Termination of Probationers for Unsatisfactory Performance or Conduct, 5 C.F.R. § 315.804.

13. 5 C.F.R. § 315.804 and Suitability Determinations, 5 C.F.R. § 731.201.

14. *Jaeger v. Freeman*, 410 F.2d 528 (1969).

15. *Toohey v. Nitze*, 429 F.2d 1332 (1970), *cert. denied*, 400 U.S. 1022 (1971).

16. S.F. Fox and C.J. Fox, Merit systems and personnel appraisals in local government, *Baseline Data Report* 22 (November/December 1990): 1–12.

17. D.M. Daley, *Performance Appraisal in the Public Sector: Techniques and Applications* (Westport, Conn.: Quorum, 1992).

18. G.L. Morrisey, *Performance Appraisals in the Public Sector: Key to Effective Supervision* (Reading, Mass.: Addison-Wesley Publishing Company, 1983).

19. K.R. Murphy and J.N. Cleveland, *Performance Appraisal: An Organizational Perspective* (Needham Heights, Mass.: Allyn & Bacon, 1991).

20. Commission on Organization of the Executive Branch of the Government (First Hoover Commission), *Personnel Management* (Washington: U.S. Government Printing Office, 1949), 33.

21. D. Thompson, Performance appraisal and the Civil Service Reform Act, *Public Personnel Management* 10 (1981): 281–288.

22. M.E. Giffin, Personnel research on testing, selection, and performance appraisal, *Public Personnel Management* 18 (1989): 127–137.

23. S.Y. Yeager, et al., Employee perceptions of state and local government evaluation and reward systems, *State and Local Government Review* 16 (1984): 60.

24. First Hoover Commission, *Personnel Management*, 33.

25. A.W. Procter, *Principles of Public Personnel Administration* (New York: D. Appleton and Co., 1921), 162–164.

26. J.F. Kikoski and J.A. Letterer, Effective communication in the performance appraisal interview, *Public Personnel Management* 12 (1983): 33–42.

27. D. McGregor, An uneasy look at performance appraisal, *Harvard Business Review* 35 (May–June 1957): 89–94.

28. D. Daley, Performance appraisal as a guide for training and development: A research note on the Iowa Performance Evaluation System, *Public Personnel Management* 12 (1983): 159–166.

29. G.R. Herbert and D. Doverspike, Performance appraisal in the training needs analysis process: A review and critique, *Public Personnel Management* 19 (1990): 253–270.

30. F.J. Landy, et al., The bottom line in performance evaluation, *Public Productivity Review* 6 (1982): 78–92.

31. K. Callahan and M. Holzer, eds., Symposium on new approaches to productivity, *Public Productivity and Management Review* 15 (1991): 107–279.

32. M.R. Edwards, Productivity improvement through innovation in performance appraisal, *Public Personnel Management* 12 (1983): 13–24.

33. R.E. Robson and D.H. Nelson, Supervisor and nonsupervisor agreement and dissonance regarding performance appraisal, *Review of Public Personnel Administration* 11 (Fall 1990–Spring 1991): 121–130.

34. G.A. Graham, Personnel practices in business and governmental organizations, in *Problems of the American Public Service*, ed. C.J. Friedrich, et al. (New York: McGraw-Hill Book Company, 1935): 397.

35. M.S. Schinagl, *History of Efficiency Ratings in the Federal Government* (New York: Bookman Associates, 1966).

36. D. Daley, Performance appraisal in North Carolina municipalities, *Review of Public Personnel Administration* 11 (Summer 1991): 32–50.

37. R.M. Guion, *Personnel Testing* (New York: McGraw-Hill Book Company, 1965).

38. F.J. Landy, *Psychology of Work Behavior*, 4th ed. (Homewood, Ill.: Dorsey Press, 1989).

39. J.P. Campbell, et al., The development and evaluation of behaviorally based rating scales, *Journal of Applied Psychology* 57 (1973): 15.

40. II.S. Feild and W.II. Holley, Traits in performance ratings Their importance in public employment, *Public Personnel Management* 14 (1985): 327–330.

41. U.S. Office of Personnel Management, *Performance Standards Handbook: A Reference for Managers and Supervisors* (Washington: U.S. Government Printing Office, 1981): 1–15.

42. _____, *Evaluating Elements and Standards* (Washington: U.S. Government Printing Office, 1985).

43. F.H. Lopez, *Evaluating Employee Performance* (Chicago: Public Personnel Association, 1968): 202.

44. "Probst Service Report Form," in *Public Personnel Administration*, ed. W.E. Mosher and J.D. Kingsley (New York: Harper & Brothers, 1936): 438.

45. Schinagl, *History of Efficiency Ratings*, 50–51.

46. P.C. Smith and L.M. Kendall, Retranslation of expectations: An approach to the construction of unambiguous anchors for rating scales, *Journal of Applied Psychology* 47 (1963): 149–155.

47. F.J. Landy and R.M. Guion, Development of scales for the measurement of work motivation, *Organizational Behavior and Human Performance* 5 (1970): 93–103.

48. H.J. Bernardin and P.C. Smith, A clarification of some issues regarding the development and use of behaviorally anchored rating scales (BARS), *Journal of Applied Psychology* 66 (1981): 458–463.

49. P.W. Hom, et al., Effectiveness of performance feedback from behaviorally anchored rating scales, *Journal of Applied Psychology* 67 (1982): 568–576.

50. W.C. Borman and M.D. Dunnette, Behavior-based versus tract-oriented performance ratings: An empirical study, *Journal of Applied Psychology* 60 (1975): 562.

51. U.S. Office of Personnel Management, *Performance Standards Handbook*, I-6.

52. L.L.J. Trunzo, Performance appraisal at commerce, *International Personnel Management Association News* (August 1985): 4.

53. Performance Management System, 5 C.F.R. § 430.

54. D.A. Kravitz and W.K. Balzer, Context effects in performance appraisal: A methodological critique and empirical study, *Journal of Applied Psychology* 77 (1992): 24–31.

55. B.P. Maroney and M.R. Buckley, Does research in performance appraisal influence the practice of performance appraisal? Regretfully not! *Public Personnel Management* 21 (1992): 185–196.

56. G.E. Roberts, Linkages between performance appraisal system effectiveness and rater and ratee acceptance, *Review of Public Personnel Administration* 12 (May–August 1992): 19–41.

57. First Hoover Commission, *Personnel Management*, 32.

58. U.S. General Accounting Office, *Performance Appraisal Information from Selected Federal Agencies* (Washington: U.S. Government Printing Office, 1985).

59. R.J. Harvey, The future of partial correlation as a means to reduce halo in performance ratings, *Journal of Applied Psychology* 67 (1982): 171–176.

60. P.R. Sackett, et al., Tokenism in performance evaluation, *Journal of Applied Psychology* 76 (1991): 263–267.

61. P.R. Sackett and C.L.Z. DuBois, Rater-ratee race effects on performance evaluation: Challenging meta-analytic conclusions, *Journal of Applied Psychology* 76 (1991): 873–877.

62. U.S. General Accounting Office, *Performance Measurement: Appraisal and Promotion Results at the U.S. Customs Service* (Washington: U.S. Government Printing Office, 1990).

63. D.A. Kravitz and W.K. Balzer, Context effects in performance appraisal: A methodological critique and empirical study, *Journal of Applied Psychology* 77 (1992): 24–31.

64. M.L. Fehrmann, et al., The Angoff Cutoff Score Method: The impact of frame-of-reference rater training, *Educational and Psychological Measurement* 51 (1991): 857–872.

65. W.C. Borman, Effects of instructions to avoid halo error on reliability and validity of performance evaluation ratings, *Journal of Applied Psychology* 60 (1975): 556–560.

66. R.M. McIntyre, et al., Accuracy of performance ratings as affected by rater training and perceived purpose of rating, *Journal of Applied Psychology* 69 (1984): 147–156.

67. B.S. Steel, Participative performance appraisal in Washington, *Public Personnel Management* 14 (1985): 153–171.

68. C.W. Langdon, Evaluating performance of federal employees, *Marquette Business Review* 15 (1971): 206.

69. G.A. Marcoulides and R.B. Mills, Employee performance appraisals: A new technique, *Review of Public Personnel Administration* 8 (Summer 1988): 105–115.

70. Mosher and Kingsley, *Public Personnel Administration*, 431–432.

71. D.B. Fedor and M.R. Buckley, Issues surrounding the need for more frequent monitoring of individual performance in organizations, *Public Personnel Management* 17 (1988): 435–442.

72. D.A. Hofmann, et al., Mapping individual performance over time, *Journal of Applied Psychology* 77 (1992): 185–195.

73. U.S. General Accounting Office, *Performance Management: How Well Is the Government Dealing with Poor Performers?* (Washington: U.S. Government Printing Office, 1990).

74. D.C. Martin and K.M. Bartol, The legal ramifications of performance appraisal, *Employee Relations Law Journal* 17 (1991): 257–286.

75. D.M. McCabe, Labor relations, collective bargaining, and performance appraisal in the federal government under the Civil Service Reform Act of 1978, *Public Personnel Management* 13 (1984): 133–146.

76. C.A. Bowsher, *Performance Measurement: An Important Tool in Managing for Results* (Washington: U.S. Government Printing Office, 1992).

77. U.S. General Accounting Office, *Office of Personnel Management: Better Performance Information Needed* (Washington: U.S. Government Printing Office, 1990).

78. R. Boyle, *Managing Public Sector Performance* (Dublin, Ireland: Institute of Public Administration, 1989).

79. S. Cohen and R. Brand, Total quality management in the U.S. Environmental Protection Agency, *Public Productivity and Management Review* 14 (1990): 99–114.

80. M.E. Milakovich, Total quality management for public sector productivity improvement, *Public Productivity and Management Review* 14 (1990): 19–32.

81. D.N. Ammons, Executive satisfaction with managerial performance appraisal in city government, *Review of Public Personnel Administration* 8 (Fall 1987): 33–48.

82. D.N. Ammons and A. Rodriguez, Performance appraisal practices for upper management in city governments, *Public Administration Review* 46 (1986): 460–467.

83. J.L. Perry, Merit policy by trial and error: Merit pay in the federal service, *Policy Studies Journal* 17 (1988-89): 389–405.

84. J.L. Perry, et al., Federal merit pay, round II: An analysis of the Performance Management and Recognition System, *Public Administration Review* 49 (1989): 29–37.

85. U.S. Merit Systems Protection Board, *Performance Management and Recognition System: Linking Pay to Performance* (Washington: U.S. Government Printing Office, 1988).

86. U.S. General Accounting Office, *Performance Management Recognition System Performance Awards* (Washington: U.S. Government Printing Office, 1986).

87. U.S. Office of Personnel Management, *Appraising Managerial Performance: Suggested Elements and Standards for Executives, Managers and Supervisors* (Washington: U.S. Government Printing Office, 1984).

88. Performance Management and Recognition System Amendments of 1991, P.L. 102-22, 105 Stat. 71.

89. U.S. General Accounting Office, *A 2-Year Appraisal of Merit Pay in Three Agencies* (Washington: U.S. Government Printing Office, 1984).

90. _____, *Pay for Performance: Interim Report on the Performance Management and Recognition System* (Washington: U.S. Government Printing Office, 1989).

91. H.A. Frank, Volcker versus Niskanen: Reflections on the limited use of financial incentives in the public sector, *Public Productivity and Management Review* 13 (1990): 353–368.

92. G.T. Gabris and W.A. Giles, Improving productivity and performance appraisal through the use of noneconomic incentives, *Public Productivity Review* 7 (1983): 173–189.

93. Panel questions merit of pay-for-performance, *PA Times* 15 (February 1, 1992): 3.

94. E.J. Bacciocco, Jr., Survey of West Coast cities with merit pay systems, *Public Productivity and Management Review* 13 (1990): 405–411.

95. S.F. Fox, Intergenerational differences, merit pay, and loyalty in state and local government, *Review of Public Personnel Administration* 9 (Spring 1989): 15–27.

96. W.C. Lawther, et al., Implications of salary structure and merit pay in the fifty American states, *Review of Public Personnel Administration* 9 (Spring 1989): 1–14.

97. P.M. Swiercz and M. Icenogle, Incentive pay in the public sector: A discriminant analysis of professional employee responses, *Review of Public Personnel Administration* 11 (Fall 1990–Spring 1991): 71–83.

98. U.S. General Accounting Office, *Pay for Performance: State and International Public Sector Pay-for-Performance Systems* (Washington: U.S. Government Printing Office, 1990).

99. G. Gabris, ed., Why merit pay plans are not working, *Review of Public Personnel Administration* 7 (Fall 1986): 1–89.

100. L. Weber and J. McBee, Teacher evaluation instruments for merit pay decisions: Is their use justifiable? *Evaluation Review* 14 (1990): 411–426.

101. L.B. Prewitt, et al., Merit pay in academia: Perceptions from the school of business, *Public Personnel Management* 20 (1991): 409–417.

102. R.L. Taylor, et al., Merit pay in academia: historical perspectives and contemporary perceptions, *Review of Public Personnel Administration* 11 (Summer 1991): 51–65.

103. Naval Personnel Management Demonstration Project, *The Effects of Performance-Based Pay on Employee Attitudes* (Washington: U.S. Office of Personnel Management, 1985).

104. R.M. Glen, Performance appraisal: An unnerving yet useful process, *Public Personnel Management* 19 (1990): 1–10.

105. B.W. Schay, Effects of performance-contingent pay on employee attitudes, *Public Personnel Management* 17 (1988): 237–250.

106. Constance Horner, director, U.S. Office of Personnel Management, letter to George Bush, president of the Senate, July 7, 1986, and appended draft "Civil Service Simplification Act."

107. G.T. Milkovich and A.K. Wigdor, eds., for the Committee on Performance Appraisal for Merit Pay, National Research Council, *Pay for Performance: Evaluating Performance Appraisal and Merit Pay* (Washington: National Academy Press, 1991).

108. K.C. Naff and R. Pomerleau, Productivity gainsharing: A federal sector case study, *Public Personnel Management* 17 (1988): 403–419.

109. J. Uhren and L. Reese, Collective bargaining and merit pay: A case study, *Public Administration Quarterly* 14 (1990): 230–244.

110. D.L. Balfour, Impact of agency investment in the implementation of performance appraisal, *Public Personnel Management* 21 (1992): 1–15.

111. U.S. Merit Systems Protection Board, *Federal Personnel Management since Civil Service Reform* (Washington: U.S. Government Printing Office, 1989).

Chapter 7

Careers and Career Development

Continuity in an organization is provided by members remaining with it over time. The problems that can result when such continuity is eliminated have been demonstrated in nations that have undergone revolutions or have shifted abruptly from colonial to independent status. Career public servants can maintain stability of services during political turmoil, as was the case in France after World War II. Careerists are essential in maintaining continuity from one political administration to another.

The subject of careers extends the time frame involving the relationship between government and its workers. The preceding chapters considered issues such as how to attract people into government service and how to evaluate their performance, particularly during probation. This chapter focuses on:

1. the concept of a career and career patterns in general
2. executive careers
3. the role of education and training in career development

CAREERS IN GOVERNMENT

A dictionary definition of "career" is "a field for or pursuit of consecutive progressive achievement." Often implicit in the term is an assumption of upward mobility in an organization, usually through a series of promotions. A common bias is that a career, or at least a successful one, involves advancement. A related bias is that careers are for persons holding positions in the upper strata of an organization. Executives and professionals are said to have careers, whereas laborers have only jobs. Advancement, however, need not be achieved solely by promotion. Advancement or growth can be accomplished in the same position held for many years as well as in different jobs that have the same organizational rank or status. Moreover, careers are not only for executives, although this discussion emphasizes some of the special problems associated with executive career development.

Because government's first priority must be to meet societal needs through the efficient and effective delivery of services, employees' careers must be less than first priority. The argument can be made that government needs careerists only at middle and higher levels in the bureaucracy or only a small cadre of careerists located at all levels. As in industry, many government jobs involve routine work that does not require large numbers of career personnel. For these types of positions, high turnover rates may not be particularly troublesome, although daily changes obviously would hamper efficient operations.

Governments generally take a middle ground between indifference and complete commitment to employee career development. If for no other reason, such a commitment is justified as humane on the theory that employees should be treated as individuals who need to develop their potential. Governments, however, usually are not involved in extensive career planning and development for each worker. Although government does provide both formal and informal career counseling, materials on how to plan careers, and advice on how to qualify for government training and how to apply for promotions, the ultimate responsibility for such planning rests largely with the individuals.[1-3]

Career ambitions often must be tempered by career opportunities. Dead-end position classification systems frequently thwart advancement by career employees (see Chapter 3). On the other hand, high turnover rates, sometimes due to large numbers of retirements, can create opportunities for younger workers.[4] Personal factors may lead to some employees deciding to quit their jobs and temporarily dropping out of the labor market; although the vacancies they create may provide opportunities for other workers, those who resign may delay their career advancement.[5] Some positions may be viewed as placing workers on a "fast track" for advancement; the Presidential Management Internship Program sometimes has been advocated as a vehicle for rapid career advancement (see Chapter 6).[6] Baby boomers, namely those people born in the post–World War II era, may be at a disadvantage in career advancement in that their numbers far exceed the number of high-level positions available in the public, nonprofit, and for-profit sectors.[7,8] Discrimination, although generally outlawed, is a reality and thwarts the career development of minorities, women, people with handicapping conditions, and the like.[9]

Given all the uncertainties that characterize the labor market, one plausible view is that employees should not be particularly concerned about career planning and instead should learn to capitalize on career opportunities as they arise. In such a situation, government agencies might be less concerned with advising employees about career advancement opportunities and more concerned with helping workers gain psychological satisfaction with the jobs they now hold rather than prospective jobs.

Attempting to manage one's own career involves difficult choices that must be made without complete information. In starting a career, a person may have applied for positions with several different governments or agencies within a government. Should the first job offer be accepted while other applications are pending? If a career objective is to become a city manager, should the person accept a position as an analyst in a city housing department or wait until an assistant city manager position is offered?

Whatever the choice, the first job after completing one's education will influence future opportunities. Experience in a city housing department will tend to qualify the person for higher-level housing positions. If the first job is with a state, opportunities with that state usually will be greater than with other governments because the worker will have more information about job openings and application procedures for that jurisdiction.

Subsequent job decisions present similar problems of uncertainty. Should an assistant city manager accept an offer for assistant manager in a larger city, a job that involves greater responsibilities and pay, or pursue only city manager positions? Accepting a new position at higher pay also can reduce real income, considering moving expenses and cost-of-living variations among cities, so that some advancement opportunities may not be particularly attractive.

Procedures for promotion vary greatly among and within jurisdictions. Some state and local governments fill all positions through a standard examination process; persons already in government take the same examination as outsiders. Other governments give preference to promoting current employees. In these situations, the current work force of the government is treated as an internal labor market.[10] At the federal level, agencies develop their own promotion programs in conformance with policies established by the Office of Personnel Management (OPM). Some promotions are made on a "career" basis, by which individuals are promoted without competing with others. This is the case with such personnel as foresters, Internal Revenue agents, and air traffic controllers. In other instances, depending upon the agency and the type of job involved, an examination may be given.

Filling a job begins with announcing the vacancy to agency employees. They can apply for the position and submit information about their qualifications to update their personnel files. A panel, including a representative of the agency's personnel office, often is responsible for reviewing candidates' credentials, such as education, experience, and performance evaluations. The panel provides a ranked list of candidates to the person responsible for filling the position. Job interviews follow, and an individual subsequently is selected. Many variations on this procedure are possible. Sometimes vacancies are not posted, but all eligible employees are given consideration. Selection lists often are not ranked. Depending upon the jurisdiction, veterans preference may or may not be given in promotions. Some jurisdictions use promotability ratings, in which candidates are rated by their peers and higher officers in terms of their likelihood of success in high-level positions; this type of rating is prospective in comparison with performance evaluations that review prior performance.[11,12]

When an agency cannot identify an appropriate person in house, the next step may be to open the position to employees in other agencies and later to those outside the government. It should be understood that the vast majority of positions in government are filled through promotions, not external recruitment.

The laws and regulations that govern promotion procedures may encourage or discourage legal challenges. In the United States, administrators have considerable latitude in selecting employees for promotion, and as a consequence promotions produce relatively few legal challenges. Australia, in contrast, allows employees who were not selected for promotion to challenge a decision on the grounds of inefficiency and that the most qualified candidate was not selected. In such a case, the employee who was selected has the burden of proof in showing that he or she was indeed most qualified.[13]

Given the uncertainties involved in job opportunities, most careers probably are not planned carefully. Instead, they tend to evolve as employees are exposed to different types of work. Sometimes careers are advanced through mentoring, in which more experienced workers provide important advice and help locate advancement opportunities for more junior workers.[14,15] Many careerists did not plan initially to spend their working lives in government. Decisions over whether to stay in government undoubtedly were influenced by perceptions about their current positions, prospects for promotion, and job opportunities outside government. In other instances, the impetus to leave government stems from layoffs or what are called "reductions in force" (RIFs). RIF procedures are discussed in Chapter 8, but it should be noted here that workers who are displaced may find other positions in their own agencies or in others. Some workers who are terminated must seek positions with other employers.

There are at least six different types of job mobility: intra-agency, interagency, interorganizational, geographic, occupational, and social class mobility.[16] Intra-agency mobility, as the term suggests, involves movement from one job to another within an agency. The movement can be vertical (up or down) or lateral (from one job to another with the same organizational status). Military personnel are one of the most intra-agency–mobile types of government employees.[17]

Interagency mobility involves movement from one agency or department to another in the same government.[18] Promotion opportunities within an individual's occupational field, whether within an agency or between agencies in a government, are limited by the number of positions available. Governments sometimes emphasize promotion opportunities for their workers when in fact there is little "room at the top." Whether a person is an attorney, an engineer, or a budget analyst, the number of high-ranking positions in these fields in any government is extremely limited. If the persons holding those higher positions are relatively youthful, are competent, and show no interest in competing for other positions, then promotion avenues are blocked.

The third type of mobility, interorganizational, includes movements between governments and between government and private corporations. Intergovernmental job changes can be at the same level, such as interlocal, and between levels, as in state-local mobility. Some occupations may require intergovernmental mobility. City managers seeking positions of greater responsibility are forced to change employers, typically moving to larger cities.

Mobility between the public and private sectors often is associated with corporate interests in obtaining government contracts. Private firms hire government workers to enhance their pool of personnel qualifications, and undoubtedly there is an underlying assumption that such employees will be able to "deliver" government contracts. The opposite flow also occurs, with people moving from industry to government (see Chapter 8 for a discussion of conflicts of interest).

Interorganizational and interagency mobility have been the center of continuous controversy. Some personnel systems are structured to discourage or even prohibit these forms of mobility, requiring that a person enter at a low-level position to be eligible for higher positions. These restrictions are said to encourage career development and to guarantee that supervisors and managers are fully aware of operations at lower echelons. New York City in the 1920s basically prohibited both interagency and interorganizational mobility. A supporter of the system wrote, "Some of the most highly compensated men and women in this part of the service entered originally as office boys or typewriting copyists."[19]

The federal government makes both career and noncareer appointments, particularly at the top levels. The term "career" in this context refers to the method of appointment, not to length of government service. Noncareer appointments are often, but not always, "political." By their nature, they frequently are filled from outside the service. For career appointments, on the other hand, federal agencies first attempt to fill higher positions through promotions.

Several criticisms can be made of practices that discourage mobility. Government agencies can become walled-in empires that are not receptive to new ideas or even exposed to them. Such systems can deny agencies superior talent and force them to promote persons with mediocre skills. Barriers to persons outside government can provide unwarranted opportunities to current employees.

The fourth type of mobility is geographic. This often occurs in association with another type of mobility, such as when workers change employers or make intra-agency and interagency changes. Movement is common between the central office and regional offices of large state and federal agencies. There may be a reluctance to move, however, because of the problems of finding new housing, making new friends, changing the children's schools, losing the spouse's job, and the like. Employees also may be reluctant to move because of career considerations. Those in the central office may fear they will be overlooked for promotion if they move to a regional office.

Occupational job changes are the fifth type of mobility. These changes can be dramatic, as when a nurse leaves the profession, returns to college, and develops a new career, perhaps in computer operations. Position classification and qualifications standards greatly limit occupational mobility opportunities. An experienced personnel analyst who prefers to shift to budgetary work may not be able to meet the experience requirement for higher-level budgeting positions and may be forced to accept an entry-level position in that field. Perhaps the most common type of occupational change is into administration. Frequently, the management shift is within a substantive field, for example a nurse's becoming a hospital director of nursing or a social worker's becoming the administrator of a county social services agency.

Social class mobility is the sixth form of mobility. Government employment has been an important route for persons to move from the working class to the middle class.

At some point in a career, promotions cease, and a tongue-in-cheek but nevertheless plausible explanation is the Peter Principle.[20] Promotions are awarded to productive workers, who are expected to be equally effective in positions of greater responsibility. Eventually, individuals are promoted to positions for which they are not well qualified, so that further promotions are not forthcoming. In other words, workers tend to be promoted until they reach their individual levels of incompetence.

More seriously, career plateauing has come to be recognized as a major problem for workers who seek hierarchical advancement.[21-23] Because only one person can be promoted to the top position in an organization, many are bound to be disappointed. Lack of self-esteem may develop, along with feelings of having been unsuccessful. A countermeasure can include recognizing the significance of one's own position and one's accomplishments in that position. Opportunities for personal growth and development in an existing position also are important.

At the end of a career is retirement, a subject that is attracting increasing attention. One concern is that employees are not prepared psychologically for retirement, which typically constitutes an abrupt change in lifestyle.[24] Although preretirement counseling often has been used to encourage early retirement for less productive workers, counseling now is being advocated to aid workers in adjusting to retirement life. This form of counseling is being used in industry and can be expected to become more extensive in government.

Another issue is compulsory retirement. These measures have been introduced to force the superannuated to leave government, but they often have debilitating effects on persons who could continue to be productive. A counterargument has been that forcing the elderly to retire opens opportunities for other workers to advance their careers and allows government to attract young persons. According to federal law, state and local governments may not have a compulsory retirement age except in selected cases, and there is no compulsory point for federal employees. Elderly workers, however, may be forced to retire when they are unable to perform the duties of their jobs.

Many government workers simply do not retire when they officially retire. As noted in the discussion of retirement benefits in Chapter 4, retired military personnel and state and local police officers often find other jobs. The military uses an up-or-out system in which persons not promoted are forced to retire. Information is not available about the extent to which retired federal military and civilian workers find state and local government employment, but their number certainly is substantial. Not only is the practice beneficial to the individuals involved, but it often provides state and local governments with exceptional talent that they otherwise might not be able to afford. Other retirees accept part-time or full-time employment with private corporations, particularly those dealing with government, or develop their own consulting agencies. Many military retirees accept federal civilian jobs, where they are known as "double-dippers." Other federal retirees take part-time federal employment under contract.

CAREER EXECUTIVES

Although the terms *executive, administrator, manager,* and *supervisor* generally are used interchangeably in this book for convenience, at this point it is necessary to distinguish "executive" from other types of administrative positions. An executive, like other administrators, is expected to supervise subordinates but has an additional responsibility, participating in the policymaking process of a department or government. All public workers inevitably have some influence on policy, but executives can be said to have policy as a primary function. Prescribed procedures may limit the area of subordinates' activities, while executives are presumed to have greater latitude in molding governmental programs.[25,26]

At the highest level of the executive branch is a chief executive—president, governor, or mayor—under whom are political executives. These individuals serve at the pleasure of the chief executive and are expected to be compatible, personally and philosophically, with the top leader. Department heads, deputy secretaries, and assistant secretaries also are political executives.[27-30]

Directly below them in the organizational hierarchy are career executives, who generally remain in office regardless of changes in political administrations. Indeed, by their continuing in office through such changes, career executives help provide continuity in government programs. These careerists, who are only a small fraction of all public workers, constitute the interface between partisans and the rest of the government bureaucracy. It has been said that career executives make perhaps 90 percent of the important decisions in government, and precisely because of this, tension exists between career and political executives.[31-33]

One frequent assumption is that government does not sufficiently utilize the executive talent available within its own ranks simply because of an inability to identify that talent. Potentially excellent executives are overlooked when critical positions are to be filled. In response, numerous efforts have been made to be more thorough in the search for outstanding persons within the government. Some federal agencies have computerized their personnel files, which are searched when vacancies need to be filled. This type of effort dates back at least to 1940, when the U.S. Civil Service Commission established the Interdepartmental Placement Service, which used punch cards to record important data about nearly a million federal employees.[34] During the 1960s and 1970s, some governments established executive inventories that contained information about executives and could be searched for qualified candidates. In the 1990s, governments may use a combination of sources of information in seeking executives, including consulting firms that conduct searches outside the jurisdictions.[35-38]

Beyond personnel inventories are more fundamental proposals for reform.[39] The British use of rank-in-person has received wide attention.[40-42] The British administrative class has been considered a "permanent brain trust" into which are recruited young persons who are expected to become career executives.[43] Two key features of the British system are that it is based on recruitment at an early age and is closed to entry at higher levels. The administrative class historically has consisted largely of graduates in history, classics, and humanities from Cambridge and Oxford Universities. These persons serve as generalists and are not expected, before entry, to be trained in either a relevant substantive field or administrative practices. The rigorous examination process used for entry has concentrated on reasoning powers and verbal skills rather than on substantive knowledge.

The administrative class and, more generally, a closed career executive system have been severely criticized. In Britain, the Fulton Committee of 1968 characterized the administrative class as consisting of amateurs who preferred to move from one position to another, who delegated their responsibilities to the lower-status executive class, and who tended to make decisions without seeking information and advice from knowledgeable subordinates.[44] Career public servants in other classes, especially the executive class, generally were denied opportunities to join the administrative class. A major criticism has been that the system resists political leadership through such means as leaking unfavorable information to the news media.[45-47]

Other major criticisms of the British system have been that it is elitist and founded on the false assumption that generalists make good executives. The testing system employed by the British effectively screened out all but those who had graduated from the most prestigious universities, thereby working to the disadvantage of the middle and working classes. Individuals appointed to the administrative class supposedly developed a crown prince mentality concerning their role in government. Moreover, members of the administrative class were presumed to have general administrative skills that would qualify them for dealing with a wide range of problems. They could be reassigned periodically to wherever their talents were needed. Because rank was in the person, reassignment did not require matching a person's current position in terms of rank with a new position. The generalist concept is criticized on the grounds that current problems in government are technical in nature and require substantive expertise. Contemporary executives cannot be transferred suitably from one field to another, such as from education to defense.

Reforms have been instituted in Britain. The administrative, executive, and clerical classes were consolidated into the administrative group that became part of the general class. Others include the scientific, professional and technology, and training classes. The objective of reducing some of the career barriers between the old administrative and executive classes appears not to have been accomplished fully, however.[48,49]

Rank-in-person is used selectively in the United States. The U.S. Foreign Service and the military are prominent examples. The Forest Service and the National Park Service use the rank-in-person concept to some extent. The Foreign Service sometimes has been criticized as elitist, drawing heavily from Ivy League universities; similarly, the military has been criticized for relying heavily on military academy graduates for filling high command posts. Police and fire departments at the state and local levels use ranks. An advantage of these systems, like the career executive idea more generally, is that officers can be assigned to special positions or problems irrespective of their ranks. This advantage, however, is not unique to rank systems in that other merit systems allow for temporary assignment of personnel to deal with special problems.

Proposals to extend the rank-in-person concept to cover larger numbers of public workers have been common in the United States since the 1930s. In 1935 the Commission of Inquiry on Public Service Personnel recommended the establishment of a generally closed career system in which persons would be recruited for low-level positions and developed into career executives.[50,51] The First Hoover Commission (1949) emphasized the need for structuring positions in ways that would help groom employees for executive positions.[52] The Second Hoover Commission (1955) recommended the creation of a Senior Civil Service, but the recommendation, although discussed extensively, was never implemented.[53] President Eisenhower by executive order attempted to create a Senior

Civil Service, which failed because of lack of congressional funding.[54] In 1971, President Nixon recommended the establishment of a Federal Executive Service (FES), but Congress did not accept the proposal.[55]

Late entry and an open system have characterized the career executive proposals made in the United States in recent decades. The emphasis has been to change the way career executives are treated rather than the routes by which they become executives. Individuals would have opportunity to advance through promotions into executive status or could come from outside government into executive positions. Some state and local governments have established career executive systems along these lines.[56,57]

Action at the federal level came in 1978 with passage of the Civil Service Reform Act, which established the Senior Executive Service (SES).[58,59] It covers most positions previously classified at the GS-16, GS-17, and GS-18 levels along with levels IV and V of the Executive Schedule and provides for six pay levels. Some exceptions exist, such as positions in government corporations, the General Accounting Office, and intelligence agencies including the Federal Bureau of Investigation, the Central Intelligence Agency, the Defense Intelligence Agency, and the National Security Agency. OPM, in consultation with the Office of Management and Budget, authorizes SES positions for each agency.

The SES, made up of between 7,000 and 8,000 executives, consists of four types of appointments and two types of positions. Most of the executives are from the career ranks. The other three types of appointments are noncareer (political), and limited term and limited emergency. Noncareer appointees may constitute no more than 10 percent of the total SES. Some positions are "career reserved," meaning that they may be filled only by career appointees. In the Department of Housing and Urban Development, for example, career-reserved positions include the Chief Financial Officer, the Deputy Director of the Office of Personnel and Training, the Director of the Office of Public Housing, and the managers of the department's regional offices.

General qualifications for appointment to the SES are set by OPM, with more detailed qualifications being set by each agency. Lower-level managers may be selected into a candidate development program that helps prepare them for becoming executives. In these development programs, candidates receive exposure to departmentwide and governmentwide practices in policy development, human resources, program implementation, finance, and the like. Each agency has one or more "executive resources boards" responsible for reviewing candidates, and OPM has one or more "qualifications review boards" that certify qualifications for initial appointment of career appointees into the Senior Executive Service. Career appointees serve a 1-year probation and may be reassigned by their agencies within the same commuting area upon 15 days' written notice, except that the career appointee cannot be reassigned involuntarily within 120 days of the appointment of a new agency head or a new immediate supervisor.

The Senior Executive Service stresses executive performance. Performance appraisals are based on such factors as improvements in efficiency, cost savings, reduction in paperwork, improvements in effectiveness of subordinates super vised by the executives, and the meeting of affirmative action goals. The 1978 legislation requires that summary appraisal ratings include one or more fully successful levels, a minimally satisfactory level, and an unsatisfactory level.

An unsatisfactory rating can result in removal from the SES; two unsatisfactory ratings in a 5-year period require removal. A person receiving less than the fully successful rating twice in any 3-year period must be removed. Agency "performance review boards" are responsible for performance appraisal. Career appointees who are removed from the SES may have an informal hearing before a representative of the Merit Systems Protection Board. A career employee removed from the SES is entitled to a GS-15 position or above.

Career members, as provided under the Ethics Reform Act of 1989, must be recertified every 3 years.[60] In being recertified, SES careerists must demonstrate excellence in planning for policy goals and objectives, implementing policy and improving the quality of services, ensuring that high-quality services are provided in a timely fashion, and demonstrating accomplishments in technical, scientific, or professional fields. The recertification process is under the direction of the Office of Personnel Management.

Rewards are an important component of the SES. Career appointees are eligible for paid sabbatical leaves for up to 11 months.[61] All appointees are guaranteed a minimum pay rate equivalent to the minimum pay of the Senior Level (formerly GS-16). Up to half the executives may be eligible for performance awards or bonuses of as much as 20 percent of their base pay. In addition, the president may award the rank of "meritorious executive" to up to 5 percent of the Senior Executive Service in any one year; this award, which an individual can receive only once every 5 years, provides a $10,000 cash payment. Even more prestigious is the rank of "distinguished executive," providing a cash bonus of $20,000. A total of about 400 executives receive these awards each year. Although these awards of $10,000 and $20,000 are substantial, they have depreciated in value as a result of inflation since being put in place in the 1970s.[62]

The intent of the SES is to help both political and career executives. Political executives have greater flexibility in assigning career personnel. Management "teams" to implement administration policies can be assembled more readily. Career executives are supposed to be offered challenging assignments coupled with financial rewards; this is a high risk–high reward system. A career executive, however, does not relinquish all job security upon becoming a member of the SES.

Several issues have emerged with the implementation of the Senior Executive Service. One involves the use of performance evaluations. There have been complaints that standards of performance are both vague and unreasonable and that the appraisal process is more related to bureaucratic politics than to actual performance. Surveys have shown that half or more of the executives are dissatisfied with this aspect of the system.[63-65] A Merit Systems Protection Board survey of personnel specialists found that half (54 percent) thought the SES appraisal system had no impact and that another 20 percent thought it had a harmful impact.[66]

Pay is another issue. In its early years, the pay cap was so severe that a large segment of the entire SES received the same salary. A frequently expressed concern was that the cap was forcing the resignation or retirement of some of the government's most experienced and knowledgeable workers.[67,68] A related problem was that from implementation in 1979 until the congressional amendments of 1984, any excess over Executive Level I pay for bonuses and awards could not be deferred, meaning that bonuses could not be paid. Another complaint stemmed from Congress cutting the percentage of executives eligible for bonuses to 20 percent from 50 percent. Later, the 50 percent figure was restored, but OPM instructed agencies to keep bonuses to 30 to 35 percent. Bonuses have been awarded primarily to those in the higher pay levels of the SES. For example, the Merit Systems Protection Board found that 65 percent of executives at the top level received bonuses compared with only 7 percent at the bottom level.[69] Another complaint was that these rewards often were not based on merit.

A critical aspect of the SES is the interface or nexus between career SES executives and political appointees.[70] Whether the SES has been politicized is of major concern. Before the reform legislation, a common complaint was that the bureaucracy was not responsive to political leadership. Under the SES system, favorable performance evaluations, pay increases, and bonuses can be used as rewards for career executives who are supportive of the political leadership. Conversely, reassignment and sometimes removal may be used to discipline or penalize other executives rather than being used positively, such as for finding more challenging positions for executives.

The Civil Service Reform Act originally required only 15 days written notice for reassignments; for example, an executive working in Washington could have only that much notice of transfer to his or her agency's San Francisco office. The 1984 amendments retained the 15-day period within the same commuting area but imposed a 60-day notice period for job changes that would require executives to change their residences.

In the Merit Systems Protection Board survey cited above, 40 percent of the respondents said they personally had observed executives being shelved through reassignment, efforts being made to force them to resign as a result of reassignment, arbitrary lowering of a performance rating, arbitrary demotion, or structuring of a cutback in an agency's work force in such a way as to remove an executive.[71] A 1991 survey conducted by the General Accounting Office, however, found that less than 10 percent of career executives had observed such abuses of the merit principle.[72]

By the early 1990s, satisfaction among career executives had improved on many factors but remained low on some items. Satisfaction with salaries had increased from only 11 percent in 1989 to 77 percent in 1991, reflecting a large 1991 salary increase. Career SES members were satisfied with job security, the respect they received from coworkers, their duties, and the challenge of their work (between 78 and 92 percent). On the other hand, they expressed dissatisfaction with the public image of federal employees, their chances for promotion, and their health benefits (between 11 and 36 percent satisfaction rate).[73]

The agendas of political appointees often are at variance with those of career executives.[74,75] Political or noncareer SES members usually have a short-term perspective, whereas careerists think in longer terms.[76] On average, noncareer appointees have lasted only 1.7 years in their positions.[77] The short tenure is a function of being frustrated in dealing with the career bureaucracy and the lure of higher salaries in the private sector.[78] The frustrations of high-level jobs, of course, is to be found at all levels of government, not just the federal level.[79] Noncareerists may have been appointed to "shake up" their agencies and may have little or no relevant substantive backgrounds; indeed, lack of knowledge is sometimes seen as a virtue by those who make the appointments. Careerists, however, tend to think of noncareerists as ill prepared for the demands of their jobs. In a survey of former career executives, 25 percent or less thought noncareerists had valuable prior experience, possessed good leadership skills, and had a good grasp of management qualities.[80] The need for higher-qualified political appointees has been voiced often.[81]

More generally, low morale has been a problem for the Senior Civil Service as a result of these and other factors. Public statements made by presidents, other political figures, and the media have denigrated career workers, including career executives. Sometimes these individuals feel they are being used as scapegoats for most of the problems government faces. Executives have had to preside over RIFs, and it is difficult to be "upbeat" when one's work involves telling others that their jobs have been eliminated. Surveys of career executives have shown that a majority would not recommend the public sector to anyone beginning a career.[82,83]

There is no easy answer to the question, is the Senior Executive Service a success? Executives clearly are more responsive to their political bosses. Political leadership has greater flexibility in structuring the executive cadre to accomplish its missions. Beyond that, however, there are unknowns about the impact of the system on this critical tier of personnel in the bureaucracy.[84–86]

TRAINING AND EDUCATION

Although government may be interested in providing training and education programs as part of an overall strategy for employees' "growth" and career development, the fundamental purpose is to improve their work performance in current and future jobs. If government jobs are becoming increasingly complex and the number of people in the labor market with such skills is becoming increasingly scarce, then training may be an important option in developing the personnel talent needed by government.[87]

Sometimes a distinction is made between training and education, with the former suggesting a close relationship between instruction and the job performed and the latter a more general intellectual endeavor that may not have a simple, direct connection with the work. The distinction probably is most applicable to low-level positions; the type of training needed by persons in higher positions blends into education. The argument can be made that education is the appropriate alternative for managers and executives. For convenience, however, the terms "education" and "training" are used interchangeably here. A more general term is "development," which can include education and training but also other activities such as patterned assignments. A person may be assigned different duties or assigned temporarily to different jobs in the interest not of mastering the particular tasks involved but more generally of enhancing the individual's knowledge, skills, and abilities.

Training both before and after entry into government has become standard. As discussed in Chapters 3 and 5, minimum education requirements often are imposed by position classification and testing systems. The Volcker Commission recommended that Congress establish a public service scholarship program that would fund students to attend college in return for a commitment that they would enter the public service upon graduation.[88] Many states set educational standards for local government employees as well as for themselves. For example, states specify educational requirements for certification of school teachers and impose additional educational standards for retaining the certifications. States also impose training requirements for municipal police. At the federal level, the Government Employees Training Act of 1958 has made training opportunities widely available to federal employees. Each year about half of all federal executives receive training, and on average these executives each receive more than 1 week of training.[89] On the other hand, many state and local governments may find their budgets so severely strained that few employees receive any training at all.

The objective of improving employee performance can be achieved through both substantive and process training. Substantive training can include such fields as health, defense, education, and transportation. Given changes in technology, employees can become out of date, so that training is needed to update their knowledge. Process training, on the other hand, refers to the ways in which work is carried out. A training program might explain to employees how to request data from a newly established information system or how to use a new accounting system. The distinction between substance and process often is difficult to specify, and no rigid dichotomization should be attempted.

Also to be considered is whether the purpose of training is general awareness or skill development. A training program for program analysts might instruct them in research design and statistical analysis, whereas one for managers might concentrate mainly on making them aware of research methodology and what types of statistical measures are suitable for various analytical problems. The objective would not be to teach the managers how to conduct analyses.

General awareness training programs in the management field often follow popular trends. As management techniques come into vogue, training programs are established to introduce them to government workers. Since the 1960s popular topics for training have included planning-programming-budgeting systems (PPBS), management by objectives (MBO), organizational development (OD), productivity improvement, zero-base budgeting (ZBB), cutback management, and total quality management (TQM).

Some training has a psychological foundation (see Chapter 11). These behavior-oriented programs tend to stress appreciation of the needs and attitudes of oneself and others and make extensive use of groups or teams.[90] T-groups (the T is for "training") are used in which persons interact with each other, often for several days, attempting to gain a better understanding of why people behave as they do. Sensitivity training may be of a general type or directed at a specific problem.[91-93] For instance, a welfare agency might have its staff use role playing to gain a better understanding of how welfare clients react to agency personnel. This training also may be focused on internal problems, such as racial friction among agency personnel. The training may be directed at assisting employees in coping with the necessarily unpleasant aspects of their jobs, such as helping police officers cope with enforcing unpopular laws and with being ridiculed by the public. Assertiveness training has been used to teach workers to demand their own rights while not violating the rights of others.

Lengthy internships are another form of training. In some instances, the government providing the internship may have no long-term commitment to the intern, but a growing number of internships are being used to recruit and train workers, particularly individuals who will move into management positions. As noted in Chapter 6, OPM administers the Presidential Management Internship Program.[94] Many state executive and legislative branches and numerous cities have established paid internship programs that lead to full-time, permanent employment.

One of the most important forms of training is designed to prepare employees for broadened responsibilities, particularly in management. Early in an Army career, for instance, a soldier may be sent to weapons school, such as an artillery school, but later will be sent to schools that deal with battle strategies and even later to those dealing with war strategies and global politics. Similarly, a criminal investigator in a municipal police department may be sent to a police management training program.

Given that training is presumed to be critical in maintaining and improving its operations, government heavily subsidizes such programs. Employees sometimes must pay part of the cost, but government often pays the entire amount. OPM training programs are operated much like a business, with agencies being charged for each "student." This encourages OPM to develop training courses that agencies consider important. State governments often provide training to local government employees as well as to their own.

A standard prescription in training literature is that a needs assessment should be made before programs are undertaken.[95–97] Training should be considered only one possible option. Another option might be the provision of technical assistance to deal with a specific problem. State agencies often offer such aid to local governments, and the federal government provides some assistance to states and localities. Private consulting firms are another source of technical help. Other options may be redesigning work flow, an agency's structure, or staffing patterns. Rather than employees being trained to cope with problems, the problems may be resolved through redesign efforts.

Training needs can be assessed by analyzing agency performance, observing interpersonal relations of staff members, and reviewing their training, education, and experience. Performance appraisals can be used to help identify the training that employees need.[98] In practice, comprehensive reviews of training needs are rarely performed. It is more common for employees and their supervisors to be asked what types of training they think are needed.[99] A major problem of such surveys is that government workers may not be fully aware of what their training needs actually are, so that the survey results should be interpreted with care. Also, employees may think they need one form of training, but their supervisors may think they would benefit from other forms.[100] From the assessment of needs coupled with the objectives to be served, a training strategy can be devised. This produces a curriculum that specifies the extent of each type of training to be provided. The mode of the training and its extent will be governed by costs and expected results.

Greater emphasis is given to assessing the development needs of executives and soon-to-be executives than of other public workers, although a strong case certainly could be made for extensive training of newly elected officials as well.[101,102] Candidates for entry into the SES are supposed to have prepared for them individual development plans that identify needed training and experience, but this practice is often waived because of the education and experience of the candidates or agencies' constraints that preclude releasing candidates to attend training activities.[103] Such development plans also may be used for those in the SES.

Who is trained in any particular program is determined by the program's objectives and content. General orientation training for new employees obviously would be inappropriate for experienced workers. All departmental secretarial workers, however, both new and experienced, might jointly attend a training program involving new agency procedures. Programs aimed at reorienting attitudes of workers, such as those dealing with racial friction among staff members, might include everyone in a bureau or division, secretarial, professional, and managerial.

Many training programs include personnel from different agencies; this allows participants to compare practices across departmental lines. One complaint about such courses is that they may not be directly applicable to any one agency. A general course in personnel management, for example, may include many topics not relevant to some participants or may explain procedures not used by some participants' agencies.

Time is another variable. Training ranges from a 1-hour session to a year's internship to years of study in earning advanced academic degrees. An 8-hour training program can be held in 1 day or once a week for 1 hour over 2 months. The intensive 2- to 5-day workshop is popular, particularly at the federal level. For example, OPM offers a 5-day course on legislative operations, a 3-day course on writing effective letters, and a 2-day course on total quality management. Costs per participant generally range from under $200 to $700 and more.

A wide variety of training providers exists. Within a large government, departments, as well as the civil service commission, may provide training programs. At the federal level, OPM acts as a coordinator among agencies. Standardized courses in such fields as supervision, midlevel management, and executive management are offered by many departments. Departments also have special schools, such as the FBI Academy. The Defense Department operates the National Defense University (including the National War College and the Industrial College of the Armed Forces), the Armed Forces Staff College, and the Defense Systems Management School. Each regional office of OPM provides additional courses. OPM also has three executive seminar centers, in Denver, Colorado, Lancaster, Pennsylvania, and Oak Ridge, Tennessee. OPM's Washington office conducts the Women's Executive Leadership Program, which extends over many months and consists of both residential and other forms of training; the program is open to both women and men in GS-11 and GS-12 positions.

The Federal Executive Institute (FEI) in Charlottesville, Virginia, is OPM's capstone residential training facility.[104] The FEI conducts programs for officers above GS-14 and for selected state, local, and foreign government executives. The FEI's major training program is the 4-week Leadership for a Democratic

Society Program, which costs more than $6,000 per participant. FEI conducts other training, including a follow-on program for alumni. From time to time, recommendations have been made that FEI be expanded into a broad-based national civil service academy, but given the restrictive budget situation at the federal level, prospects are dim for such a proposal.

Universities also provide important training services.[105–107] Public administration programs not only are important in pre-entry training/education but also provide midcareer training. Government workers may be integrated with other students in regular degree programs, or they may constitute a separate student body as either a special midcareer degree program or a noncredit training program.

Some schools offer their programs only at their main campuses, while others operate at branch locations, such as the University of Southern California in Washington, DC, or at government installations, as in the case of the University of Oklahoma, which offers courses at military bases throughout the world. The variety of schools and modes of instruction prohibits cataloging here. For information about public administration programs, contact the National Association of Schools of Public Affairs and Administration, Washington, DC.

Other training programs are provided through affiliations of governments and government officials and through private for-profit and nonprofit agencies. The Council of State Governments, the National League of Cities, the International City/County Management Association, the Government Finance Officers Association, and the International Personnel Management Association all sponsor training programs.[108] Training programs can be operated on a multicity basis, on a multicity basis crossing state lines, and on a multilevel basis. Private corporations offer an abundance of training programs, either courses designed especially for a jurisdiction or standardized courses.

Other training is provided by experience on the job. Rotational assignments every few months are common for internships, as mentioned earlier, and for entry-level positions. Developmental assignments are the fundamental tool of executive development in the federal service. For example, an executive might be attached temporarily to the agency's budget office as a means of broadening the individual's understanding of the agency's operations.[109,110]

The federal government has been instrumental in encouraging the use of special assignments between governments and between government and the private sector. Hundreds of federal staff members have been placed in state and local governments for up to 2 years each while state and local officials, many of them from colleges and universities, were assigned to federal agencies. This program, administered by OPM, is part of the federal government's emphasis on state and local capacity building.

The diversity of training providers and training modes has produced a largely uncoordinated subsystem in the personnel field. Although many observers have suggested the need for careful planning of training programs, little has been accomplished in integrating specific efforts into an overall design. One approach would be to analyze carefully how people learn, beginning with fundamental concepts pertaining to learning psychology, and then to develop a complex set of strategies for delivering effective training services. David A. Kolb's work on learning theory has received wide attention in this respect.[111–114] According to Kolb, people have different approaches to learning, and these differences must be taken into account when one is designing educational and training programs.

Despite these calls for careful planning, what often exists may be described as a hodgepodge of training activities.[115] The absence of any comprehensive approach to training results in part from the absence of a consensus about what constitutes quality training. Quality in this field is an ambiguous commodity because comparatively few rigorous attempts are made to determine specific training objectives and to evaluate whether those objectives are met.

Training effectiveness can be influenced by the instructor, the participants, their supervisors, and the training materials, facilities, and techniques. A common complaint is that professional trainers know how to conduct a class but often lack depth of knowledge and experience in course content. The qualifications of persons from outside government also may be challenged for the same reason. Professors of public administration, professional psychologists, and others may be viewed by the trainees as not being adequately prepared. Complaints of this type may be justified sometimes, but they also may be a smoke screen for other influences on the participants. Individuals often are sent to the training programs without being consulted about whether they wish to attend.[116] Sometimes the most expendable or the most deficient employees are chosen, and their resulting resentment discourages effective training. In other situations, successful completion of a training course may be considered a requirement for promotion. Some employees seek appointment to such a course but view it more as a troublesome hurdle than as an opportunity to learn.

The reactions of administrators to training, and agencies' overall mode of operations, can reduce training effectiveness.[117] For example, trainees may be instructed in how to use the team approach to work, but on return to their agencies they may find that supervisors and peers oppose that approach. It may be unrealistic to expect much change when perhaps only one person is trained out of a unit of twenty-five. Indeed, a newly trained employee might be ill advised to use what was learned if it was contrary to the supervisor's preferences because this could result in lower performance evaluations and could harm the employee's chances of promotion. On the other hand, training may be highly effective if it is part of a larger plan to bring about organizational change.[118]

Materials, facilities, and techniques can influence training effectiveness, although perhaps mainly in a negative sense. Inadequate materials and facilities can result in ineffective training, but adequate instructional support will not by itself produce benefits. As for instructional techniques, there is no one best way. Lectures, group discussions, workshop sessions that have assigned tasks to accomplish, multimedia presentations, role playing, and the like all can be useful.

Evaluation of training programs usually is done by testing participants and/or having participants complete a questionnaire at the end of the course.[119,120] Examinations often are given at the end of training programs, just as they are in regular college courses. On rare occasions, actual experiments are conducted in which one group of employees receives training and a control group does not.[121]

Participants are asked for their assessments of the course, such as whether the instructor explained its objectives adequately, whether the instructor's presentations were well integrated with assigned readings, and similar questions. This type of evaluation necessarily is subjective, and the extent to which an instructor is entertaining can have a great influence on rater reactions. Participants may respond favorably in part because they enjoyed the social interaction with each other. Holding courses at resort locations can result in favorable ratings that have little to do with training effectiveness.

The ultimate evaluation of training is whether employees perform differently after a course experience than they did before. To gauge this, one approach is to ask the trainees' supervisors several weeks or months later to assess changes in performance stemming from the course. A related approach is to compare personnel ratings of trained and untrained persons.

Objective evaluations are easiest to perform for training programs geared to routine work. Since that type of program is intended to instruct employees in following a routine, variations from the routine can be considered a sign of lack of total training success. Many government jobs involve the processing of paper, such as procurement procedures or applications for welfare payments. By sampling the work product of trained and untrained employees, supervisors can assess whether trained workers perform better than those not trained.

Objective evaluations are more difficult when training focuses on nonroutine work and are especially difficult for managerial work.[122] How is the effectiveness of a training program for first-line supervisors to be gauged? Even more difficult is assessing executive development programs. These often are not intended to have an immediately noticeable effect on behavior. Proponents of such training claim that benefits are long term and defy objective measurement. To what extent, then, can the superior performance of an executive today be credited to a 7-week training program 10 years ago?

Executive training, moreover, is challenged as to whether it ever can be effective except in a few special cases. Management courses tend to stress problem-solving skills but may be incapable of teaching how to identify and define problems and how to be imaginative in developing alternative solutions.

Another alleged weakness is that only persons with specified personal characteristics can benefit from executive training.

Since measuring the value of training is difficult, training units often are at a disadvantage in competing for resources. Training programs for which it can be shown that benefits outweigh costs are likely to be guaranteed funding, but these constitute a small minority of all such programs. To many persons, training is considered a luxury that can be curtailed drastically or eliminated in tight budget periods. Although few would reject the principle that training is desirable, the absence of demonstrable results makes training a likely candidate for budget cuts.

SUMMARY

Governments support the concept of career development for their employees but are less than fully committed to its implementation. Employees are expected to be mainly responsible for their own career planning. Career advancement within a jurisdiction is affected by promotion procedures, with some jurisdictions using open competitive examinations for all persons and others providing advantages to current employees. Job mobility includes intra-agency, interagency, interorganizational, geographic, occupational, and social class mobility. Emerging issues concern the last step in the career process: retirement.

Concerns for promoting careers for executives have led to the use of personnel inventories and to proposals for career executive systems separate from the personnel systems for other government workers. Rank-in-person systems are defended as allowing greater flexibility in assigning responsibilities to individuals and as fostering professionalism in administration. The federal government took a major step in this direction by establishing the Senior Executive Service.

Training is extensive in government and is provided in many different forms. Variations exist in the types of training provided, the personnel participating, the length of the program, and the organizations that provide the training. Although training programs are considered an important aspect of employee career development, they generally have not been integrated into a comprehensive design.

NOTES

1. E.P. Cook, Annual review: Practice and research in career counseling and development, 1990, *Career Development Quarterly* 40 (1991): 99–131.

2. K. Kernaghan, ed., Symposium on career public service and administrative reform, *International Review of Administrative Sciences* 57 (1991): 323–440.

3. D.L. Thompson and J. Zulich, A decade of career development research: Implications for theory, practice, and research, *Journal of Employment Counseling* 27 (1990): 122–129.

4. U.S. Merit Systems Protection Board, *Who Is Leaving the Federal Government? An Analysis of Employee Turnover* (Washington: U.S. Government Printing Office, 1989).

5. G.B. Lewis and K. Park, Turnover rates in federal white-collar employment: Are women more likely to quit than men? *American Review of Public Administration* 19 (1989): 13–28.

6. G. Johnson, *Recruiting, Retaining and Motivating the Federal Workforce* (New York: Quorum, 1991).

7. D.T. Hall and J. Richter, Career gridlock: Baby boomers hit the wall, *Executive* 4 (August 1990): 7–22.

8. G.B. Lewis and M. Ha, Impact of the baby boom on career success in federal civil service, *Public Administration Review* 48 (1988): 951–956.

9. K. Bremer and D.A. Howe, Strategies used to advance women's careers in the public service: Examples from Oregon, *Public Administration Review* 48 (1988): 957–961.

10. T.A. DiPrete, *The Bureaucratic Labor Market: The Case of the Federal Civil Service* (New York: Plenum Press, 1989).

11. D. Cederblom, Promotability ratings: An underused promotion method for public safety organizations, *Public Personnel Management* 20 (1991): 27–34.

12. T. Cox, Jr., and S.M. Nkomo, Candidate age as a factor in promotability ratings, *Public Personnel Management* 21 (1992): 197–210.

13. R.D. Lee, Jr., Merit protection in the Australian public service: A comparative perspective, *Review of Public Personnel Administration* 11 (Fall 1990–Spring 1991): 84–94.

14. G.F. Dreher and R.A. Ash, A comparative study of mentoring among men and women in managerial, professional, and technical positions, *Journal of Applied Psychology* 75 (1990): 539–546.

15. B.R. Ragins and J.L. Cotton, Easier said than done: Gender differences in perceived barriers to gaining a mentor, *Academy of Management Review* 34 (1991): 939–951.

16. P.P. Van Riper, Basic factor and issues, *Public Administration Review* 27 (1967): 359–372.

17. M.W. Fields and J.B. Shaw, Transfers without trauma, *Personnel Journal* 64 (May 1985): 58–63.

18. F.T. Hebert and D.S. Wright, State administrators: How representative? How professional? *State Government* 55 (1982): 22–28.

19. T.C. Murray, Promotion in the public service, *Annals* 113 (May 1924): 354.

20. L.J. Peter and R. Hull, *The Peter Principle: Why Things Always Go Wrong* (New York: William Morrow & Company, 1969).

21. J.M. Bardwick, *The Plateauing Trap* (New York: American Management Association, 1986).

22. G.T. Chao, Exploration of the conceptualization and measurement of career plateau, *Journal of Management* 16 (1990): 181–193.

23. J.F. Wolf, Career plateauing in the public service: Baby boom and employment bust, *Public Administration Review* 43 (1983): 160–165.

24. G. Sheehy, *Passages: Predictable Crises of Adult Life* (New York: E.P. Dutton, 1976).

25. H. Cleveland, *The Future Executive* (New York: Harper & Row, 1972).

26. Y. Dror, *Public Policymaking Reexamined* (San Francisco: Chandler, 1968): 246–259.

27. D.E. Mann with J.W. Doig, *The Assistant Secretaries: Problems and Processes of Appointment* (Washington: Brookings Institution, 1965).

28. H. Heclo, *A Government of Strangers: Executive Politics in Washington* (Washington: Brookings Institution, 1977).

29. H. Kaufman, *The Administrative Behavior of Federal Bureau Chiefs* (Washington: Brookings Institution, 1981).

30. J.W. Macy, et al., *America's Unelected Government: Appointing the President's Team* (Cambridge, Mass.: Ballinger Publishing Co., 1983).

31. I.M. Sugarman, as quoted in T.B. Clark, Senior executive service: Reform from the top, *National Journal* 10 (1978): 1,546.

32. L.E. Lynn, Jr., *Managing the Public's Business: The Job of the Government Executive* (New York: Basic Books, 1981).

33. P. Lorentzen, Stress in political–career executive relations, *Public Administration Review* 45 (1985): 411–414.

34. W.P. Lehman, The interdepartmental placement service, *Personnel Administration* 4 (November 1941): 1–7.

35. W.R. Monat, et al., Pennsylvania cultivates the capacity to manage, *State Government* 62 (1969): 247–255.

36. J. Birkenstock, et al., Career executive assignments—Reports on a California innovation, *Public Personnel Management* 4 (1975): 154–155.

37. G.D. Garson, The Job Skills Data Bank: A microcomputer simulation in public personnel administration, *Review of Public Personnel Administration* 6 (Spring 1986): 72–77.

38. D.N. Ammons and J.J. Glass, Headhunters in local government: Use of executive search firms in managerial selection, *Public Administration Review* 48 (1988): 687–693.

39. J.L. Bodiguel, Political and administrative traditions and the French Senior Civil Service, *International Journal of Public Administration* 13 (1990): 707–740.

40. R.A. Chapman and A. Dunsire, eds., *Style in Administration: Readings in British Public Administration* (London, England: Allen & Unwin, 1971).

41. H.E. Dale, *The Higher Civil Service of Great Britain* (New York: Oxford University Press, 1941).

42. H. Finer, *The British Civil Service* (London, England: Fabian Society and Allen & Unwin, 1937).

43. H.M. Stout, *Public Service in Great Britain* (Chapel Hill, N.C.: University of North Carolina Press, 1938), 77–113.

44. Chairman Lord Fulton, *The Civil Service* (London, England: Her Majesty's Stationery Office, 1968).

45. G.K. Fry, The development of the Thatcher government's "grand strategy" for the civil service: A public policy perspective, *Public Administration* 62 (1984): 322–335.

46. N. Johnson, Change in the civil service: Retrospect and prospects, *Public Administration* 63 (1985): 415–433.

47. W. Plowden, What prospects for the civil service? *Public Administration* 63 (1985): 393–414.

48. K.T. Leakston and G.K. Fry, Britain's administrative elite, *Public Administration* 67 (1989): 129–147.

49. G.K. Wilson, Prospects for the public service in Britain, *International Review of Administrative Sciences* 57 (1991): 327–344.

50. Commission of Inquiry on Public Service Personnel, *Better Government Personnel* (New York: McGraw-Hill Book Company, 1935).

51. L.D. White, *Government Career Service* (Chicago, Ill.: University of Chicago Press, 1935).

52. Commission on Organization of the Executive Branch of the Government (First Hoover Commission), *Personnel Management* (Washington: U.S. Government Printing Office, 1949).

53. _____, (Second Hoover Commission), *Task Force Report on Personnel and Civil Service* (Washington: U.S. Government Printing Office, 1955).

54. M.H. Bolster, The strategic deployment of exceptional talent: An account of the career executive roster's short history, *Public Administration Review* 27 (1967): 446–451.

55. R.M. Nixon and the U.S. Civil Service Commission, The federal executive service, *Public Administration Review* 31 (1971): 235–252.

56. D.G. Carnevale, Florida's senior management system: Performance in a decentralized administrative context, *Public Personnel Management* 18 (1989): 65–74.

57. J. Rehfuss and D. Furtado, Executive management reform—The case of California, *State Government* 55 (1982): 43–49.

58. Civil Service Reform Act, P.L. 95-454, 92 Stat. 1111, Title IV (1978).

59. Personnel Management Project, *Final Staff Report* (Washington: U.S. Government Printing Office, 1977), 181–200.

60. Ethics Reform Act, P.L. 101-194, 103 Stat. 1716 (1989).

61. U.S. General Accounting Office, *Senior Executive Service: The Extent to Which SES Members Have Used the Sabbatical Program* (Washington: U.S. Government Printing Office, 1988).

62. E.G. Goldberg, ed., *The Civil Service Reform Act of 1978: Tenth Anniversary Review and Assessment* (Fort Washington, Pa.: LRP Publications, 1988).

63. U.S. General Accounting Office, *An Assessment of SES Performance Appraisal Systems* (Washington: U.S. Government Printing Office, 1984).

64. U.S. Merit Systems Protection Board, *The 1984 Report on the Senior Executive Service* (Washington: U.S. Government Printing Office, 1984).

65. _____, *The Senior Executive Service: Views of Former Federal Executives* (Washington: U.S. Government Printing Office, 1989).

66. _____, *Federal Personnel Management since Civil Service Reform: A Survey of Federal Personnel Officials* (Washington: U.S. Government Printing Office, 1989).

67. A. Gaul, Why do executives leave the federal service? *Management* 2 (Fall 1981): 13–15.

68. U.S. General Accounting Office, *Federal Executive Pay Compression Worsens* (Washington: U.S. Government Printing Office, 1980).

69. U.S. Merit Systems Protection Board, *Senior Executive Service: Pay Setting and Reassignments* (Washington: U.S. Government Printing Office, 1989).

70. J.L. Perry and T.K. Miller, The Senior Executive Service: Is it improving managerial performance? *Public Administration Review* 51 (1991): 554–563.

71. U.S. Merit Systems Protection Board, *The 1984 Report,* 50.

72. U.S. General Accounting Office, *Senior Executive Service: Opinions about the Federal Work Environment* (Washington: U.S. Government Printing Office, 1992).

73. *Ibid.*

74. Task Force on the Relations Between Political Appointees and Career Executives, "Politics and Performance," in *Leadership for America: Rebuilding the Public Service,* ed. National Commission on the Public Service (Volcker Commission) (Washington: The Commission, 1989), 157–190.

75. D. Olshfski, Politics and leadership: Political executives at work, *Public Productivity and Management Review* 13 (1990): 225–243.

76. P.C. Light, "When Worlds Collide: The Political-Career Nexus," in *The In-and-Outers: Presidential Appointees and Transient Government in Washington,* ed. G.C. Mackenzie (Baltimore, Md.: Johns Hopkins University Press, 1987), 156–173.

77. C. Ban and P. Ingraham, Short-timers: Political appointee mobility and its impact on political-career relations in the Reagan administration, *Administration and Society* 22 (1990): 106–124.

78. P.G. Joyce, An analysis of the factors affecting the employment tenure of federal political executives, *Administration and Society* 22 (1990): 127–145.

79. E.C. Hargrove and J.C. Glidewell, eds., *Impossible Jobs in Public Management* (Lawrence, Kan.: University of Kansas Press, 1990).

80. U.S. Merit Systems Protection Board, *The Senior Executive Service: Views,* 20.

81. Task Force on the Senior Executive Service, Twentieth Century Fund, *The Government's Managers* (New York: Priority Press, 1987).

82. U.S. General Accounting Office, *Senior Executive Service: Executives' Perspectives on Their Federal Service* (Washington: U.S. Government Printing Office, 1988).

83. _____, *Senior Executive Service: Reasons Why Career Members Left in Fiscal Year 1985* (Washington: U.S. Government Printing Office, 1987).

84. F.D. Ferris, Is the Senior Executive Service viable? *Public Personnel Management* 18 (1989): 355–373.

85. M.W. Huddleston, Is the SES a higher civil service? *Policy Studies Journal* 17 (1988–89): 406–419.

86. U.S. General Accounting Office, *Evaluation of Proposals To Alter the Structure of the Senior Executive Service* (Washington: U.S. Government Printing Office, 1985).

87. T. Newell, The future and federal training, *Public Personnel Management* 17 (1988): 261–271.

88. Task Force on Education and Training, in *Leadership for America,* 113–155.

89. U.S. General Accounting Office, *Federal Workforce: Data on Training Received by Agency Executives, Managers, and Supervisors* (Washington: U.S. Government Printing Office, 1987).

90. R.J. Magjuka and T.T. Baldwin, Team-based employee involvement programs, *Personnel Psychology* 44 (1991): 793–812.

91. R.T. Golembiewski and A. Blumberg, eds. *Sensitivity Training and the Laboratory Approach: Reading about Concepts and Applications,* 2d ed. (Itasca, Ill.: F.E. Peacock Publishers, 1973).

92. M.E. Gist, et al., Self-efficacy and post-training intervention on the acquisition and maintenance of complex interpersonal skills, *Personnel Psychology* 44 (1991): 837–861.

93. R. Ware, et al., Subjective changes in small group processes: An experimental investigation, *Small Group Behavior* 24 (1982): 395–401.

94. A.K. Campbell and L.D. Strakosch, The Presidential Management Intern Program: A new approach to selecting and developing America's future public managers, *Public Administration Review* 39 (1979): 232–336.

95. L.R. Flanders and D. Utterback, The Management Excellence Inventory: A tool for management development, *Public Administration Review* 45 (1985): 403–410.

96. D. Olshfski and A. Joseph, Assessing training needs of executives using the Delphi technique, *Public Productivity and Management Review* 14 (1991): 297–301.

97. C.E. Schneier, et al., A practical approach to conducting and using the training needs assessment, *Public Personnel Management* 17 (1988): 191–205.

98. C. Nanry, Performance linked training, *Public Personnel Management* 17 (1988): 457–463.

99. T.T. Baldwin, et al., The perils of participation: Effects of choice of training on trainee motivation and learning, *Personnel Psychology* 44 (1991): 51–65.

100. P.J. Haas, A comparison of training priorities of local government employees and their supervisors, *Public Personnel Management* 20 (1991): 225–232.

101. D.W. Henderson, Enlightened mentoring: A characteristic of public management professionalism, *Public Administration Review* 45 (1985): 857–863.

102. G.T. Galeris, Educating elected officials in strategic goal setting, *Public Productivity and Management Review* 13 (1989): 161–175.

103. U.S. General Accounting Office, *Senior Executive Service: Training and Development*.

104. P.C. Buchanan, ed., *An Approach to Executive Development in Government: The Federal Executive Institute Experience* (Washington: National Academy of Public Administration, 1973).

105. S.R. Faerman, et al., Bridging management practice and theory: New York State's public service training program, *Public Administration Review* 47 (1987): 310–319.

106. F.P. Sherwood, Institutionalizing executive development and attendant problems, *Public Productivity and Management Review* 15 (1992): 449–461.

107. C.J. Spindler, University-based public sector management development and training, *Public Productivity and Management Review* 15 (1992): 439–448.

108. T. Dugan, The Statewide Association's role in training and development for local government, *State and Local Government Review* 13 (1981): 51–56.

109. M.S. Taylor, et al., Participants' reactions to special assignment programs, *Public Personnel Management* 18 (1989): 430–439.

110. U.S. General Accounting Office, *Personnel Practices: Federal Employees Detailed from DOD to the White House* (Washington: U.S. Government Printing Office, 1988).

111. D.A. Kolb, *Experiential Learning* (Englewood Cliffs, N.J.: Prentice-Hall, 1984).

112. _____, *Learning Style Inventory*, rev. ed. (Boston, Mass.: McBer, 1985).

113. R.R. Sims and S.J. Sims, Improving training in the public sector, *Public Personnel Management* 20 (1991): 71–82.

114. J.B. Wells, et al., Management development training and learning styles, *Public Productivity and Management Review* 14 (1991): 415–428.

115. J.K. Conant, *Management Education and Training in Wisconsin* (Madison, Wis.: LaFollette Institute of Public Affairs, University of Wisconsin, 1992).

116. M. Wiseman, Resistance to training, *Public Productivity and Management Review* 13 (1989): 89–97.

117. C. Ban and S.R. Faerman, Issues in the evaluation of management training, *Public Productivity and Management Review* 13 (1990): 271–286.

118. T. Newell, et al., Rescuing training: Joining learning and application in a federal agency training program, *Public Personnel Management* 17 (1988): 303–313.

119. R.D. Arvey, et al., The relative power of training evaluation design under different cost configurations, *Journal of Applied Psychology* 77 (1992): 155–160.

120. D.A. Bownas, et al., A quantitative approach to evaluating training curriculum content sampling adequacy, *Personnel Psychology* 38 (Spring 1985): 117–131.

121. S.G. Miller, Effects of a municipal training program on employee behavior and attitude, *Public Personnel Management* 19 (1990): 429–441.

122. D.N. Ammons and P.A. Niedzielski-Eichner, Evaluating supervisory training in local government: Moving beyond concept to a practical framework, *Public Personnel Management* 14 (1985): 211–230.

Chapter 8

Employee Rights and Responsibilities

A common assumption throughout the history of the public service is that when people accept government jobs they relinquish some of the rights they would have as private citizens and assume responsibilities concerning their conduct that would not necessarily be expected of them in the private sector. That assumption has been challenged for decades and is under increasing attack on the grounds that government employees as individuals and as citizens should not be assigned second-class status in society. Yet absolutes are difficult to prescribe. Employee rights must be considered in context with the needs of society in general and of particular interests, such as the clients of governmental programs. Values are in competition with each other, placing public employees in ambiguous positions as to the type of behavior society expects of them and they expect of themselves.

This chapter highlights some of these competing pressures. The word "highlights" is used deliberately to indicate that the subject involves fundamental issues that could be treated thoroughly only in book-length form. The three sections discuss:

1. some of the competing values concerning ethical conduct of employees both on and off the job
2. civil liberties and civil rights as reflected in loyalty and security issues, freedom of speech for public workers, and the political activities of public personnel
3. approaches used in holding employees accountable for their actions, such as suits against employees, reductions in force (RIFs), and adverse actions

ETHICAL STANDARDS AND AMBIGUITIES

Public employees are expected to be exemplars of moral or ethical conduct. Although the concept of ethics is difficult to define, ethics can be considered as differentiating between good and bad or between right and wrong behavior.[1-6] Justice Holmes, in a famous 1892 Massachusetts case, declared that a person "has no constitutional right to be a policeman."[7] That pronouncement has been interpreted to mean that government may prescribe strict standards of conduct and greatly curtail the constitutional rights of public workers.

Holmes' position now is undergoing substantial revision. Although most people demand a high standard of behavior from government employees, there is increasing pressure to afford them greater latitude in their own conduct. Increasing employee militancy is a partial reason for this trend. Employees as individuals and collectively through labor unions are insisting on greater freedoms. This section considers ethical standards relating to behavior both on and off the job.

On-the-Job Conduct

One instance in which ethical standards are relatively unambiguous is the prohibition against corruption in both the private and public sectors. Although definitions of "corruption" vary widely, the concept generally involves some personal gain on the part of officeholders (in the words of George Washington Plunkitt of New York's Tammany Hall, "I seen my opportunities and I took 'em"[8]). Corruption can be limited to only one person, as in the case of a government worker who misappropriates property by taking it home for personal use. Corruption often implies more widespread and systematic activity, however, such as a group of workers who organize to steal supplies on a prolonged basis.

Unethical behavior can occur in both high- and low-level positions. Consider the behavior of President Nixon and his associates in the Watergate cover-up; President Bush's first chief-of-staff John Sununu, who used government aircraft for personal purposes such as dentist appointments; and state and local officials who have willingly accepted bribes in sting operations conducted by the Federal Bureau of Investigation. Lower-level types of corruption include janitors stealing supplies and office workers removing typewriters and other equipment.

The directorship of the U.S. Office of Personnel Management (OPM) is not immune from such problems. When Director Donald J. Devine's 4-year term expired in early 1985, he was renominated by President Reagan and needed Senate confirmation.[9] While awaiting congressional action, Devine served as executive assistant to the director, and Loretta Cornelius, OPM's deputy director, served as acting director. Before stepping down, however, Devine signed a delegation of authority that seemingly delegated many of the director's duties to the assistant director, the position he assumed. This delegation was kept in a closed file, and when its existence became known later, Devine asked

Cornelius to perjure herself by saying that she had known of the document. The reaction by the Senate Governmental Affairs Committee was extremely negative, and Devine was forced to ask that his name be withdrawn from nomination.

Corruption often includes government workers in collusion with persons outside government. Contracting provides great opportunities for this form of corruption. Government sometimes needlessly spends millions or even billions of dollars because of a lack of competitive bidding, faulty or inflated costs being charged to projects, and generally inefficient management that results in cost overruns.

Both military and civilian programs are subject to corrupt practices. The process of awarding defense contracts is frequently criticized, and on several occasions defense contractors have been found padding contract costs, with government administrators having allowed the practice to go unchecked. The U.S. Department of Housing and Urban Development (HUD) was embroiled in major scandals in the 1970s and 1980s. In the 1970s, Federal Housing Administration (FHA) inspectors, operating in collusion with real estate and banking interests, approved substandard housing units for FHA loans. The result was that home buyers eventually defaulted on their mortgages, forcing HUD to become the largest single owner of slum housing in the country. In the 1980s and into the 1990s, HUD was embroiled in a scandal involving favoritism in the awarding of contracts and grants.[10,11]

The personal gain in unethical activity usually has a monetary value. Members of Congress periodically are implicated in alleged acceptance of bribes for favorable legislative action. In 1977, "Koreagate" became a major scandal in which members of Congress allegedly accepted gifts from a Korean government representative in return for voting on legislation favoring that country. Congress in the early 1990s was embroiled in the Keating Five case, in which five senators apparently received financial contributions in return for assisting Charles H. Keating, Jr. of the Lincoln Savings and Loan of California.[12] Scandals involving the excessive use of check overdrafts, or check kiting, in the House of Representatives' bank and the laundering of funds through the House of Representatives' post office led to the closing of these facilities, to the creation of an administrative director's office intended to improve the quality of management in the House, and to the retirement of many members of the House rather than their running for re-election in 1992.[13]

The devices used for personal gain are seemingly limitless. Sometimes employees are able to tamper with payroll systems to provide themselves with "extra" paychecks. Bribes and kickbacks on contracts are obvious examples of the monetary rewards of unethical behavior. The payoffs of corruption can be "in kind," such as free trips to resort areas, or "gifts," such as freezers in the Truman administration and vicuña coats in the Eisenhower administration. The Iran-Contra affair of the Reagan administration included an element of government officers personally gaining financially while working to obtain arms for Iran and funds for the Contras in Nicaragua.

The financial benefit may be in employment. The "lure of future employment" is equally important. Administrators whose jobs involve dealing with private corporations may be tempted to make decisions that will enhance their job opportunities in those firms when they leave government. The same type of behavior can occur between governments. A local government may lure a state official to accept a city job in the hope that the result will be more favorable treatment by a state agency.

Corruption need not be exclusively monetary. Watergate is one of the best examples.[14,15] The break-ins, dirty tricks in campaigning, cover-ups, and other abuses of the Nixon administration provided few immediate financial benefits to the principals involved; instead, the primary reward was remaining in power. Although financial considerations certainly were at stake, the main motivator seems to have been to ensure the re-election of the president in 1972.

Nonfeasance in office, whether deliberate or unintended, constitutes a form of corruption. During the 1980s, savings and loan associations went on a spree of making high-risk loans that ultimately led to the failure of many thrift institutions and government having to pay billions to cover investors' deposits. Government regulators clearly failed in fulfilling the trust placed in them by the citizenry.[16]

Wasteful use of resources is another kind of unethical behavior. Agencies sometimes seek to aggrandize their operations to the point of consuming resources far beyond what they need. Depending upon one's views, the defense establishment may have been particularly guilty of consuming tax dollars far beyond what it needed to deter and defend against potential aggressor nations during the Cold War. Another form of waste is the lack of concern some employees show for government property; some have little sense of wrongdoing when they abuse government property because they seem to believe it belongs to no one.

Statutes, executive orders, and ethics codes have been adopted to clarify what activities should be avoided. The Ethics in Government Act of 1978 and the Ethics Reform Act of 1989 set requirements for the federal government and are enforced by the Office of Government Ethics, which was once part of OPM and is now an independent agency.[17-20] Ethics codes have been adopted by Congress, the International City/County Management Association, and the American Society for Public Administration, to name only a few.[21] Executive Order 12674, issued by President Bush, establishes principles of ethical behavior for federal employees, and in response to the executive order the Office of Government Ethics has issued generally applicable ethical standards.[22] Typical prohibitions include using public office for private gain, accepting gifts from private citizens or corporate clients with whom the employee works, and having a direct or indirect financial interest in whatever the employee manages. The appearance of a conflict of interest is prohibited, as is an actual conflict. Knowing where to draw the line is not always easy in potential conflict situations. Although a state official certainly should not accept an offer of an expensive vacation trip from a government contracting firm, should the official make a point of buying his or her own meal at a business luncheon?[23] Violation of conflict-of-interest standards can lead to dismissal and prosecution; at the federal level, the Justice Department is responsible for bringing suit in conflict-of-interest cases.[24,25]

To dramatize the importance of ethics in his administration, President Clinton signed Executive Order 12834 on the day of his inauguration, January 20, 1993. This order requires senior executives and trade negotiators to sign an ethics pledge and provides additional powers to the Office of Government Ethics.[26]

An employee who resigns a government position may be barred from accepting a job with a corporation that received a contract with which the individual was involved. A former employee also may be prevented from representing a corporation or person before a former government employer. Although these types of restrictions apply, the Supreme Court has allowed corporations to pay sizeable severance bonuses to employees who resign their positions to accept government jobs; one case involved employees of Boeing, a major defense contractor, who accepted positions with the Department of the Navy.[27]

Public officials and employees, particularly those holding positions that can influence the awarding of grants and contracts, usually must file financial disclosure statements.[28] This requirement is common for elected and appointed officials. The courts have upheld these requirements despite the complaint that they are an invasion of privacy. Federal and state legislation commonly provides for a cooling-off period, requiring a wait of 1 year or more before some former government employees may contact their former agencies. Enforcement of these provisions sometimes is lax, which causes concern about possible conflicts of interest.

Other mechanisms for protecting against fraud and corruption include the following:

- The General Accounting Office (GAO), which is answerable to Congress, audits federal agencies to uncover financial and other fraudulent activities. Similar units exist at the state level. GAO operates a toll-free hotline for reporting fraud, waste, and abuse of government property.[29]
- The U.S. Department of Justice has a unit responsible for investigating and prosecuting federal, state, and local officials involved in fraud.[30]
- The Inspector General Act of 1978 established inspector general offices in federal agencies to ferret out fraud; additional offices were created by the Inspector General Act Amendments of 1988. Many of these offices have fraud hotlines in addition to the one staffed by GAO.[31-33]

- The Ethics in Government Act of 1978 provides for the appointment of a special prosecutor or independent counsel in situations involving possible wrongdoing by high-level federal executives. The counsel is appointed by a panel of three circuit court judges.[34,35]
- Ombudsmen have been added by many governments. Among other responsibilities, they can investigate alleged cases of fraud and waste.[36]
- The Federal Managers' Financial Integrity Act of 1982 requires agencies to strengthen accounting systems so that they are less prone to tampering.[37-39]
- The Competition in Contracting Act of 1984 establishes strict rules for competitive bidding.[40,41]
- The Office of Federal Procurement Policy Act Amendments of 1988 prohibit acceptance of gratuities, restrict postemployment, and require the disclosure of information about employees involved in government purchasing.[42]
- The Chief Financial Officers Act of 1990, which established chief financial officers in most federal agencies, is expected to bring greater control over the finances of the government.[43,44]
- Congress periodically appoints select committees to investigate the ethics of its members. The process can lead to reprimands for wrongdoing and to removal from office.

Problems in ensuring ethical behavior stem from several sources. One common view is that humans are morally frail and succumb easily to temptation. James Madison, in *The Federalist Papers,* wrote:

> If angels were to govern men, neither external nor internal controls on government would be necessary. In framing a government which is to be administered by men over men, the great difficulty lies in this; you must first enable the government to control the governed; and in the next place oblige it to control itself.[45]

The assumption is that people left unchecked will abuse authority by harming the general citizenry and by favoring themselves and their associates. Of course, not everyone subscribes to this view of the inherent corruptness of the human race (the discussion of motivation in Chapter 10 presents a more positive view of human behavior).

Ethical behavior is difficult to enforce because of government's large size and complexity. The stakes are high in big government. When major highway construction or defense contracts are to be awarded, millions or billions of dollars are involved, and certainly some individuals will be inclined to use bribery as a means of winning such contracts. Ethical problems may be more likely to arise in rapidly changing situations, particularly those in which the size of government is growing.[46]

Size also is important in that government bureaucracies become difficult to oversee. It is impossible to watch over the behavior of each of the approximately 3 million civilian workers in the federal government. Smallness, however, does not ensure ethical purity. One view has been that "the very intimacy between citizen and local government invites some corruption of government."[47] Competing special interests in large jurisdictions may cancel each other, whereas one special interest may come to dominate a small local government.

Associated with bigness is complexity. As society has grown in both size and complexity, so have governmental operations. This complexity has forced policymaking bodies, such as city councils, state legislatures, and Congress, to delegate authority to the executive branch. Delegation involves discretionary authority in making decisions within the policy framework established by laws. Discretion at the local level, for example, includes deciding the extensiveness of street cleaning and snow removal in various neighborhoods, such as in middle-class and poor areas; at the state level, discretion includes deciding who will receive welfare benefits. The corruption stemming from discretion can be deliberate in the sense of intentionally favoring some individuals, groups, or corporations over others. An equally important type of corruption, and one that is frequently overlooked, involves administrators' unintentional, capricious, or arbitrary actions in exercising discretion. The concept of fairness includes treating equals equally, whereas arbitrary action involves treating them unequally. The Internal Revenue Service, for example, has been criticized as failing to be consistent in dealing with taxpayers. These are not examples of venal corruption, but they still are a form of corruption. In other words, some behavior may be legal but nevertheless unethical.

Changes in societal values constitute another factor that complicates maintaining moral standards in government. Behavior that is considered acceptable or at least tolerable today may not be acceptable tomorrow, and the converse also is true. Post-Watergate morality has been seen as imposing stricter standards on public servants than previously. On the other hand, societal standards concerning the sex lives of government workers have been somewhat relaxed in recent years. Extramarital sexual relations that once would have been grounds for immediate dismissal often are accepted or at least tolerated, although more rigid standards continue to apply to elected officials, as evidenced by the 1992 presidential election campaign and allegations that then Arkansas Governor Bill Clinton engaged in extramarital relations.

Not only is the cultural milieu important, but so are the personality characteristics of individual employees and the responsibilities of their specific jobs.[48] Some employees may be impulsive and take expedient actions that may be considered unethical by others; in an effort to cut through bureaucratic red tape, administrators may violate important principles laid down in ethics codes. Other employees, in contrast, may feel duty bound to abide by whatever ethics restrictions are imposed even if that results in their never really meeting the demands of their jobs.

A frequently heard expression is that society expects higher ethical standards of public workers than of those in the private sector. Giving special discounts to friends is accepted practice in business, whereas favoritism is taboo in government. Small business owners sometimes may use company vehicles for personal purposes and may even have employees make repairs on their residences. Again, that behavior would not be acceptable in the public sector.

This double standard, however, should not be overemphasized. Corporate ethics is a major concern in the private sector.[49,50] What is different are the relative powers of the two sectors. Corporations indeed are powerful in determining what products appear on the market and what prices are charged. Still, the consumer does have some choice; this is not true in the public sector, which exercises coercive powers. Unethical public administrators can exercise the powers of government to compel citizen obedience.

Public servants are expected to adhere to several ethical standards, each of which may seem innocuous but when applied to specific situations may be in competition with others and pose dilemmas in determining an appropriate course of action.[51,52] Public servants are expected to treat equals equally, to be professionals, to give government a fair day's work, and to be efficient and effective. Each profession has its own set of standards about what is good practice. Professionals consider themselves experts in their particular fields, and their application of that expertise is expected to further the public interest. Moral dilemmas are created by administrators being required to implement cutbacks in their programs when professional standards may suggest that more funding, rather than less, is urgently needed.

The dilemmas that can arise in pursuing professionalism can be seen in terms of client relations. Social workers may have professional standards as to family counseling that cannot be met because of excessive caseloads. High caseloads can result in social workers treating clients as numbers and not as people. Government, then, can become cold and indifferent to human problems. What is the proper course of action for the social worker? Should that practitioner provide substandard counseling to all families, selectively provide counseling to some families while largely ignoring others, complain publicly of the caseload, or resign in protest?

Similar problems are involved in the following examples:

- Should therapists in a mental hospital be required to treat patients who in the professionals' judgment cannot benefit from treatment?

- Should teachers be expected to give passing grades to students who have not mastered the subject matter because the school district does not want a high dropout rate?
- What should police officers do when they think courts are excessively lenient in sentencing persons convicted of narcotics trafficking?

Is there any single, obvious ethical course of action to take in these instances?

The value of allowing for citizen participation can conflict with the value of professionalism.[53,54] On the one hand, professionals in government consider themselves the embodiment of expertise and think they should be given relative freedom in applying that expertise. On the other hand, in a democratic society citizens not only should have access to government but also should be involved in policy deliberations. Administrators presumably should think of themselves not as distinct from the citizenry but rather as a part of it.[55] Local school officials continually confront this problem. Those who have undergone professional training can be said to know what types of education are needed for children, yet citizen and parental pressures are strong in demanding a say in the curriculum. For example, what should be the relative roles of school board members, administrators, teachers, students, parents, and citizens in determining the extent to which schools should teach sex education or more specifically, education about AIDS and the use of condoms? Administrators and teachers are likely to consider all the others amateurs, not suitably informed to deal with these kinds of issues. A professionally dominated agency or government can deny the general public the opportunity for democratic direction and decision making.

Government workers are said to be public servants, but what does that mean? There is no operational definition of this concept, and without such a definition individual workers can rationalize almost any behavior as being in the public interest. Police officers and prison guards may consider that brutality furthers the value of public safety. State highway officials acting in the public interest may disregard the problems of families forced to vacate their residences because of freeway construction.

Loyalty to a political administration is another competing value.[56] Woodrow Wilson, in an 1887 essay, proposed a science of administration in which bureaucrats would exercise their professionalism while remaining politically neutral.[57] Chapter 7 discussed career executive systems in which high-level career administrators are permitted to become involved extensively in policymaking yet are expected to remain flexible in changing policy directions when new, partisan administrations begin. The potential for conflict between the values of unquestioning obedience and professionalism is obvious. Should professionals in the Department of Defense be expected to accept administration policies that they believe will jeopardize national security? At the local level, "good" politics may require curtailing municipal expenditures for sewage treatment, but "good" sanitary engineering may dictate higher outlays. Administrators simultaneously are expected to follow orders and to provide leadership, to be subservient and to exercise initiative. Failure to take the initiative can be considered passive immorality, but exercising initiative when this would be contrary to the preferences of political administrators can be considered disloyal.[58]

Workers in both the public and private sectors must confront difficult choices between meeting the demands of their jobs and upholding their family responsibilities.[59–61] Hourly workers may be able to operate within fixed time schedules, but administrative, professional, and technical workers often are expected to spend long hours on the job at the expense of their personal lives. An obvious solution does not exist for dealing with the situation in which job demands become excessive.

A common prescription is that workers need to be trained in ethical behavior. Such training occurs in pre-employment situations, as in graduate education. The National Association of Schools of Public Affairs and Administration strongly encourages its member institutions to include ethics as part of the curriculum of their master's degree programs in public administration. Training also is provided current workers through government training units.[62] The effectiveness of these measures is uncertain. Teaching someone what is legally right and wrong may be relatively simple, but developing values about what is and is not ethical behavior is a far more challenging assignment.[63,64]

Government Demands and Responsibilities

If government has a right to demand ethical standards of its workers, do not workers have a similar right to demand that government adhere to standards? Governments may be expected to take a positive stance rather than a grudging one in recognizing the rights of public servants. Employee rights may include treating workers with respect, including them in decision-making processes, and providing fair pay and benefits.[65,66]

One of the most compelling values is that workers are citizens and are entitled to some degree of privacy.[67–69] That value sometimes conflicts sharply with the needs of government. For instance, automated information systems can be probed to develop highly detailed profiles on workers, such as how often they are ill and on what days of the week, what types of illnesses they encounter, the jobs and employers of their spouses, and the like.[70] Dress codes are used to help develop a positive image of government among the citizenry and may specifically focus upon curtailing employees who otherwise would wear sexually provocative clothing, but these codes, while permissible, can lead to excessive regimentation.[71-73] Grooming standards relating to length of hair or, for men, the wearing of beards and mustaches can create morale and enforcement problems. The Supreme Court has upheld the power of governments to impose regulations on haircuts and the like for police officers.[74] The Court reasoned that short haircuts help make the police recognizable to the public and help build esprit de corps among the officers.

The use of polygraph or lie detector tests is another source of invasion of privacy. The Employee Polygraph Protection Act of 1988 basically prohibits employers from using lie detector tests.[75-77] The law permits these tests, which measure respiration, heart rate, blood pressure, and perspiration, to be administered to government employees involved in national security, intelligence, and top secret activities; other exceptions pertain to law enforcement. Although these tests may not be used with most workers or prospective workers, so-called honesty or integrity tests are in use (see Chapter 5).

Another area of rightful concern is the extent to which government has an obligation to provide a healthy and safe working environment.[78] Employees sometimes are exposed to asbestos in government buildings and to dangerous conditions, such as at construction sites for water and sewer lines. The Supreme Court ruled that the Fourteenth Amendment does not guarantee a safe working environment to workers.[79] Although constitutional protections may be unavailable, some protections are afforded workers by state right-to-know laws, which require public and private employers to inform employees about materials and supplies used on the job such as cleaning supplies, insecticides, and the like.

Another aspect of a healthy work environment is making buildings smoke free.[80,81] Many governments, including the federal government, ban smoking in most parts of public buildings as a protective measure for nonsmokers. Such smoking bans, however, are sometimes challenged as infringing upon the rights of smokers. Some employers may be tempted to hire only nonsmokers because smokers tend to be much greater users of health benefit programs, but such a selection strategy could be subject to judicial sanction.

Still another concern has been how to deal with acquired immune deficiency syndrome (AIDS).[82-84] Should mandatory testing be imposed on employees? Some jurisdictions require such tests of their health and public safety workers.[85] When workers test positive for the virus, may they be dismissed? Although the Supreme Court has not ruled directly on this issue, it has held that organizations receiving federal aid may not routinely dismiss employees with contagious diseases, declaring that these workers are protected under the Rehabilitation Act.[86] To remove a worker, an employer must have evidence that the person's condition threatens the health of others. OPM has issued guidelines that instruct federal agencies to treat AIDS-infected workers as they would other seriously ill workers.[87] The regulations bar noninfected workers from refusing to work with infected workers.

How to deal with workers with chemical dependencies or who are considered substance abusers is a particularly controversial matter. Alcohol and illegal drug usage lead to inefficiency on the job, high absenteeism, and citizens' loss of confidence in government. Firefighters, health workers, and transportation workers inadvertently can kill themselves, their coworkers, and citizens through the use of drugs. Police officers who use narcotics are unlikely to be effective in policing drug traffic and may well be "on the take."

Governments have taken steps to deal with what is seen as a growing drug abuse problem. Employee assistance plans (EAPs) have been initiated to help workers with chemical dependencies. Regulations have been stiffened regarding disciplinary proceedings against abusers.

Most controversial, however, have been drug testing programs, which usually involve urine analyses but can include blood and saliva tests.[88-90] The issue is whether government has a right to impose such tests to ensure a drug-free work place or whether employees' privacy rights include the right to refuse to take these tests. In 1986, President Reagan signed Executive Order 12564, which provides for urine testing of employees who hold what are deemed "sensitive positions."[91] Presidential appointees, law enforcement officers, and national security workers are covered by the order. The Drug-Free Workplace Act of 1988 applies to federal government contractors, including state and local governments, and the Omnibus Transportation Employees Testing Act of 1991 applies to public transit workers in the public and private sectors.[92,93] The latter law provides for testing for alcohol and controlled substances in job applicants, when reasonable suspicion exists, and after an accident; also, random testing is permissible. The Supreme Court has upheld drug testing when there is a demonstrated need and when safeguards are taken to minimize infringements on employee privacy.[94,95] The GAO has recommended that a single agency be responsible for managing drug testing for the federal government. Under such an agency, procedures would be standardized across agency lines, greater care and privacy could be maintained in the taking of urine samples and in testing the samples, and the unit cost of such tests might be lower than if each agency conducted its own tests.[96,97] Regardless of what procedures are used, many employees think testing invades their privacy, and available evidence suggests that testing may have a negligible impact on the goal of creating a drug-free work environment.[98,99]

In addition to these topics already discussed, several others exist. Do workers have a right to privacy regarding their desks and work areas? The Supreme Court has ruled that searches of these areas are permissible when illegal drugs are being sought.[100] Do public employers have a right to "twist the arms" of employees to have them contribute to the United Fund and other charitable agencies?

Although the need for governments to have comprehensive policies regarding employee rights seems reasonable, if not essential, probably few governments have such policies. Indeed, most governments are unlikely to take a comprehensive approach to employee ethics, and few take a broader perspective that encompasses other areas such as drug testing and AIDS in the work place.[101]

Off-the-Job Conduct

Expectations as to government employee behavior cover matters off the job as well as on. A once common requirement at the local level was that women employees remain unmarried as a condition for retaining their jobs. The justification was that married women belonged at home and should not be permitted to deny jobs to men who needed to support their families. A sometimes enforced rule, especially for school teachers, has been that employees should not be seen frequenting public drinking establishments. Church attendance, if not a requirement, often has been considered a highly recommended practice for public workers.

Governments screen applicants for possible criminal records. From a criminal justice viewpoint, rehabilitation of ex-offenders often depends on their ability to obtain employment, and practices barring the hiring of ex-offenders thwart rehabilitation. For that reason, the federal government has had a limited program for helping ex-offenders obtain jobs in the government.

Where an individual lives is another aspect of private life that government may control.[102] Local governments frequently require workers to reside within the employing jurisdiction; the issue of residency, however, is moot at the federal level and largely so at the state level. Residency requirements are justified on several grounds. Municipal employees, by living within their city, supposedly gain a better understanding of the mores and problems of the community. In jurisdictions that require applicants to be residents, would-be interlopers are denied jobs. One assumption is that employees residing within the jurisdiction will spend their incomes there, thereby stimulating local business. The requirement that public safety workers live within the jurisdiction can facilitate fast response to emergencies during their off-duty hours.

Racial considerations are involved in residency requirements. As nonwhites have increased in numbers in central cities and whites have moved to suburban communities, there has been increasing pressure to adopt residency requirements. Proponents contend that, without these requirements, a city's population could be predominantly nonwhite but the government's work force would be predominantly white. The issue has produced tensions between white and nonwhite employees. Despite efforts to overturn residency requirements, they have been upheld by the courts, although these requirements are being challenged in court as being discriminatory.[103]

Government imposes standards on employees' sex lives, although the standards vary greatly from one jurisdiction to another. Workers sometimes are expected to have the morals of "a little old lady from Dubuque."[104,105] The law is unsettled as to what types of restrictions are permissible. One court may uphold the dismissal of an unwed school teacher for having a man spend the night in her home, while another court may disallow the firing of an unwed teacher for becoming pregnant. Restrictions on sexual and other behavior generally must be shown to be job related, or a nexus must be demonstrated between that behavior and work performance. For example, a supervisor convicted of child molesting might be dismissed because employees object to working with such a person. Another stipulation is that standards must not be so vague that employees cannot determine what behavior is acceptable. This vagueness standard, however, did not protect a school teacher who each night turned on the outside lights of his home and performed "unnatural" acts on a mannequin on his lawn.[106]

A man and woman living together without being married was once grounds for dismissal if one or both people were government employees. The abandonment of that value has created an ironic situation regarding antinepotism regulations. Governments often have rules that prohibit a married couple from working together, particularly in a situation where one is the superior and the other a subordinate, but these rules generally do not apply to couples who are unmarried.[107]

Inquiries into employees' sex lives and other investigations into off-duty conduct can threaten the constitutional right to privacy. *Griswold v. Connecticut* is a landmark case that established the right to privacy (the case dealt with a private citizen, not a government employee).[108] Personality tests ask questions that can be considered beyond the appropriate area of governmental inquiry. The Minnesota Multiphasic Personality Inventory is one such test, asking people the extent to which the following statements reflect their attitudes: "I am happy most of the time. I get mad easily and then get over it soon. I believe in the second coming of Christ. I wish I were not bothered by thoughts about sex."[109] The Defense Department, which has generally banned homosexuals from military service, has grilled suspected Gays and Lesbians in great detail about their personal lives.

Governments impose extensive controls over employees' and officials' personal finances in the hope of avoiding conflict-of-interest situations, but these restrictions can greatly curtail what these individuals may do.[110] The ban on using one's government position for personal gain often precludes officials from accepting honoraria and expenses for speaking engagements and for writing articles and books. Such bans can prevent someone from making a speech to an important organization because the organization is barred from funding it and the governmental agency is without sufficient funds to cover the travel costs of the official. Exceptions to outside income are made, however, as in the case of full-time medical doctors on government payroll who are allowed limited private practices; this outside income is regarded as essential for helping physicians in government have incomes comparable with those of private physicians.

Ethical problems abound in this area of outside income. Should a city manager be allowed to accept fees for consultative services provided to other city managers in the same state or other states? Should someone who works in computer information systems in government be permitted to resign to accept employment with a computer vendor? The Ethics Reform Act of 1989 provides a cooling-off period that restricts postemployment opportunities for federal workers; with these restrictions in mind, one should think carefully about accepting a government job lest career opportunities be curtailed in the future.

CIVIL RIGHTS

The United States Constitution prescribes civil rights for all citizens, and since its adoption in 1789 there has been continuing debate over what limits should be placed on those freedoms. It is recognized that rights rarely are absolute. Unfettered freedom of speech could be disastrous, as in the case of a person "falsely shouting fire in a theater and causing a panic."[111]

The problem, however, is more complicated when applied to public employees, who are expected to assume responsibilities when accepting government positions. This section explores three aspects of the problem: the rights of employees vis-à-vis loyalty and security issues, employees' exercise of their constitutional right to free speech, and their right to participate in the political process.

Loyalty and Security

Loyalty and security regulations have been used since the Revolutionary War but have become a standard aspect of public service only since the 1930s.[112–114] The House Un-American Activities Committee, chaired by Martin Dies (Democrat of Texas), held hearings in the 1930s and 1940s alleging that disloyalty within the federal bureaucracy was widespread. Senator Joseph McCarthy (Republican of Wisconsin) assumed the same type of role in the 1950s.[115] The concern over ferreting out subversives was equally common at state and local levels. States passed laws against treason, rebellion, insurrection, sedition, criminal syndicalism, criminal anarchy, displaying communist flags, and sabotage. Several states even passed laws against the wearing of disguises in public.[116] All levels of government demanded loyalty of both private citizens and government employees.

The reasons for the anticommunist movement of the 1950s are numerous. There was a sincere concern that communists, under the presumed direction of the Soviet Union, were attempting to create unrest within the United States, were directing sabotage activities, and were attempting to steal secrets about nuclear weapons technology, military strategies, and the like. Political considerations also were at stake, with those out of power challenging those in power as being too lenient with subversives.

Espionage and subversion are not relics of the past, but how these topics are looked upon has changed dramatically in recent years. During the 1980s, there was a rash of cases of active and retired federal employees leaking government secrets to the Soviet Union. The case of the Walker family involving the Navy over a period of many years was particularly prominent. With the collapse of the Soviet Union and East European communist governments, however, the threat of communism greatly diminished. China is the only major nation that advocates communism.

Despite the revolutionary reforms of governments that occurred worldwide in the late 1980s and early 1990s, laws and executive orders curtailing the activities of those who would seek the violent overthrow of the government remain in force in the United States. The Hatch Act of 1939 bars federal workers from "membership in any political party or organization which advocates the overthrow of our constitutional form of government." Executive Order 10450, issued by President Dwight D. Eisenhower in 1953, remains the governing policy of the federal government on loyalty and security matters. State level "Little Hatch Acts" also have loyalty provisions.

The words *loyalty* and *security* are not synonyms. Loyalty refers to being faithful to the existing form of government and not seeking its overthrow through violent means. A person can be loyal and yet endanger national security. A loyal employee who has friends who are subversives may inadvertently leak government secrets.

Executive Order 10450 provides for dismissing an employee who may be subject to "coercion, influence or pressure." Employees who had relatives in what once were called the communist-block countries could be dismissed on the grounds that they could be blackmailed into leaking government secrets under threat that the relatives might be harmed or even killed. Similarly, people who keep their homosexuality secret may become subject to blackmail. Alcoholics and drug addicts may be security risks in that they may divulge secret information when under the influence. The same executive order proscribes "any criminal, infamous, dishonest, immoral, or notoriously disgraceful conduct, habitual use of intoxicants to excess, drug addiction or sexual perversion."[117]

Loyalty and security procedures differ. Loyalty programs typically apply to all government employees and security programs only to sensitive positions. Sensitive positions involve the handling of information related to national security and can include clerical as well as higher-level positions. Loyalty programs often require the employee to take or sign an oath affirming allegiance to the government. A relatively superficial investigation of the person's background may be made, such as a routine check of FBI files. Forms may be sent to the person's former employers asking whether there is any reason to believe the individual is disloyal. The person's loyalty is presumed unless negative information is reported.

Security, on the other hand, involves more extensive and continuous investigation.[118] At the federal level, a full-field investigation is required of persons being considered for sensitive positions. Federal investigators personally interview the candidate's current and former employers, friends, teachers, and neighbors. Once appointed, the individual may be reviewed periodically. Each time the person is promoted and/or assigned different responsibilities, another investigation will be undertaken. Although these distinctions between loyalty and security exist, they produce confusion. Persons dismissed through security proceedings often are considered disloyal when that is not the case.

Loyalty and security programs have been challenged as violating various constitutional provisions.[119] The First Amendment to the Constitution guarantees freedom of speech and the right to assemble peaceably. This amendment and the others that make up the Bill of Rights have been applied largely to state and local governments through the Fourteenth Amendment: "No State shall make or enforce any law which shall abridge the privileges or immunities of citizens of the United States." Loyalty and security programs at all levels of government have been challenged as infringing on employees' rights to speak freely and to associate with persons of their own choosing.

The protection from being a witness against oneself or self-incrimination is part of the Fifth Amendment. The rights provided by this amendment are important when authorities attempt to force employees to testify by threatening their dismissal if they fail to do so.[120] The Fifth Amendment protects not only against self-incrimination but also against being "deprived of life, liberty, or property without due process of law." The same protection is afforded to citizens against state governments, as provided in the Fourteenth Amendment.

In criminal cases, the Sixth Amendment gives a person the right to know the "nature and cause of accusation" and to "be confronted with the witnesses against him." Among the varied aspects of due process are:

- the presentation of specific charges against a person
- the presentation of evidence that substantiates those charges
- the right to cross-examine evidence and witnesses and to present additional evidence and witnesses
- the right to representation by counsel

- the impartiality or objectivity of the person or persons responsible for reaching a decision
- the adherence to procedures prescribed by law and administrative regulation
- review of the action by an appellate body (usually a court)

The courts have applied these protections in varying degrees in cases involving the dismissal of public employees for loyalty or security reasons.

Due process considerations affect private workers as well as public ones. Private employees working under contracts with the government, such as defense contracts, or working in sensitive industries, such as arms production or nuclear energy, must pass security clearances. Failing such clearance checks results in dismissal and may prevent a person from pursuing his or her occupation.[121]

Although the furor over loyalty and security programs generally has subsided, the difficult task of reaching a balanced perspective on efforts to ensure employee loyalty and to protect national security remains. Probably few would deny government the power to protect itself from disloyalty and carelessness among its own employees, but providing that power while ensuring the liberties of employees is a difficult assignment. Loyalty programs in earlier times destroyed the careers of many loyal persons both in and out of government and encouraged orthodoxy in thinking.

Freedom of Speech

Issues involving employees exercising their constitutional right to free speech arise not only in loyalty and security cases. Employees may be unquestionably loyal and present no risk to security but, as will be seen, may choose to speak on matters that become the center of controversy. In the United States, government employees generally have the freedom to resign their positions and then freely criticize their former agencies and the individuals involved and write highly critical articles and books. This practice is in contrast with the British system, in which the Official Secrets Act precludes both current and former employees from divulging information about government agencies. Resigning in protest is not a financially feasible alternative for many government employees. Even when finances do not present a problem, an employee might not want to resign, being generally satisfied with his or her government position.

Therefore, the critical issue is: What speech rights can employees exercise without losing their jobs? There are different types and purposes of speech. Speech may be internal to the agency, as in a confrontation between employee and supervisor. Courts have held that some degree of courtesy is required and that reckless, intemperate, insulting, and vituperative speech is not protected.[122]

The Supreme Court has ruled for limited internal speech involving employees criticizing their governments. The Court ruled that a school teacher had a right to allege that a school district policy was racially discriminatory when meeting privately with a supervisor[123] but did not support an employee circulating a questionnaire among office staff members concerning agency transfer policy, morale, and the need for a grievance committee.[124] In another case, the Court upheld the right of a worker to tell a coworker that if a second attempt to assassinate President Reagan was made she "hope[d] they [would] get him."[125] In that instance, the Court found that the worker had not intended to endorse assassination of the president but was expressing an opinion against the president.

Speech involving persons external to an agency usually includes whistle blowing, when employees seek to embarrass superiors and/or to instigate changes in agency policies and practices.[126,127] The speech may be covert, such as a state employee privately telephoning a legislator, or overt, such as an employee writing a letter to a newspaper or even holding a news conference. Whistle blowing usually is considered intentional, but it can be unintentional.

In intentional cases a conflict exists between administrative loyalty and loyalty to a "higher cause." The merit principle includes the concept that the employee should serve political administrations loyally and not create problems by leaking information to opponents. The merit principle also includes the idea that employees should serve the public interest, however, and it is likely that every administration conducts some activities that some people can consider not in the best interests of society.

Whistle blowing requires courage because a person can lose a job in the process, but whistle blowers should not automatically be accorded the status of hero.[128-130] In acting on their own initiative, the whistle blowers have appointed themselves judges of what should be brought to the public's attention. Whistle blowers frequently may not be in possession of the full facts and sometimes are motivated more by malice than by serving the public interest. Were every employee to act in this manner, government bureaucracies would become chaotic. Yet unqualified condemnation of whistle blowing is equally inappropriate because the practice has brought to public attention important situations that otherwise would have been kept secret. Whistle blowers exist in private corporations as well as in government agencies.[131]

Free speech can be individual or collective. Whistle blowers often act as loners. By contrast, in some instances groups of employees have complained of government action. During the Vietnam War, some federal employees organized protest groups that issued newsletters and other publications against the war. Workers in the then Department of Health, Education, and Welfare (HEW) and in other departments participated in antiwar parades and other demonstrations. It should be noted, however, that these employees were exercising their speech rights without using classified information. HEW employees had access only to information generally available to the public. A different situation would have existed had Department of Defense employees been involved.

Employees who have not completed a probationary period have limited protections in dismissal proceedings, but one right is the freedom of speech. This was made clear in a 1977 Supreme Court case involving an untenured school teacher who had done several things that displeased school officials, such as swearing at students and arguing with school cafeteria employees in front of students.[132] The teacher called a local radio station to complain about a proposed dress code for the school district, and the board dismissed him, citing these incidents, including the telephone call.

The Court held that he could not be dismissed for contacting the radio station, that this was a constitutionally protected form of speech. The Court noted that, as an untenured employee, the teacher could have been dismissed without being given any reason. The school board did not have the power to fire an employee for an unconstitutional reason. The decision did not reinstate him, however. The Court remanded the case to a district court to determine whether the school board would have dismissed him for reasons other than the telephone call.

Agency reaction to whistle blowers and other outspoken employees may not be so direct as outright dismissal. Firing someone may not be an option if the someone covertly has leaked information. In response, stricter security measures may be imposed on the control of information. Where information leaks have been frequent, attempts are made to uncover the persons involved. The Nixon administration "plumbers" used extreme measures in plugging leaks. Columnists, notably Jack Anderson, were put under surveillance in an effort to uncover who was releasing information to the press.

If the whistle blower no longer is a government employee, dismissal obviously is precluded. The tactic, then, may be to undermine the individual's credibility, as was the case for Daniel Ellsberg, who released the secret Pentagon Papers on the Vietnam War.[133] His psychiatrist's office was entered illegally, apparently in the hope that information could be obtained to discredit him.

In other instances, reorganization and RIFs can be used to oust the employee who has met with agency disapproval. This approach certainly seems to have been used against A. Ernest Fitzgerald, an Air Force employee.[134] In the late 1960s he released information to Congress about cost overruns on the Air Force transport C-5A being built by Lockheed Aircraft Corporation. Shortly thereafter, Fitzgerald's job was eliminated. Through a series of administrative and court proceedings he was able to require the Air Force to reinstate him in a position of comparable grade, but the process took years and was extraordinarily expensive.

The federal Civil Service Reform Act of 1978 includes protection for whistle blowers through the Merit Systems Protection Board (MSPB), and the Whistleblower Protection Act of 1989 charges the MSPB's special counsel with a primary role of protecting employees, especially whistle blowers.[135,136] Other whistle-blowing avenues include the inspector general offices in federal departments and the GAO's fraud hotline. Nevertheless, problems still exist. A survey of federal personnel officials sponsored by the MSPB revealed that only about half thought adequate protections were afforded employees "attempting to expose prohibited personnel practices."[137]

Political Activities

Government employee involvement in many types of political activities has been prohibited for generations. Have those prohibitions unjustly denied employees their constitutional rights? Do such prohibitions make political eunuchs of public workers? Is it possible to relax legal provisions to allow for increased political activities by employees and simultaneously preserve the merit concept?[138,139]

In 1802 President Thomas Jefferson issued a circular providing for the political neutrality of federal employees, and ever since they have been limited in exercising their political rights. The Pendleton Act of 1883 commonly is cited as formally establishing the merit principle in the federal government, and with that law the Civil Service Commission established procedures for restricting political activities.

The reform effort was further strengthened in 1907, when President Theodore Roosevelt issued Executive Order 642. By 1939, the Civil Service Commission, operating under that order, had dealt with 3,000 cases of alleged involvement of federal workers in proscribed political activities. In that year Congress passed the Hatch Political Activities Act, further detailing what forms of political activity were prohibited. The legislation also adopted as policy the 3,000 rulings of the Civil Service Commission.[140] The following year Congress extended coverage to state and local employees who were substantially funded with federal monies.[141]

The Hatch Act prohibitions on political activities are wide ranging in their application[142]:

- Employees cannot "take an active part in political management or in political campaigns" or interfere with or affect an election.
- Money for political purposes can be neither received nor given between federal employees.
- An employee cannot "coerce the political action" of others.
- An employee cannot be forced to provide "political service" and cannot be dismissed for refusing to aid a campaign.

The law does not prohibit all political activity. Government workers retain their right to vote. An employee has the right "to express his opinion on political subjects and candidates" and to engage in voter registration drives, provided that such activities are nonpartisan. An employee may participate in nonpartisan elections, even by being a candidate for office. Federal employees may participate in partisan elections in communities designated by OPM; the employees activities must be of a nonpartisan nature, however, such as running as a nonpartisan candidate or campaigning for one. For the most part, excepted communities are in the Washington, DC, area, but some communities in Alaska, Georgia, Washington, and a few other states are included.

The Federal Election Campaign Act Amendments of 1974 reduced federal restrictions on political activities of state and local employees by deleting the prohibition against political management and political campaigning. Whether this change had any effect is unclear because state and local employees still must abide by the prohibitions in the states' so-called "Little Hatch Acts."[143]

How these rights mesh with the prohibitions has been clarified to some extent through administrative regulations[144]:

- Federal employees may publicly state their views on political candidates but cannot express those views before political conventions or rallies.
- They may act as election judges or clerks but not as poll watchers for political parties.
- They may attend a political convention but not as delegates or alternates.
- They may not make financial contributions to other federal employees, but they may contribute to political parties.
- They may wear campaign buttons and display political posters, but they may not drive voters to the polls.
- They may sign a partisan nominating petition but may not circulate petitions for others to sign.

Violating the law results in dismissal. The Hatch Act provides for removal unless OPM decides on a lesser penalty. The minimum penalty is 30 days' suspension without pay. Employees must be notified in writing of the charges against them and are entitled to an oral hearing, where they may be represented by an attorney. State and local employees charged with violating the Hatch Act have similar rights. Although OPM cannot directly remove state and local violators, it can force their dismissal by threatening to curtail federal grant monies to the jurisdiction.

The courts have generally rebuffed accusations that the Hatch Acts and the "Little Hatch Acts" are unconstitutional because they limit First Amendment rights, because they violate state rights, and because they are excessively vague.[145–148] Court decisions have not settled these controversies, however, with critics contending that Congress and state legislatures should adopt new laws permitting greater participation.[149]

At stake is the issue of balance between the rights of government to have an administrative process untainted by the partisan considerations of its workers and the rights of those workers as citizens of the nation and the states. Studies have shown that workers probably would increase their political involvement were restrictions eased.[150] For some observers, that is an indication of fundamental rights being denied workers, and for others it is an indication that opening the door to political activity could greatly increase the political aspects of administration. Congress passed bills in 1976 and 1990 that would have expanded the political rights of public employees. Presidents Ford and Bush, respectively, vetoed the bills, and Congress was unable to muster sufficient votes to override the vetoes. The 1990 bill would have permitted workers to hold office in political parties, engage in fundraising activities, participate in political meetings, and distribute political literature. The failed legislation was criticized for opening the federal bureaucracy to political abuse. Employees who previously could have turned down requests for campaign assistance on the grounds that they were "Hatched" now might be pressured into campaign activities.

EMPLOYEE ACCOUNTABILITY

Employees are held accountable for their actions both directly to the public and internally through disciplinary or adverse actions. This section considers (1) the routes available to citizens in general and to clients in particular for holding public officials accountable and (2) discusses adverse actions and the protections afforded public workers accused of misconduct and ineffective job performance.

Direct Accountability

Secrecy in government is understandable in that few people wish to have their failures or mistakes made public. Even when there is nothing to hide or cover up, public administrators may prefer to work outside the public spotlight because their activities then can be conducted in relative tranquility, thereby theoretically promoting efficient operations. Openness, however, helps hold government directly accountable to the citizenry and reduces the need for such practices as whistle blowing.

Legislation has been passed to counteract tendencies toward secrecy in government.[151] The federal Freedom of Information Act (FOIA) of 1966, as amended, takes the affirmative stance that whenever possible citizens should have access to public records.[152] The Privacy Act of 1974 allows individuals to have access to records about themselves maintained by federal agencies.[153] The 1976 Government in the Sunshine Act opened many federal agency meetings to the public.[154] Numerous states have laws comparable to the FOIA and the Sunshine Act. Through these mechanisms, the public can learn about what is occurring within government agencies and in turn can hold officials answerable for those actions.

Another approach has been the establishment of government ombudsman offices. These offices, based on a concept introduced first in Scandinavian countries, serve as mediators between government agencies and citizens. When a citizen has a complaint about the action of an agency and its workers, the ombudsman investigates and seeks to mediate the problem. Although seldom having any enforcement powers, the ombudsman can bring pressure on the agency to correct a situation.

Since the 1960s, the public increasingly has used direct confrontation with government officials. Demonstrations were used extensively in the 1960s, such as in the picketings and sit-ins over school desegregation and the Vietnam War. Prison inmates not only have gone on hunger strikes and rioted but also have negotiated procedures to be used in resolving grievances over prison management practices. In establishing their rights, prisoners have reduced the extent to which officials may act unilaterally.

Courtroom confrontations have become a particularly popular approach to holding government officials responsible for their actions.[155] Courts frequently have decided in favor of agency clients who allege that government has violated their rights. For example, the Supreme Court has held that, as part of the freedom of expression, high school students had a right to wear black armbands in school to protest the Vietnam War and that school officials had violated the Constitution by prohibiting the armbands.[156] Although there is no constitutional right to an education, the courts have held that states have created a property right to education and that education cannot be denied students through suspension from school without adherence to due process standards.[157] A state government may not halt payments to welfare recipients without first providing them an opportunity to defend themselves in an administrative hearing, where adverse witnesses may be cross-examined.[158]

Courts, however, have set some limits on the scope of government liability. One tragic situation involved a young child who endured years of physical abuse inflicted by his father, eventually resulting in severe mental retardation. The child's mother sued the local welfare agency, alleging that it knew of the situation and failed to take action. The Supreme Court held that, although county officials may have had sufficient information to warrant concern, the county did not have a responsibility in this situation; namely, it did not have a responsibility to protect one citizen from another citizen.[159]

One barrier to suits against government is the concept of sovereignty, which presumes that government is all powerful and can do no wrong. In practice, of course, wrongful acts are committed by government officials at times, and in the process citizens are harmed. In 1946, Congress passed the Federal Tort Claims Act, which allows cases in tort against the government.[160] As a result the government has been held accountable for such things as allowing a lighthouse light to burn out, resulting in a barge running aground and damaging its cargo.[161] In another case, the government was found negligent in its supervision of the private manufacture of live polio vaccine; a person had contracted polio from vaccine that had not been processed properly.[162]

Suits against state and local governments in their state courts have been more difficult than those against the federal government because many states do not have legislation comparable to the Federal Tort Claims Act. States have been protected by the concept of sovereign immunity, which holds that no one has a right to sue an all-powerful government. Local governments have been protected by the concept of governmental immunity, a doctrine that bars suits to avoid possibly bankrupting a government. In recent years, however, some states have greatly limited the application of these concepts, and at the same time federal courts have expanded their domain over cases involving these governments.[163-165]

Because suing a government may be blocked in many instances, citizens have taken an alternative legal route: suits against federal, state, and local officials as individuals. A disadvantage of this approach is that governments are known to have deep pockets; that is, they can use their taxing power to raise large sums of money to pay claimants, whereas individuals have far fewer funds to be tapped.[166] Some individuals basically are immune from suit, such as judges when acting in their official capacity, prosecutors, and the president.[167-169] When A. Ernest Fitzgerald attempted to bring suit against President Nixon for his alleged involvement in Fitzgerald's dismissal from the Air Force, the Supreme Court held that the president was immune to the "outer perimeter" of his duties. Another protected group is military officers; to ensure discipline in the military, officers may not be sued by their subordinates.[170]

An early example of a successful suit against federal officers as individuals is *Bivens v. Six Unknown Named Agents of the Federal Bureau of Narcotics* (1971).[171] Narcotics agents entered Bivens' apartment without a warrant and without probable cause, manacled him, threatened to arrest his wife and children, and used excessive force in taking him to their office for questioning. The Supreme Court ruled that Bivens could sue these officers for violating his Fourth Amendment protection against unreasonable searches and seizures. A *Bivens* remedy, therefore, is one option for an injured person.[172]

Cases of officer tort liability are possible in federal courts under the Civil Rights Act of 1871, which makes liable "every person, who under color of any statute, ordinance, regulation, custom or usage, of any State or Territory," deprives one of "any rights, privileges, or immunities" guaranteed by the Constitution.[173] Cases under this Act are called Section 1983 cases, because the pertinent language is in Section 1983 of Title 42 of the United States Code. A landmark Section 1983 case is *Monroe v. Pape* (1961), in which Chicago city policemen were held liable for violating the rights of citizens.[174,175] The policemen had entered a home, forced people to stand naked in the living room while the house was searched, and denied them the right to see an attorney when they were taken to jail.

Section 1983's original intent was to protect the recently freed slaves from state and local officials who might attempt to subjugate them. The law has been interpreted broadly by the courts, however, and now applies to high- as well as low-ranking officers at the state and local levels. In 1974, the Supreme Court dealt with the liability issue involving Ohio's governor and other executives in the killing of Kent State University students by National Guardsmen.[176] The Court held that only limited (not absolute) immunity was possible if it could be shown that substantial discretion was involved and that the officers acted in good faith. The Court, however, has held that citizens are barred from using Section 1983 in cases of simple negligence; in one case, for instance, a person had injured himself because a deputy sheriff had left a pillow on a flight of stairs.[177]

In certain situations, public officials can be held personally liable and cannot be financially assisted by their governments. In 1991, the Supreme Court ruled that Pennsylvania State Auditor General Hafer acted in an official capacity but did not commit an act of the state when she dismissed eighteen employees upon her taking office.[178] The employees were not dismissed because of incompetence and probably were dismissed because of their political affiliations. The Court decided that Section 1983 was passed for this type of situation and that Hafer could be held personally liable for damages.

To avoid a *Hafer* type situation occurring at the federal level, Congress passed the Federal Employees Liability Reform and Tort Compensation Act of 1988.[179] When a suit is filed against an employee of any of the three branches of government—legislative, executive, or judicial—the employee may request the attorney general to invoke the 1988 legislation and have the suit converted to one against the government, in which case the Federal Tort Claims Act takes effect. If the attorney general declines to take action, the employee may petition a federal court to act. In situations where a federal employee is being sued in a state court, the law provides that the case is transferred to a federal court. President Bush in 1991 issued Executive Order 12778, which requires federal agencies to seek out-of-court settlements to avoid costly litigation.

What is the public interest in these cases? Certainly they seem to present dilemmas. Government officials need to be restricted so that abuses cannot go undetected. On the other hand, officer tort liability suits can reduce public officials to timid creatures fearful of either taking or not taking action.

RIFs and Adverse Actions

Job security generally is greater in government than in the business world, but sizable numbers of government employees still lose their positions each year. One reason is reductions in force (RIFs) when an agency shrinks its work force. Another cause is the adverse action of termination, removal, or simply firing. Adverse actions are disciplinary in nature and can be less severe than termination, such as demotion, suspension, or reassignment.

RIFs have become commonplace. Proposition 13, passed by California voters in 1978, mandated severe cuts in property taxes, which in turn led to cutbacks in local programs and personnel. Other states followed California's lead and were faced with a compounded problem in the early 1980s when the nation experienced one of the worst recessions since the 1930s.[180,181] This reduced revenues, forcing cuts in personnel as state and local governments struggled to meet legal requirements that their budgets be balanced. Other RIFs resulted from changes in program priorities, most notably at the federal level, where President Reagan sought to scale down domestic programs and expand the defense effort. Major defense cutbacks began during the Bush administration in response to a greatly changed world situation, in which the Soviet Union no longer existed and posed no threat to national security and further massive cuts occurred during the Clinton administration. Still other layoffs result from privatization, when government shifts from providing a service and begins contracting for it with a private firm.

Procedures vary among governments, but there are some obvious similarities. The positions to be vacated must be identified, and policies must be established as to how affected workers will be treated. Some type of ranking system is used, with higher ranked employees having opportunities to be reassigned to other positions of comparable or reduced rank. "Bumping rights" exist, allowing one worker with more seniority to displace another with less. The federal government also provides "retreat" rights, allowing a worker to move back to a position held earlier, and assists displaced workers in finding positions in other agencies of the government. Governments sometimes provide assistance to displaced workers in obtaining employment in other governments or the private sector.[182,183]

The factors to be taken into account in ranking workers for a RIF are highly controversial. For many years, the federal government has used four items: tenure of employment (probationary or nonprobationary), veterans preference, seniority, and performance appraisals.[184] The controversy lies in how these items are weighted. Organized labor consistently has stressed seniority, arguing that government should strive to retain its most experienced workers. In 1986, regulations went into effect giving greater weighting to performance appraisals than had been the case. The change was praised as rewarding excellence in performance and was criticized as a means by which supervisors could exercise favoritism in deciding who would retain their jobs.[185,186] Employees may be notified up to 6 months in advance that they will lose their jobs, and during that time they may receive retraining and placement services.

Another sensitive aspect of RIFs is that they tend to affect women and minorities disproportionately because of the seniority provisions. This is the problem of "last hired, first fired." RIF procedures have come in conflict with court orders requiring increasing the proportion of minorities in government employment. The issue was addressed by the Supreme Court in a case involving Memphis firefighters (1984).[187,188] The city had been under a court order to increase minority employment, particularly in higher-level positions. When Memphis decided it had to lay off firefighters for budgetary reasons, it announced that the RIFs would be based on seniority. A federal district court blocked this action on the grounds that it would result in layoffs primarily among African-Americans. The firefighters' union challenged this action as a form of reverse discrimination. The Supreme Court ruled in favor of the union, holding that Title VII of the Civil Rights Act condones the use of bona fide seniority systems.

More generally, governments should deliberate thoroughly before initiating RIF procedures. They should consider other options such as hiring freezes, shrinking the size of an agency through attrition, and temporary furloughs.[189] RIFs are disruptive and can be costly in terms of the harm done to morale and productivity. Savings expected from RIFs often do not materialize. A common practice is allowing workers to retain their salaries when they are bumped to lower-level positions; that results in government paying more for less complex work.[190] In planning for a RIF, agencies need to consider how operations will be conducted with fewer employees and whether the remaining employees will need retraining.[191]

Employees have rights in both nondisciplinary and disciplinary situations. Nondisciplinary situations can involve RIFs, assigning other duties, or reassignment to other geographical locations. An employee may have appeal rights concerning not only whether the new assignment carries the same grade and pay as the original position but also whether the levels of responsibility of the two positions are truly comparable. When individuals have any complaint about their employment, they can file grievances.

A disciplinary situation involves an adverse action against an employee. Sometimes different procedures are used for poor performance and misconduct.[192,193] The former refers to an employee not completing work satisfactorily; the latter involves such actions as using intemperate language with peers or a supervisor, drinking alcoholic beverages or using narcotics while on duty, arriving late for work, or coming to work drunk or "high" on drugs. In situations involving poor performance, the supervisor usually meets with the employee to discuss an unsatisfactory rating and to set a period of time for correcting the behavior; if the employee's behavior is not corrected, then removal from office is the ultimate step.

Discipline procedures typically provide for a progression of actions. Oral and written reprimands are first used; when these measures fail to bring results, short-term (less than 14 days) and then long-term suspensions without pay may be used. Demotions and reductions in pay follow, with removals obviously being the most severe form of action. How these measures are used varies widely among supervisors and managers and from case to case within the same work setting. Managers may be reluctant to engage in disciplinary action to avoid unpleasant interpersonal situations, to avoid having to defend actions taken before a merit appeals body, and to avoid devoting scarce time to personnel problems when other matters seem more pressing. Suggestions have been made that management needs to establish systems of discipline in which employees understand clearly what punishments will be meted out for specific behaviors and patterns of behavior.[194] Others suggest that discipline needs to be cast in a positive framework, namely that management is seen as working with workers to help them correct unacceptable behavior.[195]

Adverse actions are governed by procedures established by statute, executive order, and administrative regulations.[196] Action may be taken against merit employees only for "just cause," in distinction from "at-will" employees, who can be disciplined simply at the prerogative of management. At the federal level, the Lloyd-LaFollette Act of 1912 has been the primary legislation; it provided that an employee "may be removed or suspended without pay only for such cause as will promote the efficiency of the service."[197,198] In passing the Veterans Preference Act of 1944, Congress granted special appeal rights to veterans in adverse actions.[199] Presidential executive orders have been used to require agencies to establish adverse action procedures for all employees and to provide for a system of appeals. The 1978 Civil Service Reform Act substantially revised the processes involved but retained the fundamental principle of allowing adverse actions only when they would "promote the efficiency of the service."[200]

The steps in the federal appeal process are presented in Figure 8–1.[201] This process does not apply to minor disciplinary actions, such as being suspended without pay for 14 days or less, or to RIFs or reductions in rank. When an employee is to be removed, suspended for more than 14 days, or reduced in grade or pay, the process begins with giving the individual 30 days' written notice of the proposed action. The worker has a right to respond to the proposal both orally and in writing; the law permits (but does not require) agencies to provide a formal hearing at this step. The employee may have an attorney in the oral session.

The next step is to appeal to the Merit Systems Protection Board (MSPB).[202] The board may hear the case itself, or, more likely, it may assign the case to an administrative law judge or other MSPB employee skilled in hearing procedures. At this point, the employee has a right to a formal hearing and may have an

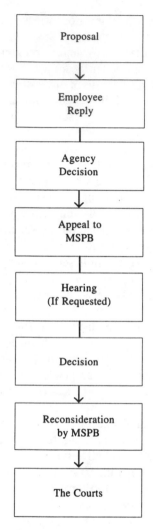

Figure 8-1 Federal Adverse Action Appeal System.

---

attorney to assist in the case. The agency decision is to be upheld unless it is shown that in cases of alleged unacceptable work performance there was not substantial evidence to support the charge. In cases other than unacceptable performance, there must be a preponderance of the evidence; this is a stricter standard of proof in that the agency must convince the MSPB that the employee probably is guilty as charged. The agency's actions can be overturned if it is shown that it did not follow established procedures and that its error may have substantially prejudiced the employee's case.[203]

The director of OPM may intervene in cases where in that official's opinion "an erroneous decision would have a substantial impact on any civil service law, rule, or regulation." After the decision of the administrative law judge, the MSPB may reconsider the case either on its own initiative or at the request of the employee, the agency, or OPM. If a decision is in favor of the employee, the agency may be required to pay the worker's attorney fees. If the decision is against the employee, the individual may appeal to a U.S. circuit court of appeals or, if pay is involved, to the U.S. Court of Claims.

Several appeal systems can exist in any large government.[204] Some agencies may have personnel systems independent of the jurisdiction's civil service commission and thus may have independent appeal systems. Collective bargaining in government provides additional appeal routes. A state employee who has been notified of a proposed adverse action may have a choice of using the state civil service commission procedure or one established by a collective bargaining agreement. An employee who thinks the chances are better with the union grievance procedures obviously will take that route. A worker unsuccessful in the collective bargaining appeal route still may have the option of shifting to the civil service procedure. In instances where federal employees have such a choice, the choice is irrevocable.

Grievance procedures under collective bargaining normally culminate in arbitration. Anyone covered by the agreement, regardless of whether that person is a member of the union, has a right to union representation. The Supreme Court has ruled that when a union fails to assist an employee it can be held partially liable for any award made to the worker; in one instance the union was required to pay part of the back salary that was owing to the employee.[205,206]

Another area in which alternative appeals procedures sometimes exist involves cases of alleged discrimination. Employees may be able to appeal to the jurisdiction's civil service commission and to the agency responsible for enforcing equal employment opportunity (how such cases are handled at the federal level is discussed in Chapter 9).

Pay usually is at stake in appeals proceedings. Removal obviously results in loss of income. Appeals in nondisciplinary cases frequently arise over the downgrading of positions. Grade creep, or inflation, can become a serious problem, and when a government seeks to correct the situation, many employees will be downgraded (see Chapters 3 and 4). Because OPM sets standards for classification of federal positions, appeals may be made to that agency by employees who think their positions are classified too low. When employees successfully appeal adverse actions, they receive back pay. The federal Back Pay

Act is for such adverse action cases and cannot be used in other cases, such as when an employee's position is found to be graded lower than it should be.[207]

Courts have been active in delineating the rights of employees who are subjected to disciplinary actions. The earlier discussion of loyalty and security, free speech, and political activities indicated some of the protections the courts have afforded employees, as well as many of the limitations. One of the major hurdles for employees seeking judicial redress has been proving that some legal right is at stake. Aside from the First Amendment cases discussed above, the due process clauses of the Fifth Amendment pertaining to the national government and the Fourteenth Amendment pertaining to the states have been the primary avenues for employees seeking judicial review. These clauses, however, do not guarantee due process in all instances; rather, it is restricted to situations that deprive a person of life, liberty, or property. Since one's life obviously is not threatened by being dismissed from government employment, the reasoning necessarily hinges on deprivation of liberty and property.

Two cases decided in 1972 by the Supreme Court illustrate this problem of defining liberty and property. *Perry v. Sindermann* involved a junior college professor who had been employed for 10 years by the college and then was dismissed without explanation and without an opportunity to defend himself in a hearing.[208] The Court ruled that, although the professor technically was nontenured, the college had a de facto tenure system that had the effect of providing him with a property right. Due process, including a hearing, was required in such a dismissal.

Board of Regents v. Roth also dealt with the dismissal of a nontenured faculty member, but it had a different outcome.[209] The Court ruled that neither an explanation for the professor's nonreappointment nor a hearing was required. The Court held that without Roth's having tenure there could be no property interest and that Roth had not proved that his liberty had been denied. Roth was free to seek employment elsewhere. In the view of the Court, had the university in its dismissal stigmatized the faculty member, such as by finding him incompetent, then his freedom to seek new employment might have been deprived. The three dissenting justices contended that all dismissals have a stigmatizing effect.

The Court again dealt with this liberty and property issue in 1976 in *Bishop v. Wood*.[210] A municipal policeman was dismissed after successfully serving a probationary period and becoming classified as a permanent employee. In interpreting the city regulations that governed dismissal of permanent employees, the Court held that in actuality such persons had no right to be retained, in effect ruling that permanent employees did not have a property right. The policeman, therefore, could not claim that due process had been denied when he was not granted a hearing. Moreover, the Court suggested that courts should not be involved extensively in these kinds of issues:

The federal court is not the appropriate forum in which to review the multitude of personnel decisions that are made by public agencies. We must accept the harsh fact that numerous individual mistakes are inevitable in the day-to-day administration of our affairs. . . . The Due Process clause of the Fourteenth Amendment is not a guarantee against incorrect or ill-advised personnel decisions.[211]

The dissent in the case reasoned that, because the policeman had been dismissed for "causing low morale" and for "conduct unsuited to an officer," the dismissal constituted a "badge of infamy" that infringed on his property and liberty rights.

The timing of when a hearing takes place and when an adverse action is implemented is important. If an employee is removed and the hearing is conducted later, that situation can place a severe financial burden on a possibly falsely accused person; of course, if the charge is not upheld in the hearing, the employee will be entitled to back pay. On the other hand, if an employee cannot be removed until after a hearing, an incompetent worker not only might be kept on the payroll but also might cause extensive confusion and inefficiency in the agency.

The Supreme Court has taken the middle ground on this issue.[212] In one case, a school security guard was dismissed for stating falsely on a job application that he had not been convicted of a felony. In another a school bus driver was removed for failing an eye examination. Both workers sought a hearing before being removed. The Court held that they were entitled to notification of the charges and an opportunity to respond, but it did not go so far as to require a pretermination hearing.

The administrative process in adverse actions does not have all the trappings of courtroom proceedings, but basic standards of due process or perhaps simply fair play have emerged. One requirement is that agencies abide by their own rules, although that is not a rigid rule. Hearsay evidence, which usually is not admissible in a court, frequently is admissible in an administrative hearing. For example, a court upheld the dismissal of an Internal Revenue Service agent under the Lloyd-LaFollette Act based on newspaper accounts that he had fatally shot a woman, even though he later was acquitted of murder.[213]

Administrative hearings should not be biased against the employee.[214] In a dismissal proceeding against an investigator in the United States Bureau of Narcotics and Dangerous Drugs, the officer who was to judge the case and the prosecutor flew together to the hearing city, stayed in the same hotel, rode in the same automobile to the hearing, and discussed the case privately on several occasions.[215] This practice was held to be biased against the employee.

Other important rights include the cross-examination of witnesses and representation by legal counsel. The employee and not the government is expected to pay legal fees. As part of the due process requirement, the dismissal must be based on some reason and cannot be arbitrary.

Agency failure to meet the due process standards does not reinstate employees who have been dismissed. If a court holds that the procedure was biased, that an unacceptable level of hearsay evidence was used, or that the employee was not permitted to cross-examine witnesses, the person does not regain the job. Instead, a new hearing is conducted, and there is a good chance that the employee will be dismissed a second time.

Criticisms of adverse action proceedings abound. Greater safeguards for employees supposedly have limited the authority of managers to manage. Workers often are not dismissed as early as they should be because managers must build a case that will withstand court review. In the disciplinary hearing, the supervisor often seems to be the one accused rather than the employee. Both employees and managers complain that adverse proceedings are excessively time consuming. The delays result in part from courts' insistence on protecting employees by giving them due process.

SUMMARY

Efforts have been made to balance the rights of government and its employees. No longer is it assumed that government may prescribe whatever behavior it chooses for its workers. Public servants do not automatically relinquish their rights as citizens when they are hired by government. At the same time, absolute rights cannot be granted to employees because that would seriously handicap the government in serving the citizenry. The concept of balancing government and employee rights sounds good as a general principle, but applying that concept to specific situations is difficult.

Government demands high ethical standards of its employees. Corruption and conflicts of interest are grounds for dismissal. Dilemmas develop over matters such as whether employees should follow the dictates of their chosen profession in the delivery of services or whether they should remain loyal to a political administration even though its actions run counter to professional standards. Employees are expected to serve the public interest and to execute statutes, but often they must exercise considerable discretion or judgment, deciding on their own, to some extent, what is in the public interest. Government establishes standards for employee conduct both on and off the job. Employees may be required to live within the jurisdiction they serve. Alcoholics and former criminal offenders are unlikely to be hired, and employees who become alcoholics or are convicted of crimes may be dismissed. The sex lives of employees also are subject to some government restrictions.

The presumed right of government to protect itself from employees who would subvert it either by leaking national security information or by advocating its violent overthrow has come into direct conflict with the rights of government workers as citizens. Loyalty and security charges have destroyed the careers of many public employees. The freedoms of speech and peaceful assembly as guaranteed in the First Amendment have been used selectively to protect public workers, but the judicial system has been unwilling to provide blanket protections. The due process clause has provided additional protections for employees dismissed for loyalty or security reasons.

Public workers have considerable free speech rights. Whistle blowing is common both for employees who choose to remain in government and for those who resign in protest. While whistle blowing helps keep government accountable, it can lead to employees acting on their own. Laws and regulations pertaining to limits on speech are expected to be specific so that employees know what is prohibited, although a lingering question is whether existing statutes are in fact sufficiently clear. An employee who exercises the constitutional right to free speech may be technically protected from dismissal, but other means, such as RIFs, can be used to seek that employee's dismissal.

Unresolved is the issue of whether public employees should be permitted to participate in political activities. The Hatch Act and its counterparts at the state level have been defended as providing for political neutrality in government administration and for protecting workers from attempts to coerce them into partisan activities. The courts have not found these laws to violate First Amendment rights or to be unconstitutionally vague. The federal government may impose political restrictions on state and local employees who are funded substantially by federal monies. Although these limitations on public servants are constitutional, existing laws could be rewritten to allow for greater involvement of public employees in the political process.

Several methods are used to hold civil servants directly answerable to the citizenry. Laws require the release of government information and that meetings on policy and regulations be held in public. Ombudsman offices help mediate problems between citizens or clients and government agencies. Through legislation, the federal government has allowed for liability suits against itself, but this is far less common at the state and local levels. In response, citizens have filed Section 1983 suits against individual government officials, holding them personally liable for their actions.

Employees have protection when government shrinks its work force through RIFs and when superiors attempt to demote, suspend, reassign, or remove them. Seniority is a major factor in RIF procedures, but there is increasing interest in relying on performance appraisals for deciding who stays and who is forced out.

Appeal procedures are provided by statutes, executive orders, and administrative regulations. The courts have moved away from the concept that government employment is a privilege and have recognized that property and liberty rights may be at stake in adverse actions. When such rights are involved, due process standards must be observed, providing for an oral hearing, an attorney to represent the employee, an opportunity to cross-examine witnesses, and the like. The procedures used are extremely time consuming and, depending on one's point of view, do not adequately protect employees, severely handicap the ability of public managers to manage, or both.

The issues in this chapter are of immense importance. To facilitate the discussion, the chapter is divided into sections and subsections, but these should not be considered independent of one another. All the issues relate to the rights of employees and their employers. What is in the best interest of society: protecting government's ability to function, or protecting the rights of government employees? The desirable approach would be to protect both, but achieving that objective is difficult.

NOTES

1. J.S. Bowman, ed., *Ethical Frontiers in Public Management* (San Francisco: Jossey-Bass, 1991).

2. W.J.M. Cody and R.R. Lynn, *Honest Government: An Ethics Guide for Public Service* (Westport, Conn.: Praeger Publishers, 1992).

3. T.L. Cooper, *The Responsible Administrator: An Approach to Ethics for the Administrative Role*, 3d ed. (San Francisco: Jossey-Bass, 1990).

4. Council on Governmental Ethics Laws, *Blue Book* (Lexington, Ky.: Council of State Governments, 1992).

5. C. Lewis, *The Ethics Challenge in Public Service* (San Francisco: Jossey-Bass, 1991).

6. L.C. Gawthrop, The ethical foundations of American public administration, *International Journal of Public Administration* 16 (1993): 139–163.

7. *McAuliffe v. New Bedford*, 155 Mass. 216, 29 N.E. 517 (1892).

8. W.L. Riordon, *Plunkitt of Tammany Hall* (New York: E.P. Dutton, 1963), 3.

9. Senate Committee on Governmental Affairs, *Renomination of Donald J. Devine: Hearings*, 99th Cong., 1st sess. (Washington: U.S. Government Printing Office, 1985).

10. R.C. Moe, The HUD scandal and the case for an office of federal management, *Public Administration Review* 51 (1991): 298–307.

11. House Committee on Government Operations, Subcommittee on Employment and Housing, *Abuses, Favoritism, and Mismanagement in HUD Programs: Hearings*, 101st Cong, 1st sess. (Washington: U.S. Government Printing Office, 1991).

12. J.R. Crawford, et al., Decision in Keating Five case settles little for Senate, *Congressional Quarterly Weekly Report* 49 (1991): 517–523.

13. J. Hook, Paralysis grips Congress as scandals spread, *Congressional Quarterly Weekly Report* 50 (1992): 775–776.

14. B. Woodward and C. Bernstein, *All the President's Men* (New York: Simon & Schuster, 1974).

15. F.C. Mosher, et al., *Watergate: Implications for Responsible Government* (New York: Basic Books, 1974).

16. House Committee on the Judiciary, Subcommittee on Criminal Justice, *Prosecuting Fraud in the Thrift Industry: Impact of the Financial Institutions Reform, Recovery, and Enforcement Act of 1989: Hearing*, 101st Cong., 2d sess. (Washington: U.S. Government Printing Office, 1990).

17. Ethics in Government Act, P.L. 95-521, 92 Stat. 1824 (1978).

18. Ethics Reform Act, P.L. 101-194, 103 Stat. 1716 (1989).

19. President's Commission on Federal Ethics Law Reform, *To Serve with Honor* (Washington: U.S. Government Prinnting Office, 1989).

20. J.D. Carroll, "If men were angels": Assessing the Ethics in Government Act of 1978, *Policy Studies Journal* 17 (1988–89): 435–447.

21. Code of Ethics for Government Service, P.L. 96-303, 94 Stat. 855 (1980).

22. Principles of Ethical Conduct for Government Officers and Employees, E.O. 12674 (1989), modified by E.O. 12731 (1990).

23. R.N. Roberts and M.T. Doss, Jr., Public service and private hospitality: A case study in federal conflict-of-interest reform, *Public Administration Review* 52 (1992): 260–269.

24. U.S. General Accounting Office, *Ethics Enforcement: Results of Conflict of Interest Investigations* (Washington: U.S. Government Printing Office, 1988).

25. _____, *Employee Conduct Standards: Some Outside Activities Present Conflict-of-Interest Issues* (Washington: U.S. Government Printing Office, 1992).

26. Ethics Commitments by Executive Branch Appointees, E.O. 12834 (1993).

27. *Crandon v. U.S.*, 494 U.S. 26 (1990).

28. U.S. General Accounting Office, *Government Ethics: HUD Financial Disclosure Reports Missing or Not Reviewed* (Washington: U.S. Government Printing Office, 1990).

29. _____, *Fraud Hotline: 9-Year GAO Fraud Hotline Summary* (Washington: U.S. Government Printing Office, 1988).

30. U.S. Department of Justice, *Report to Congress on the Activities of the Public Integrity Section for 1983* (Washington: U.S. Government Printing Office, 1984).

31. Inspector General Act, P.L. 95-452, 92 Stat. 1101 (1978).

32. Inspector General Act Amendments, P.L. 100-504, 102 Stat. 2515 (1988).

33. U.S. General Accounting Office, *Inspectors General: Fraud Hotline Operations* (Washington: U.S. Government Printing Office, 1989).

34. K.J. Harriger, *Independent Justice: The Federal Special Prosecutor in American Politics* (Lawrence, Kan.: University of Kansas Press, 1992).

35. B. Nolan, Removing conflicts from the administration of justice; conflicts of interest and independent counsels under the Ethics in Government Act, *Georgetown Law Journal* 79 (1990): 1–80.

36. R.D. Lee, Jr., The ombudsman in a political context: The Commonwealth and Victoria Ombudsmen in Australia, *International Review of Administrative Sciences* 57 (1991): 441–464.

37. Federal Managers' Financial Integrity Act, P.L. 97-255, 96 Stat. 814 (1982).

38. G.B. Frank and J.C. Steinhoff, Implementing the Federal Managers' Financial Integrity Act, *GAO Review* 20 (Spring 1985): 14ff.

39. U.S. General Accounting Office, *Financial Integrity Act: The Government Faces Serious Internal Control and Accounting Systems Problems* (Washington: U.S. Government Printing Office, 1985).

40. Competition in Contracting Act, P.L. 98-369, 98 Stat. 1175 (1984).

41. J.A. Sukol, The Competition in Contracting Act's automatic stay provision and judicial review, *Administrative Law Review* 43 (1991): 439–454.

42. Office of Federal Procurement Policy Act Amendments, P.L. 100-679, 102 Stat. 4055 (1988).

43. Chief Financial Officers Act, P.L. 101-576, 104 Stat. 2838 (1990).

44. R.A. Pewanick and J.C. Steinhoff, The Chief Financial Officers Act of 1990: A new approach to solving federal financial management problems, *International Journal of Public Administration* 15 (1992): 1,151–1,168.

45. J. Madison, "Federalist Paper No. 51," in *The Federalist Papers*, ed. A. Hamilton, et al. (New York: New American Library of World Literature, 1961), 322.

46. D.C. Menzel and J.E. Benton, Ethics complaints and local government: The case of Florida, *Journal of Public Administration Research and Theory* 1 (1991): 419–435.

47. P.H. Appleby, *Morality and Administration in Democratic Government* (Baton Rouge, La.: Louisiana State University Press, 1952), 58–59.

48. H.F. Gortner, *Ethics for Public Managers* (New York: Greenwood Press, 1991).

49. R.D. Gatewood and A.B. Carroll, Assessment of ethical performance of organization members: A conceptual framework, *Academy of Management Review* 16 (1991): 667–690.

50. S.J. Harrington, What corporate America is teaching about ethics, *Academy of Management Executive* 5 (February 1991): 21–30.

51. C.N. Callender and J.C. Charlesworth, eds., Ethical standards in American public life, *Annals* 280 (1952): 1–157.

52. F.C. Mosher, *Democracy and the Public Service* (New York: Oxford University Press, 1968).

53. K.G. Denhardt, The management of ideals: A political perspective on ethics, *Public Administration Review* 49 (1989): 187–193.

54. R.C. Kearney and C. Sinha, Professionalism and bureaucratic responsiveness: Conflict or compatibility? *Public Administration Review* 48 (1988): 571–579.

55. T.L. Cooper, *An Ethic of Citizenship for Public Administration* (Englewood Cliffs, N.J.: Prentice-Hall, 1991).

56. J.P. Dobel, Integrity in the public service, *Public Administration Review* 50 (1990): 354–366.

57. W. Wilson, The study of administration, *Political Science Quarterly* 2 (1887): 197–222; reprinted in *Political Science Quarterly* 56 (1941): 481–506.

58. G.A. Graham, *Morality in American Politics* (New York: Random House, 1952): 193–198.

59. S.J. Carroll, The personal is political: The intersection of private lives and public roles among women and men in elective and appointive office, *Women & Politics* 9 (1989): 51–67.

60. C.M. Johnson and G. Duerst-Lahti, Private lives and public work: Professional careers in state civil service, *Review of Public Personnel Administration* 12 (September–December 1991): 14–32.

61. U.S. Merit Systems Protection Board, *Balancing Work Responsibilities and Family Needs: The Federal Civil Service Response* (Washington: U.S. Government Printing Office, 1991).

62. U.S. Office of Government Ethics, *How To Keep Out of Trouble*, 2d ed. (Washington: U.S. Government Printing Office, 1989).

63. A. Hejka-Ekins, Teaching ethics in public administration, *Public Administration Review* 48 (1988): 885–891.

64. L.C. Mainzer, Vulgar ethics for public administration, *Administration and Society* 23 (1991): 3–28.

65. S. Black, et al., Perspectives on the implementation of employee rights programs, *Employee Responsibilities and Rights Journal* 1 (1988): 247–261.

66. U.S. General Accounting Office, *Employee Involvement: Issues for Agencies to Consider in Designing and Implementing Programs* (Washington: U.S. Government Printing Office, 1988).

67. J.D. Bible and D.A. McWhirter, *Privacy in the Workplace: A Guide for Human Resource Managers* (New York: Quorum, 1990).

68. K.H. Decker, *A Manager's Guide to Employee Privacy: Laws, Policies and Procedures* (New York: John Wiley & Sons, 1989).

69. House Committee on Government Operations, Subcommittee on Legislation and National Security, *Privacy Rights of Federal Employees: Hearing,* 101st Cong., 1st sess. (Washington: U.S. Government Printing Office, 1990).

70. G.S. Taylor and B.A. Spencer, Ethical implications of human resource information systems, *Employee Responsibilities and Rights Journal* 3 (1990): 19–30.

71. *Goldman v. Weinberger,* 475 U.S. 503 (1986).

72. J.S. Bowman, Dress standards in government: A national survey of state administrators, *Review of Public Personnel Administration* 12 (January–April 1992): 35–51.

73. C.R. Easterling, et al., Perceived importance and usage of dress codes among organizations that market professional services, *Public Personnel Management* 21 (1992): 211–219.

74. *Kelley v. Johnson,* 425 U.S. 238 (1976).

75. Employee Polygraph Protection Act, P.L. 100-347, 102 Stat. 646 (1988).

76. B.V. Driscoll, The Employee Polygraph Protection Act of 1988: A balance of interests, *Iowa Law Review* 75 (1990): 539–566.

77. L.S. Kleiman, et al., Legal issues concerning polygraph testing in the public sector, *Public Personnel Management* 19 (1990): 365–379.

78. Senate Committee on the Judiciary, Subcommittee on Courts and Administrative Practice, *Government Observation of Safety and Health Standards: Hearing,* 101st Cong., 2d sess. (Washington: U.S. Government Printing Office, 1990).

79. *Collins v. City of Harker Heights,* 112 S.Ct. 1061 (1992).

80. M.H. Bowers, What labor and management need to know about workplace smoking cases, *Labor Law Journal* 43 (1992): 40–49.

81. L.W. Short, The legal implications of workplace smoking policies, *Employee Responsibilities and Rights Journal* 5 (1992): 65–73.

82. *AIDS Law and Litigation Reporter* (Frederick, Md.: University Publishing Group, looseleaf service).

83. W.F. Banta, *AIDS in the Workplace: Legal Questions and Practical Answers* (New York: Lexington Books, 1992).

84. J. Mitchell, The response to AIDS in the workplace among public, private, and non-profit employers, *Review of Public Personnel Administration* 11 (Fall 1990–Spring 1991): 28–37.

85. C.D. Curran, Mandatory testing of public employees for the human immunodeficiency virus: The Fourth Amendment and medical reasonableness, *Columbia Law Review* 90 (1990): 720–759.

86. *School Board of Nassau County, FL, v. Arline,* 480 U.S. 273 (1987).

87. U.S. Office of Personnel Management, *Acquired Immune Deficiency Syndrome (AIDS) in the Workplace,* Federal Personnel Manual Bulletin 792-42 (Washington: U.S. Government Printing Office, March 24, 1988).

88. J.F. Atwood, Applicant drug testing: An intriguing odyssey, *Public Personnel Management* 21 (1992): 119–132.

89. D.E. Klingner, et al., Drug testing in public agencies: Public policy issues and managerial responses, *Review of Public Personnel Administration* 10 (Fall 1989): 1–10.

90. N.M. Riccucci, Drug testing in the public sector: A legal analysis, *American Review of Public Administration* 20 (1990): 95–106.

91. U.S. General Accounting Office, *Employee Drug Testing: Status of Federal Agencies' Programs* (Washington: U.S. Government Printing Office, 1991).

92. Drug-Free Workplace Act, P.L. 100-690, 102 Stat. 4304 (1988).

93. Omnibus Transportation Employees Testing Act, P.L. 102-143, 105 Stat. 952 (1991).

94. *National Treasury Employees Union v. Von Raab*, 109 S.Ct. 1384 (1989).

95. *Skinner v. Railway Labor Executives' Association*, 109 S.Ct. 1402 (1989).

96. U.S. General Accounting Office, *Employee Drug Testing: A Single Agency Is Needed To Manage Federal Employee Drug Testing* (Washington: U.S. Government Printing Office, 1991).

97. _____, *Employee Drug Testing: Estimated Cost To Test All Executive Branch Employees and New Hires* (Washington: U.S. Government Printing Office, 1992).

98. C.E. Labig, Jr., Supervisory and nonsupervisory employee attitudes about drug testing, *Employee Responsibilities and Rights Journal* 5 (1992): 131–141.

99. F.J. Thompson, et al., Drug testing in the federal workplace: An instrumental and symbolic assessment, *Public Administration Review* 51 (1991): 515–525.

100. *O'Connor v. Ortega*, 480 U.S. 709 (1987).

101. J.S. Bowman, Ethics in government: A national survey of public administrators, *Public Administration Review* 50 (1990): 345–353.

102. R.A. Gonzalez, et al., Municipal residency laws: Effects on police employment, compensation, and productivity, *Journal of Labor Research* 12 (1991): 439–452.

103. *McCarthy v. Philadelphia Civil Service Commission*, 424 U.S. 645 (1976).

104. House Committee on Post Office and Civil Service, *Right to Privacy of Federal Employees, Hearings*, Lawrence Speiser's testimony, 93d Cong., 1st and 2d sess. (Washington: U.S. Government Printing Office, 1974), 38.

105. M.A. Woronoff, Public employees or private citizens: The off-duty sexual activities of police officers and the constitutional right of privacy, *University of Michigan Journal of Law Reform* 18 (1984): 195–219.

106. *Wishart v. McDonald*, 500 F. 2d 1110 (1974).

107. C.M. Reed and L.J. Cohen, Anti-nepotism rules: The legal rights of married co-workers, *Public Personnel Management* 18 (1989): 37–44.

108. *Griswold v. Connecticut*, 381 U.S. 479 (1966).

109. Minnesota Multiphasic Personality Inventory, as quoted in L.H. Mirel, The limits of governmental inquiry into the private lives of government employees, *Boston University Law Review* 46 (1966): 18.

110. U.S. General Accounting Office, *Employee Conduct Standards*.

111. *Schenck v. United States*, 249 U.S. 47 (1919).

112. E. Bontecou, *The Federal Loyalty-Security Program* (Ithaca, N.Y.: Cornell University Press, 1953).

113. W. Gellhorn, *Security, Loyalty, and Science* (Ithaca, N.Y.: Cornell University Press, 1950).

114. National security and civil liberties, *Cornell Law Review* 69 (1984): 685–924.

115. J. McCarthy, *McCarthyism: The Fight for America* (New York: Devin-Adair, 1952).

116. W. Gellhorn, ed., *The States and Subversion* (Ithaca, N.Y.: Cornell University Press, 1952).

117. Executive Order 10450, as amended, Security Requirements for Government Employees, 5 U.S.C. § 7311 (1953).

118. U.S. General Accounting Office, *Security Clearances: Due Process for Denials and Revocations by Defense, Energy, and State* (Washington: U.S. Government Printing Office, 1992).

119. U.S. General Accounting Office, *Security Clearances*.

120. *Slochower v. Board of Higher Education of the City of New York*, 350 U.S. 551 (1956).

121. House Committee on Government Operations, Subcommittee on Environment, Energy, and Natural Resources, *Problems in the Nuclear Regulatory Commission's Personnel Security Clear-*

ance Program: Hearings, 101st Cong., 1st sess. (Washington: U.S. Government Printing Office, 1989).

122. *Pietrunti v. Board of Education,* 128 N.J. Super. 149, 319 A.2d 262 (1974).

123. *Givhan v. Western Consolidated School District,* 439 U.S. 409 (1978).

124. *Connick v. Myers,* 461 U.S. 138 (1983).

125. *Rankin v. McPherson,* 483 U.S. 378 (1987).

126. J.S. Bowman, Whistle blowing: Literature and resource materials, *Public Administration Review* 43 (1983): 271–276.

127. M. Aron, Whistleblowers, insubordination, and employee rights of free speech, *Labor Law Journal* 43 (1992): 211–220.

128. P.H. Jos, et al., In praise of difficult people: A portrait of the committed whistleblower, *Public Administration Review* 49 (1989): 552–561.

129. U.S. General Accounting Office, *Whistleblower Protection: Survey of Federal Employees on Misconduct and Protection from Reprisal* (Washington: U.S. Government Printing Office, 1992).

130. D.P. Westman, *Whistleblowing: The Law of Retaliatory Discharge* (Washington: Bureau of National Affairs, 1991).

131. L.K. Trevino and B. Victor, Peer reporting of unethical behavior: A social context perspective, *Academy of Management Journal* 35 (1992): 38–64.

132. *Mt. Healthy City School District Board of Education v. Doyle,* 429 U.S. 274 (1977).

133. G. Gold, et al., eds., *The Pentagon Papers: As Published by the New York Times* (New York: Bantam Books, 1971).

134. A.E. Fitzgerald, *The High Priests of Waste* (New York: W.W. Norton & Company, 1972).

135. U.S. Merit Systems Protection Board, *Questions and Answers about Whistleblower Appeals* (Washington: U.S. Government Printing Office, 1991).

136. Whistleblower Protection Act, P.L. 101-12, 103 Stat. 16 (1989).

137. U.S. Merit Systems Protection Board, *Federal Personnel Management since Civil Service Reform: A Survey of Federal Personnel Officials* (Washington: U.S. Government Printing Office, 1989).

138. J.R. Bolton, *The Hatch Act: A Civil Libertarian Defense* (Washington: American Enterprise Institute, 1976).

139. R. Christopherson, *Regulating Politicial Activities of Public Employees* (Chicago, Ill.: Civil Service Assembly, 1954).

140. Hatch Political Activities Act, P.L. 76-252, 53 Stat. 1147 (1939).

141. Hatch Political Activities Act, P.L. 76-753, 54 Stat. 767 (1940).

142. Office of the Special Counsel, U.S. Merit Systems Protection Board, *Political Activity and the Federal Employee* (Washington: U.S. Government Printing Office, 1990).

143. Federal Election Campaign Act Amendments, P.L. 93-443, 88 Stat. 1263 (1974).

144. 5 C.F.R. § 733 for federal employees, 5 C.F.R. § 151 for state and local employees.

145. *United Public Workers of America v. Mitchell,* 330 U.S. 75 (1947).

146. *Oklahoma v. United States Civil Service Commission,* 330 U.S. 127 (1947).

147. *United States Civil Service Commission v. National Association of Letter Carriers,* 413 U.S. 548 (1973).

148. *Broadrick v. Oklahoma,* 413 U.S. 601 (1973).

149. L.L. Boyle, Reforming civil service reform: Should the federal government continue to regulate state and local government employees? *Journal of Law and Politics* 7 (1991): 243–288.

150. W.M. Pearson and D.S. Castle, Liberalizing restrictions on political activities of state employees: Perceptions of high-level state executives, *American Review of Public Administration* 21 (1991): 91–104.

151. J.G. Jabbra and O.P. Dwivedi, eds., *Public Service Accountability: A Comparative Perspective* (West Hartford, Conn.: Kumarian Press, 1988).

152. Freedom of Information Act, P.L. 89-487, 80 Stat. 250 (1966).

153. Privacy Act, P.L. 93-579, 88 Stat. 1896 (1974).

154. Government in the Sunshine Act, P.L. 94-409, 90 Stat. 1241 (1976).

155. D. Jaegal and N.J. Cayer, Public personnel administration by lawsuit: The impact of Supreme Court decisions on public employee litigiousness, *Public Administration Review* 51 (1991): 211–221.

156. *Tinker v. Des Moines Independent Community School District*, 393 U.S. 503 (1968).

157. *Goss v. Lopez*, 419 U.S. 565 (1975).

158. *Goldberg v. Kelly*, 397 U.S. 254 (1970).

159. *DeShaney v. Winnebago County Department of Social Services*, 489 U.S. 189 (1989).

160. Federal Tort Claims Act, P.L. 79-CH 753, 60 Stat. 842 (1946).

161. *Indian Towing Co. v. United States*, 350 U.S. 61 (1955).

162. *Griffin v. United States*, 351 F. Supp. 10 (1972), 353 F. Supp. 324 (1973).

163. *Monell v. Department of Social Services of New York City*, 436 U.S. 658 (1978).

164. *Maine v. Thiboutot*, 448 U.S. 1 (1980).

165. *Community Communications Co. v. City of Boulder*, 455 U.S. 40 (1982).

166. J.A. Swanke, Jr., *Public Officials Liability Insurance: Understanding the Market*, 2d ed. (Washington: International City Management Association, 1989).

167. *Stump v. Sparkman*, 435 U.S. 349 (1978).

168. *Imbler v. Pachtman*, 424 U.S. 409 (1976).

169. *Nixon v. Fitzgerald*, 457 U.S. 731 (1982).

170. *Chappell v. Wallace*, 461 U.S. 296 (1983).

171. *Bivens v. Six Unknown Named Agents of the Federal Bureau of Narcotics*, 403 U.S. 388 (1971).

172. *Siegert v. Gilley*, 111 S.Ct. 1789 (1991).

173. Civil Rights Act, P.L. 41-CH 99, 16 Stat. 433 (1871).

174. *Monroe v. Pape*, 365 U.S. 167 (1961).

175. *Hudson v. McMillan*, 112 S.Ct. 995 (1992).

176. *Scheur v. Rhodes*, 416 U.S. 232 (1974).

177. *Daniels v. Williams*, 474 U.S. 327 (1986).

178. *Hafer v. Melo*, 112 S.Ct. 358 (1991).

179. Federal Employees Liability Reform and Tort Compensation Act, P.L. 100-694, 102 Stat. 4563 (1988).

180. C.H. Levine, Retrenchment, human resource erosion, and the role of the personnel manager, *Public Personnel Management* 13 (1984): 249–263.

181. P.J. May and A. Meltsner, Limited actions, distressing consequences: A selected view of the California experience, *Public Administration Review* 41 (1981): 172–179.

182. U.S. General Accounting Office, *Reduction-in-Force: Information on the Office of Personnel Management's Reduction-in-Force Rules* (Washington: U.S. Government Printing Office, 1986).

183. W.C. Rich, ed., Reduction-in-force policy: Issues and perspectives, *Public Administration Quarterly* 10 (1986): 3–109.

184. U.S. Merit Systems Protection Board, *Reduction in Force: The Evolving Ground Rules* (Washington: U.S. Government Printing Office, 1987).

185. Reduction in Force, 5 C.F.R. § 351.

186. S.H. Shapiro, "Appealable Actions," in *Federal Civil Service Law and Procedures: A Basic Guide*, 2d ed., ed. E.M. Bussey (Washington: Bureau of National Affairs, 1990): 81–118.

187. *Firefighters Local Union No. 1784 v. Stotts*, 467 U.S. 561 (1984).

188. R.N. Roberts, The public law litigation model and *Memphis v. Stotts, Public Administration Review* 45 (1985): 527–532.

189. F. Best, *Reducing Workweeks To Prevent Layoffs* (Philadelphia: Temple University Press, 1988).

190. U.S. General Accounting Office, *Recent Government-Wide Hiring Freezes Prove Ineffective in Managing Federal Employment* (Washington: U.S. Government Printing Office, 1982).

191. D.S. Cochran, et al., Designing a developmental assessment center in a government agency: A case study, *Public Personnel Management* 16 (1987): 145–152.

192. Performance Based Reduction in Grade and Removal, 5 CFR § 432.

193. Adverse Actions, 5 CFR § 752.

194. R.C. Kearney and F. Whitaker, Behaviorally anchored disciplinary scales (BADS): A new approach to discipline, *Public Personnel Management* 17 (1988): 341–350.

195. N.M. Riccucci and G.R. Wheeler, Positive employee performance: An innovative approach to employee discipline, *Review of Public Personnel Administration* 8 (Fall 1987): 49–63.

196. R.D. Lee, Jr., Merit protection in the Australian public service: A comparative perspective, *Review of Public Personnel Administration* 11 (Fall 1990–Spring 1991): 84–94.

197. Lloyd-LaFollette Act, P.L. 62-CH 389, 37 Stat. 555 (1912).

198. Adverse Action by Agencies, 5 C.F.R. § 752.

199. Veterans Preference Act, P.L. 78-359, 58 Stat. 387 (1944).

200. Civil Service Reform Act, P.L. 95-454, 92 Stat. 1111 (1978).

201. U.S. Merit Systems Protection Board, *Questions and Answers about Appeals*.

202. _____, *A 10 Year Retrospective of the MSPB, 1978–1988* (Washington: U.S. Government Printing Office, 1989).

203. *Cornelius v. Nutt*, 472 U.S. 648 (1985).

204. W.V. Luneburg, The federal personnel complaint, appeal, and grievance systems: A structural overview and proposed revisions, *Kentucky Law Journal* 78 (1989–90): 1–128.

205. *Bowen v. U.S. Postal Service*, 459 U.S. 212 (1983).

206. C. Feigenbaum, The relationship between arbitration and administrative procedures in the discipline and discharge of federal employees, *Labor Law Journal* 34 (1983): 586–598.

207. Back Pay Act, P.L. 89-554, 80 Stat. 477 (1966).

208. *Perry v. Sindermann*, 408 U.S. 593 (1972).

209. *Board of Regents of State College v. Roth*, 408 U.S. 564 (1972).

210. *Bishop v. Wood*, 426 U.S. 341 (1976).

211. _____, 426 U.S. 349.

212. *Cleveland Board of Education v. Laudermill and Parma Board of Education v. Donnelly*, 470 U.S. 532 (1985).

213. *Wathen v. United States*, 527 F.2d 1191 (1975), *cert. denied*, 429 U.S. 821 (1976).

214. *Hortonville Joint School District #1 v. Hortonville Education Association*, 426 U.S. 482 (1976); discussed in Critique.

215. *Brown v. United States*, 377 F. Supp. 530 (1974).

Chapter 9

Equal Rights and Affirmative Action

Discrimination in government employment has existed for a long time. "In 1802 Postmaster General Gideon Granger warned that if Negroes were allowed to carry the mail, it would pose a threat to security because they might coordinate insurrectionary activities and acquire subversive ideas. For example, they might learn 'that a man's rights do not depend on his color.'"[1] As recently as 1913, regulations barred married women from the postal service.[2] The liberals of the day, who advocated hiring African-Americans and women, often based their positions on being able to pay them less than other workers, thereby increasing government efficiency.[3-5] People have been discriminated against on the basis of their race, sex, marital status, ethnicity, age, and religion. The physically handicapped, mentally retarded, mentally ill, and obese as well as homosexuals also face discrimination barriers.

This chapter pursues the same theme as the previous one, namely the rights that people have in obtaining government jobs, in developing careers in government, and in not being discharged. The concern is their right to be treated the same as other persons with like skills rather than being discriminated against for a non–job-related reason. Although the possible bases for discrimination are infinite, the chapter concentrates largely on discrimination based on sex and race. Four topics are covered:

1. the distribution of minorities and women in government jobs
2. legal remedies available to eliminate discrimination and the agencies that enforce relevant statutes
3. how discrimination affects various aspects of personnel administration
4. affirmative actions to increase the numbers of women and minorities in public employment

MINORITIES, WOMEN, AND OLDER WORKERS

The federal government and state and local governments are remarkably similar in the extent to which they employ minorities and women (the data discussed in this section are from sources cited in Tables 9–1 through 9–5). Table 9–1 shows that in 1990 the work forces of these governments consisted of about 25 percent minorities and 40 percent women. African-Americans constituted about 17 percent of the government work force, a figure that is slightly higher than that in the private sector. Hispanics held 5 to 7 percent of the jobs in each sector. These figures, being averages, do not reflect the great geographical variations that exist. Minority employment is concentrated in areas where minorities are common, such as large central cities.

Minorities and women tend to be concentrated in low-ranking positions at all levels of government. Among General Schedule or similar federal positions, minorities held more than half the GS-2 positions but only about 5 percent of the Senior Executive Service positions in 1990.[6]

As Table 9–2 indicates, white men and all types of minority men on average are paid better by the federal government than women, and the same is largely true for men and women in state and local government. White men earned on average about $40,000 in 1990 compared with only $27,000 for white women and $25,000 for African-American and Hispanic women. In state and local government, white men earned about $28,000 compared with $22,000 for white and Hispanic women and $21,000 for African-American women.

Minorities and women are concentrated in some occupations. Table 9–3 shows the distribution of state and local minorities and women by occupation for 1990. It is not surprising that nearly 90 percent of administrative support or clerical jobs were held by women, accounting for nearly 40 percent of all state and local jobs held by women. Paraprofessional jobs, which include library assistants, home-

Table 9–1 Percentage Distribution of Minorities and Women in the Private Sector Work Force and in Federal and State and Local Employment, 1990

Group	Private Sector	Federal	State and Local
Minorities	22.4	26.7	27.1
African-Americans	12.5	16.5	18.5
Hispanics	6.7	5.3	6.1
Asians, Pacific Islanders	2.7	3.5	2.0
Native Americans, Alaskan Natives	0.4	1.5	0.5
Women	46.5	41.9	42.8

Source: Data from *Indicators of Equal Employment Opportunity: Status and Trends*, pp. 12, A-4, A-5, U.S. Equal Employment Opportunity Commission, U.S. Government Printing Office, 1991.

Table 9–2 Average Salaries of Federal and State and Local Employees by Sex and Race/Ethnicity, 1990

Group	Federal	State and Local
White men	$40,005	$28,166
Asian men	37,925	34,111
Native American men	33,296	24,064
Hispanic men	32,676	25,998
African-American men	30,721	23,351
Asian women	28,220	28,962
White women	27,334	22,005
African-American women	24,696	20,963
Hispanic women	24,486	21,578
Native American women	23,546	20,453

Source: Data from *Indicators of Equal Employment Opportunity: Status and Trends,* pp. 40 and 42, U.S. Equal Employment Opportunity Commission, U.S. Government Printing Office, 1991.

Table 9–3 Distribution of State and Local Minorities and Women as a Percentage of Occupations, 1990

Occupation	Minorities	Women
Officials and administrators	15.3	31.3
Professionals	21.6	49.8
Technicians	23.6	40.7
Protective service workers	23.0	13.2
Paraprofessionals	37.8	72.3
Administrative support	29.8	87.3
Skilled craft workers	23.8	4.2
Service, maintenance	42.0	20.9

Source: Data from *Indicators of Equal Employment Opportunity: Status and Trends,* p. A-6, U.S. Equal Employment Opportunity Commission, U.S. Government Printing Office, 1991.

maker aides, and child support workers, were another major area of female concentration. Minorities, in comparison, were concentrated in service and maintenance jobs (42 percent of such positions) and paraprofessional jobs (38 percent). These occupations combined—service, maintenance, and paraprofessional—accounted for about 30 percent of all state and local jobs held by minorities. Minorities and women, however, are different in higher-level occupations. Women held about a third of the official/administrator positions in state and local government and nearly half the professional positions compared with only 15 percent and 22 percent, respectively, for minorities.

Concentrations of minorities and women are found in certain departments and functional areas. Table 9–4 shows that in 1990 half or more of state and local workers were women in the functions of financial administration, public welfare, hospitals and sanitoriums, health, and employment security. Minorities held a majority of the jobs in only one functional area: housing. They also held about 40 percent of jobs in the utilities/transportation and sanitation/sewage fields.

Great variation among federal departments also is common. In 1990, for instance, four of ten workers at the Department of Housing and Urban Development were minorities. The Office of Personnel Management (OPM) had 32 percent minorities, and the Department of Agriculture had only 17 percent.[7]

These patterns are in part a reflection of education. If a state department of agriculture needs to hire an agronomist, it must select among individuals with the appropriate education, and neither women nor minorities have tended to concentrate in agronomy. Similarly, only a small fraction of graduates from civil engineering are women, so a state or local department of highways will have difficulty in hiring women. As for minorities, fewer go to college than whites, which means the latter have an advantage in winning high-level positions.

A well-known fact is that the U.S. work force is aging, and government is affected by this trend. An examination of Table 9–5 reveals that the age distributions of federal executive branch employees and the civilian work force in general are similar. A majority of federal workers (53 percent) are above

Table 9–4 Percentage Distribution of State and Local Minorities and Women by Functional Area, 1990

Function	Minorities	Women
Financial administration	25.8	59.3
Streets and highways	20.2	16.2
Public welfare	36.5	75.0
Police protection	21.6	25.6
Fire protection	16.1	5.2
Natural resources	21.7	28.7
Hospitals and sanitoriums	35.1	72.6
Health	30.6	69.5
Housing	51.1	35.9
Community development	22.5	45.2
Corrections	30.5	32.6
Utilities and transportation	38.7	19.8
Sanitation and sewage	41.4	10.8
Employment security	27.9	61.5
Other	22.3	53.8

Source: Data from *Job Patterns for Minorities and Women in State and Local Government*, pp. 27–69, U.S. Equal Employment Opportunity Commission, U.S. Government Printing Office, 1991.

Table 9–5 Percentage Age Distribution of Employed Civilians and Federal Executive Branch Employees, 1990

Age	Employed Civilians	Federal Executive Branch Employees
Under 31	} 69	17
31–40		30
41–44		15
45–49	10	14
50–54	8	11
55–59	6	8
60–64	4	4
65–69	2	1
70 and above	1	<1
Total	100	100

Sources: Data from *Employment and Earnings*, Vol. 9, No. 5, p. 10, U.S. Bureau of Labor Statistics, U.S. Government Printing Office, 1992; and *Federal Civilian Workforce Statistics: Affirmative Employment Statistics*, p. 219, U.S. Office of Personnel Management, U.S. Government Printing Office 1992.

age 40. As the work force ages, allegations of age discrimination can be expected to rise. Some state human rights commissions already report that the number of age discrimination cases has surpassed the number of race discrimination cases.

The work forces of governments, of course, include people with disabilities. Accurate information about the number of disabled workers is lacking because many disabilities can go undetected unless workers report them. In 1990, disabled workers constituted 7 percent of the federal government's work force.[8] The most common disabilities involved nonparalytic orthopedic impairments (24 percent of those workers with disabilities) followed by hearing loss (12 percent) and vision impairment (9 percent). Seven of ten disabled workers were employed by the Department of Defense or the Department of Veterans Affairs.

OUTLAWING DISCRIMINATION

Discrimination has been outlawed through a variety of means.[9,10] Courts have interpreted state and federal constitutional provisions as protecting against discrimination. State and federal statutes have furthered the antidiscrimination cause. Presidents and governors have issued executive orders for the same purpose. As this section demonstrates, each of these legal routes has differing effects. Some are sweeping, protecting numerous groups from discrimination; others are limited to one classification, such as protecting against sex discrimination.

The United States Constitution can provide protection against discrimination through the Fifth and Fourteenth Amendments. Both include the due process clause, and it is possible to contend that without having been granted due process an individual has been denied a property right, as in not receiving equal pay. The Fourteenth Amendment, which applies to the states, has the additional guarantee of equal protection of the laws.

The chance of winning a suit under the Fourteenth Amendment depends in part on what type of test the courts choose in determining whether a given practice is discriminatory. The "rationality" test holds that if a policy is found to have some rational basis or purpose it will be held constitutional even though it has an adverse effect on some groups. The "strict scrutiny" test is more probative and is more likely to overturn a given practice as discriminatory. However, this test is limited to what the courts call "suspect classes," namely groups that have had "a history of purposeful unequal treatment." A policy that had adverse effects on African-Americans, therefore, would be likely to be subject to the strict scrutiny test, whereas a policy adverse to older employees would not.[11]

Another difficulty with using the Fifth and Fourteenth Amendments is that they place a heavy burden of proof on the person challenging the government's action. The Supreme Court has held that simply showing that a government's practice negatively affects African-Americans is insufficient proof that African-Americans are the victims of discrimination.[12] When claiming discrimination under the Fifth Amendment, intent to discriminate must be shown. For example, the Court concluded that, although African-Americans were affected adversely by the process used to select Washington, DC, police officers, there was no contention that the city had discriminated intentionally against African-Americans; indeed, the government had actively recruited them.

Because of the difficulties in winning a suit under the Fourteenth Amendment, other legal routes are used, including Sections 1981 through 1983 of Title 42 of the United States Code. Those sections are part of the Civil Rights Acts passed by Congress after the Civil War. Section 1981, guaranteeing equal rights under the law, and Section 1982, providing property rights to all citizens, protect only against racial discrimination and thus cannot be used in cases involving sex and age. Supreme Court decisions in 1987, however, greatly broadened the application of Sections 1981 and 1982 by redefining "race" to include ethnicity.[13] The Court concluded that legislative intent after the Civil War was to ban discrimination not just against African-Americans. In the 1987 cases, persons of Arab extraction and Jews brought suit and won, but it is anticipated that Hispanics ultimately will utilize this route of litigation more than any other group. Section 1983, which is not restricted to race, protects against state officials who "under color of any statute, ordinance, regulation, custom, or usage" deprive one of "rights, privileges, or immunities" (see discussion of Section 1983 in Chapter 8).[14,15] All these provisions—Sections 1981, 1982, and 1983—have the drawback that they may not be used in any federal employment cases involving discrimination.[16]

The Civil Rights Act of 1964 was a landmark in the effort to eliminate discrimination. That law established the Equal Employment Opportunity Commission (EEOC), and Title VII empowered the EEOC to prosecute cases of discrimination in private employment. The law also reaffirmed the policy of nondiscrimination in federal employment. In 1965 President Johnson issued Executive Order 11246 prohibiting discrimination involving federal contracts; the order also included a provision against discrimination in federal employment. It was amended in 1967 by Executive Order 11375, extending coverage to discrimination based on sex.

In 1969 President Nixon issued Executive Order 11478, "Equal Employment Opportunity in the Federal Government." Encouraged by Title VII and the executive orders, persons who claimed that they had been discriminated against in federal employment attempted to bring suit in federal courts but were turned away repeatedly. Courts held that such suits were precluded because Congress had not yielded sovereign immunity[17,18] (sovereign immunity is discussed in Chapter 8). A Catch-22 situation had arisen in that it was illegal for the federal government to discriminate and yet no one could sue the government for having done so (states also can raise the immunity defense in their own and federal courts).[19–21]

The situation was changed in 1972 by the Equal Employment Opportunity Act. This legislation extended coverage of Title VII to the federal, state, and local governments. The law protects against discrimination based on race, color, sex, religion, and national origin but not on age or handicap. Those legislative changes led to much controversy. Some complained that implementation of the law was ineffective, and state and local governments claimed that they were being subjected to conflicting pressures from various federal agencies pursuing equal opportunity.

Important changes in the federal government's approach were approved in 1978. First, President Carter's Reorganization Plan No. 1 reassigned equal employment responsibilities among federal agencies. Second, that plan was clarified in part by a series of executive orders. Third, the Civil Service Reform Act was passed, prohibiting discrimination based on "political affiliation, race, color, religion, national origin, sex, marital status, age, or handicapping condition." The important changes made by all these documents were intended to resolve many of the problems that had been evident since passage of the Equal Employment Opportunity Act of 1972.[22–24]

Before the reorganization, the process of handling discrimination complaints had involved equal employment opportunity (EEO) counselors in each agency, with appeals being directed to a review board of the then Civil Service Commission. This had produced many problems:

- EEO counselors often were located in their agency personnel offices, giving the impression that they were apologists or defenders of the agency rather than advocates of equal opportunity.

- EEO staff members were not sufficiently trained in personnel administration and therefore could not provide effective assistance in protecting against discrimination.
- Complainants often were not informed of their rights, such as having their names kept secret while the EEO staff investigated their complaints.

President Carter, in his reorganization message to Congress, said the Civil Service Commission had been "lethargic in enforcing fair employment."[25] The administrative process for investigating discrimination charges was shifted to the EEOC, with persons claiming discrimination retaining the right to appeal unfavorable decisions in court. This shift was supported on the grounds that the EEOC would be more assertive in guaranteeing equal opportunity and would not have mixed loyalties (i.e., support of equal opportunity versus support for agency personnel actions). The reorganization would provide for consistency in that the federal government would be brought under the same set of standards as was used by the EEOC in state and local cases.

One potential problem with the Carter plan was that it created two parallel investigation and hearing processes, one for discrimination cases and one for other personnel matters. For example, an African-American woman denied a promotion could appeal the decision through the process of the Merit Systems Protection Board (MSPB); she also could allege discrimination and seek redress through the EEOC.

The Civil Service Reform Act of 1978 provided a mechanism for dealing with this problem. Cases exclusively involving alleged discrimination may be appealed to the EEOC. In so-called mixed cases involving discrimination and an action that is subject to appeal before the MSPB (see Chapter 8), the appeal route is through the board and not the commission. Should the individual not be satisfied with the board's decision, the case may be carried to either a court of appeals or the EEOC. In the latter instance, the EEOC may concur in the board's decision or issue a different opinion if it thinks the board misinterpreted the law. If the commission and the board are in disagreement, the case is submitted to a special panel consisting of a representative from each agency and a chairperson appointed by the president with Senate approval. The chairperson serves a 6-year term and "may be removed by the president only for inefficiency, neglect of duty, or malfeasance." Decisions of the special panel may be appealed in court.[26]

The mandated appeals process has been criticized as being time consuming and overly rigid. In a 1976 case involving alleged racial discrimination in promotion decisions, the Supreme Court disallowed a Title VII suit simply because it had been filed 12 days too late.[27] That case is particularly important because the Court held that the 1972 legislation that extended Title VII to cover the federal government constituted the exclusive route for federal discrimination cases. In other words, if an individual fails to meet one of the prescribed deadlines in the process, the entire case will be lost.

Another issue concerning the appeals process has been the extent to which courts should review federal discrimination charges. If a trial de novo were required, then the court would hear all the evidence in the case as though it were new, whereas a more limited approach would involve simply reviewing the record. The argument against the de novo approach was that complainants would get the equivalent of two trials or chances to prove their cases: a formal hearing and then a full court trial. The argument in favor was that the administrative hearing could be biased and therefore a person should be granted a court trial. The Supreme Court resolved the issue in 1976, holding that a trial de novo was required.[28,29] The Civil Service Reform Act guarantees this right.

The Equal Employment Opportunity Act of 1972 also was extended to state and local governments. If a person feels discriminated against by a state or local government, he or she can complain to the EEOC, which will refer the case to an entity at that level such as a state human relations commission. If the matter is not resolved, the EEOC may initiate its own investigation. In the event the commission concludes that there is little grounds for complaint, it can close the case but also can issue a letter to the individual involved permitting the filing of a private civil suit in a federal court. If the EEOC concludes that there are grounds for a suit, it refers the case to the Justice Department with a recommendation to file suit.

The major criticisms of this process are that it is excessively cumbersome and that coordination among agencies often is lacking. A person who feels discriminated against is likely to be frustrated by the seemingly endless steps. State and local EEO agencies have been criticized for relying upon the EEOC to investigate; in defense, those agencies have claimed that they do not have sufficient staff to investigate such cases, although that problem has lessened because of federal financial assistance for that activity.

A disadvantage for processing individual discrimination complaints is that only one abuse may be resolved. A person who successfully alleges discrimination in a job interview or performance appraisal may be the only one who receives redress. Therefore, the extensive energy required to correct one case of discrimination may have a negligible overall impact. An alternative is to permit class action administrative proceedings and legal suits where large groups of persons allege discrimination.[30] This has been used, for example, by African-Americans claiming that a civil service test discriminated against them. The result can be a court order to halt the use of the test, thereby affecting many people.

Another alternative is for the government to file a "pattern or practice" case alleging that discrimination within a jurisdiction is widespread. These types of cases involve elaborate analyses of statistics used to demonstrate that women,

African-Americans, or other minorities have been the subject of systematic discrimination. When these cases involve private employers, they are the responsibility of the EEOC. When state and local governments are involved, however, the Justice Department has jurisdiction. Deciding how to divide limited legal resources in enforcing individual cases and pattern cases is a difficult problem. The EEOC has been criticized as devoting too many resources to high-profile individual cases at the expense of pattern cases that would redress the wrongs inflicted on many people.[31]

Beginning in 1986, the Supreme Court began a series of rulings that gave narrow interpretations to civil rights legislation and made challenges to employers' actions difficult to pursue in court. In response to these decisions and after much debate and conflict, Congress and President Bush were able to support passage of the Civil Rights Act of 1991.[32,33] The law amended the Civil Rights Acts of 1866 (Section 1981), the Civil Rights Act of 1964, and several other important laws. Section 1981 was amended to state that it protects against discrimination in regard not only to hiring but to basically all aspects of employment. Protections were extended to congressional employees and the personal staffs of state and local elected officials. The 1991 law allows courts to award punitive damages when plaintiffs win in addition to already existing compensatory damages, such as back pay. When these damages are being requested, a plaintiff is entitled to a jury trial; this provision is regarded as important because juries are thought to be more sympathetic than judges in these types of situations. The law established a Glass Ceiling Commission to study and recommend changes for situations that tend to prevent women and minorities from being promoted into higher-level positions.

The 1991 legislation contains several important provisions regarding the procedures used in discrimination cases; these provisions have the effect of overturning several Supreme Court decisions from the late 1980s. In presenting a case, a complainant has the burden of proof in showing that a disparate impact has occurred, namely that the employer's action has the effect of harming some groups and favoring others (e.g., the hiring process results in whites being hired and minorities being rejected).[34] The burden of proof then shifts to the employer to rebut the discrimination argument. Also, in so-called mixed motive cases, in which employers are found to have used both legitimate and discriminatory practices in the same situations, the employers are liable for damages.[35] The law restricts challenges to consent decrees, contrary to a Supreme Court decision that had allowed a challenge to a decree in which a public employer agreed to take corrective action involving long-term discrimination.[36]

Antidiscrimination legislation does not end with the Civil Rights Acts of 1964 and 1991 and the Equal Employment Opportunity Act of 1972. The Equal Pay Act of 1963 prohibits sex discrimination on pay; in 1974 that protection was extended to cover public employees.[37-39] Title IX of the Education Amendments of 1972 prohibits sex discrimination in institutions receiving federal aid, and the Supreme Court has ruled that the law covers employment discrimination.[40] The Court also ruled, however, that only that part of an institution affected by federal aid must meet the Title IX requirements.[41] In a case involving a private college, the Court held that only the financial aid program of the school had to comply with federal standards.[42] This decision was overturned by Congress through passage of the Civil Rights Restoration Act of 1987, which became law despite President Reagan's veto.[43] That law also amended laws pertaining to older and disabled workers and more generally amended the Civil Rights Act of 1964.

The Age Discrimination in Employment Act (ADEA) was passed in 1967 to cover private sector employees and was extended in 1974 to cover public employees.[44,45] The law protects persons beginning at age 40. Amendments in 1978 eliminated a compulsory retirement age for federal employees and in 1986 for most other public and private employees. Age discrimination in federal employment is handled by the EEOC and at the state and local levels by the U.S. Department of Labor.

Handicapped persons are protected under the Rehabilitation Act of 1973 and the Americans with Disabilities Act (ADA) of 1990.[46-49] The Supreme Court earlier held that only areas affected by federal aid must meet Rehabilitation Act requirements, but that decision was overturned by the Civil Rights Act of 1991.[50] The ADA is landmark legislation that protects disabled people in employment and mandates access to government services, access to public accommodations (theaters, shopping centers, etc.), and other areas. People with physical and mental impairments are covered, as are people who are regarded as impaired, such as people with diabetes, epilepsy, and cosmetic disfigurements. People with acquired immunodeficiency syndrome (AIDS) or those infected with the human immunodeficiency virus are protected, but transvestites and pedophiles are not. Drug users are not covered, but the law does treat as disabled people who are in or have completed drug rehabilitation programs.

The ADA provides several ground rules regarding employment.[51] Medical examinations may not be used before a job offer is made, although pre-employment drug testing is not regarded as a medical examination and may be permissible. People who are qualified for work may not be turned down because of their disabilities, and employers are required to make reasonable accommodations, such as modifying facilities, restructuring jobs, and providing readers for sight-impaired workers.[52] Reasonableness depends on such factors as the nature of the work, the cost of the accommodations, and the resources of the employer.

In addition to the legislation already cited, state and local governments are expected to meet antidiscrimination requirements imposed through federal grant and contract programs. Title VI of the Civil Rights Act prohibits discrimination by recipients of federal assistance, including state and local governments.[53] The Intergovernmental Personnel Act of 1970, administered by OPM, requires recipient agencies to have merit systems, including protection against discrimination. This brings OPM into oversight of state and local governments. An amendment requires that standards "minimize Federal intervention in State and local personnel administration."[54]

The Office of Federal Contract Compliance Programs (OFCCP) in the U.S. Department of Labor, as provided in Lyndon Johnson's Executive Order 11246 (1965) as amended, has the responsibility for enforcing equal opportunity involving federal contracts, including those with state and local governments.[55] Contract compliance enforcement had been decentralized among federal agencies, resulting in these agencies sometimes having overlapping powers and conflicting policies. This procedure was changed by Jimmy Carter's Executive Order 12086 (1978), which amended Executive Order 11246 to provide for direct administration by the OFCCP.

Confusion at the state and local levels sometimes results from these diverse pieces of legislation and the array of federal agencies involved. The EEOC is intended to serve in a leadership and coordination role in dealing with possible overlapping responsibilities of federal agencies. The Civil Service Reform Act, moreover, gives the EEOC responsibility for establishing guidelines for recruiting minorities and for determining where underrepresentation exists in the federal government. OPM is responsible for administering the minority recruitment program.

Besides all the federal protections against discrimination, state governments have antidiscrimination laws that apply both to themselves and to their local governments. Although these are similar to federal laws, specific provisions vary. It is possible to commit an act that does not violate federal law but does violate a state law; conversely, redress may be possible in federal court but not state court.[56,57] Although the legal protections against discrimination are extensive, some categories of people do not constitute protected groups. Homosexuals are generally not protected as a class, but an employer in most instances cannot deny someone employment simply because the person is Gay or Lesbian.[58,59] Obesity is not protected, and it is clear that many Americans are denied employment opportunities simply because they are overweight.[60] Employees with cancer or people recovering from cancer often face job discrimination and may have limited rights.[61] Religious institutions, such as churches and religious colleges and universities, may discriminate in employment based upon religious beliefs.[62,63]

DISCRIMINATION IN VARIOUS ASPECTS OF PERSONNEL ADMINISTRATION

Discrimination can occur in all aspects of personnel administration. This section considers discriminatory practices as they relate to selection, on-the-job activities, and terminations.

Selection and Discrimination

The concept of validity in the selection process of a jurisdiction is discussed in Chapter 5. A valid testing program is one that selects employees who will be superior workers and rejects less qualified ones. The concern here is that testing programs can have the effect of discriminating against some groups of individuals. Paper-and-pencil tests can discriminate against qualified applicants who are visually impaired; alternative techniques, such as the use of large print, Braille, cassette tapes, and readers, can alleviate this problem. A landmark case is *Griggs v. Duke Power Company* (1971), in which the Supreme Court rejected the requirements for a high school diploma and a satisfactory intelligence test score as conditions for employment.[64] Although no corporation intent to discriminate had been shown, the Court held that the diploma and IQ test requirements were discriminatory against African-Americans and were in violation of Title VII of the Civil Rights Act. The Court noted that these requirements had been imposed without examining their validity.

It should be recalled that the courts apply different approaches in reviewing charges of discrimination. They require the use of validity tests for civil service examinations in cases brought under Title VII but not necessarily under the Fifth and Fourteenth Amendments. In 1976, for example, the Supreme Court did not require a validity test of the examination used to select police academy recruits. Because the case was brought under the Fifth Amendment, the Court was satisfied that there was a relationship between test scores and performance in the police academy and did not insist on proof that the police examination was related to job performance.[65]

Since the *Griggs* decision, differential validity has become a major concern.[66–68] The purpose of differential validity tests is to determine whether the selection process varies in its effects on selected groups. For example, a test might be valid for both men and women but to differing degrees; a test score of 90 could correlate more strongly or more weakly with job performance for men than for women. The procedures involved in differential validity are complex and have been difficult to apply for lack of adequate numbers of test scores for subgroups.

The differential validity concept led to the practice of race norming, in which employers used different cutoff scores for different groups. In the selection process, the top three minority candidates might be considered along with the top three scorers on the test, even though the minority candidates' scores were substantially lower. The Civil Rights Act of 1991 specifically prohibits the use of norming in regard to "race, color, religion, sex, or national origin."

The governing regulation pertaining to validity in both private and public employment is the "Uniform Guidelines on Employee Selection Procedures."[69,70] Adopted in 1978, the guidelines were developed jointly by the EEOC, the Civil Rights Commission, the then Civil Service Commission (now OPM), and the

Department of Justice and the Department of Labor. The guidelines allow for the use of content, construct, and criterion validity. The guidelines were particularly useful in resolving differences among federal agencies in their approaches to selection procedures.

The "bottom-line" approach to selection was adopted as part of the guidelines. Employers had complained that they were expected to undertake expensive validation studies of each component of their selection process when that process as a whole—the bottom line—had no adverse impact. The written test portion might have an adverse impact, but that was compensated for by other portions of the testing and selection program. In adopting the bottom-line principle, the participating federal agencies agreed not to prosecute such employers but said they would prosecute in cases where the bottom line was an adverse impact.

Although federal agencies have used the bottom-line approach, federal courts have used a different one. In *Connecticut v. Teal* (1982), the Supreme Court dealt with Connecticut's multihurdle testing program for promotions to welfare supervisory positions.[71] Minorities challenged the procedures, using Title VII of the Civil Rights Act of 1964, in that 80 percent of whites passed the written examination but only 54 percent of African-Americans did so. Connecticut used a bottom-line defense, arguing that, regardless of written test results, the overall testing program was not discriminatory; only 14 percent of the whites received promotions compared with 23 percent of the African-Americans. The Supreme Court ruled five to four that individual portions of a testing program could be challenged, even though the bottom line did not evidence any discrimination.

In state and local cases involving testing programs, the normal procedure is for the federal government to establish before a court a prima facie case of discrimination. This means that, at least on the face of the matter, the testing program appears to discriminate. The prima facie situation is shown by reviewing the composition of the jurisdiction's personnel and particularly the extent to which the examination process screens out some groups more than others. The "Uniform Guidelines" define an adverse impact as one in which the selection rate for a group is below 80 percent of the rate of the highest group. The jurisdiction then has the burden of showing that the test program is valid. In "pattern or practice" suits (discussed earlier), the jurisdiction might show that a disproportionately low percentage of African-Americans was not the result of the selection process but rather stemmed from discriminatory practices before 1972, when local governments were not subject to Title VII.[72]

In addition to paper-and-pencil tests, other aspects of testing can be discriminatory. For example, physical fitness or agility tests used for firefighters and police officers often emphasize anaerobic abilities (strength and speed), in which men excel, and downplay aerobic qualities (stamina), in which women excel. Despite these problems, such tests are used widely, have been validated, and have been upheld by the courts.[73,74]

Experience and educational requirements also create problems. Requiring 5 years of experience in addition to an apprenticeship to qualify for a city bricklayer job has been held to be discriminatory.[75] Requiring an excessive educational background can be discriminatory, although courts have allowed the use of educational standards, such as requiring a high school education for police and corrections officers and requiring forty-five semester credits of college studies with at least a C average for police officers.[76,77] Background investigations need to have explicit standards so that they cannot be used for discriminatory purposes.[78] Establishing criteria for professional positions is especially difficult in that some subjectivity often is appropriate; for example, there is no objective means for determining which of three candidates for a supervisory position is best qualified. Yet such subjectivity opens the door to discrimination charges.

Height and weight requirements constitute a particularly sensitive issue in that they tend to have an adverse effect on women and some racial and ethnic groups. The height and weight issue was brought before the Supreme Court in *Dothard v. Rawlinson* (1977), involving correctional officer jobs in Alabama penitentiaries.[79] A woman had been unable to qualify because of the minimum weight requirement of 120 pounds; the state also had a minimum height requirement of 5 feet 2 inches. The Court held that the practice was discriminatory in that the combined height and weight requirement would exclude 40 percent of all adult women and only 1 percent of adult men. Alabama was unable to show that the requirements were job related, and the court suggested that if physical strength was required then a strength test should be used rather than height and weight requirements.

The Court, however, went on to base its decision on another aspect of the Civil Rights Act, namely the bona fide occupational qualification, or "bfoq." Alabama not only had a height and weight requirement but specifically disqualified women from holding correctional officer positions in male prisons. The law permits discrimination where a bfoq exists. The court decided that such discrimination was appropriate, given the nature of the prisons. Sex offenders were part of the prison population. The prisoners routinely were required to remove all their clothing for searches. Bathroom facilities provided no privacy. In the words of the Court, "The environment in Alabama's penitentiaries is a peculiarly inhospitable one for human beings of whatever sex." Therefore, the bfoq requirement was met, limiting hiring to men. Gender was held not to be a bfoq in another Supreme Court case in which an employer prohibited most women from jobs involving lead exposure; for a woman to be appointed to one of these jobs, she had to provide medically documented evidence that she was infertile.[80,81] The Court held this practice to be discriminatory.

Another illustration of the bfoq standard involves age. In one case, a city refused to consider applicants for security guard positions who were 40 or older.

The city contended that age was a bfoq in that guards needed to be in good physical condition. A district court held that this was not a bfoq because the city allowed guards who reached the age of 41 to remain on their jobs. The city could not claim that guards needed to be relatively young and at the same time allow its guards to remain on the job past 40.[82–84]

Veterans preference is an aspect of personnel administration that frequently is criticized as negatively affecting women. All levels of government provide advantages to veterans in personnel testing programs.[85,86] Because most veterans are men, women have claimed that they are being denied equal protection under the law.

In attacking veterans preference, critics have held that, although there is no right to a public job, government has a responsibility to treat people equally once a job is created. The defense is that preference is due veterans, who risked their lives in defending the country, and that women are eligible for the same preference as men. The Supreme Court dealt with the issue in *Personnel Administrator of Massachusetts v. Feeney* (1979).[87] In that case, a state law required that veterans who passed a civil service test had to be considered for appointment before nonveterans. Women challenged this procedure because men with much lower scores who were veterans were being appointed before women. The Court upheld the process, failing to find it discriminatory.

Being Gay or Lesbian may be grounds for being passed over for a position. School boards sometimes contend that a homosexual teacher is an unfit role model for impressionable pupils. Military recruiters, until President Clinton came into office in 1993, routinely asked prospective recruits about their sexual preferences. The Clinton administration vowed to open the military to Gays and Lesbians and not to use sexual preference as a condition for employment or as a basis for dismissal. The administration's view was that Gays and Lesbians already were serving in the military, albeit in the closet, and that they were as effective as other personnel. Of course, both so-called straights and Gays are expected to avoid sexual behavior during duty hours. Critics of the Clinton administration proposal contended that the lack of personal privacy common in military life and the close quarters in which people often work, such as aboard naval vessels, require that personnel not be homosexual.[88]

Citizenship frequently has been imposed as a condition of employment. In 1973 the Supreme Court held that New York State's requirement that only citizens could qualify for permanent positions violated the equal protection clause of the Fourteenth Amendment.[89] The state law was held to "sweep indiscriminately" without evidence of any "substantial state interest." From 1973, therefore, state and local governments were precluded from such discrimination, but the U.S. Civil Service Commission continued to enforce its regulation against hiring aliens for permanent federal positions. Federal prohibitions against hiring aliens were brought before the Supreme Court in 1976 in *Hampton v. Wong.*[90] In a five-to-four decision, the Court ruled against the commission and pointed to the need to avoid a double standard for federal jobs in comparison with state and local jobs. It held that no "overriding national interest" had been shown to warrant discriminating against aliens. The Court's decision, however, was nullified by President Ford, who issued Executive Order 11935, prohibiting hiring aliens as being in the national interest and thereby continuing a double standard between the levels of government.

In 1978 the Supreme Court seemed to reverse partially its earlier position prohibiting discrimination against aliens in state and local employment (*Foley v. Connelie*).[91] The Court held that the equal protection clause did not prevent New York State from barring aliens from its police force. The Court said that policymaking was considered the exclusive responsibility of citizens and that police officers had a policymaking function in that they exercised discretion in law enforcement. In subsequent cases, the Court has upheld citizenship requirements for school teachers and probation officers.[92,93]

A related issue is state and local governments' preference in hiring their own residents for public jobs and for private ones supported partly or entirely with public monies. Sometimes applicants must have been residents for as much as 3 years to be eligible for appointment. Although the Supreme Court has not ruled on such provisions, it has upheld state and local preference for residents in government contracting.[94]

One other subject of controversy in the selection process has been the rule of three (see Chapter 5). That practice can have a negative effect on hiring minorities and women if they tend to score lower than others on civil service examinations, and when veterans receive added preference points they often do score lower. The EEOC has encouraged state and local governments to expand the rule of three or perhaps to select three candidates at random among all persons passing an examination. That practice would increase the chances of selecting minorities and women.

Oral examinations and job interviews are fraught with discrimination problems. Women often are less outspoken or assertive than men, placing the women in a double bind.[95] On the one hand, they may be regarded as weaker candidates because of being less assertive, and if they are assertive they can be discriminated against as being aggressive or threatening. In job interviews, employers are expected to ask only job-related questions, but this requirement often is neglected, with employers asking whether a woman is married, what her husband does for a living, how many children she has, and how the children will be cared for if she is offered a position.

Employers must exercise caution not only in the selection of workers but in their initial job placement. For instance, in hiring men and women analysts, the employer must avoid systematically placing either group in positions that are likely to lead to advancement at the expense of the other group.[96]

Discrimination on the Job

Discrimination does not end with the selection process. Once on the job, a person may be subjected to numerous discriminatory practices. Some of these are blatant. St. Louis fire stations, for instance, once had supper clubs where white firefighters cooked their meals but excluded African-American coworkers.[97] Other practices are somewhat more subtle, such as passing over older workers or Hispanics for training opportunities. Minority workers can be alienated when the majority of employees largely ignore them. An employee may be typecast as the bureau's African-American or the bureau's official woman. Agency clients sometimes encourage this typecasting; for example, African-American clients may openly expect more favorable treatment from an African-American employee than from a white one.

Performance appraisal and promotion practices are subject to discriminatory abuses. Some administrators responsible for rating employees undoubtedly take into account, positively or negatively, the sex or race of an individual, but trying to prove such discrimination is difficult. Promotion decisions easily can be used to discriminate against older workers or women.[98,99] A woman may be passed over for promotion, with the job being given to a man, yet there is nothing in writing to suggest that sex was the basis for the decision.

Proving discrimination thus is difficult because the mere appointment of a man to a vacant position does not by itself show discrimination based on sex. In individual discrimination cases, the aggrieved employee attempts to show that others of less qualification were promoted and that a practice has emerged blocking further promotions for this person. The Supreme Court has allowed for use of disparate impact analysis in such cases, whereby the plaintiff presents a prima facie case of discrimination by presenting statistical data pertaining to a group of workers, such as data showing that a large percentage of whites but only a small percentage of African-Americans are being promoted.[100] In investigating individual cases, the EEOC has extensive access to records and other forms of information. In the case of a woman faculty member at the University of Pennsylvania claiming that she had been discriminated against in a tenure decision, the Supreme Court held that the EEOC had access to her file, the files of five men who had been granted tenure, and materials that the university considered highly confidential, such as evaluation letters and deliberative records kept by the faculty committees that reviewed the tenure cases.[101,102]

Sexual harassment, another forbidden form of discrimination, is defined as "unwelcome sexual advances, requests for sexual favors, and other verbal or physical conduct of a sexual nature" that influences the work environment.[103–106] Harassment can include sexual compliments or personal inquiries, leering, notes in desks or on bulletin boards, and physical behavior such as blocking one's passage. "The behavior (with the exception of sexual assault) is 1) repetitive,

2) one-sided, 3) unwelcome, 4) involves power (or intimidation) and 5) the victim cannot get the offender to stop."[107] Power typically is involved in that an employee attempts to force a relationship on another.[108] Women are the usual victims of sexual harassment, but men also experience such pressures.

The Supreme Court for the first time dealt with sexual harassment in 1986 in *Meritor Savings Bank v. Vinson.*[109,110] Not only did it uphold the concept that harassment is a form of sexual discrimination, but it further ruled that harassment is not limited to "economic" or "tangible" matters. A victim does not have to show that pay or job was threatened but only that a "hostile environment" exists, such as sexually derogatory language being used frequently, posters of nudes being prominently displayed in offices, and the like. Controlling sexist speech, such as men referring to women's breast sizes, poses problems in First Amendment rights that guarantee free speech.[111] Employers can be held responsible for the behavior of their employees on the grounds that they knew or should have known that workers were being harassed sexually. It is imperative that employers establish work environments where everyone understands that sexual harassment is not tolerated.

The subject of sexual harassment has gained increased attention since events of 1991 and 1992. In 1991, the nation was caught up in the testimony of Anita F. Hill in the Senate confirmation hearings for Clarence Thomas as Associate Justice of the Supreme Court. She alleged that Thomas had sexually harassed her while he headed the EEOC.[112] The following year, the Navy faced a scandal in which male officers apparently sexually assaulted and harassed female officers at the Tailhook convention, an annual event for naval aviators; Navy Secretary Lawrence Garrett was forced to resign over how he handled or failed to handle the situation.[113]

An emerging issue is whether courts will adopt the "reasonable woman" standard in harassment cases involving women. The problem stems from the fact that people look on behavior in different ways and what may seem acceptable to one person is highly objectionable to another. According to a federal district court, a male bias tends to exist when a "reasonable person" standard is used, and what may be reasonable for most men is not necessarily reasonable for most women.[114,115] Under the reasonable woman standard, an employer could be liable for sexual harassment resulting from coworkers and supervisors making well-intentioned compliments to an offended woman.

Not only may employees file sexual harassment charges, but so can clients in some situations; the Supreme Court has held that a high school student could sue her school district for the sexual harassment inflicted by a coach-teacher.[116] The case was filed under Title IX of the Education Amendments of 1972 mentioned earlier.

Equal pay for equal work has been a major issue. Cases have arisen over differing pay rates for different shifts (days, evenings, and nights) and over pay increments for some workers for no additional work.[117] The Equal Pay Act, as noted earlier, prohibits pay discrimination based on sex, and Title VII of the Civil Rights Act provides broad protection against sex discrimination.[118] Until 1981 pay discrimination cases were difficult to prove because courts insisted that individuals show that their pay was below that of someone of the opposite sex performing identical work. In *County of Washington v. Gunther* (1981), however, the Supreme Court held that Title VII cases were permissible in situations involving similar but not equal jobs.[119] In the Washington County case, male prison guards were paid more than women guards, but male guards supervised more prisoners, and female guards had some clerical duties that male guards did not.

An idea that is relatively simple is shaking the job markets in both the public and private sectors: Employees should be paid according to what they contribute in work to an organization. This is known as "comparable worth" or "pay equity."[120-123] The issue of discrimination is involved in that women dominate some occupations in which pay is lower than in other fields. In government, women are dominant as clerical workers, teachers, librarians, social workers, and nurses, to name just a few fields. The contention is that analysis of what these workers contribute to an agency will show they are greatly underpaid in comparison with occupations dominated by men, such as carpentry, truck driving, and the like. A stark reality is that, at all levels of government and in the private sector, women simply are paid less than men. Proponents of comparable worth contend that this imbalance is inequitable and a form of discrimination, and opponents argue that the differences are a result of career choices and market demands. Critics suggest that women could earn as much as men if they chose more lucrative occupations.

The question of what constitutes pay equity raises many of the same issues discussed earlier in regard to position classification; namely, what criteria should be used in examining positions, and what ranges should be set for those criteria? Pay equity studies, whether done in house by a government or conducted through a consulting firm, usually involve criteria such as knowledge, problem solving, and responsibility, with a rating scale being established for each. As with the Factor Evaluation System (see Chapter 3), a total number of points is assigned to each job with the understanding that higher-rated jobs should receive higher pay. Any error in procedure can substantially thwart efforts to establish equity. The potential for error is particularly great in crossing occupational lines, as in comparing laboratory technicians with groundskeepers.[124-126]

National attention focused on Washington State, the scene of a protracted legal battle over comparable worth. In 1983, the American Federation of State, County, and Municipal Employees (AFSCME), a union affiliated with the American Federation of Labor–Congress of Industrial Organizations successfully sued the state in U.S. district court on the grounds of sex discrimination covered by Title VII of the Civil Rights Act of 1964.[127] Of significance legally was that the district court ruled that Title VII in its existing form guaranteed comparable worth. The case was appealed and eventually reversed by a circuit court, which held that the state had a right to base compensation rates on a competitive labor market. If secretaries in the private sector generally were paid less than other workers, then Washington could pay secretaries less.[128] The EEOC and the U.S. Department of Justice maintained that Title VII in its current form did not guarantee comparable worth.

Although the concept of comparable worth experienced a legal setback in the Washington State case, significant progress was made. The state reached an agreement with AFSCME and began systematically upgrading salaries in occupational groupings dominated by women.[129] Several states and cities launched comprehensive job evaluation projects that would compare all jobs in all occupations in an effort to identify and correct pay inequities in their personnel systems. Minnesota, for instance, not only passed legislation mandating comparable worth for state government but followed up with similar legislation for local governments. Michigan, another example, established what it called an Equitable Classification Plan. By the early 1990s, the topic of comparable worth was receiving less nationwide attention. Left unanswered was whether pay inequities were being corrected.

At the national level, efforts to adopt legislation requiring pay equity of all employers have been unsuccessful. Neither the Reagan nor the Bush administration was supportive of the idea, preferring to have the labor market determine compensation levels. OPM's director, Constance Horner, said in 1986 that any inequities that existed would be largely resolved in time as women had greater opportunities and expectations.[130] If pay equity were mandated by federal law, sweeping changes clearly would cost billions of dollars. Employers, both public and private, dislike the costs involved, but proponents argue that costs should not be a deterrent in treating employees fairly.

Various other aspects of daily work can lead to charges of discrimination. Workers may wish to wear religious garb that is not part of an approved uniform, such as a police officer's uniform, or that more generally violates a dress code. Some people's religious beliefs may lead them to ask for leave far beyond what is provided workers; the Supreme Court has held on this matter that a reasonable accommodation is to allow leave but without pay.[131,132] Language can create problems. Does an employee wish to be referred to as Black or as an African-American? A person undergoing psychological treatment may object to office use of the word *crazy*, and native Americans may object to remarks about people being like "wild Indians."

Employee benefits are another area of discrimination. In *Frontiero v. Richardson* (1973), the Supreme Court dealt with medical benefits and housing allowances available to Air Force officers.[133] Although men automatically were granted these benefits, married women were required to show that they provided more than half the financial support in their marriages. The Court ruled that this violated the due process clause of the Fifth Amendment.

One of the most controversial benefit issues is whether government should cover pregnancy expenses. The subject is particularly important for several reasons. The topic has the potential of affecting most women because it is estimated that 85 percent of employed women are likely to become pregnant while employed.[134] Many women are single parents and need to retain their positions and benefits; other women are members of dual-income families that depend on their continued employment and benefits. Before 1978, the Supreme Court had ruled that employers could not arbitrarily require pregnant women to take extended unpaid leaves of absence before and after delivery. It also had held that employers were not necessarily required to provide medical benefits for pregnancies even though other elective procedures (cosmetic surgery and vasectomies) were covered.[135–137]

The 1978 Pregnancy Discrimination Act changed the situation: "Women affected by pregnancy, childbirth, or related medical conditions shall be treated the same for all employment-related purposes, including receipt of benefits under fringe benefit programs, as other persons not so affected but similar in their ability or inability to work."[138] Using this law, the Supreme Court has ruled that it is discriminatory for an employer to provide pregnancy benefits to female employees but not to spouses of male employees.[139]

The Court also has reviewed whether a state can require greater protections for pregnant workers than required by federal law. A California law was challenged for requiring employers to provide extended maternity leave for women after childbirth and later to reinstate the women in the same or comparable jobs. The Court ruled that such laws are permissible, adding that states may require protection beyond minimum levels set by federal law.[140]

Pregnancy also is protected in the private sector with regard to retirement benefits. The Retirement Equity Act of 1984, which amended the Employee Retirement Income Security Act (see Chapter 4), holds that retirement systems cannot penalize persons for leaves of absence associated with pregnancy, childbirth, care for a child after birth, and adoption.[141] The law does not apply to public employers.

According to the Older Workers Benefit Protection Act of 1990, older workers are protected regarding retirement plans; namely, these plans may not discriminate against some workers based on their age. The law was passed to overturn a Supreme Court ruling that held that challenges to retirement plans under the ADEA could be made only if discrimination existed in some other aspect of employment.[142,143]

More generally, retirement benefits for men and women have been a major area of controversy. The problem stems from the simple fact that women live longer than men. If the same dollar retirement benefits are paid each month to men and women, women on the average will receive greater total benefits in their lifetimes. In response, some jurisdictions required female employees to make greater contributions to the retirement system, but in 1978 the Supreme Court found this practice to violate Title VII of the Civil Rights Act.[144] The Court also has ruled that retirement programs that give lower monthly benefits to women than to men are discriminatory.[145,146]

Terminations and Discrimination

Discrimination complaints in terminations have involved dismissals, compulsory retirements, and layoffs. Dismissal cases have involved mental illness, religious beliefs, and homosexuality. For example, what protection from dismissal does an employee have who becomes partially disabled through mental illness? One case involved a female U.S. Treasury Department employee who was dismissed because she became "hysterical, throwing currency in the air, intermittently sobbing and laughing unnaturally." The department had assisted the employee in obtaining psychiatric help, but the court left undecided whether the department had made "every reasonable effort" to retain the employee.[147]

In 1977 the Supreme Court dealt with whether a collective bargaining agreement providing for seniority had a religious discriminatory effect (*Trans World Airlines v. Hardison*).[148,149] According to a union contract with Trans World Airlines, the most senior employees had first choice of job and shift assignments. As a result, an employee with little seniority was required to work on Saturday even though that was the Sabbath for him. The union insisted that the company abide by the labor contract requiring junior employees to accept whatever shift was available, and the company refused to allow the employee to work only a 4-day week (that is, the regular 2 days off plus Saturday). The employee was dismissed and sued on the grounds of religious discrimination under Title VII of the Civil Rights Act. The Court ruled that the dismissal had not been discriminatory: "Absent a discriminatory purpose, the operation of a seniority system cannot be an unlawful employment practice even if the system has some discriminatory consequences." The Court reasoned that, had the airline made special arrangements for this employee, the action would have discriminated against all other employees.

Estate of Thornton v. Caldor (1985) posed a different religious discrimination question for the Supreme Court: Is it permissible for a state to prohibit employers from forcing their workers to work on their Sabbath?[150] Connecticut had passed such a law, giving Sabbath observers an "absolute and unqualified right" not to work. The Court decided that the law violated the constitutional provision against the establishment of religion. In 1987, the Court held that persons dismissed for refusing to work on their Sabbath were entitled to unemployment compensation, which usually is provided only to those who lose their jobs through no fault of their own.[151]

Other cases have dealt with motherhood and drug addiction. The Supreme Court has ruled that airlines may not routinely ground flight attendants when they become mothers; similar practices by public employers would be prohibited.[152] At the same time, it is permissible to dismiss transit workers when they are discovered to be on methadone for treatment of drug addiction; public safety is the rationale for such termination.[153]

Homosexuals generally cannot be dismissed or denied employment for their homosexuality per se but may be removed when it adversely affects their work.[154,155] One major exception has been the military, where simply being Gay or Lesbian was grounds for dismissal.[156,157] Another exception is the Central Intelligence Agency, where homosexuals may be dismissed on the grounds that they are security risks (i.e., that they might be subject to blackmail were someone to learn of their sexual orientation).[158,159] The logic here is difficult to follow: If a person is known to be a homosexual, what opportunity exists for blackmailing him or her?

The judicial system has been divided over the extent to which such an employee may publicly express support for homosexuality. On the one hand, courts have recognized this as public speech protected by the First Amendment; on the other hand, courts have held that employees do not have the right to flaunt their homosexuality. The issue was brought before the Supreme Court in 1985; the justices were divided evenly (four to four), which had the effect of upholding the lower court's ruling.[160] That court had decided against an Oklahoma law that allowed school boards to fire teachers for advocating or promoting homosexuality. In instances of overt acts of homosexuality, the courts have required proof that those acts reduced the employee's work performance.

Some of the most difficult situations have involved school teachers who were homosexuals but who did not promote homosexuality. The concern has been that a homosexual teacher provides an inappropriate model for impressionable children. Homosexuals, however, have contended that their homosexuality does not interfere with their teaching performance.

For example, when school authorities learned that an eighth-grade teacher was a homosexual, he was transferred from a classroom position to a nonteaching job. At that point, he made public his homosexuality, and the school district dismissed him. A lower federal court decision, which was not overturned by the Supreme Court, held that a "homosexual teacher need not become a recluse, nor need he lie about himself."[161] The decision said, however, "discretion and self-restraint" should be exercised in speaking in support of homosexuality. The conclusion was that the school board had acted properly in dismissing the teacher because he had failed to exercise such self-restraint.

Even more controversial was the case of a school teacher who was dismissed for being a homosexual and who had not publicized his homosexuality. He had not performed overt homosexual acts and had been an outstanding teacher for a dozen years, yet he was dismissed when it was learned that he was a homosexual. A state court held that he was immoral, which impaired his teaching ability. The Supreme Court declined to hear the case, letting his dismissal stand.[162]

Age discrimination is prohibited, but mandatory retirement based on age was permissible until the latter part of the 1980s. Federal law generally had limited compulsory retirement to age 65 or above until 1978, when the ceiling was raised to 70. That limit applied to state and local governments and private employers, but there was no compulsory retirement age for most federal employees.[163,164] In 1986, Congress amended the ADEA to eliminate the ceiling. Employees who choose not to retire can be forced to do so if it can be shown that they are not meeting the duties of their positions. The results of an individual physical fitness examination can be used to force the retirement of any worker in government or industry.[165] People elected to office and appointed to policymaking positions are not protected by the ADEA and may be forced to retire.[166,167]

Mandatory retirement before age 70 is permissible in some cases. If a retirement plan requiring early out was in effect before the ADEA was adopted, the plan may continue.[168] Otherwise, according to the Supreme Court, a bona fide occupational qualification (bfoq) must be established linking age with satisfactory job performance.[169] To use a compulsory retirement age below 70, an employer must show "it is highly impractical for the employer to insure by individual testing that its employees will have the necessary qualifications for the job."[170] Many court cases have involved early retirement ages for police officers and firefighters. Courts sometimes have accepted these age limits on the grounds that physical examinations would not necessarily detect potential health problems such as coronary heart disease.[171,172]

A remedy for unfounded forced retirement is the use of front pay, "generally defined as an award of prospective damages measured from the date a judgment is entered to the date of natural retirement."[173] Rather than the individual obtaining a court order for reinstatement in a position, the individual is awarded the pay that would have been earned had the person remained on the job until "natural retirement" at age 70. The advantage of front pay is that the worker who wins in court is not expected to return to a hostile work environment.

Sex discrimination in terminations is another issue. Military officers are required to advance in rank or resign their commissions. Should male and female officers have the same time period to gain promotions before being discharged? That issue was brought to the Supreme Court when a male naval officer claimed discrimination in that he was discharged after 9 years of service, having been passed over twice for promotion, while female officers were allowed 13 years before being removed.[174] The Court ruled that the Navy's up-or-out policy did not discriminate in that men and women performed different functions and that women needed a longer period of time to demonstrate their abilities and earn promotions.

Seniority systems, although deemed acceptable by the Civil Rights Act, can operate against efforts to eliminate discrimination. "Last hired, first fired" is a familiar slogan describing the plight of minorities. Because of discrimination, minorities often have been among the last to be hired, which gives them the least seniority; the result is that when layoffs occur, they are the first to go. EEO and affirmative action efforts have been directed toward increasing minority and female employment, but when a jurisdiction has seniority rules (often embedded in collective bargaining agreements) and layoffs are necessary, then those efforts can be negated. Labor unions seek to protect their members and prefer to use seniority in layoffs, but such a stance gives the appearance of supporting discrimination. The Supreme Court has ruled that courts may not mandate that race be taken into account during a reduction in force if a bona fide seniority system is in effect.[175]

AFFIRMATIVE ACTION

Administrative and judicial actions against discriminatory practices may affect only one individual, a group, or hundreds of people. Persons who prove discrimination against themselves in terms of pay might only win a court order correcting the situation. In other cases, the court decision might be broader in scope, requiring a revision of the jurisdiction's pay practices or ruling that a jurisdiction no longer may use a given civil service examination, thereby affecting a large number of persons.

Some collective relief is retroactive. The Supreme Court held in 1975 that back pay can be used as a remedy for compensating for discrimination.[176] Persons paid less than others because of discrimination can receive financial compensation back to the effective date of the Civil Rights Act of 1964. The Supreme Court has held that retroactive retirement benefits are permissible where employees have been discriminated against and that such orders for retroactive benefits may be imposed upon state and local governments.[177]

The previous section described how layoffs based on seniority work against efforts to increase the number of minorities and women in government. One factor that can alleviate this problem is the granting of retroactive seniority. The Supreme Court has held that in cases where discrimination has been proved, African-Americans may receive seniority back to the date when they applied for a position.[178,179] If they are granted retroactive seniority, minorities and women are not necessarily the most junior employees and need not be the first to be laid off.

Collective relief includes not only measures to eliminate discrimination but also positive actions to increase minority and female employment in government. The objective is to have the public bureaucracy reflect the composition of the general population. This objective of a representative bureaucracy is one of the merit principles in the Civil Service Reform Act of 1978.[180] Positive actions in hiring minorities and women result from court orders and from actions by governmental employers. Affirmative action is defined as "those actions appropriate to overcome the effects of past or present practices, policies, or other barriers to equal employment opportunity."[181]

As with antidiscrimination efforts, responsibility for affirmative action is divided among organizations.[182–185] OPM has regulations on "Affirmative Employment Programs" applying to federal agencies. The EEOC has regulations on "Affirmative Action Appropriate under Title VII" applying to all employers and regulations on EEO in the federal government.[186–188] State and local governments also must comply with regulations of other federal agencies that provide funds to such governments as well as meet standards in state laws.

All governments prepare affirmative action plans. In the federal government, each agency is responsible for developing an agencywide and regional plan. State and local governments, in addition to preparing such plans, must report annually to the EEOC on the characteristics of their employees, and a sample of smaller jurisdictions is selected each year for reporting information about their employees.

Although EEO or affirmative action plans vary in format among jurisdictions, they have a common overall design. They begin with a policy statement supporting affirmative action and proceed to identify existing problems. Characteristics of the jurisdiction's work force by occupation are compared with those of the immediate labor market. In the terms of the EEOC, the analysis looks for instances of underrepresentation, manifest imbalance, or conspicuous absence of protected groups.[189] A problem would be identified if the agency's clerical staff were almost exclusively white when private sector clerical personnel included large numbers of nonwhites and Hispanics. Once problem areas are determined, the plan attempts to identify the causes of racial imbalance. All aspects of the personnel system are considered, such as whether the testing program is screening out minorities or whether the performance appraisal process serves as a barrier to women seeking promotions. Exit interviews conducted when employees resign can help determine why minorities and women quit.

The methods used to implement affirmative action focus on recruiting persons who have been underrepresented and then working to keep them in government and helping them develop careers. Recruiting literature is directed at minorities and women. Outreach recruiting is used, such as having recruiters visit colleges and universities whose student bodies are predominantly nonwhite or female.

Recruiters meet with community groups whose members are largely African-American, Asian, Hispanic, or female.[190]

Testing and selection procedures may be adjusted, such as by replacing the rule of three with the rule of the top 25 percent of the list. Minority recruits sometimes are tutored before they take a civil service examination. Selective placement may be used, as in the case of the physically handicapped or mentally retarded; the requirement for passing the civil service test may be waived, allowing such persons to prove themselves on the job on a provisional basis. Mentors may be used to help in efforts to retain individuals. Affirmative action plans, however, are expected to provide for selecting only qualified candidates for positions.

Differences exist among the targeted groups for EEO recruitment, although the danger of stereotyping individuals should be stressed. A barrier in recruiting women, especially those of middle age, may be their reluctance to seek employment after not having worked for some years. Women also must overcome previous assumptions that their proper role is that of mother and homemaker and early socialization that taught them to defer to men rather than being more assertive.

Women with school-age children face the additional problem of being expected to work from 8 A.M. to 5 P.M. yet feeling that they should be home when their children return from school in the afternoon. To reduce this problem in federal employment, Congress in 1978 passed the Federal Employees Part-Time Career Employment Act, which requires agencies to establish part-time positions rather than rely almost exclusively on full-time employees and permits workers to share full-time positions.[191,192] It also authorized flexitime (see Chapter 11).

Other factors may be that African-Americans and Hispanics may have limited skills and education, which reduces their usefulness in jobs; that Hispanics often have difficulty with English; and that facilities pose problems, such as the absence of restrooms for women at military installations and the lack of wheelchair ramps and elevators for the physically handicapped.

Once minorities and women are recruited into government, affirmative action efforts concentrate on developing careers for them. This often is called upward mobility. Such efforts include career counseling aimed at making employees aware of promotion opportunities, inventorying their skills, and devising individualized plans for training to allow them to qualify for higher-level positions. Training can be directed at supervisors and managers to help break down any privately held prejudices against minorities and women.

Job restructuring is used to reduce promotion barriers.[193] As discussed in Chapter 3, position classification systems often include many deadend jobs. One aspect of restructuring is eliminating or reducing unwarranted education and experience requirements so that a greater number of persons can qualify for positions. Restructuring includes redesigning the work done in given positions to provide opportunities for workers to learn skills for higher-level jobs. A critical aspect of restructuring is providing bridges that enable employees to move from one job series to another. Clerical workers might be exposed to work that would allow them to qualify for technician positions, and, with additional training, the technicians could qualify for professional positions.

Restructuring of positions is used for the physically handicapped. Clerical positions can be adjusted to accommodate the blind, such as having them act as public receptionists and answer telephone inquiries. Work is redistributed among employees, with the handicapped person working equally hard as other workers. Deaf persons may be particularly well suited to working in noisy facilities, such as in a printing pressroom.

Problems abound with job restructuring. The traditions associated with position classification tend to discourage broad-based job classifications that would allow for greater career opportunities. Any restructuring may be viewed with skepticism by those holding the positions. Will the change threaten the employee's security, and is the job redesign merely a disguise for attempting to get more work out of the employee with no increase in pay? There necessarily are limits on such an approach. Unbridled restructuring can result in widespread upward reclassification of positions, so that there are more generals and colonels than corporals and privates (or their civilian equivalents).

EEO is not the sole purpose of upward mobility. That effort is intended to provide career opportunities for all employees, whereas affirmative action concentrates on minorities and women. Upward mobility often is handled by administrative units largely independent of affirmative action units, which can result in limited coordination between the two programs. Upward mobility programs may have the effect of helping white men as much as women and minorities, so that the latter see no appreciable improvement in their relative status in government.

One of the most controversial issues associated with affirmative action efforts involves the use of goals and quotas in hiring. Goals commonly refer to targets or objectives, such as increasing the number of nonwhites by X percent in a given group of government jobs within a specified number of years. Quotas, in contrast, establish requirements for filling positions based on race, sex, or ethnicity, with a percentage of all new appointments being designated for these groups.

Proponents contend that real change will result only when quotas are used to force that change. If only goals are used, administrators will find reasons why minorities and women could not be hired, so that each year the goals will not be met, and each year the pattern of past discrimination will be perpetuated. The need for quotas is said to be particularly acute given the merit system itself and the fact that government accounts for about 14 percent of the employed labor force.

Moreover, the adoption of merit systems has closed the doors to many jobseekers.[194] In an earlier day, when patronage was standard practice, large groups of minorities (particularly ethnics) were assured government jobs as a way of winning votes. Entry into the system was easier than it is now, when one must earn a high score on a civil service examination to be considered for appointment. African-Americans and Hispanics who score comparatively low have little hope of winning a government job, even though they might constitute a large segment of the electorate.

The argument for goals instead of quotas rests on the concepts of equality and merit. Quotas are antithetical to equality because they give preference to some individuals and deny jobs to others. This is termed reverse discrimination, which, if carried out by state and local governments, violates the Fourteenth Amendment's guarantee of equal protection of the laws. Quotas also are said to run counter to merit because they may have the effect of incompetent or less competent workers being hired when more competent ones are available. If jobs are reserved for African-Americans but no highly qualified African-Americans are available on civil service lists, should persons with inferior skills be hired, or should the positions go unfilled? Critics of quota systems note that Title VII of the Civil Rights Act specifically states that preferential treatment in pursuit of affirmative action is not required:

> Nothing contained in this subchapter shall be interpreted to require any employer, employment agency, labor organization, or joint labor–management committee subject to this chapter to grant preferential treatment to any individual or to any group because of race, color, religion, sex, or national origin of any such individual or group.[195]

Governments use a combination of goals and quotas. Goals are most common, but courts have imposed quotas to redress gross imbalances in the racial composition of agencies such as local fire departments.[196] These cases have involved jurisdictions where there have been no or virtually no minorities on the staff; in other words, quotas have been reserved for extreme situations. The court orders have required, for example, that one minority person must be hired for every two or three positions that are filled until the court is satisfied that sufficient progress has been made in achieving some racial balance. The jurisdiction is not required to hire anyone, but if it does hire it must follow the quota system. In 1987, the Supreme Court, by the narrowest possible vote (five to four), approved the use of court-imposed quotas.[197,198] In 1992, the Court let stand a lower court ruling that the Philadelphia police academy was required to admit African-American candidates into the academy based on the percentage of African-Americans taking the entrance examination rather than on their scores on the examination. In other words, if 50 percent of the examinees were African-Americans, then 50 percent of those admitted would be African-Americans.[199]

The Supreme Court has made several important rulings on the legality of strong affirmative action measures, including the use of quotas that were not mandated by courts. In 1978 the Court dealt with the use of quotas for college students in the famous case of *Regents of the University of California v. Bakke.*[200] The question in that case was whether quotas established for admitting minority students to the Davis Medical School had the effect of discriminating against whites (Bakke was white). In a five-to-four vote, the Court agreed that a quota system was a form of reverse discrimination. In another part of the decision, however, one of the justices switched sides to produce a five-to-four majority in favor of affirmative action. The Court thus decided that, although rigid quotas for admitting students are unconstitutional, race can be taken into account to ensure that minorities are admitted.

The following year the Court, in another important ruling, *United Steelworkers of America v. Weber,* upheld an agreement between an employer and a union to reserve half of all places in training programs for African-Americans.[201] The Court did not find this practice to be a form of reverse discrimination in violation of Title VII.

In the mid-1980s, the Supreme Court handed down rulings that provided mixed signals. It let stand a circuit court decision that had condoned a practice in New York State that added points to civil service test scores of minorities. The state had chosen to do this voluntarily, as distinguished from being under a court order.[202] The Court also approved the use of quotas as "reasonable race-conscious relief" for the Cleveland Fire Department, again even though no court had determined that discrimination existed.[203] Quotas also were approved for worker entry into a union and its apprenticeship program.[204]

In still another five-to-four vote, however, the Court disapproved a layoff plan developed for the school district in Jackson, Michigan.[205] The plan called for restricting minority layoffs to the percentage of minorities working for the district when a reduction in force took effect. The Court ruled that this violated the equal protection clause. For the plan to be upheld, the Court said, it expected a proof of a "compelling state purpose," such as correcting previous discrimination. In another case, it allowed affirmative action plans to provide job preferences for women, even in situations where there was not proof of previous discrimination.[206,207] The case involved a woman being promoted rather than a man who had a higher promotion test score. The Court ruled that taking gender into account was permissible given the objective of correcting underrepresentation and that this policy had been incorporated into an affirmative action plan and was not simply an ad hoc decision.

Quotas imposed by governments independent of court orders are being attacked in courts as constituting reverse discrimination. The governing case is *City of Richmond v. J.A. Croson Company* (1989), which involved a city-imposed quota of 30 percent funding to minority businesses in city contracts.[208]

Without admitting to having engaged in discrimination, the city in adopting the policy had noted that half the city's population was African-American but that only 1 percent of prime contracts went to minority businesses. The Court held that the city had not shown a compelling reason for the policy and that the policy would allow race-based decision making essentially limitless in scope and duration. The Richmond policy, as viewed by the Court, violated the equal protection clause of the Fourteenth Amendment. In another case, the Court did permit preference being given to minority businesses in the awarding of radio station licenses; the Court considered this practice a form of benign race consciousness that promoted programming diversity and was in keeping with policy set by Congress.[209,210]

It should be noted that affirmative action, at least at the federal level, is a fragile commodity in terms of the executive and judicial branches. Although the Congress has a relatively consistent pattern of supporting EEO and affirmative action, the White House and Supreme Court have not been so consistent. Many Supreme Court decisions have been based on five-to-four votes, suggesting that future Court rulings could change if the composition of the Court changes.

The Reagan administration made a concerted effort to downplay the use of quotas, with the president saying he wanted a color-blind society. The administration sought and won from Congress a restructuring of the Civil Rights Commission, a body that is primarily advisory and has no enforcement duties.[211] Previously, nominees to the commission required confirmation by the Senate, but now four of the eight members can be appointed directly by the president, who also may designate the chair. The result was a turnabout, with the Commission taking a stand in opposition to quotas.[212] During the Bush administration, Commission Chair Arthur A. Fletcher promised to restore the commission as the conscience of the nation, but critics contended that the commission was basically without direction, and even strong advocates of EEO questioned the commission's utility. The Clinton administration pledged increased commitment to creating a representative bureaucracy.

With all the efforts to eliminate discrimination and to increase the number of minorities and women in positions of responsibility, substantial changes might be expected in the mix of the public work force. Have those changes materialized?[213] Between 1970 and 1990, minorities increased their share of General Schedule jobs from 14 percent to 27 percent, for a gain of 13 percentage points, and women increased theirs from 33 to 43 percent, a gain of 10 points. Earlier in this chapter it was noted that minorities and women tended to be overrepresented in low-level positions and underrepresented in high-level positions.[214] At the federal level, for instance, white men hold less than 20 percent of the GS-2 positions, with the remainder being held by women and minorities, whereas white men hold more than 80 percent of the positions in the Senior Executive Service.[215]

Was this imbalance worse at an earlier time? Changes for selected years in higher-level jobs are reported in Table 9–6 for the private sector, the federal government, and state and local governments. Generally all the minority groups increased their overall share of administrative and professional jobs. For example, state and local governments lead the private sector and the federal government in the proportion of professionals who are from minority groups (22 percent compared with 13 and 17 percent, respectively). The federal government leads in the hiring of minority administrators (21 percent compared with 10 percent for the private sector and 15 percent for state and local governments). Women account for about half the professional positions in state and local government and between 30 and 40 percent of other higher-level positions in the federal, state, and local governments.[216,217]

African-Americans constitute about 12 percent of the U.S. population and are at about that number for federal administrators, state administrators, and professionals but are below that number for federal professionals and in the

Table 9–6 **Percentage Distribution of Minorities and Women in the Private Sector, Federal Government, and State and Local Governments in Official, Administrator, and Professional Positions, 1990 and Selected Earlier Years**

Job Category	Year	All Minorities	African-Americans	Hispanics	Asians and Pacific Islanders	Native Americans and Alaskan Natives	Women
Private sector							
Officials and managers	1978	6.9	3.7	2.0	0.8	0.4	17.3
	1990	10.4	5.2	3.0	1.9	0.3	29.3
Professionals	1978	9.2	4.0	1.8	3.2	0.2	33.9
	1990	13.1	5.2	2.6	5.0	0.3	47.6
Federal							
Administrators	1982	16.6	10.7	3.5	1.4	1.0	31.0
	1990	20.6	12.8	4.5	2.1	1.2	39.0
Professionals	1982	12.7	5.9	2.5	3.5	0.8	23.5
	1990	17.4	7.5	3.5	5.5	0.9	31.7
State and local							
Officials and administrators	1974	7.5	5.3	1.4	0.4	0.2	18.0
	1990	15.3	10.2	3.4	1.3	0.4	31.3
Professionals	1974	12.4	7.9	2.1	1.6	0.3	38.4
	1990	21.6	13.2	4.2	3.7	0.5	49.8

Source: Data from *Indicators of Equal Employment Opportunity: Status and Trends*, pp. 14, 16, 18, U.S. Equal Employment Opportunity Commission, U.S. Government Printing Office, 1991.

private sector. Hispanics, although constituting about 8 percent of the population and being one of the fastest growing segments of the population, remain at less than 5 percent in any of the categories shown in Table 9–6. On the other hand, these numbers can be used to suggest considerable progress in achieving a representative bureaucracy.[218] For example, Hispanic administrators in state and local government increased from 1.4 percent to 3.4 percent between 1974 and 1990, an increase greater than double.

Are there factors that are related to the success or lack of success in achieving representative bureaucracies? Earlier, the U.S. Civil Service Commission was regarded as neutral toward, if not opposed to, affirmative action, and reformers of the 1970s thought that greater priority would be given to affirmative action by shifting many responsibilities to the EEOC. Available evidence indicates that this shift to the EEOC did not necessarily have any major impact.[219] Since the reforms of 1978, the government was led for 12 years by Republican administrations that were not champions of affirmative action. Clearly, political conditions at the EEOC affected its operations.[220] Also at the federal level, agency size has been found to be inversely related to the achievement of racial balance.[221] Public employee unions have played mixed roles, sometimes defending the status quo and other times supporting affirmative action. At the local level, the progress made by women, African-Americans, and Hispanics in acquiring public jobs and gaining promotions has been found to be related to the composition of the city council, the race of the mayor, and the racial mix of the general population.[222–225] If a city has an African-American mayor and/or an African-American police chief, African-Americans will be represented in greater numbers on the police force than in cities without such mayors or police chiefs.[226]

Women are said to encounter a glass ceiling in advancing their careers; that is, that promotions become difficult to attain, resulting in men dominating the upper levels of government. As of 1992, one of four supervisors were women in the federal government, and only one of ten executives were women. According to the MSPB, the problem women face is not advancing once they are in the supervisory and executive ranks but rather getting into those ranks in the first place. Women have received fewer promotions at the critical levels of GS-9 and GS-11 than men, suggesting that the ceiling is at this point rather than at higher reaches in the civil service.[227]

Affirmative action remains one of the most controversial topics in the field of public personnel management. Does affirmative action bring about social equity, or is it a form of reverse discrimination? Does it penalize today's male white workers for discriminations of the past?[228,229] On the other hand, some affirmative action plans have been implemented successfully and have made progress in correcting imbalances, and the progress has been achieved with a minimum of conflict.[230]

SUMMARY

Employment patterns for minorities and women across sectors—private, federal, and state and local—are similar. Women constitute somewhat more than 40 percent of the three work forces and minorities about a quarter. These workers tend to be clustered in low-paying positions. Minorities in state and local governments tend to get jobs as service or maintenance workers and paraprofessionals, and women are concentrated in clerical positions.

Numerous legal routes exist for reversing discriminatory practices. The Fifth and Fourteenth Amendments to the Constitution have been used, along with the Civil Rights Acts adopted after the Civil War. The Civil Rights Act of 1964 as amended by the Equal Employment Opportunity Act of 1972 serves as the primary legal route in discrimination cases. The Civil Rights Act of 1991 added several new features to the field. Other important laws include the Equal Pay Act of 1963, the Age Discrimination in Employment Act of 1967, and the Americans with Disabilities Act of 1990.

Discrimination occurs in all aspects of public personnel administration. In selection, one of the biggest issues has been the validity of tests as they pertain to race, sex, and ethnicity. Veterans preference has been alleged to be discriminatory, as are height and weight requirements. On-the-job discrimination is evidenced in not providing equal pay for equal work. Employee benefits have been the subject of much controversy, especially in terms of whether benefits packages work in favor of one sex. Compulsory retirement has been attacked as discriminating against older employees. Seniority systems, which often are key elements of collective bargaining agreements, are being challenged when used in layoffs because the effect can be to remove a disproportionate number of minorities and women.

Affirmative action plans are used to increase minority and female representation in government. Recruiting and testing procedures are changed. Upward mobility programs and job restructuring are designed to encourage the promotion of minorities and women in government. The most controversial issue is whether goals or quotas should be used in seeking to increase minority and female employment.

Whether affirmative action plans have had an appreciable effect on the public work force is debatable. Some observers contend that progress is being achieved. Others attack affirmative action as a form of reverse discrimination, saying that if it does alter the racial and sex composition of the work force, an injustice is being perpetrated. Still others contend that, despite the numerous court cases and the flurry of activity associated with affirmative action, little real change has occurred.

NOTES

1. D.H. Rosenbloom, *Federal Service and the Constitution: The Development of the Public Employment Relationship* (Ithaca, N.Y.: Cornell University Press, 1971), 124.

2. Rosenbloom, *Federal Service and the Constitution*, 129.

3. S. Krislov, *The Negro in Federal Employment: The Quest for Equal Opportunity* (Minneapolis: University of Minnesota Press, 1967).

4. L.F. McMillin, *Women in the Federal Service*, 3d ed. (Washington: U.S. Government Printing Office, 1941).

5. P.P. Van Riper, *History of the United States Civil Service* (Evanston, Ill.: Row, Peterson, 1958), 159–60.

6. U.S. General Accounting Office, *Federal Workforce: Continuing Need for Federal Affirmative Employment* (Washington: U.S. Government Printing Office, 1991).

7. U.S. Office of Personnel Management, *Federal Civilian Workforce Statistics: Affirmative Employment Statistics, 1990* (Washington: U.S. Government Printing Office, 1992).

8. _____, *Federal Civilian Workforce Statistics*, 182–183.

9. P.A. Brandin and D.A. Copus, *In Defense of the Public Employer: Case Law and Litigation Strategies for Discrimination Claims* (Chicago, Ill.: American Bar Association, 1988).

10. K.K. Tummala, ed., *Equity in Public Employment across Nations* (Lanham, Md.: University Press of America, 1989).

11. *Massachusetts Board of Retirement v. Murgia*, 427 U.S. 307 (1976).

12. *Washington v. Davis*, 426 U.S. 229 (1976).

13. *St. Francis College v. Al-Khazraji*, 481 U.S. 604 (1987) and *Shaare-Tefila Congregation v. Cobb*, 481 U.S. 615 (1987).

14. *McDonald v. City of West Branch, MI*, 466 U.S. 284 (1984).

15. M.A. Mazzuchi, Section 1983 and implied rights of action: Rights, remedies, and realism, *Michigan Law Review* 90 (1992): 1,062–1,118.

16. *Brown v. General Services Administration*, 425 U.S. 820 (1976).

17. *Beal v. Blount*, 461 F.2d 1133 (1972).

18. *Ogletree v. McNamara*, 449 F.2d 93 (1971).

19. *Atascadero State Hospital and California Department of Mental Health v. Scanlon*, 473 U.S. 234 (1985).

20. *Equal Employment Opportunity Commission v. Associated Dry Goods Corporation*, 449 U.S. 590 (1981).

21. *Ford Motor Company v. Equal Employment Opportunity Commission*, 458 U.S. 219 (1982).

22. Reorganization Plan No. 1 of 1978, 5 U.S.C., Appendix 1.

23. Executive Orders 12067 (1978), 12068 (1978), 12086 (1978), 12106 (1978), and 12144 (1979) in 42 U.S.C. § 2000e.

24. Civil Service Reform Act, P.L. 95-454, 92 Stat. 1111 (1978).

25. J. Carter, *Message from the President of the United States: Reorganization Plan No. 1 of 1978*, 95th Cong., 2d sess., H. Doc. 95-295 (Washington: U.S. Government Printing Office, 1978).

26. Equal Employment Opportunity in the Federal Government, 29 C.F.R. § 1613.

27. *Brown v. General Services Administration*, 425 U.S. 820 (1976).

28. *Chandler v. Roudebush*, 425 U.S. 840 (1976).

29. U.S. General Accounting Office, *Federal Workforce: Agencies' Estimated Costs for Counseling and Processing Discrimination Complaints* (Washington: U.S. Government Printing Office, 1992).

30. *General Telephone Company of the Southwest v. Falcon*, 457 U.S. 147 (1982).

31. W.J. Moore, On the case, *National Journal* 23 (1991): 501–504.

32. Civil Rights Act, P.L. 102-166, 105 Stat. 1071 (1991).

33. V.J. Apruzzese, Selected recent developments in EEO Law, *Labor Law Journal* 43 (1992): 325–337.

34. *Wards Cove Packing Company v. Atonio*, 490 U.S. 642 (1989).

35. *Price Waterhouse v. Hopkins*, 490 U.S. 228 (1989).

36. *Martin v. Wilks*, 490 U.S. 755 (1989).

37. Equal Pay Act, P.L. 88-38, 77 Stat. 56 (1963).

38. M.M. Hale and R.M. Kelly, eds., *Gender, Bureaucracy, and Democracy: Careers and Equal Opportunity in the Public Sector* (New York: Greenwood Press, 1989).

39. U.S. Department of Labor, *A Working Woman's Guide to Her Job Rights* (Washington: U.S. Government Printing Office, 1992).

40. *North Haven, CT, Board of Education v. Bell*, 456 U.S. 512 (1982).

41. Education Amendments, P.L. 92-318, 86 Stat. 235 (1972).

42. *Grove City College v. Bell*, 465 U.S. 555 (1984).

43. Civil Rights Restoration Act, P.L. 100-259, 102 Stat. 28 (1987).

44. Age Discrimination in Employment Act, P.L. 90-202, 81 Stat. 602 (1967).

45. Age Discrimination in Employment Act Amendments, P.L. 95-256, 92 Stat. 189 (1978).

46. Rehabilitation Act, P.L. 93-112, 87 Stat. 355 (1973).

47. Americans with Disabilities Act, P.L. 101-36, 104 Stat. 327 (1990).

48. S.L. Percy, U.S. Advisory Commission on Intergovernmental Relations, *Disability Rights Mandates: Federal and State Compliance with Employment Protections and Architectural Barrier Removal* (Washington: U.S. Government Printing Office, 1989).

49. G.B. Lewis and C.L. Allee, The impact of disabilities on federal career success, *Public Administration Review* 52 (1992): 389–397.

50. *U.S. Department of Transportation v. Paralyzed Veterans of America*, 477 U.S. 597 (1986).

51. P.A. Susser, The ADA: Dramatically expanded federal rights for disabled Americans, *Employee Relations Law Journal* 16 (1990): 157–176.

52. H.R. Boller and D. Massengill, Public employers' obligation to reasonably accommodate the disabled under the Rehabilitation and Americans with Disabilities Acts, *Public Personnel Management* 21 (1992): 273–300.

53. *Guardians Association v. Civil Service Commission of New York*, 463 U.S. 582 (1983).

54. Intergovernmental Personnel Act, P.L. 91-648, 84 Stat. 1909 (1970).

55. *Fullilove v. Klutznick*, 448 U.S. 448 (1980).

56. *Oscar Mayer and Company v. Evans*, 441 U.S. 750 (1979).

57. *Astoria Federal Savings and Loan Association v. Solimino*, 111 S.Ct. 2166 (1991).

58. *Bowers v. Hardwick*, 478 U.S. 186 (1986).

59. E.M. Wagner, A kinder, gentler workplace for lesbians and gay men, *Journal of Individual Employment Rights* 1 (1992–93): 115–134.

60. S.A. McEvoy, Fat chance: Employment discrimination against the overweight, *Labor Law Journal* 43 (1992): 3–14.

61. _____, Cancer and employment discrimination, *Labor Law Journal* 41 (1990): 323–336.

62. *Corporation of the Presiding Bishop of the Church of Jesus Christ of Latter-Day Saints v. Amos*, 483 U.S. 327 (1987).

63. L.S. Underkuffler, "Discrimination" on the basis of religion: An examination of attempted value neutrality in employment, *William and Mary Law Review* 30 (1989): 581–625.

64. *Griggs v. Duke Power Co.*, 401 U.S. 424 (1971).

65. *Washington v. Davis*, 426 U.S. 229 (1976).

66. J.H. Blits and L.S. Gottfredson, Employment testing and job performance, *Public Interest* 98 (1990): 18–25.

67. S.B. Green, et al., Racial differences on job analysis questionnaires: An empirical study, *Public Personnel Management* 20 (1991): 135–144.

68. W.R. McKinney and J.R. Collins, Jr., The impact on utility, race, and gender using three standard methods of scoring selection examinations, *Public Personnel Management* 20 (1991): 145–169.

69. Uniform Guidelines on Employee Selection Procedures, 29 C.F.R. § 1607.

70. C. Daniel, Selection's uniform guidelines: Help, hindrance, or irrelevancy? *Review of Public Personnel Administration* 9 (Spring 1989): 68–78.

71. *Connecticut v. Teal*, 457 U.S. 440 (1982).

72. *Hazlewood School District v. United States*, 433 U.S. 299 (1977).

73. *Zamlen v. City of Cleveland*, 906 F.2d 209 (1990), *cert. denied*, 111 S.Ct. 1388 (1991).

74. M.A. Hughes, et al., A content validation methodology for job related physical performance tests, *Public Personnel Management* 18 (1989): 487–504.

75. *Crockett v. Green*, 534 F.2d 715 (1976).

76. *Aguilera v. Cook County Police and Corrections Merit Board*, 760 F.2d 844 (1985), *cert. denied*, 474 U.S. 907 (1985).

77. *Davis v. City of Dallas*, 777 F.2d 205 (1985).

78. *United States v. Chicago*, 549 F.2d 415 (1977), *cert. denied*, 434 U.S. 875 (1977), 631 F.2d 469 (1980).

79. *Dothard v. Rawlinson*, 433 U.S. 321 (1977).

80. *International Union, United Automobile, Aerospace, and Agricultural Implement Workers of America v. Johnson Controls, Inc.*, 111 S.Ct. 1196 (1991).

81. D.L. Kirp, The pitfalls of fetal protection, *Society* 28 (March/April 1991): 70–76.

82. *Rodriguez v. Taylor*, 569 F.2d 1231 (1977), *cert. denied*, 436 U.S. 913 (1978).

83. *Equal Employment Opportunity Commission v. County of Los Angeles*, 706 F.2d 1039 (1983), *cert. denied*, 464 U.S. 1073 (1984).

84. J.M. Pellicciotti, Exemptions and employer defenses under the ADEA, *Public Personnel Management* 20 (1991): 233–261.

85. Vietnam Era Veterans' Readjustment Assistance Act, P.L. 94-508, 88 Stat. 1578 (1974).

86. K.K. Tummala, Veterans' preference in the state of Montana: Equal employment or affirmative action, *Public Personnel Management* 16 (1987): 159–171.

87. *Personnel Administrator of Massachusetts v. Feeney*, 442 U.S. 256 (1979).

88. D.C. Morrison, Gay groups were left in the dust, *National Journal* 25 (1993): 343–344.

89. *Sugarman v. Dougall*, 413 U.S. 634 (1973).

90. *Hampton v. Wong*, 426 U.S. 88 (1976).

91. *Foley v. Connelie*, 435 U.S. 291 (1978).

92. *Ambach v. Norwick*, 441 U.S. 68 (1979).

93. *Cabell v. Chavez-Salida*, 454 U.S. 432 (1982).

94. *United Building and Construction Trades Council v. Mayor and Council of Camden*, 465 U.S. 208 (1984).

95. A.M. Rizzo and C. Mendez, Making things happen in organizations: Does gender make a difference? *Public Personnel Management* 17 (1988): 9–20.

96. Y. Haberfeld, Employment discrimination: An organizational model, *Academy of Management Journal* 35 (1992): 161–180.

97. *Firefighters Institute for Racial Equality v. St. Louis*, 549 F.2d 506 (1977), 588 F.2d 235 (1978), 616 F.2d 350 (1980), 434 U.S. 819 (1977), 443 U.S. 904 (1979), 452 U.S. 938 (1980).

98. *Lehmon v. Nakshian*, 453 U.S. 156 (1981).

99. *U.S. Postal Service Board of Governors v. Aikens*, 460 U.S. 711 (1983).

100. *Watson v. Fort Worth Bank and Trust*, 487 U.S. 977 (1988).

101. *University of Pennsylvania v. Equal Employment Opportunity Commission*, 493 U.S. 182 (1990).

102. W.T. Burke, III, and F.J. Cavaliere, Equal employment opportunity on campus: Strengthening the commitment, *Labor Law Journal* 42 (1991): 19–27.

103. U.S. Equal Employment Opportunity Commission, Sexual Harassment, 29 C.F.R. § 1604.11.

104. S.G. Mezey, *In Pursuit of Equality: Women, Public Policy, and the Federal Courts* (New York: St. Martin's Press, 1992).

105. M.A. Paludi and R.B. Barickman, *Academic and Workplace Sexual Harassment: A Resource Manual* (Albany: State University of New York Press, 1991).

106. D.E. Terpstra and D.D. Baker, Outcomes of federal court decisions on sexual harassment, *Academy of Management Journal* 35 (1992): 181–190.

107. J. James, Sexual harassment, *Public Personnel Management* 10 (1981): 404.

108. D.M. Stringer, et al., The power and reasons behind sexual harassment: An employer's guide to solutions, *Public Personnel Management* 19 (1990): 43–52.

109. *Meritor Savings Bank v. Vinson*, 477 U.S. 57 (1986).

110. W.L. Woerner and S.L. Oswald, Sexual harassment in the workplace: A view through the eyes of the courts, *Labor Law Journal* 41 (1990): 786–793.

111. M. Strauss, Sexist speech in the workplace, *Harvard Civil Rights–Civil Liberties Law Review* 25 (1990): 1–51.

112. J. Biskupic, Thomas drama engulfs nation; Anguished Senate faces vote, *Congressional Quarterly Weekly Report* 49 (1991): 2,948–2,949ff.

113. The Tailhook factor, *Congressional Quarterly Weekly Report* 50 (1992): 1,977.

114. *Ellison v. Brady*, 924 F.2d 872 (1991).

115. P.S. Greenlaw and J.P. Kohl, Proving Title VII sexual harassment: The courts' view, *Labor Law Journal* 43 (1992): 164–171.

116. *Franklin v. Gwinnett County Public Schools*, 112 S.Ct. 1028 (1992).

117. *Corning Glass Works v. Brennan*, 417 U.S. 188 (1974).

118. Y.S. Lee, Shaping judicial response to gender discrimination in employment compensation, *Public Administration Review* 49 (1989): 420–430.

119. *County of Washington v. Gunther*, 452 U.S. 161 (1981).

120. M.R. Killingsworth, *The Economics of Comparable Worth* (Kalamazoo, Mich.: W.E. Upjohn Institute for Employment Research, 1990).

121. R.H. Lowe and M.A. Wittig, eds., Symposium on approaching pay equity through comparable worth, *Journal of Social Issues* 45 (1989): 1–246.

122. R.T. Michael, et al., eds., *Pay Equity: Empirical Inquiries* (Washington: National Academy Press, 1989).

123. S.M. Neuse, ed., Symposium: From comparable worth to pay equity: Into the 1990s, *International Journal of Public Administration* 14 (1991): 763–922.

124. R.W. Scholl and E. Cooper, The use of job evaluation to eliminate gender based pay differentials, *Public Personnel Management* 20 (1991): 1–18.

125. J. Tompkins, et al., Designing a comparable worth based job evaluation system: Failure of an *a priori* approach, *Public Personnel Management* 19 (1990): 31–42.

126. D.M. Werwie, *Sex and Pay in the Federal Government: Using Job Evaluation Systems To Implement Comparable Worth* (New York: Greenwood Press, 1987).

127. *American Federation of State, County, and Municipal Employees v. State of Washington*, 578 F. Supp. 846 (1983).

128. *AFSCME v. Washington*, 770 F.2d 1401 (1985).

129. U.S. General Accounting Office, *Pay Equity: Washington State's Efforts To Address Comparable Worth* (Washington: U.S. Government Printing Office, 1992).

130. OPM's Horner speaks on comparable worth, *IPMA News* (February 1986): 9.

131. *Ansonia Board of Education v. Philbrook*, 479 U.S. 60 (1986).

132. R.M. Preer, Jr., Reasonable accommodation of religious practice: The conflict between the courts and the EEOC, *Employee Relations Law Journal* 15 (1989): 67–99.

133. *Frontiero v. Richardson*, 411 U.S. 677 (1973).

134. M. Jacobson, Pregnancy and employment: Three approaches to equal opportunity, *Boston Law Review* 68 (1988): 1,019–1,045.

135. *Cleveland Board of Education v. LaFleur*, 414 U.S. 632 (1974).

136. *Gedulig v. Aiello*, 417 U.S. 484 (1974).

137. *General Electric Company v. Gilbert*, 429 U.S. 125 (1976).

138. Pregnancy Discrimination Act, P.L. 95-555, 92 Stat. 2076 (1978).

139. *Newport News Shipbuilding and Dry Dock Company v. Equal Employment Opportunity Commission*, 462 U.S. 669 (1983).

140. *California Federal Savings and Loan v. Guerra*, 479 U.S. 272 (1987).

141. Retirement Equity Act, P.L. 98-397, 98 Stat. 1426 (1984).

142. Older Workers Benefit Protection Act, P.L. 101-433, 104 Stat. 978 (1990).

143. *Public Employees Retirement System of Ohio v. Betts*, 492 U.S. 158 (1989).

144. *City of Los Angeles, Department of Water and Power v. Manhart*, 435 U.S. 702 (1978).

145. *Arizona Governing Commission for Tax Deferred Annuity and Deferred Compensation Plans v. Norris*, 463 U.S. 1073 (1983).

146. *Florida v. Long*, 487 U.S. 223 (1988).

147. *Doe v. Hampton*, 566 F.2d 265 (1977).

148. *Trans World Airlines v. Hardison*, 432 U.S. 63 (1977).

149. *Logan v. Zimmerman Brush Company*, 455 U.S. 422 (1982).

150. *Estate of Thornton v. Caldor*, 472 U.S. 703 (1985).

151. *Hobbie v. Unemployment Appeals Commission of Florida*, 480 U.S. 136 (1987).

152. *Zipes v. TVA*, 455 U.S. 385 (1982).

153. *New York City Transit Authority v. Beazer*, 440 U.S. 568 (1979).

154. K.L. Karst, The pursuit of manhood and the desegregation of the Armed Forces, *UCLA Law Review* 38 (1991): 499–581.

155. S.K. Ray-Holmes, Discrimination based on one's sexual preference: Should strict scrutiny apply? *Howard Law Journal* 34 (1991): 341–366.

156. *High Tech Gays v. Defense Industrial Security Clearance Office*, 895 F.2d 563 (1990) and 909 F.2d 375 (1990).

157. F. Hernandez, Homosexuals in public service: A new suspect class? *Labor Law Journal* 42 (1991): 800–806.

158. *Webster v. Doe*, 486 U.S. 592 (1988).

159. M.D. Hoerrner, Fire at will: The CIA director's ability to dismiss homosexual employees as national security risks, *Boston College Law Review* 31 (1990): 699–748.

160. *Board of Education of Oklahoma City v. National Gay Task Force*, 470 U.S. 903 (1985).

161. *Acanfora v. Board of Education of Montgomery County*, 359 F. Supp. 843 (1973).

162. *Gaylord v. Tacoma School District*, 559 P.2d 1340 (1977), *cert. denied*, 434 U.S. 879 (1977).

163. *Vance v. Bradley*, 440 U.S. 93 (1979).

164. *Johnson v. May and City Council of Baltimore*, 472 U.S. 353 (1985).

165. A.L. Finkle, Physical unfitness: Using medical expertise in personnel adjudication, *Public Personnel Management* 20 (1991): 339–346.

166. *Gregory v. Ashcroft*, 111 S.Ct. 2395 (1991).

167. A.L. Bushlow, Mandatory retirement of state-appointed judges under the Age Discrimination in Employment Act, *Cornell Law Review* 76 (1991): 476–509.

168. *United Air Lines v. McMann*, 434 U.S. 192 (1977).

169. *Equal Employment Opportunity Commission v. Wyoming*, 460 U.S. 226 (1983).

170. *Western Air Lines v. Criswell*, 472 U.S. 400 (1985).

171. *Equal Employment Opportunity Commission v. City of Bowling Green, KY*, 607 F. Supp. 524 (1985).

172. *Equal Employment Opportunity Commission v. State of New Jersey*, 631 F. Supp. 1506 (1986).

173. M.K. Kemler, Front pay as an appropriate remedy under the Age Discrimination in Employment Act, *Wayne Law Review* 32 (1985): 116.

174. *Schlesinger v. Ballard*, 419 U.S. 498 (1975).

175. *Firefighter Local Union No. 1784 v. Stotts*, 467 U.S. 561 (1984).

176. *Albemarle Paper Company v. Moody*, 422 U.S. 405 (1975).

177. *Fitzpatrick v. Bitzer*, 427 U.S. 445 (1976).

178. *Franks v. Bowman Transportation Company*, 424 U.S. 747 (1976).

179. *International Brotherhood of Teamsters v. United States*, 431 U.S. 324 (1977).

180. L.R. Wise, Social equity in civil service systems, *Public Administration Review* 50 (1990): 567–575.

181. U.S. Equal Employment Opportunity Commission, "Affirmative Action Appropriate under Title VII of the Civil Rights Act of 1964, as Amended," 29 C.F.R. § 1608.

182. R. Nieli, ed., *Racial Preference and Racial Justice: The New Affirmative Action Controversy* (Washington: Ethics and Public Policy Center, 1991).

183. R.K. Robinson, et al., Affirmative action plans in the 1990s: A double-edged sword? *Public Personnel Management* 21 (1992): 261–272.

184. R. Turner, *The Past and Future of Affirmative Action* (New York: Quorum, 1990).

185. H. Orlans and J. O'Neill, eds., Affirmative Action revisited, *Annals* 523 (1992).

186. U.S. Office of Personnel Management, "Affirmative Employment Programs," 5 C.F.R. § 720.

187. U.S. Equal Employment Opportunity Commission, 29 C.F.R. § 1608.

188. _____, "Equal Employment Opportunity in the Federal Government," 29 C.F.R. § 1613.

189. U.S. General Accounting Office, *Federal Affirmative Action: Better EEOC Guidance and Agency Analysis of Underrepresentation Needed* (Washington: U.S. Government Printing Office, 1991).

190. D.G. Carnevale, Recruitment strategies in the federal government: Missing links and representative bureaucracy, *Review of Public Personnel Administration* 11 (Fall 1990–Spring 1991): 112–120.

191. Federal Employees Part-Time Career Employment Act, P.L. 95-437, 92 Stat. 1055 (1978).

192. U.S. Office of Personnel Management, *Job Sharing for Federal Employees* (Washington: U.S. Government Printing Office, 1990).

193. T.A. DiPrete, *The Bureaucratic Labor Market: The Case of the Federal Civil Service* (New York: Plenum Press, 1989), 197–230.

194. F. Gottfried, *The Merit System and Municipal Civil Service: A Fostering of Social Inequality* (New York: Greenwood Press, 1988), 53–91.

195. Civil Rights Act of 1964, 42 U.S.C. § 2000 c–z.

196. *Kirkland v. New York State Department of Correctional Service*, 520 F.2d 420 (1975), *cert. denied*, 429 U.S. 823 (1976).

197. *United States v. Paradise*, 480 U.S. 149 (1987).

198. J. Nalbandian, The U.S. Supreme Court's consensus on affirmative action, *Public Administration Review* 49 (1989): 38–45.

199. *Fraternal Order of Police Lodge No. 5 v. Philadelphia*, 112 S.Ct. 1668 (1992).

200. *Regents of the University of California v. Bakke*, 438 U.S. 265 (1978).

201. *United Steelworkers of America v. Weber*, 443 U.S. 193 (1979).

202. *Bushey v. New York State Civil Service Commission*, 733 F.2d 220 (1984), *cert. denied*, 469 U.S. 1117 (1985).

203. *Local Number 93, International Association of Firefighters v. City of Cleveland*, 478 U.S. 501 (1986).

204. *Local 28, Sheet Metal Workers' International Association v. Equal Employment Opportunity Commission*, 478 U.S. 421 (1986).

205. *Wygant v. Jackson Board of Education*, 476 U.S. 267 (1986).

206. *Johnson v. Transportation Agency, Santa Clara County, CA*, 480 U.S. 616 (1987).

207. M.I. Urofsky, *A Conflict of Rights: The Supreme Court and Affirmative Action* (New York: Charles Scribner's Sons, 1991).

208. *City of Richmond v. J.A. Croson Company*, 448 U.S. 469 (1989).

209. *Metro Broadcasting v. Federal Communications Commission*, 110 S.Ct. 2997 (1990).

210. Y.S. Lee, Affirmative action and judicial standards of review: A search for the elusive consensus, *Review of Public Personnel Administration* 12 (September–December 1991): 47–69.

211. U.S. Commission on Civil Rights Act, P.L. 98-183, 97 Stat. 1301 (1983).

212. _____, *Toward an Understanding of Stotts* (Washington: U.S. Government Printing Office, 1985).

213. G.B. Lewis, Progress toward racial and sexual equality in the federal civil service? *Public Administration Review* 48 (1988): 700–707.

214. U.S. General Accounting Office, *EEO at Justice: Progress Made but Underrepresentation Remains Widespread* (Washington: U.S. Government Printing Office, 1990).

215. _____, *Federal Workforce: Continuing Need*, 3.

216. K. Bremer and D.A. Howe, Strategies used to advance women's careers in the public service: Examples from Oregon, *Public Administration Review* 48 (1988): 957–961.

217. R.M. Kelly, et al., Public managers in the states: A comparison of career advancement by sex, *Public Administration Review* 51 (1991): 402 411.

218. A. Sisneros, Hispanics in the Senior Executive Service: Continuity and change in the decade 1980–1990, *Review of Public Personnel Administration* 12 (January–April 1992): 5–25.

219. J.E. Kellough, *Federal Equal Employment Opportunity Policy and Numerical Goals and Timetables* (New York: Praeger Publishers, 1989).

220. B.D. Wood, Does politics make a difference at the EEOC? *American Journal of Political Science* 34 (1990): 503–530.

221. J.E. Kellough, Integration in the public workplace: Determinants of minority and female employment in federal agencies, *Public Administration Review* 50 (1990): 557–566.

222. S. Ballard and G. Lawn-Day, Affirmative action in municipal government: Anatomy of a failure, *Review of Public Personnel Administration* 12 (May–August 1992): 5–18.

223. K.R. Mladenka, Blacks and Hispanics in urban politics, *American Political Science Review* 83 (1989): 165–191.

224. _____, Barriers to Hispanic employment success in 1,200 cities, *Social Science Quarterly* 70 (1989): 391–407.

225. R.L. Warner and B.S. Steel, Affirmative action in times of fiscal stress and changing value priorities: The case of women in policing, *Public Personnel Management* 18 (1989): 291–309.

226. W.G. Lewis, Toward representative bureaucracy: Blacks in city police organizations, 1975–1985, *Public Administration Review* 49 (1989): 257–267.

227. U.S. Merit Systems Protection Board, *A Question of Equity: Women and the Glass Ceiling in the Federal Government* (Washington: U.S. Government Printing Office, 1992).

228. R.A. Epstein, *Forbidden Grounds: The Case against Employment Discrimination Laws* (Cambridge, Mass.: Harvard University Press, 1992).

229. F.R. Lynch, *Invisible Victims: White Males and the Crisis of Affirmative Action* (New York: Greenwood Press, 1989).

230. A.J. Jones, Jr., *Affirmative Talk, Affirmative Action: A Comparative Study of the Politics of Affirmative Action* (New York: Praeger Publishers, 1991).

Chapter 10

Motivation Theory

One of the greatest unknowns is why people behave the way they do. Understanding human behavior in organizations is critical in that inappropriate policies can affect conduct to the detriment of workers, the organization, and especially the public. Motivation theories, then, attempt to explain the forces that influence employee behavior. It should be emphasized at the outset that, although each motivation theory may make some contribution to an understanding of the subject, none definitively explains human behavior.

Motivation is a component of public personnel systems because it pertains to how people work. An understanding of the alternative theories is important if for no other reason than that people in government operate as though one or more theories are valid. An understanding of behavior requires an understanding of the principles or theories that guide people in their daily work. If the theories are valid, individuals can use these ideas to deal more effectively with their subordinates, peers, and superiors.

Personnel administrators may play a small role in motivation, but the main responsibility rests with managers and the workers themselves. Motivation, or the lack of it, occurs on a daily basis throughout any government. The people in a central personnel agency will not have continuous and extensive contact with employees throughout the government. Personnel administrators, however, should be aware of contemporary motivation theories in order to consider their compatability with specific personnel practices such as position classification, pay, and promotion procedures.

This chapter and the next sample some of the vast literature that attempts to explain human motivation in organizations, with this chapter concentrating on theories of motivation, especially as they relate to individuals.[1-5] Chapter 11 discusses the applications of theories and expands the focus to include group behavior. This chapter discusses:

1. some of the theories of human personality
2. what the literature calls content theories of motivation, that is, theories that attempt to explain what common characteristics in humans motivate their behavior
3. process theories that suggest the methods by which workers become motivated

DETERMINANTS OF PERSONALITY

A person hired by a government or any other organization brings to that entity something more than a physical body and a set of knowledge, skills, and abilities. That additional ingredient is personality, which is a hypothetical construct. Although numerous alternative definitions exist, personality is defined here simply as the properties or traits of an individual. This section reviews both old and contemporary approaches to personality. Although most of these theories are not part of the mainstream of motivation, they are included to provide an appreciation of the wide range of concepts that can plausibly explain behavior. Indeed, many of these theories are only at the periphery of current research at best.

Defining motivation is as difficult as defining personality, in part because the theories start from different premises, with the result that motivation does not have the same meaning for all researchers. Motivation, like personality, is a hypothetical construct, as noted, and is presumed to account for behavior. The motivation within a person will influence the type and quality of behavior. If an employee begins to work on a difficult project, motivation will determine whether that person still is working on it an hour later and with what vigor.

Job satisfaction is not the same as motivation. Satisfaction and dissatisfaction are attitudes about jobs and influence approach–avoidance behavior. In other words, an employee who approaches work may want to avoid going to work because of dissatisfaction. On the other hand, an employee who is satisfied eagerly comes to work. Satisfaction is important in having an employee come to work on time, and motivation influences behavior on the job.[6] This and the next chapter concentrate on motivation, with job satisfaction receiving less attention but being integrated into the discussion.[7]

The relative importance of heredity and environment—nature versus nurture—is at the core of the debate on personality development.[8-10] One view is that humans are malleable and that environmental influences determine personality. The argument is supported by comparisons of cultures; for example, women in one society may play submissive roles, whereas in others they are equal to or dominant over men. Within a single society, the importance of the environment is evident. Mark Twain's *The Prince and the Pauper* is a fictional case study of the importance of the environment. In postcommunist countries, efforts have been made to change work environments that apparently discouraged competitiveness and industriousness. China also has made some effort to change the work environment, including the introduction of a modest private sector.[11] Japanese firms operate in a culture different from the cultures of other nations, and when these firms have established operations in the United States and other countries, they have had to modify their approaches to personnel management.[12,13]

Although few would deny that environment affects human development and behavior, others have suggested that there are innate physiological and psychological properties that do have an influence. The physiological requirement for sleep not only produces drowsiness but can lead to irritable behavior. Hormonal changes have important effects on behavior. Beyond these physiological matters are other properties assumed to be innate in humans. If these properties exist and constitute a predisposition toward some behaviors and against others, then it becomes important to understand them so that organizations do not attempt the impossible, that is, expect a type of behavior that is antithetical to the individuals' inherent properties.

Freud's psychoanalytic model of personality has had an immeasurable impact on how human behavior is perceived.[14-20] Freud suggested that there are conflicting forces within each person, with each force attempting to assert control over behavior. The id, which is the most primitive of these forces, seeks pleasure in sexual relationships, comfort, and aggression. A critical aspect of the id is that the individual is unaware of this force because it is the unconscious.

Freud's second force is the ego, the conscious and rational part of the personality. The ego keeps the id in check through the reality principle. Because in reality one cannot always be satisfying pleasure drives, the ego serves to postpone gratification. The ego is not a morality or ethical force but rather a rational force. A woman may want to hit her boss, but the ego constrains her; hitting the boss could result in dismissal from the job.

Freud's third aspect of personality is the superego, the conscience, representing values of right and wrong; the superego is largely unconscious and is learned rather than inherited. In the case of the woman considering hitting her boss, the superego also may prevent such behavior because of a value that superiors are to be respected no matter how wrong they may be.

Associated with Freud were Jung and Adler, who later developed their own approaches to personality. Jung, like Freud, promoted the concept of instincts as determiners of behavior but put less emphasis on sex as a motivator.[21-23] Jung wrote of archetypes or model images that were passed from one generation to another through nonenvironmental means. Evolution from lower animals was thought not to be complete in that properties of those animals exist within each individual. Adler deemphasized the role of instincts but stressed the pleasure principle, especially in terms of power.[24-26] According to Adler, having power over individuals is pleasurable. Adler also emphasized that cooperativeness was an important aspect of personality.

The theories of Freud, Jung, and Adler rarely are applied in their pure form to the study of organizational behavior, but many of their ideas are to be found in contemporary theories of motivation. Freud's id, ego, and superego concepts have been translated by Eric Berne into the roles of child, adult, and parent in a technique known as "transactional analysis" (see Chapter 11).[27,28] The pleasure principle and the unconscious are important components of contemporary theories. Freud's concept of defense mechanisms also is important. He contended that when the desire for pleasure is unsatisfied, it produces internal tensions that are transformed into behavior patterns. Repression is one such mechanism; if a desire cannot be gratified, the individual may repress that desire so that in effect it seems not to exist.

These theories of Freud, Jung, and Adler suggest that to some extent human behavior is preset or determined, that in some situations an individual will not have any choice of conduct. Instincts or innate drives trigger behavior. As the individual matures, the combination of instincts and acquired behavior patterns stemming from exposure to environmental conditions will have a great influence on what that person will do when confronted with a given situation.

Although these theories may seem largely deterministic, it is important to recognize that the three psychologists did allow for human choice in selecting behavior. Jung particularly introduced the concept of self-actualization, suggesting that as one grew older there was more conscious control over behavior. He did not provide an operational definition of self-actualization, but, as will be seen, contemporary theories rely heavily upon that concept.

Beyond the theories of these three giants of psychology is a seemingly infinite number of other theories, most of which cannot be reviewed here. One such theory that has been popular from time to time is that body type affects or reflects personality type. The major proponent of this theory has been Sheldon, who in the 1940s identified three temperaments that presumably correspond with three body types.[29-31] The three somatotypes are:

1. endomorphy, a rounded and fat body with small hands and feet
2. mesomorphy, a body shape that is square, with the body having large bones and being muscular
3. ectomorphy, a body that is slight or fragile with drooped shoulders and small face

Paralleling these three body types are three temperaments:

1. The viscerotonia temperament, associated with endomorphy, involves the seeking of physical comfort, the love of eating, and tolerance of others.

2. The somatotonia temperament, related to mesomorphy, is assertive, energetic, competitive, and aggressive.
3. The cerebrotonia temperament, paralleling ectomorphy, is characterized by emotional restraint and enjoyment of privacy and contemplation.

Sheldon did not suggest that body type determined personality but that the two factors correlated strongly. It follows, however, that if one has little control over one's body one also may have little control over one's personality, which suggests that personality is somewhat predetermined. Today, Sheldon's ideas receive little attention in motivation literature.

A persistent strain of thought has been that humans are inherently evil and/or aggressive. The biblical story of Adam and Eve can be interpreted as meaning that humans were pure of mind until that first bite of the apple, after which evil would always be a part of them. More currently, Milgram's experiments in the 1960s suggested that people are readily willing to harm others.[32] The experiments involved subjects who were told they were participating in a study of punishment. An accomplice was strapped into an electric chair, and the experimenter told the subject to administer electric shocks at increasing voltage whenever the accomplice made a mistake. The accomplice, of course, did not receive shocks that could have been fatal. The studies demonstrated that people will follow instructions of an authority figure even though they could result in severe harm to others.

Evolution has been used in support of the aggression theory. Ardrey suggested that, rather than evolving from herbivorous apes, humans evolved from aggressive, carnivorous apes.[33,34] To obtain food, these apes bludgeoned other animals to death with stones or bones. If the aggression theory is valid, it follows that such behavior is innate and always will arise in individuals—and in organizations.

Ardrey also suggested that aggression frequently is focused on protecting territory.[35] Drawing on the behavior of lower animals and on human evolution, he maintained that animals protect geographical areas from other animals of the same species. This imperative to protect territory is of such force that it can override concerns for personal and family safety. When this theory is applied to organizational behavior, individuals are seen as struggling with each other to protect their spheres of responsibility, and this behavior is the result of human evolutionary heritage.

It should be noted that Ardrey's aggression and territory theories are viewed with great skepticism. The aggression theory has been criticized from two perspectives:

1. There are alternative explanations of aggression. Fromm has suggested that aggression results from childhood experiences; Hitler's aggressive-

ness, for instance, could be explained by his lack of warm relationships as a child, particularly with his mother.[36-38]

2. Humans may have evolved from killer apes, but the purpose of the killing was not aggressive. Apes killed for food, not for pleasure.

Another line of inquiry has been whether society and organizations impose controls that are unnatural and therefore produce undesirable behavior. Morris has suggested that humans, having evolved from apes, find themselves frustrated by societal controls.[39] He has compared human behavior with animal behavior in captivity. Because animals in zoos often exhibit atypical behavior, Morris concludes that organizations are a form of captivity for humans and that human captivity produces atypical behavior.

One of the most persistent and controversial theories has been that intelligence varies among races. Although this is not a theory of personality, it does suggest that human behavior will vary among races because of innate capabilities. In recent years, Jensen has been the chief proponent of the theory, arguing that African-Americans as a group are intellectually inferior to whites and Asians in the United States.[40-42] As would be expected, Jensen's concept has been attacked strongly.

CONTENT THEORIES

Categorizing theories of motivation is artificial in that they greatly overlap. To facilitate discussion, however, some categorization is necessary. One useful approach is to classify theories as to content or process.[43,44] Content theories pertain to the substance of motivation. What is in people and their environments that serve as motivators? Process theories, on the other hand, pertain to the methods or processes by which individuals are motivated. This section discusses content theories, and the next considers process theories.

Content theory stems in part from the work of Frederick W. Taylor.[45,46] He viewed humans as inherently lazy and assumed that they could be motivated by financial incentives. In designing jobs (see Chapter 3), Taylor sought to make workers more efficient and coupled increased efficiency with increased pay. Another aspect of Taylor's content theory was that human performance frequently was reduced by fatigue. Job design, then, was intended to improve work processes to avoid worker fatigue.

In large part following Taylor's assumptions about fatigue, Elton Mayo and a team of researchers undertook a series of studies that revolutionized the way worker motivation was perceived. Mayo and his staff conducted a series of experiments at the Western Electric Hawthorne plant in Chicago between 1927 and 1932. In the first experiment, lighting was adjusted to find an optimal level of illumination that would avoid fatigue. Efficiency rose as lighting was increased. Later, however, when lighting was reduced to equal ordinary moonlight, there was no reduction in efficiency.[47–49] This finding led the researchers to conclude that social and psychological factors were important in influencing worker behavior.

Subsequent Hawthorne experiments involved rest breaks and wage incentive systems. The experimenters adjusted the frequency and length of rest breaks as well as the length of the workday. Wage incentive systems were introduced so that, by adjusting their behavior, individual workers could increase their pay. Neither of these approaches seemed to have much influence on performance. Sometimes when the experimenters expected performance to decline because of changes they had introduced, it increased. They concluded that performance sometimes increased because workers enjoyed being part of the experiment and not because of the experiment itself. Today this is known as the Hawthorne effect.

The bank wiring study was one of the most important Hawthorne experiments. The study involved experimenters' observing interpersonal relations while workers constructed telephone terminals. The conclusion was that the employees acted not as isolated individuals but as part of informal work groups that determined the level of performance. Groups set standards for what was a fair day's work. A worker performing above that level was a rate buster, and one performing below was a chiseler.

The main content theme of the Hawthorne studies and the resulting human relations approach to motivation is that workers have a need to belong. Informal work groups satisfy that need, especially because managerial approaches tend to ignore the need. Advocates of human relations theory have concluded that informal work groups can affect performance both positively and negatively (Chapter 11 discusses some approaches to utilizing this body of theory for the betterment of workers and organizations).

The Hawthorne experiments have been subjected to severe criticisms as well as lauded as a major breakthrough in motivation research. Judging the experiments by today's standards, the methodology had many flaws. For example, some of the outcomes may have been a result of the types of people recruited to participate in the experiments. Less willing participants might have performed much differently. Some of the experiments were not well controlled. Personnel changes while the experiments were in progress might have contributed to some of the results. Mayo and his researchers have been criticized for ignoring alternative explanations of performance and dogmatically concluding that groups were the primary determinant of performance. The Hawthorne studies also have been criticized for ignoring the Depression and the rise of unions as possible influences on workers' motivations.[50,51]

A hierarchy of human needs, as suggested by Maslow, is another form of content theory.[52–54] Basing his theory on psychological clinical experience,

Maslow proposed that human behavior is the result of unsatisfied needs and that needs lead to the search for gratification. He suggested five sets of needs:

1. Physiological needs involve maintaining the body's normal balances of water, oxygen, salt, and the like (homeostasis). Deprivation of a needed item, such as water, will result in behavior to satisfy the need.
2. Safety needs include not only protection from physical dangers but also the sense of safety that comes with routine behavior.
3. Belongingness and love needs entail the sense of being part of a social group.
4. Esteem needs involve the desire to differentiate oneself from others. Although belonging needs may have the effect of submerging one in a group, esteem needs make one distinct from others in the group.
5. The need for self-actualization entails self-fulfillment or maximizing one's potential.

According to Maslow, these five sets of needs are hierarchical or constitute a hierarchy of needs; that is, one level precedes the other in importance. The term used to describe this is *prepotency*. Physiological and safety needs must be satisfied before an individual can direct attention to belongingness needs. Although Maslow's theory has been extremely popular, research efforts have not substantiated its prepotency aspect. Cross-sectional studies that compared workers at different levels in an organization indicate that some groups of employees may emphasize some needs more than others.[55,56]

A variant of Maslow's theory is ERG theory, proposed by Alderfer.[57,58] He combined Maslow's physiological and safety needs into existence needs (E), combined love and esteem needs into relatedness needs (R), and relabeled the self-actualizing need as a growth need (G). Unlike Maslow, Alderfer does not contend that these needs are hierarchical but rather suggests that two of the needs may be operating simultaneously. Both Maslow's and Alderfer's theories are weak in that the concepts of need and self-actualization/growth have not been made operational. It is unclear whether these needs are assumed to be psychological and/or physiological and what is meant by a need being satisfied (i.e., whether the need continues after being satisfied). Similarly, self-actualization is an elusive concept. How can one tell when an individual is being motivated by the need to self-actualize?

Another proponent of self-actualization theory has been Argyris. Like Maslow and others, Argyris has suggested that people have natural development patterns. According to Argyris, people develop along seven continua, and these can be regarded as motivators.[59-62] People tend to develop:

1. from passivity to activity
2. from dependence to independence

3. from behaving in few ways to behaving in many ways
4. from shallow interests to deep interests
5. from having a short time perspective to having a longer one
6. from subordinates to equals and superordinates
7. from lack of awareness of self to control of self

Like the other content theories, this one suggests that these tendencies are inherent in individuals. It would follow, then, that organizations should recognize these needs and should attempt to assist employees to develop accordingly rather than present obstacles to such development.

Herzberg's two-factor theory offers still another explanation of worker motivation.[63-65] Herzberg has suggested that there is one set of factors that can motivate only in a negative sense in that they produce job dissatisfaction. When these factors are satisfied, they become neutral, much like Maslow's needs, which when satisfied no longer motivate behavior. Herzberg calls this first set hygiene factors. The second set are motivators and are particularly important as positive motivators. These include:

- achievement, or the feeling of having accomplished a job
- recognition, or having someone praise or blame one for performance
- work itself, or a perception of the nature of the job
- responsibility, or having the duty for one's own work and possibly the work of others
- advancement, or changing one's position in the hierarchy of the organization

A characteristic common to these motivators is that they all relate to work and that employees derive satisfaction from their work.

Hygiene factors, in contrast, can be dissatisfiers but not motivators. Herzberg includes as hygiene factors "supervision, interpersonal relations, physical working conditions, salary, company policies and administrative practices, benefits, and job security."[66] Perhaps most controversial in this list is salary or pay. Financial incentives have long been thought of as prime motivators, yet Herzberg's research found pay not to be a motivator. If pay was perceived to be too low, dissatisfaction could result, but an adequate level of pay was a neutral factor. Although there are many proponents of the two-factor theory, there is no consensus among researchers about the role of pay as a motivator.

The two-factor theory has been widely accepted but also has been subjected to severe attack. One issue has involved the methodology employed in Herzberg's research. Workers were asked to recall a time when they felt positively or negatively about their jobs. Then, through a series of questions, the researchers explored what series of events led to that positive or negative feeling. Responses later were coded by the researchers into the factors that have been mentioned. This raises the question as to how this coding was conducted because Herzberg's factors seem to overlap. An altercation between worker and supervisor could involve the factors of recognition, supervision, and interpersonal relations, the first of these being one of Herzberg's motivators and the two others being hygiene factors. The substance of that same argument between worker and supervisor could involve the factors of the work itself (a motivator) and physical working conditions (a hygiene factor).

A prescription that emerges from virtually all the content theories is that employees should be encouraged to develop and that this is to be accomplished through meaningful work situations. Intrinsic motivators are viewed as being more effective than extrinsic ones, such as pay and job security. The traditional view of the manager has been that of a severe taskmaster who must oversee workers lest they become lazy and nonproductive. McGregor has labeled this approach to management Theory X.[67] Content theories, on the other hand, suggest that people are better motivated by forces within them. They need and want to develop their capabilities, and organizations can help meet these human needs by providing work. Bureaucracy should be more humane to encourage self-development or, as McGregor puts it, should use Theory Y. Ouchi has suggested a variant that he calls Theory Z.[68,69] In organizations operating with this theory, the emphasis is participation, belongingness of workers, and productivity. It has been suggested that one reason for Japan's phenomenal economic success has been its reliance on Theory Z.

PROCESS THEORIES

Process theories are nonsubstantive in that they do not attempt to explain what forces motivate people. Where the content theories focus on different types of needs as motivators, the process theories are concerned with the means by which people are motivated to act.

Stimulus–response theories are process theories. An assumption is made that a stimulus results in some form of behavior. Infants inherit this mechanism for basic bodily functions, so that hunger produces the response of crying and a full bladder produces the response of urination. As the infant develops, more elaborate stimulus–response patterns are developed and/or learned. Pavlov's experiments with conditioning a dog to salivate at the sound of a bell is a well-known example of learned response patterns.[70–72]

Thorndike developed what he called the law of effect, which in brief terms holds that the probability of a response recurring will increase when a previous stimulus–response event has been pleasurable or satisfying.[73] Hull, building on Thorndike's theory, suggested that effort is a function of habit strength and drive.

Habit strength refers to the probability of a response recurring because of previous pleasurable experience; drives are needs, especially the primary needs of food, water, oxygen, and the like.[74-76] Many of the ideas of Pavlov, Hull, and Thorndike underlie contemporary process theories.

Field theory was developed at about the same time as drive theory. Lewin conceptualized the person as part of the environment, just as an atom can be understood as part of its environment or field.[77-79] Emphasis was given to the forces within the environment that stimulate the individual to act. Rather than using the stimulus–response model, however, Lewin used a cognitive model, seeing the individual as a thinking or perceiving organism. Individuals act in accordance with what they expect to happen. The stimulus–response theory emphasizes past experience, but Lewin's expectancy theory focuses on the future. Lewin's theory recognizes choice in behavior. The worker asks, "Should I do X or not?"

The concept of expectancy has been coupled with that of instrumentality into what Vroom has called the V-I-E theory (Valence-Instrumentality-Expectancy).[80] An individual considering a possible behavior questions whether it is likely to produce a desired outcome. The possible behavior is considered an instrument for satisfaction. Valence refers to the strength with which one desires an outcome or wishes to avoid it; valences range from + 1 to −1. A valence of 0 means that the individual is indifferent about the outcome. Any single behavior can have two or more outcomes, each of which will have its own valence. A worker who persistently compliments a supervisor may expect this to result in a promotion (positive valence), but that same behavior might destroy friendships among the employee's peers (negative valence). As with the Thorndike theory, expectancy theory emphasizes probabilities: What are the probabilities of various possible outcomes as a result of contemplated behavior?[81]

Porter and Lawler built upon the expectancy model in an attempt to explain worker performance. As noted in the previous section, the content theories tend to assume that job satisfaction affects performance: High satisfaction yields high performance. Porter and Lawler suggest that the opposite is true: Performance or the accomplishment of tasks produces extrinsic and intrinsic rewards that lead to job satisfaction. The model also uses effort as a variable that influences performance in conjunction with role perceptions and abilities.[82]

Just as all other theories have been criticized, so has expectancy theory.[83,84] It is more difficult to apply than the need theory. With content theories, if it is known what needs are important to workers, the organization can emphasize those needs. Expectancy theory, on the other hand, does not indicate what type of performance is likely to lead to satisfaction or explain what expected rewards would energize the individual.

Another criticism is that expectancy theory does not have a time perspective. It does not consider how values were acquired in the past, yet those values will influence an individual's decision about what rewards seem desirable. Neither does expectancy theory take into account future time perspectives, which vary among individuals. In selecting behavior, one worker may be involved with only the immediate future, whereas another is concerned with how current behavior will produce rewards in 5 years. Another major criticism is that research often has been unable to confirm the model. Correlations between V-I-E data and measures of performance have been weak.

Perhaps the most critical problem with expectancy theory is its reliance on hedonism, namely, that individuals seek to maximize pleasure and to minimize pain. Hedonism is deterministic in that it suggests that people always are motivated by a desire for pleasure. This cannot always be the case because people often do things that are not pleasurable for them. Moreover, they may seek results that provide rewards but not the maximum possible rewards. This is known as satisficing behavior.[85] Without having to accept all facets of Freudian psychology, it is possible to accept the concept of the unconscious, which influences behavior without the individual's awareness or without the individual being able to choose behavior solely on the basis of the pleasure principle. Finally, expectancy theory considers pleasure and pain opposite ends of the same spectrum, yet being motivated by a desire for pleasure and being motivated by a desire to avoid pain would seem to be substantively different.

Other process theories emphasize the function of human perception in influencing behavior; these, like expectancy theory, concentrate on cognitive processes. At least four sets of theories are important here: cognitive dissonance, exchange, attribution, and equity.

Cognitive dissonance theory, developed by Festinger, posits that an individual cannot tolerate being confronted by two or more mutually exclusive alternatives and will seek to reduce the dissonance by choosing one alternative.[86] Once the decision is made and the behavior is carried out, the individual will avoid (repress) thoughts that the wrong decision was made. A worker feeling unfairly criticized by the boss in front of peers might perceive two choices: forgetting the event, or speaking out against the boss. Should the latter choice be selected and some adverse action be taken, according to the cognitive dissonance theory the worker will continue to believe that the choice was correct.

A second type of theory emphasizing perception involves the concept of exchange. The idea was developed primarily by Homans to explain group behavior (discussed in Chapter 11).[87] Homans conceptualized that groups form when individuals make exchanges with each other. As people interact with each other, they exchange rewards and costs. A friendship may grow because the individuals involved perceive favorable exchanges.

A third type of theory based on perception is attribution theory. Developed by Heider, the theory explains behavior in terms of attributing motives to others.[88,89] If a manager returns from lunch and ignores others in the office, workers will generate reasons for that behavior. One worker may think the boss is simply engrossed in work, whereas another may think the behavior is typical in that the supervisor is perceived as a basically unfriendly person. The workers thus respond to a situation according to their differing attributions.

A fourth theory, which includes elements of the three others, is equity theory. According to this theory, proposed by Adams, an individual compares the effort on the job with the rewards of the job in relation to the effort and the rewards of persons in comparable positions.[90-93] The theory focuses on workers' perceptions of whether they are receiving equal pay for equal work. Although rewards may be other than financial, such as having a large carpeted private office, the reward of pay has been the main focus of research on equity theory.

Changes in behavior are motivated when workers perceive inequities. The perception of being underpaid results in their decreasing the quality and/or quantity of work; overpayment results in the opposite change in behavior. In some instances when inequities are perceived, behavior changes may not occur because workers revise their standards to bring their perceptions into an equitable balance. Workers may initially think they are overpaid but upon further reflection conclude that they are not because they perceive themselves to be performing duties not performed by others. Although this rationalizing process is needed in the theory, it reduces the power of equity theory to predict performance.

Equity theory is based on the concept of balance, as is the related theory of cognitive consistency proposed by Korman.[94-96] He contended that people select behaviors that are consistent with their perceptions of themselves (self-esteem). If they perceive themselves to be capable workers, they will be motivated to perform well; low performance would be incompatible with high self-esteem.

Organizations can influence self-perceptions. An organization with rigid policies tells its workers in effect that they are inadequate and therefore must be controlled. The resulting low level of self-esteem will produce a low level of job performance. If a worker becomes increasingly effective in performance over time, this is largely because of internal attributions of outcomes. A reduction in effectiveness is likely to be caused by external attributions. Research findings have not fully confirmed the Korman theory.

The last theory considered here brings the discussion back to the stimulus–response theory described at the beginning of this section and to the nature–nurture controversy at the beginning of the chapter. The theory is behaviorism, or operant conditioning, as advanced by Skinner.[97-99] Skinnerian psychology, which has been both well accepted and criticized frequently, is sometimes used to explain behavior in organizations. One of the first to suggest the applicability of Skinnerian theory was Nord, who contended that the theories of Maslow and others had received a disproportionate amount of attention.[100] According to Skinner, behavior is acognitive and is shaped by the environment. Skinner, however, does not view animals and people as operating on a simple stimulus–response basis. The stimulus–response mechanism is based on reflex motions in which the behavior is uncontrolled. A person does not decide consciously whether to kick a leg when tapped on the knee. "Classical" conditioning might be able to make the person kick involuntarily at the sound of a bell.

Operant conditioning, on the other hand, involves conditioning behavior to operate on the environment to produce a consequence. Rather than being a reflexive action, behavior is selected. Skinner experimented with animals and provided rewards when desired behavior was achieved. For example, a pigeon was conditioned to raise its head high and, as a result, to receive food. The food is a reinforcer of the behavior, in this case a positive reinforcer. Reinforcement also can be negative, although its effects may be more limited. An example of negative reinforcement is when a supervisor nags an employee for failing to complete an assigned task on time. A negative reinforcer may need to be actually present to prevent a behavior, whereas a positive reinforcer need only have a greater than 0 probability of occurring. A person may be motivated to act even if the possibility of receiving a reward has low probability (gambling is a good example). Much of the research in this area has focused on the frequency of rewards, such as providing the reward every fifth time the correct behavior is elicited.

Critics of Skinnerian psychology see dangers in emphasizing extrinsic rewards at the expense of intrinsic ones. Earlier the individual may have been willing to act for intrinsic satisfaction, but now the individual needs an external reward. Employees may be willing to work past quitting time without extra compensation because their jobs are interesting. Once an overtime pay system is introduced, however, they may be unwilling to work even a minute extra without additional pay. Another form of extrinsic reward is expressions of approval or praise. If workers are conditioned to expect praise, will their performance decline if praise no longer is given for a well-done job?

The main line of attack on Skinnerian psychology is its emphasis on behaviorism. Nord writes: "Modern Americans, especially of the managerial class, prefer to think of themselves and others as being self-actualizing creatures near the top of Maslow's need-hierarchy, rather than as animals being controlled and even 'manipulated' by their environment."[101] The contention is that humans are complex organisms and should not be compared with rats in a Skinnerian conditioning box. Skinnerian psychology, as with need theories, is criticized as being deterministic, that is, as declaring that human behavior is determined by environment. Skinner has written that operant conditioning should not be confused with learning. The concept of learning the behaviors that produce rewards does not need to be used in explaining behavior. This argument disturbs those who see humans as thinking organisms who consciously select behaviors.

Neither the content nor the process theories specifically address the question of whether important differences exist between the public and private sectors.

The theories are posited to be of general applicability, with research then testing whether that is the case. Motivation in the public sector has been suggested as being rational, norm based, and/or affective.[102] First, people enter public service because it is a rational means of achieving their objectives, such as serving as advocate for a particular special interest. Second, people also enter public service to serve what they regard as the public interest. Third, people pursue public service careers because of a sincere commitment to a particular program or service. Studies comparing public and private sector employees have had mixed results, with some finding greater employee job satisfaction in the public sector and others finding little difference or greater satisfaction in the private sector.[103-105] When congruency exists between the values of the organization and the employees' values, then job satisfaction is likely to be high and turnover low.[106]

SUMMARY

Theories on human motivation abound. Some focus largely on personality. The internal conflict theory of Freud continues to be an important influence on how human personality is perceived. Other theories relate to human evolution, suggesting that aggressive behavior and defense of territory are innate qualities. Body type has been related to variations in personality.

Content theories attempt to explain behavior in terms of the types of forces that motivate people. Human relations theory has stressed the need for interpersonal relations. A hierarchy of needs, culminating in the need for self-actualization, has been one of the most popular theories in recent years; the theory suggests that humans arc motivated by unmet needs that, when satisfied, lead to the arousal of other needs. Another popular approach has been the two-factor theory, suggesting that hygiene factors can be dissatisfiers but not motivators and that positive motivators involve satisfaction with work itself.

Process theories, being nonsubstantive, focus on the methods by which people are motivated. Early concepts that serve as the foundation for contemporary process theories include stimulus–response theory, the law of effect, drive theory, and field theory. Especially popular has been expectancy theory, which suggests that behavior results from individuals calculating whether a possible behavior will be instrumental in providing a desired outcome. Cognitive dissonance stresses the desire of individuals to resolve problems by making a choice and then not reassessing the decision they made. Exchange theory sees human behavior as based on interactions: Favorable interactions increase the probability of more of these interactions. Attribution theory involves the process of attributing motives to others and then acting in response to those attributions. Equity theory is concerned with the relationship between effort and reward for one person in comparison with the same relationship for others. Cognitive consistency concentrates on the balance between self-esteem and behavior. Behaviorism suggests that behavior is acquired by operating on the environment to produce a desired consequence.

None of the theories discussed here provides an all-encompassing approach to explaining human motivation, yet to some extent each has been propounded by its champions as the ultimate explanation. Frankly, the field of motivation has had an ample number of dogmatists. Social research in the last several decades has made remarkable strides in understanding human behavior, but there still is much to be learned. This will become apparent in the next chapter, which considers the limitations involved in applying motivation theories to real-world situations.

NOTES

1. R.C. Beck, *Motivation: Theories and Principles*, 3d ed. (Englewood Cliffs, N.J.: Prentice-Hall, 1990).

2. F.J. Landy, *Psychology of Work Behavior*, 4th ed. (Homewood, Ill.: Dorsey Press, 1989).

3. H.L. Petri, *Motivation: Theory, Research, and Application*, 3d ed. (Belmont, Calif.: Wadsworth Publishing Company, 1991).

4. R.M. Steers, *Motivation and Your Work Behavior*, 5th ed. (New York: McGraw-Hill Book Company, 1991).

5. J.A. Wagner, III, and J.R. Hollenbeck, *Management of Organizational Behavior* (Englewood Cliffs, N.J.: Prentice-Hall, 1992).

6. Landy, *Psychology of Work Behavior*.

7. C.J. Cranny, et al., *Job Satisfaction: How People Feel about Their Jobs and How It Affects Their Performance* (New York: Lexington Books, 1992).

8. R.D. Arvey, et al., Job satisfaction: Environmental and genetic components, *Journal of Applied Psychology* 74 (1989): 187–192.

9. R. Cropanzano and K. James, Some methodological considerations for the behavioral genetic analysis of work attitudes, *Journal of Applied Psychology* 75 (1990): 433–439.

10. T.J. Bouchard, Jr., et al., Genetic influences on job satisfaction: A reply to Cropanzano and James, *Journal of Applied Psychology* 77 (1992): 89–93.

11. J.B. Miner, et al., Theory testing under adverse conditions: Motivation to manage in the People's Republic of China, *Journal of Applied Psychology* 76 (1991): 343–349.

12. U. Dicle, et al., Human resources management practices in Japanese organizations in the United States, *Public Personnel Management* 17 (1988): 331–339.

13. J.R. Lincoln and A.L. Kalleberg, *Culture, Control, and Commitment: A Study of Work Organization and Work Attitudes in the United States and Japan* (Cambridge, England: Cambridge University Press, 1990).

14. S. Freud, *The Basic Writings of Sigmund Freud*, trans. and ed. A.A. Brill (New York: Modern Library, 1938).

15. _____, *The Standard Edition of the Complete Psychological Works of Sigmund Freud*, trans. J. Strachey in collaboration with A. Freud (London: Hogarth, 1961).

16. _____, *Civilization and Its Discontents*, trans. and ed. J. Strachey (New York: W.W. Norton & Co., 1962).

17. _____, *Beyond the Pleasure Principle*, trans. and ed. J. Strachey (New York: Liveright Publishing Corp., 1961).

18. _____, *The Ego and the Id*, trans. J. Riviere, ed. J. Strachey (New York: W.W. Norton & Co., 1962).

19. _____, *Group Psychology and the Analysis of the Ego*, trans. and ed. J. Strachey (New York: Modern Library, 1950).

20. _____, *The Interpretation of Dreams*, trans. A.A. Brill (New York: Modern Library, 1950).

21. C.G. Jung, *The Collected Works of C.G. Jung,* eds. H. Read, et al. (multivolume, publishers and dates vary).

22. _____, *The Integration of the Personality*, trans. S. Dell (London: Routledge & Kegan Paul, 1950).

23. _____, *The Undiscovered Self*, trans. R.F.C. Hull (New York: American Library, 1958).

24. A. Adler, *The Individual Psychology of Alfred Adler*, ed. and annot. H.L. Ansbacher and R.R. Ansbacher (New York: Basic Books, 1956).

25. _____, *Understanding Human Nature*, trans. W.B. Wolfe (New York: Greenberg, 1927).

26. _____, *The Practice and Theory of Individual Psychology*, trans. P. Radin (New York: Harcourt, Brace and Company, 1924).

27. E. Berne, *Games People Play: The Psychology of Human Relationships* (New York: Grove Press, 1967).

28. H.D. Lasswell, *Psychopathology and Politics* (Chicago, Ill.: University of Chicago Press, 1930).

29. W.H. Sheldon, *The Varieties of Human Physique* (New York: Harper & Brothers, 1940).

30. _____, *The Varieties of Temperament* (New York: Harper & Brothers, 1942).

31. L.A. Tucker, Physical attractiveness, somatotype, and the male personality, *Journal of Clinical Psychology* 40 (1984): 1,226–1,234.

32. S. Milgram, Some conditions of obedience and disobedience to authority, *Human Relations* 18 (1965): 57–76.

33. R. Ardrey, *African Genesis: A Personal Investigation into the Animal Origins and Nature of Man* (New York: Atheneum Publishers, 1961).

34. _____, *The Hunting Hypothesis* (New York: Atheneum Publishers, 1976).

35. _____, *The Territorial Imperative: A Personal Inquiry into the Animal Origins of Property and Nations* (New York: Atheneum Publishers, 1966).

36. E. Fromm, *The Anatomy of Human Destructiveness* (New York: Holt, Rinehart & Winston, 1973).

37. A. Alland, Jr., *The Human Imperative* (New York: Columbia University Press, 1972).

38. R. Claiborne, *God or Beast: Evolution and Human Nature* (New York: W.W. Norton & Co., 1974).

39. D. Morris, *The Human Zoo* (New York: McGraw-Hill Book Company, 1969).

40. A.R. Jensen, How much can we boost IQ and scholastic achievement, *Harvard Educational Review* 39 (1969): 1–123.

41. _____, *Genetics and Education* (New York: Harper & Row Publishers, 1972).

42. E. Mensh and H. Mensh, *The IQ Mythology: Class, Race, Gender, and Inequality* (Carbondale: Southern Illinois University Press, 1991).

43. J.P. Campbell, et al., *Managerial Behavior, Performance, and Effectiveness* (New York: McGraw-Hill Book Company, 1970), 340–383.

44. For an alternative classification, see R.A. Katzell and D.E. Thompson, Work motivation: Theory and practice, *American Psychologist* 45 (1990): 144–153.

45. F.W. Taylor, *The Principles of Scientific Management* (New York: Harper & Row, 1911), 42–48, 621–667.

46. C.D. Wrege and R.G. Greenwood, *Frederick W. Taylor: The father of scientific management* (Homewood, Ill.: Business One Irwin, 1991).

47. F.J. Roethlisberger and W.J. Dickson, *Management and the Worker* (Cambridge, Mass.: Harvard University Press, 1939), 17.

48. T.N. Whitehead, *Leadership in a Free Society* (Cambridge, Mass.: Harvard University Press, 1937).

49. G.C. Homans, *Fatigue of Workers* (New York: Reinhold, 1941).

50. H.A. Landsberger, *Hawthorne Revisited: Management and the Worker, Its Critics, and Developments in Human Relations in Industry* (Ithaca, N.Y.: Cornell University, 1958).

51. A. Carey, The Hawthorne studies: A radical criticism, *American Sociological Review* 32 (1967): 403–416.

52. A.H. Maslow, *Motivation and Personality* (New York: Harper & Row, 1954).

53. _____, A theory of human motivation, *Psychological Review* 50 (1943): 370–396.

54. _____, *Eupsychian Management: A Journal* (Homewood, Ill.: Richard D. Irwin, 1965).

55. J.P. Wanous and A. Zwany, A cross-sectional test of need hierarchy theory, *Organizational Behavior and Human Performance* 18 (1977): 78–97.

56. B.T. Loher, et al., A meta-analysis of the relations of job characteristics to job satisfaction, *Journal of Applied Psychology* 70 (1985): 380–389.

57. C.P. Alderfer, An empirical test of a new theory of human needs, *Organizational Behavior and Human Performance* 4 (1969): 142–175.

58. _____, *Existence, Relatedness, and Growth: Human Needs in Organizational Settings* (New York: Free Press, 1972).

59. C. Argyris, *Personality and Organization: The Conflict between System and the Individual* (New York: Harper & Row, 1957), 50.

60. _____, Organizational man: Rational and self-actualizing, *Public Administration Review* 33 (1973): 354–357.

61. _____, *Strategy, Change and Defensive Strategies* (Boston: Pitman Publishing, 1985).

62. H.A. Simon, Organizational man: Rational or self-actualizing? *Public Administration Review* 33 (1973): 346–353.

63. F. Herzberg, et al., *The Motivation To Work*, 2d ed. (New York: John Wiley & Sons, 1964).

64. E.A. Maidani, Comparative study of Herzberg's two-factor theory of job satisfaction among public and private sectors, *Public Personnel Management* 20 (1991): 441–448.

65. C. Park, et al., Testing Herzberg's motivation theory in a comparative study of U.S. and Korean public employees, *Review of Public Personnel Administration* 8 (Summer 1988): 40–60.

66. Herzberg, et al., *The Motivation To Work*, 113.

67. D. McGregor, *The Human Side of Enterprise* (New York: McGraw-Hill Book Company, 1960).

68. W.G. Ouchi, *Theory Z* (Reading, Mass.: Addison-Wesley Publishing Company, 1981).

69. J.S. Bowman, Japanese management: Personnel policies in the public sector, *Public Personnel Management* 13 (1984): 197–247.

70. I.P. Pavlov, *Conditioned Reflexes: An Investigation of the Physiological Activity of the Cerebral Cortex*, trans. and ed. G.V. Anrep (London: Oxford University Press, 1927).

71. _____, *Experimental Psychology and Other Essays* (New York: Philosophical Library, 1957).

72. _____, *Lectures on Conditioned Reflexes*, trans. W.H. Goutt, Vols. 1 and 2 (New York: International Publishers, 1963).

73. E.L. Thorndike, *Animal Intelligence* (New York: The Macmillan, 1911).

74. C.L. Hull, *Principles of Behavior* (New York: Appleton-Century-Crofts, 1943).

75. _____, *Essentials of Behavior* (New Haven, Conn.: Yale University Press, 1951).

76. _____, *A Behavioral System* (New Haven, Conn.: Yale University Press, 1952).

77. K. Lewin, *The Conceptual Representations and the Measurement of Psychological Forces* (Durham, N.C.: Duke University Press, 1938).

78. _____, *Field Theory in Social Science: Selected Theoretical Papers*, ed. D. Cartwright (New York: Harper & Row, 1951).

79. _____, *Principles of Topological Psychology*, trans. F. Heider and G.M. Heider (New York: McGraw-Hill Book Company, 1966).

80. V.H. Vroom, *Work and Motivation* (New York: John Wiley & Sons, 1964).

81. M.R. Fusilier, et al., A within-person test of the form of the expectancy theory model in a choice context, *Organizational Behavior and Human Performance* 34 (1984): 323–342.

82. L.W. Porter and E.E. Lawler, III, *Managerial Attitudes and Performance* (Homewood, Ill.: Richard D. Irwin, 1968).

83. E.A. Locke, Personnel attitudes and motivation, *Annual Review of Psychology* 26 (1975): 457–480.

84. L.L. Cummings, Organizational behavior, *Annual Review of Psychology* 36 (1985): 573–611.

85. J.G. March and H.A. Simon, *Organizations* (New York: John Wiley & Sons, 1958).

86. L. Festinger, *A Theory of Cognitive Dissonance* (Stanford, Calif.: Stanford University Press, 1957).

87. G.S. Homans, *The Human Group* (New York: Harcourt, Brace & World, 1950).

88. F. Heider, *The Psychology of Interpersonal Relations* (New York: John Wiley & Sons, 1958).

89. _____, Attitudes and cognitive organization, *Journal of Psychology* 21 (1946): 107–112.

90. J.S. Adams and S. Freedman, Equity theory revisited: Comments and annotated bibliography, *Advances in Experimental Social Psychology* (1976): 43–90.

91. J.S. Adams, Toward an understanding of inequity, *Journal of Abnormal Psychology* 67 (1963): 422–436.

92. J.W. Harder, Equity theory versus expectancy theory: The case of major league baseball free agents, *Journal of Applied Psychology* 76 (1991): 458–464.

93. D. Katz, et al., eds., *The Study of Organizations* (San Francisco: Jossey-Bass, 1980).

94. A.K. Korman, Organizational achievement, aggression, and creativity: Some suggestions toward an integrated theory, *Organizational Behavior and Human Performance* 6 (1971): 593–613.

95. _____, Hypothesis of work behavior revisited and an extension, *Academy of Management Review* 1 (January 1976): 50–63.

96. _____, *Career Success, Personal Failure* (Englewood Cliffs, N.J.: Prentice-Hall, 1980).

97. B.F. Skinner, *Science and Human Behavior* (New York: Free Press, 1953).

98. _____, *Beyond Freedom and Dignity* (New York, Alfred A. Knopf, 1971).

99. _____, *Upon Further Reflection* (Englewood Cliffs, N.J.: Prentice-Hall, 1987).

100. W.R. Nord, Beyond the teaching machine: The neglected area of operant conditioning in the theory and practice of management, *Organizational Behavior and Human Performance* 4 (1969): 375–401.

101. Nord, Beyond the teaching machine, 376–377.

102. J.L. Perry and L.R. Wise, The motivational bases of public service, *Public Administration Review* 50 (1990): 367–373.

103. D.L. Balfour and B. Wechsler, Organizational commitment: A reconceptualization and empirical test of public–private differences, *Review of Public Personnel Administration* 10 (Spring 1990): 23–40.

104. B.E. Blunt and K.A. Spring, MPA graduates and the dilemma of job satisfaction: Does crossing the sector line make a difference, *Public Personnel Management* 20 (1991): 449–456.

105. B.S. Steel and R.L. Warner, Job satisfaction among early labor force participants: Unexpected outcomes in public and private sector comparisons, *Review of Public Personnel Administration* 10 (Spring 1990): 4–22.

106. W.R. Boxx, et al., Organizational values and value congruency and their impact on satisfaction, commitment, and cohesion: An empirical examination within the public sector, *Public Personnel Management* 20 (1991): 195–205.

Chapter 11

Motivation in Daily Operations

Getting the right people for the right jobs might solve all motivational problems. If a job is intrinsically dull and the supervisor of that job is a tyrant, then a worker to be recruited should be one who thrives on boring work and is submissive. Although there may be virtues in such an approach, it is impractical when applied to all positions. Instead, there is much emphasis now on finding techniques that can motivate workers both for increasing their own satisfaction and for improving the productivity of the organization.

This chapter discusses techniques used in organizations to motivate workers based on the theories discussed in Chapter 10:

1. motivation efforts directed at individual employees, particularly efforts that provide increased worker autonomy
2. work groups and leaders, especially leaders who are managers
3. techniques emphasizing performance and organizational change
4. practical problems associated with applying motivation theory to daily management problems

INDIVIDUAL WORKERS AND AUTONOMY

Frederick Taylor, Elton Mayo, and other early researchers were concerned about the work environment affecting worker performance, and that concern continues. Studies are conducted as to how office settings can facilitate good worker relationships.[1] Ergonomics, the study of engineering as it relates to biology, involves designing office equipment such as video display terminals to meet the "human" needs of workers. These efforts concentrate on reducing employee fatigue and creating a pleasant work environment but do not necessarily stimulate workers to be productive.

Incentive systems are more focused on the motivation of workers to perform. Educational incentives are one of the most common forms in government; some jurisdictions provide released time from work in addition to covering tuition costs. Many provide incentives for unused sick leave in the form of cash bonuses, conversion of sick leave to annual leave, or application of sick leave toward early retirement. Cash awards for money-saving suggestions and for good performance also are used. A problem with these, however, is administering them fairly to avoid complaints that "favored" employees unfairly receive bonuses. Merit pay, discussed earlier, is an illustration of using money as a motivator.[2]

Several of the theories discussed in Chapter 10 either explicitly or implicitly suggest that worker motivation and/or job satisfaction improves as employees gain control over themselves. This concept holds that work should be redirected to recognize employees as individuals rather than as robots programmed to perform tasks. Increased autonomy will provide them with greater respect for management and the organization.[3] In turn, workers will become more creative in dealing with the problems of their jobs. Whereas a robot simply performs as it was programmed, "liberated" workers develop more efficient and effective means of performing tasks. At least, that is the assumption.

McGregor's Theory Y is an example of the worker autonomy philosophy; the traditional Theory X involves close supervision of workers. According to McGregor, "physical and mental work is as natural as play or rest." Employees are not inherently lazy. A worker will seek responsibility and will "exercise self-direction and self-control in the service of objectives to which he is committed."[4] Providing workers with greater autonomy, freedom, or self-control will encourage them to utilize their intellectual abilities more fully.

Increasing autonomy requires rethinking traditional roles of management. The next section considers alternative management or leadership styles, but it should be noted here that one approach to motivation is to reduce the intensity of supervision. One such method is management by exception. This technique sees the manager as dealing primarily with problems as they arise. Employees have great freedom to organize their work except when problems develop, at which point the manager intervenes. A requirement of management by exception is that considerable authority must be delegated to lower levels in the bureaucracy, permitting workers to take actions without having to obtain prior approval from their supervisors. This process is known as empowering employees.

Because management by exception is only a style or conceptualization of how supervisory personnel should perform, it can be resisted by those in authority. Therefore, organizational changes can be made to increase the likelihood of using the system. One alternative involves expanding the span of control—the number of persons and the types of work performed under any given manager. Span of control has been a recurrent topic of discussion in the study of administration. An assumption has been that the span of control over personnel should be relatively narrow when employees perform substantially different types of work.[5] A manager with twenty employees all doing different work cannot provide careful supervision. The attitude in the early 1990s, however, was that, if an organization chose to further the use of management by exception and to empower employees, it should expand the span of control. Such an approach forces managers to delegate responsibilities to subordinates. Similarly, assistants to administrators should be kept to a minimum. A bureau chief without deputy chiefs or administrative aides will have limited time to supervise subordinates.

Flexitime

Adjusting working hours is another method for increasing worker autonomy. The federal government uses the term *alternative work schedule* to refer to plans that differ from the familiar 5-day, 8-hour-per-day week.[6,7] Compressed work schedules involve 4-day or, in some cases, 3-day work weeks. Employees usually work the same total number of hours as in a 5-day week; obviously, 4 10-hour days are the same as 5 8-hour days. One variation is for workers to continue working 8-hour days but to alternate between 4-day and 6-day weeks so that their average work week remains 40 hours. Compressed work schedules do not by themselves greatly increase worker freedom on the job but obviously do enhance freedom off the job. Workers still must arrive and leave at specified times.

Flexible time, or flexitime, can be used with compressed schedules but more often is considered an alternative to them. In most flexitime systems, employees work the same number of hours each day in a 5-day week, but flexibility is allowed as to what those hours are. Flexitime systems have core time periods when all employees are expected to be at work. Figure 11–1 shows core times between 9 and 11 A.M. and between 1 and 3 P.M. Flexible bands or quiet times, when the office load may be lighter, precede the morning core time and follow the afternoon core time. Some flexitime systems have a set lunch break, such as noon to 1 P.M., whereas others have a flexible band then.

Figure 11-1 shows three possible work schedules. Workers A and B might be husband and wife. Worker A begins work later so as to be home before the children go to school, and worker B quits at 3:30 P.M. to be home about the time the children return from school. Worker C, in comparison, begins the day at 7 A.M. and does not quit until 5 P.M. but gets a 2-hour midday break for shopping, physician's appointments, or whatever.

Flexitime plans vary in their adaptability. Not only may lunch periods be fixed or flexible, but so can the workday. Some systems require an 8-hour day, others an 8-hour day averaged over 1 week, 2 weeks, or in some cases 2 months. Where that flexibility exists, an employee who wanted a 3-day weekend to take a trip

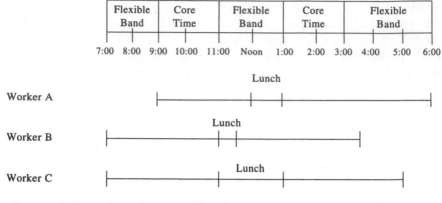

Figure 11-1 Sample Work Schedules Using Flexitime.

could decide to work 4 10-hour days in that week, as in the compressed work schedule.

Some systems allow workers to decide each day when they will begin and quit work; an employee can choose each morning whether to sleep an extra hour and not report to work until later. That can pose severe problems for the manager, however, who never knows how many persons will be working any day at any particular hour, and it can quickly lead to widespread disorganization and loss of control. Other systems require each employee to select a starting and quitting time to be followed for a month or perhaps indefinitely.

Flexitime and compressed work schedules have both advantages and disadvantages. Because the total working day is stretched from 8 hours to possibly 11 hours, employees frequently operate without immediate supervision, thereby increasing their control over their work (or giving them the opportunity to waste time). Delegation of authority may be inevitable under such plans. This increased independence is said to improve morale and job satisfaction.

A possible negative morale factor is that more detailed recordkeeping on hours worked may be required under flexitime than under conventional arrangements. Employees may have to maintain time cards, in contrast to the system in which everyone begins and ends work at the same time so that specific hourly records are not kept. Employees can view the time cards as evidence of management's unwillingness to trust them. Another drawback is that supervision is not always available when it is needed. If many employees report for work at 7 A.M. but the supervisor does not begin until 9 A.M., some work may be done differently from what the manager expects or wants. By the same token, support staff members sometimes are not present when they are needed early or late in the normal working day.

A major claim in favor of flexitime and compressed scheduling is that they increase productivity. In a 4-day work week, employees require less start-up and shutdown time, so that their time is utilized more effectively. Attitudinal surveys have found that employees think their productivity increases, and there is some evidence using objective criteria (such as the number of forms processed by clerical workers) to show that flexitime does improve output.

There is competing evidence to suggest that, when the workday is extended, productivity does not increase. Possible gains in productivity may be offset by worker fatigue. Supervisors tend to be skeptical about the effects on productivity. There is suspicion that workers goof off when the boss is not around. Supervisors tend to complain that key workers frequently are not available when they are needed. If a problem arises at 3:30 P.M. during the flexible band, the manager may have to postpone action until the next morning's core time. Although flexitime is usually overwhelmingly popular among workers, managers frequently have major concerns about its utility.[8]

Proponents of flexitime contend the opposite, namely that key personnel will tend to stagger their schedules so that someone with the needed skills is available from 7 A.M. to 6 P.M. This also means that more hours will be available for dealing with the public and agency clients. Although worker productivity may be increased, some operating costs may also rise. Heating and lighting costs may go up, and additional personnel may be needed to staff telephone switchboards and to operate other support services.

Flexible hours are said to reduce absenteeism and turnover and to improve employee recruitment.[9-11] A worker who becomes ill on the job can leave early and make up lost time in a day or two. This aspect of the plan, however, along with overtime, has caused problems with labor unions. If the worker makes up all lost time, sick leave in effect is denied. The simple solution is to debit the time from sick leave rather than require it to be made up. Similarly, should a worker who elects to work a 10-hour day be paid overtime rates for 2 of those hours? Some unions have insisted on such overtime.

Another limitation of flexitime is that it is inappropriate when employees work as a team. When they perform jobs largely independent of one another, there is little need for them all to be present at the same time. For example, for routine processing of state income tax returns, some employees could work effectively between midnight and 9 A.M. In other situations, such as road maintenance crews, workers must operate as a unit.

In addition to flexitime, governments as well as private employers are experimenting with flexiplace, which allows employees to work at home or any other suitable location.[12] The potential use of flexiplace has increased with the advent of greater computer applications in government work. Employees may telecommute via computer rather than waste time commuting to work. Transportation costs are reduced, and presumably workers impose fewer burdens on transportation systems and the environment by working at home rather than at a government office or other installation. Flexiplace reduces child care problems and may make employment possible for some people with severe physical handicaps. On the negative side, workers sometimes feel isolated by working out of their homes, and managers complain that they are unable to supervise the workers for whom they are responsible.

Changing the work schedules may improve worker satisfaction only marginally. The 4-day week simply may please a worker because there is 1 day less a week to perform a dull and unpleasant job. Neither a compressed schedule nor flexitime makes fundamental changes in the work performed. Some observers contend that more far-reaching changes are needed, with one set of proposals involving job enrichment or enlargement.

Job Enrichment

Job enlargement or enrichment is an old idea that regained prominence starting in the 1960s. In simple terms, the process involves redesigning jobs to make them more interesting for workers. The assumption is that this will increase job satisfaction, motivation, and performance. Enlargement means expanding the number of tasks to be performed in any one job to provide the worker with varied responsibilities. Most work involves routines and is cyclical. If the cycle is short, the worker frequently repeats the same operations. If a worker begins and completes the processing of a form in 1 minute and begins another form the next minute, the cycle is short, and the job is narrow rather than large. The assumption is that this short cycle will result in worker boredom, dissatisfaction, poor performance, absenteeism, and possible turnover.

On the other hand, job enlargement provides the worker with greater autonomy and responsibility.[13] In the case of processing a form, the employee may be assigned responsibility for reviewing not just a part of the form but all of it, and if its data are to be entered into a computer, the worker may be given the responsibility for transposing data onto machine-readable worksheets or inputing the data directly into a computer. The employee may be given discretion as to when each of these tasks is completed. One worker might process a form thoroughly before beginning another, whereas another worker might handle them in batches at each step in the cycle.

The critics of this type of job enlargement contend that only "horizontal loading" has occurred, tasks of the same level of responsibility have been combined. The work is no more interesting than before.[14] As a result, "vertical loading" is advocated in the name of job enrichment. Herzberg's two-factor theory is cited as the theoretical foundation for job enrichment. If the work is to be more satisfying, job redesign must concentrate on motivators. Herzberg contends that jobs should encourage employee growth by providing opportunities for increased knowledge, understanding, and creativity; workers should have an "opportunity to experience ambiguity in decision making" and "to individuate and seek real growth."[15-17] Enrichment involves having employees learn why they perform certain tasks so that they are aware of the importance of their work. Administrative regulations should be relaxed, giving the worker freedom to experiment with alternative methods for doing the assigned job. Supervision should be less intensive, so that employees are their own supervisors to an extent. In job enrichment, some of the responsibilities of higher-level positions are reassigned to ones at lower levels.

Techniques have been developed for gauging the motivational quality of existing jobs and potentially redesigned jobs. Turner and Lawrence developed the Requisite Task Attribute Index, which measures the attributes of variety, autonomy, required interaction, optional interaction, knowledge and skill required, and responsibility.[18] Building on that index and other models, Hackman and Oldham produced the Job Characteristics Model of Work Motivation and the Motivating Potential Score (MPS).[19] The model is expressed as follows:

$$\text{MPS} = \frac{\text{Skill variety} + \text{Task identity} + \text{Task significance}}{3} \times \text{Autonomy} \times \text{Feedback}$$

Variety, identity, and significance are seen as having an additive effect in determining whether the work is meaningful. Variety involves the number of different activities performed. Identity is the extent to which a whole or identifiable set of work is completed, and significance involves the effect of the work of a given job on others in or outside the organization. Autonomy is having responsibility for outcomes of the work, and feedback is obtaining information about the result of the work. Given the equation's structure, autonomy and feedback are extremely important; a score near 0 on either one will yield a motivating potential score near 0.

Job enrichment cannot be applied to all types of work. Some jobs may be essentially boring, yet the work needs to be performed. In such cases, substitution of machines for people may resolve the problem. Another option is to rotate responsibilities. In any large government office building, for example, a great volume of mail comes in each day and must be sorted. If the sorting and delivery are considered uninteresting, one approach is to have office workers take turns handling the mail so that no one employee has that assignment as a full-time responsibility.

Another approach is to use teams to handle the work, with the team members deciding who will do which job and when. Perhaps the team approach is the best that can be done in manufacturing, where technology dictates some form of assembly line. The team method, however, seems to conflict in part with the underlying theory of job enrichment. Giving a team some discretion may increase autonomy for a group of employees but not necessarily for any single one, yet job enrichment stresses the value of worker autonomy. The team approach stresses interpersonal relations, which is a hygiene factor, whereas job enrichment focuses on motivators.

Efforts to enrich jobs have concentrated on lower-level positions, with insufficient attention being given to supervisory positions. If enrichment means vertical loading, it follows that supervisors necessarily lose some powers. Such changes obviously can be threatening and, at the very least, require those in positions of authority to play different roles in managing their workers, roles that not only may be unfamiliar but also may not be preferred by the supervisors. The problem may be resolved by enriching managers' jobs as well as those of their subordinates. When it is applied throughout an organization, job enrichment becomes an equivalent of decentralization of authority. A midlevel manager yields some responsibility to lower levels and takes on additional responsibility from higher levels.

Staff functions, particularly personnel and budgeting, can be used for enrichment purposes. Midlevel supervisors can be assigned responsibility for budgeting for their agencies and for operating within their budgetary ceilings. In the same manner, personnel matters can be decentralized so that lower-level supervisors are assigned the responsibilities of selecting and disciplining employees. The result may be a reduction in staff size for personnel and budget offices. The extent to which staff functions can be decentralized depends on the need for consistency. To what extent should discretion in disciplining employees be delegated, since discretion can produce inconsistent or nonstandardized actions? Extensive delegation of this responsibility can result in some managers being severe and others being lenient in disciplining employees for the same type of wrongdoing.

If job enrichment accomplishes what its proponents claim, then more work can be accomplished by the same number of employees. If more work is not needed, then a surplus of staff develops, although such workers usually are reassigned to other areas of an organization. Nevertheless, job enrichment holds the potential for layoffs, which can reduce employee morale and arouse labor union opposition.

Another area of concern is how job enrichment relates to pay and promotion practices.[20] Using equity theory, an employee who, through job enrichment, becomes more productive but is not granted a pay increase will consider the situation inequitable, leading to a slackening in performance to bring effort and pay into balance. If pay increases are not awarded, then organized labor can contend that job enrichment is simply a speed-up scheme by management to get more work out of each employee without additional pay. For these reasons, enrichment programs may require pay increases, which can result in a rise in total personnel costs. Not only must pay systems be adjusted, but so must promotion systems to recognize that a worker is performing at a higher level of responsibility. Promotional systems that rely heavily on seniority can retard the effectiveness of job enrichment, yet it is these seniority rules that are particularly popular among unions, thereby creating one more reason for organized labor's opposition to or at least skepticism about job enrichment.

Although much of the job enrichment research and experimentation has found positive results in worker performance, job satisfaction has not always been increased. One possible explanation is that many employees have become alienated, do not seek self-actualization on the job, and cannot find work itself to be interesting. The bureaucrat bashing of political leaders may have created worker anomie that devastates motivation, job satisfaction, and productivity.[21] Another explanation is that job enrichment may encourage greater expectations, so that the level of satisfaction remains unchanged.

The effects of job enrichment on individuals and interpersonal relations have not been well researched. Role overload can develop when workers' jobs are excessively enriched. Enrichment advocates ignore interpersonal relations in that such relationships are considered only hygiene factors, but it is debatable whether that reaction is warranted. Enrichment may create role ambiguities, so that workers are not told the full limits of their authority and disagree about who has responsibility for what. This ambiguity also is a reason for union opposition. Unions prefer to make responsibilities explicit through labor contracts, whereas job enrichment encourages fluidity.

There is one other unsettled aspect of job enrichment: Change in responsibilities may have as great an influence on performance as enrichment. Simply changing a person's duties without enlarging the job can have positive effects.

GROUPS AND LEADERS

People are individuals, but they also are part of social systems known as groups. The preceding section concentrated on liberating workers or giving them increased autonomy as a means of increasing their individualism; this section emphasizes how people behave in groups. An important aspect of group behavior is the role performed by leaders.

Group Theory

A group can be defined as "a plurality of individuals who are in contact with one another, who take one another into account, and who are aware of some significant commonality."[22] Groups have a history or past and continue over time. A number of people in an elevator may interact briefly, but they would not be considered a group. Groups vary in size, with the term *small group* usually being reserved for those with ten or fewer members. Most of the discussion here concentrates on small groups.[23-25]

A distinction commonly is made between formal and informal groups. An informal group is one that emerges from interaction among people and has no official or formal designation; when workers interact on the job, they become an informal group. A formal group, in contrast, has prescribed members. Informal work groups can lead to the establishment of a labor union or grievance committee, which takes on the characteristics of a formal group. Organizations create formal groups known as committees. A characteristic of these committees is that the members usually have been chosen by someone in authority, whereas informal groups largely select their own members and leaders.

Formal and informal groups constitute dynamic subsystems in an entity. Although any one group may continue over time, membership varies as people enter and leave the organization and as people change jobs within it. Groups can have overlapping memberships. A person might be a member of several formal standing committees of an agency, of one or more interagency committees, and of numerous informal work groups. This field of group theory, then, sees the individual in a social system composed of a myriad of groups, in contrast to other theories that concentrate on the individual.

One possible explanation of why groups emerge is that people have an inherent need to be with others and that organizations themselves fail to meet this need, resulting in worker anomie and alienation. In the 1840s, Marx popularized such a view, claiming that industrialization had separated workers from the products of their work, alienating employees from their employers.[26] Mayo's school of human relations, based on the findings of the Hawthorne studies, saw workers as isolated individuals who find a sense of belonging in neither old social institutions nor industrial organizations. The report on the Hawthorne studies, however, did not go so far as to suggest that informal work groups always will arise. In one of the experiments a group did not develop, and the reason suggested was that individual autonomy coupled with an incentive pay system obviated the need for group formation.[27,28] This raises a question of whether worker autonomy techniques discussed in the preceding section would militate against group formation.

Maslow's needs hierarchy is another theory that is compatible with the belongingness stimulus for group formation; belongingness needs presumably arise after satisfaction of physiological and safety needs (see Chapter 10). Whyte's *Organization Man*, a best seller of the 1950s, portrayed organizations conveying to workers the need to belong, to be committed to a social ethic rather than to an ethic based on individualism.[29]

A cluster of theories about group formation concentrates on the interactive communication among individuals. Homans, who was associated with Mayo and the human relations school of thought, conceptualized groups in terms of four sets of variables[30]:

1. Groups involve activities, whether the activities are work related or leisure oriented.
2. Groups involve interaction among members.
3. Groups have sentiments, or feelings, that may be happy, sad, and the like.
4. Groups have norms, or standards of what is considered proper and improper behavior.

Norms are discussed shortly, but at this point the main concern is that Homans stressed interactions. Groups emerge as people meet, speak, and work with each other and have positive feelings about those interactions. Field theory, developed by Lewin, takes a similar approach, emphasizing how people interact in spatial arrangements (see Chapter 10). Exchange theory is still another related approach that describes interaction as exchange between and among people.[31] Smiles, compliments, derogatory comments, and physical punches are among the repertoire of exchanges. When exchanges are viewed as favorable, the probability of additional exchanges increases, and a group will be formed.

Groups have structures and communication networks or grapevines.[32,33] Not all members interact with each other with equal frequency and in the same ways. Some members may speak to each other only periodically throughout the day, whereas others are in nearly continuous communication. The organizational structure prescribes various interaction, but informal networks of communication overlie the formal structure. Analyses of these networks usually begin with a focus on two-person, or dyadic, relationships; linkages among the dyads then are identified. The results of such analyses are social diagrams or sociograms, which schematically display the grapevine of a group or organization: A speaks with B, who in turn relays information to C and D, who together talk with E, and so forth back to A.

One aspect of a group's structure is the varied roles that people play. "Roles describe specific behavior associated with given positions; they develop originally from task requirements."[34] Group members develop expectations about how each other member is to behave. These ideas are called expected roles. Some members may be submissive, whereas others are dominant or serve as leaders. Some may serve as mediators between aggressive members. Some may be major sources of new information for the group, and others are major disseminators of that information. Some may be heavily task oriented, and others stress human and leisure aspects of groups activities. When a member deviates from an expected role, other members will experience uncertainty about how to respond to the aberrant behavior.

Roles can be portrayed in a dynamic manner through the use of Bales Interaction Process Analysis (IPA).[35] Groups are conceptualized as problem-solving entities. Interactions, then, relate to how the group moves toward a decision in resolving a problem. Bales proposed twelve basic types of interactions. His technique entails observing the frequency of these communications as the group moves toward a decision. The communications can be verbal or nonverbal, such as smiling or pounding on a desk. The communication types include asking for an opinion, showing solidarity with the group, and expressing agreement or passive acceptance. Researchers have attempted to use the Bales approach to distinguish different phases in the decision process.

Groups have norms or rules about behavior that generally apply to all members. Norms simplify interaction in that members know what is expected of them. Norms are restricted to behavior—verbal or nonverbal—and do not encompass thoughts. Only behavior that is perceived by the group to be important is controlled by norms; less important matters are left to the discretion of each member. Norms are applied differently among the members, with leaders usually being permitted greater deviation from the group standards. One problem with the concept of norms is that a hollow explanation of behavior can develop: Group A behaves in one way because of its norms, and group B behaves differently because it has a different set of norms.

The concept of norms has led to concern that groups impose uniformity on their members and may diminish independent thinking. Laboratory experiments have demonstrated that members sometimes will accept the group's position even though they know it to be false. One interpretation is that group decisions tend to be mediocre, but a conflicting view is that individuals acting as a group tend to take greater risks than when acting autonomously. The latter is exemplified by the lynch mob, where responsibility for an extreme action is diffused through the group. Janis has labeled the process "groupthink."[36]

Group goals involve some desired future state, condition, or location. In work groups, these goals often are ambiguous or nonoperational. A group's goal may be to operate with greater independence of management, but because it does not subscribe to total independence the group may have difficulty in determining its reaction to a new set of management directives. Each member brings goals to the group and wants the other members to accept them as group goals. In some cases these may be generally accepted, but that does not mean all members accept any one goal with the same intensity.[37]

The term "cohesiveness" is used to express the extent to which group members are pulled together, see themselves and behave as a unity, and remain as members. Cohesiveness sometimes is viewed as a form of loyalty or simply the extent to which members like each other.[38] A broader conceptualization of cohesion is the extent to which members are in agreement on the roles, norms, and goals of the group. Members could like one another, but the group could disintegrate for lack of agreement on its goals.

A group clearly affects the behavior of its members. An individual may conform to the wishes of the group simply because the person wishes to remain a member. Groups interpret new information for their members, such as whether a proposed agency reorganization will be beneficial to them. Groups have ambient stimuli that affect all members; these stimuli include the individuals of the group and the various aspects of its surroundings. This might be considered the general personality, sometimes called the syntality, of the group.[39] Simply being in the presence of other members can have the effect of psychological arousal when one thinks the others have the potential for evaluating performance or behavior. This arousal will stimulate a person to be deliberative or more conscious in selecting behaviors.

Discretionary stimuli are selective in that they are directed at individual members in the group. These stimuli can be thought of as the rewards and penalties meted out to individuals. Penalties, actual and threatened, are used to reduce the probability of deviant behavior. Skinner's operant conditioning stresses the importance of positive reinforcement: "The reinforcing consequences generated by the group easily exceeded the sum of the consequences which could be achieved by the members acting separately. The total reinforcing effect is enormously increased."[40]

This influence of the group on an individual creates tension and anxiety when a person is part of two or more groups that expect different types of behavior. One group may penalize the individual for a given behavior, and another might reward the same behavior. An employee's willingness to work during the lunch hour, for example, may be supported by one group and opposed by another. This situation is known as role conflict.

Groups are influenced by the characteristics of their individual members. Myers-Briggs Type Indicators, which are based upon concepts developed by Jung, are used to identify the orientations of individuals as gauged by four factors[41,42]: (1) Is an individual an extrovert (other worldly) or an introvert? (2) Does a person rely largely on sensing (relying on the five basic senses) or intuition? (3) Does the person favor thinking (logical sequencing) or feeling? (4) Does an individual prefer judgment (thinking or feeling) or perception (sensing or intuition)? From these factors emerge sixteen types into which individuals can be classified. The mix of types in a group can influence its effectiveness. Myers-Briggs Type Indicators are used for career counseling and numerous other purposes.

Effects of Leadership

One of the most important roles in a group is that of leader, and much research has been devoted to leadership and power.[43-45] Both of these are relational concepts; that is, they concern how people relate to one another in a social context. Power usually is considered the ability of one person to influence the behavior of another or to have control over another. Leadership is the ability to move a group toward its goals.

A leader stimulates action by the group through the exercise of power. French and Raven suggest that there are at least five types of power[46-48]:

1. Reward power involves the ability to dispense or withhold tangible and intangible things valued by a group member.
2. Coercive power is the ability to compel a group member to behave in a way desired by the leader.
3. Referent power is based on the desire of a group member to behave like the leader (to model oneself after the leader).
4. Expert power comes with having knowledge unavailable to others; the leader is respected for technical competence.
5. Legitimate power involves the acceptance by group members of the idea that a leader has a right to issue instructions and that the members have the obligation to comply.

This last factor, legitimate power, is equivalent or closely related to what others call authority, and problems arise in the application of the concept to organizational behavior. In a government agency, a bureau chief has organizational authority to supervise employees to accomplish whatever tasks are expected of the unit. The chief is likely to have at least some legitimate power in that subordinates accept the chief's role as a superior. At the same time, the informal work group may have its own leader, who is different from the bureau chief. An informal leader emerges who has not been selected by the organization. Michels has suggested an iron law of oligarchy, namely that in any social setting one or a few individuals will emerge as having greater power.[49] The result can be dual leadership, in which there is an ascribed leader who holds a position designated as supervisor and an achieved leader who has emerged from the group. There is obvious potential for conflict between these leaders.

If the organization expects managers or supervisors to perform leadership roles, a question arises about what specifically is to be done. Barnard, in his classic work *The Functions of the Executive*, saw the leader as providing technical and moral competence.[50,51] Barnard and others emphasized that the leader is responsible for overseeing workers so that essential activities are completed; leadership is considered critical for meeting organizational goals.

The leader is also responsible for overseeing interpersonal relationships, especially coordinating workers and resolving conflicts among them. Leaders must make allocations among members, as in the case of managers assigning budgets to subordinates, and in doing so are expected to function in an equitable fashion.[52] Motivating workers to excel is assumed to be a major responsibility. Leaders often use contingent reward techniques—commendations, pay increases, or promotions—for preferred behavior.[53]

One of the most important functions of the leader is to deal with the environment external to the work group. Groups have boundaries, and the leader deals with boundary transactions.[54] Much of the leader's time is spent not with subordinates but rather with peers, superiors, and others external to the organization. One of the most important aspects of this external function is obtaining resources (a budget) for the organizational unit. "The leader's job is to *test* the environment to find out which demands can become truly effective threats, to *change* the environment by finding allies and other sources of external support, and to *gird* his organization by creating the means and the will to withstand attacks."[55]

Because leadership is considered central to organizational effectiveness, research has concentrated on finding what constitutes effective leadership. Trait theory, once popular, is based on the idea that great leaders have common traits. Through the study of effective leaders, especially those who had influenced history, it was thought that common traits could be identified. Once these characteristics were identified, then managers could be selected "scientifically."

The trait approach has been largely abandoned, although researchers remain intrigued with why some leaders are charismatic and how they use their charisma.[56] Leaders with charisma are able to inspire group members and in the work setting may greatly increase worker motivation. Charisma also has a darker side, in which group members may be expected to be submissive to the will of the leader.[57]

Pioneering experimental research of the 1930s was an important factor in the deemphasis of leadership traits. Lippitt and White, under the direction of Lewin, experimented with alternative leadership styles in boys' groups.[58,59] The styles were autocratic, democratic, and laissez faire (freedom with little leadership direction or interest). Both morale and group performance were influenced by style; democratic leadership was particularly popular. The implication drawn from the research was that leadership style need not be inborn but could be selected by managers to improve worker satisfaction and productivity.

During the 1940s and 1950s important leadership studies were conducted by researchers at Ohio State University and the University of Michigan.[60,61] Although there were important differences in their approaches, both groups focused on two basic leadership styles. Leadership that concentrated on organizing work and accomplishing tasks was labeled "initiating" at Ohio State and "job centered" at Michigan; it also was termed "instrumental." Leadership that showed concern for employee well-being was called "consideration" at Ohio State and "employee centered" at Michigan. The research of these groups and others that followed seemed to suggest that democratic, humane, or employee-concerned leadership increased worker satisfaction.

Likert, who directed much of the research at the University of Michigan, concluded that a new conceptualization of organizations was needed, along with a new approach to supervision.[62,63] Organizations should be seen as a series of hierarchical, overlapping groups. The supervisor/leader of one group was a subordinate/follower of a higher-level group. The supervisor was seen as a "link pin" between groups. As for supervision, there were four styles or systems ranging from autocratic to employee centered; the latter, called System 4, was seen as the most effective. In System 1, the leaders lack confidence in employees; in System 2, there is confidence but in a condescending manner; in System 3, there is confidence but remaining concern on the part of leaders to maintain control of decisions; and in System 4, leaders have complete confidence and trust in subordinates. In addition to confidence levels, the Likert model used other variables to illustrate how the style of management could be modified.

To some extent, democratic or participative leadership has become a dogma, but a lingering doubt remains about whether happy workers are necessarily productive workers.[64,65] An experimental study in the 1950s, for example, demonstrated that effective leaders are not always well liked by their subordinates.[66] Research continues to show that democratic leadership is effective in some situations but not in all.

One response to this uncertainty about the effectiveness of democratic leadership has been the managerial grid developed by Blake and Mouton.[67–70] The grid is a matrix, with one axis ranging from low to high concern for production and the other axis ranging from low to high concern for employees. Blake and Mouton were careful not to suggest that the high end of both scales, the so-called 9–9 style, was the ideal form of leadership, but grid training typically has attempted to instruct managers in being concerned simultaneously with the needs of the organization and those of the employees.

Contemporary approaches to leadership tend to stress its situational aspect, that one leadership style may be effective for one situation but not for others.[71] Research is concerned with identifying what styles are most effective in what situations. For example, it has been suggested that autocratic leadership may be most effective when employees do not seek self-actualization.[72] Workers may come to expect autocratic leadership, as in the case of local police officers, and may function well with such leadership.[73]

The situational concept is fundamental to Fiedler's contingency theory of leadership effectiveness.[74–76] The theory suggests that style depends on the extent to which the leader has power, the tasks of the unit are unambiguous, and the leader and members have good relationships. Using these three sets of variables, eight combinations are derived, and Fiedler has suggested which style is most effective for each of the eight situations. For instance, when leader power is weak, the task is unstructured, and relations are good, then a considerate or employee-centered style is appropriate; when power is strong, the task is unstructured, and relations are good, then structured leadership is needed.

Vroom and Yetton have developed a leadership model that attempts to provide explicit advice for managers on how to handle situations.[77,78] Without getting into the details of the model, it should be noted that five different styles are included delineating the extent to which the manager should handle a situation with employee involvement. Like the Fiedler model, this one is concerned with whether the task is structured, but the Vroom-Yetton model also focuses on whether the manager has adequate information without involving employees and whether workers have internalized the organization's goals.

A related contingency approach to leadership is path–goal theory.[79–81] The theory involves four leadership styles: directive, supportive, participative, and achievement oriented. Research has concentrated on when a manager should use any of them. The theory assumes that a manager will use each style from time to time.

Another factor to consider is how leaders and groups function over time.[82] Leader behavior is affected by previous events in an organization.[83] In a situation where an autocratic manager may have been replaced, workers may react negatively to any authoritarian behavior of the new manager. Organizations with managers who have long been in their positions may function differently than organizations with short-tenure managers.[84]

Particularly popular in the 1990s has been Covey's suggestion that effective leaders and other successful individuals exhibit common habits or characteristics, including being proactive, keeping the end or objective in mind, and seeking first to understand and then to be understood.[85] Covey's prescriptions, when applied to organizational behavior, presumably suggest how managers can be effective in working with their subordinates, peers, and superiors.

PERFORMANCE AND ORGANIZATIONAL CHANGE

Partly in response to criticisms that participative management may lose sight of organizational objectives, techniques have been developed that attempt to focus simultaneously on the needs of workers and the needs of the organization. Leadership research has concentrated largely on styles. Attempts have been made to identify which styles increase employee satisfaction and performance, but leadership styles are not the same as systematic management systems that can be implemented as agency policy. This section, therefore, considers more systematic approaches to managing: management by objectives (MBO), quality circles (QCs), organization development (OD), and total quality management (TQM).

It should be noted first that other techniques and processes are used to improve and/or increase the results of government programs, but they are not particularly based on employee motivation theory. Performance measurement and evaluation techniques focus upon gauging the accomplishments of public organizations in achieving goals and objectives.[86-90] Cost-benefit and cost-effectiveness analyses are specific techniques utilized in program evaluation. Program budgeting, or what was called planning-programming budgeting (PPB) in the 1960s, uses the budget process to relate costs to program accomplishments; funds are allocated in terms of achieving desired objectives.[91,92] Zero-base budgeting, (ZZB), popular during the Carter administration, makes the assumption that programs should not necessarily continue over time; emphasis is placed on identifying low-priority programs whose budgets can be reduced or eliminated. "Productivity" is a term that has been popular in the public sector.[93-95] Generally, productivity improvement efforts are aimed at providing greater levels of work and output with no increase in the use of resources, particularly human resources. Some productivity improvement efforts are linked to wage incentive systems and thus might be considered a form of Taylorism. Strategic planning has attained prominence. It emphasizes examining the mission of an organization and then determining how to change the entity to fulfill those missions.[96]

All these techniques—performance measurement, program evaluation, program budgeting, zero-base budgeting, productivity, and strategic planning—tend to deemphasize the roles of individuals. Some performance measurement efforts, however, deal with gauging the quality of the work force and in turn measuring the quality of individual worker performance. The Merit Systems Protection Board and the Office of Personnel Management have encouraged federal agencies to engage in work force quality measurement that, among other topics, examines the linkage between worker output and the quality of leadership or supervision.[97] An obvious concern is whether individual performance evaluation procedures can be used to correct worker deficiencies and to increase organizational performance.[98]

Management by Objectives

A basic premise of management by objectives, or MBO, is that managers should manage for results. The beginning of MBO can be traced to the du Pont Company and General Motors after World War I.[99] Drucker in 1954 and McGregor in 1960 popularized the concept; they were followed by Odiorne in 1965.[100-102] By the 1970s, MBO had become a well-known concept in industry and by late in that decade in federal, state, and local government.[103]

There are several theoretical bases for MBO. One is that workers will tend to work harder when they have internalized the organization's goals. If an employee understands how a set of activities will lead toward goal attainment, and if the goal is perceived as legitimate, the worker will become motivated. Ryan has suggested that behavior is purposive; that is, once workers have accepted goals, activity will continue until the goals are accomplished.[104] Locke has shown that, when difficult goals are suggested to people and they accept them, performance will tend to be higher than it would have been had less difficult goals been established.[105] Locke has maintained that individuals will set goals for themselves if the organization does not supply them. Management by objectives, sometimes called goal setting, thus attempts to use a process by which goals are established for workers (and for programs). Critics suggest that MBO is manipulative in its attempt to have workers accept goals that they otherwise might not accept.[106]

MBO defies an explicit explanation of the process involved because many variations exist. All such systems, however, begin with the identification of goals and/or objectives. Some systems use these terms interchangeably, and others reserve the term "goal" for the long range and "objectives" for short-range measurable events. An operational MBO system establishes measurable results to be accomplished within a specified time period, often a year. The process encourages planning because in setting goals/objectives organizations and managers must consider what is feasible within the next 12 months. Individual worker autonomy or group autonomy can be increased when there is agreement on what is to be accomplished within that time period; in other words, workers are empowered to act independently.[107] Under MBO, work units have objectives that are factored into subobjectives for each employee. This allows individuals to know what is expected of them, thereby increasing role clarity.

There are differing opinions about how objectives should be established. The top-down approach has top-level management set overall objectives for each major unit; these then are factored into subobjectives for subunits and ultimately into objectives for individual workers (see Chapter 3). Such an approach is seen as being appropriate, given management's responsibility to manage. The opposing view is that a top-down system can be detrimental by reducing worker autonomy and by blocking employee drives for self-actualization.

The alternative is a bottom-up approach, in which objectives originally are proposed by employees to their supervisors, after which workers and supervisors negotiate an agreement on objectives. The process continues up the organizational hierarchy. MBO is seen as a form of decentralization, allowing considerable employee independence and encouraging the satisfaction of higher-level needs as defined by Maslow. Critics of that approach suggest that suboptimization is likely; that is, lower units will perform according to their needs and not those of the organization as a whole.

Regardless of whether a top-down or bottom-up approach is used, MBO systems stress face-to-face interaction between supervisor and employee. In the top-down approach, the manager discusses with each worker what is expected to be accomplished in the coming year. It is assumed that the employees will gain a better understanding of their roles and will internalize the organization's goals/objectives. The bottom-up approach emphasizes greater participation by employees, presumably increasing the likelihood that they will accept objectives that are beneficial to the organization.

An important element of management by objectives is feedback. Performance is reviewed periodically. Employees who have not met their objectives are expected to explain why. Management is expected to help identify each worker's problems in meeting objectives and to help the individual overcome them through employee development plans that give special emphasis to training. MBO often is tied closely to performance appraisal.[108,109] Rather than being evaluated on the basis of initiative, enthusiasm, or other traits, employees are rated in terms of whether they accomplish the tasks expected of them.

Part of the feedback also involves decisions on pay and promotions. The Scanlon plan, used in industry, provides financial rewards for productive workers and encourages employees to suggest changes that will increase productivity.[110] Under management by objectives, employees who can meet difficult objectives will have an advantage in gaining promotions. Once the performance in meeting objectives has been reviewed with the worker, the cycle is repeated. New objectives or targets are set, performance is monitored, and feedback is provided.

MBO systems have different orientations, depending on the organizational locus of responsibility. Where it has been introduced through the personnel system, MBO usually emphasizes the performance of individual workers. A complaint about this approach is that agency management largely ignores the process in making important decisions. The other orientation is to use MBO as a decision process. That type of system usually is under the direct control of top management. Government has tended to use this approach, with MBO being handled by an agency head or possibly the agency budget office. Government MBO systems have put less emphasis on individual objectives and accomplishments and have focused more on organizational unit performance.

Implementing management by objectives is more difficult in government than in private corporations. Governments tend to have less freedom in personnel decisions; their workers typically cannot readily be fired for failing to reach objectives, nor can promotions and salary increases be awarded simply because objectives have been met. Establishing explicit objectives is complicated because government objectives usually are less tangible. Government lacks simple measures, such as increasing sales volume, percentage of a market, or return on investments. Unlike the private sector, government produces few tangible products, and its decision systems are more diffuse, so that it is difficult to obtain a fixed commitment to specified objectives.

One problem shared by government and industry is excessive paperwork. If objectives are made explicit under MBO, considerable paperwork will be generated. The complaint is that employees are so busy filling in forms that they have little time for productive work.

Quality Circles

Quality circles (QCs), like MBO, emphasize participation by workers in problem solving but, in contrast to MBO, emphasize group rather than individual decision making. QCs developed in Japan in the 1950s and 1960s, spread to American firms in the 1970s, and gained considerable popularity in the public sector in the 1980s and 1990s.[111] This management technique is based on Theory Z, which simultaneously stresses worker participation and achievement of results.[112,113]

A quality circle normally consists of four to fifteen workers who interact with each other on a regular basis. Most QCs involve workers and first-line supervisors, with the latter serving as leaders of the groups. The QCs meet once a week, usually during regular working hours and for a limited time, often 1 hour.

The purpose of these meetings is to identify problems and resolve them. When several problems arise, the QC must decide which to address first. For example, an office that processes client forms might identify a problem of a growing backlog of unprocessed forms. The group would help identify how the backlog developed and propose alternatives for resolving the difficulty. The discussion might well consider options for reassigning personnel to increase staffing on the task or hiring additional staff. In some situations the circle could take corrective action on its own initiative; in others it would need to make a recommendation to higher authority. Once a decision was reached, the QC would be responsible for implementation.

Where quality circles have been successful, the benefits have been substantial. Work products often improve in both quality and quantity. Because workers know their jobs better than anyone else, they may be in an excellent position to recommend improvements. Communication in the organization also improves greatly. More harmonious relations develop between managers and workers. Morale improves along with worker self-esteem, and absenteeism and turnover are reduced.[114,115] Of course, these positive results are not always realized when governments launch QC programs.[116,117]

Essential first steps in implementing quality circles include management's committing itself to the technique and providing training for all individuals. If management views QCs as a cosmetic application to make workers merely think they are being included in decision making, there is little likelihood of success and an excellent chance that employees will react negatively. Trainers are needed, especially at the first several meetings, to help a QC learn how to conduct its business. Workers need to know how to identify problems without offending others in the group, who could become defensive, as well as how to identify and evaluate alternative solutions.

Quality circle programs sometimes are linked to group incentive programs. As a QC improves its performance, all group members benefit through increased pay. This process, known as gainsharing, faces the same obstacles as individual pay incentives of MBO applications in the public sector, namely that rigid pay plans may prohibit pay incentives.[118]

One of the most difficult tasks is to train managers to adopt a participative style of leadership when they are accustomed to being *the* boss. Quality circles may want to delve into personnel and budgetary matters that managers think are their own domain.

Another problem involves adopting QCs to the culture of organizations and more generally to the work culture of a society.[119–121] In Japan, quality circles have been popular in part because of the country's cultural emphasis on group behavior as distinguished from individualism. Another factor is that workers in Japan tend to have greater commitment to their employers than employees in the United States because Japanese employment usually is with one organization for a lifetime, unlike the situation in U.S. organizations (both private and public), where employees leave either voluntarily or involuntarily.

A final problem with quality circles is integrating them with unions when collective bargaining agreements exist. It may be essential first to get a provision in a union contract authorizing QCs. Issues will arise over whether the QCs are making recommendations contrary to the prevailing contract or are interfering in the authority granted the union. Quality circles may be viewed by organized labor as a means of getting more work out of employees with no benefits for them. Another view may be that management is using QCs to improve employees' morale and to avoid having them vote to have a union represent them in collective bargaining.

Quality circles may or may not be part of an organization's effort to improve the quality of work life (QWL). The latter is intended to make working a humane endeavor. QWL programs can include QCs but also may concentrate on such matters as making the work environment more pleasant through the installation of carpeting, new furniture, and the like.[122] QWL programs, like QCs, usually are intended to increase productivity.[123–126]

Organization Development

Like QCs, MBO, and job enrichment, organization development (OD) is an approach to changing organizations.[127] It has been defined as a process aimed at "increasing the ability of the organization to do more effectively what it is mandated to do—perform its work."[128] It can be considered an intervention strategy whereby existing methods of operations are examined to find improved methods. Organization change is considered essential, given the need to respond to a continuously changing environment. An organization that is static will become antiquated, so there is a need for continuous renewal. OD specialists, therefore, stress that a long-range commitment to continuing change must be made.

The underlying premise of OD is that change comes about through a learning process. Lewin's field theory suggests that vectors or forces push people in certain directions within a field or environment (see Chapter 10). Organization development maintains that vectors that encourage the individual to learn should be strengthened and that those that discourage learning should be muted. The process is seen as unfreezing mind sets, moving the individual to a new learning mind set, and then refreezing the vectors so that learning continues at an increased level. This may be considered a strategy to release creativity in employees.[129,130]

Rogers, another important contributor to OD theory, stressed that individuals seek learning when they accept that concept or internalize it.[131] In other words, participation by employees is assumed to be essential for organization change. In the 1940s, Coch and French experimented with alternative approaches to change and came to the conclusion that worker resistance could be overcome through participation.[132,133]

Organization development normally is considered to have emerged almost accidentally from the work of Lewin, Lippitt, Bradford, and Benne in a 1946 laboratory training session in Connecticut.[134,135] Lewin, who had established the Research Center for Group Dynamics at the Massachusetts Institute of Technology, was conducting a training program for community leaders and was approached by the participants for permission to attend a meeting of the training staff concerning their observations on how the group members were interacting. The participants were allowed to attend, and the result was seen as positive in that members received feedback on their performance. The following year, the National Training Laboratory (NTL) was established in Bethel, Maine, and since then the laboratory training approach has gained great prominence. A similar movement emerged about the same time in England at the Tavistock Institute.[136]

Numerous techniques are associated, directly or indirectly, with OD. Sensitivity training has been one of its most popular aspects. Other techniques discussed here include transactional analysis (TA), survey feedback, and team building.

The laboratory approach uses sensitivity training, encounter groups, or T-groups (T is for training). Individuals leave their normal work settings to spend a weekend or longer in residence at a training center. Group size varies, but often there are about ten members. In its pure form, sensitivity training is unstructured, unlike other forms of training in which participants might be expected to learn specific bodies of knowledge. The absence of structure creates a social vacuum. People are together with no assigned tasks.[137] The vacuum, being uncomfortable to the members, stimulates group discussion. Emphasis is given to becoming sensitive or aware of how one views oneself and how others view each other. Authenticity in interpersonal relations is stressed, so that members are encouraged to say what they think of each other. The objective is not to get all group members to like each other but rather for them to learn to respect each other as individuals. OD specialists differentiate their work from group therapy. Whereas therapy focuses largely on the past, sensitivity training concentrates on the here and now. In a T-group, Ms. A is encouraged to describe how she feels about Mr. B's behavior in the group.

Although laboratory training does not strive to build friendships among the group members, supportive relationships are expected to emerge, and it is assumed that these will encourage creativity. Members are encouraged to give and receive feedback. Feedback should be immediate; a member should not wait an hour or more before saying that a comment made by another was annoying. The feedback should avoid value judgments of right and wrong and should emphasize emotional reactions, such as anger or pleasure. The receiver of the feedback needs to learn to listen attentively. From this type of feedback, members develop a sense of belonging and trust and learn to respect each other. This supportive atmosphere encourages members to explore new ideas and feelings, the presumed key to learning.

There are great variations among T-groups as to the types of participants and the purposes of the training. Some sensitivity groups focus primarily on the individual, seeking to unleash human potentials. Techniques include Rolfing, bioenergetics, biofeedback, and transcendental meditation. For these types of groups, participants normally do not know each other before the session and normally pay their own training fees. T-Groups that are part of OD, however, tend to stress developing interpersonal competencies in a group setting. A corporation or government agency may pay to have its midlevel managers attend a laboratory training program to learn to deal more effectively with each other and with others in the organization. Managers are often suspected of being barriers to developing a more participative organization culture and, therefore, especially in need of sensitivity training.[138]

Emphasis is sometimes given to family group sensitivity training in response to complaints that training one stratum of workers may produce negligible results. For example, if only junior-level supervisors receive this training, they will have difficulty applying their new capabilities because the rest of the organization has been left unchanged. The family group is the work group, involving all the personnel in a given organizational unit. OD specialists claim that focusing on the family group will create a better organizational climate.

Besides having members simply talk with one another, sensitivity training can use other techniques. Members may act out a skit (role playing) and then discuss their views on what occurred. The group from time to time may be broken down into two-person dyads, whose members interview each other. Members may be removed temporarily from their groups and reassigned to others. Physical contact among the members may be used to break down psychological interpersonal barriers. So-called trust falls are used, in which a member trustingly falls backward into the arms of another, expecting to be caught before hitting the floor. Interspersed among the informal sessions may be more structured lectures on group behavior.

The role of trainer is pivotal in a sensitivity group. The trainer is the change agent, the catalyst, for getting the members to abandon set ways and explore alternatives. The trainer can be largely nondirective, providing feedback largely of an inquiring nature. The trainer might ask a member why she said what she did, or why she has said nothing. Other trainers take a more directive approach, perhaps telling one member that what he has said has hurt the others' feelings.

Transactional analysis (TA), although not specifically a part of OD, is a technique that can be utilized. In *Games People Play* and *The Structure and Dynamics of Organizations and Groups,* Berne has translated Freudian psychology into a group framework.[139-141] Freud's id becomes Berne's child, the ego becomes a parent, and the superego becomes an adult. TA is concerned with how people relate to each other. The actions may be complementary, as in the case of Mr. A and Mr. B each acting as an adult. In other instances, Mr. A may act as parent and Mr. B as child. A seeming assumption of TA is that training should strive to have members relate to one another as adults, although Berne suggests that all of us at some time need to act as parents and children. What might be considered an offshoot of transactional analysis is assertiveness training, which is aimed at teaching people to demand their own rights and not to be submissive while at the same time respecting the rights of others. Bradshaw has contended that people need to reach the child within them as a source of potency and rejuvenation.[142]

Survey feedback is another technique of organization development but it is different from the laboratory approach or sensitivity training. Survey feedback begins with consultants obtaining information about the organization, usually by administering questionnaires to managers and employees. The questionnaire concentrates on satisfaction/dissatisfaction with how the agency operates. The organizational climate is identified through this process. The consultants use work groups to feed back the information. In this process problems are identified, and solutions presumably emerge. Fishbowling may be used, in which work group 1 discusses its reactions to work group 2 while that group watches; work group 2 then fishbowls before work group 1. In other words, the emphasis is intergroup relations. Fishbowling also can be used for improving relations between a work group and clients, as in the case of social workers and welfare clients.

Team building in organization development stresses problem solving over interpersonal relations. Although team building may use sensitivity training as part of the overall strategy, it concentrates on identifying and resolving problems of the organization. Survey feedback may be used to collect and critique data, but team building takes the additional step of developing a plan of action to meet the problems. The focus is how employees relate to each other as a team in carrying out the unit's responsibilities.[143]

It must be asked whether organization development accomplishes what it is supposed to and whether there are negative as well as positive effects. On the negative side, there has been continuous concern that OD is manipulative, that management may use it to the detriment of the individual. Sensitivity training has been seen as potentially dangerous in that the intense peer pressures of the group can upset the mental stability of individuals. Problems can arise that the trainers are not suited to handle and that should be dealt with by persons trained in psychotherapy. Some aspects of organization development, and particularly sensitivity training, have acquired a "kooky" reputation. A common criticism is that when OD stresses psychological aspects of behavior, there is a tendency to use "touchy-feely" training techniques that are of dubious utility.

Evaluation results have not been clear as to whether OD is effective in bringing about organization change. Its effectiveness must be considered undetermined because few thorough evaluations have been made. Persons completing sensitivity training may look favorably upon their cathartic experience, but there is justification to doubt whether that experience has any effect on their work behavior. As has been seen, OD concentrates on encouraging people to be creative or innovative, but it is not known whether innovative ideas can be absorbed by organizations. It is highly possible that agencies never use the best ideas generated through OD. The literature on OD is largely silent on the issue of power and authority. A person who may lose power through organizational change is likely to resist. Another weakness is that OD has paid little attention to the role of labor unions, which surely have the potential for aiding or hindering its efforts.

Total Quality Management

Like MBO, quality circles, and various forms of organization development, total quality management (TQM) focuses upon the end product of work. TQM emphasizes that organizations need to be concerned with the continuous improvement of their services and products, a process that is sometimes called continuous quality improvement or CQI.

TQM has its roots in the private sector, where firms compete for customers by producing better goods and services.[144,145] W. Edwards Deming, who is from the United States but gained notoriety through his accomplishments in working with companies in Japan, is usually credited with developing TQM. Other names associated with the technique include Joseph M. Juran in the United States and Kaoru Ishikawa in Japan.[146-148] The methods developed are intended to be comprehensive, involving all aspects of an organization, and utilize both technical knowledge about production processes and knowledge about human behavior in organizational settings.

Deming prescribes fourteen points for a total quality management system[149,150]:

1. Create constancy of purpose toward improvement of product and service.
2. Adopt the new philosophy, we are in a new competitive age.
3. Cease dependence on inspection . . . and build quality into the product in the first place.
4. Minimize total cost. Move toward a single supplier for any one item.
5. Improve constantly and forever the system of production and service.
6. Institute training on the job.
7. Institute leadership. The aim of supervision should be to help people and machines and gadgets do a better job.
8 Drive out fear, so that everyone may work effectively.
9. Break down barriers between departments.
10. Eliminate slogans, exhortations, and targets for the work force asking for zero defects and new levels of productivity.
11. Eliminate work standards (quotas) . . . and management by objectives. Substitute leadership.
12. Remove barriers that rob the hourly worker [and] . . . people in management and engineering of their right to pride of workmanship. This means, *inter alia*, abolishment of the annual or merit rating and management by objective.
13. Institute a vigorous program of education and self-improvement.
14. Put everybody . . . to work to accomplish the transformation.

Above all else, the system keeps management's and workers' attention upon satisfying customer demands through the delivery of high-quality goods and services.[151,152] Strategic planning and management are emphasized in which long-term goals are identified. TQM stresses constancy in the pursuit of these goals and discourages short-term thinking; in the private sector, U.S. firms are encouraged to adopt the views of Japanese firms that have focused on producing quality products that will establish market shares rather than on short-term objectives, such as sales quotas for the next 3 months.

Quality is expected to be built into a product or service from the outset, a process that prevents errors from occurring. Prevention, then, is stressed rather than inspection processes that detect errors and correct them. TQM shuns massive inspection programs on the assumption that prevention will reduce the need for inspections.

The system is driven by data and uses a variety of familiar management techniques. Various forms of charting methods are used, including flow charts, pareto charts, fishbone diagrams, and histograms.[153] The system, however, emphasizes only collecting those data needed for decision making and monitoring and discourages the use of some management information systems that seemingly collect data for the sake of it. Although data are used extensively, numerical quotas are discouraged. When workers have quotas to meet, attention may turn to the quantity of production rather than quality. Deming specifically suggests that MBO systems be abolished.

Achieving quality is seen as being highly dependent on workers at all levels of the organization. In TQM systems, training workers is a high priority, whereas in other settings training is often considered an expensive and largely needless activity. Top-level managers need to be trained in strategic thinking and need to keep their attention on overall missions; lower-level workers need to be encouraged to suggest improvements and to be given authority to act without having to obtain clearance from higher levels of authority. Workers are organized as teams and are encouraged to develop pride in their work.[154] Employees should not be motivated primarily through wage incentives and especially not individual incentives because these have the effect of giving individuals higher priority over work groups.

Customers are also empowered because feedback is essential regarding what customers want and what they like and dislike about existing services. In public sector TQM applications, citizens or voters are seen as customers that government seeks to serve.

Any successful management system requires top management's understanding of the system, commitment to it, and actual use of it. If management establishes a total quality management system but makes policy decisions outside the established processes, the system is a hollow one. WhereTQM has been implemented with some success, the system has been directly linked with central administration and rarely has been administered out of the personnel or human resource offices, which often lack the prestige and authority required to instigate the sweeping changes entailed in TQM.[155]

Criticisms of TQM abound in the public, nonprofit, and private sectors. All have experienced budget problems resulting in layoffs, which hardly produce situations that nurture employee involvement and participative management. Indeed, labor unions are often skeptical at best of TQM systems because they may pose threats to job security, may result in employees working harder for no increase in pay, and may weaken unions in their role of representing employees in grievance situations.[156] A frequent criticism is that TQM, by emphasizing employee involvement, creates delays in action and fosters excessive paperwork, all of which are translated into increased production costs rather than the savings usually expected from TQM. More generally, a common complaint is that TQM simply does not yield expected results, although advocates of TQM would respond by emphasizing the need for patience and that immediate results should not be expected.

TQM faces special problems when applied to the public sector. Government generally produces services and, unlike the private sector, manufactures few products. Devising a total quality management system for products may be more easily accomplished because product quality measurement frequently is easier than service quality measurement. TQM was devised in the private sector in response to highly competitive markets, but governments do not compete with one another in the same way that companies compete. The emphasis on commitment and constancy of leadership on a long-term basis is difficult to entertain in the public sector, where political leaders are always concerned about the upcoming elections and what will help them win votes. Implementing TQM can be difficult in the public sector, where programs and activities are embedded in law. Workers cannot be empowered to take action when laws prescribe what must be done.

As a final comment on the subject, some observers criticize total quality management as being only a repackaging of familiar ideas with little systematic linkage among components and as being a fad that will wane like any other fad. The concepts discussed here are not foreign or strikingly different from those discussed above, and critics suggest that TQM merely restates old concepts but fails to provide a clear direction in linking the components. For instance, changing managers' perceptions about their roles, empowering workers within a team setting, and measuring the performance of the organization are frequently heard prescriptions for organizational reform, but how these objectives are to be achieved simultaneously is not explained by TQM in any detail. Instead, far too often the advocates of TQM espouse the system from deep faith, almost as though it is a cult.

Before closing this discussion, two other sets of proposals are worth noting. First, Bayett and Conn have suggested that a revolution is occurring in the private sector and that the work place in the year 2000 will be quite different from that of the 1990s.[157] They envision organizations with fewer bureaucratic layers and organizational units with more flexible powers and responsibilities. Organizations, to liberate worker creativity, will provide employees with greater control over their work through the use of groups or teams. Second, Osborne and Gaebler have suggested that government needs to restructure or reinvent itself to encourage entrepreneurial behavior.[158] Competition for the delivery of quality services needs to be fostered, and citizens should have greater direct control over their governments. Just as with TQM, the emphasis should be achieving agencies' missions, and personnel systems should be modified to motivate workers in a competitive milieu.

LIMITATIONS ON MOTIVATION

The field of motivation and, more generally, the field of management have been characterized by fads. Management by objectives may be popular one year and TQM the next. If the fad is short lived and produces no appreciable results, harm can be done. Employees who have been subjected to one new technique after another will only yawn when the agency announces that it will begin implementing still another new process. On the other hand, the fads may have some utility, even if they are only short lived. Any change—whether it be flexitime, job enrichment, fishbowling, or strategic planning—may be refreshing. It would follow, therefore, that introducing even a seemingly ludicrous change, such as having employees wear roller skates, could be as effective as more conventional motivation techniques.

Motivation theories and techniques, as noted, generally share the weakness of having overlooked the role of labor unions (Chapter 12 discusses labor–management relations, including the role of unions in decision making and their influence on productivity). The dimension of time also is largely missing from motivation literature. Organizations have histories. The organization climate, of particular interest to OD specialists, does not just exist; rather, it has emerged over a period of time. Changing that climate may be difficult. Workers are likely to keep the same behavior patterns even after an autocratic manager has been replaced by an employee-centered one. An organization simply may not be ready to accept new approaches to motivation and management.[159,160]

Motivation is influenced by current affairs. In recent times, baiting bureaucrats has been a popular sport for politicians, including presidents. Such attacks may have severe repercussions because employees may begin to doubt their own self-worth when criticisms of them frequently are heard on news broadcasts and are displayed in newspapers. Another reaction may be anger at having to withstand such criticisms while simultaneously being expected to put in long hours on the job.[161]

Cutbacks or retrenchments in government programs constitute another negative factor. These may be desirable from the standpoint of shrinking the size of government or enhancing its efficiency, but motivation problems are part of the package deal. Fear sets in as rumors spread that a reduction in force is to occur; valuable time is wasted as workers compare notes on the latest rumors. The employee grapevine works overtime during stressful periods.[162,163] Employees who bump others and accept lower-level positions may be less efficient in carrying out their new responsibilities and may feel that government has treated them unfairly. Managers may feel that they are being expected to produce more with fewer workers[164,165] (see Chapter 8 for a discussion of reduction-in-force procedures). In such situations, efforts to motivate may be almost pointless.

Theorists have sought general theories of motivation but in doing so have tended to disregard the great variation among individuals. People are not a uniform mass, all motivated by self-actualization and not by hygiene factors. Presthus has suggested that workers can be classified into three types: the upward mobiles, the indifferents, and the ambivalents.[166] Although this may not be a perfect typology, it at least suggests that different individuals are motivated in different ways. Some employees may be incapable of being motivated. Voltaire remarked, "They go but faintly to work . . . with one buttock."[167] Many individuals have interest patterns that cannot be satisfied vocationally. For example, a person with mediocre artistic talent but intense interest cannot expect that interest to be supported in the labor market. In such a case, work is apt to be regarded solely as an economic necessity, with all the individual's motivation being channeled into a hobby. Employees bring their personal problems to work. One may be on the verge of a divorce, another is losing the battle against alcoholism, a third is distraught over the death of a child, and a fourth fears he may be infected with the human immunodeficiency virus.

Stress on and off the job can result in what is called burnout.[168] Major tension can exist between the demands made on an employee to spend long hours on the job and demands from family members to spend so-called quality time with them. Stress occurs from situations in which an employee has too many duties with short deadlines or has to deal regularly with life-threatening situations, as in the cases of police officers, firefighters, and hospital personnel in intensive care units or emergency departments.[169] Burnout can lead to low motivation and high absenteeism.[170,171]

Some government agencies have initiated wellness programs that, among other things, seek to reduce stress. Efforts include exercise programs and limits on how many hours a person may work in a day. Dealing with burned-out employees is difficult because they may find little pleasure or satisfaction in their work. They may complain often about seemingly unimportant matters, develop psychosomatic illnesses, and abuse sick leave privileges. In some situations, the best option for a burned-out worker may be for him or her to seek employment at another agency and perhaps in a somewhat different field.[172,173]

It should be recognized that some workers are simply difficult people.[174–176] They may have a basic tendency to look negatively on almost everything. If the manager of a unit discusses with the staff options for dealing with a problem, the negative employee can recite several good reasons why every option will fail. Other employees are major procrastinators: They enthusiastically accept numerous duties but manage to delay in carrying them out. Still others may have unrealistically high views of their capacities and chronically are dissatisfied with any rational assignment of duties. Of course, the supposition here is that the difficult workers meet job requirements enough to avoid disciplinary action other than an occasional reprimand. In addition to general workers, managers can be difficult people and may create dysfunctional situations for worker motivation and organization success in achieving objectives.[177] The theories do not explain how motivation techniques are to work in these situations.

Among the most important concepts that current motivation theories overlook are the phases of adult life and the phases of jobs (probation and permanent status) and careers.[178,179] Workers in their 20s have a considerably different view of their jobs and their agencies than employees who are 40 years old or older. The younger workers may see their current positions only as steppingstones to better jobs and may have limited commitment to the agency. The older persons may have more commitment, or they may be unhappy because their careers seem to have reached a deadend.

Are approaches to motivation cost effective? The proponents of MBO, QCs, OD, TQM, and other techniques would suggest that their methods can be no less cost effective than authoritarian approaches, but it is difficult to put a price tag on implementing motivation techniques. The use of sensitivity training is expensive not because of consultant fees but because of the employee and managerial time required. There is a lingering feeling that the time might be better spent working than attending committee meetings. The agency that has committees layered upon committees may be incapable of responding to the environment. Internal participation is achieved at the expense of being able to adapt to the external, real world.

Approaches to motivation have had difficulty in accommodating the idea that conflict in organizations can be functional.[180,181] Most theorists insist that conflict has utility, but many of the prominent theories implicitly suggest that interpersonal and intergroup cooperation is the ideal toward which organizations should strive. Conflict can have positive effects, however: It can stimulate learning and creativity.

Motivation theory can become its own trap when it attempts to explain all behaviors. The person committed to job enrichment as a technique tends to look at every situation with low worker performance as an opportunity for job redesign and enrichment. More generally, all performance problems tend to be seen as motivation problems when there may be other explanations. Patching of potholes may be ineffective not because the road crews have low motivation but because of inferior patching materials.

Motivation theories are difficult to apply in the public sector because of the constraints that abound. Laws specify what an agency can and cannot do, regardless of whether some alternative might be more effective. Because of personnel and budget ceilings, a manager may be forced into assigning work to an employee who is not fully qualified to do the job. Putting square pegs in round holes is not uncommon. Rigid civil service systems sometimes hinder removing unproductive workers or providing financial incentives to productive employees.

Public managers are busy people who have little time to contemplate how best to help each employee self-actualize. Managers are expected to be bosses and to see that work is done on time, yet motivation theory stresses that they should be friends to employees and encourage their participation in decision making. Managers are expected to be managers, but should they be expected to be psychologists as well?

Important ethical and value issues are associated with motivation. The earlier Mayo approach has been criticized as being manipulative: Techniques seemed to have been developed to be used by management in handling its marionette employees. Do contemporary approaches have the same underlying purposes? Proponents of MBO, TQM, and other techniques defend them as being humanizing, for the benefit of both workers and the organization.

The rights and responsibilities of employees and managers have not been well integrated with motivation theories. Public employees may be said to have a right to be treated humanely, but what rights do they have to participate in agency decision making? It is possible to envision a system in which the employees make decisions that are at the expense of the public and are paid for through taxes. If employees have rights to participate, do not citizens have similar rights? TQM advocates would give a strong affirmative response. What is the professional manager's role? Does the manager abdicate leadership responsibilities by encouraging employee participation? (Managers have been known to hide behind committees.)

Motivation must be considered within the context of an increasingly diversified work force.[182–185] Part-time and full-time employees work together and may have different reasons for why they are employed.[186] Many employees are delaying their retirements, and as a consequence the age spread among employees is growing. Motivating older workers may present challenges different from those involved in motivating other workers.[187,188] Greater diversity is occurring with regard to gender, race, and ethnicity. Motivation theories generally disregard the fact that women and men may have different concerns about their jobs and each other and that both white workers and people of color may harbor biases against one another.[189,190]

This critique on the limitations of motivation should not be interpreted as an argument against all such theories and techniques. The appropriate interpretation is that the current state of the art is less than perfect but that certainly more is known today than in the 1920s or 1930s. Much is still to be learned about why people behave the way they do, why some are creative and innovative while others are not, and why some organizations are receptive to change and others are not.

SUMMARY

Some techniques aimed at motivating workers stress their autonomy. Flexitime has been advocated not only because it gives employees a choice about when they work but also because it releases them from close supervision. Managers are forced to delegate responsibilities because some workers will be at their jobs when the managers have not yet arrived or have left for the day. Flexitime is defended as increasing productivity. Critics claim that without direct supervision workers often are less productive and that long working hours under compressed scheduling increase fatigue and reduce productivity.

Job enrichment also increases worker autonomy and gives each employee a greater range of responsibilities. By seeing how their work relates to the total effort of an organization, employees may become more motivated and productive. Enriching jobs throughout an organization has the effect of decentralizing responsibilities. If job enrichment is to be used, pay and promotion practices need to be changed.

Although some motivation theories emphasize the individual, others stress the importance of groups and group leaders. At the core of group theories are dyadic relationships, in which two people relate to one another. Groups have structures and communication networks. The networks of informal work groups may differ substantially from the organization's formal communication channels. Members play different roles in the group, which establishes behavior norms. Through the use of penalties and rewards, groups exert major influences on members' behavior.

One of the most important roles in a group is that of leadership. Managers often are assumed to perform the role of leading their subordinates toward meeting the organization's goals. The trait approach to leadership has been abandoned, and research now concentrates on effective styles for motivating workers. The prescription that has emerged is that supervisors should be concerned about the needs of their employees and not just those of the organization. The contingency approach suggests that different styles should be used, depending on the situation at hand.

Management by objectives, or MBO, is a management technique that stresses the setting of goals and/or objectives with worker involvement. Participation is seen as encouraging employees to internalize or accept the organization's goals. Through MBO, workers come to understand what is expected of them, and managers can manage on the basis of results.

Quality circles are groups of workers who meet, usually once a week, to identify and resolve problems in order to improve their output. QCs originated in Japan, spread to corporations in the United States, and now are used in many governmental agencies. Managers are expected to serve as team leaders rather than use an autocratic management style.

Organization development, or OD, seeks to help organizations adjust to their changing environments. Sensitivity training, T-groups, or encounter groups attempt to improve how people relate to each other. By becoming sensitive to others, people develop supportive relationships that encourage them to explore new ideas.

Total quality management, or TQM, attained considerable popularity starting in the 1980s. Emphasis is given to long-term commitments to mission and the continuous improvement of the quality of services or products produced. TQM is not compatible with MBO and stresses the need for managerial leadership and worker involvement.

Although much has been learned about how and why people behave as they do in organizations, much still is unknown. The theories and techniques discussed in this and the preceding chapter should not be considered a set of panaceas. Criticisms of these theories and techniques include that they often are faddish, that they tend to ignore the role of unions, that they tend to deemphasize the great variations among people, and that they tend to advocate cooperation and regard conflict as dysfunctional. Left unspecified is the extent to which public employees should be allowed to participate in decision making vis-à-vis the responsibilities of public managers and the rights of the citizenry they serve.

If the discussion in this and the preceding chapter has been followed carefully, a sense of confusion may have developed. This is unavoidable because the field of motivation is itself confused. There is a myriad of theories of motivation and techniques for motivating employees but no consensus about what works and what does not. Some degree of skepticism is warranted when one hears great claims that any one technique is superior to all others.

NOTES

1. G.R. Oldham and N.L. Rotchford, Relationships between officer characteristics and employee relations, *Administrative Science Quarterly* 28 (1983): 542–556.

2. G.B. Lewis, Pay and job satisfaction in the federal civil service, *Review of Public Personnel Administration* 11 (Summer 1991): 17–31.

3. N.K. Grant, et al., Perceived utilization, job satisfaction and advancement of police women, *Public Personnel Management* 19 (1990) 147–154.

4. D. McGregor, *The Human Side of Enterprise* (New York: McGraw-Hill Book Company, 1960), 47–48.

5. L. Gulick and L. Urwick, *Papers on the Science of Administration* (New York: Institute of Public Administration, 1937).

6. U.S. General Accounting Office, *Alternative Work Schedules for Federal Employees* (Washington: U.S. Government Printing Office, 1985).

7. J. Naisbitt and P. Aburdene, *Re-Inventing the Corporation* (New York: Warner Books, 1985).

8. M.R. Buckley, et al., A note on the effectiveness of flextime as an organizational intervention, *Public Personnel Management* 16 (1987): 259–267.

9. D.R. Dalton and D.J. Mesch, The impact of flexible scheduling on employee attendance and turnover, *Administrative Science Quarterly* 35 (1990): 370–387.

10. J.C. Latack and L.W. Foster, Implementation of compressed work schedules, *Personnel Psychology* 38 (1985): 75–92.

11. J.B. McGuire and J.R. Liro, Absenteeism and flexible work schedules, *Public Personnel Management* 16 (1987): 47–59.

12. W.H. Joice, Home based employment: A consideration for public personnel management, *Public Personnel Management* 20 (1991): 49–60.

13. M.A. Campion and C.L. McClelland, Interdisciplinary examination of the costs and benefits of enlarged jobs: A job design quasi-experiment, *Journal of Applied Psychology* 76 (1991): 186–198.

14. C.S. Wong and M.A. Campion, Development and test of a task level model of motivational job design, *Journal of Applied Psychology* 76 (1991): 825–837.

15. F. Herzberg, *Work and the Nature of Man* (Cleveland, Ohio: World Publishing Company, 1966), 177.

16. K.O. Alexander, On work and authority: Issues on job enlargement, job enrichment, worker participation and shared authority, *American Journal of Economics and Sociology* 34 (1975): 43–54.

17. G.M. McEvoy and W.F. Cascio, Strategies for reducing employee turnover: A meta-analysis, *Journal of Applied Psychology* 70 (1985): 342–353.

18. A.N. Turner and P.R. Lawrence, *Industrial Jobs and the Worker* (Cambridge, Mass.: Harvard University Graduate School of Business Administration, 1965).

19. J.R. Hackman and G.R. Oldham, Motivation through the design of work: Test of a theory, *Organizational Behavior and Human Performance* 16 (1976): 250–279.

20. H.G. Rainey, et al., Reward expectancies and other work-related attitudes in public and private organizations, *Review of Public Personnel Administration* 6 (Summer 1986): 50–72.

21. A. Wildavsky, Ubiquitous anomie: Public service in an era of ideological dissensus, *Public Administration Review* 48 (1988): 753–755.

22. M.S. Olmsted, *The Small Group* (New York: Random House, 1959), 21.

23. D. Coursey and H.G. Rainey, eds., Symposium on organizational behavior and processes in the public sector, *Public Productivity and Management Review* 14 (1991): 351–413.

24. J.A. Wagner, III, and J.R. Hollenbeck, *Management of Organizational Behavior* (Englewood Cliffs, N.J.: Prentice-Hall, 1992).

25. S.P. Robbins, *Essentials of Organizational Behavior*, 3d ed. (Englewood Cliffs, N.J.: Prentice-Hall, 1992).

26. W.J. Heisler, "Worker Alienation: 1900–1975," in *A Matter of Dignity: Inquiries into the Humanization of Work*, ed. W.J. Heisler and J.W. Houck (Notre Dame, Ind.: University of Notre Dame Press, 1977), 65–84.

27. F.J. Roethlisberger and W.J. Dickson, *Management and the Worker* (Cambridge, Mass.: Harvard University Press, 1939), 155–156.

28. H.A. Landsberger, *Hawthorne Revisited* (Ithaca, N.Y.: Cornell University, 1958), 61–62.

29. W.H. Whyte, *The Organization Man* (New York: Simon & Schuster, 1956).

30. G.C. Homans, *The Human Group* (New York. Harcourt, Brace and Company, 1950).

31. J.W. Thibaut and H.H. Kelly, *The Social Psychology of Groups* (New York: John Wiley & Sons, 1959).

32. J.B. Harvey, Some thoughts about organizational backstabbing, *Academy of Management EXECUTIVE* 3 (1989): 271–277.

33. P.K. Manning, *Organizational Communication* (New York: Aldine de Grayter, 1992).

34. D. Katz and R.L. Kahn, *The Social Psychology of Organizations*, 2d ed. (New York: John Wiley & Sons, 1978), 43.

35. R.F. Bales, *Interaction Process Analysis* (Cambridge, Mass.: Addison-Wesley Publishing Company, 1950).

36. I.L. Janis, *Groupthink*, 2d ed. (Boston: Houghton Mifflin Company, 1983).

37. D. Cartwright and A. Zander, eds., *Group Dynamics: Research and Theory*, 3d ed. (New York: Harper & Row, 1968).

38. R. Likert, *New Patterns of Management* (New York: McGraw-Hill Book Company, 1961), 20–34.

39. R.B. Cattell, Concepts and methods in the measurement of group syntality, *Psychological Review* 55 (1948): 48–63.

40. B.F. Skinner, *Science and Human Behavior* (New York: Free Press, 1953), 312.

41. I.B. Myers and M.H. McCaulley, *Manual: A Guide to the Development and Use of the Myers-Briggs Type Indicator* (Palo Alto, Calif.: Consulting Psychologists Press, 1985).

42. I.F. Tucker, Predicting scores on the Rathus Assertiveness Schedule from Myers-Briggs Type Indicator categories, *Psychological Reports* 69 (1991): 571–576.

43. R.E. Kaplan, ed., Symposium on character and leadership, *Journal of Applied Behavioral Science* 26 (1990): 417–442.

44. E.H. Schein, *Organizational Culture and Leadership*, 2d ed. (San Francisco, Calif.: Jossey-Bass, 1992).

45. M.L. Vasu, et al., *Organizational Behavior and Management*, 2d ed. (New York: Marcel Dekker, 1990).

46. J.R.P. French, Jr., and B.H. Raven, "The Bases of Social Power," in *Studies in Social Power*, ed. D. Cartwright (Ann Arbor: Institute for Social Research, University of Michigan, 1959).

47. R. Lachman, Power from what? A reexamination of its relationships with structural conditions, *Administrative Science Quarterly* 34 (1989): 231–251.

48. C.A. Schriesheim, et al., Can ipsative and single-item measures produce erroneous results in field studies of French and Raven's (1959) five bases of power? An empirical investigation, *Journal of Applied Psychology* 76 (1991): 106–114.

49. R. Michels, *Political Parties: A Sociological Study of the Oligarchical Tendencies of Modern Democracy* (New York: Dover Publications, 1959).

50. C.I. Barnard, *The Functions of the Executive* (Cambridge, Mass.: Harvard University Press, 1938).

51. W.F. Whyte, *Streetcorner Society* (Chicago: University of Chicago Press, 1943).

52. J.R. Meindl, Managing to be fair: An exploration of values, motives, and leadership, *Administrative Science Quarterly* 34 (1989): 252–276.

53. D.A. Waldman, et al., Adding to contingent-reward behavior: The augmenting effect of charismatic leadership, *Group and Organizational Dynamics* 15 (1990): 381–394.

54. G.I. Susman, *Autonomy at Work: A Sociotechnical Analysis of Participative Management* (New York: Praeger Publishers, 1976).

55. P. Selznick, *Leadership in Administration: A Sociological Interpretation* (New York: Harper & Row, 1957), 145.

56. R.J. House, et al., Personality and charisma in the U.S. presidency: A psychological theory of leader effectiveness, *Administrative Science Quarterly* 36 (1991): 364–396.

57. J.M. Howell and B.J. Avolio, The ethics of charismatic leadership: Submission or liberation, *Academy of Management EXECUTIVE* 6 (1992): 43–54.

58. K. Lewin, et al., Patterns of aggressive behavior in experimentally created "social climates," *Journal of Social Psychology* 10 (1939): 271–299.

59. R. Lippitt and R.K. White, "The 'Social Climate' of Children's Groups," in *Child Behavior and Development*, ed. R.G. Barker, et al. (New York: McGraw-Hill Book Company, 1943), 485–508.

60. R.M. Stogdill and A.E. Coons, eds., *Leader Behavior: Its Description and Measurement* (Columbus: Bureau of Business Research, Ohio State University, 1957).

61. D. Katz, et al., *Productivity, Supervision, and Morale in an Office Situation* (Ann Arbor: Survey Research Center, University of Michigan, 1950).

62. R. Likert, *The Human Organization* (New York: McGraw-Hill Book Company, 1967).

63. _____, *New Patterns of Management*.

64. R.J. Bullock, *Improving Job Satisfaction* (New York: Pergamon Press, 1984).

65. D.M. Daley, Humanistic management and organizational success, *Public Personnel Management* 15 (1986): 131–142.

66. R. Bales, "The Equilibrium Problem in Small Groups," in *Working Papers in the Theory of Action,* ed. T. Parsons, et al. (New York: The Free Press, 1953).

67. R.R. Blake and J.S. Mouton, Managerial facades, *Advanced Management Journal* 31 (July 1966): 30–37.

68. _____, An overview of the grid, *Training and Development Journal* 29 (May 1975): 29–37.

69. _____, *Executive Achievement* (New York: McGraw-Hill Book Company, 1986).

70. R.R. Blake, et al., *Grid Approaches for Managerial Leadership in Nursing* (St. Louis, Mo.: C.V. Mosby Company, 1981).

71. F.E. Berman and J.B. Miner, Motivation to manage at the top executive level, *Personnel Psychology* 38 (1985): 377–391.

72. C. Argyris, *Integrating the Individual and the Organization* (New York: John Wiley & Sons, 1964).

73. G.H. Bruns and I.G. Shuman, Police managers' perception of organizational leadership styles, *Public Personnel Management* 17 (1988): 145–157.

74. F.E. Fiedler, *A Theory of Leadership Effectiveness* (New York: McGraw-Hill Book Company, 1967).

75. _____, Engineer the job to fit the manager, *Harvard Business Review* 43 (September–October 1965): 115–122.

76. L.H. Peters, et al., Fiedler's contingency theory of leadership, *Psychological Bulletin* 97 (1985): 274–285.

77. V.H. Vroom and P.W. Yetton, *Leadership and Decision-Making* (Pittsburgh, Pa.: University of Pittsburgh Press, 1973).

78. R.H.G. Field, A test of the Vroom-Yetton normative model of leadership, *Journal of Applied Psychology* 67 (1982): 523–532.

79. B.S. Georgopoulos, et al., A path–goal approach to productivity, *Journal of Applied Psychology* 41 (1957): 345–353.

80. T.C. Mawhinney and J.D. Ford, The path–goal theory of leader effectiveness: An operant interpretation, *Academy of Management Review* 2 (1977): 398–411.

81. C. Schriesheim and M.A. Von Glinow, The path–goal theory of leadership: A theoretical and empirical analysis, *Academy of Management Journal* 20 (1977): 398–405.

82. H.P. Sims, Jr., and P. Lorenzi, *The New Leadership Paradigm: Social Learning and Cognition in Organizations* (Newbury Park, Calif.: Sage, 1992).

83. W. Boeker, The development and institutionalization of subunit power in organizations, *Administrative Science Quarterly* 34 (1989): 388–410.

84. S. Finkelstein and D.C. Hambrick, Top-management–team tenure and organizational outcomes: The moderating role of managerial discretion, *Administrative Science Quarterly* 35 (1990): 484–503.

85. S.R. Covey, *The Seven Habits of Highly Effective People* (New York: Simon & Schuster, 1989).

86. C.A. Bowsher, *Performance Measurement: An Important Tool in Managing for Results* (Washington: U.S. Government Printing Office, 1992).

87. N. Carter, et al., *How Organisations Measure Success: The Use of Performance Indicators in Government* (London: Routledge, 1992).

88. L.P. Jones, *Performance Evaluation for Public Enterprises* (New York: World Bank, 1991).

89. U.S. General Accounting Office, *Office of Personnel Management: Better Performance Information Needed* (Washington: U.S. Government Printing Office, 1990).

90. J.S. Wholey and H.P. Hatry, The case for performance monitoring, *Public Administration Review* 52 (1992): 604–610.

91. R.D. Lee, Jr., and R.W. Johnson, *Public Budgeting Systems*, 4th ed. (Gaithersburg, Md.: Aspen Publishers, 1989).

92. *Public Budgeting & Finance*, selected issues.

93. *Public Productivity and Management Review*, selected issues.

94. A.C. Hyde and G.R. Gilbert, eds., Symposium on productivity improvement in the public sector, *Public Personnel Management* 14 (1985): 319–453.

95. E. Morley, *A Practitioner's Guide to Public Sector Productivity Improvement* (New York: Von Nostrand Reinhold Company, 1986).

96. P.C. Nutt and R.W. Backoff, *Strategic Management of Public and Third Sector Organizations: A Handbook for Leaders* (San Francisco: Jossey-Bass, 1992).

97. Advisory Committee on Federal Workforce Quality Assessment, *Federal Workforce Quality: Measurement and Improvement* (Washington: U.S. Government Printing Office, 1992).

98. U.S. General Accounting Office, *Performance Management: How Well Is the Government Dealing with Poor Performers?* (Washington: U.S. Government Printing Office, 1990).

99. P.F. Drucker, What results should you expect? A users' guide to MBO, *Public Administration Review* 36 (1976): 12.

100. _____, *The Practice of Management* (New York: Harper & Brothers, 1954).

101. D. McGregor, *The Human Side of Enterprise* (New York: McGraw-Hill Book Company, 1960).

102. G. Odiorne, *Management by Objectives* (New York: Pitman Publishing Corp., 1965).

103. R. Rodgers and J.E. Hunter, A foundation of good management practice in government: Management by objectives, *Public Administration Review* 52 (1992): 27–39.

104. T.A. Ryan, *Intentional Behavior* (New York: Roland, 1970).

105. E.A. Locke, Toward a theory of task motivation and incentives, *Organizational Behavior and Human Performance* 3 (1968): 157–189.

106. D. Halpern and S. Osofsky, A dissenting view of MBO, *Public Personnel Management* 19 (1990): 321–330.

107. D.E. Bowen and E.E. Lawler, III, The empowerment of service workers: What, why, how, and when, *Sloan Management Review* 33 (Spring 1992): 31–39.

108. D. Daley, Performance appraisal and organizational success: Public employee perceptions in an MBO-based appraisal system, *Review of Public Personnel Administration* 9 (Fall 1988): 17–27.

109. U.S. Office of Personnel Management, *Management by Objectives in Performance Appraisal Systems* (Washington: U.S. Government Printing Office, 1985).

110. N.Q. Herrick, Cooperative self-interest: Learning from Joe Scanlon, *Public Productivity Review* 6 (1982): 19–34.

111. S. Watanabe, The Japanese quality control circle: Why it works, *International Labour Review* 130 (1991): 57–80.

112. W.G. Ouchi, *Theory Z* (Reading, Mass.: Addison-Wesley Publishing Co., 1981).

113. D.J. Watson and B.B. Burkhalter, Developing a Theory Z culture in local government, *Public Personnel Management* 21 (1992): 401–409.

114. J.S. Bowman, Quality circles: Promise, problems, and prospects in Florida, *Public Personnel Management* 18 (1989): 375–403.

115. B.S. Romzek, Employee investment and commitment: The ties that bind, *Public Administration Review* 50 (1990): 374–382.

116. J.S. Larson, Employee participation in federal management, *Public Personnel Management* 18 (1989): 404–414.

117. R.P. Steel, et al., Quality circle problem solving and common cents: Evaluation study findings from a United States federal mint, *Journal of Applied Behavioral Science* 26 (1990): 365–381.

118. D.L. Deadrick and K.D. Scott, Employee incentives in the public sector: A national survey of urban mass transit authorities, *Public Personnel Management* 16 (1987): 135–143.

119. P. Bate, Using the culture concept in an organizational development setting, *Journal of Applied Behavioral Science* 26 (1990): 83–118.

120. J.R. Lincoln and A.L. Kalleberg, *Culture, Control, and Commitment: A Study of Work Organization and Work Attitudes in the United States and Japan* (Cambridge, England: Cambridge University Press, 1990).

121. U.S. General Accounting Office, *Organizational Culture: Techniques Companies Use To Perpetuate or Change Beliefs and Values* (Washington: U.S. Government Printing Office, 1992).

122. D.G. Carnevale, Physical settings of work: A theory of the effects of environmental form, *Public Productivity and Management Review* 15 (1992): 423–436.

123. J.J. Accordino, Quality-of-working-life systems in large cities: An assessment, *Public Productivity Review* 12 (1989): 345–360.

124. A.E. Eaton, et al., The impact of quality of work life programs and grievance system effectiveness on union commitment, *Industrial and Labor Relations Review* 45 (1992): 591–604.

125. M.W. Fields and J.W. Thacker, Influence of quality of work life on company and union commitment, *Academy of Management Journal* 35 (1992): 439–450.

126. R.T. Golembiewski and B.C. Sun, QWL applications in public agencies: Do success rates reflect a positive-findings bias? *International Journal of Public Administration* 15 (1992): 1,263–1,276.

127. W.L. French and C.H. Bell, Jr., *Organization Development: Behavioral Science Intervention for Organization Improvement*, 4th ed. (Englewood Cliffs, N.J.: Prentice-Hall, 1990).

128. E.J. Giblin, Organization development: Public sector theory and practice, *Public Personnel Management* 5 (1976): 108.

129. K. Lewin, *Field Theory and Social Science* (New York: Harper & Brothers, 1951).

130. K.W. Black, *Beyond Words: The Story of Sensitivity Training and the Encounter Movement* (New York: Russell Sage Foundation, 1972).

131. C. Rogers, *Client Centered Therapy* (New York: Houghton Mifflin Company, 1951).

132. L. Coch and J.R.P. French, Jr., Overcoming resistance to change, *Human Relations* 1 (1948): 512–532.

133. G. Gardner, Worker's participation: A critical evaluation of Coch and French, *Human Relations* 30 (1977): 1,071–1,078.

134. W.G. Bennis, *Organization Development: Its Nature, Origins, and Prospects* (Reading, Mass.: Addison-Wesley Publishing Co., 1969).

135. N. Levine and C.L. Cooper, T-Groups—Twenty years on: A prophecy, *Human Relations* 29 (1976): 1–23.

136. R.P. Rugel and D.J. Meyer, The Tavistock group: Empirical findings and implications for group therapy, *Small Group Behavior* 15 (1984): 361–374.

137. K.D. Benne, et al., "The Laboratory Methods," in *T-Group Theory and Laboratory Method: Innovation in Re-Education*, ed. L.P. Bradford, et al. (New York: John Wiley & Sons, 1964), 15–44.

138. J. Gilberg, Managerial attitudes toward participative management programs: Myths and reality, *Public Personnel Management* 17 (1988): 109–123.

139. E. Berne, *Games People Play* (New York: Grove Press, 1964).

140. _____, *The Structure and Dynamics of Organizations and Groups* (New York: Grove Press, 1963).

141. J.A. Bradford and R. Guberman, *Transactional Awareness* (Reading, Mass.: Addison-Wesley Publishing Co., 1978).

142. J. Bradshaw, *Homecoming: Reclaiming and Championing Your Inner Child* (New York: Bantam Books, 1990).

143. T.H. Patten, *Organizational Development through Teambuilding* (New York: John Wiley & Sons, 1981).

144. J.R. Jablonski, *Implementing Total Quality Management* (San Diego, Calif.: Pfeiffer, 1991).

145. A.C. Hyde, ed., Symposium on implications of total quality management for the public sector, *Public Productivity and Management Review* 16 (1992): 23–75.

146. J.M. Juran, *Juran on Planning for Quality* (New York: Free Press, 1988).

147. K. Ishikawa, *What Is Total Quality Control? The Japanese Way* (Englewood Cliffs, N.J.: Prentice-Hall, 1985).

148. M.E. Milakovich, Total quality management for public sector productivity improvement, *Public Productivity and Management Review* 14 (1990): 19–32.

149. W.E. Deming, *Quality, Productivity, and Competitive Position* (Cambridge: Massachusetts Institute of Technology Center for Advanced Engineering Study, 1982).

150. _____, *Out of the Crisis* (Cambridge: Massachusetts Institute of Technology Center for Advanced Engineering Study, 1986), 23–24.

151. A.C. Rosander, *Deming's 14 Points Applied to Services* (New York: Marcel Dekker, 1991).

152. J.E. Swiss, Adapting total quality management (TQM) to government, *Public Administration Review* 52 (1992): 356–362.

153. J.J. Kline, Total quality management in local government, *Government Finance Review* 8 (August 1992): 7–11.

154. S. Cohen and R. Brand, Total quality management in the U.S. Environmental Protection Agency, *Public Productivity and Management Review* 14 (1990): 99–114.

155. D.E. Bowen and E.E. Lawler, III, Total quality-oriented human resources management, *Organizational Dynamics* 20 (Spring 1992): 29–41.

156. M.J. Levine, Labor management response to total quality management, *Labor Law Journal* 43 (1992): 107–116.

157. J.H. Bayett and H.P. Conn, *Workplace 2000: The Revolution Reshaping American Business* (New York: E.P. Dutton, 1991).

158. David Osborne and T. Gaebler, *Reinventing Government: How the Entrepreneurial Spirit Is Transforming the Public Sector* (Reading, Mass.: Addison-Wesley Publishing Co., 1992).

159. D.F. Harvey and D.R. Brown, *An Experiential Approach to Organization Development*, 4th ed. (Englewood Cliffs, N.J.: Prentice-Hall, 1992).

160. U.S. General Accounting Office, *Employee Involvement: Issues for Agencies To Consider in Designing and Implementing Programs* (Washington: U.S. Government Printing Office, 1988).

161. B. Adams, The frustrations of government service, *Public Administration Review* 44 (1984): 5–13.

162. J.L. Garnett, Coping with rumors and grapevines: Tactics for public personnel management, *Review of Public Personnel Administration* 12 (May–August 1992): 42–49.

163. J. Mishra, Managing the grapevine, *Public Personnel Management* 19 (1990): 213–228.

164. P.W. Ingraham and C. Barrilleaux, Motivating government managers for retrenchment, *Public Administration Review* 43 (1983): 393–402.

165. C.H. Levine, Retrenchment, human resources, erosion, and the role of the personnel manager, *Public Personnel Management* 13 (1984): 249–263.

166. R. Presthus, *The Organizational Society* (New York: Vintage Books, 1962).

167. Voltaire as quoted in R.T. Golembiewski, *Men, Management, and Morality: Toward a New Organizational Ethic* (New York: McGraw-Hill, 1965), 61.

168. R.T. Golembiewski, et al., Centrality of burnout in a public agency: Multiple measurements supporting common conclusions, *Review of Public Personnel Administration* 9 (Fall 1988): 28–44.

169. J.R. Edwards, A cybernetic theory of stress, coping, and well-being in organizations, *Academy of Management Review* 17 (1992): 238–274.

170. R.C. Gardiner, Tracking and controlling absenteeism, *Public Productivity and Management Review* 15 (1992): 289–307.

171. S.R. Rhodes and R.M. Steers, *Managing Employee Absenteeism* (Reading, Mass.: Addison-Wesley Publishing Co., 1990).

172. R.A. Cooke and D.M. Rousseau, Stress and strain from family roles and work-role expectations, *Journal of Applied Psychology* 69 (1984): 225–260.

173. C.L. Vash, *The Burnt-Out Administrator* (New York: Springer Publishing Co., 1980).

174. R.M. Bramson, *Coping with Difficult People* (Garden City, N.Y.: Anchor Press, 1981).

175. G.J. Shaw and W.L. Bransford, *The Federal Manager's Handbook: A Guide to Rehabilitating or Removing the Problem Employee* (Washington: MPC Publications, 1992).

176. W. Ury, *Getting Past No: Negotiating with Difficult People* (New York: Bantam Books, 1991).

177. F.S. Hall, Dysfunctional managers: The next human resource challenge, *Organizational Dynamics* 20 (Autumn 1991): 48–57.

178. G.F. Shea, *The New Employee* (Reading, Mass.: Addison-Wesley Publishing Co., 1981).

179. G. Sheehy, *Passages: Predictable Crises of Adult Life* (New York: E.P. Dutton, 1976).

180. D.R. Dalton and R.A. Cosier, eds., Symposium on positive conflict, *Employee Responsibilities and Rights Journal* 4 (1991): 1–85.

181. K.K. Smith, The movement of conflict in organizations: The joint dynamics of splitting and triangulation, *Administrative Science Quarterly* 34 (1989): 1–20.

182. J.P. Fernandez, *Managing a Diverse Work Force: Regaining the Competitive Edge* (Lexington, Mass.: Lexington Books, 1991).

183. S.E. Jackson, et al., *Diversity in the Workplace: Human Resource Initiatives* (New York: Guilford Publications, 1992).

184. M. Loden and J.B. Rosener, *Workforce America!: Managing Employee Diversity as a Vital Resource* (Homewood, Ill.: Business One Irwin, 1991).

185. U.S. General Accounting Office, *The Changing Workforce: Comparison of Federal and Nonfederal Work/Family Programs and Approaches* (Washington: U.S. Government Printing Office, 1992).

186. D.C. Feldman and H.I. Doerspinghaus, Missing persons no longer: Managing part-time workers in the '90s, *Organizational Dynamics* 21 (Summer 1992): 59–72.

187. N. Hale, *The Older Worker: Effective Strategies for Management and Human Resource Development* (San Francisco: Jossey-Bass, 1990).

188. G.F. Shea, *Managing Older Employees* (San Francisco: Jossey-Bass, 1991).

189. M.G. Fine, et al., Cultural diversity in the workplace, *Public Personnel Management* 19 (1990): 305–319.

190. K.D. Scott and E.L. McClellan, Gender differences in absenteeism, *Public Personnel Management* 19 (1990): 229–253.

Chapter 12

Labor–Management Relations

The subject of labor–management relations has been placed near the end of this book not because of its unimportance but because of its importance. The relationships between workers and their supervisors pervade all aspects of personnel administration, and therefore one cannot fully appreciate the scope of labor–management relations without understanding the scope of personnel administration. The discussion here emphasizes the relationships between employee organizations or unions and management, and not the more general relationships between workers and their supervisors.[1-5]

"Labor–management relations" is a broader term than "collective bargaining." The latter refers to employee unions negotiating agreements about conditions of work. From the perspective of organized labor, collective bargaining includes negotiations over pay rates and the right of workers to strike when the two parties cannot reach an agreement. As will be seen, comparatively few public workers have such bargaining rights. For convenience purposes, however, the discussion here uses the term "collective bargaining" to refer generally to negotiations regardless of whether pay is negotiable or whether workers may strike.

This chapter covers three topics:

1. the growth of public employee unions and the emergence of collective bargaining
2. collective bargaining processes
3. the impact that public employee unions and collective bargaining have had on government administration

THE EMERGENCE OF UNIONS AND BARGAINING

The concept of sovereignty has been a major impediment to the rise of public employee unions and public sector collective bargaining. Just as sovereignty has been used to protect government from legal suits (see Chapter 8), so has it been used to protect government from its employees. Under the concept of sovereignty, government asserts that it is omnipotent and can do no wrong. If government is all powerful, then by definition it cannot be forced to negotiate with its employees. Public workers as servants of the citizenry cannot assert a right to be treated by the government as coequals in bargaining. Three distinct but related issues are involved:

1. whether public employees have a right to organize
2. whether employee associations or unions may bargain
3. whether they may strike

The sovereignty issue has been asserted most strongly with regard to strikes, but for a long time government used it as well to defend against employees organizing and seeking negotiating rights.

At the federal level, employee unionism developed among blue collar workers and in the postal system and has since spread throughout the government.[6,7] Laborers and mechanics in the 1830s organized in Navy yards and federal arsenals. Postal workers, who organized in the 1880s and 1890s, focused their effort less on collective bargaining rights and more on influencing federal legislation in their behalf. As a result of this activity, the executive branch imposed "gag" rules, prohibiting employees from lobbying in Congress. These rules were overturned in 1912 by the Lloyd-LaFollette Act, a measure strongly supported by the American Federation of Labor and its president, Samuel Gompers. That act permitted lobbying activities, and the provision protecting against removal except for cause (see Chapter 8) was included, in part to protect workers from being fired for union activities (the Civil Service Reform Act of 1978 reaffirmed the right of employees and employee organizations to petition Congress). From 1912 onward there were numerous efforts to reorient the federal government's position in labor–management relations, but no major change occurred until 1962, when President Kennedy issued Executive Order 10988. That order greatly expanded unionism in the federal government.

Political involvement of public employee unions has existed since their emergence, and controversy has centered on that fact as well. Unions have lobbied for legislation favoring collective bargaining, have endorsed candidates for office, have mobilized voters, and have provided financial contributions to candidates for political office. Although the Hatch Acts have greatly restricted such activities (see Chapter 8), they have not barred political action committees from engaging in these activities.[8,9] In a survey of cities conducted in the late 1980s, 45 percent reported that police unions engaged in political activity, including the endorsement of candidates; the comparable figure for firefighter unions was 39 percent.[10] The question frequently raised is whether collectively public employees should be allowed to influence the political outcomes of their employers.

Numerous unions represent federal workers, with a substantial majority of the employees being in bargaining units of affiliates of the American Federation of Labor-Congress of Industrial Organizations (AFL-CIO). Table 12–1 shows 1991 union representation in agencies whose labor relations are under the jurisdiction of the Federal Labor Relations Authority and in the U.S. Postal Service, which is under the jurisdiction of the National Labor Relations Board. The American Federation of Government Employees (AFGE) represents the largest number of federal workers and is followed by the American Postal Workers Union (APWU) and the National Association of Letter Carriers (NALC). These AFL-CIO unions are followed by the nonaffiliated National Treasury Employees Union (NTEU) and the National Federation of Federal Employees (NFFE). About 60 percent of the federal workers are organized in exclusive bargaining units. About half the General Schedule positions and more than 90 percent of the trades and labor positions are covered by such agreements. The number of employees in exclusive units rose from only 180,000 in 1963 to 1.24 million in 1979 and has remained at about that level into the 1990s.[11]

Table 12–1 Union Representation in the Federal Government, 1991

Union	Employees*
Exclusive recognition	
American Federation of Government Employees, AFL-CIO	642,315
National Treasury Employees Union	151,736
National Federation of Federal Employees	146,113
National Association of Government Employees	69,501
Metal Trades Council, AFL-CIO	63,063
International Association of Machinists and Aerospace Workers, AFL-CIO	28,869
Other	149,180
Subtotal	1,250,777
U.S. Postal Service	
American Postal Workers Union, AFL-CIO	333,940
National Association of Letter Carriers of America, AFL-CIO	234,405
National Rural Letter Carriers of America	85,247
National Association of Post Office Mail Handlers, Watchmen, Messengers, and Group Leaders, AFL-CIO	50,716
Other	1,967
Subtotal	706,275

*Figures do not include employees represented by unions in nonappropriated fund activities (Department of Defense and National Aeronautics and Space Administration) and other jurisdictions (selected units of Agency for International Development, Department of State, Tennessee Valley Authority, U.S. Information Agency).

Source: *Union Recognition in the Federal Government*, U.S. Office of Personnel Management, U.S. Government Printing Office, 1991.

Federal departments vary considerably in the extent to which they have exclusive bargaining units. In the Treasury Department, for example, well over 80 percent of the white collar employees are in such units compared with only about 30 percent in the Interior Department. Virtually all wage employees are covered in the Departments of Energy, Labor, and Treasury compared with about 60 percent in the Agriculture Department and the Environmental Protection Agency.

Union representation and membership are not the same. A union has responsibility for representing all employees within a bargaining unit, even though some individuals are not union members. As a result, membership almost always is lower than the number of employees represented. Estimates of union membership in federal bargaining units range between 30 and 40 percent. AFGE, for example, represents well over 600,000 federal workers but has a membership of about 250,000; NFFE represents nearly 150,000 and has a membership of only 50,000.[12]

Unionization has become common in state and local governments, too. In a 1988 survey of cities, nearly 90 percent reported that they engaged in collective bargaining with some of their employees.[13] Table 12-2 shows that nearly half of all full-time state and local workers are organized. Township workers are the most organized (61 percent), and county and special districts are the least organized (34 percent). The National Education Association (NEA) is the dominant employee organization in school districts and is followed by the American Federation of Teachers (AFT), an affiliate of the AFL-CIO. The American Federation of State, County, and Municipal Employees (AFSCME), also an AFL-CIO union, has about 1.2 million members. Within general purpose local governments, firefighters are the most highly organized (65 percent), and the largest union representing them is the International Association of Fire Fighters (IAFF), an AFL-CIO union.

Table 12-2 State and Local Organized Full-Time Employees, 1987

Jurisdiction Type	Organized Employees	
	Number	Percentage
State governments	1,221,413	40
Local governments	3,732,995	48
Counties	558,149	34
Municipalities	1,058,145	51
Townships	138,576	61
School districts	1,837,165	53
Special districts	140,960	34
Total	4,954,408	45

Source: Public Employment: Labor-Management Relations, U.S. Bureau of the Census, U.S. Government Printing Office, 1991.

Several factors account for the rise of public unions. Poor working conditions have been a major and persistent reason. In the 1890s, mail clerks were required to work in unsanitary and dangerous railroad mail cars, with a resulting high accident rate.[14] More recently, public workers have sought guaranteed rest breaks, and teachers have demanded time out of the classroom to prepare their lessons. Low pay has been a frequent reason; this led to the famous Boston police strike of 1919. Some observers have suggested that there is an almost inherent tendency to organize: "Whenever any sector of the labor force became sufficiently aware of its collective presence and power, it sooner or later organized to make itself seen and heard."[15]

The growth of government unions and their militancy in the 1960s can be explained by additional factors. Some groups of workers came to the conclusion they were not part of one big happy family. Teachers most notably wrestled with whether as professionals they should demand collective bargaining rights or whether bargaining was more appropriate for blue collar workers. NEA initially seemed opposed to collective bargaining but shifted dramatically to meet the challenge of AFT.[16] Police also became more militant, in part because of the evident public hostility against them.[17] Race was another reason. African-Americans were concentrated in certain departments of local governments, and the civil rights movement extended into their ranks.[18]

The growth in public employment presented new organizing opportunities for unions; with unionism in the private sector at a standstill in the 1960s, organized labor turned to the public sector. Private sector union membership grew by only 4 percent between 1968 and 1976, whereas public sector membership grew 40 percent.[19]

By the second half of the 1980s and into the 1990s, union expansionism had faltered in the public sector and showed signs of decline. The percentage of organized employees in state and local governments had slipped from 50 percent to 39 percent. Only at the federal level were unions not seeing erosion. Among executive branch workers, union representation in exclusive bargaining units remained constant (in the 60 percent range). Nearly 90 percent of the 825,000 postal workers are in exclusive bargaining units.

Several factors may account for this recent pattern.[20] Overall, participation of workers in unions is influenced by perceptions about employers (particularly supervisors) vis-à-vis perceptions of unions and their leaders.[21] If unions are perceived as having the ability to represent workers effectively in negotiating over pay and benefits and, later, in representing individual workers in grievance cases, support for collective bargaining is likely to be strong. If the employing agency is perceived as treating workers unfairly, again, support for unions is likely to be strong. On the other hand, general trends also influence the situation. The general public mood, which seems to be at best lukewarm toward unions, necessarily influences public workers' attitudes. An explanation of the continued strength in unions in the federal government may be that these organizations are seen as protective forces in the reduction-in-force situations that have been common.

To cope with rising demands for collective bargaining and to avert strikes by public workers, governments have turned to various devices for labor–management relations. The approach at the federal level was to use an executive order rather than a statute to establish such a process. In 1962 President Kennedy issued Executive Order 10988, which was a stimulus or legitimizing force for unionization at state and local levels as well as at the federal level. That order was replaced by President Nixon in 1969 with Executive Order 11491, which was amended by Executive Order 11838 issued by President Ford in 1975.

President Carter recommended in 1978 that Congress replace the executive orders with a statute, which was accomplished through Title VII of the Civil Service Reform Act of 1978, which the AFL-CIO endorsed.[22,23] A collective negotiation process established by statute was seen as providing permanent rights to workers, whereas under the previous system a president unilaterally could alter the process by issuing a new executive order.

The law itself did not appreciably change employee union rights, but, as will be seen, it has been interpreted in ways that have expanded the areas for bargaining. Organizational responsibilities were altered through both the president's reorganization process and the reform legislation. The existing Federal Labor Relations Council was replaced by the independent Federal Labor Relations Authority (FLRA), and most functions previously performed by the assistant secretary of labor for labor–management relations were transferred to the authority.

At the state and local levels, labor–management relations are governed by a variety of measures: state statutes, attorney general opinions, executive orders, and state court decisions. As employees have organized and demanded bargaining rights, states have shifted toward reliance on statutes. These vary as to whether they include local as well as state employees. Some statutes permit local governments to enter into collective bargaining agreements, whereas others require collective bargaining if a majority of the employees request it. Some laws provide separate processes for school teachers and for public safety workers (police officers, prison guards, and firefighters). The administrative unit that oversees the process commonly is a labor relations board, but in some cases a civil service department may have responsibility, or a separate state board may be established for a selected group of workers, such as teachers. As of 1992, forty-one states reported having labor relations legislation covering some or all of their state and local government workers.[24] The legislation varies greatly, with some states such as Mississippi, Nebraska, and Virginia granting few rights to organized labor and others such as Hawaii, Massachusetts, and Rhode Island being more supportive.[25] Highly restrictive legislation on public sector employee bargaining does not necessarily deter unions and local governments from participating in negotiations, as evidenced by bargaining in North Carolina.[26]

The diversity among the states and their local governments has led to the suggestion that federal legislation is needed. Such a law presumably would reduce the confusion within and among states. Expertise in labor–management relations could be transferred from jurisdiction to jurisdiction—difficult now because of the wide variations in state laws. Public employee unions, including AFSCME and the NEA, have supported national legislation as a means of providing workers with the rights they deserve. Even if the measure never is passed, merely proposing such a bill has had the effect of encouraging state and local officials to be more receptive to negotiations.

Representatives of state and local governments have expressed misgivings about the proposed federal legislation covering their turf. They do not want the federal government to interfere in their relationships with their employees. Until 1985, the Supreme Court adhered to that view. However, the *Garcia* case of that year, in which the Court ruled that Congress had almost unlimited power to impose restrictions on state and local governments, seems to have opened the door to a wide range of federal legislation affecting state and local employment and possibly including labor relations (see Chapter 4 for a discussion of the case).[27]

It may be unlikely that federal legislation will ever be passed, but three options are possible:

1. Remove the clause in the 1947 Taft-Hartley Act that specifically excludes state and local workers; that would have the effect of bringing these workers under the jurisdiction of the NLRB, which already oversees private labor relations and postal labor relations.
2. Create an agency that would be concerned solely with public labor relations; the presumed advantage would be that it would recognize the unique character of public employment.
3. Set minimal standards and allow each state to pass separate legislation in conformance with those standards.

COLLECTIVE BARGAINING PROCESSES

Although public jurisdictions differ greatly in how they handle labor–management relations, there are processes that are common to collective negotiations. This section discusses (1) the steps that must be taken before bargaining can commence, (2) various aspects of the bargaining process, and (3) a review of procedures used when the two sides cannot agree.

Preliminary Steps

Before bargaining can begin, agreement must be reached as to what group of employees will be in a bargaining unit. A union typically will request that specified jobs constitute a unit, but management may not agree. Therefore, some administrative agency is given power to determine the unit's boundaries. At the federal level this is the FLRA, consisting of three members appointed by the president with Senate approval.[28] The members have 5-year terms, may not hold other positions in the government, and may be removed by the president only upon notice and hearing and only for "inefficiency, neglect of duty, or malfeasance in office." The FLRA is responsible for interpreting the governing legislation, including the provisions for unit determination. In states having labor-relations policies, unit determination for both state and local governments usually is the responsibility of the state labor relations board.

Each bargaining unit, providing that its members opt to have a union represent them, will be authorized to negotiate an agreement with management. The agreement can be for 1 year or more. In any given year, about 700 major state and local agreements involving between 2 and 3 million employees expire.[29]

Great variations exist among governments as to the number of bargaining units and their sizes. Table 12–3 shows that in 1991 the federal government had recognized 2,236 units, excluding those in the Postal Service and selected other agencies. The Defense Department alone had nearly 1,500. Size varied, with the average unit having about 560 employees. Of the major agencies, the Treasury had the highest average (nearly 2,500 employees per unit). On the other hand, there were some extremely small ones. For example, the National Park Service had a one-person unit at its Crater of the Moon Park in Arco, Idaho, and the National Aeronautics and Space Administration had an eight-person unit at its sprawling Johnson Space Center in Houston. AFGE represented the largest number of bargaining units (962), followed by NFFE (370) and the National Association of Government Employees (NAGE; 195).[30]

Similar variations are found at the state and local levels. Table 12–4 shows that in 1987 there were more than 36,000 such bargaining units, with an average of 160 employees each. State governments tend to have larger bargaining units (about 1,200 persons per unit in 1987) than either the federal government (560) or local governments (120). Among local governments, townships have the smallest average size (38 employees) and counties the largest (157). Even though state bargaining units are considerably larger than local ones, state governments tend to have many more units, unlike the local level, where there may be only four or five. A local government might have separate units for police officers, firefighters, labor and trades, and clerical employees.

Criteria for identifying the boundaries of a bargaining unit are established by statute or executive order. Some agencies are excluded by law. Excluded from

Table 12–3 Federal Government Exclusive Recognition Units by Department, 1991

Departments*	Exclusive Units	Average Size of Unit
Defense	1,458	437
Army (546)		
Navy (557)		
Air Force (172)		
Other (183)		
Interior	154	179
Health and Human Services	98	687
Transportation	86	411
Agriculture	77	447
Veterans Affairs	66	2,493
Commerce	52	489
Treasury	39	305
General Services Administration	24	3,533
Other	182	653
Total	2,236	559

*Excludes U.S. Postal Service and other agencies footnoted in Table 12–1.

Source: Union Recognition in the Federal Government, U.S. Office of Personnel Management, U.S. Government Printing Office, 1991.

Table 12–4 State and Local Government Bargaining Units, 1987

Jurisdiction Type	Number of Governments	Governments with Labor Relations Policy	Bargaining Units Number	Average Size
State governments	50	43	1,097	1,213
Local governments	82,934	14,381	35,314	119
Counties	3,042	891	4,083	157
Municipalities	19,227	2,894	8,944	134
Townships	16,685	1,413	4,313	38
School districts	14,710	8,047	16,317	125
Special districts	29,270	1,136	1,656	93
Total	82,984	14,424	36,411	163

Source: Public Employment: Labor-Management Relations, U.S. Bureau of the Census, U.S. Government Printing Office, 1991.

the federal Civil Service Reform Act labor relations process are the Federal Labor Relations Authority, the Federal Bureau of Investigation, and the Central Intelligence Agency. Although congressional units such as the Library of Congress and the Government Printing Office are covered, the General Accounting Office is excluded. The Tennessee Valley Authority also is excluded.

The most important and most common criterion applied in determining the bounds of a bargaining unit is that of a "community of interest." This refers to employees having common concerns.[31] Included are such factors as whether the workers interact with each other and perform similar tasks. One of the reasons for the multitude of federal bargaining units is geography: There is little sense of community when agency employees work throughout the country or even the world. Bargaining units, then, are established at regional or community levels. The Civil Service Reform Act also provides that the unit should "promote effective dealings with, and efficiency of the operations of, the agency involved." An aspect of effectiveness is whether a unit larger than what has been proposed would provide greater expertise in the bargaining process. Efficiency might be increased with a larger unit by reducing the number of agreements to be negotiated.

Other factors exclude certain types of employees from a unit. Professionals are not to be in the same unit as nonprofessionals unless the former agree to such a unit. The federal system prohibits units consisting of workers who hold nonclerical personnel jobs or intelligence positions related to national security. Also common is the exclusion of confidential employees; these might be administrative assistants, some clerical workers, and chauffeurs.

Supervisory personnel are not included in bargaining units with other personnel but may have their own units with limited rights.[32,33] Perhaps a quarter of all cities grant exclusive recognition to supervisory employees.[34]

Recognizing that workers differ greatly as to whether they support collective bargaining, unions sometimes favor small units. For example, a union might not be able to win the support of all clerical workers but might gain backing from selected groups of them. If units can be established for those groups, then the union has an excellent chance of being able to engage in collective bargaining.

Management, on the other hand, prefers not to have numerous units and, in some instances, not to have any collective negotiations. If a large unit can be established, management's chances of having the employees reject collective bargaining are increased. The federal government and many states prohibit the establishment of a unit simply because employees in the proposed group are organized.

Although gaining approval of small units may seem an attractive tactic for unions in elections, the strategy can dilute their capability in representing workers. Federal unions have had difficulty effectively representing small bargaining units that are dispersed geographically throughout the country. Since 1975, when President Ford issued Executive Order 11838, federal policy has encouraged the use of larger bargaining units; the Ford provision was incorporated in the 1978 reform legislation. When the union or unions representing two bargaining units agree to a consolidation and the agency also agrees, they may request approval of the FLRA. The consolidation can be accomplished without holding an election. Possibly reflecting this factor, average unit size grew from 330 employees in the mid-1970s to 520 in the 1980s and to 560 in the 1990s.

At the state and local levels, an alternative to fragmented bargaining units is multiemployer bargaining. For example, several local governments can bargain jointly with a union. Multiemployer bargaining can be advantageous for a union in that the union is not required to negotiate separate agreements with numerous jurisdictions. Both management and labor can afford better expertise under multiemployer bargaining. From management's perspective, such bargaining eliminates union whipsawing, whereby the union wins a major settlement in one jurisdiction and uses that agreement as leverage in negotiating similar deals with other jurisdictions. A disadvantage is that individual jurisdictions lose direct control over the bargaining process.

Rejection or approval of collective bargaining is by secret ballot. A union must petition for an election and must demonstrate that it has substantial support among the employees involved by having them sign cards requesting an election. At the federal level, a union must show that at least 3 percent of the workers want collective bargaining. Depending on the jurisdiction, once an election is called, other unions may be placed on the ballot, provided that they too can show employee support. The workers have the choice of voting for one of the unions or voting for no representation. If neither a union nor the "no representation" choice wins a majority vote, a runoff election is held for the two with the most votes.

The election process is handled at the federal level by the FLRA. State and local elections usually are conducted by state labor relations boards. For a union to participate in an election at the federal level, it must submit financial and other information certifying that it is "free from corrupt influences and influences opposed to basic democratic principles." A union must not have officers who are communists or members of other totalitarian movements.

Charges of unfair labor practices can develop in all aspects of labor–management relations, but particularly in the period before an election. An unfair labor practice simply is some action that violates the rights of workers, management, or unions. Employees have a right to information about unions, and unions have rights in soliciting worker support. Management has the right to be able to manage. Issues develop over where and when unions may talk with employees and distribute literature. Managers have an obligation not to intimidate employees either directly or implicitly, but they also have a right to inform employees about how management views labor relations. A worker may not be dismissed for participating in union activities, and management may not imply that an employee will be denied a promotion because of union involvement.

Charges of unfair labor practices are filed with the administrative unit responsible for supervising the election. At the federal level, the general counsel of the FLRA is responsible for investigating charges of unfair labor practices against both management and unions and serves as prosecutor in such cases brought before the FLRA.

Remedies may be granted when a practice has been found to be unfair. Management can be ordered to reinstate a person dismissed for union participation, and the individual will receive back pay. A union can be ordered to stop soliciting employees during regular working hours. Many unfair practice charges never really are pursued but rather are part of election strategies. The union and management each may claim that the other is engaging in unfair practices as a means of persuading employees to vote one way or the other.

The Bargaining Process

Once a bargaining unit has been determined and a union has been elected to represent the workers, bargaining can commence. A key aspect is that the union becomes the exclusive representative for those employees, and unions are careful to protect that exclusivity. One case of exclusivity that came before the U.S. Supreme Court involved a Wisconsin school board that permitted a nonunion teacher to speak against a union-supported measure at a board public meeting.[35] The issue in that 1976 case was whether the board had entered into negotiations with someone other than the union. The Court held that barring the board from hearing the nonunion teacher would violate the teacher's First Amendment right of free speech. In 1984, however, the Court ruled that an employer was required to confer with the elected union on a series of matters and could not meet with other groups of employees or individual employees.[36,37]

On one side of the bargaining table will be union representatives, but who sits on the other side? Labor–management relations in the public sector involve more than labor and management. The process must in some way acknowledge the powers of the legislative branch. For example, the legislative body cannot be ignored when a labor settlement involves money because the executive branch has no independent spending powers. A mayor might negotiate an agreement that includes a salary increase, but the city council could refuse to provide the necessary funds. Therefore, a settlement between the executive branch and a union may have to be submitted to the legislative body for ratification. At the federal level the comptroller general, who heads the General Accounting Office and is an agent of Congress, has the authority to nullify some provisions in labor agreements. Legislatures, of course, are not solely a negative force that can reject negotiated agreements. Unions historically have scored end runs around the executive by gaining from the legislative body what they could not get from the executive.

A bargaining team usually represents the government. At the federal level, bargaining is decentralized so that agency managers have choices as to who will serve on the team. One rule of thumb applying to all levels of government is that the manager of the unit should not be on the team because that may encourage confrontation situations. At the state level a labor relations unit may be established as the government's agent in bargaining; this unit takes an advocacy role, unlike the employee relations board, which sides with neither management nor union.

The advantage of having a central agency responsible for representing management is that expertise can be developed along with a consistent policy across bargaining units. A possible disadvantage is that the central agency may not be in tune with the daily problems of line managers and as a result may not effectively represent their needs. The bargaining team needs personnel expertise, budgetary expertise to understand the financial implications of various proposals, and legal expertise to interpret the language of any proposed agreement.

The arrangements for bargaining sometimes constitute an issue themselves. A generally accepted practice is that employees on the bargaining team will be released from work to prepare for and engage in bargaining; this is known as "official time." Federal workers have demanded that per diem allowances and travel expenses also be covered by the government. If an employee from San Francisco is on a bargaining team scheduled to meet in Washington, the union has said that the government should cover the worker's travel expenses. The FLRA supported this view, but the Supreme Court overturned the authority's ruling.[38]

When the two sides sit down at the bargaining table, labor may have rights to "meet and confer," to negotiate a contract, or a combination of these two. "Meet and confer" involves discussion of various issues but does not mean an agreement must be reached. In some instances, where only meet and confer rights are granted, one union may not have exclusivity; representatives from two or more unions collectively may speak for the employees. Meet and confer rights can result in a written letter of understanding, but only if management agrees to this practice. A letter of understanding, unlike a contract, is nonbinding.

Sometimes, one group of employees in a government has negotiation rights for a contract while other groups have only meet and confer rights. Supervisors often are granted only meet and confer rights, although their subordinates may have negotiation rights. The justification for limiting supervisors' rights is that to allow them to bargain would create conflicts of interest. For example, supervisory officers in a police department may tend to side with employees on wage increases but with management on enforcement of administrative regulations.

The scope of bargaining is the extent to which various topics are subject to collective negotiations. Three categories of topics relate to scope: mandatory, permissible, and prohibited. In other words, state statutes and the federal Civil Service Reform Act prescribe some topics as mandatory, and if management refuses to bargain on these, a union may file an unfair labor practice charge with the unit responsible for administering the bargaining process. Other subjects are permissible, meaning that either side may refuse to bargain. Prohibited items are those excluded from the bargaining process even though labor and management may be willing to negotiate on them.

These three types of provisions are found in the Civil Service Reform Act. The mandatory provision requires negotiations on conditions of employment, defined as "personnel policies, practices, and matters . . . affecting working conditions." Permissible items are "the numbers, types, and grades of employees or positions assigned to any organizational subdivision, work project, or tour of duty." The two sides may agree to bargain on the "technology, methods, and means of performing work."

Prohibited items at the federal, state, and local levels relate to the rights of managers.[39] The Civil Service Reform Act states that federal management must retain the right[40]:

1. to determine the mission, budget, organization, number of employees, and internal security practices of the agency; and
2. in accordance with applicable laws—
    (a) to hire, assign, direct, lay off, and retain employees in the agency, or to suspend, remove, reduce in grade or pay, or take other disciplinary action against such employees;
    (b) to assign work, to make determinations with respect to contracting out, and to determine the personnel by which agency operations shall be conducted;
    (c) with respect to filling positions, to make selections for appointments from—
        (i) among properly ranked and certified candidates for promotion; or
        (ii) any other appropriate source; and
    (d) to take whatever actions may be necessary to carry out the agency mission during emergencies.

In addition, the statute provides that the agreements cannot be contrary to laws or any governmentwide rule or regulation, which has the effect of greatly restricting the scope of bargaining. Pay rates, because they are governed by statute, are beyond the scope of federal negotiations with some major exceptions. Employees in the Postal Service, Tennessee Valley Authority, and the Department of Defense Dependent Schools have the right to bargain over wages.[41]

The FLRA interprets the management rights provisions when issues arise. Starting in 1979, it adhered to precedents established under the earlier executive orders, but since then it seemingly has extended what may be negotiated. For example, assigning workers to shifts is a management right, but the FLRA has ruled that requiring notification of an employee 2 weeks in advance about shift changes is negotiable. Performance appraisal generally is the domain of management, but the frequency of appraisals, according to the FLRA, is negotiable, along with limiting appraisals only to critical and noncritical job elements. Negotiated agreements are possible on a wide range of topics, including position classification, outside employment, goals for affirmative action, training, and time clocks.[42,43] Some critics contend that the FLRA is biased in favor of organized labor, but the agency's rebuttal is that it is mandated to further collective bargaining, which means allowing for negotiations whenever possible. When either management or labor disagrees with an FLRA ruling, a court suit may ensue.

Similar provisions on scope of bargaining are to be found at the state level. For example, Pennsylvania law for state and local governments (excluding public safety workers) provides for bargaining on "wages, hours, and conditions of employment."[44] A management rights clause provides that employers need not bargain in "such areas of discretion or policy as the functions and programs of the public employer, standards of services, its overall budget, utilization of technology, the organizational structure, and selection and direction of personnel." This provision was tested as it pertained to twenty-one different items in school negotiations. The court held nonnegotiable such issues as teachers chaperoning at athletic activities, maximum class size, maximum number of hours of teaching each week, and the availability of adequate instructional materials.[45] Items that are not negotiable, however, are subject to meet and confer provisions. Another area for negotiations is grievance procedures, including possible grievance arbitration (this is discussed in the last section of the chapter).

Provisions for union security have been a major area of controversy in public sector bargaining. An individual cannot be required to join a union, but the union as the exclusive representative is required to work on behalf of all employees. Because union survival is dependent on dues collected, unions have sought negotiated agreements that prevent so-called "free rides" by nonunion employees. In an open shop, a union may represent employees, but they have no financial obligation to the union. An agency shop agreement, in contrast, requires nonunion workers to pay the union, usually an amount approximately equal to membership dues.[46] Although the agency shop is permitted in some state and local governments, it is not permitted at the federal level.[47]

An agency shop agreement for Detroit schools was reviewed in 1977 by the Supreme Court as to whether it violated teachers' constitutional rights.[48] In accordance with Michigan law, the union had negotiated an agency shop clause. Some teachers objected that they were being compelled to fund the union's political and ideological activities. The workers contended that the union contract violated their rights of free speech and association as guaranteed under the First and Fourteenth Amendments (see Chapter 8 for a discussion of these amendments). The Court ruled unanimously that these funds could be used only in conjunction with labor relations matters, such as the bargaining process itself, contract administration, and grievance procedures. In another case, the Court approved fees to cover refreshments at union business meetings and publishing a monthly union magazine.[49] The Court also has held that procedural protection must be afforded a nonunion member who challenges the use of a union's fees.[50]

Another important Michigan case was ruled upon by the Supreme Court in 1991.[51] The case involved a group of faculty members at Ferris State College objecting to having to make payments to the union that represented them. The Court held that freedom of speech rights were not infringed by requiring faculty to contribute toward such activities as sending delegates to state and national union conventions, preparing a publication concerning teaching and job opportunities, and even preparing for a strike in a situation where strikes were banned. The Court, however, ruled against fees used to support the teaching profession in general and lobbying and political activity fees unless they are directly linked to contract ratification.

In 1992, President Bush issued Executive Order 12800, Notification of Employee Rights Concerning Payment of Union Dues or Fees. The order states that employees may only be required to pay union fees to cover the costs of "collective bargaining, contract administration, and grievance adjustment."

The checkoff is another method for providing union security. Under the checkoff system, union dues are deducted automatically from payroll checks, eliminating the need for the union to collect dues. If the checkoff is agreed upon by labor and management, a charge normally is made for administrative costs. The Supreme Court has held that, where an agency shop does not exist, a city cannot be required to collect dues from the union's members.[52] The Court agreed that a reasonable standard was used for making deductions: only when they affected all members of a department. The city of Charlotte, North Carolina had refused to collect dues because the union's members constituted only 65 percent of the city's firefighters.

Although the scope of bargaining greatly affects the outcome of the process, the abilities of the negotiators also are influential. Negotiators on both sides need to have done their homework before the sessions begin, need to have bargaining skills, and need to develop strategies. An important aspect of doing one's homework is knowing what agreements have been negotiated elsewhere. A union representing clerical workers will collect information to show that their salary scales are low in comparison with other jurisdictions and with private enterprise. At the federal level, the Office of Personnel Management (OPM) has provided negotiating guidance to management. Unlike the earlier Civil Service Commission, which was expected to be neutral, OPM openly takes a promanagement stance.

Bargaining is not strictly a rational process, and negotiators need to know how to cope with the histrionics that develop. Unions sometimes can be expected to make unrealistic demands, in part simply to satisfy their constituents. Union negotiators need to be able to report back to their members about how they confronted management. Both sides need training in the bargaining process. Knowing when to make demands, how to make demands, and when to make concessions is important. If labor relations are not to be hostile over the life of a contract, it becomes important for both sides to avoid having an attitude of attempting to defeat the other side. If one side considers itself the loser, animosity is likely to develop. "Win/win" bargaining is said to be better than "win/lose" bargaining.[53]

Both sides need to assess what they want in the agreement and should anticipate each other's proposals. This can be called "collective bargaining by objectives," in which one side identifies what it desires in the agreement and assesses the likelihood of its being accepted by the other team.[54,55] In anticipating the other side's proposals, a team needs to be prepared with counteroffers; this is an essential aspect of good-faith bargaining. If bargaining over wages is mandatory, management is not permitted to sit back and simply reject every union demand; it must offer an alternative wage settlement.

The strategy devised will include some low-priority demands that can be used as bargaining chips. A police union might yield on its demands for improved overtime provisions and uniform allowances in return for a large wage increase. Management may try to persuade the union to accept a low wage increase for substantially increased retirement benefits. The advantage of this is that the immediate impact on the budget will be less with retirement increases than with wage increases (see discussion of pension problems in Chapter 4). Winning a multiyear instead of a 1-year contract may be an important objective of management, but to achieve that concession it will need to offer an attractive package.

Unions and management have had to become skilled in budgeting.[56,57] When labor makes a demand with financial implications, management needs to be able to determine the likely costs. For example, what will be the cost of providing an additional paid holiday? What will be the future impact on the budget if a major health benefits plan is approved? A union can anticipate management's claiming to be too poor to afford what has been proposed. At that point, the labor negotiators need to be able to show that there is a budget surplus. One technique that unions have used is to strive to create surpluses. If a state teachers union effectively lobbies for increases in state aid to school districts, school managers throughout the state may be unable to argue persuasively that they cannot meet labor's demands for salary boosts.

When public sector negotiations became prominent in the 1960s, unions justified demands for wage increases largely as a means of catching up with salary scales in the private sector. Since then, parity has been reached in many instances and there is increasing emphasis on productivity bargaining.[58] Detroit,

Michigan; Orange, California; and Tacoma, Washington are just a few of the local governments that have engaged in this form of bargaining.[59] Management's position is that it cannot afford large pay raises unless workers become more productive. Some of the bargaining can be seen as management reasserting its right to manage. Previous labor contracts may have tied management's hands in being able to direct workers. Various job rules and minimum sizes of work crews that unions have won in bargaining agreements obviously curtail management flexibility and can be impediments to improving productivity.

For some state and local governments, productivity bargaining has focused on wage incentive plans: If productivity is increased, the financial savings can be used for salary increases or bonuses. Productivity bargaining linked with pay raises has several fundamental problems, however. One is the issue of how to measure productivity. In the private sector, where products are manufactured, productivity is measured more easily than in the public sector, which is largely a service field. How can productivity be measured for workers in a city building permits office or in a state department of education bureau that works with local school districts on curriculum development? Another problem is that productivity agreements commonly have treated all workers equally, regardless of whether some have become more productive than others. Such agreements may provide little incentive for government's better employees. Still another problem is that productivity bargaining may be seen by labor as simply a way of making workers work harder and harder. Wage incentive systems tied to productivity also can be challenged as focusing on hygiene factors (see Chapter 10). Productivity gains may have to be made more through increased motivation than by wage incentive arrangements in labor contracts.

Bargaining in many locales has focused not on wage increases but on concessions from labor, ranging from reducing the number of paid holidays to freezing or cutting wages.[60] Jurisdictions faced with major financial problems have insisted that workers concede some wage matters. In 1984, the U.S. Postal Service attempted to gain approval of a new wage rate for entering employees that was several thousand dollars below what was in use at the time. When the union refused to accept the proposal, the Postal Service attempted to institute it unilaterally but was blocked by Congress. Later, a special panel approved a plan that did provide for a somewhat lower pay scale.[61]

One other major influence on how negotiations are carried out is what will happen should the two sides not reach an agreement. Part of the bargaining process involves establishing a record or position that will be advantageous should an impasse occur (impasse procedures are addressed next). Assuming for the moment that an agreement is reached, the negotiated settlement put into written form is submitted to the workers for their approval. Rejection of the agreement sends the negotiators back to the bargaining table. Having a well-written document is valuable in avoiding problems once the contract is in effect.

Sometimes, however, ambiguous language is used deliberately to gloss over some differences between the two sides, or simply because the negotiators were nearing exhaustion when agreement was reached.[62]

Impasse Procedures

When the two sides cannot reach an agreement on a contract, an impasse occurs. The general rule of organized labor is "no contract—no work" and a strike ensues. In the public sector, however, strikes usually are prohibited. The courts have held that government may ban strikes, although it cannot prohibit a union's asserting the right to strike because that would violate the First Amendment's guarantee of free speech.[63,64]

The penalty for striking can be severe.[65] Employees may be suspended or removed permanently. Union officials can be jailed, and the unions can be fined. The courts have upheld these measures, although some procedural protections are provided to employees. The Supreme Court dealt with such a situation in 1976 in the *Hortonville* case.[66] Teachers in a Wisconsin school district went on strike in violation of the state's employee relations law. The school board held a hearing and dismissed the teachers. The teachers claimed in court that their Fourteenth Amendment due process rights had been violated in that the board had been biased. The Court agreed with the teachers that they were entitled to an impartial hearing but held that there was no evidence that the board had been biased. In explaining its position, the Court noted that, although board members had made public statements opposing the strike, those statements could not be construed to mean that the board members were unwilling to change their views; the board had not necessarily come to a decision to dismiss the teachers before holding the hearing.

Despite the prohibition against strikes, they still occur, and with considerable frequency. When they do, governments must decide whether to enforce legal provisions that may call for the fining of a union and dismissal of workers. Labor leaders often think that an illegal strike is worth the risk in that management would be unwilling and possibly unable to fill large numbers of jobs vacated through dismissals.

That "hypothesis" was tested in 1981, when air traffic controllers followed their union, the Professional Air Traffic Controllers Organization (PATCO), and struck, demanding improvements in working conditions, including across-the-board pay increases of $10,000. President Reagan acted swiftly by dismissing those on strike. The strike and dismissals resulted in temporary chaos for air travelers, but the president had sent a signal that the administration would not be intimidated by strikes.[67,68]

Strikes are viewed as problems. During a strike, services to the public in general and to agency clients are disrupted. Workers must survive without pay.

Future labor–management relations may be harmed because of negative attitudes generated. For these reasons, procedures have been established to resolve impasses and thereby to seek to avert strikes. Third-party intervention is the typical approach, with a party other than labor or management attempting to resolve the conflict.

Mediation is the first step in impasse resolution procedures.[69-71] The mediator is a neutral who performs the role of diplomat, seeking to find areas of agreement between the parties and to develop compromised positions on the key issues. A mediator meets jointly and separately with the parties, talks bluntly with them about their respective positions, and keeps them talking in the hope of finding a compromised position that both will accept.[72] Mediation essentially is a weak process in that the mediator does not have authority to compel the parties to agree to anything.

For the federal government, this function is handled by the Federal Mediation and Conciliation Service (FMCS), an independent agency. The FMCS deals with more than 300 federal cases each year and also provides mediation services in private and state and local labor disputes.[73] State governments have mediation agencies with various responsibilities. Some states use the same agency for both public and private labor impasses, whereas others have separate agencies. Mediation offices may be invited to intervene by either labor or management, or they may have authority to intervene on their own initiative.

In the event that mediation fails, the next step is likely to be factfinding.[74] For state and local governments, a state labor relations board usually has the power to determine whether a case should be submitted to factfinding if that process is to be used. The board may submit a list of potential factfinders to the two parties, and one is chosen through a process of elimination, in which labor and management alternately strike names from the list until only one remains.

At the federal level, when mediation has not led to an agreement, labor and management may agree to binding arbitration (discussed below), or either side may request the Federal Service Impasses Panel (FSIP) to intervene. The seven-member FSIP is a unit within the FLRA that has considerable freedom in selecting a procedure that will resolve an impasse. One choice available to the panel is factfinding.

Factfinding is more formal than mediation. The two sides submit lists of issues to the factfinder, who determines which ones to hear. The factfinder, who can consider only topics that are within the scope of mandatory bargaining, holds a hearing at which labor and management present evidence on each of the issues. Witnesses are called to testify and may be cross-examined.

Later, the factfinder issues a report, making recommendations on each of the issues. These are only recommendations; neither side is required to accept them. The factfinder's report is submitted first only to labor and management in the hope that the recommendations will be accepted. If they are not, the report is made public as a means of bringing pressure on the parties to accept the suggested agreement. Sometimes the sides are required to bargain in public as a further means for bringing pressure on them to reach agreement.[75,76] As pressures become more intense, both sides may seek to gain media attention in hope of garnering public backing.

Factfinders use several criteria that are established by executive order and/or statute. On wages, one criterion is comparability: Are workers being paid considerably less than similar ones in other jurisdictions and in the private sector? (Wages, of course, are not the subject of factfinding at the federal level because this is a nonbargainable item.) Changes in the cost of living are a criterion, as is the ability of the jurisdiction to pay higher wages. In the hearing, labor attempts to show that money is not an obstacle to higher wages. The effectiveness and efficiency of operations are other criteria, as is the general welfare of the public.

The willingness of labor and management to accept the factfinder's report depends on their assessments of the likelihood of being successful at the next step in the impasse procedure. Where strikes are prohibited, that next step often is interest arbitration, in which a third party determines the provisions of a settlement (as distinguished from grievance arbitration, discussed in the next section).[77–79] Binding arbitration is the settlement of a dispute by the decision of a neutral third party. Many states require this procedure for police and fire impasses, where strikes are considered not in the public interest. A single arbitrator may be used, selected in the same manner as a factfinder, or a three-member arbitration panel may be established. In the latter instance, each side selects a registered arbitrator, and those two select the third member. At the federal level, the FSIP has arbitration-type authority. The Civil Service Reform Act grants it authority to "take whatever action is necessary" to settle an impasse. The arbitration procedure is similar to factfinding, including the holding of a trial-type hearing. The important difference is that the arbitration award is binding rather than only a recommendation.

Interest arbitration is a controversial subject in at least two respects. One criticism is that decisional authority is granted to an individual or individuals not directly involved. From labor's perspective, the arbitrators may be largely insensitive to the workers' needs. From management's perspective, the arbitrators may make policy and yet are not accountable to the jurisdiction's constituents.

At one time management may have preferred arbitration to the alternative of a strike, and labor may have preferred the right to strike, but those positions have been greatly eroded. Organized labor has accepted interest arbitration as an alternative to striking, but management sometimes prefers enduring a strike rather than being forced to accept an arbitration award. Management might well prefer a firefighters' strike rather than an arbitration settlement involving a large salary increase because that not only will involve higher costs for fire services but also will be used as precedent in negotiating with unions representing other bargaining units. Arbitrators' decisions can have the effect of forcing cities to raise taxes.

The other main criticism of interest arbitration is that it discourages the two sides from reaching a compromise agreement. If binding arbitration is the final step, both sides in negotiating will be concerned with establishing a record for eventual use in arbitration. For example, in negotiations a union initially may demand an 8 percent salary increase, and management may offer 2 percent; a midpoint compromise at 5 percent might seem appropriate. If in the negotiations labor reduces its demand to 6 percent while management raises its offer to only 2.5 percent, however, the arbitration award could be a compromise figure considerably below 5 percent. In other words, compulsory arbitration encourages the union and management to take extreme positions and discourages them from compromising.

One variation of interest arbitration intended to alleviate this problem is final-offer arbitration.[80] Under this procedure, the arbitration panel may not fashion its own agreement but must choose between the last offers made by management and labor. The panel may have authority to choose between each side on each issue, or it may be required to choose the complete package offer of one of the sides. With each side knowing that the arbitrators must choose one position or the other, there will be pressure to make reasonable offers rather than take extreme positions that are unlikely to be accepted by the panel. Between ten and twenty states include final-offer arbitration in their public sector labor laws.[81]

Arbitration can have a narcotic effect.[82] Once it is used, the parties expect to use it again in subsequent negotiations. If arbitration is used in negotiations for one bargaining unit, other units may come to expect that their negotiations will be unsuccessful and will ultimately lead to arbitration.

The right to strike is the primary alternative to interest arbitration. Thirteen states allow strikes among some state and local employees (Alaska, California, Hawaii, Idaho, Illinois, Minnesota, Montana, Ohio, Oregon, Pennsylvania, Rhode Island, Vermont, and Wisconsin). Usually this right is granted by state statute, but California in 1985 joined the ranks of states allowing strikes through a decision by its supreme court.[83-85] The typical requirement in state and local governments is that a strike is not permissible until mediation and factfinding have failed; even at that point, the two sides may agree to interest arbitration rather than have a strike occur.

Strikes present problems to all parties involved. Management cannot meet its responsibilities because employees are unavailable for work. Employees may be concerned with failing to meet their responsibilities and must operate for an indefinite period without paychecks. Clients and, more generally, citizens are inconvenienced to various degrees because of the lack of services. Public transit strikes produce traffic jams of nightmare proportions. School teachers' strikes cause havoc with working parents, who must make alternative childcare arrangements. Protracted teachers' strikes can prevent high school seniors from graduating and proceeding to college.[86]

Once a strike starts, it can continue indefinitely.[87] Management may resolve that it cannot afford to yield to union demands for wage increases because of the government's difficult budget situation. Labor may be equally determined, assuming that management is falsely claiming it cannot afford a substantial wage increase.

When strikes threaten the public's well-being, management may petition for a court injunction sending employees back to work. Such an injunction in Pennsylvania can be issued when a "strike creates a clear and present danger or threat to the health, safety, or welfare of the public." Other states that allow strikes have similar provisions. If employees ignore the court order, the government may fire them, and the court may fine and imprison union leaders as well as fine the union.

A court-ordered injunction against a strike, however, does not bring about a settlement. It simply orders the employees to work without a union contract. One suggestion for resolving the impasse at this point is to allow courts broad discretion, including the power to order interest arbitration. That type of impasse procedure would follow the steps of mediation, factfinding, strike, and injunction coupled with interest arbitration.

MANAGING UNDER COLLECTIVE BARGAINING

With the advent of collective bargaining, the ways in which government operates necessarily have changed. Collective negotiations leading to a written agreement between labor and management change the rules that govern how activities are carried out on a daily basis. This section considers the effects of collective bargaining on daily operations and, more generally, the impact of collective bargaining on government.

Contract Administration

Once a collective bargaining agreement has been reached, management has the obligation to implement it. An exception is in the case of arbitration awards, which management may appeal to a court on the grounds that the award violates its rights guaranteed by the governing statute or executive order. Some of the more immediate implementation responsibilities include adjusting payroll records to meet new wage and salary requirements and making any changes in withholding for health insurance benefits, retirement benefits, or union dues.

Major problems have arisen at the state and local levels over government's ability to meet the financial costs of a settlement. In some cases, management may agree to a wage settlement to avoid a strike, but then the problem of finding needed funds arises; interest arbitration awards pose the same problem. Some adjustments can be made in budgets, such as postponing proposed expenditures on equipment and large capital items, but these often cannot release sufficient funds to meet higher labor costs. At that point the argument is made that the government is unable to pay, although in reality it rarely is actually unable to pay but only unwilling to take steps that would enable it to do so. Tax increases or, as noted, deferral of capital expenditures usually are options.

When governments confront such situations, they usually attempt to avoid the higher costs. They may freeze hiring to reduce payrolls. A government may impose a freeze on wage increases despite the labor contracts, but this type of action has been overturned by courts, which insist that a government prove beyond a doubt its inability to pay. Another approach is to furlough employees temporarily, for perhaps 30 days, on a staggered basis; this has the effect of paying employees about the same as they received in the prior year. Permanently laying off some workers is another tactic. All these methods of minimizing personnel costs, however, can be challenged by unions as unfair labor practices. A union does not want to be in the position of bargaining for higher salaries at the cost of employees losing their jobs.

The meaning of clauses in labor–management contracts frequently is subject to various interpretations. Sometimes clauses are drafted hastily in the midst of negotiations, and questions later arise about what they mean. In other instances, clauses may be left intentionally vague, in part because the two sides are eager to reach an agreement and do not want a relatively minor issue to result in an impasse. Ambiguous language may result when neither side is sure what it wants to win on a given item; the assumption is that the language will gain clarity as issues arise while both sides are operating under the contract.

Both labor and management are advised to resolve disputes through informal means, but when that fails an arbitration procedure can be invoked.[88,89] In most cases, the arbitration decision is binding, although some systems use an advisory approach. Arbitration to interpret a contract is known as grievance or rights arbitration, as distinguished from interest arbitration (discussed earlier). The grievance procedure itself is a negotiable item. Activating the grievance procedure normally is the prerogative of employees, not management; should management think employees are violating the contract, its route is to initiate disciplinary proceedings or to charge unfair labor practices before the labor relations board. Management may not attempt to deter employees from using the grievance procedure, such as threatening a reduction in force if employees file numerous grievances.[90]

The scope of possible grievances is great. Workers on an hourly basis may complain that overtime is not being paid as specified in the contract. There may be complaints that the administration is not adhering to sick leave provisions. Workers may complain about inadequate safety equipment. One particularly difficult area is the disciplining of employees. Workers who feel they are being charged unfairly with failing to meet their job requirements may have the choice of initiating either the adverse action appeals procedures administered by the personnel agency (see Chapter 8) or the grievance procedure provided in the labor contract. Employees choose whichever procedure they think will work to their advantage. Unions prefer the negotiated route because it provides them an opportunity to demonstrate their effectiveness in helping workers. Personnel administrators argue that employees should not be required to use the negotiated procedure, given that some of them probably are opposed to unions even though they are in a collective bargaining unit.

In 1983, the Supreme Court handed down a controversial ruling on union responsibilities in grievance cases. In *Bowen v. U.S. Postal Service,* the Court held that a union must represent employees effectively in grievance cases. It ruled that the postal union involved, having provided inadequate representation, should pay more than half the $53,000 owed an employee who had been discharged wrongfully. One outcome is that unions may seemingly prosecute all cases regardless of their merits to avoid being hit with litigation themselves.[91,92]

The federal Civil Service Reform Act not only permits grievance procedures but also requires that they be included in negotiated agreements. The procedure must be "fair and simple" and provide for "expeditious processing." A union having exclusive representation has a right to participate in the grievance process, and employees have a right to present their own cases.

The final step in the grievance procedure within the agency is binding arbitration, which can be invoked by either the union or management. Several items are excluded from the grievance procedure:

- any claimed violation relating to prohibited political activities
- retirement, life insurance, or health insurance
- a suspension or removal
- any examination, certification, or appointment
- classification of any position that does not result in a reduction in grade or pay of an employee

Appeals may be made by either or both parties to the Federal Labor Relations Authority (see Figure 12–1).

When a prohibited personnel practice is involved, an employee must choose either the negotiated route or that of the Merit Systems Protection Board (MSPB; see Chapters 2 and 8). In other words, parallel systems exist, with one being part of the merit system and the other part of labor relations.[93,94] When employees choose the negotiated procedure, they may ask the MSPB to review the decision

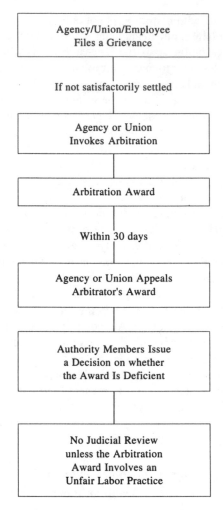

Figure 12-1 Federal Labor Relations Authority Adjudication of Appeals of Arbitration Awards. *Source:* Information from *A Guide to the Federal Service Labor-Management Relations Statute*, p. 64, Federal Labor Relations Authority, U.S. Government Printing Office, 1990.

that eventually is reached. In cases of alleged discrimination, they may ask the Equal Employment Opportunity Commission to review a decision reached through the negotiated grievance procedure.

Most negotiated grievance procedures involve several steps, beginning with the employee meeting with the supervisor to discuss the complaint. The union shop steward, who is an employee in the unit, attends this meeting on behalf of the employee. In subsequent steps, the union may provide an attorney to defend the employee. If a satisfactory settlement is not reached at the first step, the case is appealed to the department head or, in large jurisdictions, to a bureau chief and later to the department head. The last step before grievance arbitration is to appeal to a central administrative officer, such as an assistant secretary of administration.

The grievance arbitrator, usually selected by each side alternately striking names from a list until only one remains, conducts a hearing and normally must issue a ruling within a specified time period. Where the language of an agreement is ambiguous, the arbitrator attempts to determine what has been the past practice in an agency and tries to devise a ruling in conformance with that practice. Where past practice offers little guidance, the arbitrator explores with the two sides the negotiations that led to the inclusion of the phrase in the contract. The powers of the arbitrator can be enormous. At the federal level, the FLRA can accept appeals on arbitration awards but will not substitute its judgment for that of the arbitrator. Voiding such an award requires proof that it is contrary to statute or regulations. An award also can be vacated if there is proof that the arbitrator was biased or capricious or exceeded allowed authority.

Negotiated grievance procedures have posed problems for managers. Sometimes managers are not fully aware of contract provisions and take actions that prompt workers to file grievances. Managers can avoid such situations by making sure they have a thorough understanding of the contract. These procedures and collective bargaining in general may intimidate some managers. They may be reluctant to take action to avoid a possible confrontation that ultimately would result in their judgment being scrutinized by an arbitrator.

Impact of Collective Bargaining

Organized labor has had to fight hard for each power it has gained. At every point there have been attempts to exclude unions from the public sector. Yet they have won great powers that affect all aspects of government administration, not just personnel administration.

Wage determination has constituted one arena of conflict.[95,96] The argument has been that wages should be nonnegotiable in that they have direct bearing on total expenditures and ultimately on tax rates. Critics of unions have insisted that employees should not be able to gouge taxpayers' wallets. Unions have won the right to bargain over wages in many state and local governments, however, and in some areas of the federal government, most notably the Postal Service. Some unions undoubtedly have won major wage gains, and the mere threat of unionization surely has prompted impressive wage increases in some jurisdictions.

Nevertheless, available evidence suggests that there is not a perfect relationship between unionization and labor costs. Public sector salaries are influenced in part by private market salaries; local government employee wage rates are likely to be high in areas where private wages are high. The wealth of a jurisdiction has been found to be associated with the level of public wage rates; relatively poor jurisdictions do not pay as well as wealthy ones, regardless of unionization. Unions necessarily are sensitive to their political climates. Those that make wage demands that to the public seem excessive may invite taxpayer revolts.

Starting in the 1980s, many unions in state and local governments were forced into taking a defensive posture, attempting to keep pay scales up and avoiding cutbacks in public jobs. State and local governments have faced intermittent financial crises as revenues declined for three reasons:[97]

1. Tax rate cuts were mandated by voter-approved resolutions such as Proposition 13 in California.
2. Major economic recessions swept the nation in the early 1980s and again in the early 1990s.
3. Severe cuts in federal domestic programs reduced aid flowing from Washington. These affected wage and job security and led to reductions in force despite union efforts.

Unions have had to fight for a right to participate in politics. Before being allowed to bargain with management, public employee unions acted mainly as lobbyists seeking legislation for their benefit. Organized labor is increasing its role in the electoral process. Unions have lobbied, albeit unsuccessfully, for Hatch Act revisions that would permit merit employees to become active in political campaigns (see Chapter 8). Public employee unions endorse candidates for office and sometimes campaign to defeat antiunion politicians at the polls. Campaign politics is perhaps keenest in local government elections, especially in jurisdictions that have worker residency requirements. If all municipal employees are required to live within the city, they can easily influence the outcome of a mayoral election. Union influence is weaker in state and national elections, where voters are unlikely to be persuaded to vote for a gubernatorial or presidential candidate simply because of union support.

A charge frequently made about collective bargaining is that it is antithetical to the merit principle.[98,99] Unions want to negotiate on how personnel decisions are made, and critics suggest that much of the personnel process should be insulated from bargaining. A special committee of the International Personnel Management Association once suggested that most aspects of recruiting, testing, position classification, political activity regulations, and separation decisions should be nonbargainable.[100]

The case against unions on the merit issue is not as strong as it might seem. In arguing that unions are against merit, it is not accurate to suggest that unions are for patronage. As was emphasized in Chapter 2, patronage is not simply the opposite of merit. Unions are one of the major opponents of patronage because that system can threaten their members' job security. Much of the issue centers on union endorsement of seniority as a factor in personnel decisions. Seniority is considered antithetical to merit because the focus is how long one has held a job and not how well one performs a job. Unions tend to prefer that promotions, layoffs, and the like be based at least in part on seniority.

The seniority issue tends to clash with affirmative action, which itself has been criticized as antithetical to merit. Because the least senior workers often are minorities and women, these persons are less likely to be promoted and more likely to be laid off when a seniority rule is used in reductions in force. Unions often seem insensitive to the discrimination problems that women and minorities face, although some unions are active in this regard, such as advocating bridging positions that would allow women in clerical positions to move into administrative positions.[101,102]

Collective bargaining has been seen as increasing the number of personnel problems faced by administrators.[103] The question, however, is whether the bargaining process created those problems or only facilitated their surfacing. Tensions between managers and their subordinates have always existed, and unions have been able to capitalize on those problems. Labor organizations have provided a strong voice for employees.

From the line manager's perspective, few discretionary powers may seem to remain. The manager not only must abide by statutory requirements and civil service regulations but also must operate within the confines of a negotiated labor agreement. Some managers probably have become timid, fearful of taking action that might lead to a union grievance. At the same time, collective bargaining may have been helpful to managers in that agreements spell out each side's rights and obligations. Managers now manage by contract, insisting that workers meet their obligations as specified in the document.

Unions can have both positive and negative influences on employee performance.[104] From the negative standpoint, unions are seen as needlessly driving a wedge between workers and their superiors, encouraging confrontation rather than cooperation. Employees are encouraged to pledge allegiance to their union, not to the government that employs them. Unions can provide a defense or rationalization for poor performance. Employees may be encouraged to put less effort into their work because unions may say that management presumably is unconcerned about their welfare. Indeed, managers often are instructed not to grant improvements in working conditions to their subordinates because to do so is to relinquish a bargaining chip in subsequent negotiations. Labor organizations can increase worker dissatisfaction in that the union itself seems to be another source of authority that dictates what employees may and may not do. Employees resent having to abide by union rules as well as management regulations. Labor organizations are structured hierarchically and can discourage democratic decision making among their members.[105,106]

One subject on which labor and management are likely to have differing opinions is privatization or contracting out. Especially since the early 1980s, governments have become interested in alternative means of delivering public services, and contracting with private for-profit and nonprofit firms is often regarded as a viable option for service delivery. Unions' opposition to such efforts is logically based on the potential loss of public jobs and therefore union membership and influence. Unions in the federal government and the Federal Labor Relations Authority have contended that the process of contracting out is bargainable, but the Supreme Court in 1990 basically held that the process was exclusively reserved for management.[107,108] In instances where labor–management relations are particularly adversarial and even hostile, management may view contracting out as a way of avoiding altogether the problems associated with organized labor. On the other hand, a study of cities found that unions can bring political influence to bear and can diminish the likelihood that management will seriously consider the privatization of services.[109]

On the positive side, unions can foster increased worker productivity by helping develop improved methods of operation and by increasing employee motivation, although the counterview is that unions rarely are concerned with productivity or its improvement. Labor leaders in some cases have been instrumental in helping management deal with employee problems, such as habitual tardiness. Labor–management committees have been used to deal not only with personnel matters but also more generally with the operations of agencies. In 1992, the Office of Personnel Management appointed a committee of union presidents to develop recommendations on improving working conditions throughout the government.

Instead of opposing innovation, unions can help facilitate changes that increase agency and worker productivity. Management can enlist labor's support in instituting motivational and other programs.[110] Nevertheless, labor always will be concerned that innovations not lead to layoffs and that unions' authority not be eroded. Management efforts to use such techniques as quality circles and total quality management, which emphasize group involvement, sometimes are viewed by unions as threats to their right to bargain over working conditions (see Chapter 11). The Postal Service, for instance, has experienced union opposition to its effort to install quality-of-working-life committees.[111] Given the different needs of labor and management, it is doubtful whether adversarial relationships can ever be replaced permanently with cooperative ones.

The laws under which labor–management relations are conducted have important influences on behavior. In the first place, the existence of a law providing for bargaining tends to stimulate union activity.[112,113] Laws restrict the topics for negotiation and in doing so may put management in a position of wanting to bargain and cooperate with labor but being prevented from doing so.[114,115] Job security, one of organized labor's biggest concerns, is largely outside any bargaining process provided in law because security depends upon budgets, which are controlled by the chief executive and legislative body. Cutbacks in budgets lead immediately to reductions in force. The federal government's process has been sharply criticized as being too adversarial, encouraging resolutions of problems by litigation rather than negotiation, and being led by a weak FLRA, whose actions are seen as "untimely, inconsistent and unclear."[116]

SUMMARY

Despite the issue of governmental sovereignty, employee unions and collective bargaining have emerged as integral parts of public personnel systems. At the federal level, the largest unions include the American Federation of Government Employees, the National Treasury Employees Union, and the National Federation of Federal Employees, plus the American Postal Workers Union and the National Association of Letter Carriers. The American Federation of State, County, and Municipal Employees and the National Education Association are major representatives of state and local workers. Unionism arose out of dissatisfaction with pay and working conditions and a series of special factors peculiar to the 1960s. Labor–management relations are governed at the national level by legislation. States use laws, executive orders, and attorney general opinions to govern labor relations for both state and local employees.

Unit determination is essential before collective bargaining can commence. The main criterion is that employees have a community of interest. Special criteria pertain to various types of workers: supervisory, professional, and confidential. Once the unit is established, an election is held to determine whether collective bargaining is desired and, if so, what union will represent the employees. The federal government has more than 2,000 bargaining units. State and local governments differ widely on the number of bargaining units and the number of employees in each.

The bargaining process is complicated by determining who represents management, the scope of bargaining, and other factors. Sometimes the negotiated agreement must be submitted to the legislative body as well as to the employees for approval. Labor may have meet and confer rights, bargaining rights, or a combination of these. Some topics are mandatory items for bargaining, and others are only permissible or may be prohibited. In virtually every instance, there is a provision that management must retain the right to manage. Wages generally are non-negotiable at the federal level but often can be negotiated in states and localities. Bargaining strategies are developed by each side as to the concessions they wish to win.

The purpose of impasse procedures is to avert employee strikes. Mediation usually is the first step and is followed by factfinding. Interest arbitration may ensue, whereby management and labor are required to accept the award of an arbitrator or arbitration panel. Arbitration has been criticized as placing excessive powers in the hands of individuals who are not answerable to the electorate; arbitration decisions can make tax increases almost inevitable. Arbitration also may discourage the two sides from compromising, and for that reason final-offer arbitration sometimes is used. Regardless of general prohibitions against strikes, public workers increasingly have walked out. Some jurisdictions allow strikes when mediation and factfinding fail; when these strikes pose a threat to public health and safety, they can be halted by a court injunction.

Contract administration includes making budgetary adjustments to meet the higher personnel costs of a negotiated agreement and determining the precise meaning of various contract clauses. The latter involves a negotiated grievance procedure that has several steps, usually culminating in grievance arbitration.

Collective bargaining has had considerable effect on the public sector. Employee wages have risen, although there is not a perfect relationship between wage gains and unionization. Unions have increased their role in political elections as well as continuing to lobby for state and national legislation. Unions have been criticized as being opposed to the merit system, but that point is debatable. They oppose patronage and have supported some aspects of merit, but at the same time they have defended the use of seniority in personnel decisions. Collective bargaining has limited the powers of managers, so that they no longer can take many unilateral actions. Unions have had both positive and negative effects on workers. On the negative side, employees may have become alienated from management and may be discouraged from excelling in their work. On the positive side, unions occasionally have been instrumental in motivating workers and assisting in productivity improvement efforts.

NOTES

1. E.M. Bussey, ed., *Federal Civil Service Law and Procedures: A Basic Guide* (Washington: Bureau of National Affairs, 1991).
2. C.J. Coleman, *Managing Labor Relations in the Public Sector* (San Francisco: Jossey-Bass, 1990).
3. H.T. Edwards, et al., *Labor Relations Law in the Public Sector*, 4th ed. (Charlottesville, Va.: Michie, 1991).
4. Federal Labor Relations Authority, *A Guide to the Federal Service Labor–Management Relations Statute* (Washington: U.S. Government Printing Office, 1990).
5. R.C. Kearney, *Labor Relations in the Public Sector*, 2d ed. (New York: Marcel Dekker, 1992).
6. A.L. Chickering, ed., *Public Employee Unions: A Study of the Crisis in Public Sector Labor Relations* (Lexington, Mass.: Lexington Books, 1976).
7. J. Stieber, *Public Employee Unionism: Structure, Growth, Policy* (Washington: Brookings Institution, 1973).

8. M.F. Masters, Federal-employee unions and political action, *Industrial and Labor Relations Review* 38 (1985): 612–628.

9. R.L. Smith, Public employee unions and politics in American cities, *Journal of Collective Negotiations in the Public Sector* 14 (1985): 1–12.

10. R.E. Dahl and J.F. Wappel, Labor–management relations in local government: Current practices, *Baseline Data Report* 21 (May/June 1989): 6.

11. U.S. Office of Personnel Management, *Union Recognition in the Federal Government* (Washington: U.S. Government Printing Office, 1991), 21.

12. Gale Research, *Encyclopedia of Associations*, 26th ed. (Detroit: Gale Research, 1991).

13. Dahl and Wappel, Labor–management relations in local government, 2.

14. W.E. Mosher and J.D. Kingsley, *Public Personnel Administration* (New York: Harper & Brothers, 1936), 496.

15. M.R. Berube, *Teacher Politics: The Influence of Unions* (New York: Greenwood, 1988).

16. T.M. Stinnett, et al., *Professional Negotiation in Public Education* (New York: Macmillan, 1966).

17. H.A. Juris and P. Feuille, *Police Unionism* (Lexington, Mass.: Lexington Books, 1973).

18. H.H. Wellington and R.K. Winter, Jr., *The Unions and the Cities* (Washington: Brookings Institution, 1971), 45–47.

19. Labor union and employee association membership, *U.S. Department of Labor News* 77-771 (1977).

20. M.H. LeRoy, State of the unions: Assessment by elite American labor leaders, *Journal of Labor Research* 13 (1992): 371–379.

21. R.G. Fortier, An AFGE local: An examination of factors contributing to union strength in the public sector, *Public Personnel Management* 13 (1984): 265–292.

22. Civil Service Reform Act, P.L. 95-454, 92 Stat. 1111 (1978).

23. Reorganization plan no. 2 of 1978, *Weekly Compilation of Presidential Documents* 14 (1978): 953–958.

24. Kearney, *Labor Relations in the Public Sector*, 70–71.

25. J.P. Piskulich, *Collective Bargaining in State and Local Government* (New York: Praeger Publishers, 1992), 69.

26. R.G. Brown and T.L. Rhodes, Public employee bargaining under prohibitive legislation: Some unanticipated consequences, *Journal of Collective Negotiations in the Public Sector* 20 (1991): 23–30.

27. *Garcia v. San Antonio Metropolitan Transit Authority*, 469 U.S. 528 (1985).

28. D.H. Rosenbloom, The Federal Labor Relations Authority, *Policy Studies Journal* 17 (1988–89): 370–388.

29. E.J. Wasilewski, Jr., Collective bargaining in 1992: Contract talks and other activity, *Monthly Labor Review* 115 (January 1992): 3–20.

30. U.S. Office of Personnel Management, *Union Recognition in the Federal Government*.

31. J.E. Martin and R.L. Smith, Appropriate bargaining units for state employees, *Journal of Labor Research* 6 (1985): 289–305.

32. J.M. Douglas, *At the Bargaining Table: The Status of Public Sector Supervisory, Managerial, and Confidential Employees* (Alexandria, Va.: International Personnel Management Association, 1989).

33. P.M. Seviercz, Quasi-collective bargaining: Supervisory representatives in the U.S. Postal Service, *Labor Law Journal* 43 (1992): 131–141.

34. Dahl and Wappel, Labor–management relations in local government, 4.

35. *City of Madison, Joint School District No. 8 v. Wisconsin*, 429 U.S. 167 (1976).

36. *Minnesota State Board of Community Colleges v. Knight*, 465 U.S. 271 (1984).

37. *Perry Education Association v. Perry Local Educators' Association*, 460 U.S. 37 (1983).

38. *Bureau of Alcohol, Tobacco and Firearms v. Federal Labor Relations Authority*, 464 U.S. 89 (1983).

39. *Federal Labor Relations Authority v. Aberdeen Proving Ground, Department of Army*, 485 U.S. 409 (1988).

40. Civil Service Reform Act, P.L. 95-454, 92 Stat. 1111 (1978).

41. *Fort Stewart Schools v. Federal Labor Relations Authority*, 495 U.S. 641 (1990).

42. U.S. General Accounting Office, *Federal Labor Relations Authority and Administrative Roles and Case Processing* (Washington: U.S. Government Printing Office, 1986).

43. U.S. Office of Personnel Management, *Negotiability Determinations by the Federal Labor Relations Authority* (Washington: U.S. Government Printing Office, 1985).

44. Pennsylvania Public Employee Relations Act, Act 195 of 1970.

45. *State College Education Association v. Pennsylvania Labor Relations Board*, 9 Pa. Commw. 229, 306 A.2d 404 (1973).

46. W.H. Volz and D. Costa, A public employee's "fair share" of union dues, *Labor Law Journal* 40 (1989): 131–137.

47. M.F. Masters and R.S. Atkin, Public policy, bargaining structure and free-riding in the federal sector, *Journal of Collective Negotiations in the Public Sector* 19 (1990): 97–112.

48. *Abood v. Detroit Board of Education*, 431 U.S. 209 (1977).

49. *Ellis v. Brotherhood of Railway, Airline and Steamship Clerks*, 466 U.S. 435 (1984).

50. *Chicago Teachers Union, Local 1 v. Hudson*, 475 U.S. 292 (1986).

51. *Lehnert v. Ferris Faculty Association*, 111 S.Ct. 1950 (1991).

52. *City of Charlotte v. Local 660, International Association of Firefighters*, 426 U.S. 283 (1976).

53. R.J. Kuhns, Win/win negotiating—Process or philosophy? *Journal of Collective Negotiations in the Public Sector* 15 (1986): 281–287.

54. R.C. Richardson, *Collective Bargaining by Objectives: A Positive Approach* (Englewood Cliffs, N.J.: Prentice-Hall, 1977).

55. D.A. Dilts and W.J. Walsh, *Collective Bargaining and Impasse Resolution in the Public Sector* (New York: Quorum, 1988): 51–71.

56. "Guide to Costing Out Public Sector Wage and Benefit Packages," in *Public Employee Organizing and the Law*, ed. M.T. Leibig and W.L. Kahn (Washington: Bureau of National Affairs, 1987), 205–218.

57. L.M. Toulmin, The treasure hunt: Budget search behavior by public employee unions, *Public Administration Review* 48 (1988): 620–630.

58. D.N. Ammons, *Municipal Productivity* (New York: Praeger, 1984).

59. Kearney, *Labor Relations in the Public Sector*, 194–198.

60. D.J.B. Mitchell, Concession bargaining in the public sector: A lesser force, *Public Personnel Management* 15 (1986): 23–40.

61. C. Newland, Settlement reached in postal arbitration, *Public Administration Times* 8 (January 15, 1985): 1ff.

62. C. Scott and J. Suchan, Public sector collective bargaining agreements: How readable are they? *Public Personnel Management* 16 (1987): 15–22.

63. *National Association of Letter Carriers v. Blount*, 305 F.Supp. 546 (1969), *appeal dismissed* 400 U.S. 801 (1970).

64. *United Federation of Postal Clerks v. Blount*, 325 F.Supp. 879 (1971), *affirmed* 404 U.S. 802 (1971).

65. J.D. Straussman, et al., Public unions and penalties for striking across the states, *Review of Public Personnel Administration* 6 (Summer 1986): 19–33.

66. *Hortonville Joint School District #1 v. Hortonville Education Association*, 426 U.S. 482 (1976).

67. A.B. Shostak and D. Skocik, *The Air Controllers' Controversy: Lessons from the PATCO Strike* (New York: Human Sciences, 1986).

68. G.T. Sulzner, Federal labor–management relations: The Reagan impact, *Journal of Collective Negotiations in the Public Sector* 15 (1986): 201–210.

69. D.A. Dilts, et al., Mediation in the public sector: Toward a paradigm of negotiations and dispute resolution, *Journal of Collective Negotiations in the Public Sector* 19 (1990): 49–60.

70. D.A. Dilts, et al., Mediation and the path toward settlement: An analysis of union negotiator behaviors, *Journal of Collective Negotiations in the Public Sector* 21 (1992): 171–182.

71. A.M. Zack, *Public Sector Mediation* (Washington: Bureau of National Affairs, 1985).

72. D.M. McCabe, The federal sector mediation and labor management relations process: The federal sector management experience, *Public Personnel Management* 19 (1990): 103–122.

73. Bussey, *Federal Civil Service Law*, 287.

74. N.E. Nelson, How factfinders view the criteria in factfinding, *Journal of Collective Negotiations in the Public Sector* 21 (1992): 159–170.

75. R.C. Feiock and J.P. West, Public presence at collective bargaining: Effects on process and decisions in Florida, *Journal of Collective Negotiations in the Public Sector* 19 (1990): 69–82.

76. J.P. West and R.C. Feiock, Support for sunshine bargaining in Florida: A decade later, *Review of Public Personnel Administration* 9 (Spring 1989): 28–50.

77. C.R. Deitsch and D.A. Dilts, *The Arbitration of Rights Disputes in the Public Sector* (New York: Quorum, 1990).

78. G.G. Dell'Omo, Capturing arbitrator decision policies under a public sector interest arbitration statute, *Review of Public Personnel Administration* 10 (Spring 1990): 19–38.

79. C.G. Smith, The resolution of negotiation impasses in the federal service, *Journal of Collective Negotiations in the Public Service* 20 (1991): 321–339.

80. T.J. Di Lauro, Interest arbitration: The best alternative for resolving public-sector impasses, *Employee Relations Law Journal* 14 (1989): 549–568.

81. Kearney, *Labor Relations in the Public Sector*, 322–323.

82. W.A. Kleintop and J.J. Loewenberg, Collective bargaining, compulsory interest arbitration and the narcotic effect: A longitudinal study of Delaware County, Pennsylvania, *Journal of Collective Negotiations in the Public Sector* 19 (1990): 113–120.

83. *County Sanitation District No. 2 v. Los Angeles County Employees Association, Local 660*, 214 Cal. Rptr. 424, 699 P.2d 835 (1985).

84. R.L. Hogler, *Public Sector Strikes: Employee Rights, Union Responsibilities, and Employer Prerogatives* (Alexandria, Va.: International Personnel Management Association, 1988).

85. _____, Public sector strikes, labor–management relations, and the common law, *Public Personnel Management* 17 (1988): 83–90.

86. P.A. Zirkel, The academic effects of teacher strikes, *Journal of Collective Negotiations in the Public Sector* 21 (1992): 123–138.

87. D.M. Partridge, The effect of public policy on the duration of strikes by public school teachers, *Journal of Collective Negotiations in the Public Sector* 21 (1992): 111–121.

88. M.J. Duane, To grieve or not to grieve: Why "reduce it to writing?" *Public Personnel Management* 20 (1991): 83–90.

89. R.J. Schoonhoven, ed., *Fairweather's Practice and Procedure in Labor Arbitration*, 3d ed. (Washington: Bureau of National Affairs, 1991).

90. Bussey, *Federal Civil Service Law*, 233.

91. *Bowen v. U.S. Postal Service*, 459 U.S. 212 (1983).

92. R.R. Smith, From Bowen to Devine: The quandry facing federal unions, *Labor Law Journal* 35 (1984): 435–439.

93. G.W. Bohlander, Public sector independent grievance systems: Methods and procedures, *Public Personnel Management* 18 (1989): 339–354.

94. J.M. Douglas, State civil service and collective bargaining: Systems in conflict, *Public Administration Review* 52 (1992): 162–171.

95. T.J. Loney, Learning from personnel research, 1963–1988; public sector labor relations research, the first generation, *Public Personnel Management* 18 (1989): 162–175.

96. J. Tracy, *Comparisons between Public and Private Sector Union Wage Differentials: Does the Legal Environment Matter?* (Cambridge, Mass.: National Bureau of Economic Research, 1988).

97. K.G. Love, Recessional impact on local government human resource management systems: A model indicating impact of unionization, *Public Personnel Management* 13 (1984): 307–315.

98. D.I. McIntyre, Merit principles and collective bargaining: A marriage or divorce? *Public Administration Review* 37 (1977): 186–190.

99. L. Reese and J. Ohren, The impact of collective bargaining in four cities: The diversity thesis revisited, *Review of Public Personnel Administration* 8 (Fall 1987): 68–74.

100. The public's interest in personnel administration, *International Personnel Management Association News* (December 1977): 9.

101. D.M. Figart, Collective bargaining and career development for women in the public sector, *Journal of Collective Negotiations in the Public Sector* 18 (1989): 301–333.

102. N.M. Riccucci, *Women, Minorities, and Unions in the Public Sector* (New York: Greenwood, 1990).

103. R.C. Elling, Civil service collective bargaining and personnel-related impediments to effective state management, *Review of Public Personnel Administration* 6 (Summer 1986): 73–91.

104. D.T. Methe and J.L. Perry, The impacts of collective bargaining on local government services, *Public Administration Review* 40 (1984): 359–371.

105. S.M. Lipset, et al., *Union Democracy: The Internal Politics of the International Typographical Union* (Garden City, N.Y.: Doubleday, 1962).

106. A. Hyde, Democracy in collective bargaining, *Yale Law Journal* 93 (1984): 793–856.

107. *Department of the Treasury, Internal Revenue Service v. Federal Labor Relations Authority*, 110 S.Ct. 1623 (1990).

108. K.C. Naff, Labor–management relations and privatization: A federal perspective, *Public Administration Review* 51 (1991): 23–30.

109. T. Chandler and P. Feuille, Municipal unions and privatization, *Public Administration Review* 51 (1991): 15–22.

110. J.T. Barrett, *Labor–Management Cooperation in the Public Service* (Washington: International Personnel Management Association, 1985).

111. NLRB announces settlement changes against USPS' program, *Government Employee Relations Reporter* 30 (1992): 604–605.

112. J.S. Zax and C. Ichniowski, Bargaining laws and unionization in the local public sector, *Industrial and Labor Relations Review* 43 (1990): 447–462.

113. J.L. Conant, Agency problems in public sector labor relations, *Government Union Review* 10 (Summer 1989): 40–54.

114. M.J. Levine, Legal obstacles to union–management cooperation in the federal service, *Labor Law Journal* 42 (1991): 103–110.

115. R.M. Schwartz, Participative decision making and union–management cooperative efforts: Attitudes of managers, union officials, and employees, *Review of Public Personnel Administration* 11 (Fall 1990–Spring 1991): 38–54.

116. U.S. General Accounting Office, *Federal Labor Relations: A Program in Need of Reform* (Washington: U.S. Government Printing Office, 1991).

Critique

Public personnel systems consist of numerous parts and relationships that frequently seem uncoordinated with each other and with the larger governmental system. This chapter provides a perspective on the problems that exist and possible future conditions that will influence personnel systems. The main topics are:

1. the complaints frequently made about personnel systems
2. the unresolved issues that are endemic not only to personnel administration but more generally to the governmental system
3. the future of public personnel systems

A NEGATIVE VIEW

Personnel administrators are dedicated to their work, perhaps being zealots for the advancement of the merit principle. The historical development of personnel systems, however, has tended to encourage an "us-against-them" outlook on government. In the early reform period, there was a real "them," namely persons who openly supported political patronage. In the 1990s, the "them" is not so apparent because few persons would advocate a return to unlimited government patronage. Personnelists, nevertheless, remain fearful that politicians and politically appointed executives, while professing their support of the merit principle, would embrace patronage if given the opportunity. There is a perceived need to be vigilant in watching for any administrative practice that might allow for political considerations in personnel matters.

The "us-against-them" outlook persists not only because of the historical development of the field but also because of organizational arrangements and contemporary pressures. Reformers were successful in creating independent

385

civil service commissions, but that independence created a considerable degree of isolation. By insulating personnel from political pressures, reformers pushed this important function into a remote corner. Removed from the center of management, personnelists see themselves at best as being ignored and at worst as being attacked. Managers tend to consider personnelists as having no particular skills that could be helpful in improving agency operations. Personnel administrators hold the opposite view: that they have an extensive array of skills that, if they were only utilized, would facilitate more effective and efficient operations in government. Unions and collective bargaining are seen as constituting a major force that could nullify the progress that has been achieved. The demand for affirmative action is another contemporary pressure that many personnel administrators have difficulty accepting.

Perhaps the most persistent line of attack that encourages the "us-against-them" outlook is the claim that personnel systems are dysfunctional. The conclusion reached in 1975 by the Study Committee on Policy Management Assistance for the U.S. Office of Management and Budget is typical[1]:

> Civil service regulations, promulgated to guard against the ravages of unbridled patronage, limit the flexibility of policymakers and management in selecting and assigning personnel; thus, needs determination and program development become futile because implementation is compromised.

This is "the triumph of techniques over purpose."[2] By installing procedures for personnel actions, personnelists have hoped to produce systems that are based on merit, but critics contend that the procedures, better known as red tape, are not only superfluous but harmful.

The field of personnel administration has been based primarily on the input side of government. The field of budgeting originally had a similar emphasis. Early budget systems stressed how dollars were being spent, with only limited concern about the consequences of those expenditures. Contemporary budget systems, however, attempt to link expenditures with program outcomes. Are people safer because of police expenditures, and do children read better because of educational expenditures? Personnel systems, in contrast, remain committed to the inputs. The assumption has been that, if tests are constructed appropriately and administered fairly, then the "right" people will be brought into government. If performance appraisal systems are refined, then superior workers can be promoted and inferior workers removed.

Little attention has been paid to how employees influence the outcomes of governmental programs. The difficult problem entails analyzing the relationship of different types of workers in combination with supportive equipment and materials in producing governmental services that have measurable impacts.

Program evaluation has gained wide acceptance since the 1970s, but evaluations tend to concentrate on comparing the relationships between total inputs (usually expressed in dollars) with program results. For example, police expenditures are analyzed in terms of their effects on crime rates. Personnel evaluation would take the additional step of relating the mix of personnel to program results. The prospects for conducting such analyses are uncertain, as would be the results of the analyses, but the point here is that personnel administrators have largely ignored the impacts of programs, preferring to concentrate on the processes or techniques of position classification, examination, performance appraisal, and the like.

When criticisms are made of various aspects of personnel administration, the response of personnelists is to seek refinement in the techniques they use.[3] If it is alleged that incompetents achieve high scores on civil service examinations while competent individuals are screened out, the response is to redesign the tests. If there are complaints that employees are not sufficiently protected from arbitrary disciplinary action, the response is to redesign the appeals system. If the appeals system is attacked for being exceedingly slow and for providing excessive protection to workers, the response again is to redesign the appeals system.

Skeptics suggest that refining techniques is fruitless and is likely to lead to more red tape. "Refinement" of procedures is viewed as making them more detailed and complicated. Once a performance appraisal system has been refined, it becomes a cumbersome device that imposes great burdens on managers' time. The skeptics ultimately deem the refined system as no better than the system used previously. The prescription is[4]:

> Fire the whole personnel department. . . . The trouble with personnel experts is that they use gimmicks borrowed from manufacturing: inventories, replacement charts, recruiting, selecting, indoctrinating and training machinery, job rotation, and appraisal programs. And this manufacturing of men is about as effective as Dr. Frankenstein was.

There is support for the dictum, Don't make the techniques better; instead, make government better by eliminating the techniques.

Personnel offices, like budgeting and planning offices, perform a staff and not a line function. A staff function often is a thankless task. Line managers can point to the accomplishments of their agencies. A highway department can justify itself by pointing to the redesigning of major intersections or the resurfacing of deteriorated roads. A mental health agency can claim great achievements in helping its clients deal with mental disorders. But what can be claimed by a personnel agency?[5] Gauging the effectiveness of staff agencies is difficult because such agencies are facilitators rather than providers of governmental services. As noted, personnel agencies attempt to get the right people into the right jobs, but if employees perform effectively there is no obvious linkage between that success and the work of the personnel office. Line managers can claim the success as theirs and say it was accomplished in spite of civil service regulations. Managers may view personnel offices as performing nonproductive (and sometimes counterproductive) functions.

It is fashionable to attack personnel administration as being devoid of a governing theory or principle. It has been seen as "a barren area for theoretical study," being mainly "the routine application of a practitioner's 'bag of tricks.'"[6] The merit principle has been the center of personnel systems, but the concept often has been considered in a negative sense. Merit is perceived as keeping patronage out of government. The concept of merit was a useful focus for the reforms of the late 1800s and early 1900s, but, say the critics, that idea is not developed sufficiently to provide guidance in meeting contemporary problems of administration. Even worse, many personnelists define "merit" as rigid adherence to procedures of their own design. Deviation from procedures becomes a "merit system violation," even though the "violation" may have a positive effect on agency efficiency and effectiveness.

This is a harsh critique that personnelists themselves accept, at least in part. The euphoria of the early reform years has gone. In the 1890s, reformists (Carl Schurz in this case) spoke glowingly of their cause[7]:

> There are some among us who stood at the cradle of the Civil Service Reform movement. They remember the time when the practical politician looked upon the Civil Service Reformer as a visionary dreamer of singularly hopeless conceit—as little better than a harmless idiot who might be tolerated at large without the slightest danger to the existing order of things. When we remember that time, which does not lie very far behind us, and then contemplate the marvelous change that has since taken place, will the hope for the complete triumph of the cause we advocate still appear extravagantly sanguine?

Today, many would consider such language embarrassing, empty rhetoric.

A resurgence of reform has developed since the 1970s.[8] Much attention was directed at reorganization as one aspect of reform. Organization charts for personnel functions were redrawn at the federal level, and some state and local governments took similar action. Reorganization could not be expected to eliminate the persistent criticisms of personnel systems, however. Reorganization alone can be a pointless exercise. As the first century Roman, Petronius remarked, "I was to learn that later in life we tend to meet any new situation by reorganizing, and a wonderful method it can be for creating the illusion of progress while producing confusion, inefficiency, and demoralization."[9] This is not to suggest that the federal reorganization effort was pointless but to warn that reorganization is not a panacea.[10]

Reform at the federal level also has been aimed at encouraging the removal of nonproductive employees and rewarding productive ones with pay increases. The Senior Executive Service and the Performance Management and Recognition System for managers were created along with a substantially altered labor–management relations system under the Federal Labor Relations Authority.

UNRESOLVED ISSUES

Basic values that by themselves may seem unquestionably appropriate may collide when applied to specific situations. The problem is that the relative importance of each value has not been determined, so competition among values is characteristic of contemporary governmental systems. Personnel systems operate in an environment of uncertainty and under conditions far beyond their control.[11,12] The issues confronting personnel systems are numerous, longstanding, difficult to resolve, and of great magnitude to those in government and to the general citizenry.[13-15]

One of the most fundamental issues is the role of bureaucracy in a democracy.[16-18] Back in 1935, one critic wrote, "Bureaucracy is neither a system of government nor a collection of disagreeable men doing unnecessary things, but the personnel aspect of administration in all its ramifications and difficulties."[19] As society has grown and government has accepted greater responsibilities, bureaucracies have emerged to provide services. Bureaucracies have been seen as being essential to the survival of democracies. A different view, however, is that bureaucracies have become unwieldy organizations that are dehumanizing, defy anyone's control, and encourage inefficiency. Moreover, there has been a tendency for bureaucrats to aggrandize their roles, actually setting themselves up as the final arbiters of what is or is not good for the public.

Bureaucracies are characterized by red tape. Elaborate regulations are written that are unintelligible to the average citizen. The reasons for the paper blizzard are not difficult to discern. Regulations that prescribe procedures and forms that require extensive recordkeeping are imposed to set what are thought to be fair rules of the game. State and local governments complain about the information that they must supply to federal agencies about equal opportunity, but those procedures were installed to discourage discriminatory practices and to encourage equal employment opportunities for minorities and women. Managers may complain about the red tape associated with dismissing employees, but those procedures were established to protect workers against arbitrary dismissal. What is red tape to one person is not necessarily red tape to others. Employees who find themselves in a disciplinary situation are not likely to condemn the appeals procedure as mere red tape. In other words, all red tape has a purpose, and no matter how loud the complaints it will continue to characterize government in general and personnel systems in particular.[20-22]

A problem stemming from red tape is that it can become counterproductive to the main objectives of the organization. Just as extensive air pollution controls reduce the efficiency of automobile engines, extensive personnel controls and procedures can hinder agency efficiency. A police department eager to achieve racial balance in its work force may divert some of its limited resources away from the objective of controlling crime. Should a state government be advised to spend less on developing valid civil service tests and more on services that directly benefit the public?

How political leadership is to control administrative processes is a related issue. It is contended that those elected by the citizenry should have the power to govern, particularly that a chief executive should have control of the bureaucracy, including personnel.[23] Chief executive control, however, obviously arouses concern about politicizing personnel administration, a concern that will always be present.

The issue of political control is most sensitive in the higher levels of bureaucracy. Few people would contend openly that political considerations should enter into personnel actions involving clerical workers and laborers. Where there are differing views is at high levels of administration, where questions of policy inevitably arise. In 1887, in a classic essay, Woodrow Wilson proposed a science of administration that would be largely divorced from politics.[24] That view of separating politics from administration is considered unrealistic these days.[25]

Between the partisan chief executive and midlevel merit employees are two types of officials for whom no clearcut roles have been prescribed. One group consists of politically appointed executives: department secretaries, under-secretaries, assistant secretaries, and the like. Political executives often are amateur managers and have only limited support from the chief executive in the appointment process. Once political executives are appointed, they are expected to carry out their responsibilities with little support from the chief executive and immediate staff. Largely cut off from higher political authority, political executives must rely on merit-appointed workers for information and advice and for performing the tasks of their agencies. Many political executives feel trapped by their organizations and have a sense of being controlled by their bureaucracies rather than controlling them.[26,27]

The other group consists of career merit executives, who are one rung below the political executives. Career executives almost inevitably are involved in broad policy issues that have implications for partisan politics. A common recommendation has been that career merit executives should be afforded considerable job security while at the same time being responsive to political leadership. The idea of a career executive system with rank-in-person has been proposed many times, and President Carter's proposal for a Senior Executive Service was incorporated into the Civil Service Reform Act of 1978. Regardless of the specific proposals advanced for career executive systems, one fundamental issue remains. How are career executives to balance their professional judgments with the preferred policies of their immediate superiors and the possibly differing preferred policies of the chief executive?

Special status for career executives is related to a more general issue: the extent to which the public service should consist of careerists. Encouraging careers in government is justified as helping employees, government, and the public. Career systems help individuals develop their potentials. A job is not just a job but rather an opportunity for intellectual growth and the development of new skills. Career systems also are beneficial in that they supposedly increase governmental effectiveness and efficiency. The career worker is seen as being more productive than one who has been in government for only a short period. A competing value is that government jobs should be open to all qualified persons regardless of whether they currently are employed in government. Fostering careers can be an elitist approach to personnel administration: "Actually, the career system verges on the closed system."[28]

The rights of executives and managers—both political appointees and those protected under a merit system—are another center of debate, particularly in relationship to subordinates. A common theme is that personnel systems have stripped managers of the power to manage. The Committee for Economic Development took this position just before Congress passed the 1978 Civil Service Reform Act[29]:

> Perhaps the most serious charge that can be leveled at federal personnel administration under current conditions is that it is insufficiently oriented to support the management function. Under long-established civil service restraints, department and agency heads are severely handicapped by their inability to deploy manpower in ways which put the right person in the right job, at the right time, for the right reason.

Testing and selection procedures, such as the rule of three, limit managerial flexibility in personnel, as do equal employment opportunity requirements and collective bargaining contracts. Managers are given official responsibility for directing their agencies to achieve expected results. Such results can be achieved only through effective utilization of personnel, and the managers' powers in this respect are circumscribed severely.

From the perspective of employees, managerial powers should indeed be limited. Even when the vast majority of managers are dedicated to public service and are considerate of their subordinates, there may be some who would treat their workers unfairly if protective procedures did not exist. Without appeal procedures on adverse action, for example, managers might feel unfettered in dismissing employees for inconsequential reasons. These procedures, however, are incapable of guaranteeing fair treatment. Highly competent employees can be forced from their positions through reorganizations, transfers to different geographic locations, and assignment to undesirable tasks. Because the procedures do not guarantee equitable treatment, are they worth the costs they impose on managers? Have merit systems provided excessive job security for workers, so that firing incompetents is impossible? If this is the case, merit systems contribute to governmental inefficiency.[30]

There are other aspects to this issue of employee rights. One involves employees participating in the political process. Government has precluded many of its workers from being active participants in partisan elections, but:

- should acceptance of government employment require relinquishing this constitutionally protected right?
- to what extent should one's right to free speech be curtailed because of being a government employee?
- what types of outside activities create conflicts of interests that should be prohibited?[31]
- is whistleblowing a healthy phenomenon, or is it dangerous in that it subverts the political administration chosen by the electorate?
- do loyalty and security programs infringe on the right to privacy and foster timidity on the part of government employees?

There is no universally accepted formula for motivating employees to increase efficiency and effectiveness. Part of the problem is a substantive disagreement on what strategies are most likely to produce positive results. Should workers be given greater autonomy, as is encouraged by management by objectives and total quality management, or should more emphasis be given to group activities in which the manager is viewed as a leader and not the boss? Are employees motivated by being interested in the work they perform or by the financial rewards of work? Wage incentive systems, often considered in the past to have had little bearing on performance, are regaining support among some personnel reformists. Although some see these as a reform, others regard them as a return to Theory X.[32-34] Agreement may exist that public sector salaries and wages should be comparable to those in the private sector, but numerous difficult questions remain unresolved regarding how individual workers are to be compensated.[35]

Motivation also involves a value issue of what is fair play in dealing with employees. Are motivation schemes manipulative in that the "right" strings are pulled on the marionette workers, resulting in greater productivity?[36] Labor unions have feared that efforts to improve motivation are intended to get more work from employees with no increase in pay.

A generally accepted value is that workers should have some role in determining how they perform their jobs. Motivation theories suggest that such involvement leads to greater job satisfaction and improved performance. To what extent, however, should workers be permitted to organize into labor unions and bargain with government over the conditions of work?[37] To what extent are the various aspects of personnel systems appropriate subjects for collective bargaining? A traditional belief has been that bargaining is not totally compatible with merit.

Unresolved is the issue of how closely the public bureaucracy should represent the general population. Specifically, to what extent should personnel systems provide special procedures to increase the percentage of women, African-Americans, Hispanics, and other minorities in the public work force? Are policies intended to favor these groups a form of unacceptable reverse discrimination? Such favoritism would seem to conflict with the merit principle, in that skin color and sex have little bearing on how a worker performs a job. Do civil service systems originally designed to protect against political patronage have the effect of fostering social inequity, namely discouraging minorities from entering public employment and advancing their careers?[38]

Veterans constitute another group that has received special treatment. Veterans preference existed before the establishment of merit systems and has continued even though the practice conflicts with the merit concept. The use of veterans preference is under increasing attack, but some form of it is likely to continue.

Since the founding of this nation, a continuing problem has been determining the relative role of the national, state, and local governments. A continuous debate has focused on whether the federal government has gained excessive powers. This problem of intergovernmental relations is apparent in equal employment opportunity. State and local personnel systems must conform with federal requirements on affirmative action. The federal government has sought to bring state and local employees under national work standards. Congress has been pressured to adopt legislation that would set ground rules for labor–management relations at the state and local levels.

An important societal value has been that citizens should be able to play some direct roles in government, even though ours is a representative form of democracy. When this value is applied to the field of personnel, it raises the issue of whether citizens should be involved in individual personnel actions:

- Should disciplinary proceedings include the public, as in the case of citizen review boards?
- Should citizens be able to file legal suits not only against a governmental body but also against individual workers?

- How is the value of citizen rights to be balanced with the value of employee rights?
- Does allowing for citizen suits create timid government workers?
- Does protecting workers from suits make them indifferent to citizen needs?

These are only some of the fundamental unresolved issues facing government and public personnel systems. They are not a complete catalog. The point is that these basic value questions have not been resolved, with the result that public personnel systems are expected to serve simultaneously a wide range of values that are not synchronized with each other.[39] Attacking the personnel field as being devoid of theory is unwarranted. The problem is not a lack of theory but an overabundance of theories.

Personnel administration cannot be governed by a coherent set of values when society has been unable to reach consensus about the relative importance of fundamental values that affect the entire governmental system. As long as the governmental system remains as it is—that is, open or receptive to competing ideas and values—there will be no permanent resolution of this problem. Personnel systems must learn to cope with the ambiguity and not expect it to disappear.

THE FUTURE

Forecasting the future is not easy. It entails projecting what is likely to occur. Will present trends continue, and if not, what new trends will emerge? The next step is to consider whether participants in the system are likely to alter their behavior, and if the answer is affirmative the next question is, how will behavior change? Given the difficulty of making such projections and predicting reactions to projections, the process of forecasting is highly susceptible to error.[40]

One problem in forecasting is that it is difficult to predict the intensity of incentives for change. How extensive must acid rain problems become before the political system is willing to deal with them? The oil shortages of the 1970s provided stimulus for governmental action, but as supplies later increased and prices declined there was little political activity to develop comprehensive energy policies on consumption, conservation, exploration for more resources, and research for new sources of energy.

A forecast for personnel administration could begin with projecting societal and global changes and then attempting to relate those changes to personnel systems. Will the nation's growing racial and ethnic diversity eventually lead to its splintering or even disintegration?[41] Will there be unrestrained tariff wars among nations as societies come to feel that their industrial bases are threatened by international competition? Will extensive new oil reserves be located, and in what countries? Will government in the United States forge a strong alliance with business as a strategy for coping with international economic competition, or will economic competition among the United States, Japan, and Europe lead to massive economic decline here?[42] Questions of this type are extraordinarily important, but they cannot be addressed here. To open up questions of this magnitude would start a new book, not end this one, and the opportunities for error would be immense. Almost no one predicted the disintegration of the communist governments of eastern Europe, the Soviet Union, and Yugoslavia. Instead, the assumption here is that there will be a general continuation of existing global trends which will not dramatically alter the internal operations of governments in the United States. This has been called a "surprise-free projection."[43]

A Conservative View

Although the assumption can be made that external changes will be largely continuations of present trends, internal changes can be expected to be either relatively modest or more dramatic in impact. The discussion here is concerned with a situation involving only moderate change; the next section turns to a brief review of possible changes having more significant scope.

In this surprise-free projection, the assumption can be made that the problems discussed in the preceding section will persist. For instance, there is no basis for assuming that the issue of political influence in personnel matters will subside. The familiar debates about the rights of a chief executive, agency managers, and employees will not fade. The pressure for equal employment opportunity and affirmative action will continue, along with demands for collective bargaining. As noted, these unresolved issues are fundamental ones that are not subject to quickie solutions.

Beyond those issues are economic forces that are likely to influence public personnel systems. Revenues can be expected to be scarce for most governments in the foreseeable future. The federal government has amassed monumental budget deficits since the 1980s, in part as a result of major tax cuts enacted in 1981. State and local revenues have been curtailed by provisions such as Proposition 13 in California, which mandated limitations on property tax rates. Adding to the problem has been a severe realignment of the economy, resulting in losses of thousands of jobs, particularly in manufacturing and in middle management in many businesses and industries. Cutbacks in federal defense spending in the 1990s have resulted in the displacement of thousands of military personnel and civilians who worked for defense contractors. Further complicating the situation has been the aging of the population. Young people have moved out of many communities in search of job opportunities, leaving behind an older population living on fixed incomes of savings and Social Security.

Tight economic conditions create incentives for change that have repercussions on personnel systems. One immediate step is to cut back on services and to furlough employees. Reductions in force have become common in government, which once was characterized by strong job security. Another step may be increased use of contracting for services, if such contracts prove to be a less expensive means for delivering services.[44] Greater use of part-time employees may result in savings for jurisdictions because such workers commonly do not qualify for retirement and many other benefits. These factors, then, can change the character of the public work force. There may be a leveling in growth or even a decline in public employment. As a reaction, employees may turn increasingly to collective bargaining in the hope of protecting their jobs.

Another possible outgrowth of tight budgets can be increasing emphasis on productivity improvement stemming from greater use of program evaluation and personnel appraisal.[45] In other words, why fund programs and hire workers when only limited results are achieved? There may be incentives to find more cost-effective mixes of personnel. The general pressure for evaluation may encourage further development in performance appraisal systems, but if these are used for weeding out less productive workers the process will increase worker demands for job security.

Tight budgets may be an incentive for substituting machines for personnel. Labor costs in government have risen sharply, perhaps in part because of the increasing use of collective bargaining. As personnel costs rise, substitution of machines becomes more economically feasible. Low-priced computers, especially personal computers, make recordkeeping with few persons possible compared with paper-and-pencil record systems; personnel records are particularly well suited to computer applications.[46] The conversion to greater use of machines, however, is limited by the nature of governmental services. Many government jobs cannot be handled by machines.

Besides economic trends, there are sociopolitical and administrative factors that will influence the future. One unknown is the attitude that the chief inhabitant of the White House will have toward public servants. Recent presidents and other political leaders have been frequent critics of public bureaucracies. Although their criticisms in some instances may be well founded, such repeated attacks foster a negative attitude among the public and government employees and may discourage America's brightest from considering careers in government.[47] Does government become the employer of last resort for those who cannot find employment in the private sector?[48] Negativism can result in government recruiting mediocre employees and not those who could increase its effectiveness and efficiency.

Another unknown is whether the concept of comparable worth will be adopted. If advocates are able to win legislative and judicial support for comparable worth, a major restructuring of both the private and the public sector could occur. The adoption of comparable worth, which might well result in higher salaries for such occupations as teaching, nursing, and the like, would probably lead to increasing numbers of men moving into these occupations.

Government also is changing with respect to the level of complexity of work. Patronage in the 1800s could be defended on the grounds that almost anyone could adequately perform the duties of government jobs. Today government jobs are highly technical, including many clerical positions that require knowledge of computer-controlled equipment. Of course, nontechnical jobs will remain in abundance, at least until breakthroughs can be achieved in the way services are provided. Until the pothole-proof road can be built, there will be road crews and jobs that require little skill.

The increasingly technical nature of jobs creates problems. Recruiting people with the necessary skills may be difficult as government is forced to compete for these individuals with the private sector, which can offer much higher salaries and benefits. Technical jobs may tend to keep minorities out of government. Increasingly technical jobs can be threatening to other workers.[49] Some individuals will welcome the challenge of learning new skills; others will not. There will be increasing emphasis on midcareer training, although doubts about whether training has real payoffs will persist.

The increasing complexity of governmental work has been seen as a possible threat to democracy. The "administrative state," "professional state," or "technocracy" already has developed.[50,51] Many federal and state jobs require persons with college degrees in science and engineering. All levels of government require individuals with degrees in education, law, social work, and health. The Federalists were an elite of wealth; today's elite consists of professionals. To what extent do professionals virtually dictate to the public and political leaders what policies and programs are to be adopted? To what extent is that practice likely to increase?

Technocracy challenges the traditional role of the manager as boss. Expertise has long been recognized as a source of power.[52,53] The gap may be widening, however, between what managers know and what they need to know to take appropriate action. Managers are likely to become increasingly dependent on subordinate specialists. Authority based on one's position in the hierarchy may be replaced by sapiential authority, or authority based on knowledge.[54,55]

Changes in the nature of work performed—its increasingly technical nature—lend support to the idea that existing personnel practices must give way to new ones. The proposals to abandon rigid position classification systems and pay plans with a step system must be seen in this light. Such proposals would dramatically revise personnel administration far more than what occurred under the Civil Service Reform Act. The proposals would provide management with the flexibility needed in managing but also could increase opportunities for abuse, such as providing pay increases to the favored and unjustifiably denying them to others.

Theories X, Y, and Z can be seen as competing concepts in the future. The increasing role of professionals in government has led to the suggestion that Theory Y is likely to become the dominant approach to management. Professionals presumably resent hierarchical authority and perform best in situations that provide them with great autonomy. Organizations of the future might consist of temporary groups created to deal with specific problems and frequently restructured as the nature of the problems changes. Were that type of organization to emerge, there would be little need for position classification, pay plans, and other common aspects of personnel systems.

In contrast to this projection of a fluid bureaucratic structure, a forecast could just as well be made that rigidities will continue. The work ethic may be declining, so that Theory X is needed to keep employee performance from declining. A tradition of governmental systems has been to fix organizational structure, often establishing it by legislation. That tradition will be difficult to overcome.

As for Theory Z, which blends the two other concepts, there is little experience in U.S. governments upon which to base a forecast. Theory Z emphasizes group involvement in improving worker productivity, but this approach can be seen as encroaching upon the prerogatives of both management and organized labor. Whether labor and management are prepared to accept this concept is unknown.

Another look must be taken at the age-old custom of patronage. Earlier discussions have covered the growth and decline, but not the demise, of this custom. The question must be raised as to whether reforms of the future will erode some protections afforded career government workers and whether in doing so they will allow for political or nonmerit factors to influence personnel decisions.[56] For example, the Senior Executive Service has been hailed as a means of having top career officers be more accountable to political executives, but does this action place careerists in jeopardy of being dismissed every time they disagree with the political administration? Can reform proposals to make bureaucracies more fluid contribute to greater politicization of administration and personnel systems? Again, there are no answers to these questions.

The topics discussed in this and the preceding sections can be treated as individual subjects for reform, namely that labor–management relations issues can be handled separately, as can be issues regarding testing procedures. A piecemeal approach to problem solving, however, may not necessarily be a preferred option; an alternative would be a more comprehensive set of reforms that were the outgrowth of a larger vision of how personnel systems should operate.[57] Having been criticized for failing to provide substantial leadership, the Office of Personnel Management has developed a strategic plan that offers a vision for federal human resource management.[58,59] The plan proposes that the personnel system should assist agencies in recruiting and retaining a work force that serves the public's needs, satisfies the needs of government workers, and helps managers further their agencies' missions. Pay reform, total quality management, the delegation of testing and hiring authority, and the like are seen as individual steps that foster the realization of the vision. An emphasis upon such a vision was fundamental to the Volcker Commission of the 1980s at the federal level and to the National Commission on the State and Local Public Service of the 1990s.[60,61]

Wide-sweeping sets of reforms based upon well-focused visions of the future, however, may not have the essential backing of decision makers and may become interesting collectors of dust on bookshelves rather than blueprints for reforms that are implemented. If such plans are to bring about change, incentives must exist that encourage their adoption and implementation.

A More Radical View

A more radical view of the future is that governments will be confronted with serious personnel problems beyond what have already been discussed and that governments may respond either effectively or ineffectively to these challenges.

The case has been made that by the beginning of the twenty-first century government will find itself in a threatening situation stemming from demographic and technological changes. As was discussed briefly in Chapter 3 with regard to personnel planning, population trends indicate that some of government's most experienced workers will be retiring and that the new work force will be characterized by greater proportions of women, racial and ethnic minorities, and older workers.[62-65] One certainty is that public managers will need to be skilled in handling a far more diversified work force than currently exists (see Chapter 11).[66] In this diversified work setting, managers at a minimum will need to have a flexible approach to managing, or what has been called flex-management.[67]

Major difficulties are projected based on these changes in the composition of the work force and simultaneous changes in the nature of jobs, namely that they will become increasingly technical and will require increased levels of knowledge, skills, and abilities.[68] Government will need fewer employees with only a high school education and more with undergraduate and advanced degrees. The crunch results from presumably lower-qualified workers entering the job market to replace higher-qualified workers. The number of government positions is expected to grow at about the national growth rate or slightly higher, so that any presumed gap between the need for workers and their availability will not be closed by a decreased demand for workers.[69] The problem has been seen as sufficiently severe to warrant possibly rewriting immigration laws to allow greater numbers of well-trained workers into the country.[70]

Not everyone adheres to this threatening forecast. Shortages may not be as severe as predicted as a result of erroneous assumptions made in projecting census data and economic adjustments in the labor market. As the federal government reduces its military strength and reduces its purchase of military hardware and services from the private sector, many highly skilled workers will be dislocated and will be available for government employment. Critics also suggest that the projections about the increased complexity of government work are overstated, namely that although government jobs will gain in complexity the pace will be slower than many expect.[71]

If the projected threats to an available labor pool become reality, will government respond effectively, and in what ways? When government is unable to fill positions because of a lack of qualified applicants, pressures will mount for strategies to cope with shortages. Similarly, breakdowns in government services and poor quality of services, when caused by low-skilled workers, will serve as incentives for reform. At least two general types of response are possible. Government may selectively focus upon segments of the personnel system that will increase its ability to recruit and retain employees. Second, government may take a more far-reaching approach and engage not in reforms but in a revolution in personnel management systems.

The first approach entails making changes in recruiting and retaining employees. Techniques include making testing procedures more flexible so that qualified candidates need not wait months after a test before learning their test scores and being offered positions. Raising salary and wage levels to be more competitive with those in the private sector would be essential. The federal government's shift to locality-based pay for white collar workers is seen as an important step in increasing its competitiveness in attracting professional employees. Improved benefits packages, including liberalized parental leave policies, will increase the attractiveness of government employment. Government may increase its efforts to provide on-site childcare services for employees.[72] Training will be used more extensively in an effort to train existing workers for jobs that might go unfilled for lack of qualified applicants.

The second approach involves radical rethinking and reorienting of personnel systems and the governments that they are supposed to serve. One line of thinking is that bureaucracy has in some respects outlived its utility and that the challenges of today and tomorrow require a more fluid organizational configuration. This perspective, then, cannot support rigid personnel systems that are bound in red tape. Most aspects of contemporary personnel systems would need to be substantially revised and in many instances abandoned. In a nonbureaucratic organization, the classification of jobs into types of jobs and series of jobs would be a pointless exercise. Advocates of reform, such as Osborne and Gaebler, who have called for "reinventing government," suggest that government needs to foster entrepreneurship, which emphasizes customer service, a key concern of total quality management.[73] Whereas bureaucratic systems emphasize rules, reformed government agencies emphasize serving their missions.

Empowering agencies and their employees to take actions necessary in fulfilling their missions is endemic to reformed systems. Empowerment is seen as an important stimulant for employee motivation and innovation.[74] Fewer management controls and greater decentralization are required, both of which run counter to existing personnel systems. Emphasis is placed on holding employees and managers accountable for the performance of their units, and less attention is provided to following rigid rules, as in the case of personnel systems. In what Boyett and Conn have called "Workplace 2000," employees must be allowed to take charge.[75]

In addition to empowerment, competition is fundamental in a reformed workplace. Government workers cannot assume that their agencies will provide services because an alternative is to contract with private firms for service delivery. Agencies are expected to think of citizens as customers who must be sought out, just as for any private corporation, which thrives on being able to attract customers.[76] To compete effectively, government agencies must increase their efficiency through better utilization of resources, including the use of personnel. Frequent training and updating of workers is essential in a competitive environment.[77] In this new environment, workers may be financially rewarded based upon their individual performances or, as in the case of total quality management, based upon group productivity.

CLOSING COMMENT

The early personnel reformers had a cause. They looked forward to the day, as Carl Schurz put it in 1896, "when a change of party in the national Administration will no longer present the barbarous spectacle of a spoils debauch, torturing the nostrils of our own people and disgracing the Republic in the eyes of civilized mankind."[78] The cause of eliminating patronage continues, but, as has been seen, there are many other values that influence public personnel systems. These values are not totally compatible with each other and reflect a lack of consensus about how government should operate. The future of public personnel systems is uncertain because the outcomes of the struggle over values is uncertain.

Because values vary throughout society, it seems inappropriate to propose a single set of recommendations for future personnel systems. One model system could not serve the varying needs of all jurisdictions. The federal government, for instance, has replaced the civil service commission model, but that still may be effective for many state and local governments. Some jurisdictions may be able to loosen controls on political participation by government workers, whereas others that took such action would be inviting a return to political patronage.

The future obviously will bring change in public personnel systems, but what changes and for what ends are unclear. Condemning the practices of personnel administration can be great sport, but developing workable solutions to perceived problems is a formidable task.

NOTES

1. Study Committee on Policy Management Assistance, *Strengthening Public Management in the Intergovernmental System* (Washington: U.S. Government Printing Office, 1975), 23.

2. W.S. Sayre, The triumph of techniques over purpose, *Public Administration Review* 8 (1948): 134–137.

3. R.P. Biller, Where do we go from here? *Public Personnel Management* 12 (1983): 225–231.

4. R. Townsend, *Up the Organization: How To Stop the Corporation from Stifling People and Strangling Profits,* rev. ed. (Greenwich, Conn.: Fawcett Crest, 1971), 126–127.

5. S.K. Straus, Multiple constituencies activities and standards: A framework for evaluating the effectiveness of public personnel departments, *Review of Public Personnel Administration* 11 (Fall 1990–Spring 1991): 55–70.

6. D.E. Klinger and J. Nalbandian, Personnel management by whose objectives? *Public Administration Review* 38 (1978): 366.

7. C. Schurz, *The Spoils System* (Philadelphia: Altemus, 1896), 43.

8. P.W. Ingraham and J. White, The design of civil service reform: Lessons in politics and rationality, *Policy Studies Journal* 17 (1988–89): 315–330.

9. Attributed to Petronius, Arbiter of Bithynia, ca. 66, *Public Administration Review* 33 (1973): 335.

10. W.D. Heisel, Alternatives to traditional civil service, *Public Personnel Management* 12 (1983): 277–281.

11. P.W. Ingraham and D.H. Rosenbloom, eds., *The Promise and Paradox of Civil Service Reform* (Pittsburgh, Pa.: University of Pittsburgh Press, 1992).

12. D.H. Rosenbloom, with M.M. Emmet, eds., *Centenary Issues of the Pendleton Act of 1883* (New York: Marcel Dekker, 1982).

13. U.S. General Accounting Office, *The Public Service: Issues Affecting Its Quality, Effectiveness, Integrity, and Stewardship* (Washington: U.S. Government Printing Office, 1989).

14. _____, *The Public Service: Issues Affecting Its Quality.*

15. _____, *The Public Service: Issues Confronting the Federal Civilian Workforce* (Washington: U.S. Government Printing Office, 1992).

16. F.C. Mosher, *Democracy and the Public Service,* 2d ed. (New York: Oxford University Press, 1982).

17. J.P. Burke, *Bureaucratic Responsibility* (Baltimore, Md.: Johns Hopkins University Press, 1986).

18. J.L. Perry, "Challenges Confronting Public Administrators," in *Handbook of Public Administration*, ed. J.L. Perry (San Francisco: Jossey-Bass, 1989), 3–10.

19. C.J. Friedrich, "Responsible Government Service under the American Constitution," in *Problems of the American Public Service*, ed. C.J. Friedrich, et al. (New York: McGraw-Hill Book Company, 1935), 28.

20. U.S. Commission on Federal Paperwork, *Final Summary Report* (Washington: U.S. Government Printing Office, 1977).

21. H. Kaufman, The direction of organizational evolution, *Public Administration Review* 33 (1973): 300–307.

22. _____, *Red Tape: Its Origins, Uses, and Abuses* (Washington: Brookings Institution, 1977).

23. Municipal Manpower Commission, *Governmental Manpower for Tomorrow's Cities* (New York: McGraw-Hill Book Company, 1962), 106.

24. W. Wilson, The study of administration, *Political Science Quarterly* 2 (1887): 197–222.

25. F.E. Rourke, Responsiveness and neutral competence in American bureaucracy, *Public Administration Review* 52 (1992): 539–546.

26. H. Heclo, *A Government of Strangers: Executive Politics in Washington* (Washington: Brookings Institution, 1977).

27. P. Lorentzen, Stress in political-career executive relations, *Public Administration Review* 45 (1985): 411–414.

28. P.P. Van Riper, *History of the United States Civil Service* (Evanston, Ill.: Row, Peterson & Company, 1958), 554.

29. Committee for Economic Development, *Revitalizing the Federal Personnel System* (New York: Committee for Economic Development, 1978), 5.

30. D.H. Rosenbloom, Some political implications of the drift toward a liberation of federal employees, *Public Administration Review* 31 (1971): 420–426.

31. U.S. General Accounting Office, *Employee Conduct Standards: Some Outside Activities Present Conflict-of-Interest Issues* (Washington: U.S. Government Printing Office, 1992).

32. H. Kahn, et al.; *The Next 200 Years* (New York: William Morrow & Company, 1976).

33. *Futures Research Quarterly*.

34. H. Rosen, *Servants of the People: The Uncertain Future of the Federal Civil Service* (Salt Lake City, Utah: Olympus, 1985).

35. P.W. Ingraham and D.H. Rosenbloom, Political foundations of the American federal service: Rebuilding a crumbling base, *Public Administration Review* 50 (1990): 210–219.

36. U.S. General Accounting Office, *Organizational Culture: Techniques Companies Use To Perpetuate or Change Beliefs and Values* (Washington: U.S. Government Printing Office, 1992).

37. _____, *Federal Labor Relations: A Program in Need of Reform* (Washington: U.S. Government Printing Office, 1991).

38. F. Gottfried, *The Merit System and Municipal Civil Service: A Fostering of Social Inequality* (New York: Greenwood, 1988).

39. P.W. Ingraham and D.H. Rosenbloom, with J.P. Knight, *The State of Merit in the Federal Government* (Washington: National Commission on the Public Service, 1990).

40. F.C. Thayer, The president's management "reforms": Theory X triumphant, *Public Administration Review* 38 (1978): 309–314.

41. A.M. Schlesinger, *The Disuniting of America* (New York: Norton, 1992).

42. L. Thurow, *Head to Head: The Coming Economic Battle among Japan, Europe, and America* (New York: Morrow, 1992).

43. H. Kahn and B. Bruce-Briggs, *Things To Come* (New York: Macmillan, 1972), 39–40.

44. C.H. Levine, The federal government in the year 2000: Administrative legacies of the Reagan years, *Public Administration Review* 46 (1986): 195–206.

45. A.C. Hyde and G.R. Gilbert, eds., Productivity improvement in the public sector, special issue, *Public Personnel Management* 14 (1985): 319–454.

46. T. Hunt, Futurism and futurists in personnel, *Public Personnel Management* 13 (1984): 511–520.

47. U.S. General Accounting Office, *Federal Employment: How Federal Employees View the Government as a Place To Work* (Washington: U.S. Government Printing Office, 1992).

48. National Commission on the Public Service, *Leadership for America* (Washington: the Commission, 1989).

49. A. Toffler, *Future Shock* (New York: Bantam, 1971).

50. D. Waldo, *The Administrative State: A Study of the Political Theory of American Public Administration* (New York: The Ronald, 1984).

51. _____, The administrative state revisited, *Public Administration Review* 25 (1965): 5–30.

52. R. Michels, *Political Parties: A Sociological Study of the Oligarchical Tendencies of Modern Democracy,* trans. E. Paul and C. Paul (Glencoe, Ill.: Free Press, 1949).

53. W.G. Scott, The theory of significant people, *Public Administration Review* 33 (1973): 308–313.

54. R. Theobald, *An Alternative Future for America* (Chicago, Ill.: Swallow, 1970), 76–83.

55. V.A. Thompson, *Modern Organization: A General Theory* (New York: Knopf, 1962).

56. B. Rosen, Crises in the U.S. civil service, *Public Administration Review* 46 (1986): 207–214.

57. L.M. Lane and J.F. Wolf, *The Human Resource Crisis in the Public Sector* (New York: Quorum, 1990).

58. U.S. General Accounting Office, *Managing Human Resources: Greater OPM Leadership Needed To Address Critical Challenges* (Washington: U.S. Government Printing Office, 1989).

59. U.S. Office of Personnel Management, *Strategic Plan for Federal Human Resources Management* (Washington: U.S. Government Printing Office, 1990).

60. National Commission on the Public Service, *Leadership for America.*

61. The National Commission on the State and Local Public Service is chaired by William F. Winter and is located at the Nelson A. Rockefeller Institute of Government at the State University of New York, Albany.

62. Hudson Institute for U.S. Department of Labor, *Workforce 2000* (Washington: U.S. Government Printing Office, 1987).

63. Hudson Institute for U.S. Office of Personnel Management, *Civil Service 2000* (Washington: U.S. Government Printing Office, 1988).

64. R.S. Fosler, et al., *Demographic Change and the American Future* (Pittsburgh, Pa.: University of Pittsburgh Press, 1990).

65. U.S. General Accounting Office, *The Changing Workforce: Demographic Issues Facing Employers* (Washington: U.S. Government Printing Office, 1992).

66. C.E. Teasley, III, and L. Williams, The future is nearly now: Managing personnel in the twenty-first century, *Review of Public Personnel Administration* 11 (Fall 1990–Spring 1991): 131–138.

67. D. Jamieson and J. O'Mara, *Managing Workforce 2000* (San Francisco: Jossey-Bass, 1991).

68. B. Wooldridge and J. Webster, The turbulent environment of public personnel administration: Responding to the challenge of the changing workplace of the twenty-first century, *Public Personnel Management* 20 (1991): 207–224.

69. R.E. Kutscher, New BLS projections: Findings and implications, *Monthly Labor Review* 114 (November 1991): 3–12.

70. B. Dicken and R. Blomberg, Immigrants—Can they provide the future labor force? *Public Personnel Management* 20 (1991): 91–100.

71. U.S. General Accounting Office, *The Changing Workforce: Demographic Issues Facing the Federal Government* (Washington: U.S. Government Printing Office, 1992).

72. _____, *The Changing Workforce: Comparison of Federal and Nonfederal Work/Family Programs and Approaches* (Washington: U.S. Government Printing Office, 1992).

73. D. Osborne and T. Gaebler, *Reinventing Government: How the Entrepreneurial Spirit Is Transforming the Public Sector* (Reading, Mass.: Addison-Wesley Publishing Company, 1992).

74. R.M. Kanter, "The New Workforce Meets the Changing Workplace," in *Personnel Practices for the '90s: A Local Government Guide,* ed J. Matzer, Jr. (Washington: International City Management Association, 1988), 34–55.

75. J.H. Boyett and H.B. Conn, *Workplace 2000: The Revolution Reshaping American Business* (New York: Dutton, 1991).

76. C. Pollitt, *Managerialism and the Public Services: The Anglo-American Experience* (Oxford: Basil Blackwell, 1990).

77. J.F. Coates, et al., *Future Work: Seven Critical Forces Reshaping Work and the Work Force in North America* (San Francisco: Jossey-Bass, 1990).

78. Schurz, *The Spoils System,* 46–47.

A Research Guide
to Personnel Literature

Aside from the subject portion of a library's central catalog, there are numerous sources that can be helpful in researching public personnel systems. This guide is designed to provide assistance in locating relevant materials. A traditional form of bibliography is not included here because the preceding chapters are footnoted extensively.

Several periodicals are of general use. *Public Personnel Management* (Washington: International Personnel Management Association) and *Review of Public Personnel Administration* (Columbia: University of South Carolina and Section on Personnel Administration and Labor Relations of the American Society for Public Administration) contain articles pertinent to all aspects of public personnel.

More general periodicals that frequently contain articles about personnel include *Public Administration Review* (Washington: American Society for Public Administration), *Journal of Policy Analysis and Management* (New York: John Wiley & Sons and Association for Public Policy Analysis and Management), *Spectrum* (formerly *State Government*; Lexington, Ky.: Council of State Governments), and *Public Management* (Washington: International City/County Management Association).

Other periodicals are geared to specific aspects of personnel, including the *Journal of Applied Psychology, Administrative Science Quarterly, Academy of Management Journal, Academy of Management Review,* and *Labor Law Journal,* to name only a few.

Perusing each of these journals to locate articles would be excessively time consuming. Therefore, the following indexes should be used: *Psychological Abstracts* (Washington: American Psychological Association), *Public Affairs Information Service Bulletin* (New York: Public Affairs Information Service), *Sage Public Administration Abstracts* (Beverly Hills, Calif.: Sage Publications,

Inc.), *Social Sciences Citation Index* (Philadelphia: Institute for Scientific Information), and *Social Sciences Index* (New York: H.W. Wilson).

Some annual or biennial references on state and local governments contain chapters on personnel. These include the *Book of the States* (Lexington, Ky.: Council of State Governments), which is issued every 2 years, and the *Municipal Yearbook* (Washington: International City/County Management Association).

Numerous federal documents can provide important information. Two reference works that explain government documents are L.F. Schmeckebier and R.B. Eastin's *Government Publications and Their Use*, 2d rev. ed. (Washington: Brookings Institution, 1969), and J. Morehead and M. Fetzer's *Introduction to United States Government Information Sources* (Englewood, Colo.: Libraries Unlimited, 1992). *Public Employment,* compiled annually by the Census Bureau, is an excellent source of current data on workers at all levels of government. The Office of Personnel Management and the Merit Systems Protection Board provide many useful reports, as do the Department of Labor and the General Accounting Office.

Several indexes are available for locating government reports: the *Monthly Catalog of United States Government Publications* (Washington: U.S. Government Printing Office), *Index to U.S. Government Periodicals* (Chicago: Infordata International), and *Congressional Information Service Index* (Bethesda, Md.: Congressional Information Service). The *American Statistics Index* (Congressional Information Service) is useful for locating data in government documents. *Government Reports Announcements and Index* (U.S. Department of Commerce, National Technical Information Service) indexes many reports that have been prepared for federal agencies but not published. These can be obtained in photocopy form.

Computer-based CD-ROMs (compact disk–read only memory) facilitate research. Congressional publications can be searched through *Congressional Masterfile* (Congressional Information Service), and statistics can be located through *Statistical Masterfile* (Congressional Information Service). Indexes mentioned above that are available on CD-ROMs include the *Monthly Catalog of United States Government Publications, Public Affairs Information Service Bulletin, Social Sciences Citation Index,* and *Social Sciences Index.* Other CD-ROMs are available for more specialized areas of research.

This book has emphasized legal aspects of public personnel systems because courts are assuming increasingly important roles in these systems. For the uninitiated, legal research may seem frightening, but it need not be. Two useful guides to legal research are M.L. Cohen and K.C. Olson's *Legal Research in a Nutshell*, 5th ed. (St. Paul, Minn.: West, 1992) and J.M. Jacobstein and R.M. Mersky's *Fundamentals of Legal Research*, 4th ed. (Mineola, N.Y.: Foundation Press, 1991). These books identify the main legal research tools and explain how to use them. For help understanding legal terminology, consult

D. Oran's *Law Dictionary for Nonlawyers*, 2d ed. (St. Paul, Minn.: West, 1985) or H.C. Black's *Black's Law Dictionary*, 5th ed. (St. Paul, Minn.: West, 1979).

If one is exploring a legal aspect of personnel for the first time, a place to begin is a summarization of the issues. Journal articles are helpful in identifying leading court cases. To locate appropriate articles, use the *Index to Legal Periodicals* (New York: Wilson). That index has not only subject entries but also court case entries; in other words, if a particular case is of interest, the index can be used to locate articles that interpret the case. *Corpus Juris Secundum* (St. Paul, Minn.: West) is a massive legal encyclopedia that is updated annually.

Laws also need to be researched. U.S. laws are published in their original form in the *United States Statutes at Large* (Washington: U.S. Government Printing Office). The Pendleton Act can be cited as 22 Stat. 403 (1883), with the first number being the volume and the second number the page. This is a common form of legal citation. The utility of the *Statutes at Large* is limited because the original legislation may have been amended numerous times. Therefore, to locate the current governing legislation, use the *United States Code* (Washington: U.S. Government Printing Office). This multivolume reference codifies federal statutes; in other words, statutes are arranged by subject matter. Even more useful sources are the *United States Code Annotated* (St. Paul, Minn.: West) and the *United States Code Service* (Rochester, N.Y.: Lawyers Cooperative), which follow the same format of the *U.S. Code* but in addition provide citations of court cases that interpret the legislation. Citations for the code follow a format similar to other legal citations. The title is abbreviated "U.S.C.," for the code itself, "U.S.C.A.," for the annotated code, and "U.S.C.S." for the code service. One difference in citing the code is that a section number, rather than a page number, is used; the symbol "§" precedes the number. Similar reference works on state laws are available for each state.

Administrative agencies issue regulations that interpret the legislation being enforced. At the federal level, proposed and final regulations are published in the *Federal Register*, cited as "Fed. Reg.," which is issued Monday through Friday. Once regulations are adopted, they are incorporated into the *Code of Federal Regulations*, cited as "C.F.R."

The federal government has three main levels of courts. District courts are the lowest level, and their opinions are printed in the *Federal Supplement* (St. Paul, Minn.: West) and cited as "F.Supp." The next level is the circuit courts of appeal, whose opinions can be found in the *Federal Reporter* (St. Paul, Minn.: West) cited as "F.2d," with the "2d" for second series (the first "F" series encompassed the years 1880 to 1912).

U.S. Supreme Court opinions are published in four series. The federal government prints the *United States Reports*, which is cited as "U.S." This citation has been used throughout this book except for the most recent cases, where the "U.S." citation was unavailable. In those instances, the *Supreme Court*

Reporter (St. Paul, Minn.: West) has been used; those cases have "S.Ct." citations. The third source is the *United States Supreme Court Reports: Lawyers' Edition* (Rochester, N.Y.: Lawyers Co-operative), cited as "L.Ed.2d." Both the *Supreme Court Reporter* and the *Lawyers' Edition* contain helpful research aids that are not included in the *United States Reports*. *United States Law Week* (Washington: Bureau of National Affairs) provides Supreme Court opinions and reports on other courts' decisions as well.

Important state court decisions can be found through a series of regional reporters (St. Paul, Minn.: West). The *Pacific Reporter*, for example, contains opinions from courts in Arizona, California, Colorado, and several other states. The *Atlantic Reporter* provides opinions from Maryland, New Jersey, Pennsylvania, and other states.

Several digests compile court decisions by subject. *West's General Digest* is now in its seventh series. The *Tenth Decennial Digest* (St. Paul, Minn.: West) covers 1986 to 1991. Other digests are available for the regional reporters.

Keeping up to date in the legal field can be accomplished through several sources. Reading current articles from legal periodicals is helpful. If one wants to determine the current status of a court case that was decided a few years ago, *Shepard's Citations* (Colorado Springs, Colo.: Shepard's) would be used. *Shepard's* indicates whether a lower court decision was appealed and identifies other court opinions that have cited the case that is of interest. It also identifies court cases as they pertain to sections of the U.S. code. *Shepard's Citations* are available for the regional reporters mentioned above.

The *Government Employee Relations Report* (Washington: Bureau of National Affairs) is issued weekly and is especially helpful for public sector labor–management relations law as well as for other personnel-related legal topics.

Happy reading!

Index

A

Accountability, employee, 217–228
Acquired immunodeficiency syndrome
  (AIDS), 120, 205, 249
Adams, John, 17
Adams, John Quincy, 18
Adler, A., 285–286
Administrative Careers with America
  (ACWA), 118
Administrative, professional, and technical
  employees (APT), 51–52, 67, 77, 111
Administrative class, British, 176–177
Adult life, phases of, 334
Adverse actions, 221–228
Affirmative action, 264–272
  definition, 265
  goals and quotas, 267–270
  plans, 265
  promotions and, 269
  testing and selection, 266
Age, 240–243, 253–254, 263
  See Discrimination
Age Discrimination in Employment Act, 249,
  260, 263
Agency shop, 361
Air traffic controllers, 365
Alcohol abuse. See Employee assistance
  programs
Alderfer, C.P., 290
American Association of Collegiate Schools
  of Business (AACSB), 11
American Federation of Government
  Employees (AFGE), 349–350, 352, 354

American Federation of Labor—Congress of
  Industrial Organizations (AFL-CIO),
  348–349
American Federation of State, County, and
  Municipal Employees (AFSCME),
  258–259, 350, 353
American Federation of Teachers (AFT),
  350–351
American Postal Workers Union (APWU), 349
American Society for Public Administration,
  12, 198
Americans with Disabilities Act, 249
Arbitration
  final offer, 368
  grievance or rights, 370–373
  interest, 367–369
Ardrey, R., 287
Argyris, C., 290–291
Arthur, Chester, 20
Assertiveness training, 327
Assessment centers, 126
Association for Public Policy Analysis and
  Management (APPAM), 12
Australia and promotions, 172
Authority, delegation of, 306
Autonomy and worker, 303–311

B

Back pay, 248
Back Pay Act, 225–226
Background investigations, 120
Bakke case, 269
Bales, R.F., 314

411

Barnard, C.I., 316–317
Bayett, J.H., 331–332
Behaviorally anchored rating scales (BARS), 151–152
Behaviorism, 295–297
Behaviors, 148
Benefits, 88–102
    See Discrimination
    family-related, 99–100
    financial security, 99
    fringe, 88
    health, 90–93
    holidays, 89
    other, 100–101
    retirement and death, 93–99
    sick leave, 91
    vacation, 90
    work hours and work days and, 89–90
Benne, K.D., 325
Berne, E., 286, 327
Bishop v. Wood, 226
Bivens v. Six Unknown Named Agents of the Federal Bureau of Narcotics, 219
Blake, R.R., 318
Blue Cross-Blue Shield, 92
Board of Regents v. Roth, 226
Bona fide occupational qualification (bfoq), 253-254, 263
Bonuses, 160, 179, 304
Bottom line, selection and, 252
Bottom up, organizational design, 43–44
Bowen v. U.S. Postal Service, 371
Boyett, J.H., 401
Bradshaw, J., 327
Branti v. Finkel, 23
British career service, 176–177
Buckley Amendment, 116
Budgeting, 21, 30–31, 51, 68, 77, 183, 310, 320, 363, 377, 386, 395–396
Bumping rights, 221
Bureaucracy
    growth of, 4–9
    role of, 389–394
Burnout, 333–334
Bush, George and Bush administration, 217, 220, 248, 259, 270, 362

C

Campbell, A.K., 33–34
Careers and career development, 169–194
    See Training
    definition, 169–170
    executive careers, 175–181
    mobility, 172–174
    plateauing, 174
    position classification and, 50
Carter, Jimmy, 29, 110, 128, 246, 250, 352, 391
Carter Reorganization Plan, 245
Centralization/decentralization, 310, 321
Certification of candidates, 130, 132
Chief Financial Officers Act, 200
China Lake pay experiment, 60, 160–161
Citizen involvement, 217–220
Citizenship, 254–255
City of Richmond v. J.A. Croson Company, 269
Civil rights, 209–217
    freedom of speech, 212–215
    loyalty and security, 209–212
    political activity, 215–217
Civil Rights Acts, 219, 222, 244–245, 248–249, 251–252, 258–259, 261, 264, 268
Civil Rights Commission, 251, 270
Civil Rights Restoration Act, 249
Civil service commission, 28–30, 37, 215
Civil service reform, early period, 20–22
Civil Service Reform Act, 25, 27, 35, 60, 85, 97, 156, 158, 178–181, 214–215, 223, 245–247, 250, 265, 348, 352, 359–360, 367, 371, 391
Civil Service Retirement Law, 94
Classification Acts, 51
Clinton, Bill and Clinton administration, 92, 201, 221, 254, 270
Coch, L., 325
Cognitive dissonance theory, 294
Collective bargaining, 31
    See also Labor-management relations; Unions
    bargaining process, 358–365
    community of interest, 356
    contract administration, 369–373
    election process, 357–358
    impact of, 373–377
    impasses, 365–369
    management rights, 360
    managing under, 369–377
    pay and, 360–361, 363–364, 373–374
    preliminary steps (bargaining units), 354–358

processes, 353–369
professional and confidential employees, 356
unit determination, 354–357
Commission of Inquiry on Public Service Personnel, 177
Committee for Economic Development, 391
Comparable worth, 258–259, 397
Compensation
    See Benefits; Salaries and wages
    public and private compared, 101–102
Competition, public and private, 2
Competition in Contracting Act, 200
Complement control, 31
Compressed work schedules, 305–307
Computer adaptive testing, 118
Computers, 66
Conditioning. *See* Motivation
Conduct (standards of). *See* Ethics
Conflict in organizations, 334
Conflict of interest, 198–199, 359
Congress, 197, 200
Congress of Industrial Organizations, 349
Conn, H.P., 331–332, 401
Connecticut v. Teal, 252
Construct validity, 124
Content validity, 121–122
Contingency theory, 318–319
Continuous quality improvement. *See* Total quality management
Contracting out. *See* Privatization
Cornelius, L., 196–197
Corruption, 196–197
Council of State Governments, 12, 186
County of Washington v. Gunther, 258
Covey, S.R., 319
Credentialism, 115
Criterion-related validity, 122–124
Critical elements, 149, 154, 159

D

Decentralization, 310, 321
Delphi technique, 67
Deming, W.E., 329–330
Desk audit, 55
Devine, D., 34, 196–197
Dies, M., 209
Difficult people, 334
Direct hire authority, 113
Disabilities, 243, 245, 249, 267

Disability insurance and retirement, 92–93
Discipline procedures. *See* Adverse actions
Discrimination
    See also Affirmative action
    adverse action and, 225
    adverse impact, 252
    age, 249, 253–254, 263
    back pay, 264
    bona fide occupational qualification (bfoq), 253–254
    bottom line, 252
    comparable worth, 258–259, 397
    handicapping condition, 243, 245, 249, 267
    height and weight requirements, 253
    intergovernmental relations, 249–250
    military and, 254, 259–260, 263–264
    on the job, 256–261
    performance evaluation and, 256
    position classification and, 59
    pregnancy, 260
    prima facie case, 252
    promotions and, 256
    race, 268–272
    reasonable woman and, 257
    religion and, 259, 261–262
    retirement, 260–261
    selection and, 251–255
    seniority and, 264–265
    sex, 248–249, 253–254, 262–263, 270–272
    terminations, 261–264
    testing and, 251–252
Dismissal. *See* Adverse actions
    probation and, 143–144
Diversity in work force, 335
    See Affirmative action
Dothard v. Rawlinson, 253
Double dippers, 175
Dress codes, 204–205
Drive theory, 292–293
Drucker, P.F., 320
Drug abuse. *See* Employee assistance programs
    termination and, 262
Drug-Free Workplace Act, 206
Due Process. *See* Fifth Amendment, Fourteenth Amendment

E

Economic Stabilization Act, 88
Economy and efficiency movement, 51

Education. *See* Position classification; Training
Education Amendments, 248–249, 257
Education requirement, discrimination and, 253
Effectiveness and efficiency, 396
Ego, 285, 327
Eisenhower, Dwight and Eisenhower administration, 177–178, 197, 210
Eligibility list, 129–130
Ellsberg, D., 214
Elrod v. Burns, 22–23
Employee accountability, 217–228
Employee assistance programs, 91, 206
Employee Polygraph Protection Act, 120, 205
Employee Retirement Income Security Act, 97, 260
Employee rights and responsibilities, 195–238, 392–393
  See Reduction in force
  Adverse actions, 221–228
  Direct accountability, 217–220
  Ethical standards, off the job, 207–209
  Ethical standards, on the job, 195–204
  Freedom of speech, 212–215
  Government demands of employees, 204–207
  Loyalty and security, 209–212
  Political activities, 215–217
Employment cost index, 83
Equal employment opportunity, 31, 239–281
  See Affirmative action
  Discrimination in personnel administration, 250–264
  Minorities, women, and older workers, 240–243
  Outlawing discrimination, 243–250
Equal Employment Opportunity Act, 245, 247–248
Equal Employment Opportunity Commission (EEOC), 33, 246–248, 251, 256, 265, 272, 372
Equal pay. *See* Salaries and wages; Discrimination
Equal Pay Act, 258
Equal protection. *See* Fourteenth Amendment
Equity theory, 310
ERG theory, 290
Ergonomics, 48, 303
Estate of Thornton v. Caldor, 261

Ethics, 195–209, 335
  capricious and arbitrary behavior, 201
  codes and standards of conduct, 198–199
  conflicts of standards, 202–203
  loyalty to political administration, 203–204
  off the job, 207–209
  public and private, 2–3
  testing and, 117
Ethics in Government Act, 198, 200
Ethics Reform Act, 198, 209
Exchange theory, 294
Examination. *See* Testing
Executive, political and career, 175–176
  See Political leaders; Senior Executive Service
Executive class, British, 176–177
Executive level, 23, 79, 86, 180
Executive orders
  642, 215
  10450, 210
  10988, 348, 352
  11246, 245, 250
  11375, 245
  11478, 245
  11491, 353
  11838, 352, 356
  11935, 255
  12086, 250
  12564, 206
  12674, 198
  12778, 220
  12800, 362
  12834, 199
Expectancy theory, 141–142, 293–294
Experience requirement, discrimination and, 253

F

Factfinding, 366–367
Factor evaluation system (FES), 53, 55, 258
Fair Labor Standards Act (FLSA), 87
Family and Medical Leave Act, 100
Family Educational Rights and Privacy Act, 116
Fatigue, 303
Featherbedding, 19
Federal Election Campaign Act Amendments, 216
Federal Employees Compensation Act (FECA), 92

Federal Employees Liability Reform and Tort Compensation Act, 220
Federal Employees Pay Comparability Act, 83–86, 131, 161
Federal Employees Retirement System (FERS), 98–99
Federal Executive Institute (FEI), 185–186
Federal executive service, 178
Federal Labor Relations Authority (FLRA), 33, 37, 157–158, 349, 352, 354–357, 359, 361, 366, 371–372, 376, 389
Federal Labor Relations Council, 352
Federal Managers' Financial Integrity Act, 200
Federal Mediation and Conciliation Service (FMCS), 33, 366
Federal Occupational and Career Information System (FOCIS), 112
Federal Pay Comparability Act, 82
Federal Political Personnel Manual, 29
Federal Prevailing Rate Advisory Committee, 84
Federal Salary Reform Act, 82
Federal Service Entrance Examination, 117
Federal Service Impasses Panel (FSIP), 33, 366–367
Federal Tort Claims Act, 219–220
Feedback, 326, 330
  survey, 327–328
Festinger, L., 294
Fiedler, F.E., 318–319
Field theory, 313
Fifth Amendment, 211, 226–228, 243–244, 251, 259–260
Final average salary, 94
Financial disclosure, 199
First Amendment, 22–23, 211, 216, 218, 226–228, 361–362, 365
Fitzgerald, E., 214, 219
Flexiplace, 307–308
Flexitime, 305–308
Foley v. Connelie, 255
Ford, Gerald, 217, 352, 356
Forecasting. *See* Future; Planning
Foreign Service, 177
Fourteenth Amendment, 22–23, 211, 218, 226–228, 243–244, 251, 268–269, 361–362
Freedom of Information Act (FOIA), 217
Freedom of speech, 212–215
French, J.R.P., 316, 325

Freud, S., 285–286, 294
Fringe benefits. *See* Benefits
Frontiero v. Richardson, 259–260
Fry v. United States, 88
Fulton Committee, British, 176
Future, 331, 394–401

G

Gaebler, T., 332, 401
Gainsharing, 81, 161
Garcia v. San Antonio Metropolitan Transit Authority, 87, 97–98, 353
Garfield, James, 20
General Accounting Office (GAO), 30, 33–34, 199, 206, 215, 355, 358
General Management (GM). *See* Performance Management and Recognition Systems
General Schedule (GS), 53, 77, 79–82, 240–243, 349
Gilbreth, F. and L., 47
Glass Ceiling Commission, 248
Goal setting, 321
Goals, affirmative action and, 267–270
Gompers, S., 348
Government Employees Training Act, 182
Government Finance Officers Association (GFOA), 186
Government in the Sunshine Act, 217–218
Grade creep and grade inflation, 59, 80
Grant, Ulysses, 20
Grievance procedures, 225
Griffenhagen, E.O., 50
Griggs v. Duke Power Company, 251
Griswold v. Connecticut, 208
Groups, 294, 311–319
  cohesiveness and, 314–315
  goals and, 314
  groupthink and, 314
  individual members and, 315
  leaders and leadership, 316–319
  quality circles and, 323–324

H

Hackman, J.R., 309
Hafer, B., 220
Haircuts, 181
Halo effect, 155
Hampton v. Wong, 254–255

Handicapping condition, 243, 245, 249, 267
Harrison, William Henry, 18, 20
Hatch Political Activities Acts, 22, 210,
    215–216, 229, 348, 374
Hawthorne studies and effect, 288–289, 312
Health insurance. See Benefits
Health maintenance organizations (HMOs),
    92
Heider, F., 294–295
Height and weight requirements, 253
Herzberg, F., 291–292, 308–309
Hierarchy of human needs, 289–290. See also
    Maslow
Hill, A., 257
Hiring goals and quotas. See Discrimination
Homans, G.S., 294, 313
Homosexuality, 208, 250, 254, 262–263
Hoover Commission, First and Second, 177
Horner, C., 60, 259
Hortonville case, 365
Housing and Urban Development, U.S.
    Department of, 197
Hudson Institute, 62–63
Hull, C.L., 292–293
Human relations, 289, 312
Human resources information systems
    (HRIS), 64–66
Hygiene factors, 333. See Herzberg

I

Id, 285, 327
Impasses in collective bargaining, 365–369
Incentive systems, 304
    See Motivation
    management by objectives and, 320–323
    total quality management and, 329–330
Individual achievement record, 118
Inspector General Act, 199
Insurance. See Benefits
Intelligence tests, 116, 251
Interaction process analysis, 314
Intergovernmental Personnel Act (IPA), 26,
    249–250
Intergovernmental relations, 36, 215–216,
    246–250, 393
International Association of Fire Fighters
    (IAFF), 350
International City/County Management
    Association (ICMA), 12, 76, 112, 186, 198

International Personnel Management
    Association (IPMA), 12, 186, 374
Internships, 140–141
Iron law of oligarchy, 316
Ishikawa, K., 329

J

Jackson, Andrew, 18–19
Janis, I.L., 314
Japanese management, 292, 324, 329
Jefferson, Thomas, 215
Jensen, A.R., 288
Job characteristics model of work motivation,
    309
Job classification. See Position classification
Job design, 46–49
    affirmative action and, 266
Job enrichment and enlargement, 308–311
Job information centers, 112
Job interviews, 131
    discrimination and, 255
Job mobility, 172–174
Job performance evaluation. See Performance
    evaluation
Job restructuring, 266–267
Job satisfaction, 304, 311
    compared with motivation, 284
Job security. See Compensation; Reduction in
    force
Job titles, inconsistent usage, 51
Jung, C.G., 285–286
Justice, U.S. Department of, 199, 252

K

Keating Five, 197
Kennedy, John, 348, 352
Kent State University, 220
Knowledge, skills, and abilities, and testing,
    114
Koreagate, 197
Korman, A.K., 295

L

Labor, U.S. Department of, 252
Labor–management relations, 347–383
    See also Collective bargaining; Unions
    benefits and, 96
    states and, 352–353

Labor Statistics, Bureau of, 83
Labor unions. *See* Unions
Lawler, E.E., 293
Lawrence, P.R., 309
Layoffs. *See* Reduction in force
Leaders and leadership, 316–319
Legislative branch and labor–management
  relations, 358
Letter of understanding, 359
Lewin, K., 293, 313, 317, 325
Liability
  employee, 217–220
  government, 217–220, 243–264
Life insurance, 93. *See* Benefits
Likert, R., 318
Lincoln, Abraham, 20
Lippitt, R., 317, 325
Little Hatch Acts, 210, 216
Lloyd-LaFollette Act, 223, 227, 348
Local governments, number of, 6–9
Locke, E.A., 321
Loyalty
  See Civil rights
  to government and country, 209–212
  to political administration, 203–204

M

Madison, James, 200
Maintenance system, 10
Management by objectives (MBO), 183,
  320–323, 329
Management rights, 360
Managerial grid, 318
Marbury v. Madison, 17–18
Marital status, 207
Maslow, A.H., 289–291, 295, 312, 321
Mayo, E., 288–289, 303, 312
McCarthy, J., 209
McGregor, D., 292, 304, 320
Mediation, 366. *See* Collective bargaining
Meet and confer rights, 359. *See* Collective
  bargaining
Merit
  concept of, 25–28
  unions and, 374–375
  violation in selection process, 132
Merit pay, 85–86, 160–162
Merit Pay System, 85, 158

Merit Systems Protection Board (MSPB), 27,
  31–35, 37, 179–180, 214–215, 223–224,
  246, 320, 371–372
Meritor Savings Bank v. Vinson, 257
Michels, R., 316
Michigan Equitable Classification Plan, 239
Milgram, S., 287
Minorities, 240–243, 270–272
  See Race
Mobility, 172–174
Monroe v. Pape, 220
Morris, D., 288
Motion and time studies, 47–48
Motivating potential score (MPS), 309
Motivation, 48, 143, 283–302, 392–393
  See Groups
  attribution theory, 294–295
  cognitive dissonance, 294
  conditioning and, 292
  content theories, 288–292
  daily operations, 303–345
  equity theory, 295
  exchange theory, 294
  expectancy theory, 293–294
  field theory, 293
  flexitime and, 305–308
  human relations, 289
  job enrichment and enlargement and,
    308–311
  job satisfaction and, 284
  leaders and leadership and, 316–319
  operant conditioning, 295–296
  prepotency of needs, 290
  process theories, 292–297
  reinforcement, 296
  self-actualization, 286
  stimulus response, 284–285, 295–296
  valence-instrumentality-expectancy
    (V-I-E), 293
Mouton, J.S., 318
Myers-Briggs type indicators, 315

N

Narcotic effect of arbitration, 368
National Academy of Public Administration
  (NAPA), 53
National Association of Counties (NACo), 12
National Association of Government
  Employees (NAGE), 354

National Association of Letter Carriers (NALC), 349
National Association of Schools of Public Affairs and Administration (NASPAA), 11, 204
National Civil Service League, 29
National Commission on State and Local Public Service, 399
National Commission on the Public Service, 75, 110, 399
National Education Association (NEA), 350–351, 353
National Federation of Federal Employees (NFFE), 349–350, 354
National Labor Relations Board (NLRB), 35, 349, 353
National League of Cities (NLC), 12, 186
National League of Cities v. Usery, 87
National Training Laboratory (NTL), 325
National Treasury Employees Union (NTEU), 349
Navy experiments, 60
Nixon, Richard and Nixon administration, 178, 196, 214, 219, 352
Nord, W.R., 295–296
Norms, groups and, 314

O

Obesity, 250
Occupational Outlook Handbook, 61
Occupational Outlook Quarterly, 60
Odiorne, G., 320
Office of Federal Contract Compliance Programs (OFCCP), 250
Office of Federal Procurement Policy Act Amendments, 200
Office of Government Ethics (OGE), 198–199
Office of Management and Budget (OMB), 30–32, 83
Office of Personnel Management (OPM), 27, 31–35, 37, 52, 83, 111, 140, 157–158, 185–186, 216, 225, 242, 250–251, 265, 320, 326, 376, 399
Official Secrets Act, British, 212
Old Age, Survivors, Disability and Health Insurance (OASDHI), 98
Older workers, 334–335
See Age; Discrimination
Older Workers Benefit Protection Act, 260
Oldham, G.R., 309

Oliver classification system, 56
Ombudsmen, 200
Omnibus Transportation Employees Testing Act, 206
One best way, 46–47
Open shop, 361
Operant conditioning, 315. See Motivation
Organization and management studies, 46
Organization development, 183, 325–328
Organizational change, 319–332
Organizational design, 43–46
Organizational structure, 28–36
Orientation of new workers, 140
Osborne, D., 332, 401
Ouchi, W.G., 292
Overtime, 86

P

Part-time employees, 335, 396
Patronage, 15–24, 397
  compared with private sector, 3
  federal positions, 23–24
  pay and, 77
  pre-patronage era, 16–18
  state and local, 20, 22–23
  strengths and weaknesses, 19–20
Pattern or practice, 247–248
Pavlov, I.P., 292–293
Pay equity. See Comparable worth
Pay-for-Performance Labor-Management Committee, 86
Pendleton Act, 20–22, 215
Pentagon Papers, 214
Performance appraisal. See Performance evaluation
Performance evaluation, 144–160, 322, 386–387, 396
  critical elements, 149
  forms of data for, 148
  halo effect and, 155
  management of, 158–160
  problems, 152–158
  purposes, 144–147
  role of unions, 157–158
  techniques, 147–152
Performance Management and Recognition System (PMRS), 77, 85, 145, 158–160, 162, 389
Performance Rating Act, 149
Perry v. Sindermann, 226

Personality, 284–288
Personnel Administrator of Massachusetts v. Feeney, 254
Personnel administrators, 385–389
Personnel literature, guide to, 407–410
Personnel planning. *See* Planning
Personnel systems. *See* Public personnel systems
Personnel theory, 388. *See* Motivation
Peter principle, 174
Physical examinations, 120
Planning, 60–69
   costs of, 69
   defined, 61
   forecasting personnel requirements, 64–66
   programs and, 67
   year 2000 and, 62–63
Political activity, 208–209, 215–217
   See Hatch Political Activities Acts
Political control, 390
Political leaders/politicians, 3, 11
Political positions. *See* Patronage positions
Political transitions, 24
Polygraph tests, 120, 205
Porter, L.W., 293
Position classification, 49–57, 397–398
   appeals and, 225
   centralization/decentralization, 58–59
   education requirements, 56–57
   experience requirements, 57
   grade creep, 80
   operational problems, 57–60
   reclassification, 132
Postal Service, 364, 371, 376
Power, 307–308
Preferred provider organization (PPO), 92
Pregnancy Discrimination Act, 260
Presidential Management Internship Program (PMIP), 111, 140, 170, 183
Presthus, R., 333
Privacy, right to, 206
Privacy Act, 217
Private sector, compared with private sector, 101–102
Privatization, 45, 66–67, 376
Probation, 139–144
   freedom of speech and, 214
   Senior Executive Service and, 178–179
   socialization theory and, 141
Probst service report, 149
Productivity, 86, 161, 320, 363–364, 392–393

Professional, Administrative, Technical, and Clerical Survey (PATC), 83–84
Professional Air Traffic Controllers Organization (PATCO), 365
Professional and Administrative Career Examination (PACE), 117–118
Promotions, 171–172
   affirmative action and, 266–267
Proposition 13, 221, 374, 395
Prune jobs, 110–111
Public employment
   economy and, 4
   federal, 4–5
   size and growth, 4–9
   state and local, 5–6
Public personnel systems. *See* Future
   bureaucratization of government labor market, 4–9
   compared with private sector systems, 1–4
   complaints frequently made about (negative view), 385–389
   defining boundaries and characteristics of, 9–13
   unresolved issues, 389–394
Public sector, compared with private sector, 1–4, 101–102, 296–297, 322, 331, 335

Q

Quality circle, 323–324
Quality of working life, 324, 376
Quotas, affirmative action and, 267–270

R

Race, 207, 240–243, 288. *See* Discrimination
   norming, 251
Ramspeck Act, 51
Rank in person, 177–178
Rating systems, 148–152
Raven, B.H., 316
Reagan, Ronald and Reagan administration, 34–35, 80, 110, 196–198, 221, 249, 259, 270, 365
Recruitment, 109–114, 396
Red tape, 389–390
Reduction in force (RIF), 76, 88, 145, 172, 181, 221–222, 229, 333, 370
Reform movement, 20–21, 37, 385–388
Regents of the University of California v. Bakke, 269
Rehabilitation Act, 205, 249

Religion. *See* Discrimination
Representative bureaucracy, 393
Requisite task attribute index, 309
Research Center for Group Dynamics, 325
Residency requirements, 207, 255
Retention, 113–114
Retirement Equity Act, 260
Retirement plans
  See also Benefits
  end of career and, 175
  investment of funds, 96
  state and local, 94
Rewards. *See* Incentives
Rogers, C., 325
Role conflict, 142–143
Roosevelt, Franklin, 22
Roosevelt, Theodore, 215
Rule of three, 130–132
  discrimination and, 255
Rutan v. Republican Party of Illinois, 23
Ryan, T.A., 321

S

Sabbatical leave, 179
Salaries and wages, 75–107, 400. *See also*
  Collective bargaining; Discrimination
  adjustments, 31
  adverse actions and, 225–226
  bonuses, 84
  collective bargaining and, 360–361,
    363–364, 373–374
  discrimination and, 264
  executive pay, 84–85
  extra compensation, 86–87
  front pay, 263
  grades and steps, 79–82
  job enrichment and, 310–311
  locality based, 83
  longevity increases, 82
  merit pay, 85–86, 160–162
  minimum wage, 87
  1993 federal salaries, 81
  overtime and collective bargaining,
    370–371
  patronage and, 77
  pay cap, 85
  pay plan, 49, 397–398
  prevailing rate system, 84
  recruitment and, 111–112

  total quality management and, 329–330
  unions and, 86
San Diego, pay experiment, 60, 160–161
Schedules A, B, and C, 23–24, 118, 160
  veterans and, 130
Schurz, C., 388, 401
Scientific management, 46–47, 50
Sections 1981, 1982, and 1983; 220, 244
Security, national. *See* Civil Rights
Selection of workers, 129–132
  discrimination in, 251–255
  promotions and, 171–172
Self-actualization, 318, 335
  See Motivation
Senior civil service, 177–178
Senior Executive Service, 77, 79, 85, 145,
  162, 178–181, 184–185, 389, 398
Seniority, 264
  discrimination and, 264–265
  reduction in force and, 222
  unions and, 375
Sensitivity training, 325–327
Sex discrimination. *See*, Discrimination;
  Women
Sex lives of workers, 208. *See*
  Homosexuality
Sexual harassment, 256–257
Sheldon, W.H., 286–287
Sick leave, 91
Simplified management system, 60, 161
Sixth Amendment, 211–212
Skinner, B.F., 295–296, 315
Social Security, 97–99
Socialization process, 141–143
Sociograms, 313
Somatotypes, 286–287
Sovereignty
  See Liability
  unions and, 347–348
Span of control, 45, 304–305
Speech, freedom of. *See* First Amendment;
  Fifth Amendment; Fourteenth Amendment
Spoils. *See* Patronage
*Standards for Educational and Psychological
  Tests*, 125
Standard Form 171, 115
Standards of conduct. *See* Ethics
Stimulus-response, 284–285, 295–296
Strategic planning, 67, 320, 329–330, 399
Strikes, 351, 365, 367–369

court injunctions and, 369
state policies and, 368
Superego, 285, 327
System, definition, 10

T

T-groups, 183, 326
Taft Commission on Economy and Efficiency, 51
Taft-Hartley Act, 353
Tailhook, 257
Tavistock Institute, 325
Taylor, F.W., 46–47, 49, 288–289, 303
Taylor-Russell tables, 123
Teachers Insurance and Annuity Association (TIAA), 95
Teams, 307, 309–310
   See Groups
   team building and, 328
Technocracy, 397
Technology and work, 49
Telecommuting, 307–308
Temperaments, 286–287
Terminations. *See* Adverse actions
Testing, 10, 114–129, 400. *See also*
   Discrimination
   administration, 125–129
   aptitude, 116, 119
   discrimination and, 251–252
   oral, 119–120, 255
   paper and pencil, 116–119
   personality, 116–117
   position classification and, 50
   types of tests, 114–121
   validity, 121–125
Theories X, Y, and Z, 292, 304, 323, 392, 398
Therbligs, 47
Thomas, C., 257
Thorndike, E.L., 292–293
Time and motion studies, 47–48
Title VII. *See* Civil Rights Acts
Top down, organizational design, 43–44
Torts, 218–220
Total quality management (TQM), 183, 329–332
Training, 182–189, 329, 400
   distinguished from education, 182
   effectiveness, 187–189
   organization development and, 325–328

performance evaluation and, 184
quality circles and, 324
raters in performance evaluation, 155–156
Training academies, 141
Traits, 148
   leadership and. 317
Trans World Airlines v. Hardison, 261
Transactional analysis, 326–327
Truman administration, 197
Turner, A.N., 309

U

Unemployment insurance, 99
Unfair labor practices, 357–360
Uniform Guidelines on Employee Selection Procedures, 125, 251–252
Union security, 361
Unions, 10, 264, 310, 373–377, 392–393
   affirmative action and, 269
   emergence of, 347–353
   flexitime and, 307
   membership, 349–351
   motivation and, 332
   patronage and, 374–375
   political activity of, 348–349, 374
   quality circles and, 324
   security of, 361
   seniority and, 264
   total quality management and, 331
United Steelworkers of America v. Weber, 269
Upward mobility, 267

V

Valence-instrumentality-expectancy theory (V-I-E), 293
Vesting, 95
Veterans preference, 4, 127–130, 254, 393
Veterans Preference Act, 128, 223
Volcker Commission, 75, 110, 399
Vroom, V.H., 293, 319

W

Wages. *See* Salaries and wages
Washington, George, 17
Washington State and comparable worth, 258
Watergate, 196, 198
Weight and height requirements, 253

Wellness programs, 90, 333–334
Whistle blowing, 213
Whistleblower Protection Act, 214
White, R.K., 317
Whyte, W.H., 312
Win/win bargaining, 363
Women, 240–243, 255, 259–260, 270–272
  See Discrimination
  comparable worth, 258–259, 397

reasonable woman, 257
Work environment, 205
Work hours and work days, 89–90. *See*
  Flexitime
Workers' compensation insurance, 92

Y

Yetton, P.W., 319

Notes

Notes

Notes

Notes

Notes

Notes

Notes

Notes

Notes

Notes

Notes

Notes